moosewood restaurant

new classics

moosewood
restaurant
new classics

350 recipes for homestyle
favorites and everyday feasts

Clarkson Potter/Publishers
New York

Moosewood Collective members contributing to this book:

Joan Adler, Ned Asta, Michael Blodgett, Laura Branca, Dave Dietrich, Tony Del Plato, Linda Dickinson, Susan Harville, David Hirsch, Nancy Lazarus, Neil Minnis, Eliana Parra, Sara Wade Robbins, Wynelle Stein, Maureen Vivino, Jenny Wang, Lisa Wichman, and Kip Wilcox.

Look for Moosewood bottled dressings at your local market or contact us at our website, www.moosewoodrestaurant.com.

Published by Clarkson Potter/Publishers, New York, New York.
Member of the Crown Publishing Group.

Random House, Inc. New York, Toronto, London, Sydney, Auckland
www.randomhouse.com

CLARKSON N. POTTER is a trademark and POTTER and colophon are registered trademarks of Random House, Inc.

Printed in the United States of America

Design by Jan Derevjanik

Library of Congress Cataloging-in-Publication Data
Moosewood Restaurant new classics: 350 recipes for homestyle favorites and everyday feasts / by the Moosewood Collective.
    1. Vegetarian cookery.   2. Cookery (Natural foods)   I. Moosewood Restaurant.
    TX837.M6745   2001
    641.5′636—dc21   2001034355

ISBN 0-609-60165-2 (hardcover)
ISBN 0-609-80241-0 (paperback)

10 9 8 7 6 5 4 3 2 1

First Edition

We dedicate our work to all of you who use our cookbooks, make Moosewood-style food for yourselves, and know intimately the pleasures of good food and good company.

acknowledgments

Over the years, we've written a lot of cookbooks, but as you might imagine, each one is unique and seems to take on a character and a life of its own. Different Moosewood Collective members are at the helm at different times, and we keep churning out food—always new and unique. Two things stay the same: There's lots of cooking and lots of writing.

Two other things for which we are grateful beyond words also stay the same: our literary agents and our editor. Like anchors, Arnold and Elise Goodman, our agents, coach us and coax us, encourage us and challenge us, laugh with us and eat with us, and never let us down. Sixteen years and still counting. We thank them for their constant backing, flexibility, and openness to change, and for their continuing effort to know us all both as a group and as individuals—not so easy.

Pam Krauss, our editor supreme, is a wizard of words and can turn a dull sentence into a shimmering metaphorical allusion with a simple turn of phrase. Her eye for detail doesn't miss a trick, making us rise to the crisp and clear. We fully appreciate her creativity, vision, and ability to competently steer the boat if it veers off course. She has been a unswerving fan of Moosewood food from the start and we couldn't do without her.

Thanks also to our amiable and innovative book designer, Jan Derevjanik, who has done a fabulous job, and the rest of the Clarkson Potter staff for their contagious enthusiasm and careful work.

Thanks to Dorothy Handelman for taking the time to come to Ithaca, for arranging the photo shoots in creative and fun settings, and for getting us to smile at exactly the right moments.

Last, but not least, we want to thank our friends, families, neighbors, fellow workers, and customers, who always love to be in on the recipe testing and always have an opinion. We need your mouths, stomachs, palates, minds, feedback, and loving inspiration. Thank you, from all of us.

contents

breakfast &
brunch

Moosewood Muffins 26
Apple Zucchini Muffins 28
Strawberry Banana Muffins 29
Maple Nut Granola 30
Stovetop Almond Oatmeal 34
Peach Oats Brûlée 35
Up-to-Date Irish Oatmeal 36
Oven Apple Oats 37
Cherry Whole Wheat Scones 38
Savory Congee 40
Sweet Spiced Congee 41
Three Tofu Scrambles 42
Sweet Potato Pancakes 46
Puffy Pancake 47
Lemon Ricotta Pancakes 48
Oatmeal Banana Pancakes 49
Vegan Oat & Walnut Pancakes 50
Smoked Cheddar Waffles 51
Whole Grain Waffles 52
Yeasted Waffles 53
Gingered Peach Butter 54
Greek Wheatberries & Peaches 55
Huevos Rancheros 56
Plum Butter with Orange 57
Tempeh Sausage 58
Quick Cinnamon Biscuits 59

soups

Vegetable Stocks 62
Minimalist Miso Soup 64
Vegetable Barley Soup 65
Thai Coconut Soup 66
Thai Carrot Soup 67
Asian Cabbage Soup 68
Valle d'Aosta Cabbage Soup 69
Artichoke Soup Provençal 70
Carolina Vegetable Soup 71
Creamy Chestnut Soup 72
Curried Spinach Pea Soup 73
Spinach Coconut Soup 74
Squash & Tomatillo Soup 75
Fennel Leek Soup 76
Potato Florentine Soup 78
Italian Bean & Squash Soup 79
Smooth Gazpacho with Greens 80
Southeast Asian Fruit Soup 81
Zero Soup 82
Scallop Chowder 84
Manhattan Seafood Chowder 85
Curried Fish Chowder 86
Spanish Bean Soup 87

salads

side vegetables

grains

wraps, rolls, sandwiches & burgers

drinks & snacks

the lighter side

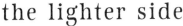

casseroles & other baked dishes

sautés, stews, skillet beans & hashes

Bibimbop 302

Chilean Bean Stew 304

Indian Ratatouille 305

Red & Green Sopa Seca 306

Sicilian Stir-Fry 307

Tilghman Island Stew 308

Spicy Broccoli Soba Sauté 310

Vegetarian Pozole 311

Tofu Stroganoff 313

Tofu in Black Bean Sauce 314

Winter Curry 316

Basic Skillet Black Beans 317

Basque Skillet Beans 318

Black Bean & Sweet Potato Hash 319

Chili with Tofu or TVP 320

Drunken Beans 322

French Ragoût Beans 323

Indian Skillet Black-Eyed Peas 324

Potato & Asparagus Hash 325

Peppers & Greens Skillet Hash 326

showstoppers

Asparagus Leek Strudel 332

Kale & Red Pepper Strudel 334

Mushroom Cheese & Tofu Strudel 336

Pizza with Three Toppings 338

Vegan Turnovers 342

Wild Mushroom Sauté 344

Fish Tostadas 346

East-West Stuffed Portabellos 347

Japanese Stuffed Eggplant 348

Moussaka-Style Stuffed Eggplant 350

Greek Lasagna 352

Pasta with Sunday Ragù 354

Pine Nut Pasta Cavalfiore 356

Sicilian Eggplant Pasta 357

Batter-Fried Vegetables & Fish 358

Cioppino 360

Elegant Oven-Poached Fish 362

Escabeche 363

Gingered Salmon-in-a-Packet 364

Fish with Artichokes & Capers 365

Thai-sStyle Scallops-in-a-Packet 366

Pecan-Crusted Fish 367

sauces, salsas & seasonings

Arrabiatta Sauce 370

Creamy Tomato Sauce 370

Avocado Wasabi Dressing 371

Black Bean Mango Salsa 372

Four Cheese Sauce 373

Garlic Scape Pesto 374

Joan's Three-Tomato Salsa 375

Light Sour Cream 376

breads

desserts

introduction

We've always been proud of the recipes that make their way into our cookbooks, surviving multiple rounds of testing and the scrutiny of both our customers and our friends and family. In our humble opinions, however, the collection you hold now is destined to become dog-eared. These are recipes that we're convinced will become classics, dishes so good that you'll make them again and again. *Moosewood Restaurant New Classics* includes our everyday favorites as well as some "showstoppers" for home-style feasts and special occasions. We expect to intrigue experienced cooks and also appeal to those with less experience or familiarity with cooking natural foods.

New vegetarians often encounter bewilderment from family and friends. Going home and announcing that you no longer eat meat can shake the cultural norms of your family—they don't know how to feed you, and they surely hope you'll get over it soon. We're here to help.

When we at Moosewood embarked on our adventure with natural foods, we were breaking away from the mainstream, meat-centered American diet. Many in our generation felt we were hot on the trail of a different way of eating that might bless us with health and longevity, but more importantly, with color, spice, and a whole new world of foods. Finding healthful ingredients wasn't hard; making them taste good was another story. We turned to the foods of the Mediterranean, the Middle East, India, Mexico, Africa, and Asia. We took a closer look at our own family roots, from down south, Italy, Armenia, China, Chile, and Philly. Then we figured out how to eliminate the meat and poultry, reduce the fat, exchange processed ingredients for natural whole foods, and we were on our way.

We love the explosion of ingredients, spices, fresh herbs, and other flavorings that are now available in markets. We applaud the proliferation of restaurants that serve food from traditional and ethnic cuisines, from Sri Lanka, Tibet, and Ethiopia to Cambodia. Life in the United States is enriched when new immigrants open restaurants and share food from home. Ethnic cuisine is a powerful means of cultural preservation, especially when you explore its origins and history.

Moosewood food has been called eclectic and cross-cultural because we serve dishes from so many different ethnic or regional cuisines. Moosewood often serves food prepared in a nontraditional way, but we're really good at preserving the intent, borrowing and adapting the central idea while maintaining the integrity of the original. We love to cook and are constantly improvising and experimenting. We want our vegetables sun-ripened, the cheeses savory and robust, the herbs freshly picked, the spices newly roasted and ground, and the grains whole and hearty. In a nutshell, we want flavors that sing.

We know that you do, too—and that you don't want to spend your days chained to the stove. We couldn't agree more. It has always amused us when our cookbooks have been acknowledged as outstanding restaurant collections. For while Moosewood *is* first and foremost a restaurant, and always has been, we've never served food that is overtly "restaurant-y." Homey, comforting, and satisfyingly familiar are the adjectives most often applied to our menu offerings, and although we are as appreciative of a beautifully plated dish as anyone, we've never emphasized architectural towers of food or applied our sauces with a squeeze bottle. In short, we cook at the restaurant much as we do at home. Customers come to Moosewood not to be stunned by our virtuosity, but to be nourished, soothed, and fortified by our food, and to have their culinary horizons broadened. These are certainly goals we all embrace in our own kitchens, and the recipes that follow are all delicious examples of this philosophy. Try a few, share them with friends, prepare them with love for family—we are certain you'll come back for seconds, thirds, and more!

food sensitivities & allergies

Over the years a growing number of Moosewood customers have brought specific food sensitivities to to our attention, and they need to know exactly what's in the food they're about to eat. For some, it can seem that food is becoming an enemy—not something we at Moosewood want to contemplate!

During the last couple of decades, the incidence of food sensitivities and allergies in the American population has increased dramatically. There are several theories that have attempted to explain this increase. Among them:

- Wider use by shippers, processors, and manufacturers of additives such as preservatives, coloring agents, flavor enhancers, and dough conditioners.

- With large industrial farming practices, fewer varieties of various crops are grown and so less variety is available for our consumption; wheat is an example of this. With less variation, our bodies may develop sensitivities more readily.

- Environmental toxins other than those found in food may result in abnormal reactions to normally benign substances.

- A greater percentage of the average person's diet consists of processed prepared foods and "fast foods," which often contain additives.

Food allergies and sensitivities are often hard to pin down. Symptoms might include joint inflammation and pain, migraine headaches, respiratory problems, temporary or long-term digestive disorders, fatigue and general malaise, and/or skin rashes. The symptoms may be dramatic and occur within minutes or even seconds of eating the offending substance. Or the onset of symptoms could occur gradually, hours or even days following ingestion, making it very difficult to make a direct association between, say, eating a sauce prepared with corn oil one day and headachey flu-like symptoms the next.

It can also be hard to pinpoint the cause of the problem when someone becomes sensitive or allergic to something that is a constant in the diet, such as wheat, corn, dairy products, yeast, common food additives, or soy. If an elimination diet (during which several common foods are not eaten at all) relieves the symptoms, then a slow one-by-one reintroduction of the eliminated foods may identify the culprit.

Although we use mostly fresh ingredients, we've found that in order to protect customers who have particular allergies or sensitivities, we must pay close attention to details and read labels closely. For example, hoisin sauce contains wheat, balsamic vinegar contains sulfites, some fresh produce has been treated with preservatives. Furthermore, labels don't always give complete information or may not be available. If you're serving food to someone with an allergy, tell them every ingredient, no matter how insignificant it may seem to you. If you have developed a sensitivity, talk to other people sensitive to the same substance to learn where they've discovered it might turn up. Then you can avoid it and save yourself from reactions.

Sulfites are one of the most common food sensitivity culprits. Used as a food preservative, they prevent discoloration and, in beer and wine, they control unwanted bacteria that may interfere with proper fermentation. Sulfites go by several names, including metabisulfite, bisulfite, sodium sulfate, and sulfiting agents. Sulfites are so pervasive and hard to identify in our foods, that we've decided to discuss them as an example of substances that may be causing discomfort in people who might not suspect a food sensitivity. Symptoms of sulfite sensitivity may include headache, joint pain, digestive disorders, fatigue, or breathing problems, and in cases of severe allergic reactions, anaphylactic shock and death.

Like other additives, sulfites are present in many prepared foods, yet are not included in the ingredient list because they "ride along" as secondary ingredients in something that *is* listed, such as dehydrated ingredients, grape juice, barley malt, wine vinegars, coconut, etc. Here's how it happens: Dehydrated garlic, for example, may be part of the formula for making a jarred pasta sauce. The manufacturer buys dehydrated garlic from various suppliers, depending on price and availability, some additive-free and others treated with additives, such as preservatives, color enhancers, or anticaking agents.

Some manufacturers do list secondary ingredients in parentheses, for example: "dehydrated garlic (may contain sodium metabisufite)," and we applaud that practice. If a label specifies "fresh" onions and garlic, you can be reasonably sure that they haven't been treated. If a label says "no preservatives," no preservatives have been added as a primary ingredient, and if the manufacturer is vigilant none of the primary ingredients will contain preservatives either. When a label says "no sulfites," you can be sure that no sulfites have been added directly, and somewhat sure that none are riding along.

foods that *usually* contain sulfites are as follows:

- shrimp (*all* shrimp: sulfites are sprayed on shrimp right in the boat.)
- beer, ale, and wine (organic wines contain naturally occurring sulfites, but unlike virtually all other wines, have no added synthetic sulfites.)
- barley malt, breads and baked goods containing barley malt, rice malt ("malt flavoring" does not contain sulfites.)
- most light-colored dried fruits, unless labeled "unsulfated" or "unsulfited" (sulfites prevent darkening and discoloration, so dark-colored fruits, such as prunes, dark raisins, and currants, aren't treated with sulfites.)
- balsamic vinegar, wine vinegar, rice wine vinegar (some balsamic vinegars, in particular, contain heavy concentrations of sulfites.)
- Dijon-style mustard and prepared mustards containing wine, garlic powder, or onion powder
- dried coconut and coconut milk (any form of coconut not fresh in the shell or specifically labeled sulfite-free probably has been treated.)
- instant and dehydrated potatoes, sauerkraut
- fresh or canned grapes (particularly white), white grape juice (sulfites prevent unwanted fermentation while grapes are held for processing. Concord grape juice is usually not treated.)

foods that *may* contain sulfites are as follows:

- pickled vegetables and onions, pepperoncini (check the ingredient list.)
- dehydrated vegetables (when sulfited dehydrated vegetables are an ingredient in canned and frozen foods, sulfites are often not listed on the label.)
- dehydrated garlic and onions (including garlic powder and onion salt)
- fresh seafood, such as scallops and some fish (ask the counter person—many are very well-informed about items likely to have been treated.)
- moonlight and other light-colored mushrooms (canned and some fresh)
- bouillon cubes, powdered stock, broth mixes, canned sauces and soups (sulfites may not be listed in the ingredient list.)
- stuffing mixes, such as seasoned bread crumbs and seasoned rice

pantry list

Having basic cooking ingredients at home saves time and makes it easier to eat well day in, day out. With a well-stocked pantry, you can whip up creative meals with items on hand and shorten your shopping list when preparing a complicated meal. Consider buying pantry items in bulk from a reliable local store where stock rotation ensures the freshness of food. That way you get the quality and quantity you want and you'll save money and consume less packaging.

The staples below are suggestions of foods good to keep on hand. None of us stocks all of them, just the things we use most regularly. We hope you'll use the list for inspiration and as a reminder when it's time to shop for food.

shelf items

GRAINS:

Barley, bulghur, buckwheat groats (kasha), cornmeal, couscous, grits, millet, oats, popcorn, quinoa, rice (arborio, basmati, brown, white).

Transfer packaged or bulk grains to glass jars with tight-fitting lids for storage: it's easier to see how much you have on hand and helps protect your grains from insects. Milled grains, like flours and meals, have a shorter shelf life than whole grains, so unless you use them up within a month, they should be refrigerated or frozen in closed containers.

BEANS:

Dried: Black turtle beans, black-eyed peas, chick peas, red kidney beans, cannellini (white beans), lentils (red, brown), limas, navy or pea beans, pintos, split peas (green, yellow).
Canned: Butter beans, black beans, chick peas, kidney beans, cannellini.

When buying dried beans, look for those with uncracked shiny coats and good color. Read the labels on canned beans. Some are sodium-free, some are organic, some have additives and preservatives.

PASTA:

Asian: Rice noodles, soba noodles, udon noodles.
Italian: Spaghetti, linguine, penne, ziti, farfalle, orzo, lasagna noodles.

Dried pasta, if stored in a well-sealed container, can last a lifetime, so stock a range of shapes and sizes: tiny pasta to add to soups and stews, chunky pasta to toss with vegetables, and long noodles for saucing.

NUTS & SEEDS:

Almonds, cashews, hazelnuts (filberts), peanuts, pecans, pine nuts, walnuts, sesame seeds, poppy seeds, sunflower seeds, tahini, peanut butter.

Nuts and seeds are terrific to have on hand for cooking, snacking, and for quick, nutritious additions to cereal, yogurt, and fruit salads. If possible, buy them in bulk, since they tend to be expensive. Check that they are crunchy, smell fresh, and have good color and sheen. Always store refrigerated.

OILS:

Canola, olive (regular and extra-virgin), dark sesame oil.

Experiment with different brands because the flavor varies. Oils that are used often can be stored in dark bottles or in a closed cupboard. Oils that are used less frequently should be stored in the refrigerator.

SPICES & HERBS:

Allspice, annatto (achiote), basil, bay leaves, black pepper, cardamom, cayenne, caraway, coriander seed, cinnamon (ground, and stick), cloves, cumin seed, curry powder, dill, fennel seed, five-spice powder, garam masala, marjoram, mint, mustard seed, nutmeg, Old Bay Seasoning, oregano, paprika, rosemary, saffron, sage, tarragon, thyme, turmeric.

An extensive spice collection is a real asset. Is there anything more frustrating than having everything you need for a recipe except one pesky herb or spice? Since the flavor and fragrance of herbs and spices fade over time, buy in small quantities or store refrigerated in well-sealed containers. For best flavor, purchase them whole and grind them as needed.

CONDIMENTS:

Chinese chili paste, Chinese fermented black beans, fermented black bean sauce, fish sauce (nuoc mam), fruit spreads, hoisin sauce, mustard (Dijon, spicy brown, yellow), soy sauce, Tabasco or other hot sauce, vinegars (apple cider, red wine, balsamic, rice wine), wasabi powder.

Condiments add depth, heat, pungency, flavor, and complexity and can make a so-so dish suddenly delicious. Those that contain fresh ingredients, oil, or high percentages of sugar or other sweeteners should be refrigerated.

CANNED & JARRED GOODS:

Artichoke hearts, capers, coconut milk (unsweetened), olives (Spanish, kalamata, black), pimientos, roasted red peppers, chipotle peppers in adobo sauce, salsa, tomato juice, tomato paste, whole tomatoes, tomato sauce, clams, clam juice.

Read the labels and experiment with different brands to find your favorites. We think canned goods that are free of additives and preservatives taste best.

WINES & LIQUEURS:
Chinese rice wine, dry red and white wines, liqueurs (amaretto, Grand Marnier, Frangelico), Marsala, mirin, sake, sherry.

    Sometimes a splash of wine or liqueur can add the perfect touch to a dish. If not used regularly, store them in the refrigerator.

FROZEN FOODS:
Black-eyed peas, lima beans, peas, corn, okra, puff pastry, filo dough, tortillas (wheat, corn), tempeh.

    Keep frozen foods well wrapped to avoid freezer burn.

miscellaneous

DRIED FRUITS (RAISINS, CURRANTS, APRICOTS, DATES, FIGS, DRIED CHERRIES): Store refrigerated in a closed container, if not using quickly.
DRIED MUSHROOMS: Store in a cool, dry place.
FRESH GARLIC: Store in a vented jar.
SEAWEED (HIJIKI, NORI): Store in a dry place.
SUN-DRIED TOMATOES: Store in a closed container or plastic wrap in the refrigerator.
VEGETABLE BOUILLON OR PACKAGED BROTH: Does not need refrigeration until opened.

storage of refrigerated items

CHEESES: Wrap tightly and keep refrigerated.
FRESH GINGER ROOT: Molds quickly if allowed to get moist, so store in an open container in the refrigerator or wrap in a paper towel and store in the produce drawer. Ginger root can also be stored in a freezer bag in the freezer.
MISO: Will keep for a long time if refrigerated in a closed plastic bag or container.
SEITAN: One variety of seitan is soft and stored in liquid; once the packaging is opened, refrigerate in a closed container, and use within 4 days. A second variety is much drier, has a longer shelf life, and can be frozen.
TOFU: Once opened, place the tofu in a closed container with water to cover and refrigerate. Change the water daily and use within 4 days.
YOGURT, COTTAGE CHEESE, RICOTTA CHEESE: Check the sell-by or expiration date. Always refrigerate.

about the recipes

Here's a bit of information you may find helpful as you plunge into this cookbook. Most of our recipes list the quantity of each prepared vegetable in cups. When the exact amount of a vegetable isn't crucial, however, we just call for "1 vegetable" and we mean a medium-sized one (not a miniature specimen or a giant garden variety one).

Peeling is often a matter of personal taste, although the eventual use of the vegetable or fruit in a specific dish and whether or not it's organic can be determining factors. We always peel carrots, parsnips, turnips, sweet potatoes, and beets. Cucumbers, eggplant, potatoes, and fruit are sometimes peeled, sometimes not: we decide case by case.

When we call for scallions, we expect you to use both the green and white parts unless otherwise indicated, and we want you to use any non-baking potato when we make no particular specification for potatoes. With canned tomatoes, you can buy whole ones and either chop them with a knife right in the can or squeeze them by hand into the pot—or use already diced tomatoes, sometimes labeled "fresh cut."

When fresh herbs in the ingredient list are followed by a dried equivalent in parentheses, either is fine, but if the fresh herb is available, it's preferable. If only the fresh herb is listed, we don't recommend using it dried at all. In some recipes, we call for dried herbs, but you can always use fresh if you prefer: just triple the dried amount and add the fresh herb near the end of the cooking process.

CBORD Group of Ithaca, New York, prepared the data for our nutritional bars. Their "per serving" analysis always applies to the largest number of servings listed when there's a range. When several choices are offered in the ingredient list, the nutritional calculations are based on the first choice that appears. Optional ingredients and garnishes for which no quantity is given are not included in the analysis. When the procedure mentions, "oil a baking pan," no amount of oil is given, since this will vary depending on the type of pan used and whether the oil is brush-applied or sprayed. In almost all cases, the amount of oil absorbed by the food from the baking pan is negligible, so the nutritional analysis does not take it into account.

the inside scoop

Where do all of the recipes come from? Here's the inside scoop on our development process. Since everyone in the Moosewood Collective is a really good cook, we take advantage of our collective talents and wisdom. We begin by asking everyone to submit unpublished recipes from among their personal favorites. We also have a team of idea people who research intriguing new products and techniques, read the latest cooking magazines and cookbooks, and generate ideas for new dishes to develop. Then we organize into teams of three or four and get together at one another's homes and then recipe testing begins.

Based on our working knowledge of each other's strengths and tastes, we know who's an artist with filo but not with pie crust, and who's a wizard with dill but can't abide cilantro. If one of us has created something special at the restaurant, we ask that person to develop a version suitable for the home cook. So many of us cook to taste, eyeing up ingredients without measuring, that standardizing amounts and documenting procedures can be a challenge. That's one of the benefits of cooking together. We keep each other on task.

We each take responsibility for developing reliable, replicable recipes, then meet for a big day of cooking with our team. Developers gather at the home of the teammate with the biggest, best-equipped kitchen. The team leader gathers all of the ingredients we will need, and then we start cooking. We note the times: how long to slice and chop, how long to sauté, simmer, bake, or chill. Later, the whole team sits down to a feast, and, sworn to be frank, shares feedback. We discuss possible substitutions for seasonal or hard-to-find ingredients and ways to simplify procedures, suggest a hint of some herb or spice or a splash of lemon, and make a note of any items to describe in the Guide to Ingredients. The developers dutifully record amounts and procedures and test the recipes again and again until they're perfect. At the end of the day, we put dibs on what we get to take home for dinner or to share with a neighbor or at a rehearsal. Our friends and families love this process.

Next, each recipe is assigned to another team who "second-tests" it to see if it works. Second-testers rate each dish and make comments. They jot down descriptive words and phrases to include in headnotes, ideas for titles, and menu suggestions. Sometimes a recipe doesn't make it to the finals. As soon as brand-new recipes are typed up, our restaurant menu-planners start raiding the files for something new to give the cooks to test-drive in quantity for that day's menu. The final verdict is left to our customers. If they like it, the dish becomes part of our treasure trove of trusted recipes. And it just keeps on growing. . . .

breakfast
& brunch

breakfast & brunch

It seems that a new study linking a good morning meal to improved concentration, mental acuity, memory, and energy is released every few months, and these findings are especially pertinent to kids.

Yet, too often our mornings are ushered in by sleeping until the last minute, cajoling and threatening late risers, then wolfing down something before dashing for buses, trains, and carpools. So much for breakfast.

The arguments for having a good meal in the morning are legion—and persuasive. The body needs nourishment, and most of us need to be alert, clear thinking, and energetic. Eating breakfast regulates food consumption. With a meal under your belt there's less temptation to snack mid-morning, or to overeat at lunch, or to make poor food choices. There is also evidence that eating breakfast essentially stokes the body, increasing metabolism and the rate at which calories are burned throughout the day.

Unfortunately, quick fixes—even toast or bagel on the run—are not good solutions for some sound physiological reasons. Breakfasts high in refined carbohydrates are fast burns, and soon leave you starving and shaky, an adrenaline response to low blood sugar. It also appears that carbohydrates alone can induce drowsiness, although when taken with the other nutrients, they play an important role in relaxation and concentration. Protein, fat, and fiber on the other hand are important starters because they provide longer lasting satisfaction and energy output, and steady glucose levels, which affect mood stability. Given the compelling connections between protein intake and brain function, the recommended wisdom is to have the bulk of one's protein for breakfast and lunch. That may mean looking at breakfast and brunch strategically and a little differently.

No time to cook for breakfast? Stretch your ideas of what's possible. Make use of leftovers. Cook enough for the weekend brunch to create "on purpose" leftovers. Reheat hot cereals in the microwave. Christine Lavin sings a song called "Cold Pizza for Breakfast," and why not? Frittatas are a great supper-into-breakfast meal, as are our savory flans, quiches, and tarts. The Greek Wheatberries & Peaches from Sunday's brunch is an ideal candidate for Tuesday's breakfast.

If you want breakfast food for breakfast, but can't see cooking on workday mornings, plan ahead a little. Our muffins, quickbreads, and whole grain, high-fiber waffles freeze beautifully, reheat well in the toaster oven, and make a meal when served with yogurt and fruit or accompanied by a fruit smoothie. Cooking can be so relaxing and fun. Do a little extra with breakfast or brunch in mind and you'll thank yourself later.

If you're an early-rising "morning person," cook extra even on workdays. After all, given what science tells us about carbohydrates, pancakes *are* the perfect supper.

moosewood muffins

Just by adding fruit, nuts, and/or chocolate chips, humble muffins can be transformed into a multisensory treat. Our basic muffin recipe leaves plenty of room for creative inspiration; over the years, early-morning Moosewood muffin-makers have tried more than two hundred variations. We've listed some of our most popular combinations. If you think of something else that appeals to you, we urge you to try it.

At Moosewood, morning customers like a muffin with their coffee, and lunch and dinner customers often check out the muffin case when it's time for dessert. The streusel topping adds a special touch. It can be stored in an airtight container in the refrigerator for a couple of weeks, so if you anticipate baking muffins regularly, make extra topping and you'll save time later.

For a vegan variation, omit the egg and use soy margarine and soy milk in place of the butter and the milk.

Yields 12 muffins
Preparation time: 30 to 35 minutes
Baking time: 30 minutes
Cooling time: 15 minutes

✂ Preheat the oven to 350°. Prepare a 12-cup muffin tin by lightly oiling the cups or placing a paper liner in each cup.

If you want a topping, mix together all of the streusel ingredients and blend with a fork until the butter is pea-sized or smaller. Set aside. In a mixing bowl, cream together the butter and sugar until smooth. Beat in the egg and then the milk and vanilla; the mixture will look lumpy. By hand with a rubber spatula, fold in the fruit and/or nuts and/or chocolate chips. Set aside.

streusel topping *(optional)*

$\frac{1}{3}$ cup unbleached white flour

$1\frac{1}{2}$ tablespoons cold butter, chopped into small pieces

$1\frac{1}{2}$ tablespoons brown sugar, packed

$\frac{1}{4}$ teaspoon ground cinnamon

pinch of nutmeg

pinch of salt

wet ingredients

6 tablespoons butter, at room temperature

$\frac{1}{2}$ to $\frac{3}{4}$ cup sugar

1 egg

$\frac{1}{2}$ cup plus 2 tablespoons milk

$\frac{1}{2}$ teaspoon pure vanilla extract

2 cups chopped fruit, and/or nuts, and/or chocolate chips*

dry ingredients

2 cups unbleached white all-purpose or pastry flour

1 teaspoon baking powder

$\frac{1}{4}$ teaspoon baking soda

$\frac{1}{4}$ teaspoon salt

$\frac{1}{4}$ teaspoon ground cinnamon or other spice (optional)

* *See the Variations for suggested flavor combinations. Use 2 cups of chopped fruit (one kind or a combination); or 1 cup fruit, $\frac{1}{2}$ cup nuts, and $\frac{1}{2}$ cup chocolate chips; or $\frac{1}{2}$ cup nuts or chocolate chips and $1\frac{1}{2}$ cups fruit.*

In a separate large bowl, sift together the flour, baking powder, baking soda, salt, and cinnamon, if using, and mix well. Add the wet ingredients to the dry ingredients and fold together with a rubber spatula without overmixing. Spoon about ⅓ cup of the batter into each muffin cup. Sprinkle each muffin with a scant tablespoon of streusel topping if you like.

Immediately place the muffins in the oven and bake for 30 to 35 minutes, until puffed and golden. After about 20 minutes, rotate the muffin tin in the oven to ensure even baking.

Remove the muffins from the oven and place the tins on a rack to cool for about 15 minutes. The hot muffins are quite soft and may fall apart if handled right away. Serve warm or cool completely and store in a sealed container at room temperature.

PER 1.75-OUNCE SERVING: 167 CALORIES, 3.1 G PROTEIN, 6.7 G FAT, 23.6 G CARBOHYDRATES, 3.9 G SATURATED FATTY ACIDS, 38.4 MG CHOLESTEROL, 169.4 MG SODIUM, 0.5 G TOTAL DIETARY FIBER

variations *Here are some of our most popular muffin varieties. Fruit should be chopped into pieces large enough to be easily recognizable.*

peach blueberry: *1 cup peeled and chopped fresh peaches and 1 cup fresh blueberries.*

apple cranberry: *1½ cups peeled, cored, and chopped Granny Smith apples, ½ cup fresh or frozen chopped cranberries (you can chop cranberries in a mini processor), and 1 additional tablespoon of sugar.*

mango banana chocolate chip: *½ cup peeled, pitted, and chopped ripe mangos, 1 peeled and chopped ripe banana, and ½ cup semi-sweet chocolate chips.*

papaya red raspberry: *1 ripe papaya, peeled, seeded, and chopped and 1 cup fresh red raspberries.*

peaches & pecans: *1½ cups peeled and chopped fresh peaches and ½ cup chopped toasted pecans.*

pear chocolate almond: *1 cup peeled, cored, and chopped ripe pears, ½ cup chopped toasted almonds, and ½ cup semi-sweet chocolate chips.*

pumpkin apple cinnamon: *¾ cup cooked mashed pumpkin (canned is fine), 1 cup peeled, cored, and chopped apples, and an additional ¼ teaspoon of cinnamon.*

pumpkin pecan chocolate chip: *¾ cup cooked mashed pumpkin (canned is fine), ½ cup chopped toasted pecans, and ½ cup semi-sweet chocolate chips.*

strawberry chocolate almond: *1 cup chopped fresh strawberries, ½ cup chopped toasted almonds, and ½ cup semi-sweet chocolate chips.*

apple zucchini muffins

Here's a muffin that's very, very low in fat, made with no butter and no oil whatsoever. We add a bit of oat bran, a nutritious touch—since oat bran has been identified as a food helpful for lowering cholesterol. The zucchini, apples, and yogurt all contribute to the moistness of the muffins, which are flavored with the tasty pairing of vanilla and cinnamon.

 Yields 12 muffins
Preparation time: 20 minutes
Baking time: 25 to 30 minutes

1 ½ cups unbleached white flour

½ cup oat bran

1 ½ teaspoons baking powder

½ teaspoon baking soda

½ teaspoon ground cinnamon

¼ teaspoon salt

2 eggs

¾ cup plain nonfat yogurt

¾ cup brown sugar, packed

½ teaspoon pure vanilla extract (optional)

1 cup grated zucchini

1 cup peeled, cored, and chopped apples

✂ Preheat the oven to 350°. Lightly oil the muffin tin. Place a paper liner in each cup.

In a bowl, sift together the flour, oat bran, baking powder, baking soda, cinnamon, and salt. Stir to mix evenly.

In a separate bowl, beat the eggs until pale yellow. Add the yogurt, brown sugar, and the vanilla, if using, and beat until thoroughly mixed. With a rubber spatula, fold in the zucchini and apples. Stir the wet ingredients into the dry ingredients until just blended.

Spoon about ⅓ cup of batter into each muffin cup. Bake for 15 minutes, rotate the muffin tin in the oven to ensure even baking, and continue to bake for another 10 to 15 minutes. When a paring knife inserted into a muffin comes out clean, the muffins are done.

Remove the muffins from the tin and place on a wire rack. Serve hot, warm, or at room temperature. Allow to cool completely before storing in a sealed container.

PER 2.75-OUNCE SERVING: 144 CALORIES, 4.1 G PROTEIN, 1.5 G FAT, 29.8 G CARBOHYDRATES, 0.4 G SATURATED FATTY ACIDS, 44.3 MG CHOLESTEROL, 164.4 MG SODIUM, 1.3 G TOTAL DIETARY FIBER

strawberry banana muffins

These wheat-free, gluten-free muffins are made with the yummy combination of strawberries and bananas. Look for potato starch in the kosher foods section of your market.

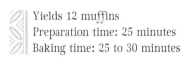

Yields 12 muffins
Preparation time: 25 minutes
Baking time: 25 to 30 minutes

1 1/4 cups rice flour

1/4 cup potato starch

1/4 cup tapioca flour

1/2 teaspoon xanthum gum*

1/4 teaspoon ground cinnamon

1 teaspoon baking soda

1 1/2 teaspoons baking powder

1/2 teaspoon salt

1/2 cup butter, softened

1/3 cup sugar

2 eggs

1/2 teaspoon pure vanilla extract

1/3 cup milk

2 bananas, peeled

1 1/2 cups stemmed and coarsely
   chopped fresh strawberries

Xanthum gum is a binding agent, found in health food stores and well-stocked supermarkets. In this recipe, in the absence of wheat gluten, it holds the muffins together.

Preheat the oven to 350°. Lightly oil a muffin tin and fill with paper liners.

In a large bowl, sift together the rice flour, potato starch, tapioca flour, xanthum gum, cinnamon, baking soda, baking powder, and salt. Stir to mix. In a separate bowl, cream together the butter and sugar until smooth. Beat in the eggs and add the vanilla and milk, stirring well. The mixture will be quite lumpy.

Mash the bananas and fold them with the strawberries into the wet ingredients. Mix the wet ingredients into the dry ingredients to form a thick batter.

Spoon a generous 1/3 cup of batter into each muffin cup. Bake for 25 to 30 minutes. After about 15 minutes, turn the muffin tin to ensure even baking. Insert a paring knife into a muffin; when the blade comes out clean the muffins are done.

Place the muffin tin on a cooling rack for a few minutes, then remove the muffins from the tin and place them on the rack or a platter. Serve warm or at room temperature. Cool completely before storing in an airtight container.

PER 3-OUNCE SERVING: 197 CALORIES, 2.8 G PROTEIN, 9.2 G FAT, 26.6 G CARBOHYDRATES, 5.3 G SATURATED FATTY ACIDS, 65.2 MG CHOLESTEROL, 341.5 MG SODIUM, 1.5 G TOTAL DIETARY FIBER

maple nut granola

Early mornings at Moosewood Restaurant, the kitchen hums with activity. The bakers are doing their wake-up baking rituals—and one of them is always making granola. Nothing tastes fresher than homemade granola; nothing makes the kitchen smell better. It makes getting up early an event to look forward to!

Serves 6
Total time: 30 to 40 minutes

4$^{1}/_{2}$ cups medium-cut organic rolled oats
$^{1}/_{4}$ cup oat bran
$^{1}/_{2}$ cup sunflower seeds
$^{1}/_{4}$ cup hulled sesame seeds
2 teaspoons ground cinnamon
$^{1}/_{2}$ cup blanched and sliced almonds
$^{1}/_{4}$ cup whole toasted cashews*
$^{1}/_{4}$ cup coarsely chopped Brazil nuts
$^{1}/_{4}$ cup coarsely chopped walnuts
$^{1}/_{3}$ cup vegetable oil
$^{1}/_{2}$ cup pure maple syrup
2 tablespoons barley malt syrup or unsulphured molasses**

Preheat the oven to 350°. Lightly oil a baking pan.

In a large bowl, mix together the oats, oat bran, sunflower seeds, sesame seeds, cinnamon, and the nuts. In a small bowl, combine the vegetable oil, maple syrup, and barley malt or molasses. Stir the maple mixture into the oat mixture and toss well to coat thoroughly. Spread the granola evenly on the prepared baking pan.

Bake for 15 to 20 minutes; stir at 5-minute intervals to ensure uniform baking, until golden brown.

*Toast cashews in a single layer on an unoiled baking tray at 350° for 5 to 10 minutes, until fragrant and golden brown.
**Barley malt is a liquid made from fermented barley and often used in baking bread. We use it here to add sweetness and moisture. If unavailable, any unsulphured molasses except blackstrap will work fine.

Remove the pan from the oven and place it on a cooling rack. Stir the granola occasionally to help dissipate heat. When completely cooled, place in an airtight container for storage. The granola will keep for 7 to 10 days.

PER 7-OUNCE SERVING: 862 CALORIES, 25.9 G PROTEIN, 41.7 G FAT, 103.7 G CARBOHYDRATES, 7.4 G SATURATED FATTY ACIDS, 0 MG CHOLESTEROL, 21.1 MG SODIUM, 15.7 G TOTAL DIETARY FIBER

moosewood granola

Moosewood granola is made from nutritious ingredients that are less refined than the ingredients in most commercial cereals, and we bake it only briefly so it retains nutrients. For the most healthful cereal, avoid using coconut, heavy vegetable oils, sweeteners, and lots of nuts, all of which can add dramatic amounts of fat, sugar, or calories.

At the restaurant, our basic recipe includes rolled oats, oat bran, sunflower seeds, sesame seeds, cinnamon, vegetable oil, maple syrup, and barley malt. We then add a pair of ingredients to distinguish each batch and offer two types of granola each day: one with a modest amount of nuts and one with dried fruit but no nuts. Adding only a pair of ingredients to the basic recipe helps create a balanced granola without competing flavors. Check out our variations for inspiration and alter ingredients as you like.

This Maple Nut Granola recipe is really popular with our customers. We serve it in bowls with milk or soy milk and use it as a crunchy topping for yogurt or ice cream. Try it with your favorite fresh fruits.

Granola doesn't take long to cook and can burn easily, so stay nearby while it bakes.

oatmeal

Recently, a morning guest described her childhood memory of poorly made oatmeal-in-a-hurry: hot, gray, watery gruel full of tough, lumpy unappetizing bits. Oh, dear. Another person lost to the delights of oatmeal due to bad preparation and, most likely, the use of quick or instant oats. Luckily, this guest has become a flexible and adventurous adult who dared to try again with "real" oatmeal—and has been thoroughly converted to the joys of steaming, nutty oats bolstered with whatever soothes: apricot preserves, bananas, blueberries, butter, brown sugar, sautéed apples, currants, you name it.

Oats flourished in the damp, cool climate of the British Isles, so it makes sense that people there learned the ins and outs of making truly delicious oatmeal. Chatting in the kitchen (or "visiting") while the aroma of cooking oats fills the air and then enjoying the warmth of both the company and the food can all be part of the charm of morning oatmeal. Almost anyone who travels in Ireland or Scotland remarks about the tasty oatmeal served there, and about the gracious hospitality of the people. Oatmeal can be hospitality itself, and you can offer it to your family, your guests, or just yourself.

It's a shame that these days we don't always take the time for hot cereal. Hot oatmeal made from steel-cut or regular old-fashioned oats sure beats cold cereal from a box, especially in the chill of early morning or in the depths of winter. Although time seems to be at a premium today in America, some things are just worth it. How the day starts matters. Besides, there are shortcuts and tricks even with something as basic as oats. Just take a look at the four recipes that follow for some ideas.

But first, a warning about shortcuts that won't take you to the same endpoint. While the American innovation of rolled oats at the end of the 1800s has reasonable merit, the next two oatmeal inventions by the breakfast industry, "quick-cooking" oats and "instant" oats, have quite limited or even questionable merit. None of these processed oats make the wonderful, nuggety, flavorful oatmeal that you get from the steel-cut (or "pinhead") oats typically available in tins like McCann's Irish Oatmeal or in the bulk section of natural food stores.

So what's the difference? Steel-cut oats are unprocessed oat groats that have been cut into pieces. They are amazingly flavorful and cook to a luscious, creamy consistency with kernels that retain a pleasant slight chewiness. If they're not soaked first, they take about a half hour to cook and we recommend minimal stirring (mostly at the end) for the best texture. Regular rolled oats are steamed oat groats that have been flattened with giant rollers. Often the rolled oats sold in bulk in natural food stores have also been flash-toasted during processing which gives them a golden hue and deeper flavor than the Quaker type. Rolled oats cook in about 10 minutes on moderately low heat, should be stirred just enough to prevent sticking, and make a substantial bowl of oatmeal with a thick, mostly uniform texture. The flavor is a bit dull but can be perked up with your favorite additions. Quick-cooking oats, which are a bit powdery, are cut smaller and rolled thinner than regular oats. Although they're ready in a minute or two, the flavorless mush turns to an unappetizing jello-like paste a few minutes later. Instant oats are rolled from cut groats that have been precooked and dried. Stir them into boiling water and instantly you have a bowl of gelled goo. Leftovers might make good glue for arts and crafts projects.

Because oatmeal is made of an unrefined whole grain, it has a lot going for it healthwise. It's full of disease-fighting antioxidants that are as protective as the ones in most fruits and vegetables and it contains lots of soluble fiber which can help lower LDL cholesterol and blood pressure when eaten regularly. Oats also provide protein, iron, calcium, zinc, potassium, magnesium, and vitamin E. And don't think the "sticks to your ribs" line is just a lot of malarkey. Studies show that oats take a long time to digest and keep you feeling full longer; one study reports that participants eating an oatmeal breakfast ate a third less calories at lunch than their cornflake-eating counterparts. So it may help you lose a few pounds, too. (Perhaps attributing the phenomenal strength of a Celtic legendary hero to his love of porridge is not so far-fetched after all!)

Now just a touch of present-day lore. Moosewood cook Maureen Vivino teaches Scottish Country Dancing, which has a history spanning several centuries and a living tradition of creating new dance figures. Sometimes, the path of a dancer suggests or resembles something (like an eight, for instance) and so the figure is named that. Relatively recently, someone choreographed a figure and named it "The Spurtle." Wouldn't you know? A spurtle, also called a thieval in some Scottish locales, is a foot-long wooden stick that somewhat resembles a tiny baseball bat and is used expressly for stirring hot porridge. The dance figure cleverly represents the clockwise stirring motion of the spurtle reaching right down to the bottom of the pot. Whether you stir with a spurtle (clockwise for good luck) or not, try taking some time for oatmeal in the morning.

stovetop almond oatmeal

All of the avid oatmeal eaters at Moosewood use regular rolled oats for quick breakfasts and steel-cut or "Irish" oats when time permits. We use quick-cooking oats only for cookies, baking, or thickening soups—but not in a real oatmeal dish. Instant oats are so inferior to true oats, it's not worth cooking them. We never use them: absolutely never.

Oatmeal made in the microwave is particularly creamy and smooth. Just be sure to use a glass or ceramic bowl that is much bigger than you would expect to need. Oatmeal goes wild in the microwave, bubbling and spurting, so give it a big container and cover the bowl with a plate, or else you'll be cleaning the microwave instead of eating oatmeal. For 1 cup of oats and 2 cups of water: heat for 2 minutes, stir well, heat for 2 minutes more, and let sit until the temperature suits you. Then stir well and eat.

Cleaning tip: Soaking your oatmeal pots in water will make them easier to clean later; it's even quicker than cleaning them right away. Daily oatmeal eaters who try to do two things at once and accidentally scorch the bottom layer of oatmeal may find this trick especially useful.

2 cups rolled oats*

4 cups water

1 teaspoon salt

1 cup whole, unblanched almonds

3 tablespoons raspberry or apricot
   preserves**

brown or white sugar and/or
   additional preserves (optional)

* *Rolled oats are sometimes labeled "old-fashioned" oats or "regular" oats; do not substitute "quick-cooking" oats.*
** *We recommend Sorrel Ridge spreadable fruit as excellent store-bought preserves.*

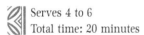
Serves 4 to 6
Total time: 20 minutes

In a pot with a tight-fitting lid, bring the oats, water, and salt to a boil; then lower the heat to medium-low and continue to cook, stirring frequently, for about 5 minutes.

Meanwhile, toast the almonds in a single layer on an unoiled baking tray at 350° for 5 to 10 minutes, until fragrant and golden brown. Finely chop in an electric grinder or food processor.

While the nuts toast, add the preserves to the oatmeal and cook, stirring frequently, for another 5 minutes, until the preserves are evenly distributed and the oatmeal is "smooth" and thickened. Let cool for 2 or 3 minutes, and serve immediately. If desired, offer the nuts with the sugar and/or extra preserves at the table.

PER 10.5-OUNCE SERVING: 315 CALORIES, 11.7 G PROTEIN, 13.5 G FAT, 39.2 G CARBOHYDRATES, 1.3 G SATURATED FATTY ACIDS, 0 MG CHOLESTEROL, 400.9 MG SODIUM, 7.3 G TOTAL DIETARY FIBER

peach oats brûlée

Here's a wonderful way to make oatmeal a centerpiece at your breakfast or brunch table. And besides the great presentation, there's almost no standing and stirring over the stove involved!

The butter and brown sugar topping, melted and crisped under the broiler, is just a flourish, but we recommend it as a traditional Irish touch, well worth the extra 5 minutes and the calories.

 Serves 4
Preparation time: 10 minutes
Baking/broiling time: 30 minutes

4 cups unsweetened peach juice*
2 cups rolled oats**
1/2 to 3/4 teaspoon salt
1 to 2 tablespoons butter
1/3 to 1/2 cup brown sugar, lightly
    packed

* We like After The Fall brand natural juices.
** Rolled oats are sometimes labeled "old-fashioned" oats or "regular" oats; do not substitute "quick-cooking" oats.

Preheat the oven to 350°.

Pour the juice into a saucepan, cover, and bring to a boil on high heat. Stir in the oats and salt and return to a boil, stirring constantly for about 1 minute.

Transfer the oat mixture to a lightly oiled, ovenproof 2-quart casserole dish that's about 9 x 6 inches. Cover and bake for 25 minutes, until the liquid is absorbed and the oats are tender and golden. Remove from the oven, dot the top with the butter, and evenly sprinkle on the brown sugar. Place under the broiler about 3 to 6 inches from the heating element and broil for 2 to 3 minutes, until the sugar is melted and bubbly. Serve hot.

PER 11-OUNCE SERVING: 493 CALORIES, 12.1 G PROTEIN, 7.4 G FAT, 97.6 G CARBOHYDRATES, 2.6 G SATURATED FATTY ACIDS, 7.8 MG CHOLESTEROL, 354.2 MG SODIUM, 8.9 G TOTAL DIETARY FIBER

variations • *Try a combination of 2 cups of apple juice and 2 cups of pear juice in place of the 4 cups of peach juice in the recipe. Other good flavor choices that work well are apple-apricot juice and apple-raspberry juice. In a real pinch, when you're out of juice, you can use water instead.*

up-to-date irish oatmeal

Here's a stovetop version of oatmeal using real Irish oats. Toasting the oats in a little oil or butter before cooking them isn't absolutely necessary, but it does enhance the nutty flavor and chewy texture. Adding salt near the end of cooking makes a creamier oatmeal by giving the starch and pentosan gums in the oats first crack at the water. The date topping can be made as the oatmeal cooks and then mixed in just before serving. Leftover, this can be a great sweet snack—just pop it in the microwave and enjoy. For a simpler dish, omit the date glaze and pass the brown sugar, maple syrup, or honey at the table.

We've made this dish with water, milk, and a combination of both, and all three ways are delicious. Using milk is the more traditional Celtic choice—but, hey, this is twenty-first century America, so the choice is yours! Be sure to stir out to the edges of the pot and, especially if you decide to use milk, stir frequently to prevent scorching. We recommend using a wooden spoon or spurtle.

oatmeal
4 cups water or milk (whole or 2%)

2 teaspoons butter or vegetable oil

1 cup Irish oats, thick oats, or steel-cut oats

1/2 teaspoon salt

date glaze
3/4 cup finely chopped dates

1/2 cup water

1/8 teaspoon ground cardamom

1/2 teaspoon pure vanilla extract

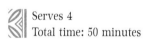
Serves 4
Total time: 50 minutes

Bring the water or milk to a boil in a saucepan. Meanwhile, in a small skillet on medium heat, warm the butter or oil. Add the oats and sauté, stirring constantly for 3 minutes, until the oats deepen slightly in color. Remove from the heat and set aside. When the water or milk boils, add the toasted oats and cook uncovered on medium heat for 20 minutes, stirring occasionally.

While the oats cook, make the date glaze. Combine the dates, water, and cardamom in a small saucepan. Bring to a low boil and then simmer for about 10 minutes, stirring now and then, until the mixture is reduced to a smooth, gooey glaze. Add a wee bit more water, if needed. Remove from the heat and stir in the vanilla. Cover and set aside.

When the oats have cooked for 20 minutes, add the salt, lower the heat to medium-low, and continue to cook for 10 minutes more, stirring frequently to prevent sticking. Mix in the date glaze until well blended. Remove from the heat and set aside for about 3 minutes, uncovered, before serving.

PER 9-OUNCE SERVING: 240 CALORIES, 6.1 G PROTEIN, 4.1 G FAT, 47.4 G CARBOHYDRATES,
1.6 G SATURATED FATTY ACIDS, 5.2 MG CHOLESTEROL, 321.4 MG SODIUM, 6.1 G TOTAL DIETARY FIBER

oven apple oats

Irish oats, sometimes called thick oats or steel-cut oats, take close to half an hour to cook on the stovetop, so baking them takes no longer and leaves your hands free from stirring over the stove. And besides the convenience, there's no need to worry about burning the oatmeal at the end.

The result is a very creamy and fluffy oatmeal that is lighter than bread pudding, but somewhat reminiscent of it. Made with milk (a longstanding Celtic tradition), this sweet combination of apples, maple syrup, and currants is one of our favorite oatmeals.

 Serves 4
Preparation time: 15 minutes
Baking time: 25 to 30 minutes

3 1/2 cups 2% or whole milk

1 cup Irish oats*

2 teaspoons pure maple syrup

1/2 teaspoon freshly grated nutmeg

1 to 1 1/2 cups peeled and diced apples

2/3 cup currants or raisins, or less to taste

1/2 teaspoon salt

Also called thick oats or steel-cut oats. Supermarkets often carry McCann's Irish Oats in decorative round tins, but your local natural foods store or health food store may have steel-cut oats in bulk at a less hefty price.

 Preheat the oven to 375°.

In a saucepan, heat the milk on medium heat until very hot but not quite boiling; stir occasionally to prevent scorching. Stir in the oats, maple syrup, nutmeg, and diced apples and continue to cook for several minutes, just until the mixture returns to a boil. Remove from the heat, add the currants or raisins and the salt, and mix well.

Spoon the oatmeal mixture into a 1 1/2-quart casserole dish, cover, and bake for 25 to 30 minutes, until all of the liquid is absorbed and the oatmeal is creamy. The oatmeal "casserole" will puff up slightly when finished.

Stir well just before dishing it up, and eat while piping hot.

PER 10.5-OUNCE SERVING: 338 CALORIES, 13.5 G PROTEIN, 6.4 G FAT, 59.9 G CARBOHYDRATES, 2.9 G SATURATED FATTY ACIDS, 14.9 MG CHOLESTEROL, 402.2 MG SODIUM, 6.5 G TOTAL DIETARY FIBER

cherry whole wheat scones

These scones are jeweled with red cherries and topped with cinnamon sugar. Currants or raisins can replace the dried cherries, but we prefer the sweet piquant cherry flavor and their lovely color. If you prefer a less sweet scone, reduce the amount of topping to taste.

Although the scones can be baked on any baking sheet, we recommend getting a baking brick, which provides even heat distribution and absorbs oven moisture.

We like to bake with whole wheat pastry flour. Its lower gluten content helps produce a more tender product than regular whole wheat flour can, but it still has the nutty flavor and nutritional benefits of a whole grain. Its finer texture makes it preferable for sweet breads and desserts.

Our cherry scones are best eaten warm, right out of the oven, but will store well for a few days.

¼ cup plus 2 tablespoons sugar
½ teaspoon ground cinnamon
2 cups whole wheat pastry flour
1 tablespoon baking powder
¼ teaspoon salt
½ cup dried cherries
2 large eggs
⅓ cup vegetable oil
⅓ cup milk

Yields 8 scones
Preparation time: 30 minutes
Baking time: about 15 minutes

Preheat the oven to 400°. Oil a baking sheet or clay baking brick.

Combine 2 tablespoons of the sugar and the cinnamon in a cup and set aside. Sift the remaining sugar, the flour, baking powder, and salt into a large bowl. If any of the bran remains in your sifter be sure to add it to the flour mixture. Add the dried cherries and stir well.

In a medium bowl, beat the eggs. Reserve 1 tablespoon of the beaten eggs for later. Beat the oil and milk into the remaining eggs. Make a well in the dry ingredients, pour in the egg mixture, and stir until just combined: The dough will be soft. Turn it onto a floured surface and pat it into a circle about 8 inches across and ½ inch thick.

Cut the circle into eight pie-shaped wedges. With a spatula, lift each wedge and arrange them on the prepared baking sheet or brick so that they're not touching. Push any errant cherries back into line. Brush the tops of the scones with the reserved egg and sprinkle generously with the cinnamon sugar.

Bake for about 15 minutes, until golden brown and firm to the touch.

PER 3-OUNCE SERVING: 268 CALORIES, 6.4 G PROTEIN, 11.8 G FAT, 37.2 G CARBOHYDRATES, 3.1 G SATURATED FATTY ACIDS, 66.8 MG CHOLESTEROL, 221.9 MG SODIUM, 4.3 G TOTAL DIETARY FIBER

congee: made savory and sweet

Congee, a thick porridge with a texture a bit like cream of wheat, is eaten for breakfast or late-night snacks in every corner of China and all across Southeast Asia and the East. There seems to be no limit to what you can stir into it. When we recently started experimenting with congee, many of us at Moosewood couldn't believe we had missed this dish in all our years of cooking. Everyone who tastes it for the first time is amazed at how deeply satisfying it is. Even some people who hate oatmeal like it!

Congee, also called jook or kitchari, dates from the Zhou Dynasty (1000 B.C.). It was historically made with either two types of rice together or, especially in Northern China, with many other grains as well: barley, wheat, millet, tapioca, sorghum, or corn. Since the same amount of raw rice, cooked longer with more water, yields three times as much congee as cooked rice, it's very possible that congee came about as a way to stretch a bag of rice to feed more mouths.

But all necessity aside, congee came to be loved (even craved) for its own wonderful texture, digestibility, and accommodating nature. The Vinayapitaka quotes the Buddha's praises of congee's nourishing qualities: "It gives life, beauty, ease, and strength as it dispels hunger." Even today, Chinese medical texts consider it very beneficial and prescribe many specific congee recipes for alleviating particular ailments.

Because the dish requires a long cooking time and the proper consistency depends upon slow, even simmering, it's best made in quantity. While you can halve the recipe for a smaller amount, the final result will not be quite as smooth and silky. Leftover congee can be stored in the refrigerator for up to a week and is easily reheated by adding a small amount of water and stirring on medium heat. It can also be reheated in the microwave, and some of us think it's quite good cold.

We offer two recipes for basic congee that illustrate different techniques for making it. One is made with long-grain white rice, cooks for about 40 minutes, and then stands for another hour. The other uses Arborio rice, cooks for 75 minutes, and yields a smoother, less chewy dish. Both are wonderful, and sweet sticky rice also works well.

Congee can be spruced up in any number of ways. Here we give one savory and one sweet possibility as part of the recipes, and list a host of other variations to try.

savory congee

Serves 8 to 10
Preparation time: 15 minutes
Cooking time: 35 to 40 minutes
Standing time: 50 to 60 minutes

Place the rice in a sieve and rinse well with cool water. Combine the rice, salt, and the water or stock in a large pot, cover, and bring to a boil—about 15 minutes. Once it boils, partially uncover to prevent boiling over, lower the heat to medium-low, and cook for 20 to 25 minutes. Remove from the heat, cover, and let stand for 50 to 60 minutes, until thickened to a chewy porridge.

When the congee is almost ready, make the savory sauce. Heat the oil in a saucepan on medium-high heat. Stir in and sauté the garlic and scallions for 4 minutes, until the garlic is golden. Add the soy sauce and mirin and continue to cook another 1 or 2 minutes. Mix in the cilantro and pepper; then spoon the sauce onto the congee. Top with roasted peanuts.

congee

1 1/2 cups long-grain white rice
1 1/4 teaspoons salt
10 cups water or vegetable stock

savory sauce

2 teaspoons peanut oil
6 garlic cloves, minced or pressed
1 1/2 cups scallions, thinly sliced
1/2 cup soy sauce
3 tablespoons mirin
1/2 cup minced fresh cilantro
1/4 teaspoon ground black pepper or
    to taste

1 cup dry-roasted, unsalted peanuts,
    whole or crushed

PER 5-OUNCE SERVING: 205 CALORIES, 6.6 G PROTEIN, 7.7 G FAT, 28.6 G CARBOHYDRATES, 1.1 G SATURATED FATTY ACIDS, 0 MG CHOLESTEROL, 942.9 MG SODIUM, 2.1 G TOTAL DIETARY FIBER

variations ❧ *Other good savory additions to congee include 1) Chinese chili paste with garlic, 2) fried shallots, 3) sautéed grated daikon topped with white vinegar, sugar, and dark sesame oil, and 4) sliced shiitake mushrooms sautéed with garlic and fresh ginger root or simply added to our Savory Sauce, above.*

sweet spiced congee

Although the majority of Asian congees are enhanced with savory additions, we've experimented with the addition of delectable fresh fruit sauces that really get those morning juices flowing. Just top the congee with the quickly made sauce or stir it in for a super breakfast treat or snack.

 Serves 8 to 10
Preparation time: 15 minutes
Cooking time: 75 minutes

Place the rice in a sieve and rinse well with cool water. Combine the rice, salt, and the water in a large pot and bring to a boil, uncovered. When it boils, cover the pot, reduce the heat to low, and simmer for about an hour, stirring occasionally, until thickened to a smooth porridge.

When the congee is almost ready, combine the apples, pears, and water in a medium saucepan, cover, and bring to a boil. Add the cinnamon, sugar, nutmeg, ginger, and allspice and cook, uncovered, on medium heat for about 15 minutes, stirring occasionally, until the fruit softens and makes a thick sauce.

Spoon about ¼ cup of the sweet sauce on top of individual bowls of congee and serve immediately. Store leftover congee and sauce separately.

congee

1½ cups Arborio rice

1¼ teaspoons salt

12 cups water

sweet sauce

5 apples, peeled, cored, and diced*

5 Bosc pears, peeled, cored, and diced*

2 cups water

2 tablespoons ground cinnamon

2 to 3 tablespoons brown sugar, packed

2 teaspoons ground nutmeg

2 teaspoons ground ginger

1 teaspoon allspice

* A total of about 9 or 10 cups of raw diced fruit works well. If you are using large apples, three may be enough. Dice the fruit into ¼- to ½-inch pieces.

PER 8-OUNCE SERVING: 178 CALORIES, 2.4 G PROTEIN, 1 G FAT, 41.6 G CARBOHYDRATES, 0.3 G SATURATED FATTY ACIDS, 0 MG CHOLESTEROL, 302 MG SODIUM, 4.1 G TOTAL DIETARY FIBER

variations ❦ *Use all apples or all pears instead of a combination. For a Peach Congee, use 9 pitted and diced peaches and reduce the cinnamon to 1 tablespoon. Try 4½ cups of cranberries for the fruit, omit the cinnamon, and use ¾ to 1 cup of packed brown sugar. Enjoy a simple New England-style congee by stirring maple syrup and butter to taste into the basic congee recipe. Add 1½ cups of currants or raisins to any of the sweet congees.*

three tofu scrambles

Tofu scrambles are quick, easy, and versatile, and soft tofu readily absorbs spices and other flavors. Serve scrambles with toast or muffins as a scrambled egg alternative for breakfast or brunch, with rice for a hearty lunch, or with rice and steamed vegetables for a light supper.

Here are three versions to try. If you have a nonstick skillet, use it. It's the best pan for these recipes. If you don't have nonstick cookware, use a wok or heavy skillet.

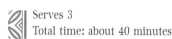 chinese tofu scramble

This scramble will warm your tongue with tiny bits of hot pepper and ginger.

Serves 3
Total time: about 40 minutes

2 tablespoons vegetable oil
1 cup chopped onions
3 garlic cloves, minced or pressed
2 tablespoons minced fresh ginger root
1 cup chopped red bell peppers
1 fresh chile, seeded and minced
16 ounces soft tofu, pressed*
4 cups chopped mustard greens
2 tablespoons light miso
2 tablespoons warm water
2 tablespoons soy sauce, more to taste
¼ teaspoon dark sesame oil
2 cups cooked rice
2 tablespoons toasted sesame seeds**

* See note on opposite page.
** Toast sesame seeds in a single layer on an unoiled baking tray at 350° for about 5 minutes, until fragrant and golden.

In a nonstick skillet, warm the oil on medium heat. Sauté the onions for about 5 minutes, until they begin to soften. Add the garlic and ginger and sauté briefly. Add the bell peppers and chiles and sauté for another 2 to 3 minutes.

Crumble the pressed tofu and carefully stir it into the vegetables. Cook the vegetables and tofu uncovered for 4 to 5 minutes, until the moisture evaporates. Gently turn the mixture over and cook for about 2 minutes. Turn off the heat.

In a saucepan or steamer, bring 1 to 2 inches of water to a boil. Add the greens, cover, and cook for about 1 minute, until limp and bright green. Drain. In a small bowl, mix the miso with the warm water until smooth. Stir in the soy sauce and sesame oil. Pour the sauce over the scramble and toss lightly.

Serve the tofu scramble on rice, topped with the greens and toasted sesame seeds.

PER 16-OUNCE SERVING: 455 CALORIES, 17.9 G PROTEIN, 19.4 G FAT, 55.6 G CARBOHYDRATES, 3.9 G SATURATED FATTY ACIDS, 0 MG CHOLESTEROL, 897.3 MG SODIUM, 3.7 G TOTAL DIETARY FIBER

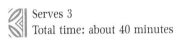

mexican tofu scramble

Here's a spectacular vegan "Huevos Rancheros." Use 6-inch or 9-inch tortillas for the best result.

Serves 3
Total time: about 40 minutes

6 small or 3 large corn or flour
   tortillas
2 tablespoons vegetable oil
1 cup chopped onions
3 garlic cloves, minced or pressed
1 cup chopped red bell peppers
1 cup chopped green or yellow bell
   peppers
1 fresh green chile, minced
1 teaspoon ground cumin
1 teaspoon ground coriander
1 teaspoon salt, or more to taste
16 ounces soft tofu, pressed*
6 tablespoons chopped fresh cilantro
1 1/2 cups salsa (page 372 or 375)

* Sandwich the tofu between two plates and rest a heavy weight on the top plate. Press for about 15 minutes; then drain the expressed liquid from the plate.

Wrap the tortillas in aluminum foil and warm in a 300° oven for 10 to 15 minutes.

In a wok or heavy skillet on medium heat, warm the oil. Sauté the onions for about 5 minutes, until they begin to soften. Add the garlic, bell peppers, chile, cumin, coriander, and salt and sauté another 2 or 3 minutes.

Crumble the pressed tofu into the vegetables and stir gently until well mixed. Cook uncovered for 4 to 5 minutes without stirring until the moisture evaporates. Gently turn over the scramble and cook for about 2 minutes. Turn off the heat.

Remove the tortillas from the oven, and fill each one with a generous mound of scramble topped with fresh cilantro. Roll up the tortillas and place them in a baking dish. Cover the dish tightly with aluminum foil and keep warm in the oven for up to 20 minutes, until ready to serve. Top each serving with 1/2 cup of salsa.

PER 17-OUNCE SERVING: 397 CALORIES, 16.2 G PROTEIN, 17.3 G FAT, 49.9 G CARBOHYDRATES, 3.4 G SATURATED FATTY ACIDS, 0 MG CHOLESTEROL, 1,367.4 MG SODIUM, 6.8 G TOTAL DIETARY FIBER

indian tofu scramble

Flavored with curry spices and brightened with yellow turmeric, this scramble is good on rice or wrapped in a soft flatbread. You can use up to 2 tablespoons curry paste to replace the curry powder in the recipe. Look for curry paste in the imported foods section of your supermarket. Curry pastes vary wildly in hotness, so add judiciously. The *Jaipur* brand has no preservatives or artificial ingredients.

Commercially made chapatis are available in the frozen food section of health food stores and specialty food shops. If you use them, wrap them in aluminum foil and warm them in a 300° oven just as you begin to cook the scramble.

Serves 3
Total time: about 40 minutes

2 tablespoons vegetable oil

1 medium onion, coarsely chopped (about 1 cup)

3 garlic cloves, minced or pressed

2 tablespoons minced fresh ginger root

1 cup chopped red bell pepper

1/2 teaspoon turmeric

1 1/2 to 2 1/2 teaspoons curry powder

1 teaspoon salt, more to taste

16 ounces soft tofu, pressed*

3 cups rinsed, stemmed, and chopped fresh spinach

2 cups cooked white or brown basmati rice, or 6 chapatis

* *Sandwich the tofu between two plates and rest a heavy weight on the top plate. Press for about 15 minutes; then drain the expressed liquid from the plate.*

In a wok or heavy skillet on medium heat, warm the oil. Sauté the onions for 5 minutes until softened. Add the garlic, ginger, bell peppers, turmeric, curry powder or paste, and salt and sauté for 3 or 4 minutes, adding a little water if the vegetables stick to the pan.

Crumble the pressed tofu into the vegetables and stir gently until well mixed. Cook the tofu and vegetables for 4 to 5 minutes without stirring. Gently turn over the scramble and cook for another 2 to 3 minutes. Place the chopped spinach on top of the scramble, cover, and steam for 1 to 2 minutes, until the spinach leaves are limp but still bright green. Remove the lid and turn off the heat.

Serve the scramble on rice or rolled up in warm chapatis.

PER 15-OUNCE SERVING: 389 CALORIES, 14.6 G PROTEIN, 15.5 G FAT, 50.2 G CARBOHYDRATES, 3.4 G SATURATED FATTY ACIDS, 0 MG CHOLESTEROL, 823 MG SODIUM, 3.1 G TOTAL DIETARY FIBER

pancakes & waffles

When we think of waffles and pancakes, we usually think of a simple, homey breakfast treat. In truth, they can be as light as air or as rich as dessert. They can be sweet and fruity or nutty and earthy, dainty and elegant or oversized and indulgent. It's a wonder packaged mixes can be so popular when pancakes and waffles are so easy to make from scratch.

tips:

1. For light, fluffy pancakes and waffles, don't overmix the batter. When combining the wet and the dry ingredients, it is better to leave a few lumps than to stir too much. For the best pancakes, don't flip them more than once and don't flatten them with a spatula.

2. After mixing, let the batter sit for a few minutes until bubbles form on top. This "rest" gives the baking powder or soda time to start working, so the pancakes or waffles will be lighter.

3. Heat the griddle well before cooking the pancakes. It is hot enough when a drop of water "dances" on the pan and evaporates quickly. If waffles stick, it may be an indication that the iron isn't hot enough.

4. To retain their crisp outer texture, serve waffles immediately and don't stack them. Serve pancakes as soon as possible; if you are making a large batch, you can keep them warm in a 200° oven in a single layer on a tray.

sweet potato pancakes

Delightfully delicate and permeated with the enticing aroma of lemon, these deep golden-brown, thin pancakes are moist inside with crisp edges.

For breakfast, serve them plain or with butter or maple syrup. For lunch or supper, top them with sour cream and put a chunky salsa on the side. For dessert, serve at room temperature drizzled with equal parts of lemon juice and honey stirred together and top with freshly whipped cream. For another simple lemon syrup, stir together 2 tablespoons of fresh lemon juice and $1/2$ cup of pure maple syrup.

For ease of cooking, combine the wet ingredients in a 1-quart measuring cup with a pouring lip, stir in the dry ingredients, and then pour the batter directly onto the hot skillet.

1 cup peeled and grated raw sweet potatoes*

$1/4$ to $1/2$ teaspoon freshly grated lemon peel

1 large egg or 2 medium eggs

1 cup milk

2 tablespoons oil or melted butter

1 cup unbleached white flour

2 teaspoons baking powder

$1/2$ teaspoon salt

2 tablespoons sugar

Serves 4
Preparation time: 10 minutes
Cooking time: 3 minutes per batch
Total time: about 35 minutes

Grate finely: use a small-holed grater or, if your grater has larger holes for shredding, use a light pressure on each stroke to produce a finer shred.

In a bowl or large measuring cup, combine the grated sweet potatoes, lemon peel, egg, milk, and oil or butter. In a separate bowl, stir together the flour, baking powder, salt, and sugar. Gently stir the dry ingredients into the wet ingredients just enough to combine. Do not beat or overstir. Set aside to rest for 5 to 10 minutes.

Warm a lightly oiled skillet, griddle, or nonstick frying pan on medium-high heat. When a drop of water bounces and sizzles on the skillet and before the oil smokes, pour on scant $1/4$ cups of batter to form round pancakes. After about 2 minutes, when the pancakes are evenly dotted with bubbles and about half of the bubbles have broken, flip the pancakes with a spatula. Cook the second side until lightly browned, about 1 minute. Continue to cook batches of pancakes until all of the batter is used.

Serve right away or keep warm in a 250° oven. If you plan to serve at room temperature or reheat later, cool the pancakes in a single layer on a flat surface and then stack for storage. If storing for more than a few hours, refrigerate.

PER 5.5-OUNCE SERVING: 278 CALORIES, 7.3 G PROTEIN, 10.2 G FAT, 39.3 G CARBOHYDRATES, 3.1 G SATURATED FATTY ACIDS, 70.4 MG CHOLESTEROL, 511.6 MG SODIUM, 1.4 G TOTAL DIETARY FIBER

puffy pancake

When we tested our baked pancake on a few enthusiastic tasters, we were surprised to discover that several people remembered eating pancakes similar to this as youngsters. The oversized pancake is sometimes called a "German Dutch Puff" or more humorously "Dutch Baby."

As a child, Moosewood employee Barbara Davidson loved these made with raisins and cinnamon. Here we top the pancake with both fruit and a simple apple syrup.

 Serves 4
Total time: 45 minutes

pancake batter

3 eggs
¾ cup milk
1 tablespoon butter, melted
1 tablespoon sugar
½ teaspoon pure vanilla extract
¾ cup unbleached white flour
¼ teaspoon ground cinnamon
¼ teaspoon salt
pinch of ground nutmeg (optional)

fruit topping

1 tablespoon butter
2 cups sliced apples
2 tablespoons brown sugar, packed
¼ teaspoon ground cinnamon
½ cup fresh or frozen blueberries or
    raspberries (optional)

apple syrup

2 cups apple cider
3-inch cinnamon stick

Preheat the oven to 425°.

Whisk together the eggs, milk, butter, sugar, and vanilla in a large bowl. Sift in the flour, cinnamon, and salt, and the nutmeg, if using. Stir just to combine and set aside.

Melt the butter in a skillet. Add the apple slices and sauté for 2 to 3 minutes. Stir in the brown sugar and cinnamon. Add the berries, if using, and cook for another 1 to 2 minutes, until the sugar has melted and the apples are hot. Remove from the heat.

Butter a 10-inch cast-iron or other oven-proof skillet. Evenly pour in the batter and top with the fruit mixture. Bake for 30 minutes, until puffed and golden around the outside and firm in the center.

Meanwhile, bring the cider and cinnamon stick to a boil in a heavy medium saucepan. Cook until the liquid has cooked down to about ¼ cup, about 30 minutes. Near the end, watch carefully to avoid burning the syrup and reduce the heat, if necessary. Remove from the heat and strain.

Serve the pancake immediately, straight from the pan, and top with the syrup.

PER 7.5-OUNCE SERVING: 341 CALORIES, 9.8 G PROTEIN, 12.1 G FAT, 49.2 G CARBOHYDRATES, 5.7 G SATURATED FATTY ACIDS, 217 MG CHOLESTEROL, 295.5 MG SODIUM, 2.8 G TOTAL DIETARY FIBER

lemon ricotta pancakes

This is a good example of the boundless possibilities of pancakes. Serve them topped with your favorite syrup, additional fruit, or fresh whipped cream. These pancakes could even be offered for dessert—try them à la mode.

Because they contain ricotta cheese, use a good-quality nonstick pan or well-seasoned griddle or skillet with even heat distribution, so the delicate batter doesn't stick or burn.

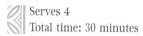 Serves 4
Total time: 30 minutes

In a mixing bowl, sift together the dry ingredients. In a separate bowl, beat the egg whites until fluffy. Thoroughly fold in the ricotta, vanilla, and lemon peel and then the fruit. Stir the dry ingredients into the wet ingredients just enough to combine.

Lightly oil a skillet or griddle and place on medium-high heat. Use about $1/4$ cup of batter for each pancake. Cook for 1 to $1^1/2$ minutes on the first side until bubbles appear on the top. Turn the pancakes and cook on the second side until golden brown, about 1 minute.

Serve hot.

dry ingredients

$2/3$ cup unbleached white flour

2 tablespoons sugar

$1/2$ teaspoon salt

$1/8$ teaspoon cream of tartar

pinch of ground cinnamon

wet ingredients

6 egg whites

2 cups ricotta cheese

$1/4$ teaspoon pure vanilla extract

2 teaspoons freshly grated lemon peel

$1/4$ cup fresh blueberries or pitted cherries*

* *Frozen blueberries also work well. Thaw before using in the recipe.*

PER 7.5-OUNCE SERVING: 287 CALORIES, 21.1 G PROTEIN, 9.2 G FAT, 29.1 G CARBOHYDRATES, 5.6 G SATURATED FATTY ACIDS, 34.9 MG CHOLESTEROL, 537.7 MG SODIUM, 1 G TOTAL DIETARY FIBER

oatmeal banana pancakes

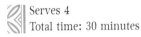

Pancakes are a great weekend morning treat. These are fairly sweet, so you may prefer a fruit topping on them rather than syrup, although good maple syrup is mighty fine on them, too. Sliced strawberries with a light dusting of confectioners' sugar is one of our top choices, providing a lovely balance of flavors.

Serves 4
Total time: 30 minutes

Sift together the flour, salt, baking powder, and nutmeg. Add the oats and mix well. In a separate bowl, stir together all of the wet ingredients. Make a well in the dry ingredients and stir in the wet ingredients just to combine.

Lightly oil a skillet or griddle and place on medium-high heat. Use about ¼ cup of batter for each pancake and cook until bubbles appear on the top, about 1 to 1½ minutes. The bananas will settle to the bottom, so you want to flip these pancakes just as soon as bubbles start to form to avoid scorching them. Cook on the second side until golden brown, about 1 minute.

Serve hot.

dry ingredients

1 cup unbleached white flour
½ teaspoon salt
2 teaspoons baking powder
¼ teaspoon ground nutmeg
¼ cup quick-cooking oats*

wet ingredients

1 egg, lightly beaten
1 cup 2% milk
1 tablespoon vegetable oil
2 tablespoons maple syrup or sugar
1 cup sliced ripe bananas

* Or use rolled oats chopped into finer pieces in a blender or food processor.

PER 6.5-OUNCE SERVING: 300 CALORIES, 8.8 G PROTEIN, 7.5 G FAT, 50.8 G CARBOHYDRATES, 2.4 G SATURATED FATTY ACIDS, 70.4 MG CHOLESTEROL, 509.1 MG SODIUM, 3.1 G TOTAL DIETARY FIBER

vegan oat & walnut pancakes

Hearty and healthful, these pancakes are made without eggs or dairy and are a great choice when your vegan friends are coming for brunch. For anyone looking for cholesterol-free recipes, this is certainly one to add to your repertoire.

Topped with fruit, this delicious pancake is a complete meal.

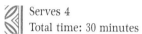 Serves 4
Total time: 30 minutes

¾ cup unbleached white flour

¼ cup whole wheat flour

½ teaspoon salt

2 teaspoons baking powder

⅛ teaspoon ground cinnamon

⅛ teaspoon ground nutmeg

¼ cup toasted and finely chopped walnuts*

¼ cup quick-cooking oats**

1⅓ cups plain or vanilla soy milk or almond milk

1 tablespoon vegetable oil

1 teaspoon pure maple syrup or sugar

In a large bowl, sift the flours, salt, baking powder, cinnamon, and nutmeg. Stir in the walnuts and oats. In a separate bowl, stir together the milk, oil, and maple syrup or sugar. Make a well in the dry ingredients and pour in the wet ingredients. Stir just until combined.

Lightly oil a skillet or griddle and place it on medium-high heat. Use about ¼ cup of batter for each pancake and cook on the first side until bubbles appear on the top, about 1 to 1½ minutes. Turn the pancakes and cook on the other side until golden brown, about 1 minute.

Serve right away or keep warm in a 250° oven.

* Toast walnuts in a single layer on an unoiled baking tray at 350° for 5 to 10 minutes, until fragrant and golden brown.
** Or pulse about 6 tablespoons of rolled oats in the blender or food processor to make ¼ cup of oat flour.

PER 4.5-OUNCE SERVING: 243 CALORIES, 7.8 G PROTEIN, 10.6 G FAT, 31.1 G CARBOHYDRATES, 1.7 G SATURATED FATTY ACIDS, 0 MG CHOLESTEROL, 469.5 MG SODIUM, 3.9 G TOTAL DIETARY FIBER

smoked cheddar waffles

The smoked Cheddar, Dijon mustard, and scallions in these very savory buttermilk waffles are good paired with poached or scrambled eggs and salsa. Go right ahead and pile the eggs and salsa on top of the waffles; you won't be sorry. If you use a deeper "Belgian" type waffle maker, the yield will be six or seven waffles instead of eight. Be sure not to overmix the batter.

For a nice complement, try with steamed asparagus or broccoli on the side.

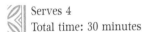
Serves 4
Total time: 30 minutes

^{2}/$_3$ cup unbleached white flour
^{2}/$_3$ cup rye flour
^{1}/$_4$ teaspoon baking soda
1 teaspoon baking powder
^{1}/$_2$ teaspoon salt
2 eggs
1 cup buttermilk
2 tablespoons melted butter
2 tablespoons chopped scallions
^{1}/$_2$ teaspoon Dijon mustard
^{3}/$_4$ cup grated smoked Cheddar cheese

In a large bowl, sift together the two flours, baking soda, baking powder, and salt. In a separate bowl, beat the eggs lightly and stir in the buttermilk, butter, scallions, mustard, and grated cheese. Add the egg mixture to the dry ingredients and stir just until combined. Let the waffle batter sit for about 10 minutes, until you see some bubbles on top.

Meanwhile, preheat the waffle iron. Use ^{1}/$_3$ cup of batter for each waffle and bake according to the instructions that came with your waffle iron.

PER 5.5-OUNCE SERVING: 346 CALORIES, 15 G PROTEIN, 17.2 G FAT, 33.2 G CARBOHYDRATES, 9.5 G SATURATED FATTY ACIDS, 172 MG CHOLESTEROL, 741.4 MG SODIUM, 3.4 G TOTAL DIETARY FIBER

whole grain waffles

It's your day off, maybe even the first day of vacation. You've turned off your cell phone. You got up early, not to make a hurried dash out the door, but to take in the unrushed pleasure of the cool morning air.

What better way to enjoy such a morning than a hardy, healthy, homey breakfast? Fill your kitchen with the aroma of waffles sizzling in the iron and coffee brewing or tea steeping in the pot. Relax and browse through page 45 for tips on making perfect waffles.

Serves 4
Preparation time: 10 minutes
Sitting time: 10 minutes
Baking time: 25 to 35 minutes

dry ingredients
1 ¼ cups unbleached white flour

½ cup whole wheat pastry flour

2 tablespoons sugar

1 tablespoon baking powder

½ teaspoon baking soda

1 teaspoon salt

¼ cup flax seeds, ground*

¼ cup cornmeal

wet ingredients
2 eggs

1 ½ cups milk

1 tablespoon vegetable oil

* *Use an electric spice or coffee grinder to grind the seeds.*

In a large bowl, sift together the white and whole wheat flours, sugar, baking powder, baking soda, and salt. Add the ground flax seeds and cornmeal and mix well. In a separate bowl, lightly beat the eggs and stir in the milk and oil. Pour the liquid mixture into the dry ingredients and stir just enough to combine. Let the batter sit for about 10 minutes before baking.

Preheat the waffle iron.

Use ⅓ cup of batter for each waffle and bake according to the directions for your waffle iron. You may want to lightly oil the iron to prevent sticking.

PER 7-OUNCE SERVING: 388 CALORIES, 14.3 G PROTEIN, 11.2 G FAT, 58 G CARBOHYDRATES, 3.3 G SATURATED FATTY ACIDS, 138.6 MG CHOLESTEROL, 1051.4 MG SODIUM, 5 G TOTAL DIETARY FIBER

yeasted waffles

Yeasted waffles are really, truly, positively wonderful. It may be said, ahem, that they rise above all others. Crisp on the outside, delicate on the inside, the extra time dedicated to making them is worth it.

Our waffles are perfect for most of the traditional toppings used on griddlecakes, but they're so good themselves that we caution you not to smother them.

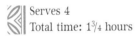

Serves 4
Total time: 1¾ hours

½ teaspoon rapid-rise yeast*

2 cups unbleached white flour

½ teaspoon salt

2 eggs

2 cups milk

¼ cup butter, melted

½ teaspoon pure vanilla extract

We use Fleischmanns brand, which is available in supermarkets.

In a large bowl, mix together the yeast, flour, and salt. In a separate bowl, beat the eggs and mix in the milk, melted butter, and vanilla. Pour the wet mixture into the dry ingredients and stir just to combine.

Cover the batter and set it aside at room temperature to rise for 1½ hours. Set the table and get ready for fun eating.

Preheat the waffle iron. Use ⅓ cup of batter for each waffle and bake according to the directions that came with your waffle iron.

PER 7.5-OUNCE SERVING: 415 CALORIES, 13.8 G PROTEIN, 17.6 G FAT, 49.3 G CARBOHYDRATES, 9.6 G SATURATED FATTY ACIDS, 171.7 MG CHOLESTEROL, 512.6 MG SODIUM, 1.6 G TOTAL DIETARY FIBER

gingered peach butter

The Pennsylvania Dutch are famous for their fruit butters—especially apple butter. Made from puréed fresh fruit and spices, they are baked until deliciously thick and smooth. Try this spread on toast, muffins, biscuits, waffles, or pancakes.

Fruit butters can be prepared in small batches in the summertime when the fruit is ripest and sweetest. Packed into glass jars and frozen until the holidays, they make absolutely perfect gifts adorned with a ribbon or two.

6 ripe peaches (about 3 pounds)
6 tablespoons brown sugar, packed
8 slices fresh ginger root
(¼ inch thick)

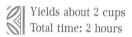
Yields about 2 cups
Total time: 2 hours

Preheat the oven to 325°.

Rinse, peel, and pit the peaches and cut them into large chunks. Place them in a nonreactive saucepan, cover, and cook on medium-low heat, stirring frequently, for about 20 minutes, until softened.

Purée the peaches through a food mill or in a food processor. Stir in the sugar and ginger slices and pour the mixture into an 8-inch square nonreactive baking pan. Bake uncovered for about 1¼ hours, stirring every 15 to 20 minutes, until it has cooked down to about half of its original volume and is thick and spreadable. Remove from the oven and discard the ginger slices. Cool.

Pack Gingered Peach Butter in a jar or plastic container with a tightly fitting lid and store in the refrigerator. It will keep chilled for up to 1 week and frozen for at least 2 months.

PER 1-OUNCE SERVING: 26 CALORIES, 0.3 G PROTEIN, 0 G FAT, 6.7 G CARBOHYDRATES, 0 G SATURATED FATTY ACIDS, 0 MG CHOLESTEROL, 1.2 MG SODIUM, 0.7 G TOTAL DIETARY FIBER

greek wheatberries & peaches

Robin Wichman and Tricia Hackett (two enthusiastic, hardworking former Moosewood employees) indulged in many wonderful varieties of creamy yogurt while bicycling in southern Europe. With their encouragement, we have re-created one of their favorites from Greece.

The chewy texture of wheatberries is a pleasant surprise and a nutritious addition. We suggest cooking extra wheatberries while you're at it—once they are cooked, this dish is very quick to assemble. You can easily double the recipe.

Greek Wheatberries & Peaches can play many roles. Try it for breakfast, as a snack or dessert, and as a side dish for a spicy curry or savory stew.

4 ripe peaches

1/8 teaspoon ground cinnamon (optional)

1/8 teaspoon ground cardamom (optional)

2 cups nonfat plain yogurt

1/2 cup cooked wheatberries (see Note)

1/4 cup sugar, or to taste

Serves 4
Total time: 20 minutes using cooked wheatberries

Peel and chop the peaches and sprinkle with the cinnamon and/or cardamom. Stir in the yogurt and wheatberries. Add sugar to taste.

Serve immediately.

PER 8-OUNCE SERVING: 216 CALORIES, 9.4 G PROTEIN, 0.7 G FAT, 45.6 G CARBOHYDRATES, 0.2 G SATURATED FATTY ACIDS, 2 MG CHOLESTEROL, 92 MG SODIUM, 2.5 G TOTAL DIETARY FIBER

note *For enough cooked wheatberries to double our recipe, soak 1/2 cup of raw wheatberries at room temperature in water to cover for 8 to 24 hours. (We tried skipping this step, but it didn't work).*

Drain and rinse the soaked wheatberries, place them in a saucepan, and add fresh water to cover by 2 inches. Bring to a boil, lower the heat, cover, and simmer about 1 to 1 1/2 hours, until tender. Drain well and chill for about 20 minutes before using in this recipe.

Drained, cooked wheatberries can be stored in a sealed container in the refrigerator for up to one week and in the freezer for several months. They make a delicious addition to pilafs, chickpea salads, brothy soups, and vegetable stews.

huevos rancheros

This is a simple version of the traditional Mexican dish. Make it easy with just tortillas, eggs, and salsa, or make it special by adding the extras. You can choose to make it with 1 or 2 eggs per person. To really go all out, add side dishes of beans and Spicy Cantaloupe Salad (page 96).

We pan-toast the tortillas, but you could also deep-fry or oven-toast them.

Serves 4
Total time: 30 minutes

In a saucepan, warm the salsa, tomatoes, and cilantro until hot but not simmering. Keep warm on very low heat.

Preheat the oven to 300°.

In a heavy skillet on medium-high heat, warm a teaspoon of oil. Add a tortilla and cook until just beginning to brown, about 30 seconds. With tongs, turn over and cook for about 10 seconds. Place the tortilla on a large sheet of foil and repeat with the remaining tortillas, adding more oil as needed. Wrap the stack of tortillas and place in the oven to keep warm.

Fry the eggs in the skillet until well set on the bottom; then sprinkle with cheese, if using. Cover the pan and cook until the eggs are set.

easy tomato salsa

1 cup commercial salsa*
1 fresh tomato, chopped
1 tablespoon chopped fresh cilantro

1 tablespoon vegetable oil
4 corn or flour tortillas (6 inches)
4 to 8 eggs

optional extras

1 cup grated Cheddar cheese
1/4 cup chopped red onions or scallions
1/2 cup sliced black or green olives
1 Hass avocado, cut into wedges
1 to 2 tablespoons chopped fresh cilantro

* Our current favorites are Herdez and Pace brands.

To serve, place a warm tortilla on each plate and top it with a fried egg and a generous portion of salsa. Sprinkle on the extras of your choice.

PER 6.5-OUNCE SERVING: 222 CALORIES, 10.6 G PROTEIN, 11.3 G FAT, 19.8 G CARBOHYDRATES, 3.1 G SATURATED FATTY ACIDS, 264.4 MG CHOLESTEROL, 360.3 MG SODIUM, 2.7 G TOTAL DIETARY FIBER

For 2 cups of homemade tomato salsa, heat 1 teaspoon of vegetable oil and sauté 1 cup of chopped onions, 5 minced garlic cloves, and 1 seeded and minced fresh chile for about 5 minutes. Add 1 teaspoon each of salt, ground cumin, and ground coriander; then stir in 3 cups of chopped fresh tomatoes and 1/3 cup of chopped fresh cilantro. Cook for about 7 minutes.

plum butter with orange

This slightly tart fruit spread is made from the magenta Santa Rosa plums that are commonly sold in supermarkets in summer and fall. It's a thick, smooth, and creamy dark purple spread—absolutely delicious on buttered toast, muffins, scones, or biscuits.

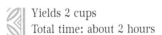 Yields 2 cups
Total time: about 2 hours

2 pounds Santa Rosa plums
(about 8)
$1/4$ cup water
$1/3$ cup sugar
1 tablespoon freshly grated
orange peel

Preheat the oven to 325°.

Rinse and pit the plums and cut them into large chunks. Place the plums, water, sugar, and orange peel in a 2-quart nonreactive pot. Cook on medium-low heat for 30 to 40 minutes, stirring frequently until softened.

Purée the plums through a food mill or in a food processor and pour into an 8-inch square nonreactive baking pan. Bake for 1 to $1^1/4$ hours, stirring every 15 to 20 minutes. When the plum butter thickens and is reduced to about half of its original volume, remove from the oven and allow to cool to room temperature.

Pack the plum butter in small covered jars or containers and chill. It will keep for up to 1 week in the refrigerator and for at least 2 months in the freezer.

PER 1.5-OUNCE SERVING: 42 CALORIES, 0.4 G PROTEIN, 0.3 G FAT, 10.2 G CARBOHYDRATES, 0 G SATURATED FATTY ACIDS, 0 MG CHOLESTEROL, 0.1 MG SODIUM, 0.8 G TOTAL DIETARY FIBER

tempeh sausage

If you grew up with sausage patties on Sunday morning and would like a vegetarian alternative to fill that niche, try these. They're dee-lish! The good cooking of Susan Jane Cheney, former Moosewood chef and forever Moosewood friend, was the inspiration for these sausages.

Tempeh has a chewy, meaty texture and readily soaks up the savory seasonings of sage, thyme, and soy sauce. What's particularly nice about these patties is that, unlike high-fat meat sausages, they are oven-baked to a lovely brown with only a little oil.

Yields 24 small patties
Preparation time: 30 minutes
Baking time: 10 minutes

16 ounces tempeh
2 1/2 to 3 tablespoons vegetable oil
1 teaspoon dried sage
1 teaspoon dried thyme
1 teaspoon salt
1/4 teaspoon ground black pepper
1 tablespoon soy sauce
2 tablespoons unbleached white flour

Preheat the oven to 400°. Generously oil a baking sheet.

Break up the tempeh and steam it in a basket steamer for about 10 minutes. When cool enough to handle, crumble it into a bowl and mix in 2 tablespoons of the oil and all of the remaining ingredients.

Form the tempeh mixture into 1-inch balls or make larger ones, if you prefer. Place the balls on the prepared baking sheet and press them down into patties about 1/4-inch thick. Brush the tops with the remaining oil.

Bake for about 5 minutes, until the tops are browned. Use a spatula to flip the patties over and then bake for 5 minutes more, or until browned.

PER 0.75-OUNCE SERVING: 52 CALORIES, 3.6 G PROTEIN, 3.5 G FAT, 2.3 G CARBOHYDRATES, 0.8 G SATURATED FATTY ACIDS, 0 MG CHOLESTEROL, 133.7 MG SODIUM, 0.1 G TOTAL DIETARY FIBER

quick cinnamon biscuits

To make most biscuits, you have to cut fat into the dry ingredients, but with these cream biscuits, the ingredients are just stirred together and patted out, a process that takes less time and results in unusually tender biscuits.

Quick Cinnamon Biscuits are best warm. Leftovers can be reheated in a toaster oven at 300°.

Yields 9 biscuits
Preparation time: 25 minutes
Baking time: about 30 minutes

cinnamon sugar mix
¼ cup brown sugar, packed

2 teaspoons ground cinnamon

1 teaspoon ground nutmeg

biscuit dough
2½ cups unbleached white flour

2 tablespoons brown sugar, packed

2 teaspoons baking powder

½ teaspoon salt

1½ cups plus 1 tablespoon heavy cream

icing
3 tablespoons confectioners' sugar

2 to 3 teaspoons milk or heavy cream

✂ Preheat the oven to 400°.

In a small bowl, combine the brown sugar, cinnamon, and nutmeg and set aside.

In a large bowl, stir together the flour, brown sugar, baking powder, and salt. Add 1½ cups of the cream and stir briskly until the dough forms a ball, about 1 minute. With your hands, fold the dough over a few times in the bowl, until all of the loose bits are incorporated and the dough is smooth.

Turn the dough out onto a lightly floured surface. Lightly flour your hands and gently pat the dough into a ½-inch-thick rectangle about 9 x 13 inches. Brush the surface of the dough with the remaining tablespoon of cream. Sprinkle evenly with the cinnamon sugar mix.

Starting from a long side, roll the dough into a cylinder. Slice into 9 equal rounds. Place the biscuit rounds, cut side down, in an unoiled 8-inch square baking dish or a pie plate. Bake for about 30 minutes, until the biscuits are lightly browned.

While the biscuits bake, prepare the icing. Mix together the confectioners' sugar and milk or cream until smooth. When you remove the biscuits from the oven, immediately drizzle them with the icing. Serve warm.

PER 3-OUNCE SERVING: 301 CALORIES, 4.1 G PROTEIN, 15 G FAT, 38 G CARBOHYDRATES, 9.2 G SATURATED FATTY ACIDS, 54.1 MG CHOLESTEROL, 224 MG SODIUM, 1.2 G TOTAL DIETARY FIBER

soups

soups ✿ Everybody loves soup. It fortifies the body and soothes the soul. It's one of those comforting first loves that quietly sustain us from infancy into venerable old age.

Soup generously stretches to help you feed a crowd. It can lend a gracious touch to an elegant, well-designed dinner. Whether nourishing the masses, impressing the VIPs, treating your friends and family well, or taking good care of yourself, when you've got good soup on hand, it's like gold.

Great soup is a cornerstone of the menu at Moosewood, where we make four or five soups every day. Our soups burst with nutrition and flavor, and we're proud of them. So far we've developed literally hundreds of soups, and there's no end in sight. When our regular customers phone, the most frequently asked question is about the soups of the day. Recently the restaurant began selling frozen soups to take home, and they're becoming very popular. You too can freeze soups. We recommend freezing in the portions you'll want to reheat.

Soup is a flexible medium that invites, even demands, the personal touch and flights of fancy; it accommodates all kinds of variation and adaptation. It's the place to be frugal and transform leftovers into a brand-new meal.

To make good soup, invest in a heavy pot with a lid. With nonstick pots, you can cook with less oil and washing is easier. A heat diffuser, also called flame tamer, is handy because it evenly distributes the heat while soups simmer or gently reheat. Almost all of our soups are okay made with water, but many, especially brothy ones, are even better if made with a flavorful stock. At Moosewood, we make a big pot of vegetable stock every night and the last chore before closing the restaurant is to turn it off and refrigerate it for use the next day. Read about how to make soup stocks at home in the pages that follow.

Most of our recipes begin with sautéing onions, garlic, and/or spices in a little oil to release and mellow their strong flavors before adding liquids. To thicken soup, we occasionally use a roux or cornstarch, but most often we prefer to make soup thick and creamy by puréeing all or a portion of it in a blender. When we want a soup to be both thick and also chunky with distinct textures, colors, and flavors, we purée only a portion of it and then stir the purée back in for creaminess. Stir in quick-cooking ingredients such as peas, mushrooms, fresh herbs, and greens very near the end of cooking to keep their colors bright and the texture perfect.

Soup can be served for any meal. Start with a breakfast of bracing Minimalist Miso Soup to fend off a cold morning and start your day with the spirit of the samurai. At mid-day, make soup the proverbial "meal in itself" with our Curried Fish Chowder, Spinach Coconut Soup, or Spanish Bean Soup. Take a delicious homemade soup to work for a comforting lift. In the evening, have a bowl of Artichoke Soup Provençal or Southeast Asian Fruit Soup as a stimulating first course, or make soup the main event with a salad and bread. Stir it up!

vegetable stocks

While many soups and stews can be made with plain water, they often taste even better when made with stock—and brothy soups, especially, can really benefit from the added flavor of a stock.

Here are four of our favorite vegetable stocks that we use at Moosewood: Basic Vegetable Stock, Garlic Peppercorn Stock, Mock Chicken Stock, and Gingery Asian Stock. Check out our Lemongrass Stock (page 66) if you're looking for a stock with Thai flair. Choose the one that best suits your needs.

There's no need to peel garlic for stock: just quickly smash it. Hold a flat wooden salad server or broad-bladed knife over the clove and give it a sharp blow with the heel of your hand. Stock is easy to make and very worth the effort. We recommend you make it a regular kitchen staple. See pages 450 and 473 for more information on bouillon and stock.

Yields about 8 cups
Preparation time: 20 minutes
Cooking time: about 1 hour

basic vegetable stock

10 cups water

2 onions, quartered

2 sweet potatoes or 4 carrots, peeled and quartered

2 potatoes, scrubbed and thickly sliced

2 celery stalks and/or a cup of mushroom stems

2 garlic cloves, smashed

2 fresh parsley sprigs

1 bay leaf

4 allspice berries

4 whole black peppercorns

$^{1}/_{2}$ teaspoon salt

garlic peppercorn stock

10 cups water

3 whole heads of garlic, broken into
  cloves

2 potatoes, scrubbed and thickly
  sliced

2 carrots, peeled and quartered

3 celery stalks, coarsely chopped

1/4 teaspoon whole black peppercorns

4 fresh parsley sprigs

3 bay leaves

1/2 teaspoon salt

1/4 teaspoon dried thyme

gingery asian stock

10 cups water

2 leeks *or* 2 bunches of scallions *or*
  2 onions

5 carrots, peeled and quartered

4 celery stalks with leaves, chopped

10 garlic cloves, smashed

5 dried shiitake mushrooms
  (optional)

3-inch piece of fresh ginger root,
  sliced

6 whole cloves

3 parsley sprigs

1/4 teaspoon Sichuan peppercorns

1/2 teaspoon salt

mock chicken stock

10 cups water

5 cups chopped onions

2 small heads of garlic, broken into
  cloves

3 potatoes, scubbed and thickly
  sliced

3 cups peeled chopped carrots

3 cups chopped celery

1/2 bunch of fresh parsley

4 bay leaves

1 teaspoon dried thyme

1 1/2 teaspoons turmeric

1/2 teaspoon salt

Combine the ingredients for your preferred stock in a large soup pot, cover, and bring to a boil on high heat. Lower the heat and, still covered, simmer for about 1 hour.

Allow to cool slightly and then strain the stock through a sieve or colander. Use it immediately, or refrigerate it in a covered container for up to 4 days, or freeze it for up to 6 months.

minimalist miso soup

This soup (affectionately known as Mini Miso) is one of the simplest versions we serve regularly at home. Made with a traditional *dashi* or stock, it's divine; but if you don't have the ingredients handy for the dashi, hot water will still make an excellent soup. Kombu is a type of dried seaweed and shiitake are dried mushrooms with a distinctive (and wonderful) flavor. While the dashi cooks, you can prepare the soup ingredients, so as soon as the dashi is ready, soup's on. Although the soup is not ruined if the broth boils, when it does, miso's highly useful digestive and antibacterial enzymes will be destroyed.

Serves 4
Total time: 25 minutes

dashi

5-inch-long piece of kombu
    (page 468)
4 dried shiitake mushrooms
5 cups cold water

soup

1 cleaned leek (page 460) or
    4 scallions, thinly sliced
1/2 cup peeled and grated carrots
2 cups hot water
1/3 to 1/2 cup miso
1 cup tiny cubes of firm tofu
    (about 5 ounces)

Place the kombu and shiitake in a saucepan and add the cold water. Cover and slowly bring to a boil; then uncover and simmer the dashi for 10 to 15 minutes.

Meanwhile, in a separate saucepan, simmer the leeks or scallions and the carrots in the water on low heat for 5 to 10 minutes, until tender. Place the miso in a small bowl, ladle in about a cup of the hot cooking water, and with the back of a spoon, press and stir to make a smooth sauce. Stir the miso back into the vegetables and broth and gently heat, being careful not to boil.

Strain the dashi through a sieve lined with cheesecloth to remove any grit. Discard the kombu. Rinse the shiitake, remove the stems, and slice the caps. Add the strained hot dashi, sliced shiitake, and tofu cubes to the soup. Serve hot.

PER 16-OUNCE SERVING: 108 CALORIES, 6.1 G PROTEIN, 2.9 G FAT, 16.2 G CARBOHYDRATES, 0.4 G SATURATED FATTY ACIDS, 0 MG CHOLESTEROL, 708.9 MG SODIUM, 2.8 G TOTAL DIETARY FIBER

vegetable barley soup

During the cold-weather months, Moosewood cooks know to make an especially large pot of this soup: both customers and staff always want big, steaming bowls of it. Nothing beats lots of vegetables, rich miso-flavored stock, and thick chewy barley, a substantive grain that helps our bodies generate warmth and energy during the long winter hours.

It's best to get the barley cooking first and then prepare the rest of the ingredients for the soup. You may even want to cook the barley the day before; then the soup can be made in about an hour.

Serves 6
Total time: 1¼ to 1½ hours

½ cup raw hulled barley*

7 cups water

3 tablespoons olive oil

2 cups chopped onions

¼ teaspoon salt

1½ cups cubed white potatoes

½ cup diced celery

1 cup diced red or yellow bell peppers

1 cup peeled and diced carrots

1 cup cut green beans (1-inch pieces)

1 cup cubed yellow or green summer
  squash

1 cup chopped mushrooms

¼ teaspoon dried marjoram

½ teaspoon dried thyme

2 tablespoons dry sherry

3 tablespoons barley miso

ground black pepper to taste

⅓ cup chopped fresh parsley

 chopped scallions

*In case you have cooked barley on hand,
 ½ cup raw yields about 2¼ cups cooked.*

Rinse the barley and place it in a medium saucepan with 3 cups of the water. Bring to a boil, cover, and simmer on low heat until tender, 1¼ to 1½ hours. Drain.

Warm the oil in a large nonreactive soup pot. Add the onions and salt and cook on medium-high heat, stirring occasionally, until lightly browned, about 8 minutes. Meanwhile, heat the remaining 4 cups of water to a simmer in a saucepan.

Stir the potatoes, celery, bell peppers, carrots, green beans, squash, and mushrooms into the onions until well coated with oil. Add the marjoram, thyme, and sherry. Cook for 2 minutes more, stirring constantly.

Pour the simmering water into the soup pot. Ladle out ½ cup of water and combine with the miso to form a smooth saucy paste; then return it to the pot. Add pepper to taste, cover, and simmer until the vegetables are tender, about 15 minutes. Add the drained barley to the soup, stir in the parsley, and cook for 5 minutes more. Serve topped with scallions.

PER 15-OUNCE SERVING: 274 CALORIES, 5.5 G PROTEIN, 8.3 G FAT, 46.5 G CARBOHYDRATES, 1.2 G SATURATED FATTY ACIDS, 0 MG CHOLESTEROL, 389.4 MG SODIUM, 7.5 G TOTAL DIETARY FIBER

thai coconut soup

Our vegetarian adaptation of this classic Thai soup uses a lemongrass stock that Moosewood cook Sara Robbins developed especially for the recipe. The stock is flavorful, yet delicate, and would be good in other Thai-style soups and sauces that traditionally use chicken stock. So while you're at it, consider making a double batch of lemongrass stock and freezing half for later. Before adding the leek to the stock, be sure to chop and thoroughly clean it to remove embedded sand.

This soup has a pleasant creamy yellow color and a wonderful coconut and ginger aroma. Make it as mild or hot as you like.

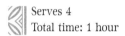
Serves 4
Total time: 1 hour

In a large soup pot, combine the water, lemongrass, celery, leeks or onions, carrots, ginger, peppercorns, salt, and coriander, if using. Bring to a boil, then reduce the heat, cover, and simmer for 35 to 45 minutes.

Drain the vegetables in a strainer and return the stock to the soup pot. Then press the vegetables, squeezing their juices into the stock. Add the coconut milk, lime juice, cayenne, and turmeric and bring to a simmer. Add the tofu, mushrooms, cilantro, and salt, and cook gently for 3 to 5 minutes.

Serve garnished with minced scallions and fresh cilantro.

lemongrass stock

6 cups water

3 fresh lemongrass stalks, coarsely chopped

2 celery stalks, chopped

1 leek or onion, coarsely chopped

1 large carrot, peeled and chopped

3-inch piece of fresh ginger root, sliced

1/4 teaspoon whole black peppercorns

1/2 teaspoon salt

1/2 teaspoon coriander seeds (optional)

soup

1 3/4 cups reduced-fat or regular coconut milk (14-ounce can)

2 tablespoons fresh lime juice

pinch of cayenne, or to taste

1/2 teaspoon turmeric

1/2 cake firm tofu, cut into bite-sized cubes (6 ounces)

1 cup thinly sliced mushrooms

1 tablespoon chopped fresh cilantro

1/2 teaspoon salt

minced scallions and fresh cilantro

PER 15-OUNCE SERVING: 151 CALORIES, 6.2 G PROTEIN, 10.8 G FAT, 8.9 G CARBOHYDRATES, 5.6 G SATURATED FATTY ACIDS, 0 MG CHOLESTEROL, 627 MG SODIUM, 1.3 G TOTAL DIETARY FIBER

thai carrot soup

Here's a soup that generated a lot of excitement at one of our Southeast Asian ethnic nights. The lemongrass stock adds the mysterious flavor that is so characteristic of Thai cuisine. If you make the stock the day before (or made a batch of lemongrass stock that's in the freezer waiting for just this moment), the soup can be ready within 35 minutes.

Creamy coconut milk gives this vibrant golden-orange vegetable soup its silken texture. The chile and ginger add exactly the right amount of spicy warmth. Serve garnished with lemon or lime wedges and sprigs of fresh cilantro or basil—Thai basil, if you can find it.

 Serves 6
Total time: 1 hour (including making stock)

2 tablespoons vegetable oil

2 cups chopped onions

2 garlic cloves, minced or pressed

1 teaspoon grated fresh ginger root

1 fresh green chile (seeded for a
  milder hot)

2 teaspoons ground coriander

1 cup chopped tomatoes

1 cup chopped red bell peppers

4 cups peeled and chopped carrots

1 teaspoon salt

1 recipe Lemongrass Stock (opposite)

1¾ cups reduced-fat coconut milk
  (14-ounce can)

2 tablespoons minced fresh cilantro
  or Thai basil

Warm the oil in a medium soup pot. Add the onions and sauté for about 10 minutes, until golden and softened. Stir in the garlic, ginger, chile, and coriander and cook for 1 minute, stirring constantly.

Add the tomatoes, bell peppers, carrots, salt, and the lemongrass stock and bring to a boil. Cover the soup pot, reduce the heat, and simmer until the carrots are soft, about 15 minutes. Remove from the heat and stir in the coconut milk.

Purée the soup in batches in a blender until smooth and creamy. Stir in the cilantro or basil and reheat gently, if needed.

PER 14-OUNCE SERVING: 195 CALORIES, 4.1 G PROTEIN, 11.1 G FAT, 22.2 G CARBOHYDRATES, 4.8 G SATURATED FATTY ACIDS, 0 MG CHOLESTEROL, 676.5 MG SODIUM, 4.8 G TOTAL DIETARY FIBER

asian cabbage soup

Slowly browned onions combined with lots of garlic and ginger and a shiitake stock give this thick, stew-like soup its deep underlying flavor. A little chili paste adds warmth without overpowering the subtler scallions, cabbage, and shiitake. If you wish, stir a few drops of sesame oil into each bowl.

To save time, you can cut the vegetables for the stock while the shiitake soak.

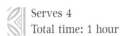

Serves 4
Total time: 1 hour

In a small saucepan, bring 2 cups of the water and the shiitake mushrooms to a boil. Remove from the heat and soak for 15 to 20 minutes, until softened. Strain the soaking liquid into a 2-quart pot, and set the shiitake aside.

Add the remaining 4 cups of water, the scallions, carrots, daikon, and ginger to the soaking liquid. Cover, bring to a simmer, and cook gently for 30 minutes. Strain and return the stock to the soup pot.

While the stock is simmering, heat the oil in a wok or heavy skillet and add the onions. Cook on medium heat for about 15 minutes, stirring frequently, until the onions are well browned but not scorched. Add the garlic and sauté for 3 minutes. Mix in the ginger, cabbage, and carrots and cook, stirring often, until the cabbage is limp and crisp-tender, about 10 minutes. Add the vegetables to the strained stock and stir in the chili paste and soy sauce.

asian-style stock

6 cups water
8 dried shiitake mushrooms
1 cup scallion tops (the green parts)
1 cup thinly sliced carrots
1 cup thinly sliced daikon
8 to 10 thin slices fresh ginger root

sauté

2 tablespoons vegetable or peanut oil
2 cups thinly sliced onions
2 tablespoons minced garlic
    (3 to 4 cloves)
1 tablespoon peeled grated fresh
    ginger root
4 cups thinly sliced napa or savoy
    cabbage
1 cup sliced carrots, cut into
    matchsticks
1 teaspoon Chinese chili paste
2 to 3 tablespoons soy sauce, or to
    taste

hijiki or sliced scallions

Remove and discard the shiitake stems. Thinly slice the caps, add them to the soup, and reheat until just boiling. Ladle the soup into bowls. Top with hijiki or scallions, or both.

PER 12-OUNCE SERVING: 272 CALORIES, 8.4 G PROTEIN, 8.1 G FAT, 49.4 G CARBOHYDRATES, 2 G SATURATED FATTY ACIDS, 0 MG CHOLESTEROL, 490.5 MG SODIUM, 10.7 G TOTAL DIETARY FIBER

valle d'aosta cabbage soup

In the Alpine region of Italy, no good cook would consider throwing away stale bread when it can be used to thicken an earthy and wonderfully delicious soup like this. Most any kind of bread will do—whole wheat, rye, sourdough, or white.

With this hearty soup, you won't need much else for a cold-weather meal. Try Pretty Beets & Carrots (page 106), Tempeh Sausage (page 58), or Roasted Caramelized Balsamic Onions (page 125). What better choice than Almond Biscotti (page 408) for dessert?

Serves 4 to 6
Preparation time: 35 minutes
Baking time: 25 to 30 minutes

4 cups cubed bread
   (about ¹/₂ pound)
5 tablespoons butter
5 to 6 cups thinly sliced or grated
   cabbage
¹/₂ teaspoon ground nutmeg
¹/₂ teaspoon ground black pepper
¹/₂ teaspoon salt, or more to taste
6 cups vegetable stock or broth
2 cups grated Fontina cheese

Preheat the oven to 350°. Bring a large pot of water to a boil.

Spread the bread cubes evenly in a 9 x 13-inch casserole dish or a 2-quart ovenproof dish. If the cubes aren't dry, toast them briefly in the oven. Melt 3 tablespoons of the butter and drizzle over the bread. Set aside.

When the water boils, blanch the cabbage just until tender, about 2 minutes. Drain well. Spread the cabbage over the bread. Melt the remaining 2 tablespoons of butter and stir in the nutmeg, pepper, and salt, and pour the seasoned butter on the cabbage and bread. Pour the stock over everything and evenly spread the cheese on top.

Bake until the cheese melts and starts to brown, 25 to 30 minutes.

Serve immediately.

PER 13-OUNCE SERVING: 374 CALORIES, 14.1 G PROTEIN, 23.2 G FAT, 28.2 G CARBOHYDRATES, 13.5 G SATURATED FATTY ACIDS, 70.1 MG CHOLESTEROL, 961.9 MG SODIUM, 3.1 G TOTAL DIETARY FIBER

artichoke soup provençal

This brothy vegetable soup shows off artichokes and the flavor combination of sherry, saffron, and citrus, which is uniquely characteristic of the Provence region of France. The other vegetables are all staple pantry items: onions, potatoes, carrots, and celery—so next time you shop, pick up some artichoke hearts, a lemon, and a juicy orange and you'll be all set to make this lovely soup.

Try serving this with Pretty Beets & Carrots (page 106) or with Green Bean & Walnut Salad (page 108).

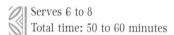 Serves 6 to 8
Total time: 50 to 60 minutes

1 tablespoon olive oil

3 cups chopped onions

1 1/2 cups chopped potatoes

2 1/2 cups peeled and chopped carrots

1/2 cup chopped celery

1 1/2 teaspoons salt

2 bay leaves

5 cups vegetable stock or water

5 artichoke hearts, cut into quarters
    (14-ounce can)*

2 tablespoons dry sherry

1/4 teaspoon crumbled saffron

1 tablespoon fresh lemon juice

1/4 cup orange juice

1/2 teaspoon freshly grated orange
    peel

ground black pepper to taste

chopped fresh parsley
thinly sliced lemon rounds

* A 9-ounce frozen package, defrosted, will also work fine, and some brands come already quartered.

Warm the olive oil in a nonreactive soup pot. Add the the onions, potatoes, carrots, celery, salt, and bay leaves and sauté on medium heat for 10 minutes, stirring often. Add the stock or water and bring to a boil; then lower the heat, cover, and simmer for about 15 minutes.

Add the artichoke hearts, sherry, and saffron to the soup pot and continue to simmer for 5 minutes. Stir in the lemon juice, orange juice, and orange peel and simmer for an additional 5 minutes. Season to taste with black pepper. Remove and discard the bay leaves.

Serve garnished with chopped parsley and thin slices of fresh lemon.

PER 10-OUNCE SERVING: 127 CALORIES, 3.6 G PROTEIN, 2.1 G FAT, 25.2 G CARBOHYDRATES, 0.3 G SATURATED FATTY ACIDS, 0 MG CHOLESTEROL, 620.2 MG SODIUM, 5.5 G TOTAL DIETARY FIBER

carolina vegetable soup

Make this hearty soup with a good, mildly smoky, prepared BBQ sauce. We are partial to locally produced sauces: Ralph's Mamma's BBQ Sauce and Dinosaur Barbeque Sauce are two favorites. We hope you have a good local favorite, too.

The flavor of this soup improves as it sits, making it a good candidate for ahead-of-time cooking.

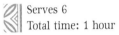
Serves 6
Total time: 1 hour

3 tablespoons vegetable oil

2 cups chopped onions

3 garlic cloves, minced or pressed

1 cup peeled and chopped carrots

1 cup peeled and cubed sweet
    potatoes

1/2 cup chopped celery

1 1/2 cups chopped zucchini

1 cup fresh, frozen, or canned lima
    beans

3/4 cup frozen corn kernels

1 1/2 cups chopped fresh tomatoes

1/2 teaspoon fresh thyme
    (1/4 teaspoon dried)

1/4 cup barbeque sauce

4 cups water

1 teaspoon salt

1/2 teaspoon ground black pepper

2 tablespoons chopped fresh parsley

Tabasco sauce or other hot pepper
    sauce to taste

2 tablespoons chopped fresh basil
    (optional)

chopped scallions

In a large soup pot, warm the oil on medium heat and sauté the onions and garlic until the onions are translucent, about 10 minutes. Add the carrots, sweet potatoes, and celery and sauté for 3 minutes. Add the zucchini, lima beans, corn, tomatoes, thyme, and barbeque sauce. Stir for a minute and then add the water, salt, and black pepper.

Cover and bring to a boil; then reduce the heat to low and cook for 20 minutes. About 5 minutes before serving, add the parsley, Tabasco sauce, and, if you wish, the basil.

Serve topped with chopped scallions.

PER 12-OUNCE SERVING: 189 CALORIES, 4.5 G PROTEIN, 8 G FAT, 27.5 G CARBOHYDRATES, 2 G SATURATED FATTY ACIDS, 0 MG CHOLESTEROL, 516.5 MG SODIUM, 5 G TOTAL DIETARY FIBER

creamy chestnut soup

Chestnuts have been used to advantage in Italian cuisine for generations. Dried and ground, they make a great bread flour or thickening agent. Here, the tender morsels grace a simple velvety soup with an elegant flavor.

Add a loaf of good bread, slices of sharp provolone, and a salad of crisp romaine and fresh juicy tomatoes tossed with a light vinaigrette, and the meal is complete.

Serves 6
Preparation time: 25 minutes
Cooking time: 35 minutes

In a soup pot, warm the butter and olive oil on medium-high heat. Sauté the leeks, garlic, and salt until the leeks are soft and tender, about 7 minutes. Add the nutmeg and rosemary and sauté for a minute or two.

Add the celery, bay leaves, potatoes, and water or stock. Bring to a boil, reduce the heat, cover, and simmer until the potatoes are tender, 5 to 7 minutes. Remove from the heat and discard the rosemary and the bay leaves.

Stir the half-and-half and ³/₄ cup of the chestnuts into the soup pot. Purée the soup in batches in a blender until smooth. Chop the remaining chestnuts into bite-sized pieces. Add them with the salt and pepper to the puréed soup.

Gently reheat and sprinkle on the parsley just before serving.

1 tablespoon butter

2 teaspoons olive oil

2 cups well rinsed and chopped leeks, the white and tender green parts

2 to 3 garlic cloves, minced or pressed

2 teaspoons salt

¹/₂ teaspoon ground nutmeg

3 sprigs of fresh rosemary, tied with string

2 cups chopped celery, stalks and leaves

2 or 3 bay leaves

4 cups diced potatoes*

3 cups water or vegetable stock

2 cups half-and-half

1¹/₂ cups dry whole chestnuts (7.4-ounce jar)

¹/₄ teaspoon salt

ground black pepper to taste

¹/₄ cup minced fresh parsley

* About 1¹/₂ pounds of potatoes will yield 4 cups diced.

PER 14-OUNCE SERVING: 328 CALORIES, 6.4 G PROTEIN, 12.9 G FAT, 48.2 G CARBOHYDRATES, 7 G SATURATED FATTY ACIDS, 33.1 MG CHOLESTEROL, 990.3 MG SODIUM, 3.4 G TOTAL DIETARY FIBER

curried spinach pea soup

There are only four main ingredients in this vivid chartreuse soup: spinach, peas, potatoes, and onions—and then a long list of curry spices. The enticing fragrance loosed in the kitchen as the soup cooks is part of its appeal. So is the color. Feel free to play with the amounts of ginger, cayenne, and lemon juice to shift the emphasis.

Penny Goldin developed this soup as a tribute to Moosewood's Tibetan employees who grew up in India—exiled from Tibet—and whose childhood memories are stimulated by these aromatic Indian fragrances.

With a soup this thick and spicy-sweet, you'll want something piquant and crisp, such as our Cucumber Peanut Salad (page 107).

Serves 6 to 8
Preparation time: 15 minutes
Cooking time: 45 minutes

5 cups water

2 teaspoons salt

4 cups diced potatoes

8 garlic cloves, peeled and left whole

1 tablespoon vegetable oil

4 cups chopped onions

1 1/2 tablespoons grated fresh
   ginger root

1 1/2 teaspoons turmeric

1 1/2 teaspoons ground cumin

1 1/2 teaspoons ground coriander

1/2 teaspoon ground cinnamon

1/2 teaspoon ground cardamom

1/8 teaspoon cayenne, or to taste

1/4 teaspoon ground black pepper

1 1/2 tablespoons fresh lemon juice

3 cups frozen green peas
   (about 15 ounces)

4 cups packed fresh spinach, rinsed
   and large stems removed

1 3/4 cups reduced-fat coconut milk
   (14-ounce can)

fresh cilantro leaves (optional)

Bring the water and salt to a boil in a large soup pot. Ease in the potatoes and garlic, cover, reduce the heat, and simmer until the potatoes are tender, about 15 minutes.

Meanwhile, in a large saucepan, warm the oil. Add the onions and sauté on medium heat, stirring frequently, until translucent, about 10 minutes. Stir the ginger, turmeric, cumin, coriander, cinnamon, cardamom, cayenne, and black pepper into the sautéed onions. Add the lemon juice and 1 cup of the potato cooking liquid, cover, and simmer for about 5 minutes.

Transfer the onion mixture to the pot of undrained cooked potatoes. Add the peas and spinach, cover, and cook for about 5 minutes, until the spinach is wilted. Stir in the coconut milk. In a blender, purée the soup in batches until smooth and creamy. Reheat gently. Serve with cilantro, if desired.

PER 12-OUNCE SERVING: 210 CALORIES, 6.3 G PROTEIN, 6.7 G FAT, 32.9 G CARBOHYDRATES, 3.2 G SATURATED FATTY ACIDS, 0 MG CHOLESTEROL, 655.7 MG SODIUM, 5.6 G TOTAL DIETARY FIBER

spinach coconut soup

This hearty and flavorful soup is a perfect example of fusion cookery. It was inspired by recipes from cultures as diverse as Southeast Asia and Australia which, themselves, bear the imprint of Indian and European cuisines.

Have a cup of this soup followed by Mixed Greens Frittata (page 244) or Mushroom Pecan Burgers (page 188), or serve it beside crunchy Cucumber Peanut Salad (page 107).

Serves 6
Preparation time: 15 minutes
Cooking time: 30 to 35 minutes

2 tablespoons vegetable oil

1½ cups chopped leeks, white and tender green parts only

4 large garlic cloves, minced or pressed

¾ teaspoon ground cumin

¾ teaspoon ground coriander

⅛ to ¼ teaspoon cayenne

½ teaspoon paprika

1 large potato, peeled and diced

½ cup raw white basmati rice

5 cups vegetable stock

pinch of salt

1¾ cups reduced-fat coconut milk (14-ounce can)

2 tablespoons fresh lemon juice

20 ounces spinach, rinsed, stemmed, and torn into large pieces

salt and ground black pepper to taste

In a 3-quart soup pot, heat the oil on medium-low heat. Add the leeks and garlic, cover, and sauté for 5 minutes, stirring occasionally. Add the cumin, coriander, cayenne, and paprika, cover, and sauté for another 5 minutes, stirring often to prevent the spices from burning.

Stir in the potatoes and basmati rice and sauté for 1 minute. Add the stock and salt. Cover, bring to a boil, lower the heat, and simmer for 15 to 20 minutes, until the rice is tender. Stir in the coconut milk, lemon juice, and spinach. When the spinach has wilted, just a minute or two, remove the soup from the heat and season with salt and pepper to taste. Serve hot.

PER 14-OUNCE SERVING: 237 CALORIES, 5.9 G PROTEIN, 11.1 G FAT, 30.3 G CARBOHYDRATES, 4.8 G SATURATED FATTY ACIDS, 0 MG CHOLESTEROL, 220.7 MG SODIUM, 3.5 G TOTAL DIETARY FIBER

squash & tomatillo soup

Mellow, sweet squash combined with tangy tomatillos and a hint of smoky chipotles in adobo sauce make this a satisfying Mexican-style soup to serve plain or with toppings. Offer the toppings in small bowls so guests can help themselves and serve with Roasted Vegetable Quesadillas (page 163) for a big enchilada of a meal.

Try butternut, Kabocha, or delicata winter squash: 2 to 3 pounds of whole winter squash will yield 6 cups peeled and cubed.

 Serves 8 to 10
Preparation time: about 40 minutes
Simmering time: 15 to 25 minutes

18 fresh tomatillos (about 2 pounds)*

4 to 5 cups chopped onions

1 tablespoon olive oil

8 garlic cloves, chopped

6 cups peeled and cubed winter squash

6 cups vegetable stock

3 cups undrained plum tomatoes, chopped (28-ounce can)

1 to 2 teaspoons minced chipotles in adobo sauce

salt and ground black pepper to taste

toppings

sour cream

chopped fresh cilantro or more minced chipotles in adobo sauce

avocado cubes, corn kernels, and/or crumbled tortilla chips

 Preheat the oven to 450°.

Remove and discard the husks of the fresh tomatillos. Rinse the tomatillos, cut them in half, and place them cut-side up in a single layer in a shallow baking dish. Roast for 30 to 35 minutes, until soft.

Meanwhile, in a soup pot, cook the onions in the olive oil on medium heat, stirring frequently for about 10 minutes, until golden. Add the garlic and cook for a couple of minutes, until fragrant. Stir in the squash, stock, and the tomatoes with their juice, cover, and bring to a boil. Lower the heat and simmer for 15 to 25 minutes, until the squash is quite tender. Add the chipotles and the roasted tomatillos.

In a blender, purée the soup in several batches and return it to the pot. Add salt, pepper, and more chipotles to taste, and gently reheat if needed.

Serve hot, with some or all of the toppings.

If you can't get fresh tomatillos, canned tomatillos are often in the Mexican section of the supermarket; Goya is a readily available brand. For this recipe, drain a 26-ounce can and add the tomatillos with the tomatoes.

PER 16-OUNCE SERVING: 129 CALORIES, 3.5 G PROTEIN, 2.1 G FAT, 27.8 G CARBOHYDRATES, 0.3 G SATURATED FATTY ACIDS, 0 MG CHOLESTEROL, 195.1 MG SODIUM, 2 G TOTAL DIETARY FIBER

fennel leek soup

When most people hear the words "Dairy Queen," they immediately think of the ice cream chain with its softy cones and ice cream cakes. But at Moosewood in the '70s, the Dairy Queen was none other than our own Linda Dickinson. Raised on a farm, Linda was never shy about using both milk *and* cream in a soup or sauce and, boy, did her food taste good!

What a switch to have her gradually become just as adept at making rich-tasting, creamy-seeming food, keeping right in step with today's health-conscious mindset. So here's LD's creamy green soup, full of spring-time flavors but, look, Ma, no dairy!

We make thrifty use of both the leek tops and the fennel's fronds and stems: Putting them in the stock intensifies and rounds out the overall flavor of the soup. To save time, you can prepare the rest of the soup ingredients while the stock simmers.

Reserve a few feathery fennel fronds to use for garnishes.

Serves 6 to 8
Total time: about 1 hour

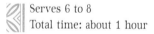

1 fresh fennel bulb, trimmed

10 cups water

3 leeks, sliced down the center and well rinsed

1 1/2 cups peeled and coarsely chopped carrots

4 cups coarsely chopped potatoes

1/2 teaspoon dried thyme

1/2 teaspoon fennel seeds

1 1/2 teaspoons salt, or more to taste

2 tablespoons olive oil

2 cups spinach, rinsed and stemmed

2 tablespoons chopped fresh dill

1 tablespoon fresh lemon juice

freshly ground black pepper to taste

thinly sliced radishes

a few fresh fennel fronds

croutons

Remove any tough outer layers from the fennel bulb, setting the tender inner bulb aside. Rinse the outer layers well and place them in a large pot with 10 cups of water. Cut off the dark green tops of the leeks, rinse well to remove any hidden sand, and stir them into the pot. Add the carrots, about half of the potatoes, the thyme, fennel seeds, and 1 teaspoon of the salt. Bring to a boil; then lower the heat, cover, and simmer the stock for about 45 minutes.

While the stock simmers, cut the fennel bulb in half and thinly slice it. Remove the root ends from the leeks, peel off the outermost layer, and chop the white and most tender green parts.

In a large soup pot, sauté the fennel and leeks in the olive oil until tender, about 10 to 15 minutes. Strain the stock and add it to the fennel and leeks. Add the rest of the potatoes and simmer until soft, about 15 minutes. Stir in the spinach, dill, lemon juice, and remaining 1/2 teaspoon of salt.

Purée the soup mixture in batches in a blender until smooth and silky. Add salt and pepper to taste and finish with a few floating radish slices, fennel fronds, and/or croutons.

PER 12-OUNCE SERVING: 157 CALORIES, 2.9 G PROTEIN, 3.9 G FAT, 29.1 G CARBOHYDRATES
0.5 G SATURATED FATTY ACIDS, 0 MG CHOLESTEROL, 633.6 MG SODIUM, 3.8 G TOTAL DIETARY FIBER

potatoes: starchy vs. waxy

Starch content is the defining factor in potato texture and usage. Russet or Idaho potatoes are the highest in starch and are best for baked potatoes, puréed soups, French fries, and potato pancakes. Waxy potatoes, such as fingerling potatoes, most red varieties, and some of the round whites, are lower in starch and hold together when cooked, an asset for salads, gratins, and stews and for roasting and boiling. Popular yellow-fleshed varieties, like Yukon Gold and Yellow Finn, are medium starchy and versatile enough for all purposes. Ashley Miller, former Moosewood member and author of *The Potato Harvest Cookbook,* gives two simple guidelines for determining a spud's starch content.

1. Cut the potato in half; if the blade is filmy or has a foamy residue, or if the spud sticks to the knife, its starch content is high.

2. If you're a science buff, make a brine of 11 parts water to 1 part salt. Drop in the potato. A high-starch potato is denser and will sink; low-starch types will float.

potato florentine soup

Comforting potato soups are among the most popular of those we serve at the restaurant. Italian flavors distinguish this beautiful creamy green soup. Serve it with Savory Cheddar Thyme Biscotti (page 400).

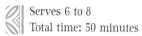
Serves 6 to 8
Total time: 50 minutes

In a soup pot, combine the oil, onions, and rosemary. Cover and cook on medium heat for 10 minutes, stirring often. Add the potatoes, salt, and water or stock and bring just to a boil. Lower the heat, cover, and simmer for about 10 minutes, until the potatoes are tender. With a slotted spoon, remove and set aside 2 cups of the cooked potatoes. To the soup pot, add the spinach, basil, and parsley, cover, and cook for 1 or 2 minutes, until the spinach is wilted but still bright green.

In a blender, purée the reserved potatoes with the Neufchâtel, grated cheese, milk, and pepper. Stir the purée back into the soup and reheat gently.

1 tablespoon olive oil
2 cups chopped onions
1/2 teaspoon crumbled dried rosemary (1 teaspoon minced fresh)
4 cups diced potatoes
1 teaspoon salt
4 cups water or vegetable stock
10 ounces rinsed, stemmed, and chopped fresh spinach
1/4 cup chopped fresh basil
1/4 cup chopped fresh parsley
1/3 cup Neufchâtel cheese
1/2 cup grated Fontina, Parmesan, or sharp Cheddar cheese
2 cups milk
1/2 teaspoon ground black pepper

PER 12-OUNCE SERVING: 179 CALORIES, 7 G PROTEIN, 6.4 G FAT, 24.5 G CARBOHYDRATES, 3 G SATURATED FATTY ACIDS, 16 MG CHOLESTEROL, 425.5 MG SODIUM, 2.8 G TOTAL DIETARY FIBER

italian bean & squash soup

Healthful, hearty, and satisfying, this attractive soup in the Southern Italian tradition is quite easy to prepare. Oregano and crushed red pepper are assertive enough flavors to balance the otherwise sweet and mild soup.

Try the soup with Green Olive & Artichoke Tapenade (page 209) or Portabello Sandwiches (page 171), or with one of the Flavored Olives (page 213) and Bread Sticks (page 394).

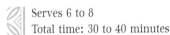 Serves 6 to 8
Total time: 30 to 40 minutes

1 tablespoon olive oil

3½ cups finely chopped onions

6 large garlic cloves, minced or pressed

1 celery stalk, preferably with some leaves, finely chopped

1¾ cups crushed canned tomatoes with their juice (15-ounce can)

1 quart vegetable broth*

1 teaspoon dried oregano

 pinch of crushed red pepper flakes

4 cups diced peeled butternut squash

3½ cups cooked pinto beans (two 15-ounce cans, rinsed and drained)

1 teaspoon salt

coarsely ground black pepper to taste

freshly grated Pecorino cheese (optional)

In a large nonreactive soup pot, heat the oil on medium heat. Add the onions, garlic, and celery and sauté until softened, about 10 minutes. Add the crushed tomatoes, broth, oregano, and red pepper flakes and bring to a simmer. Stir in the squash and cook until tender, 10 to 15 minutes. Add the beans and salt and continue to cook until the beans are thoroughly heated. Add black pepper to taste.

Serve hot topped with freshly grated cheese, if desired.

* *If you prefer a commercially produced broth, we recommend Pacific Organic or Imagine Foods brands, in aseptically packaged boxes.*

PER 12-OUNCE SERVING: 195 CALORIES, 7.7 G PROTEIN, 3 G FAT, 38 G CARBOHYDRATES, 0.5 G SATURATED FATTY ACIDS, 0 MG CHOLESTEROL, 744.6 MG SODIUM, 6.8 G TOTAL DIETARY FIBER

smooth gazpacho with greens

Gazpacho has been eaten, some say, since before Roman times! Made in hot weather from icy well water and "leftovers" (*acho* means "bits"), it remained a provincial dish until the nineteenth century, when the addition of sweet peppers and cucumbers boosted it into popular view. In Spain it's said, "There are as many types of gazpacho as there are mortars and pestles."

This recipe is quite fast and involves no cooking. With a food processor that "does the chopping for you," the soup can be prepared in 15 minutes. With a small processor or blender, you may need to purée in batches.

Because gazpacho is uncooked, it relies on top-notch vegetables and herbs to produce a vibrant flavor. Be vigilant and choose the juiciest produce and freshest herbs for this soup and allow the flavors to marry for several hours before serving.

Serves 4
Preparation time: 30 minutes
Chilling time: at least 1 hour

2 cups peeled, seeded, and chopped cucumbers
1 cup chopped ruby lettuce or romaine
2 cups chopped red and/or yellow bell peppers
¼ cup chopped scallions
3 garlic cloves, minced or pressed
1 tablespoon chopped fresh cilantro
3 tablespoons extra-virgin olive oil
2 tablespoons dry sherry
1 tablespoon cider vinegar
2½ to 3 cups tomato juice
1 cup crustless French bread cubes
½ teaspoon ground cumin
½ teaspoon salt
ground black pepper to taste
1 to 2 tablespoons minced fresh green chiles (optional)

sprinkling of fresh chives or minced yellow bell peppers
drizzle of olive oil

✳ In a food processor or blender, purée the cucumbers, lettuce, bell peppers, scallions, garlic, cilantro, olive oil, sherry, and vinegar with 2½ cups of the tomato juice to produce a saucy consistency. Add the bread cubes and let soak for 3 to 5 minutes. Stir in the cumin and salt. Purée until smooth, adding more tomato juice, if needed. Add black pepper and fresh chiles, if you like.

Chill well and serve topped with a sprinkling of chives or minced yellow bell peppers and a drizzle of olive oil.

PER 12-OUNCE SERVING: 199 CALORIES, 4 G PROTEIN, 11.5 G FAT, 21.8 G CARBOHYDRATES, 1.6 G SATURATED FATTY ACIDS, 0 MG CHOLESTEROL, 904 MG SODIUM, 3 G TOTAL DIETARY FIBER

southeast asian fruit soup

Jenny Wang is a Moosewood chef with a flair for creating unusual Asian dishes. She made this soup in an instant one steamy summer day when the melons were fragrant and lusciously ripe. Melons always vary in sweetness, so add brown sugar to taste.

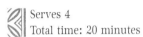 Serves 4
Total time: 20 minutes

✂ Working in batches, purée the cantaloupe, coconut milk, lemon juice, ginger, mint, almond extract, and cinnamon in a blender until smooth. Add brown sugar to taste. Chill for several hours or overnight to allow the flavors to meld.

Serve garnished with fresh mint leaves or edible flowers and lemon slices.

6 cups peeled, seeded, and cubed
   cantaloupe
1¾ cups reduced-fat coconut milk
   (14-ounce can)
2 tablespoons fresh lemon juice
2 tablespoons grated fresh ginger root
2 tablespoons minced fresh mint
1 teaspoon pure almond extract
generous dash of ground cinnamon
¼ to ½ cup brown sugar, packed

fresh mint leaves or edible flowers
lemon slices

PER 13.5-OUNCE SERVING: 245 CALORIES, 4.4 G PROTEIN, 9.5 G FAT, 38.7 G CARBOHYDRATES, 5.4 G SATURATED FATTY ACIDS, 0 MG CHOLESTEROL, 40.4 MG SODIUM, 2.2 G TOTAL DIETARY FIBER

zero soup

Perusing some vegetable soup recipes on weight loss program menus inspired us to develop one of our own. The zero refers to the fat content and the calorie count is also fairly negligible.

Prepare the vegetables one at a time and add each to the pot of simmering broth as you go. (We like the nonfat broths in asceptically packaged quart boxes by Imagine Foods and Pacific.) Use the list of "zero" vegetables on the next page to make the soup a little differently each time. Just replace or add to the vegetables called for here.

Serves 4 to 6
Preparation time: 20 to 30 minutes
Simmering time: 15 to 20 minutes

Heat the broth in a soup pot. Add the first seven vegetables one at a time, trimming and chopping as you go. Stir in the tomatoes, soy sauce, vinegar, basil, oregano, dill, thyme, and pepper. Simmer for 15 or 20 minutes, until the vegetables are tender. Add salt to taste.

PER 12-OUNCE SERVING: 97 CALORIES, 3.9 G
PROTEIN, 0.7 G FAT, 21.3 G CARBOHYDRATES,
0.1 G SATURATED FATTY ACIDS, 0 MG CHOLESTEROL,
548.8 MG SODIUM, 3.9 G TOTAL DIETARY FIBER

4 cups nonfat vegetable broth, "un-chicken" broth, or stock

2 cups diced onions

1 cup diced celery

1 cup peeled and diced carrots

1 cup cut green beans

1 1/2 cups finely chopped green cabbage

1 cup diced red bell peppers

4 garlic cloves, minced or pressed

3 cups diced tomatoes in juice (28-ounce can)

2 tablespoons soy sauce

1 tablespoon cider vinegar

1 teaspoon dried basil

1 teaspoon dried oregano

1 teaspoon dried dill

1/2 teaspoon dried thyme

1/2 teaspoon ground black pepper

salt to taste

variations *For Mexican Zero Soup, add zucchini and minced chiles and replace the herbs with cumin, coriander, and cilantro. Use lime juice instead of vinegar.*

For Hungarian Zero Soup, add mushrooms and replace the basil, oregano, and thyme with paprika, marjoram, and more dill. Top with nonfat sour cream.

For Asian Zero Soup, replace the cabbage with bok choy and add straw mushrooms. Replace the herbs with grated fresh ginger root and minced scallions. Top with mung bean sprouts.

"zero" vegetables

Artichoke hearts	Chard	Kale	Snow Peas
Asparagus	Collards	Leeks	Spaghetti squash
Beets	Cucumbers	Lettuce	Spinach
Broccoli	Eggplant	Mushrooms	Summer squash
Broccoli rabe	Endive	Okra	Tomatoes
Brussels sprouts	Escarole	Onions	Turnips
Cabbage	Garlic	Peppers	Water chestnuts
Carrots	Green beans	Pumpkin	Watercress
Cauliflower	Jicama	Scallions	Zucchini
Celery			

not "zero" vegetables

Corn	Peas	Winter squash
Parsnips	Potatoes	Yams

scallop chowder

A rich, velvety soup laden with potatoes, corn, and seafood, this is a quintessential New England chowder that's simply luscious. We use sea scallops or large bay scallops because they will remain tender and succulent.

Serve with Scandinavian Slaw (page 102) or Three Peppers Cabbage Slaw (page 104) and either Biscuits à la Focaccia (page 392) or Three Seed Whole Wheat Rolls (page 401).

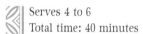 Serves 4 to 6
Total time: 40 minutes

Melt the butter in a soup pot. Add the onions, celery, thyme, and dill and sauté on medium-high heat until the onions are soft and translucent, about 7 minutes. Add the potatoes, corn, and 2 cups of the water and bring to a boil; then cover and cook until the potatoes are tender, about 10 minutes.

Meanwhile, if using sea scallops, cut them into quarters. Bay scallops may be left whole. Bring the remaining cup of water to a boil in a saucepan, add the scallops, and simmer for 3 to 5 minutes, until firm and opaque. Drain the scallops, reserving the cooking liquid, and set aside.

In a blender, combine the scallop cooking liquid, the milk or half-and-half, and 3 cups of the cooked vegetables and purée until smooth. Return the vegetable purée to the soup pot and stir in the lemon juice, salt, and pepper. Add the scallops and gently reheat for a few minutes, just until the soup is hot.

Top each serving with a sprig of dill or parsley or a few minced chives and accompany with a lemon wedge on the side for a little added zing.

2 tablespoons butter

1 cup chopped onions

1 cup chopped celery

1 1/2 teaspoons minced fresh thyme
    (1/2 teaspoon dried)

1 1/2 teaspoons minced fresh dill
    (1/2 teaspoon dried)

2 large potatoes, cut into bite-sized
    cubes

2 cups fresh or frozen corn kernels

3 cups water

1 pound sea scallops or large bay
    scallops

1 cup milk or half-and-half

2 tablespoons fresh lemon juice

1 teaspoon salt

1/4 teaspoon ground black pepper

sprigs of fresh dill or parsley or
    minced chives

a few lemon wedges

PER 12-OUNCE SERVING: 216 CALORIES, 13.3 G PROTEIN, 5.8 G FAT, 31.2 G CARBOHYDRATES, 3 G SATURATED FATTY ACIDS, 33.2 MG CHOLESTEROL, 580.8 MG SODIUM, 3.1 G TOTAL DIETARY FIBER

manhattan seafood chowder

Manhattan. The word whispers sophistication and elegance. *Chowder.* The word bespeaks that which is homespun and hearty. Reconciling this seeming contradiction has inspired chefs to new heights of creativity. This is a soup that can be either a comfort to the soul while a winter nor'easter roars down the coast, or an opening course in the most decorous of meals.

Cooking fish in soup presents a bit of a challenge. The goal is to cook it thoroughly, but not so much that it falls apart. Bite-sized chunks that maintain their integrity are ideal.

Serves 4 to 6
Preparation time: 25 minutes
Cooking time: 35 minutes

2 tablespoons olive oil

2 cups chopped onions

3 bay leaves

2 teaspoons dried thyme

1 cup chopped celery

1 cup peeled, sliced carrots*

2 cups cubed potatoes ($^1\!/_2$-inch cubes)

$1^1\!/_2$ cups uncrushed canned tomatoes with their juices (14.5-ounce can)

$^3\!/_4$ cup dry vermouth

1 teaspoon salt

 pinch of ground black pepper

4 cups water or vegetable stock

1 pound haddock or other firm white fish, cut into 1-inch cubes

1 tablespoon fresh lemon juice

2 tablespoons soy sauce

12 clams, scrubbed**

$^1\!/_3$ cup chopped fresh parsley

In a soup pot, warm the olive oil on medium-high heat. Add the onions and sauté until translucent, about 10 minutes. Add the bay leaves, thyme, and celery, cover, and cook on medium-high heat for about 5 minutes. Add the carrots, potatoes, tomatoes, vermouth, salt, pepper, and water or stock, bring to a boil, then cover and simmer for about 20 minutes, until the potatoes are almost tender.

Add the fish, lemon juice, and soy sauce. Bring the chowder to a boil and add the clams. Cover again and cook, stirring occasionally to avoid burning, until all of the clams have opened, about 5 minutes. Stir in the fresh parsley, remove the bay leaves, and serve immediately.

* *Cut the carrot lengthwise and slice crosswise into half-moons.*
** *We prefer littleneck clams. Clams should be closed before they are cooked. If the shell is open, discard it. Any clams that do not open when cooked should also be discarded.*

PER 16-OUNCE SERVING: 332 CALORIES, 26.9 G PROTEIN, 10.2 G FAT, 26.2 G CARBOHYDRATES, 1.9 G SATURATED FATTY ACIDS, 67.5 MG CHOLESTEROL, 930.9 MG SODIUM, 4 G TOTAL DIETARY FIBER

curried fish chowder

Chowders are thick seafood soups that originated in North America, and the term probably comes from the French word for stew pot, *chaudière.*

This recipe was inspired by the house soup served at Sweet's Restaurant near the Fulton Fish Market in New York City. Moosewood cook Sara Robbins remembers childhood trips with her family to enjoy the "freshest seafood in NYC." Sweet's curried chowder was always one of her family's favorite menu choices.

We've tried to capture the soup's hallmarks: its golden color, rich creaminess, and mild curry flavor. Accompany it with a mesclun salad and a crusty baguette.

Serves 4 to 6
Preparation time: 20 minutes
Cooking time: 40 minutes

1 tablespoon vegetable oil
1 cup diced shallots or onions
2 garlic cloves, minced or pressed
1 teaspoon salt
1 cup minced celery
2 to 3 teaspoons curry powder
1/2 teaspoon turmeric
1/2 teaspoon ground black pepper
4 cups diced potatoes
1 cup diced yellow squash
1/2 cup peeled and diced carrots
4 cups water or vegetable stock
1/2 cup dry sherry or dry white wine
1 pound mild white fish fillets, such
    as hake, sole, or scrod
2 tablespoons cream cheese
1 cup milk or half-and-half

minced chives or shallots
a few lemon wedges

In a soup pot, heat the oil on medium heat. Sauté the shallots or onions, garlic, and salt for 5 minutes, stirring often. Add the celery and sauté for about 5 more minutes. Add the curry powder, turmeric, and pepper and sauté for 1 to 2 minutes, stirring constantly. Add the potatoes, squash, carrots, water or stock, and sherry or wine. Cover and bring to a boil; then reduce the heat and simmer until the vegetables are very tender, about 15 minutes.

Rinse the fish fillets and cut them into bite-sized pieces. Add them to the pot, cover, and cook for 5 to 7 minutes, until the fish is no longer translucent. Remove from the heat.

In a blender, combine the cream cheese, milk or half-and-half, and 2 cups of the hot soup and purée until smooth. Stir the purée back into the soup and reheat gently, if needed. Serve hot topped with chives or shallots and with lemon wedges on the side.

PER 12-OUNCE SERVING: 266 CALORIES, 18.9 G PROTEIN, 5.7 G FAT, 32.4 G CARBOHYDRATES, 2.3 G SATURATED FATTY ACIDS, 28 MG CHOLESTEROL, 1,077.7 MG SODIUM, 3.3 G TOTAL DIETARY FIBER

spanish bean soup

Sauté soy sausage with caraway, fennel, and red pepper to give this swashbuckling bean soup a classic Mediterranean appeal. If you don't have stock on hand, you can use 4 cups of commercial vegetable broth mixed with 4 cups of water.

Serve it with a hunk of peasant bread, sharp provolone cheese, and a bottle of deep red wine.

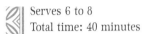
Serves 6 to 8
Total time: 40 minutes

2 garlic cloves, minced or pressed
2 cups chopped onions
1 teaspoon salt
1 tablespoon olive oil
2 teaspoons ground fennel seeds
1/4 teaspoon red pepper flakes
3 bay leaves
3 cups soy sausage, cut into chunks*
2 cups cubed potatoes (1-inch cubes)
8 cups vegetable stock
4 cups stemmed and chopped kale, collards, Swiss chard, or cabbage
1 cup chopped celery with leaves
3 cups drained cooked cannellini beans**
generous pinch of saffron
1 1/2 teaspoons salt
1/2 teaspoon ground black pepper

grated Parmesan cheese (optional)

In a soup pot, sauté the garlic, onions, and salt in the oil on medium-high heat for about 10 minutes, or until the onions are golden. Add the fennel, red pepper flakes, and bay leaves and sauté for another minute. Add the soy sausage and cook on medium-high heat, stirring often, for 5 minutes, until the sausage starts to brown.

Add the potatoes, stock, greens, and celery, cover, and bring to a boil. Then reduce the heat and add the beans, saffron, salt, and pepper. Simmer until the vegetables are cooked, about 5 minutes.

Serve topped with grated cheese, if desired.

* An 11-ounce package works well.
** To cook, soak 1 1/2 cups of dried beans in plenty of water to cover for at least 2 hours or overnight. Rinse the beans and then simmer them with 3 bay leaves in 2 quarts of water until tender, 45 to 60 minutes. Or use two 15-ounce cans, drained and rinsed.

PER 16-OUNCE SERVING: 274 CALORIES, 14.2 G PROTEIN, 9.5 G FAT, 36.7 G CARBOHYDRATES, 1.5 G SATURATED FATTY ACIDS, 0 MG CHOLESTEROL, 1567 MG SODIUM, 7 G TOTAL DIETARY FIBER

salads

salads

Salads can be the appetite-whetting, quintessential complement to a main dish or they can play the central role of the meal. Anything goes.

Three key guidelines for salads are (1) thoroughly rinse and sort the greens and vegetables, (2) take care not to overcook anything, and (3) consider composition in terms of flavor, texture, color, and contrast.

We have probably all encountered the unforgettable experience of a salad that looks divine: perky colorful greens drizzled with a special dressing and topped with fresh herbs, toasted nuts, and edible flower petals, and then—*crunch*—that unmistakable sensation of grit between the teeth. Delight plunges instantly into dismay. The lesson: Always take the time to rinse greens and vegetables and to sort beans and grains.

Cooking vegetables until just crisp-tender is a good rule of thumb. After you drain them, their residual heat will continue to cook them for a while, so either drain the vegetables when they're still a little firmer than you want and let them sit at room temperature, or drain them when they're exactly right and immediately immerse them in cold water to halt the cooking process.

Mixing herbs, fruits, vegetables, nuts, cheeses, and dressings to make salads is an art. Earthy, mellow, and sweet salads feature beans, potatoes, yams, beets, carrots, turnips, parsnips, and jicama. Lighter salads made mostly of sunny greens can range from mild to slightly bitter and from uncooked, grassy, and herblike to savory and cooked. Adding a root vegetable to a bowl of crisp greens can create a sense of wholeness: roots, stalks, stems, and leaves all take their places, contributing to the dish.

Fresh juicy fruit proclaims its close kinship with sunshine and water. Fruit salads are bright and invigorating whether they highlight one special fruit or combine many. They can be sweet or tart, or both sweet and tart! Including clementines in a "spring mix" salad may be just the sweet touch needed to balance a sharp tart dressing.

Dairy and tofu products add earthiness to salads. Cheese, marinated tofu, or tofu-kan provide a robust, dense, chewy texture and a welcome burst of flavor. Creamy dressings made with dairy products or silken tofu add lusciousness and a sense of indulgence. Toasted nuts and seeds are sharp, bitter, and rich. Sprouts are light and airy.

Seasonings add an essential bright note to an otherwise ordinary salad. Flavored vinegars and oils, minced chiles, and fresh ginger can really wake up the senses. Simply using good olive oil and freshly ground pepper can make all the difference.

Herbs, vinegars, and citrus juices can be combined in many ways. One family might be basil, marjoram, cilantro, mint, and lemon. These light flavors are perfect for green salads. Then there's the quartet of thyme, oregano, parsley, and balsamic vinegar—good for pasta and potato salads. Rosemary and sage are distinctive and solo well in a dish of assertive root vegetables.

Salads can be cool, juicy, refreshing, and crunchy or earthy, chewy, and satisfying. At Moosewood, we're never without them.

avocado & shrimp sushi salad

This free-spirited salad has all the flavors of a California roll without the roll. If you don't eat shrimp, just replace it with another avocado and a diced ripe tomato.

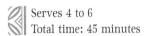 Serves 4 to 6
Total time: 45 minutes

In a small bowl, mix together all of the wasabi dressing ingredients until smooth, and set aside.

Bring the rice and water to a boil in a medium saucepan. Reduce the heat and simmer, covered, until the water is absorbed, about 20 minutes.

Meanwhile, bring a large pot of water to a simmer and cook the shrimp until it is pink and firm, about 2 to 3 minutes. Drain. In a cup, whisk together the rice vinegar, sugar, and salt until the sugar dissolves.

When the rice is cooked, place it in a large bowl and pour on the seasoned rice vinegar. Add the carrots, scallions, radish or daikon, sesame seeds, and half of the crumbled nori and toss well. Set aside to cool. Peel, pit, and slice the avocado (page 447).

To assemble the salad, line a large platter or four smaller plates with the greens. Mound the rice in the middle and arrange the shrimp and avocado slices around the outside. Pour on the wasabi dressing and sprinkle with the rest of the nori. Garnish with citrus wedges.

wasabi dressing

1 tablespoon wasabi powder

2 tablespoons water

1/4 cup rice vinegar or lime juice

1 teaspoon salt

salad

1 cup raw white rice, preferably sushi rice (page 467)

1 1/2 cups water

1 pound peeled and deveined shrimp

1/4 cup rice vinegar

2 teaspoons sugar

3/4 teaspoon salt

2/3 cup peeled and grated carrots

1/4 cup minced scallions

1/4 cup grated radish or daikon

1 tablespoon toasted sesame seeds*

1 sheet nori, toasted and crumbled**

1 ripe avocado, preferably Hass

4 to 5 cups mixed salad greens or spinach leaves

lemon or lime wedges

* Toast sesame seeds on an unoiled baking tray at 350° for 2 to 3 minutes, until fragrant and golden brown.
** Lightly toast the nori by waving it over a very low open flame for about 30 seconds, until deepened in color.

PER 11-OUNCE SERVING: 262 CALORIES, 18 G PROTEIN, 7.3 G FAT, 30.8 G CARBOHYDRATES, 1.2 G SATURATED FATTY ACIDS, 129.7 MG CHOLESTEROL, 865.2 MG SODIUM, 3.9 G TOTAL DIETARY FIBER

celery salad with blue cheese

Cool, crisp bites of celery are combined with creamy chunks of tangy blue cheese in this disarmingly simple and pleasing side dish.

Try this versatile salad beside Wild Rice Pilaf (page 147) or Breaded Polenta Cutlets (page 282).

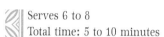

Serves 6 to 8
Total time: 5 to 10 minutes

Cut the celery crosswise into ½-inch-thick pieces to make about 4 cups sliced. Place it in a serving bowl and sprinkle in the crumbled blue cheese. Add the salt, pepper, and olive oil and toss well.

Serve chilled.

8 to 10 celery stalks
¾ cup crumbled blue cheese*
¼ teaspoon salt
coarsely ground black pepper to taste
1 tablespoon extra-virgin olive oil

* Maytag, mellow Danish, and Buttermilk Blue are all good choices of blue cheese for this dish. About 3 ounces of cheese will yield ¾ cup.

PER 1.75-OUNCE SERVING: 59 CALORIES, 2.6 G PROTEIN, 4.9 G FAT, 1.7 G CARBOHYDRATES, 2.2 G SATURATED FATTY ACIDS, 8 MG CHOLESTEROL, 256.6 MG SODIUM, 0.7 G TOTAL DIETARY FIBER

cucumber side salads

Cool and crisp, refreshing and cleansing, cucumber salads are important in cuisines around the world. At Moosewood we serve them often with Indian, Eastern European, Middle Eastern, and North African main dishes. Pour our easily prepared dressings on a few sliced cucumbers and you have a little side dish, salad, or garnish that can really make the meal.

The Arugula Caper Dressing is also good over potatoes or green beans. Try the Sushi Dressing on carrots or avocados.

cucumbers with arugula caper dressing

In order to blend the dressing well, it's necessary to make more than is needed for this cucumber salad. The remaining dressing will keep for several days refrigerated in a tightly covered container. It can also be made ahead and refrigerated until ready to use.

Serves 4
Total time: 30 minutes

3 cups cucumber crescents*

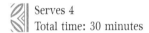

arugula caper dressing

2 slices French or Italian bread, crusts removed

2 tablespoons cider vinegar or white balsamic vinegar

1 cup fresh arugula leaves

1 tablespoon capers, rinsed

1/3 cup extra-virgin olive oil

* Peel 3 medium cucumbers, halve them lengthwise, and scoop out the seeds with a spoon. Slice crosswise into 1/2-inch-thick crescents.

Place the cucumbers in a serving bowl and set aside. Put the bread in a separate bowl, pour the vinegar over it, and let it soak for 5 minutes.

Meanwhile, place the arugula, capers, and olive oil in a blender. With your hands, gently squeeze the excess vinegar from the soaked bread and add the bread to the blender. Blend on high speed until the dressing is uniformly colored and very smooth, about 30 seconds. Scrape down the sides of the blender, if necessary.

Add about half of the dressing to the cucumbers and stir gently to evenly coat. Serve chilled.

PER 6-OUNCE SERVING: 251 CALORIES, 3.2 G PROTEIN, 19.8 G FAT, 16.4 G CARBOHYDRATES, 2.7 G SATURATED FATTY ACIDS, 0 MG CHOLESTEROL, 202 MG SODIUM, 1.8 G TOTAL DIETARY FIBER

cucumber salad with sushi dressing

This dressing is excellent made ahead and refrigerated until ready to use.

 Serves 4 to 6
Total time: 20 minutes

3 cups cucumber crescents*

sushi dressing

¼ cup rice vinegar

1 teaspoon wasabi powder

2 teaspoons sugar

1 tablespoon soy sauce

2 to 3 teaspoons minced pickled
   ginger

½ sheet toasted nori**

* Peel 3 medium cucumbers, halve them
  lengthwise, and scoop out the seeds with a
  spoon. Slice crosswise into ½-inch-thick
  crescents.
** Nori is a deep green seaweed sold in
  sheets. Toast it by waving briefly over a flame
  until the color deepens to a bright sheen.
  Toasted nori is also available pre-packaged.

Place the sliced cucumbers in a large bowl.

In a smaller bowl, stir together the vinegar, wasabi powder, sugar, and soy sauce. Add the pickled ginger. Using scissors, cut the nori into long 1-inch-wide ribbons. Bundle the ribbons of nori and hold them over the bowl. Snip them into tiny squares and stir into the dressing. Pour the dressing over the cucumbers and serve immediately.

PER 3-OUNCE SERVING: 32 CALORIES, 1.6 G PROTEIN, 0.1 G FAT, 5.7 G CARBOHYDRATES, 0 G SATURATED FATTY ACIDS, 0 MG CHOLESTEROL, 140.2 MG SODIUM, 0.6 G TOTAL DIETARY FIBER

israeli za'atar salad

This combination of vegetables is popular all over the Mediterranean and the Middle East. The za'atar seasoning mix of sesame, thyme, and sumac really delivers the goods.

While very common in Middle Eastern cooking, the maroon color and sour citrusy taste of sumac are still something of a novelty here, despite the fact that sumac trees grow wild along our hedgerows and roadways. It's worth buying conveniently packaged sumac to keep in your pantry. It's available in specialty markets and well-stocked supermarkets.

Za'atar Salad can pack a wallop in pita bread and makes a piquant side dish for Middle Eastern Lentils & Pasta (page 254). We like it best served on a bed of watercress with hard-boiled eggs, grated feta, and chickpeas. Add warm bread and one of the Flavored Olives (page 213) for a feast.

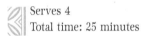
Serves 4
Total time: 25 minutes

1 cup peeled, seeded, and cubed cucumbers

2 cups cubed fresh tomatoes

1 1/2 cups chopped yellow or green bell peppers

1/2 cup diced red onions

1 tablespoon minced fresh thyme (1 teaspoon dried)

1 tablespoon toasted sesame seeds*

1 to 2 teaspoons powdered sumac, or to taste

1 tablespoon extra-virgin olive oil

2 tablespoons fresh lemon juice

1/2 teaspoon salt

ground black pepper to taste

1/4 cup minced fresh parsley (optional)

Toast sesame seeds on an unoiled baking tray at 350° for 2 to 3 minutes, until fragrant and golden brown.

In a serving bowl, combine the cucumbers, tomatoes, bell peppers, and red onions. Stir in the thyme, sesame seeds, sumac, olive oil, lemon juice, salt, black pepper, and parsley, if using. Serve at room temperature or chilled.

PER 8-OUNCE SERVING: 97 CALORIES, 2.4 G PROTEIN, 5.4 G FAT, 12.2 G CARBOHYDRATES, 0.7 G SATURATED FATTY ACIDS, 0 MG CHOLESTEROL, 312 MG SODIUM, 3.1 G TOTAL DIETARY FIBER

jicama orange salad

Jicama (HEE-kuh-muh), a rounded tuber indigenous to Central America, has a thin, light brown skin and mild, crisp, juicy white flesh. It's also known as "yam bean" because it is the bulbous root of a leguminous plant. Today it can be found in supermarkets as well as in Mexican and Chinese groceries.

In Mexico, jicama salad is served most often as an appetizer with drinks, but we find that our quick and easy version also makes a refreshing low-fat counterpoint to savory bean and cheese dishes.

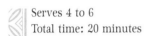 Serves 4 to 6
Total time: 20 minutes

1 small jicama (about ½ pound)

4 seedless oranges, peeled and sectioned*

1 tablespoon fresh lime juice

½ teaspoon chili powder, or to taste

½ teaspoon coarse salt, or to taste

fresh coarsely ground black pepper to taste

Peel the jicama, cut it into matchsticks, and place in a serving bowl. Add the orange sections to the bowl and drizzle on the lime juice. Sprinkle on the chili powder, salt, and pepper and mix well. Cover and refrigerate until serving time.

* *Use a sharp knife to slice off the peel, including the white pith. Working over a bowl, slice toward the center of the orange along the membrane on one side of a section and then flick the knife up the membrane on the other side to release the section. Repeat for all of the sections.*

PER 4-OUNCE SERVING: 50 CALORIES, 0.8 G PROTEIN, 0.2 G FAT, 12.4 G CARBOHYDRATES, 0 G SATURATED FATTY ACIDS, 0 MG CHOLESTEROL, 202.3 MG SODIUM, 3.5 G TOTAL DIETARY FIBER

variations *Try adding 6 thinly sliced radishes or 1 to 2 tablespoons of minced red onion. Replace the chili powder with cayenne or hot paprika. For a different look, cut the jicama into thin wedges and the oranges into thin half-rounds. Top the salad with minced fresh cilantro.*

spicy cantaloupe salad

Moosewood cook Eliana Parra created this ingenious little salad on a whim. Unconventional and refreshing, the combination of sweet, juicy cantaloupe with a spicy, peppery dressing is a dramatic sensation for the palate.

Feel free to adjust the cayenne to taste and use other greens that you like or have on hand for the endive: Red ruby lettuce is attractive. The salad can be served right away, but if it sits for a little while, the greens absorb the dressing and the intensity of the flavors can really shine. For an exotic twist, top with a cup of crumbled ricotta salata cheese.

Serves 6 to 8
Total time: 35 minutes

salad

- 2 cups rinsed and chopped curly endive
- 1 cantaloupe, seeded, peeled, and cut into 1-inch cubes
- 1 tablespoon chopped fresh cilantro (optional)
- 2 tablespoons chopped scallions

dressing

- 2 tablespoons olive oil
- 2 teaspoons cider vinegar
- 3 tablespoons fresh lime juice
- 2 teaspoons ground coriander
- 1/4 teaspoon cayenne, or to taste
- 1/4 teaspoon ground black pepper

Place the endive on a platter. In a bowl, combine the cantaloupe, cilantro, and scallions. In a separate small bowl, whisk together all of the dressing ingredients. Pour the dressing on the cantaloupe and toss well. Arrange the cantaloupe on the greens.

PER 2.5-OUNCE SERVING: 51 CALORIES, 0.7 G PROTEIN, 3.7 G FAT, 4.6 G CARBOHYDRATES, 0.5 G SATURATED FATTY ACIDS, 0 MG CHOLESTEROL, 8.7 MG SODIUM, 1 G TOTAL DIETARY FIBER

spinach with peanut dressing

This is a favorite supper of Moosewood cook Nancy Lazarus. She simply put together the flavors she loves most and the result is divine. Serve it with bread and follow it with fruit for a nice meal.

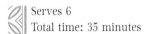
Serves 6
Total time: 35 minutes

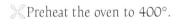Preheat the oven to 400°.

Place the sweet potato matchsticks on a baking sheet. Drizzle with the oil, toss to coat, and sprinkle with salt. Roast in the oven until crisp on the outside and tender inside, 15 to 20 minutes. Meanwhile, remove the spinach stems, chop the spinach leaves, and slice the hard-boiled eggs. If using, cut the lemon into six wedges.

For the dressing, warm the oil in a saucepan on medium-high heat. Sauté the onions for about 10 minutes, until translucent. Stir in the tomatoes, peanut butter, sugar, cilantro, and Tabasco sauce and bring to a simmer. Cook for about 5 minutes. Add salt and more Tabasco sauce to taste.

To serve, make a bed of spinach on each salad plate. Top with a generous portion of the warm Peanut Dressing, sprinkle with roasted sweet potatoes, and top with sliced hard-boiled eggs. Garnish each plate with a lemon wedge, if you wish.

vegetables

3 cups sweet potato matchsticks*

1 teaspoon vegetable oil

sprinkling of salt

10 ounces fresh spinach, rinsed

3 hard-boiled eggs

1 lemon (optional)

peanut dressing

2 teaspoons vegetable oil

1½ cups chopped onions

1¾ cups "fresh cut" tomatoes
    (14-ounce can, drained)

¼ cup peanut butter

1 teaspoon sugar

2 tablespoons chopped fresh cilantro

1 teaspoon Tabasco sauce or other
    hot pepper sauce, or more to
    taste

salt to taste

* *Julienne the sweet potatoes into 2 x ¼-inch
   pieces.*

PER 9.5-OUNCE SERVING: 232 CALORIES, 9.5 G PROTEIN, 10.9 G FAT, 26.5 G CARBOHYDRATES, 2.7 G SATURATED FATTY ACIDS, 125.2 MG CHOLESTEROL, 169.1 MG SODIUM, 4.1 G TOTAL DIETARY FIBER

tossed green salad vinaigrette

Every cookbook and every cook should have a favorite vinaigrette dressing. It's easy to make minutes before any meal and is perfect on fresh greens or steamed vegetables.

The ingredients for the vinaigrette must be top-notch. For the salad, use a variety of fresh greens: assorted lettuces, arugula, baby spinach, watercress, tender mustard (mizuna) and beet greens, curly endive, Belgian endive, radicchio. Be sure to balance the sweet and mild with the sharp and rough greens, using fewer sharp ones. For a little salad ritual, make the dressing right in the salad bowl, add the greens, toss, and serve immediately.

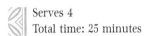
Serves 4
Total time: 25 minutes

8 cups assorted greens

2 tablespoons red wine vinegar
 dash of balsamic vinegar (optional)
2 garlic cloves, minced or pressed
$^1/_2$ teaspoon Dijon mustard
$^1/_4$ teaspoon salt
dash of freshly ground black pepper
$^1/_3$ to $^1/_2$ cup virgin or extra-virgin
  olive oil*

* *If using the smaller amount of oil, you may want to whisk in 2 tablespoons of water at the end.*

Rinse the greens well. Spin them dry in a salad spinner or pat them dry with a clean towel. Tear them into bite-sized pieces and set aside.

In a salad bowl, whisk together the vinegar(s), garlic, mustard, salt, and pepper. Continue to whisk briskly while gradually drizzling in the olive oil. Add the greens and toss to coat with dressing.

Serve immediately.

PER 6-OUNCE SERVING: 194 CALORIES, 3.1 G PROTEIN, 19.1 G FAT, 4.9 G CARBOHYDRATES, 2.6 G SATURATED FATTY ACIDS, 0 MG CHOLESTEROL, 216.6 MG SODIUM, 2.9 G TOTAL DIETARY FIBER

variations *To the basic salad add chickpeas, sliced radishes, sliced red onion, scallions, grated carrots, fresh chopped parsley, fresh minced basil, snipped chives, croutons, quartered marinated artichoke hearts, and grated cheese such as feta.*

what makes it extra-virgin?

Over the past few decades, we have witnessed the arrival of many brands of imported olive oil on the supermarket shelves. Specialty stores display a dazzling selection of Greek, Italian, and Spanish brands, along with some from California, variously labeled "virgin" and "extra-virgin," "pure" and "light."

Extra-virgin is the purest, most fruity and fragrant, and least chemically altered olive oil. It is extracted from the first pressing of the olives, producing a low-acid, high-flavor oil. Imported extra-virgin olive oil must have an acidity level of 1 percent or less, and its aroma and flavor must pass the high standards of the International Olive Oil Council.

The most distinctive and, therefore, most expensive extra-virgin olive oils are made from olives grown only on one farm and labeled "estate" or "single estate." Flavors vary from year to year due to changing weather patterns and soil conditions. Commercial bulk extra-virgin olive oil is produced from a blend of ripe and unripe oils from different farms, or even different regions and countries. Its flavor can be excellent, but it will not have the nuances of a single estate oil.

Because of its very low smoking point, extra-virgin olive oil is not recommended for sautéing. Use this strong "olivey-tasting" oil to accent salads, dips, spreads, marinades, sauces, roasted vegetables, and fish, and for dipping crusty bread.

spicy potato salad

In the United States, we're accustomed to potato salads dressed with mayonnaise or oil and vinegar. But this potato salad is both very low-fat and vegan.

This potato salad gets back to its native North American roots, using smoky, spicy condiments made from its indigenous neighbors, chipotle peppers and tomatillos. Adjust the hotness of the salad by varying the amount of chipotles you use. It's a great addition to a Tex-Mex buffet, with an assortment of goodies for tacos, burritos, and quesadillas spread across the table.

 Serves 6
Preparation time: 30 minutes
Chilling time (optional): 30 minutes

8 cups water
6 potatoes (3 pounds)

dressing

³/4 cup canned tomatillos, packed
1 to 2 canned chipotle peppers plus 1 teaspoon adobo sauce*
1 tablespoon fresh lemon juice
1 teaspoon brown sugar, packed
¹/2 teaspoon salt

1 tablespoon chopped fresh cilantro
¹/3 cup diced celery

*We recommend La Torre brand canned chipotles in adobo sauce. Look for it in small jars or cans in the ethnic section of supermarkets. The chipotles are smoked hot peppers and the adobo sauce is a spicy thick tomato purée.

Bring the water to a boil in a covered pot.

Meanwhile, peel the potatoes and cut them into 1-inch cubes. Cover with cool water until you are ready to cook them, so they won't turn brown. When the water boils, drain the potatoes, and carefully ease them into the boiling water. Cover and simmer for 15 to 20 minutes, until tender.

While the potatoes simmer, purée the tomatillos, chipotles and adobo sauce, lemon juice, sugar, and salt in a blender. When the potatoes are cooked, drain them and quickly plunge into cold water to stop the cooking. Drain again and place in a serving bowl. Add the tomatillo dressing and toss well. Stir in the cilantro and celery.

Serve warm or chill for 30 minutes before serving.

PER 8-OUNCE SERVING: 172 CALORIES, 3.9 G PROTEIN, 0.3 G FAT, 39.8 G CARBOHYDRATES, 0.1 G SATURATED FATTY ACIDS, 0 MG CHOLESTEROL, 263 G SODIUM, 3.4 G TOTAL DIETARY FIBER

warm potato salad

Warm potatoes readily absorb the piquant flavors in this dressing. We love it on arugula and also on other sharp greens, such as baby mizuna, mesclun, and watercress. And if you like a stronger, untamed cheese, try chèvre instead of ricotta salata.

Serve Warm Potato Salad as a main dish or as a side dish for baked or grilled fish or Tofu Burgers (page 182).

 Serves 6 to 8
Total time: 30 minutes

4 to 6 potatoes (2 pounds)

dressing

2 tablespoons minced shallots

1 garlic clove, minced or pressed

¹/₂ teaspoon salt

¹/₄ teaspoon ground black pepper

3 tablespoons cider vinegar or other light vinegar

¹/₂ teaspoon Dijon mustard

1 tablespoon minced fresh thyme (1 teaspoon dried)

2 tablespoons small capers

12 kalamata olives, pitted and coarsely chopped

¹/₄ cup olive oil

arugula, rinsed and stemmed

ricotta salata, crumbled or coarsely grated

Scrub the potatoes and peel them if you wish. Slice in half lengthwise and cut crosswise into ¹/₂-inch-thick semi-circles. Place them in a pot with salted cold water to cover and bring to a boil. Reduce the heat, cover, and simmer for 15 to 20 minutes, until the potatoes are just tender.

Meanwhile, in a small bowl, whisk together all of the dressing ingredients. When the potatoes are tender, drain them and place in a serving bowl. Pour on the dressing and toss well.

Serve immediately on a bed of arugula and top with ricotta salata.

PER 5-OUNCE SERVING: 186 CALORIES, 2.2 G PROTEIN, 9.4 G FAT, 24.5 G CARBOHYDRATES, 1.2 G SATURATED FATTY ACIDS, 0 MG CHOLESTEROL, 404.3 MG SODIUM, 2.1 G TOTAL DIETARY FIBER

slaws

A good slaw, like a good chutney, relish, or raita, adds balance to richer dishes. Both sweet and sharp, slaws make a meal more interesting, whether it's barbecued tofu or a fish tostada.

The word "slaw" comes from the Dutch "sla," a contraction of the French word "salade." "Cole," as in cole slaw, is the generic name for the cabbage family. Although green cabbage is often the centerpiece vegetable, slaws can be made from any vegetable or fruit that can be finely sliced or shredded. Red cabbage, broccoli, kohlrabi, and turnips are all good choices. For more delicate slaws, use napa, savoy, or Chinese cabbage. Carrots, celery, and onions are often used in traditional slaws, but don't limit yourself: We've grated parsnips and beets into slaws and sliced in fresh fennel and multi-colored bell peppers. Crisp, tart fruits like Crispin apples and Bosc pears make perfect additions.

Creamy, mayonnaise-based dressings are most familiar, but creamy dressings can also start with buttermilk, yogurt, or sour cream. Equally good are slaws tossed with sweet and sour dressings or savory vinaigrettes. When it comes to herbs and spices, your inspiration is the limit.

scandinavian slaw

Our lively slaw stays crisp because the vegetables are sliced, not grated. The dressing is an inspired buttermilk/caraway combo. Serve alongside rich or highly seasoned main dishes. If you like, line the serving bowl with decorative leaves of flowering cabbage.

Serves 6
Preparation time: 30 minutes
Chilling time: 1 hour

1½ cups thinly sliced fresh fennel

3 cups thinly sliced green cabbage

3 cups thinly sliced red cabbage

3 cups peeled, cored, and thinly sliced apples

1½ cups thinly sliced celery

⅓ cup vegetable oil

2 teaspoons ground caraway seeds

1½ cups buttermilk

2 tablespoons sugar

2 tablespoons cider vinegar

salt to taste

Place the fennel, green and red cabbage, apples, and celery in a bowl. In a separate small bowl, whisk together the oil, caraway, buttermilk, sugar, and vinegar. Pour the marinade over the vegetables and toss thoroughly. Cover and refrigerate for about 1 hour. Add salt to taste just before serving.

PER 11-OUNCE SERVING: 240 CALORIES, 4.2 G PROTEIN, 13.7 G FAT, 29 G CARBOHYDRATES, 3.6 G SATURATED FATTY ACIDS, 2 MG CHOLESTEROL, 114.5 MG SODIUM, 5.4 G TOTAL DIETARY FIBER

asian cabbage slaw

Most of the vegetables in this tangy slaw are familiar staples, but the napa cabbage may be new to you. Napa cabbage is a very pale green celery cabbage with delicate, crinkled leaves. All types of celery cabbage are popular throughout China, Japan, and Korea, but napa is the variety most commonly found here—available in most well-stocked supermarkets.

The dressing, with sesame oil, mirin, and soy sauce, adds a distinctly Asian accent to this light and satisfying dish.

Serves 6 to 8
Total time: 25 minutes

4 cups grated napa cabbage

2 cups peeled and grated carrots

3/4 cup diced red bell peppers

2 fresh green chiles, seeded and minced

1 to 1 1/2 cups diced shallots

1 garlic clove, minced or pressed

2 tablespoons chopped fresh cilantro

dressing

2 tablespoons vegetable oil

2 tablespoons dark sesame oil

3 tablespoons rice vinegar, or more to taste

2 tablespoons orange juice

1 tablespoon mirin or dry sherry

1 tablespoon soy sauce

3 tablespoons sugar, or to taste

pinch of salt (optional)

Place the cabbage, carrots, peppers, chiles, shallots, garlic, and cilantro in a bowl. In a separate bowl, whisk together the dressing ingredients. Pour the dressing over the vegetables and toss thoroughly. Taste and, if needed, add a pinch of salt or more vinegar.

Serve immediately or refrigerate until serving.

PER 5-OUNCE SERVING: 139 CALORIES, 2.1 G PROTEIN, 7.4 G FAT, 17.9 G CARBOHYDRATES, 1.5 G SATURATED FATTY ACIDS, 0 MG CHOLESTEROL, 126.2 MG SODIUM, 2.7 G TOTAL DIETARY FIBER

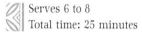

three peppers cabbage slaw

This simple cabbage slaw is only a starting point for a wide range of combinations of your own favorite vegetables. For an attractive slaw, cut the vegetables neatly and uniformly. Use a sharp knife or blade to produce a clean, crisp, cut edge, and the vegetables will absorb the dressing without wilting.

Serves 6 to 8
Total time: 25 minutes

salad

4 cups finely shredded green cabbage

1/2 red bell pepper, cut into 1-inch matchsticks

1/2 green bell pepper, cut into 1-inch matchsticks

1/2 yellow bell pepper, cut into 1-inch matchsticks

1/2 cup finely sliced scallions

3 tablespoons chopped fresh parsley

1 seeded and minced jalapeño pepper (optional)

dressing

2 teaspoons freshly grated lemon peel

2 tablespoons fresh lemon juice

1 garlic clove, minced or pressed

2 to 3 tablespoons vegetable oil

2 tablespoons white balsamic or cider vinegar

1 teaspoon sugar

1/2 teaspoon salt

Place the salad ingredients in a serving bowl. In another bowl, whisk together all of the dressing ingredients. Pour the dressing on the vegetables and toss thoroughly. Add more vinegar, sugar, or salt to taste.

Serve immediately or refrigerate for up to 3 days.

PER 3.5-OUNCE SERVING: 58 CALORIES, 1.2 G PROTEIN, 3.8 G FAT, 6.1 G CARBOHYDRATES, 0.9 G SATURATED FATTY ACIDS, 0 MG CHOLESTEROL, 161.3 MG SODIUM, 2 G TOTAL DIETARY FIBER

vietnamese root vegetable slaw

White daikon and jicama speckled with orange, red, and green make for a colorful, Vietnamese-inspired slaw that's tangy and flavorful but not spicy. If you prefer it spicy hot, add more chiles or cayenne, or include the chile seeds. Be careful when adding more cayenne, however; it can have a harsh edge, especially when not sautéed. Know your cayenne and use it with a discriminating touch. For the dressing, start with 1/4 cup of rice vinegar and add more to taste.

Other root vegetables, such as rutabagas, turnips, beets, and parsnips, can replace those we've selected, but if you're not familiar with daikon and jicama, give them a try. Daikon is a white radish that the Japanese consider a fundamental food, and jicama is a vegetable native to Mexico and the Amazon with the crisp texture of an autumn apple.

Serves 4 to 6
Total time: 30 minutes

2 cups peeled and grated daikon

1 1/2 cups peeled and grated jicama

1 cup peeled and grated carrots

1/2 cup diced red onions

1 fresh green chile, seeded and minced

1/4 cup chopped fresh cilantro

dressing

4 to 5 tablespoons rice vinegar

1 tablespoon soy sauce

1 tablespoon sugar

1 teaspoon salt, or to taste

1/8 teaspoon cayenne

Place the grated daikon, jicama, and carrots, and the red onions, chiles, and cilantro in a medium bowl. Whisk together all of the dressing ingredients in another bowl. Pour the dressing over the vegetables and toss thoroughly. Taste and add more salt or vinegar, as desired.

Serve immediately or refrigerate until serving.

PER 5-OUNCE SERVING: 53 CALORIES, 1.5 G PROTEIN, 0.2 G FAT, 11.9 G CARBOHYDRATES, 0 G SATURATED FATTY ACIDS, 0 MG CHOLESTEROL, 546.8 MG SODIUM, 3.2 G TOTAL DIETARY FIBER

pretty beets & carrots

The striking red and orange colors of shredded beets and carrots make this a bright centerpiece with a crisp, refreshing texture and tangy flavor. If you use a food processor or mouli-julienne, which is a countertop, hand-cranked grater, this can be ready in minutes.

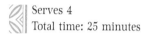
Serves 4
Total time: 25 minutes

1 large raw beet, peeled
1 large carrot, peeled
1 walnut-sized piece of fresh
    ginger root
2 tablespoons vegetable oil
3 tablespoons cider vinegar
1 garlic clove, minced or pressed
salt and ground black pepper to taste
1/4 cup minced scallions
6 green or red lettuce leaves

Coarsely grate the beet and then the carrot to yield about 1 1/2 cups of each. Place in separate bowls and set aside.

Grate the ginger finely and combine it with the oil, vinegar, and garlic. Toss the beets with half of the dressing and add salt and pepper to taste. Mix together the scallions, carrots, and the remaining dressing. Add salt and pepper, if you like.

Arrange the lettuce on a platter, mound the carrot mixture in the center, and spoon the beets around it.

Serve chilled or at room temperature.

PER 3.5-OUNCE SERVING: 97 CALORIES, 1.2 G PROTEIN, 7.2 G FAT, 8 G CARBOHYDRATES, 1.9 G SATURATED FATTY ACIDS, 0 MG CHOLESTEROL, 47.7 MG SODIUM, 2.2 G TOTAL DIETARY FIBER

cucumber peanut salad

This simple snappy salad flavored with fennel seeds and roasted peanuts can be made as spicy as you like by adding a few more chiles.

Serves 4
Preparation time: 20 minutes
Marinating time: 20 minutes

3 cucumbers, peeled, seeded, and
    sliced into ¼-inch-thick crescents
    (about 4 cups)

2 teaspoons salt

1 tablespoon brown sugar, packed

2 tablespoons fresh lemon juice

1½ tablespoons white vinegar

1 tablespoon vegetable oil

2 teaspoons fennel seeds

1 to 2 teaspoons seeded, minced fresh
    chile (optional)

½ cup crushed roasted peanuts, or
    more to taste*

Crush peanuts using a food processor, or put them in a plastic bag to keep them from scattering and use a rolling pin. About ⅔ cup whole peanuts will yield ½ cup crushed.

Stir together the cucumbers and salt, place in a colander, and drain for 10 to 15 minutes. Rinse the cucumbers well and drain again.

Meanwhile, in a small bowl, stir together the brown sugar, lemon juice, and vinegar until the sugar has dissolved.

When the cucumbers have drained, heat the oil in a small saucepan. When it's hot, add the fennel seeds and the chile, if using. Lift the pan off the heat to avoid scorching, and swirl the pan for about 30 seconds. Continue to cook on low heat for another minute, stirring continuously. Remove from the heat and set aside.

Transfer the drained cucumbers to a large shallow serving bowl and pour the hot seasoned oil over them, tossing well. Stir in the vinegar mixture. Set aside at room temperature for at least 20 minutes before serving.

Serve at room temperature or chilled. Top with the crushed peanuts just before serving.

PER 6-OUNCE SERVING: 164 CALORIES, 5 G PROTEIN, 11.9 G FAT, 12.3 G CARBOHYDRATES, 2.1 G SATURATED FATTY ACIDS, 0 MG CHOLESTEROL, 1,327.8 MG SODIUM, 2.8 G TOTAL DIETARY FIBER

green bean & walnut salad

Here is a generous, good-looking side dish suitable for a holiday meal. The dressing as well as the beans and walnuts can be prepared ahead, so it's easy to assemble the salad at the last minute.

Serve with Fennel Leek Soup (page 76) and Three Seed Whole Wheat Rolls (page 401), or pair with Lighter Lasagna Primavera (page 374).

 Serves 6 to 8 as a side salad
Total time: 30 minutes

Bring a large covered pot of water to a boil.

While the water heats, whirl the dressing ingredients in a blender until emulsified. Set aside. In a heavy skillet, sauté the walnut halves in the butter for a couple of minutes, stirring gently until lightly browned and crisped. Sprinkle with salt and pepper and set aside.

Cook the green beans in the boiling water until just tender, 5 to 10 minutes. Drain the beans and plunge them into cold water to cool. Drain and set aside. Tear the frisée or greens into bite-sized pieces.

Arrange the salad greens on a platter. Mound the green beans in the center and drizzle on half of the dressing. Scatter the walnuts on top. If you like, use a vegetable peeler or small paring knife to shave about a dozen long, paper-thin pieces of Pecorino over all.

Pass the rest of the dressing at the table.

dressing

¼ cup walnut oil
¼ cup olive oil
3 tablespoons sherry vinegar*
3 tablespoons chopped fresh parsley
1 garlic clove, pressed or minced
1 teaspoon Dijon mustard
¼ teaspoon salt

salad

1 cup walnut halves
1 tablespoon butter
salt and pepper to taste
2 pounds green beans, stem ends trimmed**
1 head frisée or 4 cups mixed salad greens
small wedge of Pecorino Romano cheese (optional)

* *Sherry vinegar is available in most groceries and supermarkets. Its particular flavor is just right for this recipe.*
***Haricots verts are especially nice.*

PER 8-OUNCE SERVING: 286 CALORIES, 5.4 G PROTEIN, 25.4 G FAT, 14 G CARBOHYDRATES, 3.4 G SATURATED FATTY ACIDS, 3.9 MG CHOLESTEROL, 110.7 MG SODIUM, 4.5 G TOTAL DIETARY FIBER

thai eggplant & tomato salad

This eye-catching salad exemplifies the complex flavors in Thai cuisine. Here, smoky roasted eggplant and crisp fresh vegetables are bathed in a marinade of mint, cilantro, basil, ginger, chiles, lime, and Southeast Asian fish sauce or soy sauce.

Because the eggplant should marinate for at least an hour, start this recipe about 2 hours before serving, or roast and marinate the eggplant the day before. Toss the salad with soba or udon noodles and top it with roasted peanuts and crunchy mung sprouts for a perfect luncheon or light supper dish.

 Serves 4 to 6
Preparation time: 30 minutes
Roasting and marinating time: 1½ to 2 hours

Preheat the oven to 450°.

Toss the eggplant with the oil, spread the cubes on a large baking sheet, and roast for about 25 minutes, stirring every 10 minutes. Meanwhile, place the tomatoes, cucumbers, bell peppers, and scallions in a bowl and set aside in the refrigerator.

Whisk all of the marinade ingredients together in a small bowl.

When the eggplant is roasted, transfer to a serving bowl, toss with the marinade, and set aside to cool and marinate for at least an hour. Just before serving, add the other vegetables and gently toss with the eggplant.

Serve at room temperature.

salad

5 cups peeled cubed eggplant (1-inch cubes)*

2 tablespoons vegetable oil

2 tomatoes, halved, cored, and cut into thin slices

½ large cucumber, peeled, halved, seeded, and cut into crescents

1 small yellow or red bell pepper, cored, seeded, and thinly sliced

2 scallions, sliced on the diagonal

marinade

¼ cup fresh lime juice

1 tablespoon freshly grated lime peel

3 tablespoons vegetable oil

2 tablespoons grated fresh ginger root

2 tablespoons fish sauce or soy sauce

1 to 2 tablespoons chopped fresh mint

¼ cup chopped fresh Thai basil

2 tablespoons chopped fresh cilantro

2 teaspoons minced fresh green chiles, or more to taste

* *1 large eggplant or two medium Japanese eggplants will yield about 5 cups.*

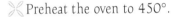

PER 5.5-OUNCE SERVING: 142 CALORIES, 1.7 G PROTEIN, 12.2 G FAT, 9.2 G CARBOHYDRATES, 3.1 G SATURATED FATTY ACIDS, 3 MG CHOLESTEROL, 393.1 MG SODIUM, 2.5 G TOTAL DIETARY FIBER

tofu salad

Miso and tahini bring rich flavor to this mock chicken salad. A bite of this tofu concoction might give you a flashback to your favorite deli. For a chewier texture, the tofu is crumbled and dried in a skillet. While the tofu cools, the vegetables and herbs can be prepared.

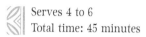 Serves 4 to 6
Total time: 45 minutes

1 cake firm tofu (16 ounces)
1 tablespoon vegetable oil
2 teaspoons soy sauce
1 1/2 teaspoons fresh lemon juice
3 tablespoons light or white miso
3 tablespoons tahini
1/3 cup prepared low-fat or regular mayonnaise
2 tablespoons Dijon mustard
1 1/2 cups peeled and grated carrots
1 1/2 cups diced red bell peppers
1 1/2 cups diced celery
1/3 cup chopped scallions
1 tablespoon chopped fresh parsley, basil, or dill
salt and ground black pepper to taste

Crumble the tofu. Heat the oil in a nonstick or heavy skillet on medium-high heat. Add the tofu and cook, stirring constantly, until the tofu becomes dry and shrinks slightly, about 5 minutes. Stir in the soy sauce and the fresh lemon juice and cook for 1 minute. Remove from the heat and set aside to cool for at least 10 minutes.

Meanwhile, whisk together the miso, tahini, mayonnaise, and mustard in a mixing bowl. Add the carrots, bell peppers, celery, scallions, fresh herbs, and the cooled tofu. Allow the flavors to meld for 15 minutes or more and then add salt and black pepper to taste.

Serve stuffed in a pita, on a baguette, or with a green salad.

PER 8-OUNCE SERVING: 192 CALORIES, 9.8 G PROTEIN, 12.2 G FAT, 14.4 G CARBOHYDRATES, 2.1 G SATURATED FATTY ACIDS, 6.2 MG CHOLESTEROL, 458 MG SODIUM, 3.9 G TOTAL DIETARY FIBER

two shredded carrot salads

Both of these bright, tart dressings complement the sweetness of shredded carrots to a tee. For a bit of a bite, include small capers; although about half the size of regular capers, they are both more flavorful and more expensive. Sometimes marked nonpareil, they can be found in the imported foods section of many grocery stores and supermarkets. For a cheerful presentation, serve this glistening salad on a big lettuce leaf or a bed of dark green spinach leaves.

Use a food processor or a hand-held grater for shredding the carrots. The food processor is quicker, but some processors grate the carrots into a soggy mass. If you don't have a food processor that will do a sharp, clean grating job that leaves the carrots relatively dry, pull the hand grater out of the drawer. It won't take that much longer and you'll be pleased with the result.

Serves 4
Total time: about 30 minutes

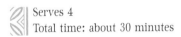Place the carrots in a serving bowl and set aside. With a whisk or in a blender, combine the ingredients for the dressing of your choice. (The Horseradish Vinaigrette will be smoother if puréed in a blender for 30 seconds.) Pour the dressing over the carrots and toss well.

Serve lightly chilled or at room temperature.

2½ cups peeled and grated carrots

Choose one of the following:

cilantro dressing

3 tablespoons olive oil

1 small garlic clove, minced or pressed

1 teaspoon minced fresh cilantro

1 tablespoon minced fresh parsley

½ teaspoon salt

2 tablespoons fresh lemon juice

pinch of cayenne (optional)

horseradish vinaigrette

3 tablespoons olive oil

4 teaspoons prepared horseradish

4 teaspoons cider vinegar

1 small garlic clove, minced or pressed

¼ to ½ teaspoon salt

1 teaspoon dried dill weed (optional)

2 teaspoons small capers (optional)

PER 4-OUNCE "CILANTRO" SERVING: 134 CALORIES, 1 G PROTEIN, 10.8 G FAT, 9.7 G CARBOHYDRATES, 1.5 G SATURATED FATTY ACIDS, 0 MG CHOLESTEROL, 330.4 MG SODIUM, 2.7 G TOTAL DIETARY FIBER

PER 4-OUNCE "HORSERADISH" SERVING: 135 CALORIES, 1 G PROTEIN, 10.8 G FAT, 9.7 G CARBOHYDRATES, 1.5 G SATURATED FATTY ACIDS, 0 MG CHOLESTEROL, 185 MG SODIUM, 2.7 G TOTAL DIETARY FIBER

perfect tomato salad

Both sweet and acidic, a tomato salad is perfect to pair with pastas, risottos, potato hashes, skillet beans, or frittatas. When tomatoes are in season, look for heirloom types, and for a truly spectacular salad, use lots of different kinds—big red beefsteaks, purple brown Brandywines or Cherokee Purples, Golden Jubilees or Yellow Taxis, and striped Green Zebra tomatoes, and a few baby tomatoes named for other fruits such as pear, grape, and cherry.

You need about $2^1/_2$ pounds of tomatoes to serve four people. Slice the big tomatoes thickly to show off their shapes. Just cut the tiny tomatoes in half. Arrange them all artistically on a big platter. Sprinkle on some salt, pepper, and finely chopped fresh basil leaves, preferably green and purple, and drizzle on a thin ribbon of extra-virgin olive oil. Or use one of the dressings that follow. Serve at room temperature.

basil pineapple dressing for winter tomatoes

When supermarket tomatoes are less than perfect, try this dressing. Fresh basil grown in greenhouses is available year round, and its quality in winter is close to its late summer glory. Pineapple adds the sweet acidity usually missing from off-season, commercially produced tomatoes.

Yields $^2/_3$ cup

3 tablespoons extra-virgin olive oil
1 tablespoon rice or cider vinegar
$^1/_4$ cup unsweetened pineapple juice*
$^1/_4$ cup chopped fresh basil leaves
$^1/_4$ cup chopped scallions
$^1/_2$ teaspoon salt
pinch of crushed red pepper flakes

* Or 1 tablespoon of pineapple juice concentrate and 3 tablespoons of water.

Purée everything in a blender until smooth. Drizzle the dressing over $2^1/2$ pounds of sliced tomatoes or tomato wedges. The dressing can be made ahead and refrigerated in a covered container until ready to use.

PER 11-OUNCE SERVING: 167 CALORIES, 2.8 G PROTEIN, 11.6 G FAT, 16.2 G CARBOHYDRATES, 1.6 G SATURATED FATTY ACIDS, 0 MG CHOLESTEROL, 326.7 MG SODIUM, 3.6 G TOTAL DIETARY FIBER

buttermilk dressings for tomatoes

We love buttermilk dressings on fresh, ripe tomatoes, but they're good on other vegetables as well. Gussy up the basic dressing with one of the variations. Dill Buttermilk Dressing and the Feta Buttermilk Dressing are also good on cucumbers or celeriac. Chopped hard-boiled egg is a delicious addition to Curried Buttermilk-dressed tomatoes. Add corn kernels and chopped scallions to tomatoes with Cumin Buttermilk Dressing.

Yields about 1 cup

basic buttermilk dressing

- ½ cup buttermilk
- ¼ cup prepared mayonnaise or plain yogurt
- 1 tablespoon vegetable oil
- 1 tablespoon cider vinegar
- salt to taste
- ¼ teaspoon ground black pepper

In a blender, combine all of the Basic Buttermilk Dressing ingredients and the variation ingredients you select and purée until smooth.

Drizzle the dressing over 2½ pounds of sliced tomatoes or tomato wedges. Extra dressing will keep covered and refrigerated for 3 to 4 days.

PER 12-OUNCE SERVING: 158 CALORIES, 3.5 G PROTEIN, 9.5 G FAT, 18.2 G CARBOHYDRATES, 1.9 G SATURATED FATTY ACIDS, 4.7 MG CHOLESTEROL, 160.5 MG SODIUM, 3.2 G TOTAL DIETARY FIBER

variations

- *For Dill Buttermilk Dressing, add 2 tablespoons of chopped fresh dill and an extra tablespoon of vinegar.*
- *For Curried Buttermilk Dressing, add 1 teaspoon curry powder, ¼ teaspoon crushed red pepper flakes, and ¼ teaspoon turmeric.*
- *For Feta Buttermilk Dressing, omit the salt and add ¼ cup crumbled feta cheese and ½ teaspoon dried oregano.*
- *For Cumin Buttermilk Dressing, add ¾ teaspoon ground cumin and ¼ teaspoon ground cardamom.*

side
vegetables

side vegetables

Okay, you're way beyond simply heating canned corn, so why does the phrase "side vegetable" still fail to arouse any resounding enthusiasm? Maybe for some people the term bears the taint of childhood obligation, of what you had to eat because it was "good for you" or because "children were starving" somewhere. Maybe a side vegetable was something you had to down in order to get to dessert?

Despite the American "kids don't like vegetables" syndrome—possibly a reaction to canned or frozen vegetables overcooked and poorly seasoned—at Moosewood, we see lots of children who grow up loving vegetables.

After a shift, some of the Moosewood staff might dish up plates of several side vegetables and make a meal of it. Creamy garlic mashed potatoes naturally harmonize with mixed greens, a spicy stir-fried savoy cabbage dish is great beside lusciously juicy corn on the cob, Asian Greens & Spring Vegetables is perfectly offset by Wasabi Mashed Sweet Potatoes.

For customers at the restaurant, we use side vegetables to create colorful and tempting finished plates. In the dead of winter, burgundy beets offset a deep orange stuffed squash; Asparagus with Red Pepper Sauce is smashing beside Mushroom Strudel. With tantalizing side vegetables, the main dish will taste better, look better, and seem more interesting. Side vegetables can provide contrasting tastes and textures that refresh the palate and ready it for the next bite. Crisp fried foods love tangy slaws, smooth mashed sweet potatoes adore spicy greens, a piping hot, creamy casserole gets a pleasant jolt from chilled, tart-sweet pickled beets.

In this chapter we've selected some less common vegetables to prepare as sides and have put some new spins on old favorites. From the looks of the many clean plates we clear from the tables, we can tell that our customers love our side vegetables as much as we do.

heirloom vegetables

Until recently, farmers and plant breeders saved the seeds of the most desirable plants from each year's harvest for the next year's crop. Gardeners gave their surplus to friends and relatives, and especially noteworthy varieties found their way to seed companies for wider distribution. Today with larger mechanized farms, fewer gardeners harvesting seeds, and more hybrids and sterile seeds, many heirloom varieties have become rare or extinct.

This amounts to more than just the old being pushed out by the new. Heirlooms are not the first choice for agribusiness where concerns of perishability, yield, shipping endurance, pest resistance, and appearance are more important than flavor. As more old varieties are lost, we also lose a broad genetic base. This creates a less diverse source of food crops that may not be as adaptable or hardy.

What can the consumer do? If you enjoy gardening, grow heirloom vegetables yourself. Patronize farmers' markets and produce stands where farmers label and promote heirlooms. Buy locally grown fresh produce to support growers who can produce a wider range of varieties than what is offered at typical supermarkets. Another option is to join Community Supported Agriculture (CSA) to encourage regional small-scale farms. CSA members buy shares in the produce they will eventually receive. Most CSAs encourage participation, including input on what to grow. For information, visit *www.reeusda.gov/csa*.

Moosewood's David Hirsch, an avid organic gardener, has come up with a few of his favorite heirloom varieties.

beans

cherokee trail of tears—*Carried by the Cherokees on their forced march west to Oklahoma. These are very tasty purple podded beans.*

kentucky wonder—*A classic green bean, excellent flavor, great fresh, frozen, or canned.*

jacob's cattle—*White beans attractively spotted with maroon. Good for all bean dishes, especially soups or baked beans.*

beets

chioggia—*Strong-growing beautiful Italian variety. Horizontal slices show alternating rings of rose pink and white. Nice in salads.*

golden beet—*Brilliantly colored roots that are also particularly sweet.*

broccoli

romanesco—*Spiraling florets form psychedelic patterns on this nutty-flavored Italian heirloom.*

cabbage

early jersey wakefield—*A very tender and sweet English variety from the eighteenth century.*

carrots

scarlet nantes—*Non-fibrous texture and sweet flavor for all uses, particularly juicing.*

corn

golden bantam—*Introduced in 1902, this is still a popular sweet corn for home gardeners.*

eggplant

rosa bianca—*Delicate flavor, smooth texture, and unusual lavender stripes on a white fruit make this Italian heirloom worth trying.*

kale

russian red (ragged jack)—*Brought to North America by Russian traders, this is our favorite variety of a very nutritious cooking green. The flat, violet-veined leaves are milder and more tender than other kales.*

leeks

blue solaise—*A cold-hardy, attractive leek. Its blue stems become violet-streaked red during the winter.*

lettuce

black seeded simpson—*A crisp, tasty, classic looseleaf with bright yellow leaves.*

forellen schluss (speckled trout)—*An Austrian heirloom with very tender, light green leaves speckled with maroon.*

mustard greens

mizuna—*A Japanese type that is versatile; baby greens are good in salad, mature leaves cook quickly for soups or stir-frys. Plant has a lovely feathery, fern-like habit.*

tatsoi—*A Chinese heirloom with deep green leaves on white stalks, similar to pak choi, but smaller. Use like mizuna.*

peas

golden sweet—*Unusual chartreuse snow pea, new to this continent but grown for centuries in India. Eat the pods before peas develop.*

swiss chard

five color silverbeet—*The flavor of this Swiss chard is not different from the green variety, but the gorgeous color range of red, pink, yellow, orange, and cream stops people in their tracks. Good in both flower and vegetable gardens as an edible ornamental.*

squash

delicata—*A nineteenth-century introduction valued today for its dry, sweet flesh. Sized just right for individual servings of stuffed squash.*

tomatoes

amana orange—*Huge slicing tomatoes with rich flavor. Combine with other colored slicers for festive platters.*

black krim—*Russian heirloom with full flavor and purplish-red fruits that turn almost black in hot weather.*

brandywine—*Large pink beefsteak, good for slicing, intense tomato-ey flavor. An Amish family heirloom that has become very popular.*

cherokee purple—*Tennessee variety reputed to be one of the sweetest. Unusually colored rose, green, and brown.*

costoluto genovese—*Italian variety good for sauce, juice, fresh eating. Somewhat tart, bright red.*

green zebra—*An introduction from the eighties that is grouped with heirlooms because of its appearance and non-hybrid status. Zesty tart-and-sweet flesh that is, not surprisingly, striped yellow to yellow-green.*

joya de oaxaca—*Mexican variety that is good both fresh and dried. Yellow flesh streaked with pink, orange, and red. Highly flavorful.*

mortgage lifter (radiator charlie's mortgage lifter)—*Huge beefsteaks that enabled the breeder to pay off his mortgage by selling the plants and seeds of this exceptional tomato.*

yellow pear—*Prolific producer of sweet, juicy small tomatoes that are low in acid and very flavorful.*

asian greens & spring vegetables

This light and elegant side dish with a mild sesame-ginger dressing can be made with almost any type of greens. At Moosewood, we like it best with bok choy, spinach, or Swiss chard. Use either snow peas or halved asparagus spears, depending upon what is available and looks most fresh and tender.

Serves 4 to 6
Total time: 20 minutes

6 ounces snow peas or 8 asparagus
   spears
4 cups sliced bok choy, or 6 cups
   rinsed and stemmed fresh
   spinach leaves
1 cup carrot matchsticks*
1/2 cup daikon matchsticks*

dressing

3 tablespoons dark sesame oil

3 tablespoons soy sauce

1 1/2 teaspoons sugar

2 teaspoons grated fresh ginger root

1/3 cup scallions, sliced on an extreme
   diagonal
1 tablespoon toasted sesame seeds**
lemon wedges

Bring 1 quart of water to a boil on high heat. Remove the strings from the snow peas, if using, and blanch for 1 to 2 minutes. (Or, for asparagus, snap off the tough stem ends, cut the spears in half on the diagonal, rinse, and simmer until tender, about 7 minutes.) Remove with a slotted spoon, drain, and set aside. Blanch the bok choy in the same water for 2 to 3 minutes (blanch spinach for 1 minute), then drain and set aside.

Meanwhile, whisk together the sesame oil, soy sauce, sugar, and ginger root.

Toss the bok choy or spinach with half of the dressing and spread on a serving platter. Toss the rest of the vegetables with the remaining dressing and arrange them on top of the greens. Sprinkle with the scallions and sesame seeds.

Serve at room temperature decorated with a few lemon wedges.

* If you prefer, use 1 cup of grated carrots and
1/2 cup of grated daikon.
** Toast sesame seeds on an unoiled baking
tray at 350° for 2 to 3 minutes, until fragrant and golden brown.

PER 10-OUNCE SERVING: 114 CALORIES, 3.3 G PROTEIN, 8.1 G FAT, 8.5 G CARBOHYDRATES, 1.1 G SATURATED FATTY ACIDS, 0 MG CHOLESTEROL, 428.1 MG SODIUM, 2.9 G TOTAL DIETARY FIBER

asparagus with red pepper sauce

In our area of the country, asparagus heralds the arrival of spring. This simple, beautiful dish provides a showcase for them. The asparagus spears are roasted and then drizzled with a bright red vinaigrette.

Look for spears that are firm, substantial, not too skinny, and uniformly green with tightly budded tips. Soaking asparagus spears in water for a few minutes before rinsing and draining them helps remove any sand or dirt embedded in the stalks.

The Roasted Red Pepper Sauce is perfect on any steamed or roasted vegetable (we especially like it on roasted green beans), or it can double as a dressing for your favorite sandwich. This recipe can be prepared with canned roasted red peppers, but roasting a fresh pepper with the asparagus provides a much better flavor.

Serves 4
Preparation time: 10 minutes
Roasting time: 25 to 30 minutes

1 pound fresh asparagus

1 tablespoon olive oil

1 large garlic clove, minced or pressed

1/4 teaspoon salt

roasted red pepper sauce

1 red bell pepper, seeded and cut into eighths

1/4 cup olive oil

1 garlic clove, minced or pressed

1 tablespoon red wine vinegar

2 to 3 teaspoons chopped fresh dill

salt and ground black pepper to taste

Preheat the oven to 400°. Oil a baking tray.

Snap off the tough stem ends of the asparagus and rinse well. Toss the spears with the olive oil, garlic, and salt and place them in a single layer on one half of the baking tray. On the other half of the tray, arrange the red pepper strips. Roast for 25 to 30 minutes, turning about every 10 minutes, until the vegetables are tender.

Place the roasted pepper strips in a blender with the olive oil, garlic, vinegar, and dill. Purée until smooth. Add salt and black pepper to taste. Arrange the roasted asparagus on a serving platter. Drizzle some of the dressing in a ribbon across the middle of the asparagus and pass the rest at the table.

Serve at room temperature.

PER 5.5-OUNCE SERVING: 196 CALORIES, 3.5 G PROTEIN, 18.2 G FAT, 7.5 G CARBOHYDRATES, 2.5 G SATURATED FATTY ACIDS, 0 MG CHOLESTEROL, 159 MG SODIUM, 2.1 G TOTAL DIETARY FIBER

braised fennel with parmesan

Fresh fennel bulbs, with celery-like stems and feathery tops, retain a mild anise flavor, whether braised, simmered in soups or stews, or sliced raw into salads. Here fennel simmers in olive oil and garlic, its classic Italian companions.

We intensified the anise flavor with the addition of ground fennel seeds. The topping of crunchy bread crumbs and Parmesan cheese makes an elegant and tasty presentation.

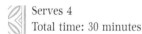
Serves 4
Total time: 30 minutes

Slice the tops off the fennel bulbs, reserving several fronds for garnish. Remove the outer layers of the bulbs if bruised or soft. Slice the bulbs lengthwise into narrow wedges about ⅛ inch wide.

In a large skillet, heat the olive oil and sauté the garlic and ground fennel for several seconds. Stir in the salt and the sliced fennel and sauté for 1 to 2 minutes. Add the water, cover, and increase the heat slightly. Simmer, stirring occasionally, for 10 to 15 minutes, until tender.

Meanwhile, make the seasoned bread crumbs. Warm the olive oil in a small heavy skillet. Add the garlic and sauté for a few seconds. Add the bread crumbs and stir until golden and crunchy, about 5 minutes. When the fennel is tender, transfer it to the serving dish and evenly sprinkle with the bread crumbs.

Serve topped with grated Parmesan, pepper, and chopped fennel fronds.

sauté
2 fennel bulbs
2 tablespoons olive oil
3 garlic cloves, chopped
1 teaspoon freshly ground fennel seeds*
1 teaspoon salt
3 tablespoons water

seasoned bread crumbs
2 tablespoons olive oil
1 garlic clove, chopped
½ cup bread crumbs**

topping
⅓ cup grated Parmesan cheese
freshly ground black pepper to taste
1 to 2 tablespoons chopped fennel fronds

* Grind the seeds with a mortar and pestle or in an electric spice grinder.
** Pulverize stale or lightly toasted whole wheat, sourdough, or French bread in a blender or food processor.

PER 6-OUNCE SERVING: 255 CALORIES, 7.6 G PROTEIN, 18.5 G FAT, 16.7 G CARBOHYDRATES, 4.2 G SATURATED FATTY ACIDS, 8.8 MG CHOLESTEROL, 945.5 MG SODIUM, 4.6 G TOTAL DIETARY FIBER

cauliflower with polonaise topping

At Moosewood, we find many ways to use cauliflower: in marinated vegetables, creamy pasta dishes, Indian curries, chunky soups. Here we top it with zesty, herbed bread crumbs and serve it as a fancy side dish.

An easy method for cutting cauliflower: Place the head stem side up on a cutting board. Pull away the leaves on the underside of the cauliflower, cut around the large core, and remove it. Once the core is removed, with a sharp paring knife, cut the desired size of florets by cutting the branches from the inside of the cauliflower.

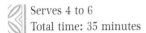
Serves 4 to 6
Total time: 35 minutes

Steam or blanch the cauliflower florets in salted boiling water until tender, 5 to 8 minutes. Drain and set aside.

Meanwhile, warm the butter or oil in a large 12-inch skillet and sauté the garlic and bread crumbs for 3 to 4 minutes, until the crumbs are golden. Mix the hard-boiled egg, if using, into the bread crumbs. Add the parsley, tarragon, chives, Dijon, and salt and mix well. Add the drained cauliflower florets to the skillet, toss with the seasoned bread crumbs, and add pepper to taste.

Serve immediately.

8 cups cauliflower florets*

2 tablespoons butter or extra-virgin olive oil

2 garlic cloves, minced or pressed

2/3 cup bread crumbs, preferably whole wheat**

1 hard-boiled egg, peeled and chopped (optional)

1 tablespoon chopped fresh parsley

1 tablespoon chopped fresh tarragon (1 teaspoon dried)

1 tablespoon chopped fresh chives

1 tablespoon Dijon mustard

1/2 teaspoon salt

ground black pepper to taste

* Two pounds of cauliflower will yield about 8 cups of florets.
** Pulverize stale or lightly toasted whole wheat, sourdough, or rye bread in a blender or food processor.

PER 6-OUNCE SERVING: 106 CALORIES, 4.2 G PROTEIN, 5.2 G FAT, 12.8 G CARBOHYDRATES, 2.6 G SATURATED FATTY ACIDS, 10.3 MG CHOLESTEROL, 363.1 MG SODIUM, 4.7 G TOTAL DIETARY FIBER

curried corn

Try making this dish when the first young ears of sweet corn appear at farm stands in your area; otherwise, frozen corn is a good substitute.

If you've found a good-quality curry powder or garam masala, use it in this dish, but if you would like to concoct your own curry spice mix, you can start with the amounts we suggest in the ingredient note for a mildly curried taste. Add more spices and cayenne for a more pungent flavor.

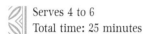 Serves 4 to 6
Total time: 25 minutes

2 tablespoons vegetable oil or butter

1 cup diced shallots or onions

2 to 3 teaspoons curry powder*

3 cups fresh or frozen corn kernels**

1³⁄₄ cups reduced-fat coconut milk
   (14-ounce can)

1 tablespoon fresh lime juice

salt and ground black pepper to taste

chopped fresh cilantro or thinly
   sliced scallions (optional)

* *For homemade curry powder, blend 1 teaspoon of ground cumin, 1 teaspoon of ground coriander, ¹⁄₈ teaspoon of ground cinnamon, ¹⁄₄ teaspoon of ground ginger, ¹⁄₈ to ¹⁄₄ teaspoon of cayenne.*
** *A pound of frozen corn kernels equals 3 cups.*

In a covered saucepan, warm the oil or butter on medium-high heat. Add the shallots or onions and sauté for 3 minutes. Add the curry powder, stir well, and sauté until the spices darken and the shallots or onions are lightly golden and soft, about 3 minutes longer.

Stir in the corn, cover, and heat for about 3 minutes. Pour in the coconut milk, cover, and heat thoroughly, but not to a boil. When the corn is tender and hot, remove from the heat and stir in the lime juice. Add salt and pepper to taste.

If you like, serve sprinkled with cilantro or scallions.

PER 6-OUNCE SERVING: 203 CALORIES, 4.5 G PROTEIN, 11.6 G FAT, 24.2 G CARBOHYDRATES, 4.9 G SATURATED FATTY ACIDS, 0 MG CHOLESTEROL, 25.6 MG SODIUM, 2.3 G TOTAL DIETARY FIBER

chilean artichokes

Eliana Parra, affectionately known as Nana, came to Moosewood in 1981 after emigrating from her native Chile. She remembers lots of artichokes growing in her grandparents' garden. Her mother used to set a big bowl of them right in the middle of the table, and the kids would gobble the leaves to see who could get to the hearts first.

When Nana moved to Ithaca, where artichokes are expensive, she bought a few, thinking her U.S.-raised kids wouldn't like them and she could eat them all herself. Not so. The love of artichokes passed down to daughter and son, and so the family race to the hearts continues.

If you're lucky enough to find them, use tender, completely edible baby artichokes. Or make the salad with canned artichoke hearts or try the vinaigrette as a dipping sauce for regular artichokes. If the vinaigrette is more than you need, save it—it's good with other vegetables, on baked fish, with shrimp or scallops, and as a salad dressing.

Serves 4
Total time: 15 to 30 minutes

vegetables

16 baby artichokes* or a 15-ounce can of artichoke hearts

lettuce or mixed baby greens

1 hard-boiled egg, chopped

1 tomato, cut into wedges

green vinaigrette

¼ cup olive oil

3 tablespoons fresh lime juice

⅓ cup chopped scallions

½ cup chopped fresh cilantro

¼ teaspoon salt

¼ cup water

* Choose small, firm, baby artichokes with tightly closed, tender leaves.

To cook the baby artichokes, bring a large nonreactive pot of water to a boil. Use a stainless-steel knife to cut off the top quarter of the artichokes and trim the stems to about an inch. Bend back the outer green leaves and snap them off at the base until you reach the leaves that are yellow. Trim the remaining green from the base.

Boil the baby artichokes for 10 to 20 minutes, until a leaf can be easily pulled out. Drain upside down. Meanwhile, spread the greens on a serving platter and arrange the chopped egg and tomato wedges on top, leaving room in the center for the artichokes. Combine all of the Green Vinaigrette ingredients in a blender and purée until smooth.

When the artichokes are cool enough to handle, halve or quarter them. If using canned artichoke hearts, quarter them. Arrange the artichokes in the center of the platter and pour the vinaigrette over them.

PER 7-OUNCE SERVING: 213 CALORIES, 5.9 G PROTEIN, 16.1 G FAT, 14.9 G CARBOHYDRATES, 2.5 G SATURATED FATTY ACIDS, 62.6 MG CHOLESTEROL, 266.3 MG SODIUM, 6.1 G TOTAL DIETARY FIBER

mixed greens

Greens, wild and cultivated, have found their way into every cuisine. In Southern cooking, greens are traditionally flavored with ham and simmered for as long as 45 minutes, until they're very soft. In Mediterranean cooking, they are often sautéed in oil and garlic for a much shorter time, leaving them brighter in color and with more of a bite.

As greens become more common on restaurant menus, the trend is to cook them more lightly, but, to do this successfully, the greens must be young and tender. More mature greens take longer to cook: completely removing the tough stems can help speed things up.

This recipe lets you cook your greens as long as you like. Just keep enough liquid in the pot so the greens stay moist, juicy, and, most important, unscorched. The pot liquor is tasty and can be soaked up with bread or cornbread.

2 tablespoons vegetable oil

2 or 3 garlic cloves, minced or pressed

3 pounds fresh greens, rinsed, stemmed, and coarsely chopped*

3 tablespoons soy sauce

3 tablespoons cider vinegar

1/2 teaspoon Tabasco sauce or other hot pepper sauce, or more to taste

1/2 cup water, plus more if needed

salt to taste

Serves 4 to 6
Preparation time: 15 minutes
Cooking time: 20 to 45 minutes

* Try 1 to 2 bunches of collard greens (about 1 1/2 pounds) and 1 to 2 bunches of kale (about 1 1/2 pounds)

In a large pot, heat the oil and sauté the garlic on medium heat for just a minute to soften it. Add the damp greens, cover, and cook on medium heat for 5 minutes, until the greens on the bottom begin to soften. Stir the greens until evenly coated with oil.

Add the soy sauce, vinegar, Tabasco sauce, and water. Stir the greens well and add more water, if needed. Simmer for about 15 minutes, stirring occasionally and tasting to sample the texture. They're done when they are as soft as you like them. Add salt and more Tabasco sauce to taste.

PER 8-OUNCE SERVING: 102 CALORIES, 4.8 G PROTEIN, 5.5 G FAT, 11.6 G CARBOHYDRATES, 1.3 G SATURATED FATTY ACIDS, 0 MG CHOLESTEROL, 437.8 MG SODIUM, 4.8 G TOTAL DIETARY FIBER

roasted caramelized balsamic onions

The intoxicating aroma of this very simple dish floating throughout the house will slowly but surely lure people into the kitchen.

Roasting with balsamic vinegar enhances the natural sweetness of many onion varieties, including Vidalia, yellow, and the common Spanish onions. If you only have smaller onions, just use a few more in place of the two large Spanish onions in the recipe. After you turn the onions over and baste them with the marinade, the inner rings will pop up in a beautiful symmetrical pattern.

Serve as a side with a hearty casserole, stew, or vegetable omelet.

2 large Spanish onions

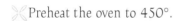
marinade
¼ cup unsalted butter
⅓ cup balsamic vinegar
¼ teaspoon dried thyme
¼ teaspoon salt
ground black pepper to taste

 Serves 4
Preparation time: 5 minutes
Baking time: 40 to 45 minutes

✂ Preheat the oven to 450°.

Cut the onions into halves at their equators. Remove the papery skin and any tough outer layers. Do not cut off the root and stem ends and be careful not to score the layers you don't remove: uncut, the outer layer will better hold the onion together as it roasts. Place the onion halves cut side down in a 9-inch square baking pan.

Melt the butter in a saucepan and stir in the vinegar, thyme, salt, and pepper. Pour over the onions. Bake for about 20 minutes, and then turn the onions over and baste them with the pan juices. Bake for another 20 to 25 minutes, until easily pierced with a paring knife and the inner rings have begun to swell and rise up.

Serve immediately or at room temperature.

PER 4-OUNCE SERVING: 132 CALORIES, 0.9 G PROTEIN, 11.6 G FAT, 6.3 G CARBOHYDRATES, 7.2 G SATURATED FATTY ACIDS, 31 MG CHOLESTEROL, 154.2 MG SODIUM, 1.3 G TOTAL DIETARY FIBER

spicy stir-fried savoy cabbage

Make this quick side dish just before sitting down to eat. Cook thinly sliced savoy cabbage with the typical Chinese flavors of ginger, soy sauce, and chili paste. For variety, try this recipe with Chinese cabbage, common green cabbage, kale, or bok choy and sample their distinctive flavors.

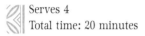 Serves 4
Total time: 20 minutes

3 tablespoons vegetable oil

2 cups sliced onions

1 tablespoon grated, peeled fresh ginger root

6 cups thinly sliced savoy cabbage

1/4 to 1/2 teaspoon Chinese chili paste

2 tablespoons soy sauce, or to taste

Heat the oil in a wok or large skillet until hot, but not smoking, about 4 minutes. Add the onions and ginger and stir-fry until the onions are limp. Add the cabbage and chili paste and stir-fry until the cabbage is crisp-cooked and the outer edges turn bright green, about 10 minutes longer. Mix in the soy sauce, toss once or twice, and serve immediately.

PER 8-OUNCE SERVING: 164 CALORIES, 4.3 G PROTEIN, 11 G FAT, 15.3 G CARBOHYDRATES, 2.8 G SATURATED FATTY ACIDS, 0 MG CHOLESTEROL, 436.2 MG SODIUM, 5.2 G TOTAL DIETARY FIBER

fat facts

The health benefits of vegetable oils are now well documented. Health-conscious eaters need not eliminate oils from their diet. In fact, oils in moderation are necessary to maintain optimum health. Many oils offer a balance of "good fat" and fatty acids that can actually help to reduce cholesterol. Olive, canola, peanut, almond, and hazelnut oils are considered the healthiest choices among vegetable oils because they contain monounsaturated fats, which are believed to reduce the progression of coronary artery disease by lowering "bad" cholesterol (LDL) without negatively affecting "good" cholesterol (HDL). Polyunsaturated fats, present in corn, safflower, sunflower, sesame, walnut, and soy oils, can also reduce LDL levels, but may reduce the positive effects of HDL. Canola and walnut oils also contain omega-3 fatty acids, which are believed to positively affect both HDL and LDL levels and to help ameliorate the symptoms of arthritis and asthma.

turnips with greens

Here in upstate New York, we have a relatively short growing season, so many of our local organic farmers grow root vegetables that sweeten in the ground as the air turns frosty. We like to feature this winter produce at Moosewood Restaurant by roasting parsnips, carrots, beets, turnips, and rutabagas to draw out their natural sweetness and flavor.

As for greens, we suggest using hardy ones that last late into the growing season, such as Swiss or ruby chard, collards, kale, turnip greens, or mustard greens.

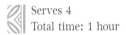 Serves 4
Total time: 1 hour

4 cups peeled turnip matchsticks*

2 cups quartered and thinly sliced onions

5 tablespoons olive oil

1 tablespoon minced fresh oregano (1½ to 2 teaspoons dried)

¼ teaspoon salt

⅛ teaspoon ground black pepper

4 garlic cloves, minced

pinch of crushed red pepper flakes (optional)

8 cups rinsed, stemmed, and sliced greens (see headnote)

chopped fresh parsley or chives

* Julienne the turnips into 2 x ¼-inch pieces.

Preheat the oven to 350°. Oil a baking sheet.

Place the turnips and onions in a bowl and toss them with 4 tablespoons of the olive oil and the oregano. Spread evenly on the baking sheet and sprinkle with the salt and pepper.

Bake for 20 to 30 minutes, or until the ends of the turnip matchsticks are golden brown and crisp. Remove from the oven and set aside.

In a nonreactive pan, cook the garlic in the remaining 1 tablespoon of olive oil just until soft. Add the crushed red pepper, if using, and the greens. Cook, stirring often, for about 15 minutes, until the greens are tender. Remove from the heat.

Serve the greens in a large shallow serving bowl or on a plate, topped with the roasted turnips and onions. Garnish with chopped parsley or chives.

PER 8-OUNCE SERVING: 222 CALORIES, 2.3 G PROTEIN, 18.2 G FAT, 14.6 G CARBOHYDRATES, 2.4 G SATURATED FATTY ACIDS, 0 MG CHOLESTEROL, 203.5 MG SODIUM, 2.4 G TOTAL DIETARY FIBER

mashed potatoes

Mashed potatoes are *the* quintessential comfort food. You may prefer them adorned only with a pool of melting butter or with rich, brown, mushroom gravy, but with their earthy flavor and creamy texture, mashed potatoes are the perfect vehicle for many other flavors. Mix your mashed potatoes with . . . fresh herbs, herbed oils, flavored oils, pestos, root vegetables, mushrooms, hard cheeses, soft cheeses, goat cheese, flavored cheeses, tofu, butter, no butter, chopped vegetables, puréed vegetables, sautéed, roasted, or steamed vegetables, leeks, onions, chives, shallots, subtle spices, strong spices, hot peppers, roasted garlic, poached garlic, sautéed garlic. You could try different combinations every day for a year without repeating!

The flavor and texture of simple mashed potatoes are largely dependent on which potatoes you choose and how you mash them. The truth is that you can mash any potato, and you can use any tool to do it. But, the results will vary from silky and smooth to lumpy and bumpy, from light and airy to substantial and hearty. Of course, some of us have a penchant for heavy, lumpy mashed potatoes, and making them that way can be intentional!

potato varieties

baking potatoes floury high-starch Russets, Idahos, etc., make for fluffy, airy mashed potatoes that readily absorb flavors and fat.

red potatoes waxy and low-starch. Mashing with skins gives extra flavor and texture. Gluey if overworked.

long white and round white (all-purpose) and yellow-fleshed potatoes, such as yukon gold and yellow finn mealy and medium-starch, making creamy and moist mashed potatoes.

blue & purple potatoes all-purpose and medium-starch. Can add a little color and fun. Peruvian Blues are especially flavorful.

old potatoes During storage, water evaporates making for fluffy mashed potatoes with a sweet flavor. Be sure to remove eyes, soft spots, and wrinkled skin.

sweet potatoes low-starch, high-sugar, making dense, but silky-smooth mashed potatoes. Dark-skinned sweet potatoes with deep orange flesh are moist when cooked; light-skinned with beige flesh are less sweet and drier when cooked.

cooking the potatoes

 First, wash the potatoes well and peel them if you wish. If not peeling, remove any eyes, rough blemishes, and green areas. Cut the potatoes into quarters or large chunks. Cut the pieces to a uniform size; otherwise smaller chunks will be mushy and overdone when the larger chunks are just right.

 Place the cut potatoes in a pot with enough cool water to cover, plus about an inch. Sprinkle with salt. If you're not cooking them right away, store them in the refrigerator covered with water and they won't turn gray.

 To cook, cover the pot, bring to a boil, and then simmer until the potatoes are tender. Start checking for doneness after about 15 minutes. A thin-bladed knife or a fork inserted into the center of a chunk should slip in and out easily.

- Drain the potatoes in a colander, reserving the liquid, if you wish, for soup stock or to use as the liquid for mashing.
- Mash the potatoes while they're hot. Once the potatoes are mashed, whisk or stir in fat (butter, oil, cream cheese) and enough liquid for the consistency you want. Warmed liquids will help keep the mashed potatoes warm.
- Possible liquids include milk, cream, buttermilk, yogurt, cottage cheese, vegetable broth, garlic broth, soy milk, potato-cooking water, vegetable purées, or dried-mushroom soaking liquid.

mashed potato *don'ts*

- **Don't undercook.** The potatoes will require over-vigorous mashing which breaks down the starch cells. Result: gummy potatoes.

- **Don't overcook.** The starch cells will break down. Result: gluey potatoes.

- **Don't "mash" in a food processor.** The blades thoroughly break down starch cells. Result: pasty potatoes.

- **Don't microwave potatoes for mashing.** Microwaved potatoes tend to be firm, requiring extra mashing. Result: gooped-up potatoes.

- **Don't beat too long with an electric mixer.** Result: dense, heavy potatoes.

- **Don't put off washing, or at least rinsing well, your mashing tool right after use.** Result: hardened-on mashed potatoes that will remind you of white school glue as you try to scrape them off.

flavor combinations
regular mashed potatoes:
(add garlic—or not—to any of these)

Chipotles in adobo sauce, minced cilantro, and Monterey jack cheese

Parmesan cheese, lemon peel, and thyme

Parmesan cheese and rosemary or saffron

Gruyère cheese and spinach

Cheddar cheese and cabbage or broccoli

Rutabaga, apples, and honey

Yogurt, curry powder, and green peas

Chèvre and chives

Leeks, cabbage, and sour cream

Cumin, cauliflower, and buttermilk

Zucchini, black olives, red bell peppers, chiles, and Cheddar cheese

Scallions, chard, and cream cheese

Caramelized onions, ricotta cheese, and Parmesan cheese

mashed sweet potatoes:

Maple syrup and ground cardamom

Bourbon, pears, pecans, and brown sugar

Coconut milk, thyme, and ground allspice or ground nutmeg

Grated fresh ginger root and ground cinnamon

Horseradish or wasabi

fennel leek mashed potatoes

A continental version of Irish Colcannon, these mildly flavored potatoes are a wonderful winter supper side dish. Or, for real potato gourmands like a few of us are at Moosewood, this is no less than a main dish for lunch. It really couldn't be easier to make, as the vegetables are cooked all together in one pot.

Freshly steamed, nutritious greens drizzled with a squeeze of fresh lemon make a good accompaniment.

Serves 4 to 6
Preparation time: 15 minutes
Cooking time: 25 minutes

4 cups cubed potatoes (1-inch cubes)
2 cups thinly sliced cabbage
1 leek, finely chopped*
1 teaspoon salt
2 tablespoons butter
1/2 teaspoon ground fennel seeds
1/2 cup warmed milk or vegetable cooking liquid
salt and ground black pepper to taste

* Use only the white and most tender, light green part of the leek near the bulb. Be sure to rinse the chopped leeks well under running water to remove sand and grit.

Combine the potatoes, cabbage, leeks, and salt in a soup pot with water to cover. Place a tight-fitting lid on the pot and bring to a boil on high heat. Reduce the heat and simmer until the vegetables are soft, about 20 minutes.

Meanwhile, melt the butter in a small saucepan. Stir in the fennel and set aside. When the vegetables are cooked, reserve about 1/2 cup of the cooking liquid if you prefer to use it in place of the milk. Then drain the vegetables, return them to the soup pot, pour the seasoned butter on them, and mash with the milk or vegetable cooking liquid. Add salt and pepper to taste.

PER 7-OUNCE SERVING: 164 CALORIES, 3.3 G PROTEIN, 4.5 G FAT, 28.9 G CARBOHYDRATES, 2.7 G SATURATED FATTY ACIDS, 11.8 MG CHOLESTEROL, 460.5 MG SODIUM, 3.2 G TOTAL DIETARY FIBER

low-fat garlic mashed potatoes

We make these garlic mashed potatoes with Yukon Gold, Butter, or any other yellow variety for the beautiful golden color and smooth texture. The potatoes and garlic are cooked together, then mashed with buttermilk for extra smoothness and a hint of that "sour cream" taste.

They're very good, they have almost no fat, and we promise you won't need any butter! Add more or less garlic, depending on how much garlicky flavor you like.

Serves 4
Total time: 25 minutes

4 cups peeled and diced potatoes
   (¼-inch cubes)
2 to 4 garlic cloves, coarsely chopped
4 to 5 cups water
1 teaspoon salt
½ cup warmed buttermilk
¼ teaspoon ground black pepper

In a covered pot, combine the potatoes, garlic, water, and salt and bring to a boil on high heat. Reduce the heat and simmer for about 10 minutes, until the potato cubes are soft and a knife can be easily inserted and withdrawn.

Drain the potatoes and transfer to a bowl. Mash the potatoes and garlic with the buttermilk. Stir in the pepper. Serve piping hot.

PER 7-OUNCE SERVING: 158 CALORIES, 3.9 G PROTEIN, 0.4 G FAT, 35.6 G CARBOHYDRATES, 0.2 G SATURATED FATTY ACIDS, 1 MG CHOLESTEROL, 484.4 MG SODIUM, 3.1 G TOTAL DIETARY FIBER

mashed potatoes with shallots

Disarmingly simple. Seductive. Divine. Build your supper around these mashed potatoes—just slice a fresh tomato onto your plate and add a single colorful side vegetable. You'll find it's all you need.

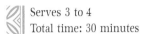
Serves 3 to 4
Total time: 30 minutes

4 cups peeled and diced potatoes
   (¼-inch cubes)

1 teaspoon salt

1 cup minced shallots

2 tablespoons butter

¼ to ½ cup milk or potato cooking
   liquid

½ cup thinly sliced fresh basil leaves

½ cup grated Parmesan cheese
   (optional)

salt and ground black pepper to taste

Combine the potatoes, salt, and enough water to cover in a soup pot. Place a snug lid on the pot and bring to a boil on high heat. Reduce the heat and simmer for about 20 minutes, until the potato cubes are soft and a knife can be easily inserted and withdrawn.

Meanwhile, gently sauté the shallots in the butter until soft, about 10 minutes, and set aside. When the potatoes are ready, reserve some of the cooking liquid if you wish to use it for mashing, then drain the potatoes and return them to the soup pot.

Mash together the potatoes, the sautéed shallots and butter, the milk or potato cooking liquid, the basil, and, if using, the cheese. Use just enough liquid to make the mashed potatoes creamy and fluffy. Add salt and pepper to taste.

Serve immediately.

PER 8-OUNCE SERVING: 233 CALORIES, 4.6 G PROTEIN, 6.3 G FAT, 41.4 G CARBOHYDRATES, 3.8 G SATURATED FATTY ACIDS, 16.6 MG CHOLESTEROL, 676.6 MG SODIUM, 3.4 G TOTAL DIETARY FIBER

tofu mashed potatoes

Here's a nutritious dish for mashed potato lovers, especially those interested in lowering milk fat and increasing protein in their diet. In these smooth mashed potatoes, the usual butter and milk are replaced with a puréed mixture of silken tofu, garlic, and celery.

The purée itself makes a very nice vegan "cream sauce" that's also good on peas, carrots, squash, or rice. When mashed into potatoes, the sauce produces a lovely creamy texture: Use all or part of the sauce to reach the consistency you like. If you're a fan of garlic, up the amount as you wish.

Serve the mashed potatoes plain or with Mushroom Gravy (page 380).

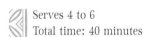
Serves 4 to 6
Total time: 40 minutes

tofu "cream" sauce

2 celery stalks, finely chopped

1 to 2 large garlic cloves, sliced

1 cup water

6 ounces silken tofu

1 teaspoon salt

6 cups peeled and cubed potatoes
ground black pepper to taste

In a small covered saucepan, combine the celery, garlic, and water and bring to a boil. Reduce the heat and simmer for about 10 minutes, until the celery is soft. Combine the celery, garlic, cooking liquid, tofu, and salt in a blender and purée to make a smooth sauce.

Meanwhile, place the potatoes in a soup pot with water to cover. Cover and bring to a boil; then reduce the heat and simmer until the edges of the potato cubes are soft and a knife can be easily inserted and withdrawn, 15 to 20 minutes.

Drain the potatoes and mash them with enough of the tofu "cream" sauce to reach your preferred consistency. Season with pepper.

PER 8.5-OUNCE SERVING: 166 CALORIES, 4.9 G PROTEIN, 1.2 G FAT, 35 G CARBOHYDRATES, 0.2 G SATURATED FATTY ACIDS, 0 MG CHOLESTEROL, 416.6 MG SODIUM, 3.3 G TOTAL DIETARY FIBER

wasabi mashed sweet potatoes

Wasabi is a hot powder or paste made from Japanese horseradish. Most of us think of it as only a sushi condiment, but we also love it in this dish. We recommend using a good-quality, preservative-free wasabi powder without artificial color.

Use about 3 pounds of the sweetest sweet potatoes—the deep orange, long sweet potatoes often called yams by growers. If your sweet potatoes aren't very sweet, add some maple syrup or brown sugar to taste.

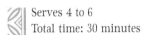
Serves 4 to 6
Total time: 30 minutes

6 cups cubed peeled sweet potatoes
water to cover
1 teaspoon salt
1 tablespoon wasabi powder
¼ cup butter
salt to taste
pure maple syrup or brown sugar to taste

In a covered pot, bring the sweet potatoes, water, and salt to a boil. Lower the heat and simmer until the sweet potatoes are very soft and easily pierced with a fork. Drain, reserving some of the cooking water.

Mix the wasabi powder with about 1½ tablespoons of the potato cooking water to make a paste. Combine the drained sweet potatoes, wasabi paste, and butter and mash well. Add a little more of the cooking water, if needed. Add salt and maple syrup or brown sugar to taste.

PER 5-OUNCE SERVING: 205 CALORIES, 2.3 G PROTEIN, 8.1 G FAT, 31.8 G CARBOHYDRATES, 4.8 G SATURATED FATTY ACIDS, 20.7 MG CHOLESTEROL, 494.4 MG SODIUM, 2.4 G TOTAL DIETARY FIBER

variation ❧ *Replace the sweet potatoes with a buttery white potato, such as Yukon Gold or Yellow Finn.*

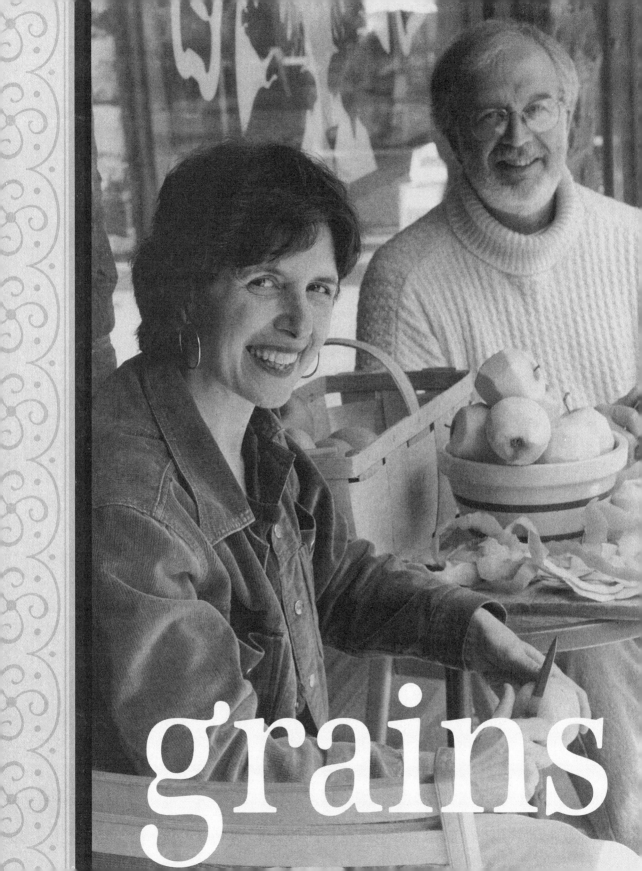

grains

grains

❧ Creating a new grain dish is always a welcome challenge, partly because most of us are crazy about starch, but also because grains are such willing vehicles for innovation.

Almost any grain or food made from grain, when prepared with just a pat of butter and a sprinkling of salt, can be perfectly satisfying. Yet most grains combine so successfully with other ingredients and seasonings that new pilafs, risottos, and salads are always on the horizon.

Brown rice, bulghur, barley, oats, and whole wheat bread have always been mainstays at Moosewood. We love the taste and depth of whole grains. They are earthy and fragrant, nutty and sweet, and they cook up creamy, chewy, or fluffy. With each new cuisine we've explored, we've discovered a new grain or variety of grain: basmati rice from India, arborio rice from Italy, black rice from Thailand, red rice from Arkansas, and wild rice from the marshy waters of Michigan, Minnesota, and Wisconsin, an ancient and present-day gift from Native American tribes. We think of quinoa as an Incan gift from Peru, oats as from Scotland, and millet from Africa by way of China. Grits were refined in the deep South and blue corn in the Southwest. We were tickled to discover that the largest U.S. grower of kasha is right in our backyard, in Penn Yan, New York.

And whole grains are nutritious. They are composed of a bran layer rich in vitamins, minerals, and fiber; a germ layer that houses most of the grain's protein and fat; and the largest layer, the endosperm, which is predominantly carbohydrates. When grain is refined or polished, the bran and germ are removed and, alas, so are many nutrients and much of the fiber.

At Moosewood, we use quick-cooking grains like bulghur, rolled oats, and cornmeal as thickeners for soups and stews. We layer cooked rice, bulghur, and couscous into casseroles, and turn to barley, wild rice, and quinoa for stuffing vegetables. We resurrect day-old whole wheat bread as croutons for soups or salads, and for bread crumbs to top our casseroles, bread fish filets, and bind tofu burgers. To revitalize a boring breakfast routine, we cook rice, barley, or millet with extra water and a bit of sweetener for creamy cereals.

Grains partner with every other food group: vegetables, cheese, legumes, fruits, nuts and seeds, seafood, and seaweed. Grains not only combine well with other foods, they mesh well with other grains. A classic is kasha and farfalle or bow-tie pasta, but we also make pilafs of red rice and long-grain brown rice, basmati rice and wild rice, and with rice and vermicelli. We make a delicious duo of grits and quinoa. It's best to stir dressing and seasonings into grains still warm from cooking, because then they absorb flavor better.

Because grains are such an integral part of our repertoire, you'll find them throughout this book. Find selection and storage suggestions in our discussion of pantry items (page 19) and information in the Guide to Ingredients (page 447).

bulghur with spinach

Easy, homey, earthy, and satisfying—there, that about sums it up. Our colorful sauté made with nut-brown bulghur and vibrant green spinach, and fragrant with garlic and dill, is excellent topped with grated feta cheese.

Bulghur is available in four grades: fine, medium, coarse, and extra-coarse—also known as "half-cut." The fine and medium grades require less time to cook and are fluffier and less chewy than the coarse grades. Don't confuse bulghur with cracked wheat, which is not precooked and must be simmered for at least 20 minutes.

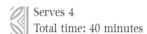
Serves 4
Total time: 40 minutes

1 tablespoon olive oil

1 cup minced scallions

2 to 3 garlic cloves, minced or pressed

1 cup medium-grain bulghur

1 1/4 cups hot water

1/2 teaspoon salt

3 cups rinsed, stemmed, and finely chopped fresh spinach

1 tablespoon chopped fresh dill (1 teaspoon dried)

freshly ground black pepper to taste

a few lemon wedges

In a heavy saucepan with a tight-fitting lid, warm the olive oil on medium heat. Add the scallions and garlic and sauté until softened and fragrant, about 2 to 3 minutes. Add the bulghur and sauté for another minute, stirring to coat the grains with oil.

Pour in the water and salt, bring to a boil, reduce the heat to low, cover, and simmer for 10 minutes. Stir in the spinach and dill and cook for 8 to 10 minutes more, until the water is absorbed but the spinach is still bright green. Stir with a fork to fluff and add pepper to taste.

Serve with lemon wedges all around.

PER 6-OUNCE SERVING: 193 CALORIES, 6.4 G PROTEIN, 4.2 G FAT, 35.8 G CARBOHYDRATES, 0.6 G SATURATED FATTY ACIDS, 0 MG CHOLESTEROL, 321.7 MG SODIUM, 9.1 G TOTAL DIETARY FIBER

bulghur with caramelized onions

Aromatic browned onions sweeten the rugged wheat flavor of bulghur in this simply prepared side dish that is excellent with North African or Middle Eastern–style grilled fish or stews. Add some chopped toasted almonds or walnuts to the pilaf and you have a great filling for stuffed cabbage rolls.

 Serves 4
Total time: 40 minutes

2 tablespoons olive oil
3 cups thinly sliced onions
$1/2$ teaspoon dried thyme
$1/2$ teaspoon salt
1 cup medium-grain bulghur
$1/4$ cup raisins or currants
$1/2$ teaspoon ground cinnamon
$1 1/3$ cups boiling water
ground black pepper to taste
salt or soy sauce to taste

Heat the oil in a large skillet. Add the onions, thyme, and salt and sauté on high heat, stirring often, until golden, about 10 minutes. Lower the heat, cover, and cook for about 15 minutes, stirring occasionally, until the onions are very soft and brown.

Stir in the bulghur, raisins, cinnamon, and boiling water. Cover tightly and simmer gently until all of the liquid is absorbed, about 15 minutes. Add pepper and salt or soy sauce to taste.

PER 8-OUNCE SERVING: 280 CALORIES, 6.9 G PROTEIN, 7.9 G FAT, 49.8 G CARBOHYDRATES, 1.1 G SATURATED FATTY ACIDS, 0 MG CHOLESTEROL, 314.6 MG SODIUM, 9.7 G TOTAL DIETARY FIBER

couscous pilaf with pine nuts

When you need a last-minute side that has a festive look, this golden pilaf, speckled with red and green vegetables and rich with pine nuts, is just the ticket.

Serve it hot as a side dish with fish or steamed vegetables. Or enjoy it cold as a salad with Escabeche (page 363) or Perfect Tomato Salad (page 112).

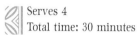

Serves 4
Total time: 30 minutes

Place the couscous, boiling water or stock, salt, and 1 teaspoon of the olive oil in a heatproof bowl. Cover and set aside for about 5 minutes. Uncover and fluff with a fork to break up any lumps. Set aside.

Meanwhile, heat the remaining 2 teaspoons of olive oil in a small skillet on medium heat. Add the garlic and sauté for 1 minute, until it begins to turn golden. Add the bell peppers and sauté for 2 to 3 minutes, stirring constantly, until tender. Remove from the heat and toss with the couscous. Stir in the scallions, parsley, basil, and lemon juice. Add black pepper to taste.

Stir in the pine nuts right before serving.

1 1/2 cups couscous
1 1/2 cups boiling water or vegetable stock
1 teaspoon salt
1 tablespoon olive oil
2 garlic cloves, minced or pressed
1 cup minced red bell peppers
1/2 cup minced scallions
2 tablespoons minced fresh parsley
2 tablespoons chopped fresh basil*
1 tablespoon fresh lemon juice
ground black pepper to taste
3 tablespoons toasted pine nuts**

* Or use 1 tablespoon of chopped fresh dill.
** Toast pine nuts in a single layer on an unoiled baking tray at 350° for 3 to 5 minutes, until fragrant and golden brown.

PER 8-OUNCE SERVING: 348 CALORIES, 11.8 G PROTEIN, 7.4 G FAT, 58.7 G CARBOHYDRATES, 0.7 G SATURATED FATTY ACIDS, 0 MG CHOLESTEROL, 604.9 MG SODIUM, 4.5 G TOTAL DIETARY FIBER

curried quinoa

The more we use quinoa at Moosewood, the more we like it. This "superfood" of the Incas is high in protein, calcium, and phosphorus, with a delicate nutty flavor and a soft yet slightly crunchy consistency. It has a naturally-occuring bitter coating which is mostly removed during processing—a quick cold-water rinse will eliminate any bitter residue that might remain.

Serves 6 to 8
Total time: 40 minutes

1 cup quinoa
1 1/2 tablespoons vegetable oil
1/2 cup diced onions
1 teaspoon grated fresh ginger root
1/2 fresh green chile, minced, or
    1/8 teaspoon cayenne
1/2 teaspoon turmeric
1/2 teaspoon ground coriander
1/4 teaspoon ground cinnamon
1/2 teaspoon salt
1 3/4 cups water
1/2 cup fresh or frozen green peas

1 or 2 tablespoons chopped fresh
    cilantro (optional)

Place the quinoa in a fine-mesh strainer and rinse it with cold water. Drain well.

In a heavy saucepan, warm the oil and sauté the onions on medium-high heat for 4 or 5 minutes. Add the ginger, chile or cayenne, and the quinoa and cook for a minute, stirring constantly. Stir in the turmeric, coriander, cinnamon, and salt and cook for another minute, stirring.

Add the water and bring to a boil. Cover, reduce the heat, and simmer for 15 minutes. Stir in the peas, cover, and cook for 4 or 5 minutes, until the peas are tender and the water has been absorbed.

Before serving, fluff with a fork and add the cilantro, if you wish.

PER 6.5-OUNCE SERVING: 216 CALORIES, 6.5 G PROTEIN, 7.6 G FAT, 31.6 G CARBOHYDRATES, 1.6 G SATURATED FATTY ACIDS, 0 MG CHOLESTEROL, 327.9 MG SODIUM, 3.9 G TOTAL DIETARY FIBER

kasha with red cabbage

Crisp cooked red cabbage and fresh dill brighten this down-to-earth side dish, which is especially welcome on a cold winter's evening.

Try this slightly nutty grain dish with Simple Baked Tofu (page 225) or Elegant Oven-Poached Fish (page 362).

Serves 4 to 6
Total time: 35 to 40 minutes

1 cup diced onions
2 garlic cloves, minced or pressed
1 tablespoon vegetable oil
2 cups finely chopped red cabbage
1/4 teaspoon caraway seeds
1/4 teaspoon salt
1 cup kasha
1 egg white, lightly beaten
2 cups water or vegetable stock
1 to 2 tablespoons chopped fresh dill
2 tablespoons chopped fresh parsley
1 tablespoon soy sauce, or to taste
ground black pepper to taste

lemon wedges
dill sprigs

In a saucepan, sauté the onions and garlic in the oil for 5 minutes on medium-high heat. Add the red cabbage, caraway seeds, and salt and sauté for another 5 minutes.

While the vegetables cook, toss the kasha with the egg white in a small bowl until all of the grains are coated. Add the kasha to the sautéed vegetables and cook, stirring constantly, for 1 to 2 minutes, adding a little more oil if necessary to prevent sticking.

Add the water or stock, cover, bring to a boil, then reduce the heat to low. Simmer for 15 to 20 minutes, until the liquid is absorbed and the kasha is tender. Stir in the dill, parsley, and soy sauce, and add pepper to taste.

Serve immediately, garnished with lemon wedges and dill sprigs.

PER 6-OUNCE SERVING: 140 CALORIES, 5.1 G PROTEIN, 3.6 G FAT, 24.2 G CARBOHYDRATES, 0.6 G SATURATED FATTY ACIDS, 0 MG CHOLESTEROL, 253.4 MG SODIUM, 2.3 G TOTAL DIETARY FIBER

risotto-style barley

While true risottos are made with rice, the chewy kernels of pearled barley with their creamy exteriors make an excellent substitute. The outer hulls of pearled barley have been removed, allowing each grain to release surface starch as it cooks, which results in a silky sauce. Although the bran and hulls have the most nutrients, pearled barley is still an excellent source of dietary fiber.

 Serves 4
Total time: 1 hour

2 1/2 cups vegetable stock
1/2 teaspoon dried thyme
1/4 teaspoon crumbled saffron
2 tablespoons olive oil
1 cup sliced and well rinsed leeks*
2 garlic cloves, minced or pressed
1 cup pearled barley
1/2 cup dry white wine
1/2 teaspoon salt
1/4 to 1/2 cup grated Parmesan cheese

* Use the white and tenderest green parts only.

In a small saucepan, bring the stock, thyme, and saffron to a boil. Cover and set aside.

Warm the oil in a medium saucepan. Add the leeks and garlic and sauté on medium heat until softened, about 5 minutes. Stir in the barley and toss to coat it with oil. Add the wine and cook, stirring often, until the wine is absorbed.

Add the hot stock and bring to a boil; then cover and reduce the heat to low. Cook the barley, stirring every 5 minutes or so, until the stock is absorbed and the barley is al dente, about 30 to 35 minutes. Add a little more stock or water if the barley is too chewy for your taste. Add the salt and 1/4 cup of Parmesan and stir until the cheese melts.

Serve at once, passing more cheese at the table, if desired.

PER 5-OUNCE SERVING: 353 CALORIES, 10 G PROTEIN, 10.4 G FAT, 52.2 G CARBOHYDRATES, 2.7 G SATURATED FATTY ACIDS, 6.7 MG CHOLESTEROL, 566.2 MG SODIUM, 9.7 G TOTAL DIETARY FIBER

rice

Rice feeds more people than any other grain on the planet. In many Asian countries, rice is so important that the words for "rice" and "meal" are almost the same. Easy to store, simple to prepare, and nutritious, rice has the highest percentage of digestible, utilizable protein of any grain and contains iron, calcium, and B vitamins. At Moosewood, we serve rice at every meal. Long- or short-grain brown rice is most usual, but we also use brown and white basmati, wehani, jasmine, arborio, glutinous "sticky" rice, and black Thai rice.

Avoid parboiled or "converted" rice, which lacks valuable water soluble vitamins, and forget about rice labeled "minute" rice, which is nothing more than a dehydrated ghost of its former self.

golden pineapple rice

Serve this sunny, fruit-flavored rice with your favorite Caribbean, Indian, or Southeast Asian dishes. For an exotic one-dish meal, top it with an assortment of sautéed or roasted vegetables and steamed or baked marinated tofu.

 Serves 6 to 8
Preparation time: 15 minutes
Cooking time: 45 minutes

1 ½ cups brown rice

2 teaspoons vegetable oil

2 garlic cloves, minced or pressed

1 ½ teaspoons grated fresh ginger root

½ teaspoon turmeric

½ teaspoon salt, or more to taste

2 ½ cups water

1 cup fresh or unsweetened drained canned pineapple chunks

¼ cup minced fresh cilantro or scallions

½ cup chopped toasted cashews (optional)*

* Toast cashews in a single layer on an unoiled baking tray at 350° for 5 to 10 minutes, until fragrant and golden brown.

In a medium saucepan with a tight-fitting lid, combine the rice, oil, garlic, ginger, turmeric, and salt. Sauté for a minute or two, stirring constantly to prevent sticking. Add the water and bring to a boil.

When the water boils, reduce the heat to low, cover, and simmer for about 45 minutes, until the water is absorbed and the rice is tender. Stir in the pineapple, cilantro or scallions, and the cashews, if using.

PER 5-OUNCE SERVING: 138 CALORIES, 2.6 G PROTEIN, 2.1 G FAT, 27.3 G CARBOHYDRATES, 0.5 G SATURATED FATTY ACIDS, 0 MG CHOLESTEROL, 151.6 MG SODIUM, 2.2 G TOTAL DIETARY FIBER

mexican red rice

With classic flavors from south of the Rio Grande, this rice dish can serve as a foil for a more highly seasoned companion, yet it's tasty enough to be enjoyed on its own. It's colorful and not at all difficult to make.

Serve it with a spicy fish, stew, or bean dish or with a creative sauté of Latin American, Caribbean, Creole, Cajun, Indian, or Southeast Asian persuasion.

Serves 4 to 6
Total time: 35 to 40 minutes

1 1/2 teaspoons whole cumin seeds
1 tablespoon vegetable oil
1/3 cup finely chopped onions
1/3 cup finely chopped red bell peppers
1 garlic clove, minced or pressed
pinch of cayenne
1 large tomato
1 cup long-grain white rice
1 cup water
1/2 teaspoon salt

Toast the cumin seeds on an unoiled tray at 350° or in a dry skillet for 1 to 2 minutes, until fragrant. Grind the seeds in a spice grinder or with a mortar and pestle and set aside.

In a saucepan with a tight-fitting lid, warm the oil on medium heat. Add the onions, peppers, garlic, cayenne, and cumin and sauté for 5 minutes. Meanwhile, in a food processor or blender, purée the tomato to make about a cup of sauce: if less than a cup, add enough water to yield a full cup.

Add the rice and tomato purée to the saucepan and stir for a minute or two. Add the water and salt and bring to a boil; then reduce the heat, cover, and simmer very gently for 15 minutes. Remove from the heat and allow to sit for 5 minutes before lifting the lid.

Stir to fluff and serve.

PER 4-OUNCE SERVING: 145 CALORIES, 2.6 G PROTEIN, 2.8 G FAT, 27.2 G CARBOHYDRATES, 0.7 G SATURATED FATTY ACIDS, 0 MG CHOLESTEROL, 204.9 MG SODIUM, 1 G TOTAL DIETARY FIBER

orange saffron rice

At Moosewood, we like to serve this golden, fragrant rice with curries, grilled vegetables, and seafood. Customers always remark on its lovely color and slightly sweet flavor. If you are pressed for time, replace the brown basmati rice with white basmati, which cooks in 15 minutes.

Try it accompanied by Black Bean Mango Salsa (page 372) and Curried Corn (page 122).

Serves 3 to 4
Preparation time: 5 to 10 minutes
Cooking time: 50 minutes

1 1/2 cups brown basmati rice
2 teaspoons vegetable oil
2 teaspoons freshly grated orange peel
1/3 teaspoon turmeric
1/3 teaspoon ground cardamom
3/4 teaspoon salt
generous pinch of saffron
2 1/4 cups water

In a small, heavy pot with a tight-fitting lid, sauté the rice with the oil, orange peel, turmeric, cardamom, salt, and saffron for 1 or 2 minutes. Stir constantly to coat the grains with oil and to prevent sticking.

Add the water and bring to a boil; then reduce the heat, cover, and cook on very low heat until all of the water is absorbed, about 50 minutes.

Fluff the rice before serving.

PER 7.5-OUNCE SERVING: 259 CALORIES, 4.9 G PROTEIN, 4.1 G FAT, 50.1 G CARBOHYDRATES, 1 G SATURATED FATTY ACIDS, 0 MG CHOLESTEROL, 450.5 MG SODIUM, 4.1 G TOTAL DIETARY FIBER

sesame rice

Toasted sesame seeds and fresh scallions add an unexpected crunch to this simple savory rice, which fits in perfectly with sautés and tofu dishes. This recipe can be easily doubled and can be the "just right" contribution that rounds out the offerings at a potluck or buffet.

Try it under our Tofu Hijiki Burgers (page 187) or with Indian Skillet Black-eyed Peas (page 324).

Serves 6
Preparation time: 15 minutes
Cooking time: 45 minutes

1 cup brown rice
1 1/2 teaspoons dark sesame oil
1 1/2 cups water
1/3 cup minced scallions
2 tablespoons toasted sesame seeds*
2 to 3 teaspoons soy sauce to taste

* Toast sesame seeds in a single layer on an unoiled baking tray at 350° for 2 to 3 minutes, until fragrant and golden.

In a saucepan with a tight-fitting lid, toss the rice with 1/2 teaspoon of the sesame oil to coat the grains. Add the water, cover, and bring to a boil, then reduce the heat and simmer until the rice is tender, about 40 to 45 minutes. Stir in the scallions, sesame seeds, the remaining sesame oil, and soy sauce to taste.

PER 4-OUNCE SERVING: 136 CALORIES, 3 G PROTEIN, 3.5 G FAT, 23.3 G CARBOHYDRATES, 0.6 G SATURATED FATTY ACIDS, 0 MG CHOLESTEROL, 90.4 MG SODIUM, 2.3 G TOTAL DIETARY FIBER

wild rice pilaf

At Moosewood, we serve this popular pilaf with roasted or stuffed vegetables, fish, and sautéed or braised greens. Wild rice adds excellent flavor and a distinctive texture and appearance to pilafs, but it's pricey. Typical mixed rice pilafs have 1 part wild rice to 2 parts brown rice, but the proportions can range from 1:1 to 1:4 without compromising the vigorous, complex flavors of the grains.

Serves 6
Preparation time: 15 minutes
Simmering time: 45 minutes
Sitting time: 5 minutes

1 cup long-grain brown rice
1/2 cup wild rice
1 tablespoon olive oil
2 1/4 cups water
2/3 cup finely diced bell peppers*
1/2 cup chopped scallions
1 tablespoon chopped fresh parsley
1 tablespoon soy sauce
1 tablespoon fresh lemon juice
pinch of salt and ground black pepper

*A mix of red, green, and/or yellow bell peppers is nice.

Rinse the brown rice and wild rice in a sieve and set aside to drain.

In a saucepan, warm the oil on medium heat and add the rice. Sauté, stirring constantly, for 3 minutes. Stir in the water, cover, and bring to a boil; then reduce the heat and gently simmer for 45 minutes, until the rice is tender and the water is absorbed.

Allow the finished rice to sit, covered, for 5 minutes. Transfer the rice to a serving bowl, stir in the bell peppers, scallions, parsley, soy sauce, lemon juice, salt, and pepper. Serve warm or at room temperature.

PER 6-OUNCE SERVING: 176 CALORIES, 3.6 G PROTEIN, 4 G FAT, 32 G CARBOHYDRATES, 0.5 G SATURATED FATTY ACIDS, 0 MG CHOLESTEROL, 306.3 MG SODIUM, 2.2 G TOTAL DIETARY FIBER

variations Substitute other herbs for the parsley to suit your menu. For example, use dill for a more Northern or Eastern European menu; cilantro and chiles for a Mexican menu; basil and oregano for an Italian menu; and mint and marjoram for a French or Greek menu.

simple asian pilaf

Colorful flecks of fresh vegetables glisten in this salad-like pilaf. Serve it chilled in lettuce-leaf cups on a summer combo plate or hot and steamy alongside almost any Asian fish or tofu dish.

Cut the vegetables close to the same small size and, if you prefer, use white basmati rice. To save time, prepare the vegetables and seasonings while the rice cooks and the hijiki soaks. This dish looks fabulous served in shiny black enameled bowls.

Try Simple Asian Pilaf with East-West Stuffed Portabellos (page 347) or Tofu in Black Bean Sauce (page 314).

Serves 4
Preparation time: 50 minutes
Sitting time: 10 minutes

1 cup brown basmati rice

2 cups water

¼ cup dried hijiki*

½ cup diced red bell peppers

½ cup diced celery

2 to 3 minced scallions

1 teaspoon vegetable oil

½ teaspoon dark sesame oil

1 tablespoon soy sauce

1 tablespoon rice vinegar

1 tablespoon grated fresh
ginger root

¼ cup toasted sesame seeds**

1 teaspoon salt, or to taste

* *Hijiki can swell to yield different amounts depending on the type. Cut hijiki swells more than uncut. If you buy cut hijiki, 2 tablespoons dried should yield about ¹/₂ cup soaked and chopped—a good amount for this dish.*

** *Toast sesame seeds on an unoiled baking tray in a conventional or toaster oven at 350° for 3 to 5 minutes, until fragrant and golden brown.*

In a saucepan, combine the rice and water. Cover and bring to a boil; then reduce the heat and simmer for about 40 minutes, until the water is absorbed and the rice is tender but firm.

While the rice is cooking, soak the hijiki in boiling water to cover for 15 minutes. Drain and chop the hijiki to make about ¹/₂ cup.

Combine the bell peppers, celery, scallions, vegetable oil, sesame oil, soy sauce, vinegar, ginger, sesame seeds, and salt in a large bowl. Add the chopped hijiki and the cooked rice and stir well. Cover the bowl and allow the pilaf to sit for 10 minutes so the flavors can marry.

PER 7.5-OUNCE SERVING: 261 CALORIES, 6.1 G PROTEIN, 7.4 G FAT, 44.2 G CARBOHYDRATES, 1.3 G SATURATED FATTY ACIDS, 0 MG CHOLESTEROL, 815.7 MG SODIUM, 5.2 G TOTAL DIETARY FIBER

the gem of the ocean

With the great influx of ethnic foods in the American marketplace and the explosion of restaurants offering cultural specialties from around the world, Americans are finally discovering seaweed. Although the English language uses the word "weed" to describe these edible marine algaes, most other languages select the more respectful "sea vegetables"—a far more accurate description.

While certain marine algae are used like herbs or spices, most sea plants are more like land vegetables. They are primitive photosynthesizing plants without true leaves, stems, or roots, but with a leaflike blade, a stemlike stipe, and a rootlike holdfast. They range widely in size and reproduce by spores, gametes, and fragmentation.

Seaweeds are divided into five groups: red algae, green algae, brown algae, blue-green algae, and yellow-green algae. Although apparently color-coded, these classifications are actually based on cell structure, food storage, reproduction, and other scientific considerations. Color does not reliably indicate which group a particular algae belongs to. For instance, a bright red algae may actually belong to the green algae family. Go figure.

Seaweed inhabits the ocean and brackish coastal waters. While it tends to cohabit with sea grasses, it is distinct from sea grasses, which are angiosperms that have seeds and flowers. Seaweed fastens itself to the sea floor by tendrils that look like, but don't function like, roots—the tendrils draw in no nourishment. Instead, seaweed feeds itself through its blades or fronds, extracting elements directly from the ocean water and eventually converting them into organic compounds that our bodies can use.

People have eaten hundreds of species of seaweed since the beginning of history, and both oral and written accounts convey our human fascination with the beauty and diversity of this ocean plantlife. In coastal regions where harsh climate or a lack of arable land exists, people naturally turned to the sea to enhance their diets. But even in areas with adequate climate and soil, seaweed was a prized food. Palmaria palmata, fresh sol or dulse, has been eaten in Iceland since about 1000 B.C. In China's Book of Poetry (800–600 B.C.), sea vegetables are praised as a delicacy fit for any honored guest, and Japanese literature regularly refers to them as a gem or gemlike. Ancient Hawaiian nobility kept limu gardens of transplanted choice edible algae. And archaeologists have found food stashes of algae in Stone Age South African dwellings.

wehani & apricot pilaf

Wehani rice is a reddish-brown hybrid of basmati rice that is available in natural food stores. Sweet, chewy apricots and a judicious sprinkling of fresh rosemary offset the nutty flavor of the rice.

Try this sweet and savory pilaf with grilled portabello mushrooms, Basic Skillet Black Beans (page 317), or Roasted Winter Vegetables (page 264).

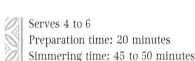
Serves 4 to 6
Preparation time: 20 minutes
Simmering time: 45 to 50 minutes

1 cup long-grain brown rice
1 cup wehani rice
$\frac{1}{2}$ cup diced onions
1 tablespoon olive oil
1$\frac{1}{2}$ teaspoons minced fresh rosemary
$\frac{1}{2}$ teaspoon salt, or more to taste
2$\frac{1}{2}$ cups water
$\frac{1}{3}$ cup diced unsulphured dried apricots

In a sieve, rinse and drain the brown and wehani rices and set aside.

In a medium saucepan with a tight-fitting lid, sauté the onions in the oil for 3 to 4 minutes. Add the drained rice, rosemary, and salt to the saucepan and sauté for another minute, stirring to coat the rice with the oil.

Add the water, cover, and bring to a boil, then reduce the heat to low and simmer until the rice is tender, 45 to 50 minutes. Stir in the apricots and set aside for 5 minutes.

Fluff and serve.

PER 6-OUNCE SERVING: 363 CALORIES, 6.4 G PROTEIN, 3.2 G FAT, 75.9 G CARBOHYDRATES, 0.5 G SATURATED FATTY ACIDS, 0 MG CHOLESTEROL, 201.5 MG SODIUM, 4 G TOTAL DIETARY FIBER

grits

Grits are good. They're good plain, with just butter and salt and maybe a little cheese stirred in. Good baked with vegetables, mushrooms, herbs, and cheese. Good sliced when cold and pan-fried or breaded and deep-fried. Good as a starch over which to ladle stews, sauces, or gravies. Good for breakfast, lunch, or supper. In short, good most any time you serve them! But you've got to know your grits.

It's a matter of personal taste whether to use white or yellow grits, commercial or stone-ground. Commercial, supermarket-variety grits have a consistent nubby texture and carry other flavors beautifully. Supermarket grits come in quick-cooking, regular (sometimes called old-fashioned), and instant varieties. Some grits gourmands disdain commercial grits, but we like them—except for "instant": never *ever* allow instant grits to pass through your lips. They are insipid in flavor and texture, and filled with chemical additives. Instant grits give grits a bad name, and since quick-cooking grits cook in just 5 to 10 minutes, the 3- to 4-minute "instant" aspect just isn't relevant. Quick grits are fine: creamy and good-tasting, without additives. Regular or old-fashioned grits cook in 15 to 30 minutes.

Commercial grits are made from dried corn, usually white, with the germ removed to increase shelf life. They are roller-ground in factories. Quaker brand grits can be found in the cereal section of most well-stocked supermarkets. Often, especially in the Southeast, smaller, more local brands are also on the shelf; one of our favorites is Dixie Lily (Box 50337, Nashville, Tennessee 37205).

Serious grits aficionados often prefer stone-ground grits made by smaller producers. Stone-ground grits are dried whole kernels of white or yellow corn crushed between millstones. They have an earthy corn flavor and a creamy-bumpy texture. Black speckles tell you that the grits were ground from whole kernels of dried corn (the base of a corn kernel is black). White grits usually contain some spots of yellow, because most stands of white corn are within bee-flying distance of yellow corn, resulting in some cross-pollination. Yellow and white grits are about the same in sweetness, flavor, and nutritional value. The various stone-ground grits we've tried take from 45 minutes to almost 2 hours to cook. They should be stored in the freezer in a well-sealed container where they will keep for several months.

grits with goat cheese & dill

At first, the idea of grits with goat cheese seemed a little strange, even to us. But then we tried it! Its creamy texture and brisk dill accent make it an unconventional but reassuringly soothing and satisfying side dish.

Any kind of grits will work here, but the cooking times will vary. It takes about 10 minutes for quick-cooking grits to cook, 25 minutes for regular grits, and about 40 minutes for stone-ground grits. Goat cheese, also called chèvre, is available at the cheese counter of most well-stocked supermarkets.

Serves 6
Total time: 20 minutes with
quick-cooking grits

4 cups water
1 cup minced celery
$^1/_2$ teaspoon salt
1 cup grits
1 cup soft goat cheese
1 tablespoon minced fresh dill
$^1/_2$ cup minced scallions or chives

In a covered saucepan, bring the water, celery, and salt to a boil. Stir or whisk in the grits, lower the heat, cover, and cook at a low simmer, stirring frequently, until thickened.

Remove from the heat and stir in the goat cheese, dill, and the scallions or chives. Serve hot from the pan.

PER 7.5-OUNCE SERVING: 157 CALORIES, 6.2 G PROTEIN, 4.4 G FAT, 23.3 G CARBOHYDRATES, 2.8 G SATURATED FATTY ACIDS, 8.7 MG CHOLESTEROL, 286.6 MG SODIUM, 0.9 G TOTAL DIETARY FIBER

grits baked with shallots

Elegant shallots transform a humble, down-home favorite into a refined and unusual side dish. The preparation time will vary depending on the type of grits you use; quick-cooking, regular, or stone-ground grits are fine for this dish, but instant grits are *not*.

 Serves 4
Preparation time: about 20 minutes
Baking time: 30 minutes

2 cups water

1/2 cup grits

1/2 cup minced shallots

2 tablespoons butter

1/2 cup plus 2 tablespoons shredded
  Parmesan or Pecorino Romano
  cheese

2 eggs, well beaten

Preheat the oven to 350°. Thoroughly butter or oil a 1 1/2-quart baking pan or soufflé dish.

Bring the water to a boil in a saucepan. While stirring briskly or whisking, gradually pour the grits into the water. Cook on low heat until thickened, stirring occasionally. The cooking time will be about 10 minutes for quick-cooking grits, 25 minutes for regular grits, and longer for stone-ground grits.

Meanwhile, sauté the shallots in the butter on medium heat until golden and soft, about 5 minutes. When the grits are done, stir in the shallots, 1/2 cup of the cheese, and the beaten eggs. Pour into the prepared baking dish and sprinkle with the remaining cheese.

Bake for about 30 minutes, until puffed and uniformly golden.

PER 7-OUNCE SERVING: 284 CALORIES, 15 G PROTEIN, 15.7 G FAT, 20.4 G CARBOHYDRATES, 8.7 G SATURATED FATTY ACIDS, 164.4 MG CHOLESTEROL, 495.3 MG SODIUM, 0.2 G TOTAL DIETARY FIBER

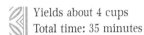

grits with quinoa

The combination of corn grits and quinoa does basic cooked grits one better. The two are excellent partners with complementary textures and flavors. The grits provide a creamy base and the quinoa adds both a protein-rich boost and a chewiness reminiscent of stoneground grits.

Serve the cooked blend as you would plain grits: Add raisins, maple syrup, or sugar for a breakfast cereal, add cheese and herbs for a savory side dish, or use in baked grits dishes and as a base for stews and sauces.

Yields about 4 cups
Total time: 35 minutes

4 cups water

1/2 teaspoon salt

3/4 cup regular or quick-cooking grits*

1/2 cup quinoa

* *If you're using quick-cooking grits, add the quinoa to the boiling water first, and then add the grits after 5 minutes.*

Bring the water and salt to a boil in a saucepan. Stirring or whisking constantly, pour in the grits. When the grits and water return to a boil, stir in the quinoa. Cover, reduce the heat to very low, and simmer for about 25 minutes, stirring frequently. If the grits begin to stick, use a heat diffuser to avoid scorching.

Remove from the heat and let sit covered for about 5 minutes. If too thick, stir in a little hot water. Serve hot.

PER 7.25-OUNCE SERVING: 181 CALORIES, 5.1 G PROTEIN, 1.5 G FAT, 37.1 G CARBOHYDRATES, 0.2 G SATURATED FATTY ACIDS, 0 MG CHOLESTEROL, 302.7 MG SODIUM, 1.5 G TOTAL DIETARY FIBER

pan-american grits

When looking for a versatile companion for Mexican, Peruvian, Southwestern, or Southern meals, we thought, "Why not grits?" Add bell peppers, corn kernels, cumin, and coriander to this New World staple, and you've got it!

This dish reheats very well in the microwave, a double boiler, or the oven.

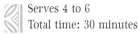

Serves 4 to 6
Total time: 30 minutes

1 recipe Grits with Quinoa
   (opposite)
1 cup chopped onions
2 tablespoons olive oil
1 cup diced red or green bell peppers
1 teaspoon ground cumin
1 teaspoon ground coriander
1 cup fresh, frozen, or drained
   canned corn kernels
1 cup grated Cheddar cheese

chopped fresh cilantro and/or
   scallions
Tabasco sauce or other hot pepper
   sauce

While the Grits with Quinoa cooks, sauté the onions in the olive oil for 3 to 4 minutes on medium-high heat. Stir in the bell peppers and continue to sauté for a couple of minutes. Stir in the cumin and coriander and sauté, stirring, for 1 minute. Add the corn and cook until all of the vegetables are tender, about 5 minutes longer. Set aside.

When the grits with quinoa are ready, stir in the sautéed vegetables and the cheese. Top with chopped cilantro and/or scallions and serve with Tabasco sauce.

PER 8-OUNCE SERVING: 283 CALORIES, 9.5 G PROTEIN, 12.5 G FAT, 35.1 G CARBOHYDRATES, 4.8 G SATURATED FATTY ACIDS, 19.8 MG CHOLESTEROL, 325.5 MG SODIUM, 2.3 G TOTAL DIETARY FIBER

At least 20 mills in the U.S. make stone-ground grits, most of them small operations with loyal customers. These mills grind and ship small orders year-round:

Nora Mill Granary
7107 South Main Street
Helen, Georgia 30545
(800) 927-2375
www.noramill.com

Falls Mill
134 Falls Mill Road
Belvidere, Tennessee 37306
(931) 469-7161
www.fallsmill.com

Adams Foods
Route 6, Box 148-A
Dothan, Alabama 36301
(800) 239-4233

wraps, rolls, sandwiches & burgers

wraps, rolls, sandwiches, and burgers ❧

Sandwiches in general, and burgers and wraps in particular, can be the perfect marriage of practicality and flavor—an easy-to-eat, all-in-one meal with no cutlery required!

For a casual meal or satisfying lunch, nothing beats a good burger with a slice of tomato and a handful of chips, and after twenty-five years, we've got burger making down to a science. In fact, at Moosewood we're proud of all our sandwiches and consider each a worthy centerpiece for a genuine sit-down dining experience.

We offer several new takes on old sandwich classics. It's not an ordinary cheese sandwich when the filling is Gruyère with caramelized onions or smoked Gouda with sautéed greens on dark pumpernickel. Meaty Portabello Sandwiches make a succulent and satisfying meal and our tofu sandwich spreads, whether Italian or Thai-style, are new favorites and blessedly simple to make. Even good old everyday egg salad gets five new ethnic interpretations.

We find inspiration for wraps, rolls, sandwiches, and burgers in a wide range of ethnic cuisines—Mexican, Italian, Creole, Indian, Thai, Greek, Japanese, Middle Eastern, and Scandinavian, to name a few. Wraps really caught the popular imagination about ten years ago. If they seem kind of ho-hum to you by this time, check out these recipes; we bet you'll find some new ideas for pleasing lunches or dinners. Maybe you've never tried a hearty Caribbean Beans & Greens Wrap? Or spicy Fajitas with Mole?

We've always been proud of our tofu burgers at Moosewood. We started making them in 1973 and they've just become more and more popular. They're full of good stuff and they taste great. Numbers of people, identifying themselves as tofu-phobic, have been completely surprised by how much they like them. We've gone on to expand our burger repertoire, developing new kinds with unexpected tasty ingredients like cremini mushrooms, pecans, hijiki, black-eyed peas and sweet potatoes.

In the restaurant, when we misjudge how many burgers to make and sell out before the end of lunchtime, the cooks are always appropriately apologetic. A chorus of groans from disappointed customers (and workers as well) greets the person who goes out to erase them from the dining room chalkboard menu. We always resolve to make more next time. We've even wondered if maybe we shouldn't post a sign out in front of the restaurant bragging about how many we've sold so far, like that *other* burger place.

asparagus egg salad wrap

Transform the classic egg salad sandwich by adding dressed-up herbed mayonnaise and the sweet bite of asparagus, and roll it up in a flour tortilla.

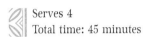 Serves 4
Total time: 45 minutes

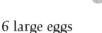

6 large eggs
1/4 cup prepared mayonnaise
2 teaspoons chopped fresh tarragon
2 teaspoons Dijon mustard
2 teaspoons fresh lemon juice
1/4 teaspoon salt
ground black pepper to taste
12 to 15 asparagus spears
4 flour tortillas (10 inches across)
4 leaves of red leaf, green leaf, or
    Bibb lettuce, rinsed and dried

Place the eggs in a saucepan with cold water to cover. Bring to a boil and then lower the heat and simmer for about 10 minutes. Drain the eggs and cover with cold water.

In a mixing bowl, combine the mayonnaise, tarragon, mustard, lemon juice, salt, and pepper. As soon as the eggs are cool enough to handle, peel and coarsely chop them. Stir the eggs into the dressing. Set aside.

Rinse and stem the asparagus. Steam or boil the spears until bright green and just tender, 3 to 5 minutes. Plunge into cold water, drain, and cut into 5-inch pieces.

Warm a large dry skillet on medium heat. Warm the tortillas one at a time for 20 to 30 seconds on each side, until softened. Lay each warm tortilla flat on a work surface. Center a lettuce leaf on each and top with about 1/3 cup of egg salad and several asparagus pieces. Fold in both sides over the filling and then roll from the bottom up to form a wrap.

Serve immediately.

PER 7-OUNCE SERVING: 339 CALORIES, 16.6 G PROTEIN, 17.7 G FAT, 28.1 G CARBOHYDRATES, 4.5 G SATURATED FATTY ACIDS, 400.3 MG CHOLESTEROL, 578.7 MG SODIUM, 2 G TOTAL DIETARY FIBER

caribbean beans & greens wrap

Filled with the warm flavors of the Caribbean—a subtle blend of thyme, allspice, and orange—this vegan wrap is both nutritious and delicious. The wrap filling is quickly prepared with canned beans and conveniently made all in one skillet. Other greens, such as kale or mustard, could be used, but we prefer collard greens.

Eat the wraps immediately or prepare some ahead and store them in the refrigerator for later. Try them with Peach Salsa (page 381) or just enjoy them plain. Mmm, mmm.

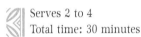
Serves 2 to 4
Total time: 30 minutes

1 cup diced onions

1 garlic clove, minced or pressed

1 tablespoon vegetable oil

1/2 teaspoon dried thyme

1/2 teaspoon ground allspice

1/2 teaspoon salt

4 cups lightly packed chopped
    collard greens

1 tablespoon water, or as needed

1 1/2 cups cooked black beans
    (15.5-ounce can, rinsed and
    drained)

3 tablespoons orange juice

4 flour tortillas (8 or 9 inches across)

In a nonreactive soup pot or skillet, sauté the onions and garlic in the oil for about 10 minutes, until translucent, stirring often. Add the thyme, allspice, salt, collard greens, and water. Cover and cook on medium heat, adding more water if necessary to prevent sticking, until the greens are tender, about 5 to 10 minutes. (The amount of time it will take depends upon how fresh and young the collards are.)

Push the greens to the sides of the pot, add the beans to the center, and mash them well with a potato masher. Add the orange juice, stir everything together, and remove from the heat.

Warm the tortillas (page 158). Place a generous 1/2 cup of filling on the bottom half of each tortilla, roll it up, and serve immediately.

PER 6.5-OUNCE SERVING: 237 CALORIES, 8.9 G PROTEIN, 6.2 G FAT, 37.4 G CARBOHYDRATES, 1.6 G SATURATED FATTY ACIDS, 0 MG CHOLESTEROL, 785.1 MG SODIUM, 8.1 G TOTAL DIETARY FIBER

note *If you're preparing these wraps ahead of time, don't warm the tortillas. Just roll them up, place in a lightly oiled baking dish, cover tightly, and refrigerate until ready to use. To serve, bake covered at 350° for 15 to 20 minutes, until hot.*

indian curried potato wrap

Chapatis, made from whole wheat flour and water, are simple Indian flat breads that are traditionally served with curries and used to scoop up the sauce and bits of vegetables.

Some of us at Moosewood have made our own from scratch. Those available in natural food stores and large supermarkets tend to be more pliable than the homemade kind, so they lend themselves to new uses, like these wraps.

Try them accompanied by Rhubarb Cherry Chutney (page 383).

Serves 4 to 6
Preparation time: 45 minutes
Baking time: 10 to 15 minutes

2 1/2 cups cubed white potatoes

1/2 teaspoon salt

1/2 cup Neufchâtel or cream cheese, at room temperature

1 tablespoon vegetable oil

1 cup diced onions

1 garlic clove, minced or pressed

1 teaspoon grated fresh ginger root

1/4 teaspoon ground cinnamon

1/4 teaspoon turmeric

1/8 teaspoon cayenne, or to taste

1/2 cup frozen green peas

1/2 cup chopped fresh tomatoes

2 teaspoons fresh lemon juice

salt to taste

6 whole wheat chapatis or flour tortillas (7 inches across)*

We recommend Cedarlane whole wheat chapatis, a flat Indian "bread" available in natural food stores and well-stocked supermarkets.

Preheat the oven to 350°. Lightly oil a baking dish.

Place the potatoes and salt in a small pot with water to cover and bring to a boil. Reduce the heat, cover, and cook for about 10 minutes, until tender. When the potatoes are tender, drain and mash them with the Neufchâtel, and set aside.

Meanwhile, warm the oil in a saucepan, and sauté the onions and garlic on medium heat for about 10 minutes, until translucent. Add the ginger, cinnamon, turmeric, and cayenne and cook for 1 to 2 minutes, stirring constantly. Add the peas and tomatoes, cover, and cook on low heat just long enough to heat through. Stir the cooked vegetables and the lemon juice into the mashed potatoes. Add salt to taste.

Place a generous 1/3 cup of the filling at the bottom of each chapati and roll it up. Place the wraps seam side down in the prepared baking dish, cover with aluminum foil, and bake for 10 to 15 minutes, until hot.

PER 6-OUNCE SERVING: 236 CALORIES, 6.2 G PROTEIN, 7.1 G FAT, 37.7 G CARBOHYDRATES, 2.6 G SATURATED FATTY ACIDS, 7.2 MG CHOLESTEROL, 409.8 MG SODIUM, 3.7 G TOTAL DIETARY FIBER

roasted pepper & onion wrap

These wraps are great for casual meals. If you prefer a simpler version of the filling, just omit the seitan and/or grated cheese and plan to make six wraps rather than eight. The result is still delicious and satisfying. Try replacing the seitan with some Lemony Baked Tofu (page 223) or add a dollop of your favorite salsa to the wrap.

Serve the filling and tortillas right at the picnic table so everyone can wrap their own. Or offer these with Drunken Beans (page 322) and Cucumber Peanut Salad (page 107) for a delicious Mexican-style menu.

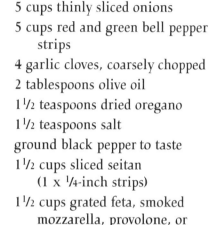

 Serves 4
Preparation time: 15 minutes
Baking time: 25 to 30 minutes

5 cups thinly sliced onions

5 cups red and green bell pepper strips

4 garlic cloves, coarsely chopped

2 tablespoons olive oil

1 1/2 teaspoons dried oregano

1 1/2 teaspoons salt

ground black pepper to taste

1 1/2 cups sliced seitan
(1 x 1/4-inch strips)

1 1/2 cups grated feta, smoked mozzarella, provolone, or Cheddar cheese

8 flour or corn tortillas
(8 inches across)

Preheat the oven to 450°. Oil a large baking tray about 12 x 18 inches.

Place the onions, bell peppers, garlic, oil, oregano, salt, and black pepper in a large bowl. Toss together to coat the vegetables evenly with oil, then spread them on the prepared baking sheet.

Bake for 10 minutes and then briefly stir the vegetables. Bake 10 minutes more and stir again. Return them to the oven and continue to bake for another 5 to 10 minutes, until the vegetables are tender and beginning to brown. Transfer the vegetables to a bowl, then mix in the seitan and grated cheese.

Warm the tortillas (page 158). Place about a cup of the filling on one half of each hot tortilla, roll up the wraps, and serve immediately. Or if you prefer, place the filling in a bowl, cover the tortillas with a towel to keep them warm, and let each person assemble and "wrap" his or her own.

PER 17-OUNCE SERVING: 527 CALORIES, 18.2 G PROTEIN, 22.9 G FAT, 66 G CARBOHYDRATES, 8.8 G SATURATED FATTY ACIDS, 37.8 MG CHOLESTEROL, 1,679.5 MG SODIUM, 6.8 G TOTAL DIETARY FIBER

fajitas

The word *fajita* comes from the Spanish word *faja*, which means belt or sash. Traditionally, grilled chicken or beef would be sliced into strips and included in a fajita. But our version features strips of tofu and vegetables roasted with olive oil and garlic and wrapped in warm flour tortillas. Bring the fajitas to the table already assembled or have the tortillas and filling ready and let everyone make their own.

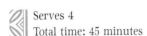
Serves 4
Total time: 45 minutes

1 cake firm tofu (16 ounces)

1 zucchini

1 onion

1 red bell pepper

2 garlic cloves, minced or pressed

2 tablespoons olive oil

1 teaspoon salt

1 cup Mole (page 379) or prepared
    salsa

4 flour tortillas (10 inches across)

Preheat the oven to 425°.

Cut the cake of tofu crosswise into 4 slices. Stack the slices and cut them into ¹/₂-inch-wide strips. Cut the zucchini in half lengthwise, slice the halves lengthwise into ¹/₂-inch strips, and cut the strips crosswise into 3-inch lengths. Cut the onion into ¹/₂-inch-thick slices. Cut the pepper in half, remove the seeds, and cut into ¹/₂-inch-thick strips.

In a large bowl, lightly toss the tofu, zucchini, onions, and peppers with the garlic, oil, and salt. Spread in an even layer on a baking sheet. Roast in the oven for 25 to 30 minutes, until the vegetables are tender and browned.

When the vegetables have been roasting for 15 minutes, simmer the Mole in a small saucepan or skillet on low heat for about 10 minutes, stirring occasionally. Cover and set aside. Heat each tortilla on a hot, dry griddle or skillet for about 1 minute, flipping it two or three times until it's hot.

To serve, put about ¹/₄ of the roasted vegetable and tofu mixture in the center of each hot tortilla, top with some of the Mole or salsa, roll it up, and serve warm.

PER 12-OUNCE SERVING: 437 CALORIES, 16.3 G PROTEIN, 22.9 G FAT, 47 G CARBOHYDRATES,
4.2 G SATURATED FATTY ACIDS, 0 MG CHOLESTEROL, 1,590.8 MG SODIUM, 7.1 G TOTAL DIETARY FIBER

roasted vegetable quesadillas

Potato sandwiches—have we no shame? These pan-grilled tortilla sandwiches stuffed with savory roasted vegetables and melted Cheddar are heavenly.

The vegetables don't have to be measured exactly for this recipe to work fine. One medium potato, a very small onion, half a bell pepper, and one small zucchini should do the trick. We give measurements in cups, because everyone's notions of "small" or "medium" differ. For the best results, cut the vegetables into quite thin slices—no more than $1/4$ inch thick.

2 cups quartered and sliced potatoes

$1/2$ cup sliced onions

$3/4$ cup sliced red or green bell peppers

$1 1/2$ cups sliced zucchini

2 tablespoons olive oil

1 garlic clove, minced or pressed

$1/2$ teaspoon dried oregano

$1/2$ teaspoon salt

$1/4$ teaspoon ground black pepper

4 flour tortillas (8 inches across)

1 cup grated Cheddar cheese

Serves 4
Preparation time: 25 minutes
Baking time: 25 to 30 minutes

Preheat the oven to 425°.

Toss all of the vegetables with the olive oil, garlic, oregano, salt, and black pepper until evenly coated. Spread them on a large baking sheet in a single layer. Roast in the oven until the potatoes are tender and beginning to brown, about 25 to 30 minutes.

Pile about $1/4$ of the roasted vegetable filling on one half of each of the tortillas, leaving a $1/2$-inch border around the outer edge. Top the filling with $1/4$ cup of the cheese. Fold the tortilla over the filling to form a half-moon shape.

Heat a lightly oiled large skillet on medium heat. When the skillet is hot, cook two of the quesadillas for 1 to 2 minutes on each side, until golden brown. Remove the quesadillas from the skillet and keep them warm while cooking the remaining two quesadillas. Slice each quesadilla in half and serve warm.

PER 8.5-OUNCE SERVING: 375 CALORIES, 12.1 G PROTEIN, 18.9 G FAT, 40.4 G CARBOHYDRATES, 7.5 G SATURATED FATTY ACIDS, 29.7 MG CHOLESTEROL, 632.2 MG SODIUM, 3.9 G TOTAL DIETARY FIBER

variations ♥ *Try adding portabello mushrooms, eggplant, or asparagus. Replace the Cheddar cheese with feta or mozzarella and accent with your favorite herbs.*

vegetable rolls

These Southeast Asian–style rolls feature bean thread noodles and sautéed vegetables seasoned with fresh tarragon and basil. They're most flavorful served at room temperature—or even warm—so if you have any cold leftover filling, reheat it before using.

The cooking goes quickly, so prepare all of the vegetables and seasonings before you start to cook. The rice-paper discs, also called spring roll wrappers, are rather fragile, so expect to break one or two. The packages contain enough to accommodate a few "casualties."

hoisin dipping sauce

$^1\!/_4$ cup hoisin sauce

1 tablespoon water

2 tablespoons rice vinegar or lemon juice

1 teaspoon dark sesame oil

$^1\!/_2$ teaspoon Chinese chili paste (optional)

Serves 4 to 6
Total time: $1^1\!/_2$ hours

12 rice paper discs (8 inches across)

$^1\!/_4$ cup chopped peanuts

* Bean thread noodles, also known as cellophane noodles, are made from mung bean flour. They become slippery and transparent as they cook and readily absorb flavors. They can be found in Asian groceries and well-stocked supermarkets.

$1^1\!/_2$ to 2 ounces bean thread noodles*

1 tablespoon peanut or other vegetable oil

2 cups grated green cabbage

2 cups sliced mushrooms

4 garlic cloves, minced or pressed

1 tablespoon grated fresh ginger root

1 cup peeled and grated carrots

1 cup thinly sliced red bell peppers

$^1\!/_2$ cup finely chopped scallions

2 tablespoons soy sauce

1 tablespoon rice vinegar

1 tablespoon chopped fresh tarragon

2 tablespoons chopped fresh basil

✳ Soak the bean threads in warm water until softened, about 10 to 15 minutes.

Meanwhile, heat the oil in a large skillet and sauté the cabbage for 3 to 4 minutes. Add the mushrooms, garlic, and ginger and continue to sauté on medium heat for another 4 minutes, until the mushrooms are soft. Add the carrots and bell peppers and cook for about 5 minutes more, until hot but still slightly crunchy. Remove from the heat.

When the bean threads are soft, drain them and cut into 3- to 4-inch lengths with scissors or a knife. Add them to the sautéed vegetables with the scallions, soy sauce, vinegar, tarragon, and basil. Stir to combine and set aside.

In a small bowl, whisk together all of the Hoisin Dipping Sauce ingredients.

Moisten the rice-paper discs a few at a time by immersing each one in a large, shallow bowl of warm water, transferring it to a clean towel, and laying it flat. Let them soften for a few minutes. Soften more as needed and as space permits.

Place about ⅓ cup of filling on the bottom half of a softened disc, fold over the sides, and then roll up from the bottom, as tightly and gently as possible. Place seam side down on a platter and repeat with the rest of the filling and discs.

Serve with the Hoisin Dipping Sauce and a sprinkling of peanuts.

PER 8-OUNCE SERVING: 391 CALORIES, 9.1 G PROTEIN, 11 G FAT, 64.8 G CARBOHYDRATES, 2.1 G SATURATED FATTY ACIDS, 0.3 MG CHOLESTEROL, 740.3 MG SODIUM, 5.4 G TOTAL DIETARY FIBER

packing up lunch

We read recently that forty percent of all meals consumed in America are eaten outside the home. We're not certain whether brown bag and boxed lunches are included in that category—they're eaten away from home, but the food may be homemade.

Most of us have vivid memories of carrying lunch to school. Comparing our lunch box contents with our schoolmates', we viewed other people's food with curiosity, relief, and occasional envy, and sharpened our swapping strategies. Some may remember when a brown bag lunch was a paper sack from home, an egg salad sandwich and an apple, eaten on a park bench. But for the last fifteen years the corporate Brown Bag Lunch is code for eating while you're meeting. While lunch was once a respite from the pressures of the workday, too often these days it's compressed to a few quiet minutes or rolled into the day's affairs.

Whether it's working lunches, wolfing down something between classes, or committee meetings from 6 to 9, we need to defend the quality of our lives against the excessive demands of work and civic duty. When you eat well, you feel it. Find alternatives to the dining hall service, ordering out, or the dreaded snack machine. Reduce the impact of a busy schedule on your health and energy by taking control of your diet before work conquers well-being.

When packing lunch for young people, always try to include fresh or dried fruit, carrots, or celery. Soups stay hot and juice, milk, or fruit smoothies stay cold in squat insulated bottles. If a healthful drink is included in the lunch pack, your kids are less likely to buy soda.

Foods that travel well to work or school settings should also meet these standards:

- You can pack it up in 5 to 10 minutes, and it won't spoil before you eat it.

- It still looks and tastes good when you're ready for lunch.

- It's not noisy to eat.

- You can look civilized and attentive to others while you eat it.

- You don't feel ashamed of your lunch; in fact, other people wish you'd share.

- It doesn't leave odd aromas or debris in the meeting room or on you.

- You're confident that you're eating well.

Here is a list of things, many of which you can find in this book, that make good meals to pack.

Muffins
Fresh fruit and fruit salad
Nori rolls and vegetable sushi
Muffuletta
Burgers
Wraps and sandwiches
Soups and stews
Main-dish salads like pasta, potato, and
    grain salads
Slaws and side-dish salads
Marinated vegetables
Roasted vegetables
Frittatas, quiches, and casseroles

cheese sandwiches for cheese lovers

When it comes to cheese sandwiches, life has more to offer than an old-fashioned grilled cheese with its slice of dill pickle on the side. These enticing sandwiches feature some of the wide variety of cheeses now available in supermarket delis. If you haven't tried them, splurge a little and introduce yourself to a few new favorites.

Use about $1/3$ to $1/2$ cup of grated cheese for each slice of bread.

sun-dried tomato pesto

Pesto and smoked mozzarella cheese baked together on bread make a scrumptious combination for a party appetizer. On crackers or small rounds of bread, this will easily serve 10 to 12.

 Serves 4 as a sandwich
Total time: 20 minutes

$1/2$ cup sun-dried tomatoes
  (not oil-packed)

$1/2$ cup chopped walnuts

2 cups packed fresh basil leaves

2 garlic cloves, minced or pressed

1 tablespoon olive oil

freshly ground black pepper

French or Italian bread, or crackers

$1 1/2$ cups sliced smoked mozzarella
  cheese

Preheat the oven to 350°.

In a small bowl, soak the sun-dried tomatoes in boiling water to cover for about 15 minutes. When the tomatoes are soft, drain them and reserve the soaking water.

Meanwhile, spread the walnuts on an unoiled baking sheet and toast in the oven for about 10 minutes, until fragrant and golden brown. Cool for 1 to 2 minutes.

Combine the sun-dried tomatoes, basil, garlic, oil, pepper, and 2 tablespoons of the reserved tomato-soaking water in the food processor and purée, scraping the sides of the bowl a few times. Add the walnuts and process until combined.

Spread a slice of bread or a cracker with pesto, top with a thin slice of mozzarella, and serve.

PER 6-OUNCE SERVING: 474 CALORIES, 19.9 G PROTEIN, 25.7 G FAT, 44.6 G CARBOHYDRATES, 8.4 G SATURATED FATTY ACIDS, 38 MG CHOLESTEROL, 919.4 MG SODIUM, 6.4 G TOTAL DIETARY FIBER

gruyère with caramelized onions

Gruyère has a robust, nutty character that perfectly complements the sweetness of caramelized onions. If using dried thyme, add it to the skillet with the salt and sugar.

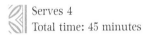
Serves 4
Total time: 45 minutes

1 tablespoon olive oil

2 cups thinly sliced onions

$1/8$ teaspoon salt

$1/4$ teaspoon sugar

1 tablespoon minced fresh thyme
   ($1/2$ teaspoon dried)

freshly ground black pepper to taste

$1 1/2$ to 2 cups grated Gruyère cheese

4 slices crusty bread

In a heavy skillet, heat the olive oil on medium-low heat. Add the onions and sauté for about 15 minutes, stirring frequently. Stir in the salt and sugar, lower the heat, cover the pan, and continue to cook for about 10 more minutes, until the onions are brown. Add the fresh thyme and pepper and continue to sauté for 5 minutes. Set aside to cool.

Preheat the oven to 350°.

Sprinkle $1/4$ of the cheese on each slice of bread. Place on a baking sheet and bake for about 10 minutes, until the cheese is melted. Top each sandwich with a quarter of the onions and serve.

PER 6-OUNCE SERVING: 408 CALORIES, 18.9 G PROTEIN, 20.5 G FAT, 37.2 G CARBOHYDRATES, 11.3 G SATURATED FATTY ACIDS, 44.6 MG CHOLESTEROL, 569 MG SODIUM, 2.7 G TOTAL DIETARY FIBER

cheddar with apple slices

Use a good sharp Cheddar, like the kind you can get in Vermont, Wisconsin, New York, or England. Choose apples that are tart and crisp.

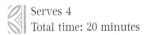
Serves 4
Total time: 20 minutes

4 slices crusty bread

 your favorite mustard to taste

2 cups grated sharp Cheddar cheese

$1 1/2$ cups thinly sliced apples

little cornichons or your favorite
   sweet pickles

Preheat the oven to 350°.

Spread each slice of bread with a little mustard. and sprinkle with $1/2$ cup of the cheese. Place on a baking tray and bake for about 10 minutes, until the cheese is melted and bubbly. Top the hot sandwiches with the apple slices and serve with cornichons or sweet pickles alongside.

PER 6-OUNCE SERVING: 425 CALORIES, 20.1 G PROTEIN, 21.7 G FAT, 38.8 G CARBOHYDRATES, 12.6 G SATURATED FATTY ACIDS, 59.5 MG CHOLESTEROL, 738.4 MG SODIUM, 4.5 G TOTAL DIETARY FIBER

smoked gouda with sautéed greens

The sweetness of the smoked gouda and the peppery flavor of the mustard greens combine well with a dark pumpernickel bread. This sandwich is more than just a snack; it's satisfying enough to make a meal.

 Serves 4
Total time: 20 minutes

4 cups mustard greens, rinsed and dried

2 tablespoons olive oil

2 garlic cloves, minced or pressed

1/4 teaspoon salt

ground black pepper to taste

4 slices pumpernickel bread

2 cups grated smoked Gouda cheese

Preheat the broiler.

Chop the greens into small pieces. In a large heavy skillet, heat the oil and garlic on medium heat until sizzling. Add the greens and sauté for about 3 minutes, until limp and tender. Sprinkle with the salt and pepper and remove from the heat.

Lightly toast the bread and top each with 1/2 cup of the grated cheese. Broil the sandwiches for 3 to 5 minutes, until the cheese is bubbly and beginning to brown. Remove and top with the sautéed greens. Serve immediately.

PER 6-OUNCE SERVING: 411 CALORIES, 19.5 G PROTEIN, 24.5 G FAT, 29 G CARBOHYDRATES, 11.2 G SATURATED FATTY ACIDS, 64.6 MG CHOLESTEROL, 997.3 MG SODIUM, 3.7 G TOTAL DIETARY FIBER

marinated feta with pita

One bite of this sandwich will instantly wake up your taste buds. Sharp feta cheese, salty sun-dried tomatoes, and piquant vinegars make a strong statement. If you like, use dill or oregano in place of the marjoram.

The marinated feta in this delicious sandwich is also a good addition to fresh greens and vegetable salads. In a sealed container in the refrigerator, it will keep for up to 1 week.

Serves 4 to 6
Preparation time: 25 minutes
Chilling time: 2 hours or overnight
Baking time: 15 minutes

3 to 4 sun-dried tomatoes
   (not oil-packed)
2 cups cubed feta cheese
   (1/2-inch pieces)
1 tablespoon chopped fresh
   marjoram (1 teaspoon dried)
2 tablespoons olive oil
2 tablespoons red wine or balsamic
   vinegar or a mix
1/4 teaspoon ground black pepper
2 to 3 pita breads (7 1/2 inches across)

Place the sun-dried tomatoes in boiling water to cover for 15 minutes, until soft.

In a small bowl, combine the feta cubes, marjoram, olive oil, vinegar, and pepper. Chop the softened sun-dried tomatoes, add them to the bowl, and mix well. Cover and chill for at least 2 hours or overnight.

Preheat the oven to 325°.

Cut the pita breads in half, divide the feta among them, and stuff it inside the pockets. Wrap the stuffed pitas in aluminum foil and bake for 15 minutes, or until hot. Unwrap and serve immediately.

PER 3.3-OUNCE SERVING: 269 CALORIES, 9.8 G PROTEIN, 13.4 G FAT, 27.7 G CARBOHYDRATES,
6.4 G SATURATED FATTY ACIDS, 33.6 MG CHOLESTEROL, 724.2 MG SODIUM, 1.5 G TOTAL DIETARY FIBER

portabello sandwiches

A portabello sandwich is simple and quick, whether it's for a workday meal or a party. Broiling, roasting, or grilling heightens the rich flavor of these succulent fungi, which can be layered with a variety of other vegetables, cheeses, and condiments for a mouthwatering sandwich. Cooked portabellos refrigerate well, so you can cook extra and consider it another sandwich waiting to be made.

Here we offer three of our favorite combinations, but we encourage improvisation. Our Easy Russian Dressing and Chipotle Mayonnaise Dressing both make about $2/3$ cup—plenty for four sandwiches.

Serve Portabello Sandwiches alone or with a cup of soup and a tossed salad.

Serves 4
Total time: 30 minutes

portabello prep for all three sandwiches

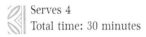

3 tablespoons olive oil

2 garlic cloves, minced or pressed

dash of salt and ground black pepper to taste

4 portabellos, rinsed and dried (about 8 ounces)

Preheat the oven to 400° or turn on the broiler.

Combine the oil, garlic, salt, and pepper in a small bowl and set aside.

Remove the stems from the portabellos and slice the caps into $1/2$- to $3/4$-inch-thick slices. Brush the portabello slices with the oil mixture and arrange at least 1 inch apart on a baking sheet.

To roast, bake on one side for 4 to 8 minutes, then turn with a spatula and bake for 4 to 8 minutes more, until tender and juicy. To broil, cook for 3 to 5 minutes, turn with a spatula, and cook for 3 to 5 minutes on the other side.

portabello reuben

Moosewood's Tempeh Reuben has been a customer favorite for years and, although its popularity never wanes, this portabello version gives it a run for the money.

easy russian dressing

1/4 cup diced tomato

1/3 cup prepared mayonnaise

1 tablespoon chopped scallions

1 teaspoon prepared horseradish

1 teaspoon cider vinegar

1/2 teaspoon salt

1/4 teaspoon ground black pepper

dash of Tabasco sauce or other hot pepper sauce

1 teaspoon tomato paste (optional)

sandwich

8 slices plain or toasted rye bread

4 sliced cooked portabellos (page 171)

1 cup drained sauerkraut

1 1/2 cups grated Swiss cheese

Preheat the oven to 400°.

Combine all of the dressing ingredients in a blender or food processor and purée until smooth and creamy. Spread Russian Dressing on 4 slices of bread and place plain side down on a baking pan. Layer each slice with 1/4 of the portabello slices, 1/4 cup of the sauerkraut, and a generous 1/3 cup of the cheese.

Top each sandwich with a second slice of bread spread with dressing, and bake for about 4 minutes, until the cheese melts. Serve immediately.

PER 8.5-OUNCE SERVING: 501 CALORIES, 18.8 G PROTEIN, 30.6 G FAT, 39.1 G CARBOHYDRATES, 10.3 G SATURATED FATTY ACIDS, 43.9 MG CHOLESTEROL, 1370.9 MG SODIUM, 5.7 G TOTAL DIETARY FIBER

portabello spinach & tomato sandwich

Inspired by BLTs, here's a sandwich for the twenty-first century.

6 ounces spinach, rinsed and stemmed

1 or 2 loaves whole grain French or Italian bread*

4 sliced cooked portabellos (page 171)

2 tomatoes, cut into 8 slices

salt and ground black pepper to taste

* Choose a loaf or loaves long enough to make four 5- or 6-inch sandwiches.

If you wish, steam the spinach until just wilted and then strain, pressing out the juice.

Cut the bread in half lengthwise and on the bottom half layer the portabello slices, spinach, and tomato slices. Sprinkle with salt and pepper. Replace the top of the loaf and cut into four sandwiches.

PER 10-OUNCE SERVING: 441 CALORIES, 12.8 G PROTEIN, 14.5 G FAT, 66 G CARBOHYDRATES, 2.2 G SATURATED FATTY ACIDS, 0 MG CHOLESTEROL, 773 MG SODIUM, 6 G TOTAL DIETARY FIBER

portabello chipotle sandwich

Our Chipotle Mayonnaise Dressing is fabulous with robust roasted portabellos. You may find yourself eating two sandwiches before you realize what you're doing! We suggest using Monterey Jack, Fontina, Muenster, or some other similarly mild cheese for the best balance of flavors.

chipotle mayonnaise dressing

- 2 tablespoons chipotles in adobo sauce*
- 6 tablespoons prepared mayonnaise
- 2 tablespoons lime juice

sandwich

- 4 multi-grain or other whole grain rolls
- 4 fresh lettuce leaves, rinsed and dried
- 4 sliced cooked portabellos (page 171)
- 1/2 red onion, thinly sliced
- 2 tomatoes, cut into 8 slices
- 2/3 pound sliced mild cheese (optional)

* We recommend La Torre brand canned chipotles in adobo sauce. The chipotles are smoked hot peppers and the adobo sauce is a spicy thick tomato purée.

Mince the chipotle peppers. Combine them with the mayonnaise and lime juice in a bowl and mix thoroughly. Slice open each roll, spread with about 1 1/2 tablespoons of the dressing, and place a lettuce leaf on one half. Layer on 1/4 of the sliced portabellos, 1/4 of the sliced red onions, 2 tomato slices, and, if you wish, a slice or two of cheese.

PER 9.5-OUNCE SERVING: 442 CALORIES, 9.7 G PROTEIN, 22.1 G FAT, 57.2 G CARBOHYDRATES, 3.3 G SATURATED FATTY ACIDS, 5.5 MG CHOLESTEROL, 603.7 MG SODIUM, 8.4 G TOTAL DIETARY FIBER

roasted vegetable sandwiches

Would the comic strip *Blondie* have achieved a cherished spot in the American psyche had it not been for our vicarious enjoyment of Dagwood's sandwich-making? His refrigerator was always stocked with *everything* you'd ever consider putting in a sandwich.

Here are two of our favorite Moosewood sandwiches with distinctly ethnic roots. So pull out the fixings and give these sandwich combos a try à la Dagwood.

french-style sandwich

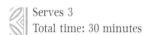

Serves 3
Total time: 30 minutes

1 cup sliced apples*
$^1/_2$ cup thinly sliced onions
1 cup thickly sliced mushrooms
1 tablespoon melted butter
1 tablespoon prepared mayonnaise
1 tablespoon chopped fresh dill
20-inch baguette
1 cup arugula
$^1/_2$ cup packed grated Gruyère cheese

* We recommend using a tart-sweet variety
like Crispin or Granny Smith.

Preheat the oven to 400°. Lightly oil a 7 x 11-inch baking dish.

Toss the apples, onions, and mushrooms with the melted butter and place them in the prepared baking dish. Roast for 15 minutes, until the apples and vegetables are tender and have released some of their juices.

Meanwhile, combine the mayonnaise and the dill in a small bowl. When the vegetables are roasted, slice the baguette in half lengthwise. Cover one half of the baguette with the arugula, spoon on the roasted mixture, and top with the grated cheese. Spread the dilled mayonnaise on the other half and put the baguette together. Slice it into thirds to make three sandwiches.

PER 9-OUNCE SERVING: 514 CALORIES, 17.6 G PROTEIN, 16 G FAT, 75.4 G CARBOHYDRATES,
8.1 G SATURATED FATTY ACIDS, 34.8 MG CHOLESTEROL, 804.3 MG SODIUM, 2.3 G TOTAL DIETARY FIBER

mediterranean-style sandwich

Serves 3
Total time: 40 minutes

vinaigrette

1/4 cup olive oil

2 tablespoons red wine vinegar

1 large garlic clove, minced or
pressed

3/4 teaspoon salt

1/4 teaspoon minced dried rosemary,
ground fennel seeds, or dried
thyme

pinch of ground black pepper

sandwich fixings

1 tiny eggplant, peeled and sliced*

3/4 cup thinly sliced red bell peppers

1/2 cup thinly sliced onions

20-inch baguette

1 1/2 cups mesclun or mixed baby
greens

1/2 cup grated smoked mozzarella,
feta, or Parmesan cheese

1 cup thinly sliced tomatoes

8 fresh basil leaves, whole or
chopped

*About 1/2 pound eggplant works well. Cut it
into 1/4- to 1/2-inch-thick rounds.*

Preheat the oven to 400°.

In a small bowl, whisk together the oil, vinegar, garlic, salt, the herb of your choice, and the black pepper and set aside. Spread the eggplant rounds in the bottom of a 9 x 13-inch or larger baking dish. Add the bell peppers and onions, keeping the vegetables in a single layer, if possible. Reserve 1 tablespoon of the vinaigrette and pour the rest over the vegetables.

Roast for 25 to 30 minutes, until the eggplant is very tender.

When the vegetables are roasted, cut the baguette in half lengthwise. Brush the cut surfaces of each half with the reserved vinaigrette. Layer one half of the baguette with the greens, place the roasted eggplant rounds along the length of the loaf, and cover with the bell peppers and onions. Top with the cheese, tomato slices, and the basil leaves. Cover with the other baguette half and slice into thirds to make three sandwiches.

PER 14-OUNCE SERVING: 611 CALORIES, 16.3 G PROTEIN, 27 G FAT, 77.5 G CARBOHYDRATES, 5.9 G SATURATED FATTY ACIDS, 18.2 MG CHOLESTEROL, 1,338.8 MG SODIUM, 3.3 G TOTAL DIETARY FIBER

soy foods ≫

The soybean is an impressive legume; there is no other as nutritious or versatile. Soybeans are almost 40 percent protein, compared to the approximately 20 percent protein content of other beans. They contain seven of the eight essential amino acids and are also a good source of iron and vitamins B_1 and B_2. Significantly higher in fat than other beans, soy provides slow-burning calories and longer-lasting energy and satisfaction.

Soybeans, which have been cultivated for at least 2,500 years, are a staple for millions of people. Soybeans are eaten whole, pressed for oil, ground for meal, and made into milk. You can get them sprouted, toasted, fermented and compressed, curdled, cultured, isolated and extruded. For centuries, soybeans have been the wellspring for soy sauce, miso, tofu, tempeh, bean sprouts, soy milk, and soy flour, and now a host of new soy products has flooded the market.

When Moosewood first opened its doors in 1973, many of the potential health benefits of soy (page 312) were not widely known. But we began right away using lots of soy products because of their versatility, malleability, and ability to absorb other flavors.

Tofu is king at Moosewood: we press, bake, braise, freeze, and shred it. We barbecue, jerk, and marinate it, and we serve it completely unadorned in miso soup. It is the primary ingredient in burgers, pita sandwiches, burrito fillings, and stuffed vegetables.

Much as we love tofu, it's only one form of soy essential in our kitchen. Soy sauce not only flavors our Asian sautés but deepens the flavor of many of our bean dishes and soups regardless of ethnicity. Miso, a salty soy paste with the consistency of peanut butter, is the key ingredient in one of our most popular salad dressings and is the secret addition to our "old-fashioned" split-pea soup. Soy milk is the basis for our favorite vegan rice pudding and can be substituted for milk in many recipes.

Indonesians first cultured soybeans to make the meaty soy food called tempeh. Ounce for ounce, tempeh's protein content is almost as high as chicken's, and it is a boon to vegetarians because it contains vitamin B_{12}, a B vitamin not otherwise found in the plant world. Tempeh, like tofu, is a magnet for seasonings. Whether spiced or marinated, baked, sautéed, or crisp-fried, it can accompany and complement a variety of dishes from around the world. It is at the heart of our Reuben sandwich.

We've included many new soy recipes throughout this book, and you'll find soy in some unlikely places, like lasagna, mashed potatoes, strudel, and frittatas, as well as in Asian fare.

muffuletta

A pungent spread of minced olives and vegetables is the exciting condiment in this extravagantly robust sandwich. The bread must have a good, thick crust to absorb the marinade and hold in the lavish layers of filling.

Bring this for lunch, and you may find yourself dreaming of Tuscany all afternoon. It's great picnic fare with cool drinks or a good Montepulciano. You can make extra olive spread and keep it for several days.

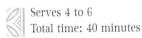 Serves 4 to 6
Total time: 40 minutes

In a bowl, combine all of the olive salad ingredients.

Using a serrated bread knife, slice the loaf of bread in half, separating the top crust from the bottom crust. Hollow out the bread halves by scooping out the soft center, leaving two shells with 1-inch-thick crusts.

Spread the olive salad evenly over the bottom shell. Layer on the deli slices, tomatoes, and cheese. Cover with lettuce leaves and top with the upper crust. Slice into four to six wedges or cross sections.

PER 7-OUNCE SERVING: 460 CALORIES, 16.7 G PROTEIN, 23 G FAT, 47.9 G CARBOHYDRATES, 6.6 G SATURATED FATTY ACIDS, 20.3 MG CHOLESTEROL, 1,777.3 MG SODIUM, 1.2 G TOTAL DIETARY FIBER

olive salad

2 tablespoons extra-virgin olive oil

2 tablespoons red wine vinegar

1 large garlic clove, pressed

1/2 cup minced kalamata olives

1/2 cup minced Spanish olives

1/4 cup minced fresh parsley

1/4 teaspoon ground black pepper

1/4 teaspoon dried oregano

1/4 cup peeled and minced carrots

1/4 cup minced celery

2 to 4 tablespoons chopped toasted pine nuts or walnuts (optional)

1/2 cup minced fresh basil (optional)

1 loaf of crusty Italian or French bread (10-inch round or a bâtard)

4 to 6 slices of meatless deli "cold cuts" made from seasoned soy protein and/or wheat gluten

4 to 6 tomato slices

4 to 6 slices of provolone, Jarlsberg, Swiss, or smoked Gouda cheese

4 to 6 leaves of green or red lettuce

variation ☙ *Preheat the oven to 400°. Assemble the muffuletta without adding the lettuce. Wrap in aluminum foil and heat in the oven for 25 to 30 minutes, until the cheese has melted. Open the top and add the lettuce before serving.*

italian tofu spread

People who still believe the cliché that vegan and dairyless dishes are austere or boring need only broaden their experience with well-prepared dishes like this one to change their minds.

At Moosewood our vegan sandwiches are sought after by vegans and non-vegans alike.

This tofu spread features a rich, multifaceted dressing and can double as a sandwich spread, salad, or dip. Serve it stuffed in pita bread, on crusty Italian bread or focaccia, or with a salad of mixed fresh greens.

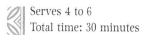
Serves 4 to 6
Total time: 30 minutes

1 cake firm tofu (16 ounces)

½ cup sun-dried tomatoes (not oil-packed)

½ cup toasted whole almonds*

3 tablespoons extra-virgin olive oil

2 large garlic cloves, minced or pressed

2 tablespoons fresh lemon juice

3 tablespoons water

⅓ cup chopped fresh basil

2 cups diced fresh tomatoes

½ teaspoon salt

ground black pepper to taste

Toast almonds in a single layer on an unoiled baking tray at 350° for 5 to 10 minutes, until fragrant and golden brown. Cool for 5 minutes or so before grinding.

Place the tofu between two plates, weight the top plate with a heavy object, and press while you prepare the other ingredients. In a small bowl, soak the sun-dried tomatoes in hot water to cover. Set aside.

Finely grind the almonds in the bowl of a food processor. Add the oil, garlic, lemon juice, and water and process to a fairly smooth consistency. Transfer to a large bowl. Stir in the basil and fresh tomatoes.

Drain the tofu, crumble it into bite-sized pieces, and add it to the tomato mixture. Drain and mince the sun-dried tomatoes. Stir in the sun-dried tomatoes, salt, and black pepper to taste.

PER 7-OUNCE SERVING: 233 CALORIES, 10.9 G PROTEIN, 16.7 G FAT, 15.1 G CARBOHYDRATES, 2 G SATURATED FATTY ACIDS, 0 MG CHOLESTEROL, 475.6 MG SODIUM, 4 G TOTAL DIETARY FIBER

variation *For a smoother-textured salad that makes a nice spread for crostini or crackers, whirl the tofu in the food processor with the oil, garlic, almonds, lemon juice, and water. Mix in the fresh and sun-dried tomatoes and the basil by hand. Top with slivers of roasted red pepper, a dab of sautéed greens like escarole or spinach, or a sprinkling of chopped fresh basil.*

thai tofu spread

Our staff and thousands of our customers agree that this sure tastes good. Some seasoned tofu is quite salty, so be sure to taste the spread before adding soy sauce—you may not need to add any.

At Moosewood, we serve this Thai Tofu Spread in toasted pita bread with lettuce and tomato slices or as an appetizer with sesame crackers or rice cakes and vegetable sticks.

Serves 8
Total time: 40 minutes

16 ounces tofu-kan or other seasoned tofu

$^2/_3$ cup diced red bell peppers

$^1/_3$ cup minced scallions

$^1/_3$ cup chopped fresh basil and/or cilantro

$^1/_2$ cup reduced-fat coconut milk

1 tablespoon grated fresh ginger root

2 tablespoons fresh lemon or lime juice

$^1/_3$ cup peanut butter

1 fresh green chile, minced (seeded for a milder hot)

soy sauce to taste

Coarsely grate the tofu-kan by hand or in a mouli-julienne; food processors turn the tofu into mush. In a bowl, toss the grated tofu with the bell peppers, scallions, and fresh basil and/or cilantro.

In a blender, combine the coconut milk, ginger, lemon or lime juice, peanut butter, and some of the minced chiles, and purée until smooth. Taste and add more of the chile if you want a spicier sauce.

Pour the dressing over the tofu mixture and toss well. Add soy sauce and more lemon or lime juice to taste.

PER 4-OUNCE SERVING: 123 CALORIES, 7.6 G PROTEIN, 8.6 G FAT, 6.2 G CARBOHYDRATES, 2.1 G SATURATED FATTY ACIDS, 0 MG CHOLESTEROL, 53 MG SODIUM, 1.4 G TOTAL DIETARY FIBER

five ethnic egg salads

We had a great time tinkering with this perennial favorite. The simplest egg salad made with fresh eggs, crisp celery, a good mayonnaise, and quality mustard is hard to beat. But hard-boiled eggs and mayonnaise are a fine vehicle for a host of other ingredients and seasonings.

Here are five egg salads that can be eaten as sandwiches, spreads, or canapés, or stuffed into ripe juicy tomatoes shells, crisp cucumber shells, or bell pepper halves.

Serve any of our egg salads as a sandwich between slices of whole wheat bread, baguette, or a coarse country-style bread with tender leaf lettuce and sliced tomato. As an appetizer, serve with sesame crackers, pita, crostini, tortilla chips, or rye crackers—depending on the particular "citizenship" of the salad.

Reduce the fat content of any of these salads by discarding the cooked yolks of five of the eggs. If you don't have a 2-quart saucepan, a larger one is okay—just use enough water to immerse the eggs completely.

 Serves 4 to 6
Total time: about 30 minutes

8 eggs
4 cups cold water

Choose one of the following:

creole
½ cup chopped celery
¼ cup diced red bell peppers
2 teaspoons minced garlic
¼ cup thinly sliced scallion greens
2 teaspoons minced fresh thyme
    (1 teaspoon dried)
¼ cup prepared mayonnaise
1 to 3 teaspoons Tabasco sauce or
    other hot sauce
½ teaspoon salt
ground black pepper to taste

greek
1½ tablespoons pitted, chopped
    kalamata olives (about 6 olives)
3 tablespoons chopped, toasted
    walnuts*
1½ tablespoons chopped fresh dill
¼ cup prepared mayonnaise
1 teaspoon fresh lemon juice
½ teaspoon salt, or to taste

* Toast on an unoiled baking tray at 350° for about 5 minutes, until golden brown.

italian
1 teaspoon minced or pressed garlic
2 tablespoons toasted pine nuts
¼ cup diced red bell peppers
3 tablespoons minced fresh basil
¼ cup diced celery
¼ cup prepared mayonnaise
1 teaspoon red wine vinegar
½ teaspoon salt, or to taste
ground black pepper to taste

mexican

1 1/2 tablespoons chopped Spanish
    olives

3 tablespoons chopped celery

3 tablespoons chopped sun-dried
    tomatoes (soaked in hot water
    if leathery)

1/4 cup prepared mayonnaise

3 tablespoons chopped fresh cilantro

1 teaspoon adobo or Tabasco sauce,
    or more to taste

1/4 teaspoon salt

scandinavian

1/4 cup chopped celery

3 tablespoons chopped fresh dill

1/4 cup thinly sliced scallion greens or
    red onions

1 tablespoon capers, drained and
    large ones chopped

1/4 cup prepared mayonnaise

1 to 2 tablespoons prepared white
    horseradish

1/4 teaspoon salt, or to taste

ground black pepper to taste

✂ Bring the eggs and water to a boil in a covered 2-quart saucepan. Reduce the heat to a rapid simmer and cook for 10 minutes.

While the eggs cook, prepare the ethnic flavorings of your choice. Submerge the cooked eggs in cold water and crack the shells to facilitate peeling. As soon as the eggs are cool enough to handle, peel them and transfer to a large bowl.

Mash the eggs well with a potato masher or fork. Add the remaining ingredients (except the salt and pepper, if you want to add them to taste). Stir everything gently to combine and serve.

CREOLE: PER 4-OUNCE SERVING: 168 CALORIES, 10.4 G PROTEIN, 11.6 G FAT, 5.2 G CARBOHYDRATES, 3 G SATURATED FATTY ACIDS, 336.3 MG CHOLESTEROL, 383.4 MG SODIUM, 0.5 TOTAL DIETARY FIBER

GREEK: PER 3.5-OUNCE SERVING: 194 CALORIES, 10.6 G PROTEIN, 15.1 G FAT, 4 G CARBOHYDRATES, 3.4 G SATURATED FATTY ACIDS, 336.3 MG CHOLESTEROL, 480.9 MG SODIUM, 0.3 G TOTAL DIETARY FIBER

ITALIAN: PER 3.5-OUNCE SERVING: 163 CALORIES, 10.2 G PROTEIN, 11.5 G FAT, 4.1 G CARBOHYDRATES, 3 G SATURATED FATTY ACIDS, 336.3 MG CHOLESTEROL, 368.5 MG SODIUM, 0.3 G TOTAL DIETARY FIBER

MEXICAN: PER 3.5-OUNCE SERVING: 177 CALORIES, 10.8 G PROTEIN, 12.1 G FAT, 6.2 G CARBOHYDRATES, 3.1 G SATURATED FATTY ACIDS, 336.3 MG CHOLESTEROL, 461.8 MG SODIUM, 0.8 G TOTAL DIETARY FIBER

SCANDINAVIAN: PER 3.5-OUNCE SERVING: 164 CALORIES, 10.2 G PROTEIN, 11.6 G FAT, 4.2 G CARBO-HYDRATES, 3 G SATURATED FATTY ACIDS, 336.3 MG CHOLESTEROL, 304.6 MG SODIUM, 0.3 G TOTAL DIETARY FIBER

tofu burgers

At nearly every Saturday lunch, we serve big baked Tofu Burgers open-faced on a thick slice of toasted whole wheat bread, with fresh lettuce beneath, a generous tomato slice on top, and homemade Easy Russian Dressing (page 172) over all, yum!

You can replace the basil with marjoram and combine the herbs in any proportion you like as long as the total amount of dried herbs equals 1 tablespoon. If using fresh herbs, the total amount should be about 3 tablespoons.

This mix can also be used to stuff portabello mushrooms or to make tofu "meatballs," which will bake in about 20 minutes. Tightly covered and refrigerated, the uncooked burger mix will keep for 1 to 2 days. Or you can form the mix into patties and freeze them: To serve, just thaw at room temperature and bake.

Serves 8
Preparation time: 30 minutes
Baking time: 30 minutes

2 cakes firm tofu (16 ounces each)
2 tablespoons vegetable oil
2 cups diced onions
1 cup peeled and grated carrots
1 cup diced bell peppers
1 teaspoon dried oregano
1 teaspoon dried basil
1 teaspoon dried dill
²/₃ cup chopped walnuts
1 cup bread crumbs*
2 tablespoons tahini
2 tablespoons light miso
2 tablespoons soy sauce
1 to 2 tablespoons Dijon mustard (optional)

* Pulverize stale or lightly toasted whole wheat, sourdough, or French bread in a blender or food processor.

Sandwich the tofu between two plates and rest a heavy weight on the top plate. Press for about 15 minutes; then drain the expressed liquid from the bottom plate.

Meanwhile, heat the oil in a frying pan and sauté the onions, carrots, peppers, oregano, basil, and dill for about 7 minutes, until the vegetables are just tender. Crumble the pressed tofu into a large bowl. Stir in the walnuts, bread crumbs, tahini, miso, soy sauce, and mustard, if using. Add the sautéed vegetables and mix well.

Preheat the oven to 400°. Generously oil a baking sheet.

Using about ¾ cup of burger mix per burger, form eight patties by hand and place them on the baking sheet about 2 inches apart. Bake for about 30 minutes, until the burgers are firm and browned. Serve hot.

PER 7.5-OUNCE SERVING: 279 CALORIES, 14.2 G PROTEIN, 17.8 G FAT, 20.1 G CARBOHYDRATES, 2.7 G SATURATED FATTY ACIDS, 0 MG CHOLESTEROL, 430.4 MG SODIUM, 3.7 G TOTAL DIETARY FIBER

dixie burgers

Colorful, tasty, and full of vitamins and minerals from sweet potatoes, greens, and tofu, these burgers are both low-fat and high-fiber. What more could you want?

Serve on a bun with one of our Two Barbeque Sauces (page 388), smoked Cheddar cheese, tomato and onion slices, and pickles. Accompany with sweet potato fries and pickled okra.

Serves 4
Preparation time: 30 minutes
Baking time: 20 minutes

1 tablespoon vegetable oil
1 cup chopped onions
4 garlic cloves, minced or pressed
pinch of salt
2 cups grated raw sweet potatoes
1/3 cup minced celery
1/4 teaspoon dried thyme
1/4 teaspoon ground allspice
1/2 cup minced red bell peppers
2 cups stemmed and finely chopped
    raw collard greens or kale
1 tablespoon soy sauce
1/4 teaspoon ground black pepper
1 1/2 cups cooked black-eyed peas
    (15-ounce can, drained)*
4 ounces firm tofu (optional)

* *1/2 cup of dried black-eyed peas will yield about 1 1/2 cups cooked.*

Preheat the oven to 350°. Generously oil a baking sheet.

Heat the oil in a heavy or nonstick frying pan. Add the onions, garlic, and salt and sauté on medium-high heat for 10 minutes, until the onions are soft and translucent. Add the grated sweet potatoes, celery, thyme, and allspice and cook for 5 minutes, stirring often. Add the bell peppers and the collard greens or kale, cover, and cook on medium-low heat for another 5 minutes, until the greens are just tender. Remove from the heat and stir in the soy sauce and black pepper.

Meanwhile, in the bowl of a food processor, pulse the black-eyed peas and, if using, the tofu until the peas are mashed, but not smooth. Combine the sautéed vegetables with the mashed mixture and form into 4 patties.

Bake on the prepared baking sheet for 20 minutes or until firm.

PER 8-OUNCE SERVING: 188 CALORIES, 6.1 G PROTEIN, 4.4 G FAT, 32.5 G CARBOHYDRATES,
1.1 G SATURATED FATTY ACIDS, 0 MG CHOLESTEROL, 490.4 MG SODIUM, 5 G TOTAL DIETARY FIBER

falafel burgers

In Israel, falafels are healthful and tasty street food. These burgers have that distinctive and appealing falafel flavor, minus the fat of deep-frying and plus the boost of protein from the tofu.

Stuff these patties in pita pockets with lettuce, tomatoes, and either fresh Yogurt Tahini Dressing, or try our bottled Moosewood Restaurant Lemon Tahini Dressing. Or arrange the burgers artfully on a bed of greens and drizzle with any Middle Eastern–style dressing.

 Yields 8 burgers
Preparation time: 30 minutes
Baking time: 30 minutes

1 cup diced onions

2 to 3 garlic cloves, minced or pressed

1 tablespoon olive oil

1 cup diced red bell peppers

1 teaspoon turmeric

1 teaspoon ground coriander

pinch of cayenne, or to taste

1 cake firm tofu (12 ounces), pressed and crumbled*

1 1/2 cups cooked chickpeas (15-ounce can, drained)

3 tablespoons fresh lemon juice

1 tablespoon soy sauce

1 teaspoon dark sesame oil

1/4 cup chopped fresh parsley

1/4 cup tahini (page 471)

1/2 teaspoon salt, or more to taste

1/2 cup bread crumbs, as needed

chopped scallions or thinly sliced red onion rings
Yogurt Tahini Dressing (page 389)

* Sandwich the tofu between two plates and rest a heavy can or book on the top plate. Press for about 15 minutes and then drain the expressed liquid.

✂ Preheat the oven to 350°. Generously oil a baking sheet.

In a 9-inch skillet, sauté the onions and garlic in the olive oil on medium heat for 5 minutes. Add the bell peppers, turmeric, coriander, and cayenne and sauté for 5 minutes, or until the vegetables are tender, stirring occasionally to prevent sticking.

While the vegetables cook, combine the tofu, chickpeas, lemon juice, soy sauce, and sesame oil in the bowl of a food processor (see Note). Process until well combined, but not a paste. It may be necessary to stir the contents once or twice, as it will be quite dry.

Transfer the tofu mixture to a large bowl and add the sautéed vegetables, parsley, tahini, and salt. Mix everything together well with your hands. If the mixture is too sticky, add up to $1/2$ cup bread crumbs. Add more salt to taste.

Shape $1/2$-cup portions of the burger mix into 8 patties and arrange on the prepared baking sheet with a bit of space between them. Bake for 30 minutes, until golden, juicy, and firm. Decorate with scallions or onion rings and top with Yogurt Tahini Dressing.

PER 5-OUNCE SERVING: 185 CALORIES, 8.2 G PROTEIN, 9.2 G FAT, 19.8 G CARBOHYDRATES, 1.3 G SATURATED FATTY ACIDS, 0 MG CHOLESTEROL, 424.5 MG SODIUM, 3.7 G TOTAL DIETARY FIBER

note ✿ *If you don't have a food processor, don't worry. Falafels have a much longer history than food processors. Vigorously mash the chickpeas with a potato masher. Blend in the liquids, and then add the tofu and tahini and persevere with the mashing. Add the remaining ingredients and mix well.*

surveying the seaweed scene

For Americans, sea vegetable cookery is a fairly new thing. Twenty years ago, the typical shopper didn't add seaweed to the grocery list, and many people tried seaweed only when feeling adventurous at an Asian restaurant. Gradually, however, seaweed is gaining a foothold in the American diet. Sun-dried seaweeds are available in health food stores and ethnic markets throughout North America. Frozen, blanched, or salted fresh seaweed is also often available. Our local Ithaca supermarkets have fresh sushi deli counters that are stocked daily and always busy.

In Japan, Korea, the Philippines, and Indonesia, and on the Hawaiian Islands, seaweed is part of the daily diet. In the Canadian maritime provinces, dulse is considered an improvement on the potato chip and sold at pubs as a snack to have with a pint. In the Ukraine, a canned beet-tomato-algae mixture called sea cabbage is widely available. Seaweed can be steamed, sautéed, baked, dried, and preserved in brine. Most types can be eaten raw and some are good frozen.

Seaweed absorbs high concentrations of elements from the sea, which gives it immense nutritive value. Rich in vitamins and minerals (A, E, C, D, Niacin, B_{12}, folic acid, phosphorus, calcium, iron, iodine), seaweed also provides a full complement of trace elements. Many seaweeds contain oils—which may keep plants from drying out between tides—but calories and cholesterol are negligible. Three ounces of dried nori supplies half the daily adult protein requirement, and 1 tablespoon of cooked hijiki is about equal to the calcium in a glass of whole milk.

Fresh seaweed is not as fishy or salty as you might expect. Most varieties have unique, delicate flavors ranging from beanlike or nutlike to a taste reminiscent of arugula or parsley with a hint of the sweetness of grapes. But you really have to try them to appreciate their variety. Abalone, cloud ears, truffles, sea grapes, Irish moss, and sea lettuce are all enticing on their own. Most fresh seaweeds keep for a few days sealed in plastic bags with a little seawater and refrigerated in the crisper bin.

A few of the most common types of Japanese dried seaweed available in U.S. markets are hijiki, konbu, nori, arame, funori, and wakame. Korean dried seaweed includes kim, tasima, parae, nongmichae, mojaban, and miyok. Chinese dried seaweed includes fah tsoi, hai dai, and chi choy. Dulse and kelp are the best-known Western varieties.

Most dried seaweeds can be rehydrated by soaking in water or steaming. Dried hijiki can be crumbled straight into the rice-cooking pot. Wakame requires a 20-minute soak before it's added to a dish, and konbu is often simmered to make a broth. Soups made with seaweed tend to be best when newly prepared.

If you haven't ventured into the seaweed scene yet, give it a try. For recipes, check out Asian or natural foods cookbooks or the Web, and see pages 148 and 187. It's hard to find a healthier habit to get hooked on.

tofu hijiki burgers

This is a good-looking burger, flecked with green, orange, and black. Moosewood's Susan Harville was inspired to create it after trying a burger at Dojo in New York's East Village.

These burgers are delicious topped with tomato slices and served alongside Cucumber Peanut Salad (page 107) and brown rice, or eat them as a sandwich on a bun slathered with Avocado Wasabi Dressing (page 371).

Serves 4 to 6
Preparation time: 40 minutes
Baking time: 30 to 40 minutes

¼ cup dried hijiki seaweed

1 cup peeled and grated carrots

2 tablespoons pressed garlic

2 teaspoons grated fresh ginger root

1 tablespoon vegetable oil

24 ounces firm tofu, pressed*

½ cup minced scallions

¼ cup sesame seeds

¼ cup light miso

1 teaspoon dark sesame oil

* *Sandwich the tofu between two plates and rest a heavy can or book on the top plate. Press for about 15 minutes; then drain the expressed liquid.*

Rinse the hijiki in a sieve or strainer, and place it in a bowl with warm water to cover and set aside to soak for 20 to 30 minutes.

Preheat the oven to 350°. Generously oil a baking sheet.

Sauté the carrots, garlic, and ginger in the oil for about 5 minutes, until the carrots are limp. In a bowl, mash or crumble the pressed tofu. Add the cooked carrots and the scallions, sesame seeds, miso, and sesame oil and stir well. Drain the soaked hijiki and then chop it and stir it into the mix. Add a little more miso, if you wish.

Use about ½ cup of the mix per burger and form into patties. Place the burgers on the baking sheet and bake until firm and golden, 30 to 40 minutes.

PER 6.5-OUNCE SERVING: 206 CALORIES, 12.4 G PROTEIN, 11.9 G FAT, 16.4 G CARBOHYDRATES, 2 G SATURATED FATTY ACIDS, 0 MG CHOLESTEROL, 376.6 MG SODIUM, 3.2 G TOTAL DIETARY FIBER

variation *Pan-fry for about 10 minutes, turning once after 5 minutes.*

mushroom pecan burgers

This is a yummy multigrain burger, high in fiber and lower in fat than many versions we've tried. Easy Russian Dressing (page 172) or Moosewood's All-Natural Honey Dijon Dressing, available in many natural food stores, are both great on these succulent burgers. Ketchup, mustard, pickles, avocado slices, alfalfa sprouts, minced red onions, and tomato slices are also good. Melt Fontina or Cheddar cheese on top for a cheeseburger.

Serves 4 to 6
Preparation time: 30 minutes
Baking time: 30 minutes

Preheat the oven to 350°. Generously oil a baking sheet.

In a medium skillet, sauté the onions in the oil. Cook on medium heat until the onions are softened, about 5 minutes. Add the marjoram, thyme, and mushrooms. Cook, stirring often, until the mushrooms are tender, 5 to 10 minutes more.

Spoon the mushroom mixture into a bowl. Add the pecans, soy sauce, bread crumbs, rice, oats, dill, and miso, if using. Mix in the tofu, mashing it with your hands or a potato masher. Add salt and pepper and mix well.

Shape the mixture into six round patties and place them on the prepared baking sheet. Bake for 30 minutes, until golden brown. Serve on toast or in a bun.

1 1/2 cups chopped onions

1 tablespoon vegetable oil

1/2 teaspoon dried marjoram

1/4 teaspoon dried thyme

4 cups chopped cremini or other mushrooms*

1/3 cup chopped toasted pecans**

2 teaspoons soy sauce

1 cup whole wheat bread crumbs

1 cup cooked brown rice

3/4 cup rolled oats

1 tablespoon chopped fresh dill

1 tablespoon miso (optional)

1 cake firm tofu, pressed (16 ounces)***

salt and ground black pepper to taste

* Cremini mushrooms give a stronger, more distinctive flavor than other mushrooms. Ten ounces of mushrooms equals about 4 cups.
** Toast pecans in a single layer on an unoiled baking tray at 350° for 5 to 10 minutes, until fragrant and golden brown.
*** Sandwich the tofu between two plates and rest a heavy weight (can or book) on the top plate. Press for about 15 minutes; then drain the expressed liquid from the bottom plate.

PER 7.5-OUNCE SERVING: 313 CALORIES, 13.5 G PROTEIN, 13.8 G FAT, 37.1 G CARBOHYDRATES, 2.1 G SATURATED FATTY ACIDS, 0 MG CHOLESTEROL, 232 MG SODIUM, 5.7 G TOTAL DIETARY FIBER

note Although we prefer these burgers baked, you can also griddle them in a lightly oiled cast-iron pan or nonstick frying pan. Cook on medium heat for 5 to 7 minutes per side.

tofu sloppy joes

At last, a novel tofu dish that is 100 percent kid-friendly—a healthy alternative to junk food that even grown-ups can enjoy!

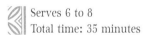 Serves 6 to 8
Total time: 35 minutes

1 cup chopped onions

1 garlic clove, minced or pressed

2 tablespoons vegetable oil

1 cup chopped bell peppers

1 cake firm tofu (16 ounces),
    crumbled or mashed

1¾ cups diced tomatoes (fresh or a
    14-ounce can)

⅔ cup tomato paste (6-ounce can)

½ cup water

1 teaspoon ground coriander

1 teaspoon ground cumin

1 teaspoon dried oregano

1 teaspoon brown sugar

pinch of cayenne

1 teaspoon salt

ground black pepper to taste

6 to 8 kaiser or hamburger rolls

In a large nonreactive pan, sauté the onions and garlic in the oil on medium heat until soft, about 5 minutes. Add the bell peppers and continue to cook for 5 minutes, stirring occasionally. Stir in the tofu, diced tomatoes, tomato paste, water, coriander, cumin, oregano, brown sugar, cayenne, and salt and simmer for 10 minutes. Add black pepper to taste.

Slice and toast the rolls. Fill each roll with about ½ cup of the sloppy joe mix. Serve immediately.

PER 9-OUNCE SERVING: 368 CALORIES, 14.7 G PROTEIN, 10.1 G FAT, 56.3 G CARBOHYDRATES, 1.8 G SATURATED FATTY ACIDS, 0 MG CHOLESTEROL, 997 MG SODIUM, 2.8 G TOTAL DIETARY FIBER

drinks&
snacks

drinks & snacks

We guess that just about everyone enjoys eating a little something between meals now and then. Snacks are fun, and when you have delicious and healthful options to choose from, you won't resort to greasy, additive-filled junk food.

Number one on our list of healthy pick-me-ups is a refreshing fruit smoothie. When we opened the cafe/bar in Moosewood Restaurant several years ago, the staff got excited (and competitive) about inventing smoothies. The drinks of the day, quickly made by blending fruits, juices, yogurt, soymilk, or even tea or coffee, were described in detail on two chalkboards, one over the bar and one out on the sidewalk. Soon our customers and even casual passersby were making their own suggestions and requests. We've included some of our favorites, along with a few other special drinks, such as Sparkling Strawberry Lemonade and Lemongrass Limeade, both perfect refreshments for a summer outdoor meal.

Of course, snacking begins at home, and it's important to have something to offer when the kids get home from school or when friends visit. Flavored Olives or Spiced Nuts are lovely to nibble on with drinks. Or try one of our flavored popcorns or a mug of chai when you relax with a movie.

Some of the most popular snacks are dips and spreads to eat with crackers, chips, or bread or with fresh vegetable sticks.

Tomatilla Guacamole is tangy and interesting, an old standard with a new twist. Once you've made Sour Cream Onion Dip fresh at home, you may never go back to the kind you can buy at the store. Some of the dips are sophisticated enough to serve as appetizers at the most elegant dinner party. Briney Green Olive & Artichoke Tapenade might be served quite formally on crisp Belgian endive leaves. Sun-dried Tomato & Chèvre Spread is wonderful on toasted baguette rounds or stuffed into giant olives or cherry tomatoes. All of these dips and spreads make fine sandwich fillings, too. Try David's Dilled Havarti Spread on rye bread with cucumber and tomato slices.

Another whole category of snack food we really go for at Moosewood is tofu, and if we do say so ourselves, tofu is one of the things we do best. Flavorful little cubes or triangles of baked tofu, whether Mexican, lemony, or curried, may just convert even the most reluctant of picky eaters. Tell them it's just a snack, not a whole meal commitment. These addictive finger foods are a great way to get more healthful tofu into your diet and love every minute of it.

teatime story

Whether a strong, robust Keemun, a fragrant Darjeeling or Ceylon, a refreshing Sencha green, or a blend of herbals, tea offerings are exciting, fascinating, and healthful. Black tea has 60 percent less caffeine per cup than coffee, and Americans' consumption of tea doubled in the past decade when news got out that the powerful antioxidants in black and green teas may help fight cancer and coronary disease. In fact, green tea, relatively little-used until a few years ago, is now featured in bottled iced teas, ice cream, and even cosmetics!

According to legend, Shen-nung, a Chinese emperor, scholar, and herbalist, discovered tea about 3,000 years ago, when a leaf from a tea plant fortuitously drifted into his pot of boiling water. It wasn't long before the leaves of the plant *Camellia sinensis* were being boiled, stewed, pickled, dried, and added to medicinal ointments. By the third century B.C., tea had become a common beverage among the Chinese people and was grown and harvested mostly by monks in high mountain monasteries.

By the seventh century A.D., tea was a valuable commodity shipped to what are now Japan, Korea, Iran, India, Afghanistan, and Arabia. By the sixteenth century, the Dutch and Portuguese had set up trade routes to the Far East and were trading in chocolate, coffee, and tea. Settlers from Europe brought tea to the British colonies in North America. In the 1700s, Britain levied high taxes on colonial tea, and colonists were so outraged that it incited the infamous Boston Tea Party. In the 1800s,

Chinese traders, more interested in opium than in European commodities, developed a lucrative opium-tea trade with India, then a British colony. When China outlawed opium and the Opium Wars broke out between China and Britain, the British set up tea plantations in their colonies of India and Ceylon, Kenya, Uganda, Tanzania, and Zimbabwe, where tea cultivation continues today.

The first tea bags were invented in the early 1900s by Thomas Sullivan, who packaged his teas in little silk bags. Commercial production of tea bags took off in the United States in the 1920s, inspiring the hit song "Tea for Two." Since smaller black tea leaves hasten the brewing, tea bags contain the smallest tea leaf particles, called "fannings" or "dusts" in the business. Hundreds of combinations of herbal teas are also available in bags and some can be found in bulk, especially in natural food stores. Today most of the three thousand varieties of tea we consume are brewed in bags.

chai

Chai rivals coffee as a stimulating pick-me-up, and brewing a fresh pot of chai with heady, exotic spices and fragrant tea leaves feels a little like stirring up a lovely magical potion. If you have a foamer, froth up the milk for a chai latté.

Be aware that commercially packaged chai, although convenient, can be quite overly sweetened.

 Serves 2
Total time: 20 minutes

3 cups water

1-inch piece of fresh ginger root, sliced

¼ teaspoon black peppercorns

½ teaspoon fennel seeds

¼ teaspoon cardamom seeds

6 to 8 whole cloves

2 heaping teaspoons black tea leaves or 2 tea bags

¾ cup milk

sugar or mild honey to taste

In a medium saucepan, boil the water and spices until the liquid has reduced to 2 cups, 10 to 15 minutes. Remove from the heat, add the black tea or tea bags, and steep for 4 to 5 minutes. Strain the tea, discard the leaves and spices, and return the tea to the saucepan. Add the milk and heat to boiling. Add sugar or honey to taste and serve.

PER 11-OUNCE SERVING: 47 CALORIES, 2.9 G PROTEIN, 1.7 G FAT, 5.2 G CARBOHYDRATES, 1 G SATURATED FATTY ACIDS, 6.4 MG CHOLESTEROL, 50.4 MG SODIUM, 0.2 G TOTAL DIETARY FIBER

green tea with ginger

Freshly brewed green tea has a clean taste and the warm fragrance of the outdoors. We think it evokes gracious feelings and calm, clear thinking. Here, ginger and honey add a delicious spicy sweetness. Because green tea has less caffeine than black tea, it's a good beverage for late afternoon or evening, but steep it for no longer than 3 to 4 minutes or its appealing bitter edge can become too strong.

For a more stimulating beverage, try using black tea—and a splash of milk, if desired.

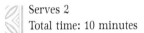 Serves 2
Total time: 10 minutes

3 cups water

1-inch piece of fresh ginger root, sliced

2 teaspoons green tea leaves or 2 tea bags

honey or sugar to taste

Bring the water to a simmer in a covered saucepan. Add the ginger and continue to simmer for 5 minutes. Add the tea or tea bags and steep for 3 to 4 minutes. Strain and serve plain or with honey or sugar.

PER 12-OUNCE SERVING: 4 CALORIES, 0 G PROTEIN, 0 G FAT, 1.1 G CARBOHYDRATES, 0 G SATURATED FATTY ACIDS, 0 MG CHOLESTEROL, 10.3 MG SODIUM, 0 G TOTAL DIETARY FIBER

what's green tea?

Green tea leaves, picked in small batches by hand or large batches by machine, are withered slowly to remove water, and then dried, steamed, or pan-fried, after which they are lightly crushed by twisting or rolling to release their flavor-producing enzymes. The shape of the leaves ranges from thin and crinkly to tight little balls to needle-like blades, and the color ranges from shades of jade to pale olive green. The most superior green tea contains only leaves and buds, while lower grades use broken leaves and stems. Green tea is best when steeped for less than 5 minutes in fresh spring water heated to just below the boiling point. In Japan, the art of making a cup of green tea for guests has evolved into a formal ceremony held in special tea rooms and is studied with masters.

fruit & herbal iced tea

Here's a perfect beverage for hot weather or any time you feel the impulse for a soft drink on ice. Try it with one type of tea or mix together two or three of your favorite flavors. We really like spearmint with apple raspberry juice, chamomile with peach juice, or lemon zinger with apple juice and the teensiest pinch of cinnamon.

Serves 4 to 6
Preparation time: 5 minutes
Steeping time: 30 minutes

4 herbal tea bags

4 cups water

2 cups apple, apple raspberry, peach, or cherry juice

In a pitcher, steep the tea bags in the water at room temperature for 30 minutes. Add the juice and chill. Serve over ice cubes with slices of lemon, orange, or lime, and a sprig or two of mint.

PER 8-OUNCE SERVING: 37 CALORIES, 0 G PROTEIN, 0.1 G FAT, 9.3 G CARBOHYDRATES, 0 G SATURATED FATTY ACIDS, 0 MG CHOLESTEROL, 6.8 MG SODIUM, 0.1 G TOTAL DIETARY FIBER

fresh sun-steeped tea

In summer and early autumn, pick your own fresh herb leaves and immediately steep them in a glass jar of water placed in the sun. After several hours you will have a wonderfully flavorful, sun-drenched tea. You'll feel like you're sipping sunshine and find yourself in an inexplicably sunny mood.

If it's cloudy or raining (a common weather condition in Ithaca), you can still go picking and just steep the herbs in boiling water or dry them for later use. Comfrey, burdock, the mints, chamomile, raspberry, rosehips, and clover are just a few common plants that make delicious infused teas.

smoothies & cold drinks

Smoothies are a quick and delicious way to give yourself a refreshing pick-me-up at any time throughout the day. They can be a simple duet of frozen fruit and soy milk or an elaborate blend of several fresh ripe fruits, juice, milk, vanilla, and peanut butter.

Combinations are endless, and the basic directions are simple: In the blender, whip up 1 to 2 cups of fruit, a cup of liquid, and maybe a teaspoon or two of a flavoring and/or sweetener. Let the suggestions below inspire you, and your smoothies will be thick, frosty, and refreshing. Refrigerate any extra and stir or re-blend if needed.

- Fruits: fresh or frozen strawberries, peaches, plums, bananas, pears, blue-berries, cherries, melons

- Liquids: orange, apple, apricot, berry, or cherry juices; soy milk, dairy milk, buttermilk, yogurt, flavored yogurt; green tea; tropical fruit "nectars" such as mango or papaya (found in the Latin American sections of supermarkets; Goya has a wide selection)

- Flavorings: pure vanilla or almond extract, chocolate syrup, cinnamon, nut-meg, peanut butter

- Sweeteners: maple syrup, sugar, honey

We like drinks that comfort—coffee and hot chocolate drinks during the wintry months, frozen drinks and fruit smoothies during the hot days of summer. The drinks that follow were developed at Moosewood's coffee and juice bar, many inspired by requests from our customers. Naming the drinks is almost as much fun as creating them: Local landmarks, favorite customers, and co-workers have all been honored with their own drink.

apple pie à la mode drink

This creamy, lip-smacking treat was developed as a drink special. Its sweet, apple 'n' spice taste will surprise you.

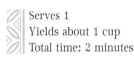

Serves 1
Yields about 1 cup
Total time: 2 minutes

¾ cup unsweetened apple juice
¼ cup soy milk or light cream
1 teaspoon sugar or pure maple syrup
¼ teaspoon pure vanilla extract
pinch of ground cinnamon
pinch of ground nutmeg

Add the ingredients to a large glass filled with ice and stir until well mixed.

PER 8-OUNCE SERVING: 120 CALORIES, 1.7 G PROTEIN, 1.3 G FAT, 25.5 G CARBOHYDRATES, 0.2 G SATURATED FATTY ACIDS, 0 MG CHOLESTEROL, 12.1 MG SODIUM, 1 G TOTAL DIETARY FIBER

autumn smoothie

Delectable says it all. We hope this smoothie inspires you to come and see the amazing colors of autumn in upstate New York for yourself. Visit in mid-October and stop in at Moosewood.

For the best flavor and consistency, use a really ripe, sweet, soft pear. If your ingredients aren't cold, add ice to the blender or your glass, but don't put ice cubes in a food processor—use crushed ice.

Serves 1
Yields about 1½ cups
Total time: 5 minutes

1 ripe fresh pear, peeled, cored, and
   chopped
½ cup unsweetened apple juice
½ cup soy milk
1 teaspoon pure maple syrup or sugar
¼ teaspoon pure vanilla extract
2 drops pure almond extract
pinch of ground cinnamon

Purée the ingredients in a blender or food processor until smooth.

PER 12-OUNCE SERVING: 170 CALORIES, 3.6 G PROTEIN, 2.7 G FAT, 34.7 G CARBOHYDRATES, 0.3 G SATURATED FATTY ACIDS, 0 MG CHOLESTEROL, 17.6 MG SODIUM, 4.2 G TOTAL DIETARY FIBER

blueberry & buttermilk falls drink

Buttermilk Falls is one of the prettiest sights in Ithaca. The gushing waterfall bubbles like sparkling buttermilk.

Try this smoothie with one of our muffins or breads for an elegant, light breakfast, or drink it solo as a midday refreshment. It's easy, thirst-quenching, and incredibly healthful.

Serves 1
Yields about 1½ cups
Total time: 2 minutes

1 cup buttermilk

½ cup fresh or frozen blueberries

2 teaspoons sugar or pure maple syrup, or to taste

Purée the ingredients in a blender or food processor until smooth.

PER 11-OUNCE SERVING: 167 CALORIES, 8 G PROTEIN, 2.3 G FAT, 30 G CARBOHYDRATES, 1.3 G SATURATED FATTY ACIDS, 7.9 MG CHOLESTEROL, 242.7 MG SODIUM, 2 G TOTAL DIETARY FIBER

elissa's egg cream

Like the classic New York specialty, this "egg cream" has no egg and no cream, but a bendy-straw and high swiveling stool might be in order. We created this drink for a couple of home-sick New Yorkers who've come back for more time and again with friends and family in tow. The flavor of this drink will only be as good as your chocolate syrup, so choose a tasty one.

Serves 1
Yields about 1½ cups
Total time: 2 minutes

3 tablespoons chocolate syrup

3 tablespoons soy milk

¼ teaspoon pure vanilla extract

1 cup sparkling water

In a 12-ounce glass filled with ice, stir together the chocolate syrup, soy milk, and vanilla. Slowly add sparkling water until the glass is filled.

PER 14-OUNCE SERVING: 139 CALORIES, 2.1 G PROTEIN, 1.3 G FAT, 29.3 G CARBOHYDRATES, 0.3 G SATURATED FATTY ACIDS, 0 MG CHOLESTEROL, 84.2 MG SODIUM, 1.3 G TOTAL DIETARY FIBER

espresso drink

Our espresso smoothie was the first drink special featured at our juice bar, and it's a great way to enjoy your morning coffee! Soy milk and banana soften the bitter edge of the espresso. For a sweeter drink, use the whole banana and add a teaspoon of sugar.

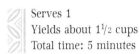
Serves 1
Yields about 1½ cups
Total time: 5 minutes

¼ cup brewed espresso
half a ripe banana, peeled and sliced
½ cup soy milk
½ cup crushed ice

Purée the ingredients in a blender or food processor until smooth.

PER 12-OUNCE SERVING: 88 CALORIES, 3.6 G PROTEIN, 2.5 G FAT, 14.4 G CARBOHYDRATES, 0.4 G SATURATED FATTY ACIDS, 0 MG CHOLESTEROL, 22 MG SODIUM, 2.7 G TOTAL DIETARY FIBER

frozen jeff

Many a customer says, "I'd like something refreshing, but not too sweet." This is it. Neil Minnis, Moosewood's man behind the bar, first developed this tangy treat for one of our favorite young Moosers, Jeff Miller, who took one sip and was hooked.

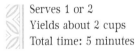
Serves 1 or 2
Yields about 2 cups
Total time: 5 minutes

1 cup orange juice
2 fresh strawberries, rinsed and
    stemmed
1 tablespoon fresh lime juice
¼ teaspoon pure vanilla extract
1 tablespoon sugar or pure maple
    syrup
½ cup crushed ice

Combine the ingredients in a blender or food processor and purée until smooth.

PER 14-OUNCE SERVING: 163 CALORIES, 1.7 G PROTEIN, 0.5 G FAT, 38.8 G CARBOHYDRATES, 0 G SATURATED FATTY ACIDS, 0 MG CHOLESTEROL, 2.8 MG SODIUM, 0.9 G TOTAL DIETARY FIBER

green tea smoothie

Fruit of any color is delicious in a smoothie made with green tea, but we lean toward pale green honeydew, and sometimes we add kiwi, too. Be sure to use a food processor when making smoothies with kiwi: Blenders are more likely to crush the bitter kiwi seeds.

Serves 1 or 2
Yields about 3 cups
Total time: 5 to 10 minutes

1 cup chilled green tea
1 banana, peeled and sliced
2 cups chopped honeydew melon
1 tablespoon honey or sugar
1 kiwi, peeled and sliced (optional)

Purée the ingredients in a blender or food processor until smooth.

PER 24-OUNCE SERVING: 276 CALORIES, 2.6 G
PROTEIN, 0.8 G FAT, 72.2 G CARBOHYDRATES, 0.3 G
SATURATED FATTY ACIDS, 0 MG CHOLESTEROL,
38.1 MG SODIUM, 4.4 G TOTAL DIETARY FIBER

hot flash cooler

This refreshing drink was first concocted by our bar staff to cool the brows of the Moosewood women, especially those in mid-life.

Soy milk combined with fruit juices is a great way to add phytoestrogens to the diet and is very beneficial to women's health. Even with this amusing title, lots of Moosewood Restaurant's male customers order the "Hot Flash Cooler" because it's so thirst-quenching and delicious. Hey, some guys get hot flashes, too, and most get hot under the collar at least once in a while. So here's how to chill.

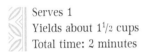

Serves 1
Yields about 1¹/₂ cups
Total time: 2 minutes

³/₄ cup chilled peach juice*

¹/₄ cup chilled soy milk**

¹/₄ to ¹/₂ teaspoon fresh lemon juice

¹/₄ to ¹/₂ teaspoon pure vanilla extract

2 teaspoons sugar

chilled sparkling water

a few ice cubes

* *Most bottled peach juices are blended, usually with white grape juice and apple juice. We use After the Fall brand peach juice.*
** *If you use vanilla-flavored soy milk, omit the vanilla extract and omit or reduce the sugar.*

In a chilled 12-ounce glass, stir together the peach juice, soy milk, lemon juice, vanilla, and sugar. Slowly stir in sparkling water until the glass is almost filled. Add the ice, close your eyes, and sip away.

PER 12-OUNCE SERVING: 147 CALORIES, 2 G PROTEIN, 1.1 G FAT, 33.4 G CARBOHYDRATES, 0.1 G SATURATED FATTY ACIDS, 0 MG CHOLESTEROL, 42.7 MG SODIUM, 1.8 G TOTAL DIETARY FIBER

sparkling strawberry lemonade

Lemonades flavored with fresh fruit are quick, elegant, and refreshing. This is one of the finest ways to capture the taste of ripe berries in their prime. Bathing the lemons in warm water for 10 minutes or zapping them in a microwave for 1 to 2 minutes before juicing will make them juicier. Is life handing you lemons? Here's what to do with 'em.

Serves 4
Total time: 15 minutes

1 cup sugar

$^1/_2$ cup water

2 cups rinsed, stemmed, and chopped strawberries

1 cup strained fresh lemon juice

24 ounces sparkling water

mint leaves

Combine the sugar and water in a small saucepan on medium heat. Stir continuously until the sugar dissolves and the liquid becomes clear. Transfer this sugar syrup to a blender, add the strawberries and lemon juice, and purée until well blended.

In a pitcher, combine the purée with the sparkling water and serve in tall glasses over ice. Or, refrigerate the purée and prepare individual glasses by mixing together equal parts of purée and sparkling water. Garnish each drink with mint leaves. Refrigerated purée will keep for about 4 days.

PER 14-OUNCE SERVING: 236 CALORIES, 0.7 G PROTEIN, 0.3 G FAT, 61.4 G CARBOHYDRATES, 0 G SATURATED FATTY ACIDS, 0 MG CHOLESTEROL, 37.6 MG SODIUM, 2.2 G TOTAL DIETARY FIBER

> "It's lemonade, lemonade, made in the shade and stirred with a spade, good enough for any old maid."
> —Tennessee Williams,
> *The Glass Menagerie*

variations *2 cups of raspberries or blackberries or 1 cup of blueberries can replace the strawberries.*

An equal amount of evaporated, unrefined cane juice (Sucanat) or $^3/_4$ cup of a mild-flavored honey can replace the sugar. The taste will vary and the color will be darker.

lemongrass limeade

Here's a sophisticated and refreshing libation to sip under a sheltering tree on a hot, breezeless day; or, a good accompaniment any day to grilled vegetables, fish, or a roasted vegetable baguette sandwich.

You'll get more juice from a lime if it's warm and soft. Chilled limes can be easily warmed up by immersing them in a bowl of hot water for 10 minutes or by briefly heating them in a microwave or regular oven. Even rolling chilled citrus back and forth on a cutting board with the palm of your hand warms and softens them. About 8 to 10 limes will yield enough juice for this limeade.

3-inch piece of fresh ginger root
  (see Note)
1 lemongrass stalk
1 cup sugar
5 1/2 cups water
1 1/2 cups fresh lime juice

Serves 6 to 8
Preparation time: 30 minutes
Chilling time: 25 minutes

Peel the ginger and slice it thinly. Trim the lemongrass stalk to about 6 inches and remove the dry outer layer. Lay the peeled stalk across a cutting board and, using the flat side of a heavy knife, whack the stalk along its length to release its fragrant oils. Then cut it into 1-inch lengths.

Combine the sliced ginger, lemongrass pieces, sugar, and 1 cup of the water in a saucepan. Bring to a boil, then reduce the heat and simmer for 10 minutes, stirring occasionally. Remove the syrup from the heat, and cool for 10 minutes. Strain the syrup into a pitcher and discard the ginger and lemongrass. Add the fresh lime juice and the remaining water to the pitcher.

Chill for about 25 minutes and serve over ice.

PER 8-OUNCE SERVING: 110 CALORIES, 0.2 G PROTEIN, 0.1 G FAT, 29.2 G CARBOHYDRATES, 0 G SATURATED FATTY ACIDS, 0 MG CHOLESTEROL, 1 MG SODIUM, 0.2 G TOTAL DIETARY FIBER

note If you'd like a more gingery drink, grate an additional inch of fresh ginger and hand-squeeze its juice into the pitcher.

pit-stop meals for recovering workaholics

There is sometimes a world of difference between how we eat when by ourselves, and the way we eat in the company of others. If we live alone, with other workaholics, or have schedules that differ radically from those of our housemates, our weeknight eating habits can border on the bizarre. There are those of us, and we know who we are, who come home feeling so beat that we're afraid that if we sit down we'll never get back up, or so wired that we're like runners cooling down from a race. These states of work pollution may result in our pacing the kitchen with a tablespoon and a jar of peanut butter and calling it supper. Have you ever stood at the open refrigerator with your fork in a pickle jar or squirted mustard into a folded slice of cheese? Pit-stop meals such as these are traditionally rounded out with a handful of raisins and a long swallow of something straight from the bottle or carton. We have first-hand accounts of such feeding rituals.

If you never sit down to eat unless you're at a restaurant, decent finger food in the fridge and cabinets really can help. If a daily dose of peanut butter is your guarantee of some protein, you could do worse. Keep a stash of unsalted, raw, or roasted nuts and raisins in a jar. Baby carrots are a blessing. They've salvaged many a life on the verge of plummeting downward in a spiral of doughnuts and barbecued potato chips. There are other ways to pull out of a nutritional tailspin. Cut some cheese or seasoned tofu into little cubes and store them in a plastic bag—you'll be more likely to eat them that way. If you want to get fancy, either buy yourself some salsa or bean dip, or make one of the many good ones in this book. Get a container of your favorite olives and a few packages of rice cakes or good crackers. With carrots, olives, cheese, seasoned tofu, crackers, and a good dip, you actually have something that begins to resemble a meal. And you can eat while you listen to your phone messages or sort the mail.

Now, assuming that anyone reading this book may have some genuine interest in cooking, there are grain, bean, pasta, and seafood salads that taste excellent stone cold. If you make pasta or grain salad on your day off, you can store it in a nonreactive container with a good tight lid for three or four days. Most supermarkets carry fresh pasta that can be stored in the refrigerator or freezer. Boil some water and throw in a few raviolis. Keep a jar of pesto or sauce on hand, or just a little bottle of olive oil and some grated Parmesan.

Fruits like apples, oranges, and grapefruit last quite a while. Bananas are risky, but working people, like most primates, seriously need bananas. Buy bananas only when you know you're not going out of town for the next four days. If you live alone, buy just three or four bananas, a yellow one for today or tomorrow and two green ones for the days after. If you get four yellow bananas, you might eat one or two, but the others will be overripe by the time you snap out of it and realize you haven't been in the kitchen since last Tuesday. If your bananas are getting too ripe to tempt you, stick them skin and all into a bag and toss them into the freezer. They'll turn black and look bad, but you can throw them into the blender frozen with some juice for very good, frosty smoothies.

Frozen bananas peel very easily; if necessary, rinse them under hot water before peeling. Frozen peaches and plums also make good smoothies, but remember to remove the pits before blending them. A frozen peach or plum will split open when you run a knife into its natural crease, exposing the pit. The fruit breaks away from the pit easily. If you're efficient, halve and pit the peaches before freezing them. Peach and plum skins will blend well, but if you prefer, you can run the frozen fruit under hot water and skin will slip off under your fingers. Keep some juice in the freezer too and, if you're really good to yourself, a bag of frozen berries.

edamame: a no-recipe snack

Edamame (ed-uh-MAH-may), young green soybeans, have been a well-loved seasonal treat in Asia for millennia but have only recently gotten their due in the United States. Now they're showing up in bars, at baseball stadiums, and in high school students' lunch bags. If you haven't yet discovered edamame for yourself, we urge you to find some and give them a try. Usually sold in the pod, the beans are simple to prepare and fun to eat as a delectable snack or appetizer. They are vibrant green, smooth-textured, and have a pleasant nutty taste, almost sweet like fresh peas. Just pop the delicious beans into your mouth and discard the empty pods. Some of us like to sprinkle the pods with salt and pepper.

Luckily, this addictive finger food has an excellent nutritional profile: low in calories, very low in fat, high in fiber, a whopping 36 percent protein, and plenty of vitamins A and C and phytoestrogens.

Occasionally you can find fresh green soybeans in the pod at farmers' markets or in the produce section of supermarkets for a limited season. Some seed catalogs offer edamame seeds, so you might try growing your own. The most dependable source for edamame, however, is the freezer of natural food stores, Asian groceries, and most large supermarkets. Oriental Mascot and Shirakiku brands come in 16-ounce packages of uniformly sized pods, parboiled and frozen. Sunrich's Hearty and Natural brand, frozen in 12-ounce bags, is certified as not genetically modified.

Optimum cooking time for fresh edamame will depend on their maturity and the time elapsed since picking. Boil them from 5 to 20 minutes, until tender. Frozen edamame take less than 5 minutes to cook in boiling water. Both make a great snack either hot, at room temperature, or chilled.

curried lentil dip

Looking for something unusual for a party or potluck dinner? When this dip is one of the choices, it's almost always gone long before the cheese dips are even half eaten. Besides, it's easily prepared and has the added attraction of being dairyless and exotically flavored. Present it along with crudités and delicate pappadams or rice crackers. Or try it with chunks or slices of pineapple and mango.

Yields about 4 cups
Total time: 30 minutes

In a medium saucepan, bring the lentils and water to a boil. Lower the heat and simmer until the lentils are very soft and most of the water absorbed, about 20 minutes.

Meanwhile, heat the oil in a skillet and sauté the onions, apples, and garlic with a dash of salt for about 5 minutes on medium heat. Add the raisins, curry powder, and the garam masala, if using, and continue to sauté for about 10 minutes, until tender.

In a food processor or blender, purée the cooked lentils and sautéed onion mixture with the coconut milk and lemon juice. Add the salt and adjust to taste.

Serve at room temperature or chilled.

1 cup red lentils
2 1/2 cups water
1 tablespoon vegetable oil
1 cup diced onions
1 1/2 cups peeled, cored, and diced apples
3 garlic cloves, minced or pressed
1/4 cup raisins
1 teaspoon curry powder
1 teaspoon garam masala (optional)*
1/4 cup reduced-fat coconut milk**
2 tablespoons fresh lemon juice
1/2 teaspoon salt

* Garam masala is a roasted spice mixture found in the Indian section of specialty stores or supermarkets. It can include cardamom, cinnamon, cloves, peppercorns, coriander, cumin, nutmeg, mace, fennel seeds, and saffron in varying proportions. The recipe in Sundays at Moosewood Restaurant (page 293) is a good place to start if you want to make your own.
** We recommend Thai Kitchen brand, which doesn't have preservatives.

PER 1-OUNCE SERVING: 34 CALORIES, 1.8 G PROTEIN, 0.6 G FAT, 5.8 G CARBOHYDRATES, 0.2 G SATURATED FATTY ACIDS, 0 MG CHOLESTEROL, 30.7 MG SODIUM, 1.7 G TOTAL DIETARY FIBER

variation For an even lower fat version of this recipe, replace the coconut milk with apple juice.

david's dilled havarti spread

Moosewood cook David Hirsch is an avid gardener who loves to grow fresh herbs. His spread has no fancy frills, but is positively addictive. It makes a simple, delicious sandwich with sliced fresh tomatoes and baby greens. However, people with bigger appetites can make a more hefty sandwich of dark rye bread or hearty pumpernickel lathered with Havarti spread and stacked with several of our suggested toppings.

Or use the spread on crackers or toasted baguette rounds garnished with attractively cut and arranged vegetables and sprouts.

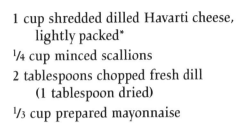

Yields 1 cup
Total time: 10 minutes

1 cup shredded dilled Havarti cheese, lightly packed*

¼ cup minced scallions

2 tablespoons chopped fresh dill (1 tablespoon dried)

⅓ cup prepared mayonnaise

If you can't find dilled Harvarti, use plain Havarti and add more dill to taste.

In a bowl, mix together the cheese, scallions, dill, and mayonnaise. In a sandwich, try with any of the following: sliced radishes, cucumbers, and tomatoes; roasted red peppers; or pickles, sprouts, shredded lettuce, or spicy mustard.

David's Dilled Havarti Spread will keep well sealed in the refrigerator for several days.

PER 1-OUNCE SERVING: 91 CALORIES, 3.5 G PROTEIN, 7.3 G FAT, 3.1 G CARBOHYDRATES, 3.1 G SATURATED FATTY ACIDS, 15.8 MG CHOLESTEROL, 147 MG SODIUM, 0.2 G TOTAL DIETARY FIBER

elegant pimiento cheese spread

Everyday Pimiento Cheese (see Variation) is just shredded cheese mixed with minced pimientos and mayonnaise, most often served Southern-style on soft white bread. But for delicious hors d'oeuvres or a wonderful sandwich on baguette or whole-grain bread, make our Elegant Pimiento Cheese.

It's a swellegant spread for sandwiches, crackers, rye or pumpernickle rounds, or crudités worthy of any occasion—even standing in front of the refrigerator with a spoon.

 Yields 3 cups
Total time: 15 minutes

2 cups grated Cheddar cheese
1 cup Neufchâtel or cream cheese
1 tablespoon fresh lemon juice
$^1/_3$ cup warm water
$^1/_2$ cup chopped pimientos or roasted red peppers (4-ounce jar, drained)
$^1/_2$ cup minced celery
2 scallions, white part only, minced
$^1/_4$ cup chopped toasted pecans*

* *Toast pecans in a single layer on an unoiled baking tray at 350° for 5 to 10 minutes, until fragrant and golden brown.*

In a food processor, whirl the Cheddar cheese, Neufchâtel, lemon juice, and water for 3 or 4 minutes, until very smooth. Transfer the cheese mixture to a bowl and stir in the pimientos, celery, and scallions.

If mixed in the spread, the pecans become soft after a couple of hours, so add them just before serving or just sprinkle them on top of each serving. This spread will keep for 4 or 5 days in the refrigerator.

PER 1-OUNCE SERVING: 63 CALORIES, 3.1 G PROTEIN, 5.3 G FAT, 1 G CARBOHYDRATES, 2.8 G SATURATED FATTY ACIDS, 13.5 MG CHOLESTEROL, 80.6 MG SODIUM, 0.3 G TOTAL DIETARY FIBER

variation *To make 1$^1/_3$ cups of easy Everyday Pimiento Cheese, stir together 2 cups of shredded Longhorn Colby or Cheddar cheese, 2 tablespoons of minced pimientos, and $^1/_3$ cup of prepared mayonnaise until well mixed.*

green olive & artichoke tapenade

Versions of briny olive paste come from all around the olive-growing lands of the Mediterranean. This one is light green, textured, and quite piquant in the style of the South of France.

At Moosewood, we usually offer this tapenade as an appetizer served in a small bowl surrounded by crackers or thin crisp toast. It's good on everything from baked potatoes, pasta, or rice to broiled fish or cauliflower and it's dynamite on a grilled cheese sandwich. Tuck a little dab of this tapenade into the centers of Roasted Carmelized Balsamic Onions (page 125).

Yields about 3 cups
Total time: 30 minutes

5 artichoke hearts (14-ounce can, drained)

1 cup toasted walnuts, chopped*

1 cup pitted green or Spanish olives

1 garlic clove, pressed or minced

2 to 3 tablespoons chopped fresh parsley

1 teaspoon freshly grated lemon peel (optional)

3 to 4 teaspoons fresh lemon juice

1/3 cup extra-virgin olive oil

cracked or ground black pepper to taste

Toast walnuts at 350° in a single layer on an unoiled baking tray for about 5 minutes, until fragrant.

In the bowl of a food processor (see Note), whirl the artichoke hearts, walnuts, olives, garlic, parsley, and lemon peel, if using, for a few seconds until everything is uniformly minced. Scrape down the sides if necessary, add the lemon juice and olive oil, and process for a few more seconds until the mixture forms a rough paste (not a smooth purée but a cohesive paste). Season with pepper to taste.

Tapenade is best served at room temperature and can be stored, covered and refrigerated, for up to a week.

PER 1-OUNCE SERVING: 77 CALORIES, 1.4 G PROTEIN, 7.4 G FAT, 2.5 G CARBOHYDRATES, 0.8 G SATURATED FATTY ACIDS, 0 MG CHOLESTEROL, 241 MG SODIUM, 1.4 G TOTAL DIETARY FIBER

note *Tapenade can be made in a blender with a little extra work. Just chop the artichoke hearts and add 1 to 2 tablespoons of the artichoke brine to the rest of the ingredients. Stop the blender several times to scrape down the sides.*

sour cream onion dip

This retro dip is still a universal favorite, so we've updated the recipe: You can actually make a great sour cream replacement using nonfat yogurt! Just drain the yogurt the night before, or at least 2 or 3 hours ahead of time. If you like, make extra yogurt cheese for other uses while you're at it. If you want to create the dip in a traditional way, ⅓ cup of the real stuff gives it that familiar flavor.

Pouring the oil on top of the onions in a hot pan thoroughly coats the onions and helps them to brown evenly.

Yields 1½ cups
Yogurt draining time: 2 to 3 hours
Preparation time: 25 minutes

1 cup nonfat plain yogurt
2 cups diced onions
½ teaspoon sugar
pinch of salt
½ cup olive oil
½ to 1 teaspoon soy sauce
⅓ cup sour cream

✂ Follow our Quick Yogurt Cheese method (page 475) using 1 cup of yogurt.

To prepare the dip, place the onions, sugar, and salt in a medium skillet on medium heat. When the pan is hot, pour the oil over the onions. Cook for about 15 minutes, shaking the pan now and then, until the edges of the onions are brown and crisp. Strain the onions through a fine sieve and, if you like, reserve the oil for another use.

Stir together the yogurt cheese, browned onions, soy sauce, and sour cream. Serve with chips or crudités.

PER 1-OUNCE SERVING: 45 CALORIES, 1 G PROTEIN, 3.7 G FAT, 2.4 G CARBOHYDRATES, 0.9 G SATURATED FATTY ACIDS, 1.9 MG CHOLESTEROL, 24.7 MG SODIUM, 0.2 G TOTAL DIETARY FIBER

sun-dried tomato & chèvre spread

Goat cheese, or *chèvre*, is a bit of an acquired taste, so here you can use all chèvre or combine it with cream cheese. We prefer fresh thyme in this spread. But if you must use dried, soften it in a tablespoon of olive oil before mixing it into the cheese. The spread tastes best after sitting for at least a half hour, if not a day or two: The chèvre absorbs the seasonings and the flavors blend.

Serve this spread with breadsticks, crackers, or slices of raw fennel, carrots, radishes, and cucumbers.

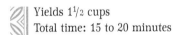
Yields 1½ cups
Total time: 15 to 20 minutes

⅓ cup sun-dried tomatoes
(not oil-packed)

1 cup soft chèvre*

1 tablespoon fresh chopped thyme
(1 teaspoon dried)

2 teaspoons freshly grated lemon peel

½ teaspoon cracked peppercorns

3 to 4 tablespoons milk

* *Using your penchant for goat cheese as a guide, make this dip with only chèvre or use a combination of chèvre and softened cream cheese.*

✖ In a small heat-proof bowl, cover the sun-dried tomatoes with boiling water and set aside to soften for about 15 minutes.

Meanwhile, in a medium bowl, combine the chèvre, thyme, lemon peel, cracked peppercorns, and enough milk to make a smooth spread. Drain and chop the sun-dried tomatoes and mix them into the cheese.

Serve immediately or refrigerate and bring to room temperature before serving.

PER 1-OUNCE SERVING: 64 CALORIES, 4.2 G PROTEIN, 4.2 G FAT, 2.9 G CARBOHYDRATES, 2.8 G SATURATED FATTY ACIDS, 9 MG CHOLESTEROL, 158.5 MG SODIUM, 0.6 G TOTAL DIETARY FIBER

tomatillo guacamole

Zesty, zippy guacamole can accompany any Latin American or Southwestern food. You can also put some in soups that are not highly flavored to add a little pizazz.

It's crucial to have perfectly ripe avocados for this dish. They should be somewhat fragrant and yield slightly to thumb pressure. When good and ripe, the flesh is soft, firm, golden-green, and can be easily separated from the peel. Dark, discolored spots are a sign of bruising and/or overripeness.

Yields about 3 cups
Total time: 25 minutes

3 ripe avocados, preferably Hass

1 pound tomatillos, husked, rinsed, and halved

2 garlic cloves, minced or pressed

½ cup chopped scallions

2 tablespoons vegetable oil

2 tablespoons fresh lime juice

1 large tomato, coarsely chopped

½ teaspoon salt

½ teaspoon ground black pepper

1 jalapeño or other fresh chile, seeded and chopped (optional)

½ cup chopped fresh cilantro (optional)

Slice the avocados lengthwise around the center, twist the halves apart, remove the pits, and scoop out the flesh with a spoon. In a food processor or blender, purée the avocado with the tomatillos, garlic, scallions, oil, lime juice, tomato, salt, pepper, and the jalapeño and cilantro, if using.

Serve immediately or chill.

PER 1-OUNCE SERVING: 31 CALORIES, 0.4 G PROTEIN, 2.7 G FAT, 1.9 G CARBOHYDRATES, 0.5 G SATURATED FATTY ACIDS, 0 MG CHOLESTEROL, 26.9 MG SODIUM, 0.9 G TOTAL DIETARY FIBER

flavored olives

Cultivated since 3000 B.C., olives were brought to North America in the sixteenth century by the Spanish. All the olives we eat first undergo a curing process which removes their natural bitterness; then they are fermented in saltwater or brine.

Here we offer you four olive snacks. All of these are great appetizers on their own or make a very tasty complement to a combination platter of sweet and savory hors d'oeuvres. And for an especially robust nibble, serve them with chewy, crusty bread for sopping up the juices of the marinades.

provençal olives

A hint of orange, the robustness of garlic and rosemary, and the sweetness of fennel and balsamic vinegar mingle together to evoke the flavors we associate with the South of France. Marinating the olives for several days before serving will allow all of the seasonings, especially the more subtle ones, to penetrate more deeply.

Yields 1 cup
Preparation time: 25 minutes

1 cup assorted brined olives

2 teaspoons fennel seeds

¼ cup balsamic vinegar

¼ cup olive oil

3 garlic cloves, peeled and chopped

1 tablespoon chopped fresh rosemary
   (1 teaspoon dried)

½ teaspoon cracked peppercorns

1 tablespoon freshly grated orange
   peel

Place the olives in a heat-proof bowl. In a small heavy dry skillet, toast the fennel seeds on low heat just until golden and aromatic. Set them aside to cool.

In a small nonreactive saucepan, bring the vinegar, oil, garlic, rosemary, peppercorns, and orange peel to a simmer. Crush or coarsely grind the fennel seeds and add them to the marinade. Simmer for at least 5 minutes and then pour over the olives.

Cool, and then cover and refrigerate. Allow the olives to marinate for at least 24 hours and up to one week before serving. Serve at room temperature.

PER 1-OUNCE SERVING: 67 CALORIES, 0.2 G PROTEIN, 6.8 G FAT, 1.8 G CARBOHYDRATES, 0.9 G SATURATED FATTY ACIDS, 0 MG CHOLESTEROL, 165.5 MG SODIUM, 0.9 G TOTAL DIETARY FIBER

spicy olive appetizer

Accompany these olives with wedges of pita bread and bite-sized chunks of feta cheese, or add them to a salad of cucumber crescents, cheese cubes, and sliced red onions.

Yields 2 cups
Preparation time: 20 minutes

2 cups brined green or black olives
¼ cup red wine vinegar
¼ cup olive oil
2 garlic cloves, peeled and chopped
½ fresh chile, chopped
freshly grated peel of 1 lemon
2 tablespoons chopped fresh oregano
1 tablespoon small capers (optional)
2 tablespoons fresh lemon juice

Place the olives in a heatproof bowl. In a small nonreactive saucepan, heat the vinegar, oil, garlic, chile, lemon peel, oregano, and the capers, if using. Simmer for 5 minutes and then pour over the olives. Add the lemon juice.

Cool, then cover and refrigerate. Allow the olives to marinate for at least 24 hours or up to one week before serving. Serve at room temperature.

PER 1-OUNCE SERVING: 45 CALORIES, 0.2 G PROTEIN, 4.4 G FAT, 1.9 G CARBOHYDRATES, 0.6 G SATURATED FATTY ACIDS, 0 MG CHOLESTEROL, 165 MG SODIUM, 0.9 G TOTAL DIETARY FIBER

kalamata olives with roasted garlic

For sensual eaters who like removing olive pits and pinching garlic skins, serve this appetizer with pits and skins intact. For more tentative guests who may not enjoy such delightful messiness, pit the olives and remove the skins from the baked garlic cloves ahead of time.

Yields about 2 cups
Total time: 40 minutes

2 heads of garlic
2½ tablespoons olive oil
2 cups kalamata olives
½ cup marsala wine
1 tablespoon chopped fresh rosemary
1 teaspoon cracked peppercorns
French or Italian bread

Preheat the oven to 350°.

Separate the unpeeled garlic cloves. Place in a small heat-proof dish and brush with ½ tablespoon of olive oil. Cover and bake for 15 minutes.

Add the olives, remaining olive oil, marsala, rosemary, and peppercorns. Cover and bake for about 15 minutes, until the garlic is soft.

About 5 minutes before the olives are ready, wrap the bread in aluminum foil and heat it in the oven. Serve the olives with the warm bread.

PER 1.5-OUNCE SERVING: 125 CALORIES, 0.9 G PROTEIN, 12.4 G FAT, 3.7 G CARBOHYDRATES, 1.4 G SATURATED FATTY ACIDS, 0 MG CHOLESTEROL, 933.2 MG SODIUM, 0.1 G TOTAL DIETARY FIBER

braised olives in tomato sauce

Use an assortment of your favorite olives in this dish. Served warm with thick slices of bread for dipping into the savory sauce, this becomes a substantial appetizer or side dish—almost a meal in itself.

 Yields about 4 cups
Total time: 15 minutes

2 cups assorted brined green and
    black olives

2 tablespoons olive oil

4 garlic cloves, peeled and chopped

2 teaspoons crushed fennel seeds

2 cups chopped fresh or drained
    canned tomatoes

4 to 6 minced sun-dried tomatoes
    (not oil-packed)

2 tablespoons chopped fresh oregano
    (2 teaspoons dried)

¼ cup red wine (optional)

¼ cup chopped fresh parsley

Rinse the olives and set them aside. In a nonreactive skillet or saucepan, warm the oil and garlic on medium heat. When the garlic begins to sizzle, add the olives, fennel seeds, tomatoes, sun-dried tomatoes, oregano, and the red wine, if using. Cover and simmer on low heat for 10 minutes.

Remove from the heat, add the parsley, and serve warm.

PER 1-OUNCE SERVING: 48 CALORIES, 0.7 G PROTEIN, 4.5 G FAT, 2.5 G CARBOHYDRATES, 0.5 G SATURATED FATTY ACIDS, 0 MG CHOLESTEROL, 443.8 MG SODIUM, 0.7 G TOTAL DIETARY FIBER

olive lore

One of the oldest known fruits of the Mediterranean shores, olives predate humans as a species. The domesticated olive tree *(Olea europaea),* an evergreen, can survive for hundreds of years in inhospitable, stony, mountainous soil. The trees flower in spring and produce berries that are ready to harvest from October to February. Spain produces large, green *manzanilla* olives, which are often pitted and stuffed with almonds, pimientos, anchovies, capers, or onions. *Liguaria, ponentine, gaeta,* and *lugano* are imported from Italy, while *kalamata* come from Greece and *niçoise* from France. California produces its own *sevillano,* a salt-cured whole or cracked olive with a meaty texture.

popcorn

Popcorn is a quick, healthful, inexpensive snack. It can be tossed with brewers' yeast, Old Bay Seasoning, gomashio, or the old standby—butter and salt. Start with 1 tablespoon of seasoning for 2 quarts of popcorn and add more to taste. Or try our flavored popcorn mixes for "gussied up" popcorn. If you are reducing your salt intake, use some fresh lime or lemon juice to replace either the salt in the Southwestern Flavored Popcorn or the cheese in the Garlic Butter & Cheese Flavored Popcorn.

We tried a variety of popcorn-making techniques. In the end, we decided that the "heavy-bottomed pot with a little oil" method was best. Use a 6-quart heavy-bottomed pot with a lid for 1/2 cup of kernels. (To pop 1 cup of kernels, use an 8-quart pot). If you want a no-oil popcorn treat, however, we recommend the electric popcorn poppers that pop the corn using just hot air. They're noisy—but they're quick and make good popcorn.

Look for packaged kernels that are organic or grown without herbicides and store them in an airtight container in a cool place. If your raw popcorn has been around awhile and looks old and shriveled, rehydrate to avoid unpopped kernels: Pour water in the jar of kernels and let soak for a few minutes; then drain and shake the jar vigorously to moisten all of the kernels. Keep the lid on the jar and let sit for a day before popping.

basic popcorn

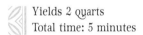 Yields 2 quarts
Total time: 5 minutes

1 tablespoon peanut or vegetable oil
¹/₂ cup raw popcorn kernels

Heat the oil and a few popcorn kernels on medium heat. When the kernels pop, add the remaining popcorn. Cover with the lid slightly ajar to allow steam to escape or use a lid with an open steam vent.

When the kernels begin to pop, shake the pot until the popping almost stops. Remove from the heat and allow the final kernels to finish popping before removing the lid.

PER 1.25-OUNCE SERVING: 171 CALORIES, 3.4 G PROTEIN, 8.3 G FAT, 22.1 G CARBOHYDRATES,
2 G SATURATED FATTY ACIDS, 0 MG CHOLESTEROL, 1.1 MG SODIUM, 4.3 G TOTAL DIETARY FIBER

southwestern flavored popcorn

These perky spices will put gusto in your popcorn without adding any fat.

2 quarts popped popcorn
1 to 2 teaspoons cumin seeds
1 teaspoon paprika
1 teaspoon chili powder
½ teaspoon salt, or more to taste

Place the popcorn in a large bowl and set aside. Toast the cumin seeds for 1 minute on a tray in a toaster oven or in a small dry skillet. Grind the seeds in a spice or coffee grinder. Combine the ground cumin with the paprika, chili powder, and salt, and thoroughly toss with the popcorn.

garlic butter & cheese flavored popcorn

Here is a rather posh gourmet popcorn that may make you want to pop a second batch, even though you've eaten enough.

2 quarts popped popcorn
3 garlic cloves, minced or pressed
3 to 4 tablespoons unsalted butter,
 olive oil, or a mixture
½ cup very finely grated Parmesan
    cheese
salt to taste

Place the popcorn in a large bowl and set aside. Sauté the garlic in the butter or oil for about 3 minutes, until golden. Pour over the popcorn and mix thorougly. Stir in the cheese, add salt to taste, and toss again.

deviled eggs four ways

Deviled eggs seem to be universally enjoyed and universally ignored, out of some misplaced dread of the ordinary. In fact, they can be as creative as anything else. Here are four recipes for fancy Moosewood deviled eggs. Displayed on a platter, they're a beautiful and irresistible appetizer. And of course, they're picnic perfect. Try presenting sampler plates of all four types.

The great challenge with deviled eggs is to get cleanly peeled, silky smooth, perfect orbs—after that, it's all fun. Here are a few tricks to help prevent eggs from cracking during cooking. Bring the eggs to room temperature and pierce the round end of their shells with a push pin before cooking them in a single layer. Stacking the eggs in a pot on top of one another can crack them accidentally. Cover the eggs with about an inch of water, bring to a rapid simmer (not a boil) on medium-high heat, then remove from the heat and let sit for 10 to 15 minutes. The simmer-and-rest method yields a tender white and creamy yolk, whereas boiling can produce a rubbery white and dry yolk. Overcooking is responsible for the grayish-green tinge of some yolks.

Older eggs, at least 1 week old, peel more easily. So do eggs just cool enough to handle. As soon as the eggs are cooked, drain them, and cover immediately with very cold or ice water to stop the cooking. Gently roll each egg on a flat surface to uniformly crack the shell, immerse in the cold water, and peel underwater. Another good rule of thumb: Cook a few extra eggs to offset the ones that crack during cooking or peeling, and the ones that, well, just vanish.

Yields 12 deviled eggs
Total time: 30 minutes

6 large hard-boiled eggs, peeled

Choose one of the following:

deviled eggs tartare

3 tablespoons prepared mayonnaise
1 teaspoon tiny nonpareil capers
1 tablespoon minced gherkin pickles
2 teaspoons minced fresh dill
   (1/2 teaspoon dried)
2 tablespoons minced chives or
   scallions
pinch of ground black pepper
garnish: 12 sprigs of fresh dill

curried deviled eggs

3 tablespoons prepared mayonnaise
1/2 teaspoon fresh lemon juice
1 teaspoon curry powder
2 tablespoons minced red bell pepper
1 tablespoon minced cilantro
1/8 teaspoon salt, or to taste
pinch of ground black pepper
garnish: 12 sprigs of fresh cilantro

puttanesca deviled eggs

¼ cup olive oil

1 teaspoon red wine vinegar

1 garlic clove, minced or pressed

¼ to ½ teaspoon red pepper flakes

2 tablespoons minced fresh basil

1 tablespoon soaked minced sun-
dried tomatoes (page 470)

1 tablespoon minced kalamata olives

1½ teaspoons tiny nonpareil capers

salt to taste

garnish: 12 small fresh basil leaves

wasabi deviled eggs

¼ cup vegetable oil

2 teaspoons rice vinegar

½ teaspoon wasabi powder (page 474)

1 tablespoon toasted sesame seeds*

2 teaspoons minced scallion greens
or chives

⅛ teaspoon sugar

¼ teaspoon salt

garnish: slivered scallions or chives

* Toast seeds in a single layer on an unoiled
baking tray at 350° for 2 to 3 minutes, until
fragrant and golden.

✂ Slice the eggs in half lengthwise. Gently scoop the yolks into a small bowl, thoroughly mash them with a fork, and set aside.

In a separate bowl, whisk together the first three ingredients of your preferred flavoring; then stir in the rest of the ingredients except the garnish. Fold the dressing into the mashed yolks. Fill the whites with the filling and serve decorated with the garnish.

TARTARE: PER 1.25-OUNCE SERVING: 62 CALORIES, 3.8 G PROTEIN, 4.3 G FAT, 1.7 G CARBOHYDRATES, 1.1 G SATURATED FATTY ACIDS, 126.1 MG CHOLESTEROL, 79.1 MG SODIUM, 0.1 G TOTAL DIETARY FIBER

CURRIED: PER 1.25-OUNCE SERVING: 61 CALORIES, 3.8 G PROTEIN, 4.4 G FAT, 1.5 G CARBOHYDRATES, 1.1 G SATURATED FATTY ACIDS, 126.1 MG CHOLESTEROL, 87.7 MG SODIUM, 0.1 G TOTAL DIETARY FIBER

PUTTANESCA: PER 1.25-OUNCE SERVING: 94 CALORIES, 3.9 G PROTEIN, 8.3 G FAT, 1 G CARBOHYDRATES, 1.7 G SATURATED FATTY ACIDS, 125.2 MG CHOLESTEROL, 101.5 MG SODIUM, 0.2 G TOTAL DIETARY FIBER

WASABI: PER 1.25-OUNCE SERVING: 93 CALORIES, 3.9 G PROTEIN, 8.2 G FAT, 0.8 G CARBOHYDRATES, 2.2 G SATURATED FATTY ACIDS, 125.2 MG CHOLESTEROL, 87.1 MG SODIUM, 0.2 G TOTAL DIETARY FIBER

spiced nuts

This appetizer will wake up your taste buds and they'll beg for more. Careful! You might eat the entire bowl and forget that there's dinner afterwards. Walnut and pecan halves, almonds, and cashews are one nice mix of nuts to try.

Serve with an icy cold drink.

Yields 2¹/₂ cups
Preparation time: 10 minutes
Baking time: 25 minutes

2¹/₂ cups mixed raw nuts

2 tablespoons butter

3 tablespoons Worcestershire sauce (page 474)

2 teaspoons Old Bay Seasoning

4 dashes of Tabasco sauce or other hot pepper sauce

Preheat the oven to 375°.

Place the nuts in a bowl. Melt the butter in a saucepan and stir in the Worcestershire sauce, Old Bay Seasoning, and Tabasco sauce. Toss the nuts with the seasoned butter and spread them out evenly on a nonstick baking sheet.

Bake for 15 minutes, turn the nuts with a metal spatula, and continue to bake for another 10 minutes, until golden brown. Check them frequently near the end of baking, so they don't burn.

Remove the nuts from the oven, loosen them with a spatula, and cool to room temperature. Store in a sealed container.

PER 1-OUNCE SERVING: 154 CALORIES, 4 G PROTEIN, 13.5 G FAT, 6.4 G CARBOHYDRATES, 2.6 G SATURATED FATTY ACIDS, 4.4 MG CHOLESTEROL, 50.3 MG SODIUM, 2.1 G TOTAL DIETARY FIBER

baked tofu sticks

These tofu sticks make a crunchy appetizer and a crisp, healthy, protein-packed alternative to those much-sought-after, greasy fishsticks of years past. For variety, try some of your favorite Asian dipping sauces, from teriyaki to ponzu. Or get creative with wild ideas for other dipping sauces: barbeque sauce, honey-mustard sauce, Ranch-style dip, or whatever strikes your fancy.

Yields 24 sticks
Preparation time: 10 minutes
Marinating time: 30 minutes
Baking time: 30 minutes

Cut the cake of tofu horizontally into three equal slices. Stack the slices and cut down through them vertically in parallel lines, dividing the cake first into halves then quarters and finally eighths, to yield 24 sticks. Arrange the tofu sticks in a baking dish in a single layer.

Mix together the soy sauce, rice vinegar, and garlic and drizzle over the tofu sticks. Set aside for about 30 minutes, turning the sticks once after 15 minutes, so the tofu will absorb the marinade evenly.

Preheat the oven to 400°. Lightly spray or oil a baking tray.

In a large shallow bowl, mix together the bread crumbs, parsley, paprika, salt, pepper, and cayenne. In a separate shallow bowl, whisk together the flour and water until smooth. Dip each marinated tofu stick into the flour mixture and then coat well with the seasoned bread crumbs. Arrange the breaded sticks on the baking tray so they're not touching and bake for about 30 minutes, until crisp and hot.

In a small bowl, whisk together the dipping sauce ingredients. Serve Baked Tofu Sticks warm, accompanied by the sauce.

1 cake firm tofu (16 ounces)
3 tablespoons soy sauce
1 tablespoon rice vinegar
1 garlic clove, minced or pressed
1 1/2 cups bread crumbs*
2 tablespoons minced fresh parsley
1 teaspoon paprika
1/2 teaspoon salt
1/2 teaspoon ground black pepper
pinch of cayenne
3 tablespoons unbleached white flour
6 tablespoons cold water

dipping sauce

1 tablespoon soy sauce
1 tablespoon rice vinegar
1 teaspoon sugar
1 tablespoon finely chopped scallions

* Pulverize stale or lightly toasted whole
wheat, sourdough, or French bread in a
blender or food processor.

PER 1.25-OUNCE SERVING: 41 CALORIES, 2.6 G PROTEIN, 1.2 G FAT, 5.3 G CARBOHYDRATES,
0.2 G SATURATED FATTY ACIDS, 0 MG CHOLESTEROL, 224.5 MG SODIUM, 0.5 G TOTAL DIETARY FIBER

curried tofu

When people claim not to love tofu, they often complain that it is bland. Not this tofu. Garlic, onions, chiles, and curry paste make this tofu deliciously spicy. Prepared curry paste is an absolutely wonderful condiment to have in the pantry: we think of it as "Curry in a Hurry" and love finding new ways to use it.

You can serve this dish as an addition to a vegetable curry or with Indian Ratatouille (page 305) or with a simple rice dish, such as Orange Saffron Rice (page 146). Or, cool it to room temperature and stuff in a pita with greens, grated carrots, yogurt, and currants.

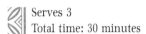

Serves 3
Total time: 30 minutes

1 cake firm tofu (16 ounces)
1 tablespoon vegetable oil
3 garlic cloves, minced or pressed
1 cup minced onions
1 fresh green chile, minced (optional)
2 teaspoons prepared curry paste*
1 teaspoon turmeric
1 teaspoon ground cumin
1 tablespoon soy sauce

Place the tofu between two plates, weight the top plate with a heavy object, and press for 15 minutes.

Meanwhile, heat the oil in a heavy cast-iron pan or nonstick skillet. Sauté the garlic, onions, and chile, if using, until the onions are golden, 10 to 15 minutes. Stir often. Mix in the curry paste, turmeric, cumin, and soy sauce and remove from the heat.

There are many good-quality brands of both Indian and Thai curry pastes. Check the label to be sure of an all-natural product with enough "heat" for your taste. We like Patak, Ashoka, Jaipur, and Tommy Tang brands.

Cut the pressed tofu into bite-sized cubes or crumble it into small pieces, whichever you prefer. Add it to the seasoned onion mixture. Cook on low heat for 10 minutes, stirring every few minutes, until the tofu is completely heated through.

PER 7-OUNCE SERVING: 200 CALORIES, 13.8 PROTEIN, 12.5 G FAT, 11.6 G CARBOHYDRATES, 2.4 G SATURATED FATTY ACIDS, 0 MG CHOLESTEROL, 407.7 MG SODIUM, 1.5 G TOTAL DIETARY FIBER

lemony baked tofu

This smooth baked tofu is delicious as a snack, sandwich filling, or topping for salads. It's packed with flavor and holds its shape well. Try it hot beside orzo and a little salad of marinated green beans and fresh tomatoes.

We offer you the choice of two very different but inviting marinades. The first has a wonderful flavor that, strangely enough, isn't quite identifiable as cilantro. The second indulges those who love rosemary above all other herbs.

Be sure to use a stainless-steel, ceramic, Pyrex, or enameled baking pan—not an aluminum one—for baking the tofu. Use the smallest baking pan you have that will hold the tofu in a single layer; an 8-inch square pan and a 7 x 9-inch pan both work fine.

Serves 2 to 4
Preparation time: 15 minutes
Baking time: 1 hour

Preheat the oven to 400°.

Cut the cake of tofu horizontally into four slices and set aside. Choose a marinade and whisk or blend together all of its ingredients until smooth. Pour half in a small nonreactive baking pan. Place the tofu slices in the pan and pour on the remaining marinade.

Bake for 45 to 60 minutes, turning the tofu once after about 30 minutes. The baked tofu should be browned, bubbling, and curling up at the edges. Remove from the oven and, with a metal spatula, transfer the tofu slices to a platter.

1 cake firm tofu (16 ounces)

Choose one of the following:

spicy cilantro lemon marinade

1/4 cup fresh lemon juice

2 tablespoons soy sauce

3 tablespoons vegetable oil

1/2 cup water

1/4 cup chopped fresh cilantro

1 tablespoon minced scallions

1 fresh green chile, seeded and minced, or 1 teaspoon Tabasco sauce or other hot pepper sauce

1/4 teaspoon ground black pepper

rosemary lemon marinade

1/4 cup fresh lemon juice

2 tablespoons soy sauce

3 tablespoons vegetable oil

1 tablespoon minced fresh rosemary (1 teaspoon dried, crumbled)

1/4 teaspoon ground black pepper

Serve hot, warm, at room temperature, or chilled. The tofu will keep in an airtight container or plastic bag in the refrigerator for up to 5 days.

PER 6.5-OUNCE SERVING: 196 CALORIES, 10.3 G PROTEIN, 15.7 G FAT, 6.4 G CARBOHYDRATES, 3.5 G SATURATED FATTY ACIDS, 0 MG CHOLESTEROL, 407.6 MG SODIUM, 0.9 G TOTAL DIETARY FIBER

mexican baked tofu

We often bake tofu in flavorful sauces at Moosewood, because tofu is very absorbent and takes on the characteristics of whatever is cooked with it. Here's a delicious way to make a Mexican-style tofu using our Mole, which is a savory spicy tomatillo and hot pepper sauce.

You can stir together the mole ingredients while the tofu is pressing. Then just mix the tofu and uncooked sauce together in a baking pan and sit back and relax. While the tofu bakes, the mole cooks.

Serve this tofu in burritos or quesadillas and as an embellishment for chili or other bean, rice, and vegetable dishes.

2 cakes firm tofu, pressed
   (16 ounces each)

1 recipe Mole (page 379),
   uncooked

Serves 4 to 6
Preparation time: 25 minutes
Baking time: 45 minutes

* *Sandwich the tofu between two plates or baking trays and rest a heavy can or book on the top. Press for about 20 minutes and then drain the expressed liquid.*

Preheat the oven to 400°.

Slice the pressed tofu into thirds horizontally. Stack the slices and then cut down through all three layers on the two diagonals, making an X, to yield 12 triangular pieces. In an unoiled 9 x 13-inch baking dish, gently toss the tofu triangles with the mole sauce.

Bake, uncovered, for 45 minutes, stirring gently at 15-minute intervals during the baking.

PER 8-OUNCE SERVING: 255 CALORIES, 15.1 G PROTEIN, 14.7 G FAT, 20.9 G CARBOHYDRATES, 2.8 G SATURATED FATTY ACIDS, 0 MG CHOLESTEROL, 817.3 MG SODIUM, 4.6 G TOTAL DIETARY FIBER

simple baked tofu

Tofu soaks up the flavor of the seasonings and develops an inviting chewy texture and golden brown color when baked. At Moosewood Restaurant, it's a favorite nosh both warm and chilled. Use it to highlight a plate of roasted vegetables or serve it as a healthy between-meal snack.

 Serves 4
Preparation time: 10 minutes
Baking time: 25 to 35 minutes

3 to 4 tablespoons soy sauce
2 tablespoons vegetable oil
1 garlic clove, minced or pressed
1 cake firm tofu, pressed
    (16 ounces)*

* *Sandwich the tofu between two plates and rest a heavy can or book on the top plate. Press for about 15 minutes and then drain the expressed liquid.*

Preheat the oven to 400°. Lightly oil a baking dish.

In a bowl, mix together the soy sauce, oil, and garlic. Cut the pressed tofu into ¾-inch cubes. Toss the cubes in the soy sauce marinade. Spread the tofu in the prepared baking dish in a single layer.

Bake for 25 to 35 minutes, stirring once or twice, until brown and chewy.

PER 4-OUNCE SERVING: 143 CALORIES, 8.9 G PROTEIN, 11.4 G FAT, 3.5 G CARBOHYDRATES, 2.5 G SATURATED FATTY ACIDS, 0 MG CHOLESTEROL, 601.8 MG SODIUM, 0.5 G TOTAL DIETARY FIBER

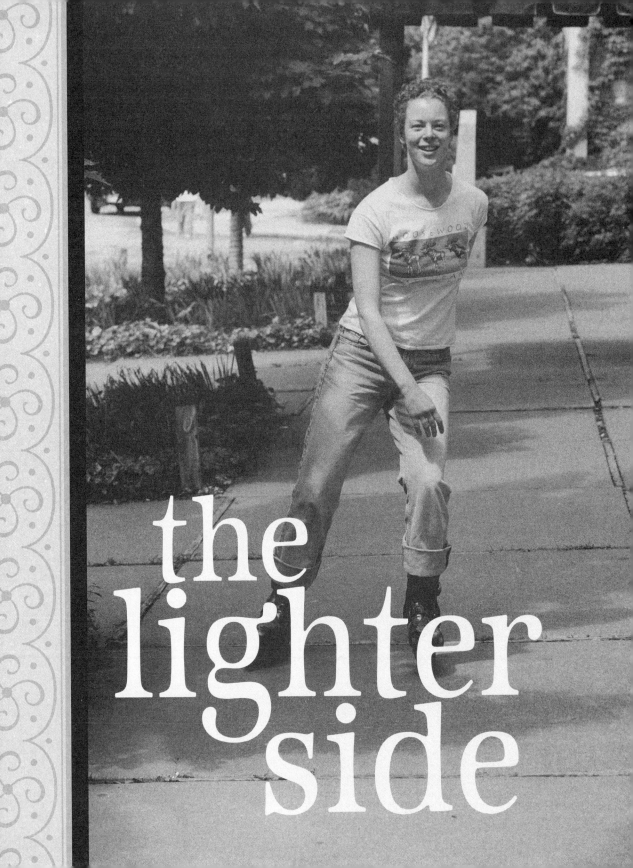

the lighter side

the lighter side

Eating light can mean many different things. Sometimes it means preparing something easy that's ready in just a few steps. It may mean cooking with less fat. Sometimes it means eating things that are easily digested and quickly metabolized into available energy. Maybe it means eating just enough and recognizing when you're full. It could even mean saving room for a really great dessert.

For many of us, ending the day with a rich, heavy meal holds little appeal. Sometimes a little light sustenance fits the bill better than a traditional "dinner." In this section, you won't find elaborate procedures, really expensive or esoteric ingredients, or fussy presentations; these are simple, straightforward, accessible recipes you will enjoy fixing during the work week for lunch or dinner.

So, what *are* you doing for dinner? How about diving into a beautiful salad like Tuscan Panzanella or Avocado & Shrimp Sushi Salad? Or stir up a steamy pot of delicate creamy Risotto Milanese. Whip up a nice Spanish Frittata and save a piece to wrap up for tomorrow's lunch. Relax on the patio with a simple bowl of Pasta with Easy Summer Sauce as the twilight falls. Listen to the evening news with a platter of succulent Moroccan Roasted Vegetables. Mix up something comforting like Orecchiette with Butter Beans or some Greens & Soft Polenta. Have fun making Lovely Low-Fat Latkes and Simplest Ever Applesauce with your mom. Surprise your housemates with Dressed-Up Salmon Cakes. Stay fit and trim with aromatic Israeli Couscous & French Lentils or fix a gorgeous platter of Antipasto with Spring Vegetables. Lighten up so that there's more time to sit back, unwind, and enjoy a pleasant, unhurried meal.

antipasto with spring vegetables

When the early spring vegetables appear on vegetable stands, don't miss the chance to enjoy them in their pristine glory—gently blanched and dressed with a simple herbed vinaigrette.

Mix up the vegetable combination as you like, using a variety of colors and textures. It's very important to cook the vegetables just until tender, or you'll miss what makes them so special—their brilliant colors and delicate young flavors. We remove the vegetables from the boiling water when they're still a little undercooked: their residual heat will continue to soften them.

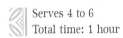

Serves 4 to 6
Total time: 1 hour

vegetables

1½ pounds baby red potatoes or fingerlings, rinsed and quartered

¼ teaspoon salt

1½ cups baby cut carrots or carrot matchsticks

12 asparagus spears, tough stem ends trimmed

1½ cups tender green beans or haricots verts, trimmed

1¾ cups diagonally sliced small yellow summer squash

1 red, orange, or yellow bell pepper, seeded and sliced lengthwise

1½ cups sliced mushrooms

1 to 1½ cups trimmed sugar snap peas or snow peas

vinaigrette

2 tablespoons minced fresh basil

1 teaspoon minced fresh summer savory or tarragon

1 or 2 garlic cloves, minced or pressed

½ cup extra-virgin olive oil

3 tablespoons red wine vinegar or cider vinegar

½ teaspoon salt, or more to taste

½ teaspoon ground black pepper

1 small head of red leaf, green leaf, Boston, or romaine lettuce

2 celery stalks, cut into slender matchsticks

12 cherry tomatoes or 2 medium tomatoes, cut into wedges

assorted olives

Bring two medium pots of water to a boil, place a large bowl of iced water in the sink, and have handy a large tray to hold the cooked vegetables.

In a separate saucepan, combine the potatoes, salt, and enough water to cover. Bring to a boil, then reduce the heat to medium and simmer until just tender, 10 to 15 minutes.

Meanwhile, cook each of the other vegetables separately in the pots of boiling water just until tender. The carrots and asparagus will take about 5 minutes, the green beans 3 to 4 minutes, and the squash, bell peppers, mushrooms, and peas only 1 to 2 minutes. When each vegetable is ready, promptly remove with a slotted spoon and plunge into the iced water. When the vegetables reach room temperature, drain and transfer to the tray.

Whisk all of the vinaigrette ingredients together or purée briefly in a blender. Spread lettuce leaves on a serving platter. When all of the vegetables are done, arrange them on the bed of lettuce. Decorate with the celery sticks, tomatoes, and olives and drizzle on the vinaigrette.

PER 15-OUNCE SERVING: 357 CALORIES, 6.6 G PROTEIN, 21.1 G FAT, 40 G CARBOHYDRATES, 2.9 G SATURATED FATTY ACIDS, 0 MG CHOLESTEROL, 473.4 MG SODIUM, 8.3 G TOTAL DIETARY FIBER

cobb salad

Cobb Salad, invented by Robert Cobb at Hollywood's Brown Derby Restaurant in 1936, has retained a certain air of glamor and sophistication ever since. Our vegetarian version is a beautiful composed salad, colorful with stripes of many different nutritious ingredients. You can use a variety of greens for Cobb Salad: try Boston lettuce, romaine, spinach, Ruby lettuce, and watercress.

Serve accompanied by Three Seed Whole Wheat Rolls (page 401) and smooth Fennel Leek Soup (page 76).

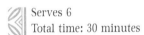
Serves 6
Total time: 30 minutes

In a small bowl, whisk together all of the dressing ingredients until blended and smooth. Set aside.

In a small covered saucepan, cook the green beans in boiling water until crisp-tender but still bright green, about 3 to 4 minutes. Drain and immerse in cold water. When cool, drain and set aside.

Spread the mixed greens on a large oval platter. Arrange the tomatoes on top of the greens in a strip lengthwise down the middle. On both sides of the tomatoes, make strips of all of the other salad ingredients, with an eye to attractive color combinations. Drizzle the dressing over all or serve the salad with the dressing on the side.

dressing

3 tablespoons red wine vinegar

3 tablespoons fresh lemon juice

1 tablespoon Dijon mustard

2 garlic cloves, minced or pressed

3 tablespoons vegetable oil

1 tablespoon Worcestershire sauce

1 tablespoon mild honey

salad

1 1/2 cups stemmed and sliced green beans*

6 cups mixed greens, torn into bite-sized pieces

1 1/2 cups diced fresh tomatoes

2 hard-boiled eggs, chopped

1 1/2 cups peeled, seeded, and chopped cucumbers

1 Hass avocado, cut into cubes**

6 ounces tofu-kan or other seasoned tofu, diced

1/2 small red onion, finely chopped

1/2 cup crumbled blue cheese

* Cut 1/2 pound of green beans into 1-inch lengths to yield 1 1/2 cups.
** Slice around the avocado lengthwise, gently twist the halves apart, and remove the pit. Cut the flesh into cubes right in the skins and scoop them out with a serving spoon.

PER 12-OUNCE SERVING: 304 CALORIES, 10.7 G PROTEIN, 19.3 G FAT, 26.2 G CARBOHYDRATES, 5.3 G SATURATED FATTY ACIDS, 90.6 MG CHOLESTEROL, 585.5 MG SODIUM, 5.1 G TOTAL DIETARY FIBER

israeli couscous & french lentils

Israeli couscous, created in the 1950s in Israel, is sometimes called pearl pasta. Its flavorfulness and tender absorbent texture are increasing its popularity in the U.S. The pieces of Israeli couscous are about the size of peppercorns, so they're good for hearty dishes. French lentils are smaller than brown or red lentils and hold their shape well when cooked.

This salad has a delicate flavor and is a good counterpart to assertively seasoned, spicy dishes. Or serve it with our Falafel Burgers (page 184) and stuffed grape leaves for a fabulous Middle Eastern-style combination platter.

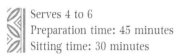
Serves 4 to 6
Preparation time: 45 minutes
Sitting time: 30 minutes

¼ cup French lentils, well rinsed

4½ quarts water

2½ teaspoons salt

1½ cups Israeli couscous

1 cinnamon stick

2 tablespoons olive oil

1 teaspoon freshly grated lemon peel

3 tablespoons fresh lemon juice

½ cup diced red bell peppers

¼ cup pitted chopped dates

1½ tablespoons minced fresh mint

¼ to ½ teaspoon ground black pepper

lemon wedges
toasted pine nuts*

* *Toast pine nuts in a single layer on an unoiled baking tray at 350° for 3 to 5 minutes, until fragrant and golden.*

In a saucepan, combine the lentils, 2 cups of the water, and ½ teaspoon of the salt. Bring to a boil; then reduce the heat, cover, and simmer for about 20 minutes or until tender. Drain well and set aside.

While the lentils simmer, bring the remaining 4 quarts of water to a rapid boil in a large covered pot. Stir in the couscous, cinnamon stick, and 1 teaspoon of salt. Cover the pot until the water returns to a boil; then uncover and cook for about 8 to 10 minutes: the couscous should be still firm in the middle. Drain, rinse with cold water, and drain again. Remove and discard the cinnamon stick.

In a serving bowl, toss together the couscous, lentils, olive oil, lemon peel, lemon juice, bell peppers, dates, mint, black pepper, and the remaining teaspoon of salt. Set the salad aside for about 30 minutes to develop the flavors.

Serve accompanied by lemon wedges and topped with toasted pine nuts.

PER 6-OUNCE SERVING: 226 CALORIES, 6.6 G PROTEIN, 5.1 G FAT, 39.2 G CARBOHYDRATES, 0.7 G SATURATED FATTY ACIDS, 0 MG CHOLESTEROL, 1,000.5 MG SODIUM, 4 G TOTAL DIETARY FIBER

tabouli with shrimp & oranges

Tabouli is traditionally a lemony parsley salad with some bulghur added for texture and interest, but here in the United States it's often prepared as a grain salad seasoned with parsley and mint. Our version has a tangy orange, mint, and olive oil dressing, fresh orange sections, and shrimp boiled until just pink.

As with any grain salad, it's important to season this tabouli to taste. The bulghur will absorb the dressing as it sits and may be spiked with additional fresh lemon juice, salt, and freshly ground black pepper just before serving. Experiment with different amounts of herbs to find the combination and intensity you prefer.

Serves 6
Preparation time: 30 minutes
Chilling time: 15 to 30 minutes

salad

3 1/2 to 4 cups cooked bulghur*
24 cooked medium shrimp, chilled
1 cup seeded and sliced cucumbers**
2 navel oranges, sectioned***
1/3 cup quartered and thinly sliced red onions
1/2 cup chopped fresh parsley
salt and ground black pepper to taste

dressing

1/4 cup extra-virgin olive oil
1 to 2 tablespoons freshly grated orange peel
3/4 cup fresh orange juice
2 tablespoons minced fresh spearmint or orange mint (2 teaspoons dried)
3 to 4 tablespoons fresh lemon juice
1/4 teaspoon ground black pepper
1/2 teaspoon salt
pinch of cayenne
1 tablespoon mild honey

4 to 6 ounces fresh spinach leaves
lemon wedges and sprigs of mint
toasted chopped walnuts (optional)

* Place 1 1/2 cups of raw bulghur in a heat-proof bowl and cover with 2 cups of boiling water. Cover the bowl and set aside to steam for 20 to 30 minutes, until the water is absorbed and the bulghur is tender.
** Peel a cucumber and slice it in half lengthwise. Scoop out the seeds and cut crosswise into 1/4-inch-thick crescents.
*** Use a sharp knife to slice off the peel and the white pith. Working over a bowl, slice toward the center of the orange along the membrane on one side of a section and then flick the knife up the membrane on the other side to release the section.

In a bowl, stir together the cooked bulghur, chilled shrimp, cucumbers, orange sections, red onions, parsley, salt, and pepper. Whisk together all of the dressing ingredients and pour over the bulghur mixture. Toss the tabouli with the dressing and refrigerate for at least 15 to 30 minutes.

When the tabouli has nearly finished chilling, rinse and stem the spinach and slice it into $1/8$-inch strips. Arrange the chiffonade of fresh spinach on a serving platter. Taste the chilled tabouli and adjust the seasonings.

Serve the tabouli on the bed of spinach, garnished with lemon wedges and mint. Top with the toasted walnuts, if desired.

PER 12-OUNCE SERVING: 324 CALORIES, 25.4 G PROTEIN, 11.1 G FAT, 32.7 G CARBOHYDRATES,
1.7 G SATURATED FATTY ACIDS, 194.6 MG CHOLESTEROL, 449.2 MG SODIUM, 6.8 G TOTAL DIETARY FIBER

mediterranean orzo salad

A local group of Italian-Americans had their first potluck dinner in the fall of 1999. As her contribution, Moosewood's Ned Asta cooked a big bowl of this orzo salad and was happy to have people asking for the recipe.

Using a mixture of olives—kalamatas, green Spanish olives, ripe black California olives—makes this salad lively in color and, in combination with the olive oil, very olive-y indeed.

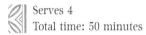 Serves 4
Total time: 50 minutes

2 tablespoons extra-virgin olive oil

4 cups cubed eggplant (1-inch cubes)*

3 or 4 garlic cloves, minced or pressed

1/2 teaspoon salt

1 cup orzo

2 teaspoons capers

1/3 cup pine nuts, lightly toasted**

1/2 cup minced red bell peppers

2/3 cup pitted chopped mixed olives

1 1/2 cups chopped fresh tomatoes

1/3 cup chopped fresh parsley

ground black pepper to taste

grated feta cheese or Parmesan cheese (optional)

* *If the eggplant skin is not tough or bitter, there's no need to peel it for this recipe.*
** *Toast pine nuts in a single layer on an unoiled baking tray at 350° for 3 to 5 minutes, until fragrant and golden brown.*

Preheat the oven to 450°. Lightly oil a 9 x 12-inch nonreactive baking pan.

Mix together the olive oil, eggplant, garlic, and salt in the prepared baking pan. Bake until the edges of the eggplant begin to brown, 20 to 30 minutes.

In the meantime, bring 2 quarts of salted water to a boil. Add the orzo and cook for about 10 minutes, until al dente, stirring occasionally. Drain well.

In a large bowl, mix together the capers, pine nuts, bell peppers, olives, and tomatoes. Add the drained pasta and toss well to coat with the vegetables. Mix in the baked eggplant cubes and parsley.

Top with some grated cheese, if desired, and serve immediately.

PER 12-OUNCE SERVING: 458 CALORIES, 12.8 G PROTEIN, 23.3 G FAT, 53.2 G CARBOHYDRATES, 2.4 G SATURATED FATTY ACIDS, 0 MG CHOLESTEROL, 1,406.8 MG SODIUM, 4.8 G TOTAL DIETARY FIBER

tuscan panzanella

Panzanella is the famous bread salad of Tuscany. Moosewood cook Laura Branca realized that this recipe could be the perfect way to use a stale loaf of bread, and when she tried it, it worked like a charm! Warm the bread in the oven until it's crisp enough to be speared with a fork, but soft enough inside to soak up the dressing.

Savory roasted peppers and squash paired with fresh asparagus and sweet sugar snaps make this a wonderful meal. For efficiency, first prepare the squash and peppers, and while they roast, prepare the rest of the ingredients. Laura wanted plenty of flavor, so her recipe makes 2 cups of the Creamy Garlic Parmesan Dressing, which would keep for a really long time if it weren't so good.

Serve the panzanella by itself or with a light, puréed soup such as Curried Spinach Pea Soup (page 73).

Serves 6 to 8
Total time: 1¼ hours

creamy garlic parmesan dressing

2 garlic cloves, minced or pressed
1 cup extra-virgin olive oil
¼ cup red wine vinegar
½ cup grated Parmesan cheese
½ teaspoon ground black pepper, or more to taste
1 teaspoon salt
½ cup 2% milk

panzanella

1 medium zucchini, cut into ¼-inch-thick slices*
1 medium yellow summer squash, cut into ¼-inch-thick slices*
1 large red bell pepper, halved and seeded
1 large green or yellow bell pepper, halved and seeded
1 tablespoon olive oil
12 to 16 fresh asparagus, stemmed and cut into 2-inch pieces
1 cup sugar snap peas, trimmed
2 cups chopped tomatoes
8 cups mesclun or mixed field greens, rinsed and drained
2 tablespoons extra-virgin olive oil
2 tablespoons red wine vinegar
salt and freshly ground black pepper to taste
2 teaspoons minced fresh basil, thyme, or parsley
1 large loaf of crusty French or Italian bread

* Cut the summer squash and zucchini crosswise on a severe diagonal for large goodlooking slices.

✂ Preheat the oven to 450°. Oil two baking sheets.

Combine the dressing ingredients in a blender or food processor, adding the milk last while you purée or process. Whirl for 30 to 45 seconds, until the dressing is the consistency of a light mayonnaise. Set aside.

Lightly brush the zucchini and squash slices and the bell pepper halves with the olive oil. Place the pepper halves on one baking tray and roast for 40 to 45 minutes, until charred with black areas. Spread the zucchini and squash on the other baking tray and roast for about 15 minutes, until they start to brown. Use a spatula to turn the slices over. Return the squash to the oven and bake for another 15 minutes, until golden brown on both sides.

Meanwhile, bring a saucepan of water to a boil. Blanch the asparagus for about 2 minutes; then add the sugar snap peas and cook for 1 to 2 minutes longer. Drain both vegetables and plunge into very cold water to cool. Drain again and set aside. Place the tomatoes and greens in a serving bowl. In a cup, stir together the olive oil, vinegar, salt, pepper, and basil or other herbs and set aside.

When the squash and peppers are roasted, remove the trays from the oven and reduce the temperature to 350°.

Place the roasted peppers in a bowl, cover, and let sit for 10 minutes. Peel off the charred skin of the peppers and then cut them into 2-inch pieces. Meanwhile, slice the loaf of bread in half lengthwise and place it in the oven for 5 to 10 minutes to crisp the crust.

Add the bell peppers, squash, asparagus, and snap peas to the serving bowl of tomatoes and greens. Just before serving, toss the salad with the reserved oil and vinegar. Finally, cut the bread into 1-inch cubes and add them to the salad.

Serve with a generous spoonful of the Creamy Garlic Parmesan Dressing.

PER 13-OUNCE SERVING: 550 CALORIES, 11.8 G PROTEIN, 39.2 G FAT, 40.8 G CARBOHYDRATES, 6.7 G SATURATED FATTY ACIDS, 8.3 MG CHOLESTEROL, 783.8 MG SODIUM, 3.7 G TOTAL DIETARY FIBER

risotto

In Italy, risotto is a familiar, home-style dish, easily made and often improvised. It is just about as easy to make as pasta and almost as versatile.

Risotto is made from plump, extremely glutinous, short- to medium-grain rice grown chiefly in the Po River Valley in Italy. Four rice varieties are typically used for risotto: Carnaroli, Vialone Nano, Baldo, and Arborio, the one easiest to find in our supermarkets. A good domestic rice is California-grown Cal-riso, which resembles Arborio but is faster cooking.

Risotto rices absorb a lot of liquid quickly and still remain al dente. Characteristically, they release a great deal of starch as they cook, which results in firm rice kernels with chewy centers suspended in a thick smooth base, giving the illusion of creaminess. Look for packages marked "ai pestelli," which means the rice was hulled with a mortar and pestle. This process leaves a powdery starch on the rice that enhances that creamy risotto texture.

Vegetables, herbs, and cheeses are flavorful additions to velvety risotto. Risotto dishes range from simple to elaborate, rustic to elegant. Nutritious and economical, risotto can be a first course, a main dish, or a side dish.

Most risottos can be prepared in less than 30 minutes. It usually takes about 20 minutes for arborio rice to cook into a creamy but al dente consistency. To make risotto, set up two pots on your stovetop. In one, keep broth or stock simmering on the back burner. Your own homemade vegetable stock, which can be frozen for convenience, is best of course, but we also like the vegetable and "un-chicken" broths available in aseptically packaged quart boxes. In a pinch, use water and bouillon cubes, as does Marcella Hazan, the luminary of Italian cooking. We like Morga brand vegetable bouillon.

On the front burner, place a heavy-bottomed, preferably nonstick, saucepan. Gently sauté onions and the rice in oil or butter. A small amount of wine is generally the first liquid addition, which is quickly absorbed by the rice. If you don't wish to use wine, substitute broth or nonalcoholic wine.

Traditionally, risotto is stirred constantly after the first addition of liquid, but we've found, especially when we use a nonstick pan, that continuous stirring isn't necessary for achieving a nice creaminess. A nonstick pot also greatly minimizes cleanup. Nonstick pots and risotto were made for each other. Always stir risotto with a wooden spoon to avoid breaking up the rice kernels.

Add the hot stock or broth about a cup or a ladleful at a time. As the stock is absorbed by the rice, add more. Stir every few minutes to see if more broth is needed, and then stir each addition well. Sometimes beginning risotto-makers are cautious and cook the rice on low heat, but with a little experience they are likely to develop a feel for just the right heat, just the right amount of stirring. Between stirrings, there's time to prep the vegetables and grate the cheese.

The last step is thoroughly stirring in the cheese. Serve the finished risotto without delay. Risotto doesn't reheat well, but try adding a beaten egg or two to cold leftover risotto and either pan-frying it for a risotto frittata or baking it for a delicious risotto cake.

red risotto

This hearty, comforting risotto comes from the lake district of northern Italy. With so many red ingredients, you can see why it's called red, but actually, the end result is a handsome mauve color. After simmering, the radicchio almost melts into the risotto and, although its bitter edge has been greatly subdued, it still provides a strong flavoring effect.

The trick to a creamy risotto is to add the stock to the sautéed rice gradually and stir often. It will take about 25 minutes for the rice to absorb all of the stock when it is added cup by cup. Using a nonstick pan helps prevent sticking and minimizes cleanup.

Start with crudités and piquant Green Olive & Artichoke Tapenade (page 209). Serve alongside dishes that don't require last-minute preparation, such as crisp Bread Sticks (page 394) and Pretty Beets & Carrots (page 106).

Serves 4 to 6
Total time: 50 minutes

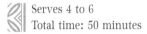

4 cups vegetable stock

1 tablespoon olive oil

3/4 to 1 cup minced red onions

1 1/4 cups arborio rice

1/2 cup dry red wine

4 cups finely shredded radicchio

2 tablespoons tomato paste

1 1/2 cups cooked small red beans (15.5-ounce can, rinsed and drained)

pinch of dried thyme

1 teaspoon salt

1/2 cup finely grated Pecorino Romano cheese

ground black pepper to taste

shavings of Pecorino Romano cheese (optional)

In a small saucepan, heat the stock to a simmer; then keep it gently simmering.

Meanwhile, in a large, heavy, preferably nonstick saucepan, warm the olive oil on medium-low heat. Add the onions and cook for about 5 minutes, until softened. With a wooden spoon, stir in the rice until well coated with the oil. Add the wine and stir for about 1 minute until it's absorbed.

Add 1 cup of the simmering stock and cook, stirring occasionally, until absorbed. Add the radicchio and another cup of stock and cook, stirring often. As each cup of stock is absorbed stir in the next. Add the tomato paste, beans, and thyme with the last ladleful of stock.

After the stock is absorbed, cook for 3 to 4 minutes more, continuing to stir, until the risotto is creamy but still al dente. Remove from the heat and add the salt. Stir in the grated cheese and pepper to taste.

Serve immediately, topped with extra cheese, if desired.

PER 7.5-OUNCE SERVING: 327 CALORIES, 12.3 G PROTEIN, 6.4 G FAT, 53.5 G CARBOHYDRATES, 2.4 G SATURATED FATTY ACIDS, 11.8 MG CHOLESTEROL, 687.6 MG SODIUM, 8.6 G TOTAL DIETARY FIBER

risotto milanese

This elegant golden-yellow risotto is probably Milan's most famous dish. We loved the idea of using a now-available "un-chicken" broth to duplicate the traditional flavor of risotto Milanese. Westbrae Natural Unchicken Broth is a canned vegetarian, semi-condensed broth found on the soup shelves in natural grocery stores. Imagine Foods and Pacific brands also make all-natural and low-fat "un-chicken" broths, which come in aseptically packaged quart boxes.

You may also use 2 vegetable bouillon cubes dissolved in 5 cups of boiling water or 5 cups of your favorite vegetable stock to replace the mock chicken broth and water in the recipe.

Pair this risotto with Roasted Winter Vegetables (page 264) or serve it as a first course, as Italians do, to be followed by Pecan-Crusted Fish (page 367) and a sautéed bitter green. If you really want to gild the lily, top each serving with a dollop of mascarpone cheese.

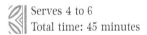 Serves 4 to 6
Total time: 45 minutes

4 cups vegetarian mock chicken broth (two 15-ounce cans)

1 cup water

¹/₂ cup diced onions

1¹/₂ tablespoons butter

1 tablespoon olive oil

¹/₂ to 1 teaspoon crumbled saffron threads

1¹/₂ cups arborio or carnaroli rice

¹/₂ cup dry white wine

¹/₂ cup grated Parmesan cheese

freshly ground black pepper to taste

In a saucepan, bring the broth and water to a low simmer. In another large saucepan, sauté the onions in the butter and olive oil on medium-high heat until golden, about 10 minutes. Add the saffron and rice, and stir thoroughly to coat the rice with the butter and oil. Add the wine and cook, stirring constantly, until it is absorbed, a minute or two.

Ladle in the simmering broth, 1 cup at a time, stirring the rice often. Let the rice absorb the broth almost completely before adding more. Continue cooking until the rice is tender but al dente, about 20 minutes.

When the rice is done, remove it from the heat and stir in the grated cheese and the pepper. Serve immediately.

PER 10-OUNCE SERVING: 290 CALORIES, 8.2 G PROTEIN, 9.3 G FAT, 41 G CARBOHYDRATES, 4.3 G SATURATED FATTY ACIDS, 16.7 MG CHOLESTEROL, 345 MG SODIUM, 3.5 G TOTAL DIETARY FIBER

spinach feta risotto

This flavorful pan-Mediterranean-style risotto is packed with good things. The amount of salt needed will depend upon the saltiness of the stock or broth you use and your own preference.

A few olives and some sliced tomatoes might be all you need to add for a lovely, light meal, although Asparagus with Red Pepper Sauce (page 119) goes well with this.

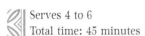

Serves 4 to 6
Total time: 45 minutes

3 cups sliced cremini mushrooms

1 garlic clove, minced or pressed

1/4 cup olive oil

1 tablespoon chopped fresh dill or thyme

2 tablespoons plus 1/2 cup dry white wine

1/4 teaspoon salt

ground black pepper to taste

5 cups vegetable stock*

1/2 cup diced onions

2 cups arborio or carnaroli rice

10 ounces fresh spinach, rinsed, stemmed, and chopped (about 10 cups)

1 cup crumbled feta cheese

*Make your own stock (page 62), use a quart of commercial broth or stock and add water to make 5 cups, or dissolve 2 vegetable bouillon cubes in 5 cups of boiling water.

In a saucepan on medium heat, sauté the mushrooms and garlic in 1 tablespoon of the oil for about 5 minutes, until the mushrooms are softened and most of the moisture has evaporated. Add the dill or thyme and 2 tablespoons of wine and cook for a minute more. Add the salt and pepper to taste. Hold on very low heat until the risotto is ready.

In a saucepan, heat the stock to a low simmer.

In a soup pot on medium-high heat, sauté the onions in the remaining 3 tablespoons of oil for about 5 minutes, until golden. Add the rice and stir with a wooden spoon until the grains are coated with oil. Add the 1/2 cup of wine and cook, stirring constantly, until the wine is absorbed.

Add the simmering stock 1 cup at a time. Cook, stirring frequently, until each cup is absorbed before adding the next. Continue until all of the stock is used and the rice is tender but still al dente, about 25 minutes. When the rice has absorbed all of the stock, add the spinach, cover, and cook for about 2 minutes, until the spinach is wilted but still bright green. Stir in the feta cheese.

Serve each portion of risotto topped with the sautéed mushrooms.

PER 13-OUNCE SERVING: 399 CALORIES, 8.8 G PROTEIN, 14.5 G FAT, 56.7 G CARBOHYDRATES, 4.1 G SATURATED FATTY ACIDS, 16.8 MG CHOLESTEROL, 466.9 MG SODIUM, 5.9 G TOTAL DIETARY FIBER

frittatas

Frittatas and omelets are similar yet different. Both use eggs and are a terrific blank canvas for the inventive cook. But while an omelet is cooked in a skillet and then folded over a filling, a frittata is layered with one filling ingredient right atop the next. Frittatas may be cooked either in the oven or on the stovetop and, unlike omelets, they're equally good hot, at room temperature, or cold. Since they are good served at any temperature, they are a good choice for a picnic or dish-to-pass meal.

Some frittatas make an excellent sandwich stuffer. Try Mixed Greens Frittata or another frittata made without a starchy filling in a long French or Italian loaf or between slices of hearty whole wheat bread.

Variations are one of the joys of making frittatas. In our time, we've made hundreds, maybe even thousands, of frittatas at Moosewood. The basic idea is usually a starch (rice, potatoes, or bread) topped with vegetables (sautéed or roasted), some cheese, and usually some herbs, all held together with egg custard. Below, we give you a bunch of ideas for vegetable-herb-cheese combinations, but we predict that the best frittatas you make will be inspirations of the moment. Begin with some leftovers or something from the vegetable bin that needs to be used and go from there. The recipes we've included here are meant to serve as models for how to make frittatas either in the oven or on the stovetop in a skillet.

In the Moosewood kitchen, we always make frittatas in the oven because we're cooking large amounts, and because once it's in the oven, it's hands-off until it's done, except to take off the cover for browning. But at home, we often make skillet frittatas on the stovetop. We've experimented with various techniques and have decided that finishing off under the broiler is easiest and makes the best-looking dish; for instructions, see page 244.

Most of the following frittata combinations can be adapted to either the oven or the skillet method. For a 7 x 11-inch or 9 x 9-inch baking pan or a 10-inch skillet, you need about 3 cups of rice or roasted potatoes, or 2 cups of croutons or toasted bread cubes for a 1-inch layer. Top with 1 to 2 cups of roasted or sautéed onions and 1 to 2 cups of other vegetables, sautéed, steamed, or roasted. One cup of cheese is usually about right. For the custard, combine 6 eggs, 1½ cups of milk, 3 ounces of cream cheese, and ½ teaspoon salt.

rice frittatas

- Green peas, sautéed mushrooms, chopped scallions or red onions; almost any fresh herb; Parmesan and/or Cheddar cheese.

- Snow peas cut crosswise into strips, celery sliced on the diagonal, carrot matchsticks, slivered scallions; tofu cubes marinated in soy sauce and dark sesame oil; hold the cheese and serve drizzled with hoisin sauce.

- Steamed or sautéed broccoli and/or cauliflower florets, strips of red onion; fresh basil and dill; Cheddar cheese.

roasted potato frittatas

- Zucchini, onions, and sun-dried tomatoes; oregano or thyme and fresh basil; mild provolone and Parmesan cheeses.

- Eggplant strips or cubes roasted with garlic, onions, bell peppers, and rosemary; Parmesan cheese.

- Kale or chard sautéed with onions and garlic; smoked cheese.

- Roasted onions and red and green bell pepper strips; fresh basil; Cheddar cheese.

bread frittatas

- Steamed or sautéed asparagus pieces, strips of red bell pepper and onions; dilled Havarti cheese.

- Sautéed yellow summer squash and onions; fresh tarragon and ground black pepper; Fontina or Gruyère cheese.

other ideas

- Grated carrots, minced bell peppers, chopped scallions or red onions, corn kernels; cumin, coriander, and fresh cilantro; Cheddar or Monterey Jack cheese. Top with tomato salsa.

- Crumbled tortilla chips or strips of tortillas; black beans or refried beans, chopped scallions, bell peppers; cumin and thyme; Cheddar or mild white cheese; top frittata with thick slices of fresh tomatoes.

mixed greens frittata

This simple, tasty, nutritious frittata contains no onions or garlic—and it's very green. Serve a wedge with a little citrus-dressed mesclun on the side, a slice of warm, buttered French bread, and bingo! What a brunch! For lunch, a cup of tomato soup, a grated carrot salad, or slices of ripe tomatoes would all make good companions.

Refrigerate leftovers for delicious sandwiches the next day.

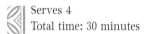
Serves 4
Total time: 30 minutes

2 cups chopped greens*
³/4 cup chopped fresh parsley
¹/4 cup chopped fresh basil
1 ¹/2 teaspoons olive oil
4 eggs, lightly beaten
¹/4 cup water
¹/4 teaspoon salt
¹/2 cup grated feta, Parmesan, or
    Cheddar cheese

* *A mixture of any greens, such as spinach, Swiss chard, collards, escarole, or kale, works fine.*

In a 10-inch ovenproof skillet, stir-fry the greens, parsley, and basil in 1 teaspoon of the oil until wilted and tender. Transfer the greens to a bowl. Rinse the skillet and set aside. In a separate bowl, whisk together the eggs, water, and salt and stir in ¹/4 cup of the cheese.

Lightly oil the skillet with the remaining ¹/2 teaspoon of oil and place it on medium-high heat. Stir the egg and cheese mixture into the greens and pour into the hot skillet. Sprinkle the top with the rest of the grated cheese. Lower the heat to medium-low and cook, without stirring, until the edges are firm and pulling away from the sides of the pan, about 5 minutes. The frittata should be mostly cooked, but with the top still slightly undercooked. Place the skillet under the broiler for 3 to 5 minutes, until the top is firm and beginning to turn golden brown.

Cut into wedges and serve, either directly from the skillet or turned out onto a large plate.

PER 4-OUNCE SERVING: 157 CALORIES, 10.6 G PROTEIN, 11.5 G FAT, 2.7 G CARBOHYDRATES, 4.4 G SATURATED FATTY ACIDS, 277 MG CHOLESTEROL, 399.4 MG SODIUM, 0.6 G TOTAL DIETARY FIBER

spanish frittata

Dense with olives, vegetables, and spices that we associate with sunny Spain, this is one of the most popular frittatas at Moosewood. Although we like to roast all of the vegetables, if you prefer, you can sauté the onions and peppers on the stovetop rather than roasting them in the oven.

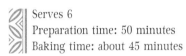
Serves 6
Preparation time: 50 minutes
Baking time: about 45 minutes

2 to 3 cups sliced potatoes
   ($\frac{1}{2}$ inch thick)
3 tablespoons olive oil
4 garlic cloves, minced or pressed
1 tablespoon paprika
2 cups thinly sliced onions
2 cups sliced bell peppers*
$\frac{1}{8}$ to $\frac{1}{4}$ teaspoon cayenne
6 eggs
3 ounces Neufchâtel or cream cheese
1 tablespoon unbleached white flour
$1\frac{1}{4}$ cups milk
$\frac{1}{2}$ teaspoon salt
$\frac{1}{2}$ cup chopped Spanish olives
1 cup grated Monterey Jack or
   Cheddar cheese

* A mix of colors is nice.

✳Preheat the oven to 400°. Lightly oil a 7 x 11-inch or a 9-inch square baking pan.

In a bowl, toss the potato slices with 2 tablespoons of the oil, half of the garlic, the paprika, and a dash of salt. Spread in an even layer on a baking sheet and roast for about 20 minutes, until tender and golden brown. In the same bowl, toss the onions and peppers with the cayenne and the remaining oil and garlic. Spread in an even layer on a second baking sheet and roast until tender and brown, about 15 minutes.

Meanwhile, combine the eggs, Neufchâtel or cream cheese, flour, milk, and salt in a blender and purée to a smooth custard.

When the vegetable are roasted, reduce the oven temperature to 350°.

Layer the roasted potatoes in the prepared baking pan. Spread on the roasted onions and peppers, sprinkle with the olives and grated cheese, and pour the custard over all.

Bake for about 45 minutes, until the custard is set and the top is golden brown. Serve hot or at room temperature.

PER 11-OUNCE SERVING: 400 CALORIES, 18 G PROTEIN, 26.5 G FAT, 24.1 G CARBOHYDRATES, 9.6 G SATURATED FATTY ACIDS, 295.5 MG CHOLESTEROL, 917 MG SODIUM, 2.9 G TOTAL DIETARY FIBER

sweet potato & zucchini frittata

The sugar and color of roasted sweet potatoes contrasts beautifully with mild, juicy zucchini and the smoked Cheddar, which adds a bacony scent and rich flavor.

Serves 4 to 6
Preparation time: 40 minutes
Baking time: 40 to 45 minutes

3 cups peeled sweet potato rounds
    ($1/2$ inch thick)
4 garlic cloves, minced or pressed
3 tablespoons olive oil
1 teaspoon salt
$1^1/2$ cups thinly sliced onions
3 cups sliced zucchini rounds
    ($1/2$ inch thick)
1 tablespoon chopped fresh marjoram
    (1 teaspoon dried)
5 eggs
8 ounces Neufchâtel or cream cheese,
    at room temperature
$1/4$ teaspoon ground black pepper
2 cups milk
1 cup grated smoked Cheddar cheese

Preheat the oven to 400°. Oil a 9 x 11-inch baking pan.

In a bowl, stir together the sweet potatoes with half of the garlic, $1^1/2$ tablespoons of the oil, and $1/2$ teaspoon of the salt until evenly coated. Spread in a single layer on an unoiled baking sheet and roast for about 15 minutes, until tender.

Meanwhile, heat the remaining $1^1/2$ tablespoons of oil in a large skillet and sauté the onions with the rest of the garlic and salt until the onions have softened, about 5 minutes. Add the zucchini and marjoram and sauté until the zucchini rounds are soft and golden brown, about 10 minutes. When the sweet potatoes are tender and brown, remove them from the oven and set aside.

Lower the oven temperature to 350°.

In a blender, purée the eggs, Neufchâtel or cream cheese, pepper, and milk to make a smooth custard. Layer the roasted sweet potatoes in the prepared pan and spread the sautéed zucchini on top. Evenly sprinkle on the smoked cheese, then pour the custard over all.

Bake for 40 to 45 minutes, until browned and firm. Serve hot.

PER 12-OUNCE SERVING: 449 CALORIES, 19.5 G PROTEIN, 29.5 G FAT, 27.3 G CARBOHYDRATES, 13.2 G SATURATED FATTY ACIDS, 274.6 MG CHOLESTEROL, 777.4 MG SODIUM, 2.6 G TOTAL DIETARY FIBER

zucchini rice frittata

In the classic, Italian-type frittata, everything is stirred together in a bowl before you pour it into the hot skillet. With dill, mint, and feta, this frittata has Greek and Balkan overtones. Use our recipe as a basic template, and try different cheeses, vegetables, or herbs, or use croutons or potatoes instead of rice—or no starch at all. If you wish, purée eight ounces of tofu in the blender with the eggs, water, and salt for a nutritious boost of soy protein.

Leftovers are good served either cold or at room temperature.

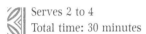

Serves 2 to 4
Total time: 30 minutes

1 cup onion slices

1 tablespoon olive oil

1 1/2 cups sliced zucchini (halved or quartered lengthwise, if large)

3/4 cup cooked brown rice

1 tablespoon minced fresh dill (1 1/2 teaspoons dried)

1 teaspoon dried mint (optional)

4 eggs

1/4 cup water

1/4 teaspoon salt, or more to taste

1/4 cup crumbled feta cheese

1/4 cup grated Parmesan cheese

ground black pepper to taste

In a 10-inch ovenproof skillet on medium heat, sauté the onion slices in the oil, stirring frequently for about 10 minutes, until the onions begin to brown. Add the zucchini and continue to sauté for about 5 minutes, until just tender. Transfer the vegetables to a large bowl and mix with the cooked rice, dill, and mint, if using.

Rinse the skillet and set it aside. In a separate bowl, whisk together the eggs, water, and salt until smooth and then whisk in the feta cheese.

Lightly oil the skillet and place it on medium-high heat. Stir the egg mixture into the vegetables and rice and spoon it into the hot skillet. Sprinkle the top with Parmesan cheese.

Lower the heat to medium-low and cook, without stirring, for about 5 minutes, until the edges are firm and pulling away from the sides of the pan. The frittata should be mostly cooked but with the top still a little wet. Place the skillet under the broiler until the top is firm and lightly browned, 3 to 5 minutes. Or, if you prefer, cover and cook on low heat until firm.

Slide the frittata onto a large plate or serve directly from the skillet in generous wedges.

PER 7-OUNCE SERVING: 245 CALORIES, 13.9 G PROTEIN, 14.6 G FAT, 14.4 G CARBOHYDRATES, 5.3 G SATURATED FATTY ACIDS, 277.4 MG CHOLESTEROL, 467.1 MG SODIUM, 1.7 G TOTAL DIETARY FIBER

pasta

Pasta is probably the first dish we think of for everyday cooking. It's economical and can be very quick and easy. You can make many pasta sauces in the time it takes to heat the water and cook the pasta, and you need little more than a salad to round out a meal. Because dry pasta is such a perfect pantry item, you can count on it for last-minute dinners or for unexpected guests. Kids will almost always eat pasta eagerly. It seems that everyone loves pasta.

Pasta is nutritious—high in B vitamins, iron, and protein (it contains 6 of 8 essential amino acids), and low in fat, sodium, and calories. Whole grain pastas are higher in protein, iron, and fiber and have fewer calories than refined flour pastas. If in the past you gave up on whole wheat pasta because of its gummy texture, try again. We've found some truly pleasing whole grain pastas with full-bodied textures and flavors. And it needn't contain wheat to be pasta; try those made from rice, buckwheat, kamut, corn, quinoa, and spelt.

Pastas can be divided into two quite different types—fresh and dried. Fresh pastas are widely available in the refrigerator case in most supermarkets. Fresh pasta is always an egg pasta with a softer texture and richer flavor than dried pasta. Take care not to overcook fresh pasta; it's usually done in just a minute or two.

Because fresh pastas don't have the "bite" and firm texture characteristic of good dried pasta, we prefer to use dried pastas at the restaurant. Made from water and semolina flour that's ground from hard durum wheat, most dried pasta is made in factories, where the extremely stiff dough is extruded at high pressure through holes in dies, a process that can't be duplicated at home.

As a rule, imported Italian dried pastas are better than those made by U.S. manufacturers because in Italy, where pasta is a national obsession, the government imposes rigid standards for ingredients, additives, and production processes, resulting in a firmer, tastier, more nutritious product. We recommend that you spend a little more to buy imported Italian pastas. At Moosewood, we like DeCecco, which is widely available in this country.

Don't let the topping overpower or disguise the pasta—the noodle should be the main attraction. There are hundreds of shapes and sizes of pastas, and the choice of which pasta to use with a particular sauce follows a certain logic. In general, long strands such as spaghetti and linguini work well with tomato sauces and pestos. Bowl-shaped cuts such as orecchietti and shells are good to serve with chunky vegetable sauces because those shapes catch and hold the pieces of vegetable. Flat noodles like fettuccine or farfalle go well with delicate cream or cheese sauces. But we would never forgo a pasta dish just because we didn't have the most proper shape on hand, and you shouldn't either.

We serve pasta in wide, shallow bowls with sloping sides. Pasta is not a dish to linger over—enjoy it while it's hot. Sophia Loren attributes her own ample charms to a lifetime of pasta. And here's her good advice on pasta etiquette: "Spaghetti can be eaten successfully if you inhale it like a vacuum cleaner."

aromatic whole wheat pasta

The simple charm of onions, carrots, celery, garlic, and parsley, along with the sharp bite of arugula, stand up well to the nutty robustness of whole wheat pasta.

The vegetables in the pasta sauce take different amounts of time to cook and we have listed them from longest cooking to shortest. To save time, sauté the first vegetable while you prepare the next; then add that one to the skillet while you dice the next.

This is quite a filling pasta, probably most appealing in cool weather. Serve with something light and refreshing, such as a tomato salad or a green salad with orange sections. Maybe figs for dessert?

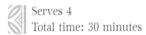
Serves 4
Total time: 30 minutes

1 tablespoon olive oil

3 cups diced onions

1 cup peeled and diced carrots

1 cup diced celery

1 tablespoon minced garlic

1/4 cup Marsala, red wine, or vegetable broth

2 tablespoons minced fresh parsley

12 ounces whole wheat pasta, preferably a chunky shape such as elbows, penne, or small shells

1 cup finely chopped arugula or Swiss chard

1 teaspoon salt

ground black pepper to taste

1 tablespoon exta-virgin olive oil

1/2 to 1 cup grated Pecorino Romano cheese

Bring a large covered pot of salted water to a boil.

Meanwhile, in a large skillet, heat the olive oil on medium heat. Add in order, the onions, carrots, celery, and garlic and sauté until the vegetables are just tender. Add the Marsala and parsley, cover, lower the heat, and gently simmer.

When the water boils, add the pasta, stir, cover the pot, and bring back to a boil. Cook the pasta until al dente. Meanwhile, add the greens to the vegetables and stir for 1 minute, until bright-colored and wilted. Add the salt and pepper, cover, and set aside.

When the pasta is al dente, drain it and toss with the extra-virgin olive oil. Spoon the vegetables over the pasta and serve immediately, passing the grated cheese at the table.

PER 16-OUNCE SERVING: 507 CALORIES, 20.8 G PROTEIN, 13.4 G FAT, 80.5 G CARBOHYDRATES, 4.2 G SATURATED FATTY ACIDS, 17.7 MG CHOLESTEROL, 859.4 MG SODIUM, 10 G TOTAL DIETARY FIBER

cabbage & noodles

We received this recipe from Alan Warshawsky, a former Moosewood cook and one of the best chefs we know. An Eastern European supper dish, full of the sweet flavors of caramelized onions and cabbage, it is nothing short of glorious comfort food. If you have the time, let the cabbage cook for an hour or more, being careful not to scorch it: the longer it cooks, the sweeter its flavor. Since this is hardly low-fat to begin with, go for a dab of sour cream on your portion and live a little.

For a warming winter meal, serve it with fresh applesauce and rye bread.

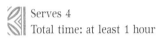
Serves 4
Total time: at least 1 hour

2 cups thinly sliced onions
¼ cup unsalted butter
1½ tablespoons paprika
8 cups finely shredded cabbage
 (about 1½ pounds)
2 teaspoons salt
12 ounces fine or medium-wide
 egg noodles
freshly ground black pepper to taste
dollop of sour cream (optional)

In a pot with a tight lid, cook the onions in the butter on medium heat until golden, about 15 minutes. Add the paprika and sauté for a few seconds more. Stir in the cabbage, add the salt, and continue to cook for 5 more minutes, stirring now and then. Cover tightly and cook on very low heat for 40 to 60 minutes, stirring occasionally, until the cabbage is very soft and brown.

When the cabbage is almost done, cook the noodles in boiling water until al dente. Drain them and toss well with the cabbage mixture. Add a generous amount of pepper and, if you like, top with a dollop of sour cream.

PER 16.75-OUNCE SERVING: 472 CALORIES, 13.7 G PROTEIN, 16 G FAT, 71 G CARBOHYDRATES, 8 G SATURATED FATTY ACIDS, 104.8 MG CHOLESTEROL, 1,224.3 MG SODIUM, 7.8 G TOTAL DIETARY FIBER

orecchiette with butter beans

The flavors of southern Italy characterize this delicious main-dish pasta. The bitter edge of broccoli rabe is somewhat tamed when combined with mild, buttery beans, mellow garlic, and aged provolone cheese. Orecchiette (little ears) is the traditional homemade pasta of Puglia, the heel of the Italian boot, but you can use any short chunky pasta. The convenience of canned beans makes this great everynight fare.

Serve with Flavored Olives (page 213), crisp breaded eggplant slices, and one of our Cucumber Side Salads (page 92). Pass extra cheese or a cruet of extra-virgin olive oil at the table, if desired.

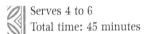

Serves 4 to 6
Total time: 45 minutes

1 large bunch of broccoli rabe
    (1 1/2 pounds)

1 tablespoon olive oil

2 tablespoons minced garlic

1/4 to 1/2 teaspoon crushed red pepper
    flakes

1 1/2 cups cooked butter beans
    (15.5-ounce can, drained)*

1 pound orecchiette or other short
    pasta shape

1 cup chopped fresh tomatoes

1/2 cup grated sharp provolone or
    Pecorino Romano

* *Cannellini or Roman beans can be substituted.*

Bring a large covered pot of salted water to a boil.

Trim any dry bottoms from the broccoli rabe stems and discard. Cut the broccoli rabe, stems, leaves, and all, into 1-inch lengths. You'll have about 9 cups of chopped broccoli rabe.

In a large, heavy frying pan, warm the oil and sauté the broccoli rabe and garlic for 7 or 8 minutes, until the broccoli rabe is bright green. Add the crushed red pepper flakes and butter beans, lower the heat, and keep warm until the pasta is cooked.

When the water boils, add the pasta, stir, and cook just until al dente. Drain and transfer to a large serving bowl. Toss the pasta with the sautéed bean mixture, the tomatoes, and the grated cheese.

Serve immediately.

PER 13-OUNCE SERVING: 414 CALORIES, 17.4 G PROTEIN, 6.7 G FAT, 71.8 G CARBOHYDRATES, 2.2 G SATURATED FATTY ACIDS, 6.5 MG CHOLESTEROL, 300.8 MG SODIUM, 7.9 G TOTAL DIETARY FIBER

pad thai

Pad Thai is probably the most popular item on most Thai restaurant menus. In Thailand, this one-dish meal can be served at any time, from an early-morning breakfast to a midnight snack. Every street vendor in Bangkok has his or her own version.

We highly recommend a healthy squeeze of fresh lime to finish this dish.

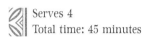
Serves 4
Total time: 45 minutes

8-ounce package of ¼-inch-wide rice stick noodles

2 tablespoons rice vinegar

2 tablespoons soy sauce

1 to 2 teaspoons Chinese chili paste

1 tablespoon tamarind concentrate (page 471)

½ cup water

3 tablespoons vegetable oil

8 ounces firm tofu, cut into ½-inch cubes

1 cup diced red bell peppers

1 cup snow peas, strings removed

2 large eggs, lightly beaten

3 tablespoons chopped fresh cilantro

chopped peanuts, mung bean sprouts, lime wedges

Soak the noodles in warm water for 20 minutes, until soft and limp. Meanwhile, combine the vinegar, soy sauce, chili paste, tamarind, and water in a small bowl and set the sauce aside. Drain the soaked noodles, rinse in cold water, and drain well again.

Have all of the prepared ingredients nearby before you begin to stir-fry.

Heat a large wok or skillet on medium-high heat. Pour in 1 tablespoon of the oil and when it's very hot, after about 30 seconds, add the tofu and stir-fry gently for 1 minute. Add the bell peppers and snow peas and stir-fry for another 2 minutes. Remove the tofu and vegetables and set aside.

Add the remaining 2 tablespoons of vegetable oil to the wok. When the oil is hot, pour the eggs into the center and stir briskly for a few seconds. Add the reserved sauce, drained rice noodles, and the tofu and vegetables, and toss well. Cook for 3 or 4 minutes, until the noodles are tender and the mixture is dry.

Transfer the Pad Thai to a large platter and sprinkle with the cilantro. Add a smattering of peanuts and mung sprouts and surround the noodles with lime wedges. Serve immediately.

PER 10-OUNCE SERVING: 433 CALORIES, 12.7 G PROTEIN, 17.2 G FAT, 57.1 G CARBOHYDRATES, 4.3 G SATURATED FATTY ACIDS, 132.2 MG CHOLESTEROL, 558.3 MG SODIUM, 3 G TOTAL DIETARY FIBER

pasta with asparagus & lemon

Adapted from a Faith Willinger recipe, this simple, fresh-tasting dish is a celebration of new spring asparagus. We've chosen penne and casarecce for this recipe because their shapes resemble bite-sized asparagus pieces. Penne is a tube-shaped pasta, and casarecce is a double-tubed pasta that looks like a miniature rolled-up scroll.

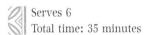
Serves 6
Total time: 35 minutes

1 ½ pounds asparagus
1 pound penne or casarecce pasta
¼ cup fresh lemon juice
¼ cup extra-virgin olive oil
 salt and black pepper to taste
¼ cup grated Pecorino or
    Parmesan cheese

Bring a large pot of salted water to a boil for the pasta.

Meanwhile, rinse the asparagus, snap off the tough lower stems, and discard them. Cut off 1 ½ inches of the asparagus tips and reserve. Chop the rest of the stems. Cook the asparagus tips in boiling water to cover for 3 or 4 minutes, until tender. Remove to a colander with a slotted spoon and set aside. In the same pot blanch the chopped asparagus stems for 6 or 7 minutes, until tender. Drain, rinse in cold water, and reserve separately.

Cook the pasta in the boiling water until al dente. While the pasta cooks, purée the asparagus stems, lemon juice, and olive oil in a blender or food processor until smooth. If necessary, add a little of the hot pasta water. Add salt and pepper to taste.

Drain the pasta and transfer it to a large bowl. Stir in the asparagus purée, the asparagus tips, and the grated cheese. If the pasta has cooled, stir it in a pot on high heat for 1 or 2 minutes, until hot. Serve immediately.

PER 12-OUNCE SERVING: 433 CALORIES, 15.4 G PROTEIN, 13 G FAT, 64.8 G CARBOHYDRATES,
2.7 G SATURATED FATTY ACIDS, 4.5 MG CHOLESTEROL, 115 MG SODIUM, 4.5 G TOTAL DIETARY FIBER

middle eastern lentils & pasta

Kosherie is the traditional name for this dish. It is made of lentils, macaroni, and rice, flavored with a hot sauce and wonderful crispy onions. It's popular in Egypt, in both city and country-side, and you might call it fast food Egyptian-style. In Cairo there are restaurants where kosherie is the only offering and small, medium, or large the only choice. Imagine the day when we can buy food like this from an American fast food chain!

Even though there are several parts to this dish, nothing is really difficult to do. Just think of it as a dance on top of the stove: Pots bubbling away on every burner waiting for the right moment to step in and take the lead. Setting a timer or two is probably not a bad idea to help you keep the rhythm.

If you prefer brown basmati rice to white, begin to cook it as your first step.

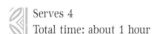
Serves 4
Total time: about 1 hour

lentils

³/4 cup lentils
3 cups water
¹/2 teaspoon salt

hot sauce

4 cups coarsely chopped fresh
   tomatoes
2 garlic cloves, minced or pressed
1 fresh green chile, chopped
1 tablespoon vegetable oil
1 tablespoon red wine vinegar
1 teaspoon salt

rice

1 cup white basmati rice
1 teaspoon vegetable oil
1¹/2 cups water
¹/2 teaspoon salt

pasta

vegetable oil for frying
4 cups thinly sliced small onions
¹/4 teaspoon salt
1¹/2 quarts salted water
1¹/2 cups elbow macaroni

In a small covered saucepan, bring the lentils, water, and salt to a boil. Reduce the heat and simmer until tender, about 40 minutes; stir occasionally. When the lentils are done, drain them if all of the water has not been absorbed.

While the lentils cook, purée the tomatoes, garlic, chile, oil, vinegar, and salt in a blender. Transfer to a small saucepan and bring to a boil. Reduce the heat and simmer briskly, uncovered, until thick, about 20 to 25 minutes. Stir occasionally as the sauce begins to cook, and more frequently as it thickens.

While the lentils and hot sauce simmer, cook the rice. Rinse the rice well in a sieve and drain. Warm the oil in a saucepan and add the rice, water, and salt. Cover and bring to a boil; then reduce the heat and simmer on very low heat, until the water is absorbed and the rice is done, about 15 minutes.

Meanwhile, pour about $1/2$ inch of oil into a medium cast-iron or nonstick skillet. On high heat, warm the oil until it is very hot, almost smoking. Add about half of the onions. Fry, stirring often, until the onions are quite brown, about 10 minutes. Remove and drain on paper towels. Sprinkle the onions with $1/8$ teaspoon of the salt. Repeat with the rest of the onions.

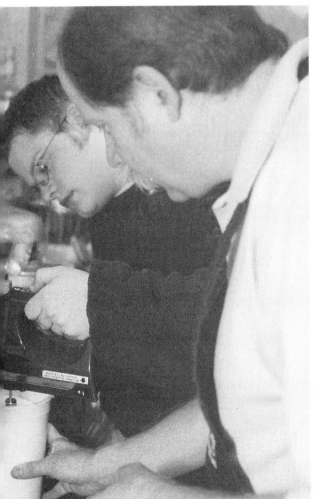

As you begin to fry the second batch of onions, bring a pot of salted water to a boil for the macaroni. By now the hot sauce has probably finished cooking, so you have a free burner! Cook the pasta until al dente and then drain.

To serve, mound the cooked lentils, macaroni, and rice in adjoining piles on a large platter. Sprinkle with the fried onions and top with some of the hot sauce.

Serve immediately and pass the rest of the hot sauce at the table.

PER 23-OUNCE SERVING: 542 CALORIES, 19.1 G PROTEIN, 7.1 G FAT, 103.3 G CARBOHYDRATES, 1.6 G SATURATED FATTY ACIDS, 0 MG CHOLESTEROL, 1,373.8 MG SODIUM, 12.1 G TOTAL DIETARY FIBER

pasta with easy summer sauce

What could be better in hot weather than a sauce that needs no cooking at all? Our Easy Summer Sauce only requires a bit of chopping, and the green beans in the recipe cook right along with the pasta.

Intensely flavorful little grape tomatoes launch the tomato season, but you can use a variety of vine-ripened tomatoes diced into ½-inch pieces. If you wish, use more tomatoes than we call for—even doubling the amount. Just for fun, try making the sauce with a multi-colored assortment of heirloom tomatoes.

Pair the pasta with Three Seed Whole Wheat Rolls (page 401), grilled zucchini slices, or Braised Fennel with Parmesan (page 120), and serve lots of juicy fruit for dessert.

Serves 4 to 6
Total time: 45 minutes

2 cups quartered grape or cherry tomatoes*
¼ cup minced fresh parsley
2 tablespoons minced fresh basil
½ cup minced red onions
1 garlic clove, minced or pressed
¼ cup chopped black olives
¼ cup extra-virgin olive oil
1 teaspoon salt
½ teaspoon coarsely ground black pepper
2 teaspoons balsamic vinegar (optional)**
1 pound farfalle or other short chunky pasta
2 cups cut green beans (2-inch pieces)
½ cup crumbled feta cheese, or more to taste

* Or any variety of tomato diced into ½-inch pieces.
** Taste the tomato mixture to decide if your tomatoes "want" the additional vinegar.

Bring a large covered pot of salted water to a boil.

Meanwhile, combine the tomatoes, parsley, basil, red onions, garlic, olives, oil, salt, pepper, and vinegar, if using, in a large bowl.

When the water boils, stir in the pasta, cover, and cook for 2 to 3 minutes. When the water returns to a boil, add the green beans and cook for 8 to 10 minutes, until the pasta is al dente and the beans are tender. Drain well.

Add the pasta and green beans to the bowl with the seasoned tomatoes. Stir in the feta cheese and gently toss everything together. Serve hot or at room temperature.

PER 13.5-OUNCE SERVING: 480 CALORIES, 13.5 G PROTEIN, 16.7 G FAT, 70.4 G CARBOHYDRATES, 3.3 G SATURATED FATTY ACIDS, 8.4 MG CHOLESTEROL, 823.4 MG SODIUM, 5.6 G TOTAL DIETARY FIBER

pasta with zucchini & mascarpone

Of course, you can make this pasta almost any time of year, but it's a really lovely, delicate dish when the zucchini is at its seasonal best: small and firm with glossy skin. A large nonstick skillet works best here, but if you don't have one, a large cast-iron frying pan will do. However, you may need to add about 3 tablespoons of the pasta cooking water to the sautéing zucchini to prevent sticking.

Accompany this pasta with a chewy bread, Perfect Tomato Salad (page 112), a side of green beans, and maybe juicy, ripe sliced peaches for dessert.

Serves 4 to 6
Total time: 40 minutes

2 teaspoons olive oil
2 cups finely chopped onions
6 cups sliced baby zucchini*
3 garlic cloves, minced or pressed
1 pound farfalle (bow-tie pasta)
2 tablespoons fresh lemon juice
1 cup mascarpone cheese
2 pinches of freshly grated nutmeg
1/4 cup grated Parmesan cheese
freshly ground black pepper
    (optional)

Slice the zucchini in half lengthwise and then cut into 1/2-inch-thick semi-circles.

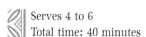Bring a large covered pot of salted water to a boil.

Meanwhile, heat the oil in a large skillet and sauté the onions on medium-high heat for about 5 minutes, stirring frequently. Add the zucchini and garlic and sauté, stirring frequently, until the zucchini is crisp-tender, 7 or 8 minutes. Cover to keep warm until the pasta is ready.

When the water boils, add the pasta, stir, and cover the pot. When it returns to a boil, uncover the pot and cook the pasta until al dente. Drain and transfer it to a large warmed bowl.

Stir the lemon juice, mascarpone cheese, and nutmeg into the sautéed zucchini. Add the skillet mixture along with all of the pan juices to the pasta and toss well. Sprinkle with the grated cheese and, if you wish, add pepper.

Serve hot.

PER 14-OUNCE SERVING: 464 CALORIES, 15.3 G PROTEIN, 13.6 G FAT, 73.6 G CARBOHYDRATES, 6.3 G SATURATED FATTY ACIDS, 28.8 MG CHOLESTEROL, 123.5 MG SODIUM, 5.1 G TOTAL DIETARY FIBER

roasted vegetables for pasta

Roasted vegetables served on a bed of pasta puts a new spin on classic comfort food. Try them topped with a sprinkling of Parmesan or feta cheese.

To ensure even cooking and a pleasing appearance, cut all of the vegetables into approximately 1-inch cubes or pieces. Seed the zucchini if it has a very seedy center. Roasted vegetables are best served soon after baking. If you're not serving them right away, leave them on the baking sheet; when hot roasted vegetables sit in a serving bowl for too long, they steam and lose some of their special roasted texture.

 Serves 4
Preparation time: 30 minutes
Roasting time: 30 minutes

2 cups chopped onions

2 cups chopped green or red bell peppers

2 cups quartered and sliced zucchini

3 cups chopped cremini or portabello mushrooms

4 cups chopped fresh tomatoes

¼ cup olive oil

4 garlic cloves, minced or pressed

1½ teaspoons ground fennel seeds

2 teaspoons salt

½ teaspoon ground black pepper

¼ cup chopped fresh basil

1 pound orzo, orecchiette, or conchigliette

Preheat the oven to 400°.

Place the onions, bell peppers, zucchini, mushrooms, and tomatoes in a large bowl. In a small bowl, whisk together the olive oil, garlic, fennel, salt, and pepper. Pour the seasoned oil over the vegetables and toss to coat well.

Spread the vegetables in a single layer on one or two nonreactive baking sheets. Roast for 15 minutes, remove from the oven, stir in the basil, and return the baking sheet to the oven. Roast for 10 minutes more, stir again, and continue to roast until the vegetables are tender and browned, about 5 minutes.

While the vegetables are roasting, bring a large pot of salted water to a boil. Cook the pasta until al dente. Drain and serve immediately topped with the roasted vegetables.

PER 26-OUNCE SERVING: 670 CALORIES, 19.3 G PROTEIN, 17.6 G FAT, 112.1 G CARBOHYDRATES, 2.4 G SATURATED FATTY ACIDS, 0 MG CHOLESTEROL, 1,222.9 MG SODIUM, 9.8 G TOTAL DIETARY FIBER

vegetable pho with shrimp

Many good Vietnamese dishes are a beautiful marriage of Southeast Asian with French and Chinese cuisines, evidence that creativity can blossom under the most adverse circumstances.

The stock may be made ahead of time, and even frozen, but the soup should be served as soon as it's ready. To garnish with fried shallots, check out the recipe in *Moosewood Restaurant Daily Special*, page 343.

Don't combine leftover soup and rice noodles: *pho* disintegrate when kept in liquid. Store *pho* and soup separately or make fresh noodles to use with reheated soup.

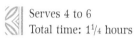 Serves 4 to 6
Total time: 1¼ hours

✳ Combine the onions, carrots, celery, garlic, lemongrass, ginger root, and 7 cups of water in a 4-quart pot. Add the shrimp shells and bring to a boil, then lower the heat, cover, and simmer for 20 minutes. Strain the stock, return it to the pot, add 1 cup of water, and set aside.

In a second pot, bring 2 quarts of water to a boil. Stir in the rice noodles and cook until al dente. Drain, rinse, and drain again. Toss with the sesame oil and set aside.

Return the stock to a simmer, add the carrots and green beans, and cook for 2 minutes. Add the shrimp and cook until pink, 2 more minutes. Remove from the heat and stir in the lime juice, cilantro, fish sauce, salt, and pepper.

Evenly apportion sprouts and noodles into soup bowls. Ladle on the soup and top with scallions, onions, or fried shallots.

stock

2 cups chopped onions

1 cup peeled and chopped carrots

⅓ cup chopped celery

4 large garlic cloves, peeled

12-inch fresh lemongrass stalk, cut into 2-inch pieces

2-inch piece of peeled ginger root

shells of ½ pound medium shrimp, shrimp reserved

soup

½ pound rice stick noodles (¼ inch wide)

1 tablespoon dark sesame oil

2 cups 1-inch carrot matchsticks

2 cups 1-inch cut green beans*

2 tablespoons fresh lime juice

2 tablespoons minced fresh cilantro

2 to 4 tablespoons fish sauce

½ to 1 teaspoon salt to taste

½ teaspoon ground black pepper

2 cups mung or soybean sprouts

minced scallions, red onions, or fried shallots

* *Or use 2 cups thinly sliced snow peas added at the same time as the lime juice.*

PER 11.5-OUNCE SERVING: 237 CALORIES, 11.1 G PROTEIN, 3.4 G FAT, 42.1 G CARBOHYDRATES, 0.5 G SATURATED FATTY ACIDS, 67.8 MG CHOLESTEROL, 730.9 MG SODIUM, 5.6 G TOTAL DIETARY FIBER

trenette al pesto

This appealing green and white dish is a regional Italian classic in Liguria, particularly in Genoa, although our version has more green beans than is typical. Trenette is a square-cut ribbon pasta, which, cooked with green beans and potatoes and coated with pesto, makes a satisfying meal.

The starch from the potatoes makes this seem almost creamy. Any potato will do, but we prefer waxier kinds, such as Yukon Gold, because they hold their shape. Choose a good firm pasta, such as DeCecco brand.

Made with purchased pesto sauce, this pasta dish couldn't be easier; however, it takes only minutes to make fresh pesto, and it tastes way better. Pesto made without cheese freezes very well, so when basil is abundant, make extra pesto and freeze some.

Serve with Flavored Olives (page 213), Bread Sticks (page 394), Perfect Tomato Salad (page 112), a glass of wine, fresh fruit, and Black Forest Biscotti (page 407) with espresso.

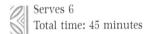
Serves 6
Total time: 45 minutes

pesto sauce

2 garlic cloves, minced or pressed

2 cups packed fresh basil leaves

1/4 cup lightly toasted pine nuts

1/2 cup grated Parmesan cheese

1/2 teaspoon salt, or more to taste

6 to 8 tablespoons extra-virgin
   olive oil

2 or 3 medium potatoes, preferably
   Yukon Gold

1 pound green beans, trimmed

1 pound pasta, such as trenette,
   linguine, or casarecce

extra-virgin olive oil and/or grated
   Parmesan cheese (optional)

Bring a large covered pot of salted water to a boil.

Meanwhile, in a food processor or blender, combine the pesto ingredients and purée until you have a rough paste, scraping down the sides as necessary. You will have about 1 cup.

Peel the potatoes. Cut them lengthwise into quarters and then crosswise into 1/4-inch slices to make about 2 cups. Cut the green beans into 2-inch lengths to make about 4 cups.

When the water is boiling vigorously, add the potatoes and then the pasta. Stir well and cover. After 2 minutes, add the green beans, stir, and cover. When the pasta is al dente, about 5 minutes, drain, reserving 2 cups of the cooking water. Test the pasta frequently to avoid overcooking.

In a large serving bowl, toss together the pasta and vegetables, the pesto sauce, and about 1 cup of the cooking water. Add more cooking water as needed to coat the pasta with a moist sauce.

Serve immediately. At the table, pass a cruet of good olive oil for drizzling over the pasta and extra grated cheese, if you wish.

PER 13-OUNCE SERVING: 552 CALORIES, 18.2 G PROTEIN, 23.9 G FAT, 68.2 G CARBOHYDRATES, 5.2 G SATURATED FATTY ACIDS, 74.3 MG CHOLESTEROL, 430.1 MG SODIUM, 7.1 G TOTAL DIETARY FIBER

variation 🌿 *Try with Garlic Scape Pesto (page 374), substitute cauliflower or fresh fava beans for the green beans, and top with diced fresh tomatoes.*

greens & soft polenta

Recently, we've seen versions of this rustic dish on several up-scale restaurant menus—traditional peasant food morphing into gourmet cuisine. Sautéed greens make a good foil for the soft polenta. Try polenta with other greens, too, such as escarole, endive, arugula, or Swiss chard.

 Serves 4 as a main dish, 6 to 8 as a side dish
Total time: 30 minutes

1 bunch of broccoli rabe

polenta
3 cups water
1 cup cornmeal
1/2 teaspoon salt
1/2 teaspoon ground fennel seeds
1/2 cup grated Parmesan cheese
    (optional)
ground black pepper to taste

1 tablespoon olive oil
2 or 3 garlic cloves, minced or
    pressed
1/4 teaspoon salt

Cut off and discard the tough bottoms of the broccoli rabe stems. Coarsely chop the broccoli rabe, stems and all, to make about 6 cups. Rinse well and set aside in a colander to drain.

Bring the water to a boil in a large pot and slowly pour in the cornmeal while stirring briskly with a whisk or a wooden spoon. Break up any lumps that form. Simmer on low heat, stirring frequently, until the polenta is thick and tastes done (see Note). Stir in the salt, fennel, and the cheese, if using. Add pepper to taste.

Meanwhile, heat the oil in a heavy pan. Add the garlic and salt and sauté on medium heat just until the garlic is golden. Add the broccoli rabe, increase the heat to medium-high, and cook, stirring frequently, for 3 to 5 minutes or until tender. Set aside until the polenta is done.

Serve the polenta in a bowl with the broccoli rabe on top or stirred in.

PER 5.5-OUNCE SERVING: 98 CALORIES, 3.1 G PROTEIN, 2.3 G FAT, 17 G CARBOHYDRATES, 0.3 G SATURATED FATTY ACIDS, 0 MG CHOLESTEROL, 237.5 MG SODIUM, 2.8 G TOTAL DIETARY FIBER

note *The coarseness of the grind, variety of corn, and whether or not it's roasted all influence the cornmeal-water ratio and the cooking time. Finely ground cornmeal might be done after just a few minutes of simmering; coarsely ground and stone-ground cornmeals may need to simmer for up to 45 minutes. With any cornmeal, you may need to add hot water during cooking.*

moroccan roasted vegetables

The colorful roasted vegetables in this recipe are softer and saucier than typical roasted vegetables, but the high heat and rapid cooking still infuse the vegetables with a roasted flavor and an intoxicating aroma.

Serve over a grain, such as couscous, topped with toasted almonds, raisins, chopped hard-cooked eggs, or grated feta cheese for a balanced, ready-to-eat meal.

 Serves 4
Preparation time: 30 minutes
Baking time: 40 minutes

1 medium onion, cut into 1/4-inch slices*

1 medium zucchini, cut into 1/4-inch-thick semi-circles*

1 small eggplant, cut into 1/2-inch-thick semi-circles*

1 large sweet potato, peeled and cut into 1/4-inch-thick semi-circles*

1 large red bell pepper, sliced into 1/4-inch strips*

2 medium fresh tomatoes, chopped*

1 1/2 cups cooked chickpeas (15.5-ounce can, drained)

3 garlic cloves, minced or pressed

2 tablespoons vegetable oil

1 tablespoon fresh lemon juice

1 tablespoon ground cumin

1 1/2 teaspoons turmeric

1 1/2 teaspoons ground cinnamon

1 1/2 teaspoons paprika

1/4 teaspoon cayenne

2 teaspoons salt

 Preheat the oven to 400°.

In a large bowl, thoroughly mix together the onions, zucchini, eggplant, sweet potatoes, bell peppers, tomatoes, chickpeas, garlic, oil, lemon juice, and seasonings.

Spread the vegetables onto an unoiled 11 x 17-inch baking tray. Bake for 20 minutes. Remove from the oven and stir well; then bake for another 20 minutes, until the vegetables are tender.

Serve warm.

If you like measuring, aim for 1 1/2 to 3 cups of each vegetable—about 11 to 12 cups total.

PER 15-OUNCE SERVING: 296 CALORIES, 8.1 G PROTEIN, 9.5 G FAT, 48.8 G CARBOHYDRATES, 2.2 G SATURATED FATTY ACIDS, 0 MG CHOLESTEROL, 1473.1 MG SODIUM, 10.3 G TOTAL DIETARY FIBER

roasted winter vegetables

Here in the Finger Lakes region of New York State, the kitchen becomes a toasty haven come the first chilly nights of autumn. As these vegetables slowly roast, the room fills with an aroma that is both earthy and divine.

The root vegetables that come in the later harvests particularly lend themselves to roasting. The sweetness of the onions and carrots intensifies as their sugars caramelize and the creamy potatoes develop a crisp crust. They are perfect partners for the sharper flavors of parsnips and turnips.

The carrots should be cut in half lengthwise and then sliced into $^1/_2$-inch semi-circles, so they'll be tender when the other vegetables are ready. For even roasting cut the parsnips, turnips, and potatoes into 1-inch cubes.

Serves 4
Preparation time: 20 minutes
Baking time: about 1 hour

$^1/_4$ cup olive oil

1 tablespoon cider vinegar

$1^1/_2$ tablespoons dried sage

2 teaspoons dried thyme

3 teaspoons salt

$^1/_4$ teaspoon ground black pepper

2 cups coarsely chopped onions

2 cups peeled and sliced carrots

2 cups peeled and cubed parsnips

2 cups peeled and cubed turnips

2 cups cubed potatoes*

grated feta, Parmesan, or Cheddar
   cheese (optional)

* *Yukon Gold, Butter, or red-skinned potatoes are creamy, waxy varieties good for roasting.*

Preheat the oven to 450°.

Whisk together the oil, vinegar, sage, thyme, salt, and pepper. Place the onions, carrots, parsnips, turnips, and potatoes in a large bowl and toss well with the seasoned oil mixture to coat the vegetables evenly. Spread in a single layer on an unoiled shallow 11 x 17-inch baking sheet or use two baking sheets.

Bake for about 1 hour, stirring every 20 minutes, until crispy, browned, and tender. Serve topped with a little grated cheese, if you wish.

PER 13-OUNCE SERVING: 323 CALORIES, 4.8 G PROTEIN, 15.2 G FAT, 45.3 G CARBOHYDRATES, 2.1 G SATURATED FATTY ACIDS, 0 MG CHOLESTEROL, 1,860.5 MG SODIUM, 5.3 G TOTAL DIETARY FIBER

lovely low-fat latkes

Latkes are a traditional favorite for the Jewish holiday of Hanukkah, but you can enjoy our delectable low-fat version any time. We use matzo meal because it makes the pancakes lighter than flour will. Some people find hand-grating the vegetables produces the very best latkes, but a good-quality food processor will also work.

To hand-grate a peeled onion, pat it dry and hold onto it with an all-purpose gripping cloth or a small dish cloth.

Serve with Simplest Ever Applesauce (page 384) or Light Sour Cream (page 376).

Serves 6 to 8
Preparation time: 15 minutes
Baking time: 25 to 30 minutes

8 cups peeled, grated, and drained potatoes (6 or 7 potatoes)*

1 cup peeled, grated, and drained onions*

2 eggs, lightly beaten

1/4 cup matzo meal

1 teaspoon salt

1 teaspoon baking powder

1/4 teaspoon ground black pepper, or more to taste

2 tablespoons minced fresh chives, Italian parsley, and/or scallions (optional)

1 to 2 teaspoons vegetable oil

We like Yukon Gold or Butter potatoes. Drain the grated potatoes and onions in a colander, pressing out as much liquid as possible with a fork: the drier the potato mixture, the lighter the latkes.

Preheat the oven to 425°. Lightly spray two nonstick baking sheets with oil.

In a bowl, mix together the potatoes and onions and stir in the eggs. Sprinkle in the matzo meal, salt, baking powder, and pepper and mix well. If you wish, add the chives, parsley, and/or scallions.

Drop well-spaced, generous tablespoons of batter onto the prepared trays. Gently flatten the batter with a spatula or the bottom of a glass: Use just enough pressure to even out the tops of the latkes.

Bake for 10 to 15 minutes, until the edges are golden brown. Remove from the oven, brush or spray the latkes with the oil, carefully flip them with a spatula, and continue to bake for 15 minutes more, until browned and crisp.

PER 7-OUNCE SERVING: 202 CALORIES, 5.6 G PROTEIN, 2.5 G FAT, 39.8 G CARBOHYDRATES, 0.7 G SATURATED FATTY ACIDS, 66.1 MG CHOLESTEROL, 364.9 MG SODIUM, 3.5 G TOTAL DIETARY FIBER

variation ❀ *Instead of baking, you can use two large nonstick, lightly oiled skillets to fry the latkes. Fry each side for about 5 minutes, spraying or brushing with oil before flipping.*

dressed-up salmon cakes

Many of us remember being served salmon cakes as children; they were mostly made with canned salmon and generally pretty bland. Here we've shifted them into a new dimension with fresh salmon and zesty herbs. Elegant, yet easy to prepare, they can also be made into appetizer-sized portions for a party.

The mix can be prepared a day ahead and refrigerated until you shape the cakes, coat them, and fry them. Accompany the cakes with wedges of fresh lemon and squeeze on the juice to taste or top with our easy Herbed Mayonnaise, which will keep in the refrigerator for 2 or 3 days.

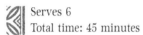

Serves 6
Total time: 45 minutes

2 1/2 cups chopped potatoes

1 cup chopped onions

1 cup peeled and chopped carrots

1 1/2 pounds salmon, skinned and cut into 1-inch pieces

1 egg

1 tablespoon prepared mayonnaise, reduced-fat or regular

1 tablespoon Dijon mustard

1 tablespoon fresh lemon juice

1 tablespoon chopped fresh herbs*

1 garlic clove, minced or pressed

1 teaspoon salt

1 teaspoon ground black pepper

1 cup cracker meal or fine, dry bread crumbs**

olive oil for frying

6 wedges of fresh lemon

herbed mayonnaise (optional)

2 tablespoons chopped fresh tarragon or dill

2 tablespoons chopped fresh chives

1 cup prepared mayonnaise, reduced-fat or regular

1 tablespoon fresh lemon or lime juice

* We suggest tarragon, thyme, or marjoram, or a mixture. Or use 2 tablespoons of chopped fresh dill.
** Cracker meal is sold in well-stocked supermarkets and makes a nice, light breading. To make dry bread crumbs, toast slices of bread in a 300° oven for about 20 minutes. Then whirl in a food processor or crush with a rolling pin.

Place the potatoes, onions, and carrots in a large covered saucepan with water to cover. Bring to a boil; then lower the heat and simmer for about 10 minutes, until the vegetables are tender. Place the fish on top of the vegetables, return to a simmer, and cook for about 7 minutes, until the fish flakes easily with a fork. Drain in a colander.

In a large bowl, mash the drained vegetables and fish with a potato masher until thoroughly mixed. Add the egg, mayonnaise, mustard, fresh lemon juice, herbs, garlic, salt, pepper, and 1/4 cup of the cracker meal or bread crumbs. Mix thoroughly.

In a skillet or frying pan, heat about 1/4 inch of oil until it sizzles. (Less oil is needed in a nonstick frying pan.) With the cracker meal or bread crumbs handy and working over a large plate, pat and shape the fish mixture into six cakes. As you finish each one, sprinkle both sides with cracker meal and carefully place it in the pan.

Fry the cakes for about 4 minutes on the first side, until golden brown and crisped. Then flip the cakes and cook for 2 or 3 minutes on the other side. Drain on paper towels to absorb some of the oil.

Serve with lemon wedges, or combine all of the Herbed Mayonnaise ingredients to offer, if you wish.

PER 8-OUNCE SERVING: 348 CALORIES, 23.6 G PROTEIN, 14.9 G FAT, 30 G CARBOHYDRATES, 3.1 G SATURATED FATTY ACIDS, 99.6 MG CHOLESTEROL, 610.4 MG SODIUM, 4 G TOTAL DIETARY FIBER

note ❧ *Salmon Cakes are a good candidate for cooking with less oil in a ridged grill pan. Spray a nonstick grill pan with a light coating of oil. Cook the cakes for about 4 minutes on each side, until golden brown.*

casseroles
&other
baked
dishes

casseroles & other baked dishes ❧

At restaurants, it's fun to order several appetizers or tapas and create a meal from an assortment of dishes. But at home, there's a lot to be said for a dinner that is one generous baking dish filled to the brim with a luscious, golden brown casserole or pie, bubbling hot. Getting hungry? Put on your oven mitts—get ready for rich gratins, baked pasta, savory pies, juicy stuffed vegetables, baked polenta, and spicy baked fish hot from the oven.

One of the best things about baked dishes is the wonderful way their flavors are absorbed and blended in the oven. The oven's heat makes them brown or crisp on top, yet moist and tender inside without a lot of oil or fat. By using lids or foil, you can control the rate of browning and reduce the liquids in the dish a little or a lot. Although many casseroles bake for quite a while, they don't take long to prepare, so you can assemble the dish and then leave it alone in the oven while you turn your attention to fixing a simple salad or dessert, or perhaps just put up your feet.

At home, some of us may be tempted to turn to baked dishes like those that follow only when there is a cold snap in the air, but at Moosewood, baked dishes like Caramelized Onion Tart and Breaded Polenta Cutlets satisfy our customers' yens year-round. Most casseroles can be partially or completely baked, and then frozen for future use. Leftovers frozen in individual portions make convenient no-fuss meals later.

Baked one-dish meals are easy to carry and retain heat well during transport. They are perfect for potluck suppers or can be assembled at home and then baked at a friend's house. And when relatives or friends are coming and you want to serve great home-cooked meals and still have time for a visit, just prepare one of the baked dishes in this section ahead of time and pop it in the oven when it's time to eat.

apple onion cheese gratin

Rich with sharp cheese and walnuts, sweet with apples and onions, this delicious and unusual gratin makes a wonderful autumn meal.

Serve it beside Wild Rice Pilaf (page 147) or Kasha with Red Cabbage (page 142) and a salad of bitter greens.

 Serves 4 to 6
Preparation time: 30 minutes
Baking time: 45 minutes

1 cup milk

1 tablespoon butter

1 tablespoon unbleached white flour

1/2 teaspoon ground nutmeg

1/2 teaspoon salt

pinch of ground cloves

4 cups peeled, cored, and sliced apples, such as Mutsu

1 cup chopped onions

2 cups grated Cheddar or Gruyère cheese

1 cup chopped walnuts

1 cup bread crumbs*

* For a slightly sweeter gratin, mix 2 table-spoons of brown sugar with the bread crumbs. This will bring out the flavor of the apples.

Preheat the oven to 350°. Lightly oil an 11 x 7-inch baking dish.

In a small pot, scald the milk, bringing it almost but not quite to a boil. In another small pot, melt the butter and whisk in the flour. Slowly add the scalded milk, whisking continuously until the sauce starts to thicken. Add the nutmeg, salt, and cloves and stir for about a minute, until thick. Remove from the heat and set aside.

Spread the apples and onions evenly in the prepared baking dish. Sprinkle on the grated cheese and pour the sauce over the top. Scatter on the walnuts and bread crumbs (seasoned with brown sugar, if you like).

Bake uncovered for 45 minutes, until the top is golden and crisp.

PER 6.5-OUNCE SERVING: 326 CALORIES, 12.1 G PROTEIN, 21.6 G FAT, 24.1 G CARBOHYDRATES, 8.3 G SATURATED FATTY ACIDS, 35.7 MG CHOLESTEROL, 437.5 MG SODIUM, 3.9 G TOTAL DIETARY FIBER

italian gratin

This easy dish has everything you might want in a great homestyle meal—a few vegetables, a little pasta, some cheese, and the cachet of sunny Italian flair.

Serve it with a romaine salad or a creamy soup, such as Fennel Leek Soup (page 76).

 Serves 6
Preparation time: 30 minutes
Baking time: 50 minutes

1 cup diced onions

3 tablespoons chopped fresh basil

1/2 teaspoon salt

3 cups undrained crushed tomatoes
(28-ounce can)

1 tablespoon olive oil

3/4 cup bread crumbs*

1 garlic clove, minced or pressed

3/4 cup raw orzo

2 cups rinsed, stemmed, and chopped
fresh spinach

4 cups sliced mushrooms

2 cups grated Parmesan cheese

* Pulverize stale or lightly toasted whole
wheat, sourdough, or French bread in a
blender or food processor.

Preheat the oven to 350°. Lightly oil an 11 x 7-inch casserole dish.

In a bowl, mix together the onions, basil, salt, and tomatoes. Set aside. Warm the oil in a small skillet and sauté the bread crumbs and garlic until the bread crumbs are lightly browned.

Spread half of the tomato mixture in the bottom of the prepared casserole dish. Sprinkle the orzo over the tomatoes. Layer the spinach, mushrooms, and 1 cup of the Parmesan cheese on top of the orzo. Top with the rest of the tomato mixture. Sprinkle on the remaining cheese and then finish with a layer of the seasoned bread crumbs. Cover tightly with foil.

Bake the gratin for 25 minutes, then uncover and bake for an additional 25 minutes, until lightly browned.

PER 9-OUNCE SERVING: 427 CALORIES, 27 G PROTEIN, 17.6 G FAT, 42.4 G CARBOHYDRATES,
9.3 G SATURATED FATTY ACIDS, 35.7 MG CHOLESTEROL, 1,281.9 MG SODIUM, 5 G TOTAL DIETARY FIBER

caribbean sweet potato gratin

This is a full-bodied main dish substantial enough for the heartiest appetite. Thinly sliced sweet potatoes are a must: they'll cook properly and release enough starch to thicken and set the gratin. Finely chopping the spinach—like the ribbons of a chiffon cut—helps disperse the flavor throughout.

 Serves 6 to 8
Preparation time: 35 minutes
Baking time: 60 minutes

1 garlic clove, minced or pressed
1½ teaspoons freshly grated lime peel
2 tablespoons fresh lime juice
2 tablespoons chopped fresh cilantro
½ teaspoon dried thyme
1½ teaspoons salt
½ teaspoon ground black pepper
2½ cups coconut milk*
4 cups peeled and sliced sweet
    potatoes** (1½ pounds)
1 cup cooked rice
1½ cups cooked black beans
    (15-ounce can, drained)
1½ cups fresh spinach, rinsed,
    stemmed, and chopped

topping

¾ cup cornmeal
1 tablespoon vegetable oil
½ teaspoon dried thyme
¼ teaspoon ground cumin
¼ teaspoon salt

Preheat the oven to 350 °. Lightly oil a 9 x 13-inch baking pan.

Combine the garlic, lime peel and juice, cilantro, thyme, salt, pepper, and coconut milk in a measuring cup. Pour one third of this mixture into the prepared baking pan. Layer half of the sweet potatoes in the bottom, topped by half of the rice, half of the black beans, and half the spinach. Pour on another third of the coconut milk mixture and repeat the layers of sweet potatoes, rice, beans, and spinach. Pour the remaining coconut milk mixture over all.

In a small bowl combine all of the topping ingredients and sprinkle over the gratin.

Bake, uncovered, for about 60 minutes, rotating the pan in the oven after 30 minutes to ensure uniform baking. When the potatoes are tender and the topping is crisp and golden brown, remove from the oven and let sit for 2 to 3 minutes until the potatoes absorb any remaining liquid.

* *About 20 ounces. Most coconut milk comes in 14-ounce cans; store extra in the freezer in a sealed container.*
** *Cut the sweet potatoes in half lengthwise, then slice them thinly.*

PER 8.75-OUNCE SERVING: 343 CALORIES, 7 G PROTEIN, 17.6 G FAT, 42.2 G CARBOHYDRATES, 13.8 G SATURATED FATTY ACIDS, 0 MG CHOLESTEROL, 708.9 MG SODIUM, 5.5 G TOTAL DIETARY FIBER

potato parsnip gratin

This creamy gratin is made in the French country tradition with a combination of root vegetables, Gruyère cheese, and herbs.

The essence of a gratin is the fusion of tastes as the slow-baking ingredients release and exchange their flavors. Slicing the potatoes and parsnips very thinly creates more surfaces that can be permeated with the flavors of the other ingredients. Try to make slices $1/16$ inch thick or less: it's the secret to success for this dish.

Our Potato Parsnip Gratin is a hearty dish well complemented by marinated vegetables, a cooked green vegetable, or a salad of bitter greens. Top off a bistro-style supper with Rustic Plum Tart (page 432).

Serves 4 to 6
Preparation time: 20 minutes
Baking time: 45 to 60 minutes

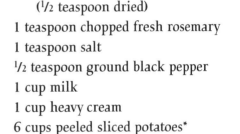

$1/2$ cup chopped shallots or onions

2 garlic cloves, minced or pressed

1 tablespoon minced fresh thyme
   ($1/2$ teaspoon dried)

1 teaspoon chopped fresh rosemary

1 teaspoon salt

$1/2$ teaspoon ground black pepper

1 cup milk

1 cup heavy cream

6 cups peeled sliced potatoes*

2 cups peeled sliced parsnips

1 cup grated Gruyère cheese, lightly
   packed

* *Cut the potatoes in half lengthwise, especially if they are large, and then thinly slice them crosswise.*

Preheat the oven to 350°. Lightly oil a 7 x 11 x 3-inch baking pan.

Combine the shallots, garlic, thyme, rosemary, salt, and pepper. Evenly sprinkle half of this mixture into the bottom of the prepared baking pan. Combine the milk and cream and pour half of it into the pan; it will disperse the other ingredients. Layer with half of the potatoes and half of the parsnips, pressing the vegetables evenly into the milk mixture. Sprinkle with the remaining shallot mixture. Layer on the rest of the parsnips and top with the remaining potatoes. Pour the last of the milk mixture over all and finish with the grated cheese.

Bake, uncovered, for 45 to 60 minutes, until the vegetables are tender and the top is crisp and golden brown. After the first 30 minutes, rotate the pan in the oven to ensure uniform baking. Remove from the oven and let stand for 2 to 3 minutes until the potatoes absorb any remaining liquid.

PER 12-OUNCE SERVING: 422 CALORIES, 11.8 G PROTEIN, 21.9 G FAT, 46.7 G CARBOHYDRATES, 13.9 G SATURATED FATTY ACIDS, 74.5 MG CHOLESTEROL, 508.1 MG SODIUM, 3.2 G TOTAL DIETARY FIBER

lighter lasagna primavera

At Moosewood Restaurant this dish is incredibly popular, and it's a great way to lower cholesterol and boost soy consumption. Whipped tofu melts unobtrusively into the cheese, so the lasagna "sets up" without the addition of eggs.

What's more, you don't have to bother with boiling water at all! Let the asparagus cook to perfection as the lasagna bakes—retaining its color and texture—and don't precook the noodles. It works like a charm.

Serves 6 to 8
Preparation time: 1 hour
Baking time: 1 hour
Sitting time: 10 minutes

tomato sauce

1 1/2 tablespoons olive oil

2 cups diced onions

6 garlic cloves, minced or pressed

1 teaspoon salt

3 cups undrained canned tomatoes, chopped (28-ounce can)

3 cups tomato purée (28-ounce can)

1/4 cup dry red wine

1/4 cup chopped fresh basil

1/4 cup chopped fresh parsley

2 teaspoons dried oregano

2 bay leaves

tofu mixture

1 cake firm tofu, crumbled (12 ounces)

1 3/4 to 2 cups low-fat cottage cheese or part skim ricotta cheese

1/2 cup chopped fresh basil

1 garlic clove, minced or pressed

1/2 teaspoon salt

ground black pepper to taste

pinch of ground nutmeg

1 cup grated low-fat mozzarella cheese

1 cup grated Parmesan cheese

1 pound fresh asparagus, rinsed, stemmed, and chopped (10 ounces frozen asparagus, thawed and chopped)

1 pound lasagna noodles

10 sliced artichoke hearts (two 14-ounce cans, drained)

Preheat the oven to 350°. Brush or spray a deep 9 x 13-inch, nonreactive baking dish with oil.

Combine the oil, onions, garlic, and salt in a nonreactive saucepan. Sauté on medium-high heat until the onions are translucent, about 10 minutes. Add the tomatoes, tomato purée, red wine, basil, parsley, oregano, and bay leaves and simmer for about 10 minutes uncovered. Discard the bay leaves.

While the sauce simmers, combine the crumbled tofu, cottage or ricotta cheese, basil, garlic, and salt in a food processor or blender and purée until smooth. Add pepper and nutmeg to taste. Transfer to a large bowl and stir in $1/2$ cup each of the mozzarella and Parmesan cheeses and all of the chopped asparagus.

Spread $1^1/2$ cups of the tomato sauce on the bottom of the prepared baking dish and top with a single layer of raw lasagna noodles. Spread on half of the tofu mixture and sprinkle with $1/4$ cup each of the remaining mozzarella and Parmesan. Repeat layers of tomato sauce, noodles, and the rest of the tofu mixture. Next, evenly distribute the artichoke hearts and sprinkle on the remaining cheese. Finish with a layer of noodles smothered with tomato sauce; you may not need all of the noodles. Set aside leftover sauce to pass at the table.

Cover tightly with aluminum foil (try to "tent" the foil so that it doesn't rest on the tomato sauce) and bake for 1 hour, or until the pasta is tender. Allow the lasagna to rest for at least 10 minutes before serving. Carefully remove the foil and serve.

PER 19-OUNCE SERVING: 517 CALORIES, 34.7 G PROTEIN, 15.6 G FAT, 63.8 G CARBOHYDRATES, 6.4 G SATURATED FATTY ACIDS, 66.1 MG CHOLESTEROL, 1,649.5 MG SODIUM, 7.9 G TOTAL DIETARY FIBER

sneaking in tofu

At Moosewood, we love tofu. We bake it, broil it, barbeque it. We like big chunks of it in sautés, stews, and sauces. We tuck it into soups, salads, sandwich spreads, smoothies, and burgers. We eat it for snacks.

But we've had to face the fact that not everyone else is as crazy about bean curd as we are (gasp!)—or not yet anyway. So, at the request of customers and friends who "know they should be eating more soy, but . . . ," we've devised a few good transitional dishes in which the tofu is disguised a bit, either mixed with cheese as in Lighter Lasagna Primavera and Macaroni & Cheese with Tofu, or unobtrusively replacing the cheese in dishes filled with other strong flavors as in Tofu Manicotti and Vegan Lasagna.

Tofu adds protein, calcium, and phytonutrients as well as a creamy-seeming bulk, but in a quiet way, without contributing much flavor of its own. Tofu's presence usually eliminates the need for eggs, which may have been used as thickeners, so that even a lasagna can be vegan.

baked ziti with roasted peppers

Impressive is just one of the glowing adjectives that describe this dish. It also is easy to assemble, holds together well, and is easy to serve. The goat cheese, roasted red peppers, and herbs make it incredibly tasty. It even reheats well. What more can you ask for?

 Serves 8 to 10
Preparation time: 1 hour
Baking time: 20 to 30 minutes

In a saucepan, warm the oil and sauté the onions, garlic, salt, and black pepper on medium heat until the onions are very soft, about 10 minutes. Add the mushrooms and cook until juicy, 5 to 8 minutes, stirring occasionally. Add the tomatoes and simmer on low heat for about 30 minutes. Add the basil just before assembling the ziti.

Meanwhile preheat the broiler. Lightly oil a 9 x 13-inch nonreactive baking pan. Bring a large, covered pot of salted water to a boil.

In a bowl, toss the bell peppers with the oil. Spread them on a baking tray and broil for about 10 minutes, until softened and slightly browned. Set aside and lower the oven temperature to 350°.

When the water boils, add the pasta and cook until al dente, about 7 minutes. While the pasta cooks, stir together the three cheeses, the garlic, basil, and oregano. When the pasta is al dente, drain it and stir it into the cheese mixture.

tomato mushroom sauce

2 tablespoons olive oil
1 cup chopped onions
2 garlic cloves, minced or pressed
1 teaspoon salt
1/2 teaspoon ground black pepper
4 cups chopped mushrooms
3 cups undrained canned tomatoes, chopped (28-ounce can)
3 tablespoons chopped fresh basil

2 red bell peppers, seeded and cut into long strips
2 tablespoons olive oil
1 pound penne or other pasta
1 cup goat cheese
2 cups ricotta cheese
2 cups grated provolone cheese
2 garlic cloves, minced or pressed
1/2 cup chopped fresh basil
1 tablespoon dried oregano

To assemble, spread 2 cups of the tomato sauce in the baking pan. Layer on the pasta and cheese, the roasted peppers, and finally cover with the rest of the tomato sauce. Bake for 20 to 30 minutes until piping hot.

PER 12-OUNCE SERVING: 442 CALORIES, 20.9 G PROTEIN, 19.9 G FAT, 45.3 G CARBOHYDRATES, 9.4 G SATURATED FATTY ACIDS, 38.5 MG CHOLESTEROL, 654.7 MG SODIUM, 2.8 G TOTAL DIETARY FIBER

macaroni & cheese with tofu

Here's everyone's favorite comfort food, good ol' macaroni and cheese, quickly prepared with an easy cheese sauce that's whipped up in the blender. The secret ingredient, tofu, adds protein and calcium to the sauce and makes it lower in fat than a traditional white sauce. And what's more, your kids won't know it's there! This is really champion mac and cheese—who knew?

Serves 4 to 6
Preparation time: 35 to 40 minutes
Baking time: 35 minutes

12 ounces pasta, such as elbows, small shells, farfalle, or any short chunky pasta

cheese sauce

12 ounces low-fat silken tofu

1/2 cup low-fat or skim milk

1/2 cup nonfat plain yogurt

1 cup grated extra-sharp Cheddar cheese, packed

1/4 cup grated Parmesan cheese

1/2 teaspoon minced or pressed garlic cloves

2 teaspoons prepared yellow mustard

1/2 teaspoon salt, more to taste

1/4 teaspoon freshly ground black pepper

1/4 teaspoon turmeric

pinch of nutmeg

1/4 cup minced onions

1/4 cup chopped fresh parsley

1/2 cup bread crumbs mixed with 1/4 cup grated Cheddar cheese

Preheat the oven to 350°. Lightly brush or spray a 2-quart baking dish with oil.

Bring a large covered pot of lightly salted water to a boil. When the water boils, stir in the pasta, cover the pot, and return to a boil. Cook until al dente. Meanwhile, in a blender or food processor, combine all of the Cheese Sauce ingredients and purée or pulse until smooth. Add more salt to taste.

Drain the cooked pasta. In a large bowl, mix together the pasta and cheese sauce. Stir in the onions and parsley and spoon the pasta into the prepared baking dish. Top with the bread crumb mixture.

Bake covered for about 30 minutes, then uncover and bake for 5 minutes more. Serve and eat!

PER 10.5-OUNCE SERVING: 435 CALORIES, 23.1 G PROTEIN, 14 G FAT, 54.3 G CARBOHYDRATES, 6.9 G SATURATED FATTY ACIDS, 31 MG CHOLESTEROL, 556.9 MG SODIUM, 2.9 G TOTAL DIETARY FIBER

tofu manicotti

Vegan! These days, customers at Moosewood request vegan dishes more often than ever, so here's a main dish to please the crowds. The filling is creamy and flavorful with plenty of body and a good balance of basil and spinach. You won't miss the ricotta cheese a bit.

If you want to use our Quick Tomato Sauce, make it first and, while the sauce simmers and the water for the pasta comes to a boil, you can press the tofu and prepare the rest of the ingredients.

Serves 4 to 6
Preparation time: 1 hour
Baking time: 25 to 30 minutes

8 ounces manicotti

10 ounces fresh spinach, rinsed and stemmed

1/2 cup chopped fresh parsley

1/2 cup chopped fresh basil

2 cakes firm tofu (16 ounces each), pressed and crumbled*

1 tablespoon minced garlic

1 tablespoon olive oil

1 teaspoon salt

1/2 teaspoon ground black pepper

1/2 recipe Quick Tomato Sauce (page 382) or 3 cups store-bought sauce

* *Sandwich the tofu between two plates and rest a heavy weight (can or book) on the top plate. Press for about 15 minutes; then drain the expressed liquid from the bottom plate. Crumble the tofu by hand.*

Preheat the oven to 350°. Lightly oil a nonreactive 9 x 12-inch baking dish.

Bring a large covered pot of lightly salted water to a boil. Add the pasta and cook until al dente. Drain carefully, rinse with cold water, and set aside.

Meanwhile, place the still-wet spinach in a large pot, cover, and cook with only the water that clings to the leaves until just wilted, 2 or 3 minutes. Drain well. In a food processor, combine the cooked spinach, parsley, basil, tofu, garlic, olive oil, salt, and pepper. Process until the mixture is creamy and resembles the texture of ricotta cheese.

Pour 1 cup of the tomato sauce into the prepared baking dish. Fill each manicotti shell with the tofu mixture and arrange the shells in the pan in a single layer. Pour the remaining 2 cups of tomato sauce over the filled manicotti, cover with foil, and bake for 25 to 30 minutes.

PER 13-OUNCE SERVING: 332 CALORIES, 19.8 G PROTEIN, 11 G FAT, 42.4 G CARBOHYDRATES, 1.5 G SATURATED FATTY ACIDS, 0 MG CHOLESTEROL, 583.4 MG SODIUM, 3.5 G TOTAL DIETARY FIBER

vegan lasagna

You don't have to be vegan to love this lasagna. It's packed with bold flavors: basil, garlic, olive oil and tomatoes, with portabello mushrooms and spinach to round out the layers. Tofu is a remarkably good stand-in for the usual cheese. If you have a yen for a little extra something on top, sprinkle on some grated soy Parmesan cheese.

 Serves 8
Preparation time: 45 minutes
Baking time: 1 hour

Warm the oil in a saucepan. Add the onions, garlic, basil, salt, and pepper and sauté on medium heat for about 5 minutes. Add the chopped mushrooms and sauté for another 5 minutes. Stir in the tomatoes and wine, bring to a boil, and simmer for 15 minutes, while preparing the filling.

Preheat the oven to 350°. Lightly oil a 9 x 13-inch baking pan.

In a blender or food processor, whirl the oil, basil, spinach, garlic, tofu, salt, and pepper to make a thick, smooth filling. Scrape down the sides with a spatula, as needed.

Spread about one fourth of the tomato sauce on the bottom of the prepared pan. Cover with a layer of noodles, then half of the filling, and ladle on another fourth of the sauce. Repeat the layers of noodles, the rest of the filling, and one fourth of the sauce. Finish with a final layer of noodles and the rest of the sauce.

Cover and bake for about 45 minutes, until the noodles are soft. Uncover and return to the oven for another 15 minutes.

sauce

1 tablespoon vegetable oil

1/2 to 3/4 cup chopped onions

3 garlic cloves, minced or pressed

1 tablespoon dried basil
  (3 tablespoons fresh)

1/2 teaspoon salt

1/4 teaspoon ground black pepper

1 cup chopped portabello or white
  mushrooms

3 cups canned tomatoes with juice,
  chopped (28-ounce can)

1/2 cup dry red wine

filling

1 tablespoon olive oil

1 cup fresh chopped basil

10 ounces fresh spinach, steamed and
  drained

3 garlic cloves, minced or pressed

2 cakes firm tofu (12 ounces each),
  cubed

1 teaspoon salt

1/4 teaspoon ground black pepper

3/4 pound lasagna noodles

PER 10-OUNCE SERVING: 302 CALORIES, 15 G PROTEIN, 9.5 G FAT, 39.5 G CARBOHYDRATES,
1.7 G SATURATED FATTY ACIDS, 40.4 MG CHOLESTEROL, 591.3 MG SODIUM, 2.8 G TOTAL DIETARY FIBER

polenta

Polenta is so synonymous with the Italian-style cornmeal mush, that most people assume polenta *means* corn. But before corn was introduced from the Americas, Italians had always made nutritious and filling polenta from ground chestnuts, wheat, barley, oats, millet, and buckwheat.

Humble polenta has inspired a multitude of dishes that are both enchanting and comforting. When topped with savory sauces, stews, beans, or cheeses, polenta becomes an excellent foundation for a main course. For a hearty side dish, serve polenta plain or fancy. Adorn it simply with butter or a sharp Italian cheese, or go vegan with no cheese but with olives, sun-dried tomatoes, or caramelized onions with ground fennel seeds. Polenta can also be made into delicious cutlets, croutons, or bite-sized appetizers. At Moosewood, we usually serve cutlets with a savory sauce.

You can make polenta with any cornmeal: yellow, white, or blue; finely ground, coarse-ground, or stone-ground; roasted corn or quick-cooking. Finely ground cornmeal makes smooth and creamy polenta; coarsely ground cornmeal gives a more solid texture. But remember, the better the quality of the cornmeal, the better the polenta.

The characteristics of the cornmeal affect the water–cornmeal ratio, the cooking time, and the flavor and texture of the polenta. We recommend starting to cook the polenta with less water and adding more hot water if needed for the consistency you want.

Things to remember when cooking polenta:

- Use your heaviest pot: cast iron, enamel-clad aluminum, stainless steel, and non-stick are all fine. Use a heat diffuser to reduce the risk of scorching.
- The rule of thumb for a basic soft polenta is 3 cups of salted boiling water to 1 cup of cornmeal. For casseroles and cutlets, 2 cups of water to a cup of cornmeal gives a thicker porridge. You can use stock or milk instead of water.
- Pour the cornmeal into the water slowly while stirring briskly with a whisk or wooden spoon.
- Lower the heat as the polenta thickens. Cook it too fast, and the polenta will be gummy. But undercook it, and it will have a raw-corn taste.
- Cooking time can vary from 15 minutes to 1 hour, depending upon the cornmeal. Cornmeal ground specifically for making polenta cooks in about 5 minutes.
- Stir often to avoid lumps and scorching.
- Store leftover polenta poured onto a flat tray and you have a head start on making polenta cutlets. Covered and refrigerated, cooked polenta will keep for up to 4 days.

polenta cutlets with olives

Black olives and sun-dried tomatoes provide little nuggets of flavor in these toothsome cutlets, which can be eaten plain or topped with cooked vegetables or a sauce.

We recommend serving the cutlets topped with Quick Tomato Sauce (page 382) alongside Green Bean & Walnut Salad (page 108) and a side of marinated vegetables, such as asparagus.

 Serves 4 as a main dish, 8 as a side dish
Preparation time: 30 minutes
Sitting time: about 20 minutes
Baking time: 20 minutes

½ cup chopped onions

2 garlic cloves, minced or pressed

½ teaspoon salt

1 tablespoon olive oil

¼ cup chopped sun-dried tomatoes (not oil-packed)

8 to 12 pitted and chopped kalamata or other black olives

1 cup cornmeal

2 cups water or vegetable stock

¼ cup grated Parmesan, mozzarella, Gruyère, or provolone (optional)

In a saucepan, sauté the onions, garlic, and salt in the olive oil on medium heat for about 10 minutes, until the onions are golden. Add the sun-dried tomatoes and the olives and cook for about 3 minutes. Add the cornmeal and stir just until the mixture is dry, less than 1 minute.

Slowly pour in the water or stock and stir briskly until the polenta thickens. Simmer, stirring frequently, until the polenta is creamy (see Note). Pour the polenta onto an oiled baking sheet or baking pans to about ¾-inch thickness. Spread with a rubber spatula for even thickness. Set aside to cool for about 20 minutes. The polenta will thicken as it cools.

Preheat the oven to 375°.

With a table knife, cut the polenta into squares, rectangles, diamonds, or other shapes. With a spatula, transfer the cutlets to a lightly oiled baking sheet and place them about an inch apart. Bake for 15 minutes. For a golden crust, turn the cutlets over, brush lightly with oil, and bake for 5 minutes longer or, if you like, sprinkle the cutlets with grated cheese for the last 5 minutes of baking.

PER 3.5-OUNCE SERVING: 114 CALORIES, 2.5 G PROTEIN, 3.7 G FAT, 18.3 G CARBOHYDRATES, 0.5 G SATURATED FATTY ACIDS, 0 MG CHOLESTEROL, 383.2 MG SODIUM, 2.1 G TOTAL DIETARY FIBER

note *For cutlets, make thick polenta that can still be poured. The amount of water needed and the cooking time will depend on the cornmeal used. Finely ground cornmeal might be done after just a few minutes of simmering; coarsely ground and stone-ground cornmeals may need to simmer for up to 45 minutes. Add more hot water during cooking if the polenta becomes too thick.*

breaded polenta cutlets

Cutting polenta into cutlets transforms it from a soothing side dish to a sophisticated main dish that has a firmer texture and a more formal presentation. Ladle on Wild Mushroom Sauté (page 344) or Roasted Red Pepper Sauce (page 119) for a perfect light dinner.

The preparation time will depend on the type of cornmeal used, so 30 minutes is a middle-of-the-road estimate. Cooked polenta will keep in the refrigerator for 3 or 4 days, so you can make it ahead, pour it out, cover it well, and refrigerate it to use later. Leftover cutlets can be frozen and reheated later.

1 teaspoon salt, or more to taste

2 1/2 cups water

1 cup cornmeal

1 cup chopped onions

1 or 2 garlic cloves, minced or
   pressed

1/2 teaspoon ground fennel seeds

2 tablespoons olive oil

1/2 cup grated Pecorino or Parmesan
   cheese (optional)

1 egg

1/4 cup milk

1 cup herbed bread crumbs*

Serves 4
Preparation time: about 30 minutes
Cooling time: at least 30 minutes
Baking time: 35 minutes

* *Pulverize stale or lightly toasted whole wheat, sourdough, or French bread in a blender or food processor. Mix in 1/4 teaspoon of mixed dried herbs, such as basil, oregano, thyme, and marjoram, and add a dash of salt and black pepper.*

Bring the salt and water to a boil. Gradually pour in the cornmeal and stir briskly with a whisk until the polenta begins to thicken. Lower the heat and simmer, stirring frequently, until the polenta tastes done (see Note).

Meanwhile, sauté the onions, garlic, and fennel in the oil on medium heat for about 7 minutes. Remove the cooked polenta from the heat. Stir in the onions and, if using, the grated cheese. Add salt to taste.

Pour the hot polenta onto an oiled baking tray or 10-inch pie pan to about a 3/4-inch thickness. Spread evenly with a rubber spatula. Refrigerate for at least 30 minutes. The polenta will thicken as it cools.

Preheat the oven to 375° and oil a baking sheet.

In a large bowl, whisk the egg until foamy and then whisk in the milk. Place the bread crumbs in a separate shallow bowl. With a table knife, cut the cooled polenta into squares, rectangles, diamonds, or other shapes. Line up in order the pan of cutlets, the egg mixture, the bread crumbs, and the oiled baking sheet.

Lift one cutlet at a time with a spatula and dip it into the egg mixture. A light coating of egg is best, so gently shake off the excess. Then dip each cutlet in the bowl of bread crumbs and coat well. Arrange the breaded cutlets on the baking sheet about an inch apart.

Bake for 35 minutes until golden brown on both sides, turning once after about 20 minutes.

PER 5-OUNCE SERVING: 163 CALORIES, 4.4 G PROTEIN, 5.5 G FAT, 23.9 G CARBOHYDRATES, 1 G SATURATED FATTY ACIDS, 33.6 MG CHOLESTEROL, 392.6 MG SODIUM, 2.4 G TOTAL DIETARY FIBER

note *A thick but pourable polenta is best for cutlets. The amount of water needed and the cooking time will vary with different cornmeals. Finely ground cornmeal might be done after just a few minutes of simmering; coarsely ground and stone-ground cornmeals may need to simmer for up to 45 minutes. Add more water, if needed, during cooking, until the cornmeal is no longer crunchy and the polenta is the consistency of thick porridge.*

variation *To fry the cutlets, heat olive oil about ¼ inch deep in a skillet and fry the cutlets for 2 to 3 minutes on each side. Serve the cutlets immediately, or keep in a warm oven until ready to serve.*

polenta lasagna

Moosewood menu planner Joan Adler recently introduced this lovely variation on a classic lasagna to the Moosewood Restaurant kitchen. It's quickly become a favorite of our cooks and customers alike. Everyone agrees that creamy polenta blends perfectly with rich mild cheeses and a vibrant tomato sauce.

Polenta Lasagna can be made ahead and kept refrigerated until baking. Or, prepare the polenta layer the night before, and assemble and bake the next evening. It also makes a good leftover.

This tomato sauce is a classic one, but if you have an old favorite recipe, don't hesitate to use it. You need about 7 cups of sauce.

Serves 6 to 8
Preparation time: 1¼ hours
Baking time: 1 hour
Sitting time: 10 minutes

polenta
4 cups water
1 teaspoon salt
1¾ cups cornmeal

sauce
3 tablespoons olive oil
2 cups chopped onions
2 tablespoons minced garlic cloves
2 teaspoons dried basil
1 teaspoon dried marjoram
½ teaspoon dried oregano
1 cup chopped red bell peppers
1 cup chopped green bell peppers
3 cups crushed tomatoes with juice (28-ounce can)
½ cup dry red wine (optional)
3 tablespoons tomato paste
1 teaspoon salt
1 teaspoon ground black pepper

1 cup Neufchâtel or cream cheese
1 large egg
2 cups rinsed, stemmed, and chopped Swiss chard, kale, or spinach
1½ cups grated mild provolone
1 cup grated Parmesan cheese

Bring the water and salt to a boil in a large saucepan. Gradually whisk the cornmeal into the boiling water. Reduce the heat to low and let the polenta simmer, stirring often, until thick but pourable (see Note). Pour the polenta onto a lightly oiled baking sheet. Use a lightly oiled spatula to spread it 1/2 inch thick or less. Refrigerate.

Warm 2 tablespoons of the olive oil in a saucepan on medium-high heat and sauté the onions for 5 minutes. Add the garlic, basil, marjoram, oregano, and bell peppers and sauté for 5 more minutes. Add the tomatoes and, if using, the wine. Bring to a simmer and add the tomato paste, salt, and black pepper. Simmer on low heat for 20 to 30 minutes, stirring occasionally.

Preheat the oven to 350°. Lightly oil a 9 x 13-inch baking pan.

Soften the Neufchâtel or cream cheese in the oven for 3 to 4 minutes. Lightly beat the egg and stir it into the softened cheese. Heat the remaining tablespoon of olive oil in a skillet or saucepan and sauté the greens until tender. Remove from the heat and set aside. Remove the polenta from the refrigerator and cut it into manageable 4 x 6-inch pieces that will fit together to make a single layer in your baking pan; a few gaps don't matter.

To assemble the lasagna, spread a third of the sauce in the bottom of the prepared baking pan and top with a layer of polenta. Add the sautéed greens to the remaining sauce and spread half of it on the polenta. Spread the softened cream cheese over the sauce and top with the provolone. Make a final layer of polenta and top with the rest of the sauce. Dust the Parmesan cheese evenly over all.

Cover the baking dish and bake for 45 minutes. Uncover and bake for 15 minutes more, until lightly browned. Remove from the oven and allow to sit for 10 minutes before serving.

PER 13-OUNCE SERVING: 420 CALORIES, 19.4 G PROTEIN, 20.4 G FAT, 41.6 G CARBOHYDRATES, 9.8 G SATURATED FATTY ACIDS, 38.8 MG CHOLESTEROL, 1,319.2 MG SODIUM, 5.3 G TOTAL DIETARY FIBER

note ♥ *For this dish, make a relatively stiff polenta. The amount of water needed and the cooking time will depend on the cornmeal used. Finely ground cornmeal such as polenta cornmeal cooks quickly and is excellent for this dish. Coarsely ground and stone-ground cornmeals may need to simmer for up to 45 minutes. Any cornmeal may need additional water; start with the amount given and add more if the polenta becomes too thick.*

tofu stuffed portabellos

Portabello mushroom caps are huge, dark, succulent, and eminently stuffable with a wonderful earthy flavor and juicy texture. How great that they're so widely available now.

This dish is a longtime favorite at Moosewood—one of our classics. The tofu stuffing is surprisingly light and turns a beautiful golden brown. We give you enough to stuff four 4½- to 5-inch mushroom caps with ¾ cup of filling each or six 3½- to 4-inch mushroom caps using ½ cup of filling each.

Serve with Mushroom Gravy (page 380) and rice, orzo, or mashed potatoes.

Serves 4 to 6
Preparation time: 20 minutes
Baking time: 25 to 30 minutes

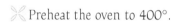

Preheat the oven to 400°.

Heat 1 tablespoon of the oil in a frying pan. Add the onions, peppers, carrots, oregano, basil, and dill and sauté on medium-high heat for about 7 minutes, until the vegetables are just tender. Crumble the pressed tofu into a large bowl. Stir in the walnuts, bread crumbs, tahini, miso, soy sauce, and the mustard, if using. Add the sautéed vegetables and mix well.

Carefully brush or wipe off any soil from the portabellos and twist off the stems. Discard the stems or use later in a soup stock. Rinse the mushroom caps gently, pat dry, and brush with the remaining oil. Place the caps, cavity up, on a nonstick or lightly oiled baking pan. Fill each one with a generous mound of the stuffing (see headnote).

Bake uncovered for 25 to 30 minutes, until the mushrooms release their juices and the filling is set and slightly golden.

3 tablespoons vegetable oil

1 cup diced onions

½ cup diced bell peppers

½ cup peeled and grated carrots

½ teaspoon dried oregano

½ teaspoon dried basil

½ teaspoon dried dill

1 cake firm tofu, pressed (16 ounces)*

⅓ cup chopped walnuts

½ cup bread crumbs**

1 tablespoon tahini

1 tablespoon light miso

1 tablespoon soy sauce

1 tablespoon Dijon mustard (optional)

4 to 6 large portabello mushrooms

* *Sandwich the tofu between two plates and rest a heavy can or book on the top plate. Press for about 15 minutes; then drain the expressed liquid.*
***Pulverize stale or lightly toasted whole wheat, sourdough, or French bread in a blender or food processor.*

PER 8-OUNCE SERVING: 247 CALORIES, 11.4 G PROTEIN, 16.7 G FAT, 17.3 G CARBOHYDRATES, 3.1 G SATURATED FATTY ACIDS, 0 MG CHOLESTEROL, 292 MG SODIUM, 3.7 G TOTAL DIETARY FIBER

italian stuffed portabellos

Portabellos mounded with vegetables and cheese are simply irresistible. They're good for an everyday supper since they're so easily prepared, yet look no further if you want something elegant enough to present at a dinner party.

This dish is nice next to Polenta Cutlets with Olives (page 281) or served on a bed of pasta topped with Quick Tomato Sauce (page 382).

 Serves 4
Preparation time: 30 minutes
Baking time: 20 to 25 minutes

4 large portabello mushrooms
   ($4^1/2$ to 5 inches)

3 tablespoons olive oil

1 cup minced onions

3 garlic cloves, minced or pressed

$2/3$ cup minced red bell peppers

3 tablespoons chopped fresh basil

$2/3$ cup ricotta cheese

1 cup grated mozzarella cheese

$1/4$ cup grated Parmesan cheese

$1/4$ teaspoon salt

2 tablespoons bread crumbs*

* *Pulverize stale or lightly toasted whole wheat, sourdough, or Italian bread in a blender or food processor.*

Preheat the oven to 400°. Lightly oil a baking dish.

Carefully brush or wipe off any soil from the mushrooms. Twist off the stems and discard. Rinse the mushroom caps and pat dry with a towel. In a skillet, warm 2 tablespoons of the olive oil and sauté the onions for about 5 minutes, until they begin to soften. Add the garlic and peppers and sauté for 5 minutes more. Remove from the heat and set aside.

In a bowl, mix together the basil, ricotta cheese, mozzarella, Parmesan, salt, and bread crumbs. Stir the sautéed vegetables into the cheese mixture. Brush the portabellos with the remaining tablespoon of oil and place them gill side up in the prepared baking dish. Mound cheese mixture in each.

Bake uncovered for 20 to 25 minutes, until the mushrooms release their juices and the cheese is melted. Serve hot.

PER 8-OUNCE SERVING: 317 CALORIES, 16.5 G PROTEIN, 22.8 G FAT, 13.8 G CARBOHYDRATES, 8.7 G SATURATED FATTY ACIDS, 40.6 MG CHOLESTEROL, 488.3 MG SODIUM, 2.3 G TOTAL DIETARY FIBER

greek stuffed zucchini

Walnuts, feta, and lemon are some of Moosewood cook Laura Branca's favorite flavors, so she created this Greek-style rice filling and then topped it off with sweet, juicy currants and a tomato sauce fragrant with sherry and cinnamon. All this adds up to an anything-but-bland zucchini dish, true to its Greek lineage.

Nibble some Flavored Olives (page 213) for starters and serve a crisp little cucumber salad as an accompaniment and the meal is complete. A good dessert might be Oya's Peaches & Pistachios (page 436).

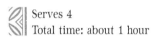
Serves 4
Total time: about 1 hour

zucchini

2 zucchini (10 inches long)
¼ cup dry sherry

cinnamon tomato sauce

2 tablespoons olive oil
1 cup chopped onions
2 garlic cloves, minced or pressed
2 tablespoons tomato paste
3½ cups chopped tomatoes with juice (28-ounce can)
1 teaspoon minced fresh oregano (½ teaspoon dried)
¼ teaspoon ground cinnamon
2 to 4 tablespoons dry sherry
 salt and ground black pepper to taste

filling

1 cup chopped onions
1 or 2 garlic cloves, minced or pressed
1 tablespoon olive oil
¾ to 1 cup finely chopped toasted walnuts*
½ cup crumbled feta cheese
¼ cup currants
3 tablespoons fresh lemon juice
2 cups cooked brown rice

⅓ cup seasoned bread crumbs (optional)
dash of olive oil (optional)
grated feta cheese
fresh oregano leaves (optional)

Toast walnuts in a single layer on an unoiled baking tray at 350° for 5 to 10 minutes, until fragrant and golden brown.

Preheat the oven to 375°. Lightly oil a baking sheet.

Slice the zucchini in half lengthwise. With a paring knife, score the flesh about $1/2$ inch deep. Place the cut sides down on the baking sheet. Sprinkle with the sherry and cover with foil. Bake for about 20 minutes, until yielding but still firm.

While the zucchini bakes, make the sauce. Heat the oil in a saucepan, add the onions and garlic, and sauté for about 10 minutes, until the onions are translucent. Add the tomato paste, tomatoes, oregano, cinnamon, and sherry. Bring to a boil; then reduce the heat and simmer for 10 to 15 minutes. Add salt and pepper to taste. Cover and set aside.

While the sauce simmers, prepare the filling. Sauté the onions and garlic in the oil for about 10 minutes, until the onions are translucent. In a bowl, combine the sautéed onions with the walnuts, feta, currants, and lemon juice. Stir in the rice.

When the zucchini is tender, use a spoon to scoop out the flesh, leaving a thin $1/4$-inch shell. Chop the flesh and add it to the filling. Mound the filling in the shells and sprinkle with seasoned bread crumbs and olive oil, if desired. Bake, uncovered, for 10 to 15 minutes, until hot.

To serve, ladle some of the tomato sauce onto each plate. Place a stuffed zucchini on the sauce and top with grated feta. Garnish, if you wish, with oregano leaves.

PER 19-OUNCE SERVING: 510 CALORIES, 11.6 G PROTEIN, 28.9 G FAT, 53.8 G CARBOHYDRATES, 5 G SATURATED FATTY ACIDS, 12.6 MG CHOLESTEROL, 484.1 MG SODIUM, 6.3 G TOTAL DIETARY FIBER

quinoa stuffed peppers

In these spicy, stuffed peppers, protein-rich quinoa, a popular grain from Peru, is combined with Cheddar cheese and Mexican-spiced vegetables for a satisfying Pan-American main dish.

Serve these with crisp Jicama Orange Salad (page 95) or refreshing Shredded Carrot Salad with Cilantro Dressing (page 111).

Serves 6
Preparation time: 1 to 1¼ hours
Baking time: 10 to 15 minutes

1 cup raw quinoa
6 medium bell peppers
3 tablespoons olive oil
1 cup chopped onions
3 garlic cloves, minced or pressed
1½ teaspoons ground cumin
1½ teaspoons ground coriander
½ teaspoon red pepper flakes
½ teaspoon salt, or more to taste
1 cup peeled and diced carrots
¾ cup diced celery
1 cup diced zucchini
1½ cups fresh or frozen corn kernels
1½ to 2 cups grated Cheddar cheese

Preheat the oven to 400°. Lightly oil a baking pan.

Place the quinoa in a fine-mesh sieve and rinse well under running water. In a covered pot, bring the quinoa and 2 cups of water to a boil. Lower the heat and simmer for about 15 minutes, until the quinoa is soft and the water absorbed.

While the quinoa cooks, cut the bell peppers in half lengthwise and, leaving the stems on, seed them. Brush the bell pepper shells with about 2 tablespoons of the oil, inside and out. Place them cut side down on the prepared baking pan and roast for 15 to 20 minutes, until softened and slightly browned, but not collapsed. When the bell peppers are roasted, reduce the the oven temperature to 350°.

Meanwhile, in a skillet, warm the remaining tablespoon of oil and sauté the onions and garlic on medium heat for about 5 minutes, until the onions have softened. Stir in the cumin, coriander, red pepper flakes, salt, carrots, celery, zucchini, and corn. Cover the pan and cook for about 10 minutes, until the vegetables are very tender.

Combine the sautéed vegetables and the cooked quinoa and add salt to taste. Turn over the roasted pepper shells and spoon filling into each half. Sprinkle each bell pepper half with some of the grated cheese and bake for 10 to 15 minutes, until the cheese is melted.

PER 10.5-OUNCE SERVING: 392 CALORIES, 14.3 G PROTEIN, 19.3 G FAT, 44.7 G CARBOHYDRATES, 7.3 G SATURATED FATTY ACIDS, 29.7 MG CHOLESTEROL, 419.5 MG SODIUM, 5.9 G TOTAL DIETARY FIBER

caramelized onion tart

It's amazing how sweet and flavorful onions become when they are cooked for a long time until golden brown and juicy. We've given you a straightforward, foolproof pie crust recipe that only takes 10 to 15 minutes to make. While it bakes, put together a tossed green salad and vinaigrette to serve alongside.

This tart packs well for picnics, school lunches, or work. Eat it any time of the day, at room temperature or hot.

Serves 6 to 8
Preparation time: 50 to 55 minutes
Baking time: 50 to 60 minutes

crust

1 1/2 cups unbleached white flour
1/2 teaspoon salt
1/2 cup chilled butter
3 to 4 tablespoons ice water

filling

1 tablespoon vegetable oil
8 cups sliced onions
1 teaspoon salt
1/2 teaspoon dried thyme
6 large eggs
1/4 cup unbleached white flour
1 tablespoon Dijon mustard
1/2 teaspoon salt
2 cups milk
1 cup packed grated Gruyère cheese

Combine the flour and salt in a large bowl. Work the butter into the flour with a pastry cutter until it resembles coarse meal. Sprinkle on the ice water and form the dough into a ball. On a lightly floured surface, somewhat flatten the ball of dough by pressing down with your palm. Roll the dough into a 13-inch circle with a rolling pin. Lift the dough into a 10-inch pie plate. Fold the edges under and crimp the edges high, because the filling is generous. Set aside in the refrigerator.

Preheat the oven to 400°.

Warm the oil in a large, heavy, preferably cast-iron skillet and add the onions and salt. Cook uncovered on medium-high heat, stirring often, for 15 minutes. Add the thyme and continue to cook for another 5 to 10 minutes. As they cook, the onions will release their juices and then start to caramelize, turning golden brown. Remove from the heat and set aside. In a blender, purée the eggs, flour, mustard, salt, and milk until smooth.

Spread the onions evenly on the bottom of the pie shell, cover with the grated cheese, and pour the milk custard over all. Bake until the filling is set and the crust is golden brown, about 50 to 60 minutes. Serve immediately or cool to room temperature.

PER 10-OUNCE SERVING: 396 CALORIES, 15.5 G PROTEIN, 22.5 G FAT, 33.4 G CARBOHYDRATES, 9.2 G SATURATED FATTY ACIDS, 217.4 MG CHOLESTEROL, 790.9 MG SODIUM, 2.2 G TOTAL DIETARY FIBER

homespun pot pie

Some of us at Moosewood remember as kids waiting for the weekends to come, when there was time for our mothers to make pot pie. Even if we weren't vegetable lovers at the time, we still loved this wonderful dish.

Our pot pie crammed with vegetables is a hearty one-dish meal that fills the house with the aroma of freshly baked biscuit dough. Simplify the preparation by cooking the vegetables in advance, then mix up the biscuit ingredients just before baking the pot pie.

Serves 6
Preparation time: 1 hour
Baking time: 25 to 30 minutes

2 cups peeled and chopped sweet
   potatoes*
2 cups chopped potatoes*
2 cups peeled and chopped parsnips
   (optional)*
1/2 teaspoon ground black pepper
3 cups water or stock
3 tablespoons cornstarch dissolved in
   1/2 cup cold water
1 cup fresh or frozen green peas
1 cup fresh or frozen corn kernels
1 tablespoon soy sauce
1/2 teaspoon salt

biscuit topping

2 cups unbleached white flour
1/2 teaspoon salt
1 tablespoon baking powder
1/2 teaspoon baking soda
6 tablespoons melted butter
1 cup buttermilk or plain yogurt
1 teaspoon chopped fresh dill
   (1 teaspoon dried)

vegetables

1 tablespoon vegetable oil
2 cups coarsely chopped onions
2 or 3 garlic cloves, minced or
   pressed
1 teaspoon salt
1 teaspoon dried thyme
1 teaspoon dried marjoram
4 to 5 cups sliced or halved
   mushrooms
1 tablespoon Dijon mustard

* *Chop the potatoes and parsnips into 1/2-inch cubes.*

variation *To make Vegan Pot Pie, use soy products instead of dairy products in the biscuit topping: replace the butter with soy margarine and replace the buttermilk or yogurt with soy milk or rice milk.*

✳ Preheat the oven to 400°. Lightly oil a 9 x 13-inch casserole dish.

Warm the oil in a soup pot. Add the onions and garlic, cover, and cook on medium heat for 10 to 12 minutes, stirring occasionally. Add the salt, thyme, marjoram, mushrooms, and mustard. Cook until the mushrooms start to release their juices, about 5 minutes.

Add the sweet potatoes, white potatoes, parsnips, black pepper, and the water or stock and bring to a boil. Then reduce the heat, cover, and simmer for 15 to 20 minutes, until the vegetables are just tender. Stir the dissolved cornstarch mixture into the simmering vegetables, stirring constantly. When the liquid starts to thicken, mix in the peas, corn, soy sauce, and salt. Pour the vegetables into the prepared casserole dish, and set aside.

In a mixing bowl, sift together the flour, salt, baking powder, and baking soda. In a separate bowl, mix together the melted butter and buttermilk or yogurt. Combine the wet and dry ingredients with as few strokes as possible to make a soft dough. Drop the biscuit batter over the vegetables in the casserole dish in six equal mounds. Sprinkle the dill over the biscuits.

Bake for 25 to 30 minutes, or until a knife inserted into the center of a biscuit comes out clean. Serve immediately.

PER 17-OUNCE SERVING: 471 CALORIES, 11 G PROTEIN, 15.5 G FAT, 74.4 G CARBOHYDRATES, 8.2 G SATURATED FATTY ACIDS, 32.3 MG CHOLESTEROL, 1,403.7 MG SODIUM, 6.8 G TOTAL DIETARY FIBER

ronald's fennel quiche

In the summer of '99, Ronald Kunis, a French-trained master chef from Haarlem, Holland, graced us with his presence, intending to learn vegetarian cookery from us. It's difficult to know who profited more. One night, he made an unforgettably delightful fennel pie. It wasn't this one *exactly*, but we tried to capture a lot of his expertise and artistry in our version. We hope you like this, Ronald.

Our pie custard has no milk in it and transforms from a rosy pink to a deeply golden-orange baked pie.

 Serves 4 to 6
Preparation time: 1 hour
Baking time: 50 minutes

crust

1 cup unbleached white flour
1/2 teaspoon salt (optional)*
1/3 cup chilled butter
2 tablespoons ice water

filling

2 tablespoons olive oil
3/4 cup diced onions
1/2 teaspoon salt
1 cup thinly sliced or diced fresh fennel
2 medium fresh tomatoes
1 cup seeded and diced zucchini
1 teaspoon ground fennel seeds
2 tablespoons minced fresh basil
1/4 teaspoon ground black pepper
4 eggs
1 1/2 cups grated feta cheese, packed
1 cup grated Swiss cheese, packed

We recommend adding the salt if you are using sweet or unsalted butter; however, it can be omitted if you're using salted butter.

Mix together the flour and the salt, if using, in a large bowl. Rapidly work the butter into the flour with a pastry cutter or your fingers until it resembles coarse meal. Sprinkle the ice water over the mixture a tablespoon at a time, and lightly mix it through the dough.

Push the dampened dough from the sides to the middle of the bowl, to form a ball that holds together. Transfer it to a clean, dry work surface. Cut the dough in half, place one half on top of the other, and press down. Repeat the cutting and pressing steps three or four times until all of the water is well distributed and the dough clings together.

Lightly flour a work surface and roll the dough into a 12-inch circle. Transfer the pie dough to a 9-inch pie plate, fold the edges under, and crimp with your fingers or a fork. Refrigerate the pie shell while you prepare the filling.

Preheat the oven to 375°.

Heat the oil in a heavy-bottomed, nonreactive skillet. Add the onions and salt, and sauté on medium heat until the onions are translucent and juicy, 8 to 10 minutes. Add the fresh fennel and sauté for another 3 to 5 minutes. The edges of the onions will begin to brown.

While the onions and fennel cook, halve the tomatoes through the stem ends and scoop out the pulp and juice, setting aside $1/2$ cup of it. Dice enough of the tomato flesh to make 1 cup and add it, with the zucchini and ground fennel, to the skillet. Cook on medium heat for 5 minutes, stirring once or twice, until the tomatoes soften and begin to fall apart. Remove from the heat and stir in the basil and pepper.

In a blender, purée the eggs, the reserved $1/2$ cup of tomato pulp and juice, and the feta to form a smooth custard. Spoon the sautéed vegetables into the chilled crust, top with the grated Swiss, and pour the custard over all. The pie will be very full.

Bake for 50 minutes, until the quiche is domed, crusty, and golden.

PER 8-OUNCE SERVING: 441 CALORIES, 17.9 G PROTEIN, 31 G FAT, 23.5 G CARBOHYDRATES,
16 G SATURATED FATTY ACIDS, 246.1 MG CHOLESTEROL, 734.8 MG SODIUM, 2.2 G TOTAL DIETARY FIBER

instant tamale pie

When you suddenly think, "We need food, pronto!," try this immensely easy and gratifying meal or munchie—Moosewood's Super Bowl half-time entertainment. With ready-made polenta, it's prepared in only 15 minutes and the rest is done by the oven.

Packaged polenta comes in 18- and 24-ounce rolls in a variety of flavors. Look for brands free of chemical additives and preservatives in health food stores, gourmet food stores, and in the Italian section of the supermarket. In this dish, use plain polenta or try San Genarro's Jalapeño Polenta with Cilantro. Wrapped and refrigerated, leftover polenta will keep for about a week.

We suggest using a medium salsa, but go for hot if faint-hearted you're not. Serve with tortilla chips, guacamole, and a garden salad.

1¾ cups pinto beans with juice (15-ounce can)

½ cup fresh or frozen corn kernels

½ cup prepared tomato salsa*

1 teaspoon ground cumin

½ teaspoon dried oregano

¼ teaspoon salt

12 ounces prepared polenta

2 to 3 tablespoons chopped fresh cilantro

1 cup grated sharp Cheddar cheese

* We like Herdez, Pace, and Enrico brands.

Serves 4
Preparation time: 15 minutes
Baking time: 30 to 35 minutes
Sitting time: 10 minutes

Preheat the oven to 350°.

Lightly oil a 10-inch cast-iron skillet or an 11-inch baking dish. Empty the beans and their juice into a large bowl and mash with a potato masher. Add the corn, salsa, cumin, oregano, and salt and mix thoroughly. Set aside.

Slice 12 ounces of the packaged polenta roll into ¼-inch-thick rounds. (Refrigerate the remainder for another use.) Arrange the rounds in the prepared skillet or baking dish slightly overlapping one another. Spoon the bean mixture evenly over the polenta, sprinkle on the cilantro, and top with the grated cheese.

Cover and bake for 15 minutes, and then uncover and bake for about 15 more minutes, until the beans are bubbling and hot. For a crisp, golden topping, place under the broiler for 2 to 3 minutes. Let sit for 10 minutes before serving.

PER 9-OUNCE SERVING: 330 CALORIES, 17.5 G PROTEIN, 10.7 G FAT, 42.5 G CARBOHYDRATES, 6.1 G SATURATED FATTY ACIDS, 29.7 MG CHOLESTEROL, 563.9 MG SODIUM, 9.8 G TOTAL DIETARY FIBER

spinach gnocchi

Traditionally, gnocchi are boiled, but if the mixture's not just right, they'll fall apart in the water. So we decided to eliminate the "falling apart" possibility—and reduce anxiety—by just baking them instead.

These lovely green dumplings are made with spinach, cheese, and just enough bread crumbs to hold them together. Baking them in a flavorful tomato sauce works just fine, and they are guaranteed not to fall apart.

Serve them alone topped with tomato sauce, use them to dress up a pasta dish, or drop them into a compatible brothy soup.

Serves 4 to 6
Preparation time: 30 minutes
Baking time: 25 minutes

10 ounces fresh spinach

3 large eggs

1 cup grated Parmesan cheese

$1/2$ cup ricotta cheese

$1 1/4$ cups bread crumbs*

2 tablespoons chopped fresh basil

$1/3$ cup chopped scallions

1 garlic clove, minced or pressed

$1/2$ teaspoon salt

$1/4$ teaspoon ground black pepper

pinch of ground nutmeg, or more to taste

$1/2$ recipe Quick Tomato Sauce (page 382) or 3 cups store-bought tomato sauce

* Pulverize stale or lightly toasted whole wheat, sourdough, or Italian bread in a blender or food processor.

Preheat the oven to 400°. Oil a nonreactive baking dish.

Rinse the spinach well and remove any large stems. Place the spinach in a large pot with only the water that clings to the leaves. Cover and cook on high heat, stirring once or twice, just long enough to wilt the leaves, about 3 minutes. Set aside to drain.

In a large bowl, beat the eggs. Mix in the Parmesan, ricotta, bread crumbs, basil, scallions, garlic, salt, pepper, and nutmeg. When the cooked spinach is cool enough to handle, gently squeeze more water from it and chop it. Stir the chopped spinach into the cheese mixture. The batter will be wet and rather soft. Drop the batter by rounded tablespoonfuls onto the prepared baking dish to make about 18 balls. Pour the tomato sauce around the gnocchi to almost cover.

Bake for about 25 minutes, until firm and beginning to brown. Serve hot with the tomato sauce ladled on top.

PER 10-OUNCE SERVING: 296 CALORIES, 20.5 G PROTEIN, 13.8 G FAT, 23.4 G CARBOHYDRATES, 6.6 G SATURATED FATTY ACIDS, 155.9 MG CHOLESTEROL, 1,189.7 MG SODIUM, 2.7 G TOTAL DIETARY FIBER

fish with cornmeal chipotle crust

Here at Moosewood, we've fallen in love with chipotles in adobo sauce. Many people who avoid spicy foods enjoy chipotles for their smoky flavor. A 7-ounce can will keep for at least a couple of weeks when transferred into a glass jar and stored in the fridge. The adobo sauce is also good on baked tofu or roasted vegetables.

For this dish, we recommend a fish such as catfish, salmon, scrod, or tilapia. Peach Salsa (page 381) or Black Bean Mango Salsa (page 372) would make an excellent topping. We often serve this dish at Moosewood with mashed potatoes (pages 130–134).

Serves 4
Preparation time: 10 minutes
Baking time: 25 minutes

4 firm fish fillets (5 to 6 ounces each)

1 tablespoon canned chipotles in adobo sauce, minced*

1 1/2 tablespoons vegetable oil

1 1/2 tablespoons fresh lemon or lime juice

1 large garlic clove, minced or pressed

1/4 teaspoon dried thyme

1/4 teaspoon salt

1/2 cup cornmeal**

lime wedges

* Chipotles in adobo sauce are available in small jars or cans in Latin American grocery stores and many supermarkets.
** 2/3 to 3/4 cup of cornbread crumbs can replace the cornmeal in this recipe. They make a wonderful crust.

Preheat the oven to 375°. Lightly oil a large baking pan for the fish. Rinse the fillets, pat dry, and set aside.

In a bowl, combine the chipotles, oil, citrus juice, garlic, thyme, and salt and stir well. For a very smooth result, whirl all of the sauce ingredients in the bowl of a food processor or mini-processor.

Pour the sauce into a shallow bowl and place the cornmeal in another shallow bowl. Dip each fish fillet in the sauce: the thicker the coating, the spicier the fish will be. Then dredge the fillets on all sides in the cornmeal and arrange them in the prepared baking pan in a single layer.

Bake uncovered for about 25 minutes, until the fillets are golden and flake with a fork. Serve with generous wedges of lime.

PER 5.5-OUNCE SERVING: 252 CALORIES, 30.8 G PROTEIN, 6.7 G FAT, 15.4 G CARBOHYDRATES, 1.6 G SATURATED FATTY ACIDS, 70.2 MG CHOLESTEROL, 249.8 MG SODIUM, 1.5 G TOTAL DIETARY FIBER

moroccan fish with cumin

Cumin, garlic, and lemon make this a zesty way to season baked or pan-fried fish. Toasting the cumin seeds before grinding intensifies and enriches the flavor of this easily prepared spice rub.

Serve the fish topped with Yogurt Tahini Dressing (page 389) or chopped fresh tomatoes, and with Orange Saffron Rice (page 146) or Bulghur with Spinach (page 138) alongside.

Serves 4
Preparation time: 20 to 30 minutes
Marinating time: 30 minutes
Baking time: 20 to 30 minutes

1 1/2 pounds mild fish fillets, such as tilapia, sole, or scrod

spice rub

1 1/2 tablespoons cumin seeds

4 garlic cloves, peeled

1/4 cup parsley sprigs, stemmed

1 tablespoon freshly grated lemon peel

3 tablespoons fresh lemon juice

1/2 teaspoon salt

1/4 teaspoon ground black pepper

Rinse the fish fillets, pat dry, and set aside in the refrigerator.

Toast the cumin seeds in a toaster oven or in a small, dry skillet for 1 to 2 minutes, until fragrant. Grind the toasted seeds in a spice grinder or with a mortar and pestle. Combine the ground cumin with the garlic, parsley, lemon peel, lemon juice, salt, and pepper in a food processor (preferably a mini one) and process until chopped fine (see Note).

Rub both sides of the fillets with the spice blend, and place them in a single layer in a very lightly oiled baking pan. Cover and refrigerate for about 30 minutes.

Pan-fry or bake the fillets, depending on your preference. We recommend baking as the better method for thick fillets. For thin fish fillets, pan-fry in a small amount of olive oil for 4 to 5 minutes, turning them once during frying. Or, cover and bake in a preheated 350° oven for 20 to 30 minutes, until the fish flakes easily with a fork.

PER 5-OUNCE SERVING: 168 CALORIES, 31.9 G PROTEIN, 2.6 G FAT, 3.1 G CARBOHYDRATES, 0.5 G SATURATED FATTY ACIDS, 87.9 MG CHOLESTEROL, 441.1 MG SODIUM, 0.8 G TOTAL DIETARY FIBER

note *You can also mince everything by hand and stir together in a bowl, if you prefer.*

sautés, stews, skillet beans & hashes

sautés, stews, skillet beans & hashes

You'll need a stew pot, a good-sized skillet, or a wok to make these stovetop recipes. Part of their beauty is that they cook up in one pot; another attraction is that they're hearty, robust, and really good for you. These one-dish meals are rich in nutrition without a lot of fat and most of them are also vegan. With a simple salad, some rice, or a piece of cornbread on the side—*voilà!*—you've got a meal.

The skillet beans, easy meals to throw together with things from the pantry, are well seasoned and stick to your ribs. They're perfect for a casual weeknight or a Saturday lunch or supper. It's great to have some warm on the stove when you come home from a bike ride, a snowball fight, or shoveling out the car. Eat a lot or a little—leftovers can be always be tossed into a soup or reheated for a snack or a side dish.

For brunch, serve Peppers & Greens Skillet Hash or Potato & Asparagus Hash. For a delightful change of pace, serve Bibimbop, a delightful Korean dish with whole fried eggs nestled on top.

Bring on a January thaw with the spicy heat of our Winter Curry. Sautés, stir-fries, and stews are easy to prepare, and they can be elegant enough for a nice dinner with company without generating a punishing stack of pots to scrub afterward. Indian Ratatouille? Tofu Stroganoff? Hey, this is Moosewood you're dealing with. A little cross-cultural cookery couldn't hurt. Check out the Sicilian Stir-Fry to discover what Marco Polo learned over in China.

bibimbop

Korean folklore has it that this dish, which could be considered rice with all the fixings, was originally served at remembrance gatherings to honor one's ancestors. After the ceremony, parts of the ritual offerings were mixed with freshly cooked rice to create a celebratory meal.

Today, bibimbop is one of Korea's famous culinary hallmarks. Usually served in flameproof, black clay pots called *tukbaege*, it arrives sizzling at the table. Inside each person's clay pot is a colorful array of julienned vegetables, mung bean sprouts, and sometimes shredded meat or nori, each arranged in a mound atop a generous portion of sticky white rice. Often a fried egg is placed in the very center. It's traditional to admire the presentation, and then mix it all up to serve. You can, however, arrange the vegetables in pretty concentric circles and serve everyone a cross section of vegetables without stirring it all together.

Our vegetarian bibimbop is beautiful and really a lot easier than it may seem at first. It's impressive with or without the fried eggs. We make it collective-style (what a surprise!) in one large pot that four people share. For a lower-fat dish, stir-fry the vegetables and eggs in a nonstick skillet using very little oil.

While medium-grain sticky rice is traditional, any plain white or brown rice cooked until soft and tender, but not mushy, will work. We give approximate times for preparing the ingredients and cooking the vegetables—50 to 55 minutes altogether—to help you decide when to start cooking the rice. Pace yourself so everything is ready to assemble by the time the rice finishes cooking.

If you don't have a large flameproof clay pot, do not despair. A 6-inch-deep stainless-steel pasta pot, a deep 10-inch casserole dish, or a standard 9 x 13-inch ovenproof dish will be fine (see Notes).

Serves 4
Preparation time: 30 minutes
Blanching & sautéing time:
  20 to 25 minutes
Total time: 1¼ hours

3 cups freshly cooked white, brown, or sticky rice*

2 ounces dried mushrooms (page 462–463)

1 cup green beans, trimmed and cut on the diagonal into bite-sized pieces

1 tablespoon vegetable oil

1 carrot, peeled and julienned**

1 red bell pepper, seeded and julienned**

½ small zucchini, julienned**

½ cup mung bean sprouts

3 scallions, thinly sliced on the severe diagonal

1 8-inch sheet of nori, toasted (page 468) and snipped into thin strips***

1 to 2 teaspoons Asian chili paste

2 teaspoons dark sesame oil

dash of salt

2 eggs (optional)

* *1 cup of raw rice will make about 3 cups cooked.*
** *Julienne all of the vegetables into matchsticks about 2 x ¼ inch.*
*** *Use scissors to cut the sheet of nori lengthwise into quarters, then stack the strips and snip crosswise at ½-inch intervals.*

Begin to cook the rice of your choice so it's ready by the time you finish sautéing and blanching the vegetables (see the Guide to Ingredients for cooking times). Immerse the dried mushrooms in boiling water, cover, and set aside to soak for 20 to 30 minutes, until soft.

Meanwhile, blanch the green beans in boiling water for 4 minutes and drain well. In a skillet, warm about a teaspoon of the oil on medium heat and stir-fry the green beans for 2 minutes. Remove from the skillet, pile on a platter, cover, and set aside. Stir-fry the julienned carrots, bell peppers, and zucchini separately until just tender, adding a teaspoon of oil, if needed. (Carrots will take about 4 minutes, bell peppers 3 minutes, and zucchini 2 to 3 minutes.) Place each stir-fried vegetable in a separate pile on the platter and keep covered.

Drain the mushrooms, trim and discard any tough stems, and thinly slice the tender caps and stems. Blanch the mung sprouts in boiling water for 1 minute and drain in a colander, pressing to eliminate water.

Oil the bottom and sides of a large flameproof clay pot, casserole dish, or stainless-steel pot. Scoop the hot cooked rice into it. On top, arrange the mushrooms, green beans, carrots, zucchini, bell peppers, mung sprouts, scallions, and nori in attractive mounds or concentric circles around the perimeter. If you wish to include the eggs, leave space at the center. Stir together the chili paste and sesame oil, drizzle it on top, and sprinkle with salt. Cover with a tight lid.

If including eggs, fry them sunny-side up in the final teaspoon of oil. While the eggs cook, place the bibimbop pot on medium heat for about 3 minutes, until the rice sizzles and everything is piping hot (see Notes). With a spatula, transfer the fried eggs to the center of the pot and serve at once.

PER 10-OUNCE SERVING: 294 CALORIES, 6.7 G PROTEIN, 6.9 G FAT, 54.1 G CARBOHYDRATES, 1.5 G SATURATED FATTY ACIDS, 0 MG CHOLESTEROL, 73.1 MG SODIUM, 5.6 G TOTAL DIETARY FIBER

notes *If your casserole dish is not flameproof, try our oven method. Preheat the oven to 500° when you begin to sauté the vegetables. Then, instead of heating the bibimbop on the stovetop just before serving, put it in the oven for about 5 minutes.*

It is customary to offer a variety of side dishes too—usually placed on separate tiny plates at the table. These can include pickled Korean radish, cucumbers in a mild vinaigrette, hot chili paste or gochu jang, sautéed sprouts, fiery cabbage kimchee, puréed anchovy paste, and cooked potatoes braised in a sweet and savory sauce. Ready-made kimchee is available in jars at Asian groceries and in many supermarkets.

chilean bean stew

The traditional name for the dish is *Porotos Granados.* Moosewood cook Eliana Parra says this is a very popular stew in the summertime in Chile, where it's made with fresh corn and fresh ivory white or red beans from the farmers' markets. She fondly remembers her whole family gathering in the kitchen on Sundays to shuck and grate the fresh corn and shell the beans.

Serve it topped with grated Cheddar cheese and accompanied by Tossed Green Salad Vinaigrette (page 98) and freshly baked cornbread.

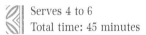

Serves 4 to 6
Total time: 45 minutes

2 tablespoons vegetable oil

2 cups chopped onions

4 garlic cloves, minced or pressed

1 1/2 teaspoons salt

1/2 teaspoon ground black pepper

1/8 to 1/4 teaspoon cayenne

3 cups water

4 cups peeled, seeded, and
    cubed butternut squash
    (about 3 pounds)

3 cups fresh, frozen, or canned corn
    kernels

3 cups cooked red pinto beans*

1/2 cup chopped fresh basil

* *Two 15-ounce cans of pinto beans, drained and rinsed, will work well, or use one can of white beans and one of red pinto beans.*

Heat the oil in a large soup pot. Add the onions, garlic, salt, black pepper, and cayenne and sauté on medium heat for 5 minutes. Add the water and the squash, cover, and bring to a boil; then reduce the heat and simmer for 10 minutes. Stir in 1 cup of the corn and the beans and basil. Cover and continue to simmer for another 5 to 10 minutes, until the squash is soft.

Ladle 2 cups of broth from the stew into a blender. Add the remaining 2 cups of corn and purée until smooth. Stir the puréed corn back into the stew.

Gently reheat before serving, if necessary.

PER 16-OUNCE SERVING: 338 CALORIES, 12.1 G PROTEIN, 6.4 G FAT, 65.6 G CARBOHYDRATES, 1.5 G SATURATED FATTY ACIDS, 0 MG CHOLESTEROL, 618.1 MG SODIUM, 10.4 G TOTAL DIETARY FIBER

indian ratatouille

This intriguing twist on a summertime classic combines Indian spices with Mediterranean flavors. A mini food processor works really well for chopping the garlic, chile, and ginger root. Since all of the dried spices go into the dish at the same time, you can just measure them into a small bowl and set them aside until needed.

Serve the ratatouille on rice or orzo or accompanied by a crusty loaf of bread. If you like, add a dollop of plain yogurt to each serving and top with fresh basil and a few toasted almonds or pistachios.

Serves 6
Preparation time: 20 minutes
Cooking time: 40 to 45 minutes

2 cups diced onions

2 tablespoons vegetable oil

2 large garlic cloves, minced or pressed

1 fresh chile, minced (seeded for a milder hot)

1 tablespoon grated fresh ginger root

1 teaspoon ground cumin

1 teaspoon ground coriander

1/2 teaspoon turmeric

1/2 teaspoon ground cinnamon

1/4 teaspoon ground cardamom

1 teaspoon salt

generous pinch of crumbled saffron

1 cup orange juice

5 cups cubed eggplant (1-inch cubes)

4 cups cubed zucchini, yellow squash, and/or pattypans

1 1/2 cups diced bell peppers

3 cups diced fresh or canned tomatoes (28-ounce can, undrained)

1/4 cup chopped fresh basil

In a stew pot, sauté the onions in the oil on medium heat until translucent, about 10 minutes. Stir in the garlic, chile, ginger, cumin, coriander, turmeric, cinnamon, cardamom, salt, and saffron and sauté for a minute, stirring constantly. Add the orange juice and eggplant, toss to coat with the spices, cover, and simmer for 10 to 15 minutes, until the eggplant is barely tender.

Add the squash, bell peppers, tomatoes, and basil. Cover and continue to simmer about 15 minutes, until all of the vegetables are tender. Add a little more orange juice or water if necessary to prevent sticking.

Serve hot or at room temperature.

PER 12-OUNCE SERVING: 146 CALORIES, 3.5 G PROTEIN, 5.7 G FAT, 23.7 G CARBOHYDRATES, 1.4 G SATURATED FATTY ACIDS, 0 MG CHOLESTEROL, 414.8 MG SODIUM, 4.6 G TOTAL DIETARY FIBER

red & green sopa seca

Mexican *sopa seca*, or "dry soup," is really a casserole made with tortillas or sometimes rice or pasta. Our version uses spinach, red bell peppers, and red or green salsa for color, and tortilla chips as a convenient option.

 Serves 6
Preparation time: 40 minutes
Baking time: about 30 minutes
Sitting time: 5 to 10 minutes

1 large yellow onion
1 large red bell pepper
1 tablespoon vegetable oil
2 cups red or green salsa*
$^{1}/_{2}$ cup water
12 corn tortillas (6 inches across), cut into 1-inch strips**
10 ounces fresh or frozen spinach
8 ounces Neufchâtel or cream cheese, softened
1 to 1$^{1}/_{4}$ cups grated Cheddar or Monterey Jack cheese

* Use your favorite commercial salsa or make a fresh salsa (page 000 or 000).
** Or use about 3 cups of crushed tortilla chips; the finished dish will be saltier. When you assemble the casserole, begin by spreading the chips on the bottom and drizzling with the salsa.

Preheat the oven to 350°.

Cut the onion and bell pepper into $^{1}/_{2}$-inch-wide strips. Place on a baking sheet and toss with the oil. Roast for 25 to 30 minutes, until soft and just browning on the edges.

Meanwhile, stir together the salsa and water. Place the tortilla strips in a bowl, pour the thinned salsa over them, and set aside. Rinse and stem fresh spinach. Blanch fresh or frozen spinach in 1 cup of boiling water just until soft and still bright green. Drain and mix it immediately with the Neufchâtel.

In an unoiled 9-inch square or 7 x 11-inch nonreactive baking pan, layer half of the soaked tortilla strips. Top with the roasted onions and peppers. Spread the spinach mixture on top and add the rest of the tortilla strips, reserving any salsa still in the bowl. Sprinkle with the cheese and drizzle on any remaining salsa.

Bake uncovered until bubbling, about 30 minutes. Remove from the oven and let sit for 5 to 10 minutes before serving.

PER 10-OUNCE SERVING: 450 CALORIES, 16.5 G PROTEIN, 22.6 G FAT, 45.9 G CARBOHYDRATES, 11.3 G SATURATED FATTY ACIDS, 48.6 MG CHOLESTEROL, 963.6 MG SODIUM, 4.4 G TOTAL DIETARY FIBER

sicilian stir-fry

We love the way stir-frying preserves the singular flavors, crisp texture, and deep vibrant colors of fresh vegetables. When we experimented with the robust Italian flavors of olive oil, garlic, fennel, and rosemary, the result was this vigorous vegetable medley that goes perfectly with polenta, bread, or orzo.

Other vegetables such as eggplant or asparagus could be included in the mix. The proportions needn't be exact as long as the total amount of raw vegetables is 10 to 12 cups. For best results, prepare all of the ingredients first. Then combine in bowls those vegetables and seasonings that will be added to the wok at the same time and place everything conveniently near the stove.

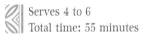

Serves 4 to 6
Total time: 55 minutes

2 tablespoons olive oil
2 cups sliced onions
1 cup thinly sliced celery or fresh fennel bulb
1 1/2 cups cut green beans (1 1/2-inch pieces)
4 garlic cloves, minced or pressed
1/4 to 1/2 teaspoon red pepper flakes
2 cups sliced mushrooms
2 cups sliced zucchini
1 cup sliced red or yellow bell peppers
1 teaspoon minced fresh rosemary
1/2 teaspoon salt
1/4 cup dry red wine
2 cups chopped fresh tomatoes
1/4 cup chopped fresh basil
1 tablespoon capers (optional)

grated Parmesan or Romano cheese (optional)
balsamic vinegar

In a wok or large sauté pan, briefly warm the oil on medium-high to high heat. Add the onions, toss to coat with oil, and cook for 2 to 3 minutes. Add the celery, green beans, garlic, and red pepper flakes and stir-fry for about 4 minutes; do not brown.

Add the mushrooms, zucchini, bell peppers, rosemary, and salt and continue to stir-fry for 2 or 3 minutes. Stir in the red wine, tomatoes, basil, and capers if using. Continue to stir-fry until the vegetables are just tender and have released their juices. Top with grated cheese, if desired.

Serve with balsamic vinegar on the side.

PER 9-OUNCE SERVING: 121 CALORIES, 3.1 G PROTEIN, 5.4 G FAT, 16.4 G CARBOHYDRATES, 0.8 G SATURATED FATTY ACIDS, 0 MG CHOLESTEROL, 227.4 MG SODIUM, 4.1 G TOTAL DIETARY FIBER

tilghman island stew

Moosewood's Dave Dietrich and Joan Adler spent their honeymoon at a beautiful waterman's village on Tilghman Island in Maryland. Inspired by the local crab and the fresh produce from the Chesapeake Bay's Eastern Shore, Dave created this stew soon after he returned to Ithaca.

There is a geological connection between the Finger Lakes region of New York and the Eastern Shore of the Chesapeake Bay. When the Ice Age glaciers that created the topography of central New York melted, the sediment washed down the Susquehanna River and collected to form the Eastern Shore, the peninsula that informs the Chesapeake Bay. We appreciate that folks there have done such good things with the soil sent down river to them.

Serve with Cornbread (page 395) or Lemon Thyme Biscuits (page 398).

Serves 4 to 6
Total time: about 1 hour

3 tablespoons vegetable oil
2 cups chopped onions
1 tablespoon minced or pressed garlic
4 bay leaves
2 teaspoons dried thyme
1 cup sliced celery
2 tablespoons Old Bay Seasoning

1 1/2 cups canned tomatoes with juice (14.5-ounce can)
4 cups peeled, cubed sweet potatoes*
6 cups water or vegetable stock
4 cups chopped kale
2 cups stemmed and halved green beans
2 cups fresh or frozen corn kernels
1 cup chopped fresh or frozen okra (optional)
1 cup chopped red bell peppers
2 cups sliced zucchini and/or yellow squash (optional)
1 tablespoon soy sauce
2 tablespoons fresh lemon juice
salt and ground black pepper to taste

grated Cheddar cheese (optional)
chopped fresh parsley or scallions

* Cube the sweet potatoes into 1/2-inch pieces and immerse them in water right away to prevent discoloration. Drain before adding to the stew.

✂ In a soup pot, warm the oil briefly on medium heat. Add the onions and sauté until translucent, about 5 minutes. Add the garlic, bay leaves, and thyme; then cover and cook for about 5 minutes, stirring occasionally. (If necessary to prevent sticking, add ¼ cup of the water or stock.) Add the celery and Old Bay Seasoning and cook for 5 minutes.

Add the tomatoes, sweet potatoes, and water or vegetable stock. Increase the heat to a moderate boil. Stir in the kale and green beans. When the stew returns to a simmer, stir in the corn and, if you wish, the okra, and cook until the green beans are just tender. Add the bell peppers and, if you like, the zucchini and/or yellow squash and cook for another 5 to 10 minutes, until all of the vegetables are tender. Stir in the soy sauce and lemon juice. Add salt and pepper to taste. Remove and discard the bay leaves.

Serve topped with grated cheese, if you like, and a sprinkling of parsley or scallions.

PER 20-OUNCE SERVING: 282 CALORIES, 6.7 G PROTEIN, 8.6 G FAT, 50.1 G CARBOHYDRATES,
2.1 G SATURATED FATTY ACIDS, 0 MG CHOLESTEROL, 255.4 MG SODIUM, 6.7 G TOTAL DIETARY FIBER

spicy broccoli soba sauté

Soba noodles, with the unique nutty flavor of buckwheat, are found in almost every little noodle house in Japan, and after tasting them, it's easy to see why the Japanese are so in love with them. Here, you can find a variety of these high-protein noodles, made from buckwheat or blends of buckwheat and wheat, as well as specialty soba with wild yam added.

Serve this richly flavored sauté with Simple Baked Tofu (page 225).

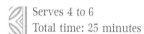
Serves 4 to 6
Total time: 25 minutes

¹/₄ cup soy sauce

2 teaspoons sugar

2 teaspoons dark sesame oil

1 tablespoon cornstarch

1 tablespoon fresh lemon juice or rice wine vinegar

¹/₂ pound soba noodles

1 tablespoon vegetable oil

3 large garlic cloves, minced or pressed

¹/₈ to ¹/₄ teaspoon cayenne

4 to 5 cups bite-sized broccoli florets

¹/₄ cup water

¹/₂ cup sake

1 carrot, peeled and grated

In a large covered pot, bring 3 quarts of water to a boil. Meanwhile, whisk together the soy sauce, sugar, sesame oil, cornstarch, and the lemon juice or vinegar until smooth, and then set aside. When the water boils, add the soba noodles and cook for 8 to 10 minutes, until al dente.

While the noodles cook, warm the oil in a wok or heavy skillet on medium heat. Add the garlic and cayenne and cook, stirring constantly, just until the garlic turns golden, a minute or less. Stir in the broccoli, water, and sake. Cover and cook for 3 to 4 minutes, until the florets are tender but still bright green. Thoroughly stir in the grated carrots and the reserved soy sauce mixture. Cook for a minute or two until the liquid thickens, then reduce the heat to low.

When the noodles are done, drain, rinse them with warm water, and drain again. Add the cooked soba noodles to the vegetables and stir until they are coated with the sauce. Place on a platter and serve immediately.

PER 7.5-OUNCE SERVING: 187 CALORIES, 8 G PROTEIN, 4.3 G FAT, 29.6 G CARBOHYDRATES, 0.9 G SATURATED FATTY ACIDS, 0 MG CHOLESTEROL, 613.1 MG SODIUM, 2.3 G TOTAL DIETARY FIBER

vegetarian pozole

Pozole or hominy is a traditional Native American food made from flint corn. Usually pozole is cooked with chiles and epazote, an herb that's widely used in Mexico to aid digestion but is nearly impossible to find in the markets in the northeastern United States, although it's as easy to grow as mint.

Our version of this stew calls for canned hominy and features chiles, delicata squash, peppers, tomatoes, and familiar herbs. If delicata squash is not available, butternut works well, too.

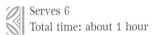
Serves 6
Total time: about 1 hour

4 teaspoons vegetable oil

2 cups chopped onions

2 garlic cloves, minced or pressed

$\frac{1}{8}$ plus $\frac{1}{4}$ teaspoon salt

$3\frac{1}{2}$ cups canned tomatoes with juice, chopped (28-ounce can)

3 to 4 cups peeled, seeded, and cubed delicata squash

4 cups coarsely chopped red or green bell peppers

4 cups drained hominy (two 15-ounce cans)

2 teaspoons fresh lime juice

2 to 3 tablespoons minced chipotles in adobo sauce*

1 tablespoon chopped fresh oregano, sage, or epazote

grated Monterey Jack, avocado cubes, crushed tortilla chips, chopped fresh cilantro, shredded lettuce, fresh lime wedges

* Chipotles in adobo sauce are smoked chiles in a spicy tomato sauce. They are available in small jars or cans in Latin American groceries and many supermarkets.

Warm the oil in a soup pot. Add the onions and sauté on medium-high heat for 5 to 7 minutes, until golden. Stir in the garlic and $\frac{1}{8}$ teaspoon of the salt and sauté for 2 minutes more. Add the tomatoes and squash and simmer for about 10 minutes.

Add the bell peppers, cover, and cook for 10 to 15 minutes, until the squash is tender. Stir in the hominy, lime juice, chipotles in adobo sauce, the remaining $\frac{1}{4}$ teaspoon of salt, and the oregano, sage, or epazote. Simmer for 5 minutes.

Serve with your favorite garnishes.

PER 18-OUNCE SERVING: 218 CALORIES, 6.3 G PROTEIN, 4.4 G FAT, 41.9 G CARBOHYDRATES, 1 G SATURATED FATTY ACIDS, 0 MG CHOLESTEROL, 312.3 MG SODIUM, 5.1 G TOTAL DIETARY FIBER

the health benefits of soy

Recently, much attention has been paid to the potential health benefits of soy. Research has been spurred by the dramatically lower rates of heart disease, certain cancers, and osteoporosis in Asian cultures where large quantities of soy are consumed. So far, the implications for heart disease have been the most promising*— so promising that the Food and Drug Administration (FDA) recommends that 25 grams of soy protein be eaten daily. The FDA also permits the labels on foods containing at least 6.25 grams of soy protein per serving to claim that their product may help reduce the risk of heart disease when consumed as part of a diet low in saturated fat and cholesterol.

It is not clear whether soy protein can help everyone, or just those who have high cholesterol. The daily standards for soy set by the FDA are lower than the daily amounts consumed in the clinical studies that demonstrated the soy protein-cholesterol lowering effect. If you are at risk for heart disease, it is wisest to discuss a higher daily intake of soy with a professional clinician. How soy lowers cholesterol is inconclusive. Is it fiber? Isoflavones? A synergy of some sort?

Scientists and nutritionists recommend soy consumption in whole food form (soybeans, soy nuts, soybean sprouts, tofu, tempeh, soy milk, and soy flour), rather than through supplements or soy products that principally contain isolated soy protein or isoflavones.

When seeking soy protein, it is important to read labels carefully. Soy sauce and soy oil contain no soy protein or isoflavones, and soy hot dogs, sausages, and bacon made with textured vegetable protein often contain only a small amount of soy or may have loads of isolated soy protein, but no isoflavones.

Here's a quick, practical guide to help you increase your intake of soy: $1/2$ cup cooked soybeans yields about 16 grams soy protein; 4 ounces of firm tofu yields 13 grams and 4 ounces of soft tofu yields 9 grams (more water, less protein); 4 ounces of tempeh yields 17 grams; 8 ounces of low-fat soy milk yields 13 grams; and $1/4$ cup of soy flour yields a whopping 47 grams.

The possible link between soy and healthy bones, and soy and cancer risk reduction is even more complex. Thus far, studies have not been conclusive, and researchers caution against comparing biologically dissimilar cultures and against consumption of a single food or of an isolate of that food. Researchers have also noted that the sexes handle chemicals differently, and that it is not understood at what hormonal point in a woman's life, if any, soy provides a protective effect.**

Soy is a good-tasting, inexpensive source of protein that is low in saturated fat, has important vitamins and minerals, and in some forms, is a good source of fiber.

* The *New England Journal of Medicine* reported a meta-analysis of about three dozen controlled studies conducted over the last twenty-five years that found that 1.5 ounces of soy protein eaten daily lowered cholesterol levels by 9 percent.

** "Eating Well" by Marian Burros, *New York Times*, January 26, 2000.

tofu stroganoff

Our vegetarian version of a classic Russian dish is composed of marinated tofu and vegetables simmered with the traditional flavors of red wine, paprika, and fresh dill. Pressing the tofu helps it maintain its integrity in the stroganoff, but if time is a constraint, you can omit this step.

Imagine our surprise when we discovered that our "fake" Tofu Sour Cream is just as good as the real stuff. Either will create a smooth, creamy stroganoff.

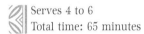
Serves 4 to 6
Total time: 65 minutes

1 cake firm tofu, pressed (16 ounces)*
3 tablespoons soy sauce
1 garlic clove, minced or pressed
1 tablespoon vegetable oil
2 cups chopped onions
1 cup chopped celery
1/2 teaspoon salt
1 tablespoon paprika
2 cups peeled and sliced carrots**
4 cups bite-sized mushrooms pieces
1/2 cup dry red wine
1 1/2 cups canned diced tomatoes with juice (14.5 ounce can)
2 cups sliced zucchini**
1 1/2 cups chopped red bell peppers
2 tablespoons chopped fresh dill
1 to 1 1/2 pounds wide egg noodles
1/2 to 1 cup sour cream or Tofu Sour Cream (page 386)

fresh dill sprigs

Cut the tofu into 3 slices. Stack the slices and make two horizontal and two vertical cuts to yield 27 cubes. Gently toss the tofu with the soy sauce and garlic. Set aside to marinate, stirring occasionally.

Meanwhile, warm the oil in a soup pot and add the onions, celery, and salt. Cover and cook on low heat, stirring occasionally, for about 10 minutes. Add the paprika and carrots, cover, and cook for about 5 minutes. Add the mushrooms and wine, cover, and cook for another 5 minutes.

Add the tomatoes, zucchini, and peppers and bring to a boil. Reduce the heat, cover, and simmer for 5 to 10 minutes, until everything is tender. Add the dill and the tofu cubes with the marinade, cover, and simmer for 2 or 3 minutes, until bubbly hot.

About 20 minutes before serving, bring a large pot of water to a boil, cook the noodles until al dente, and drain.

Sandwich the tofu between two plates. Rest a heavy can on top. Press for 15 minutes; then drain.
**Slice carrots and zucchini in half lengthwise and cut crosswise into 1/2-inch-thick semi-circles.*

Just before serving, gently stir 1/2 cup of sour cream or Tofu Sour Cream into the stroganoff. Ladle the stroganoff over the hot egg noodles in wide shallow pasta bowls. Top with dill sprigs and pass more sour cream at the table.

PER 20-OUNCE SERVING: 484 CALORIES, 20.1 G PROTEIN, 13.3 G FAT, 71.4 G CARBOHYDRATES, 4.3 G SATURATED FATTY ACIDS, 74 MG CHOLESTEROL, 747.5 MG SODIUM, 6.8 G TOTAL DIETARY FIBER

tofu in black bean sauce

At Moosewood, we love to prepare tofu bursting with assertive seasonings. With a sauce of fermented black beans, this Hunan-style dish dispels any lingering notion that "tofu is bland."

Fermented black beans, most commonly used on fish, vegetables, or poultry, undergo fermentation and are seasoned with salt, ginger, and orange to produce a flavor that's at once salty, spicy, and sweet. They go by a variety of names: salted black beans, preserved black beans, or sometimes Chinese black beans. They are available in plastic packages in Asian food stores and in the Asian section of some supermarkets. One 8-ounce package goes a long way: sealed in plastic or stored in a jar in the cupboard or refrigerator, the beans will keep for months.

Before using the beans, rinse well and chop finely to reduce the saltiness and moderate the intense flavor. Very few people would want to eat them whole by the spoonful!

This tofu is delicious spooned over a bed of rice and accompanied by a cooked green vegetable.

Serves 4
Total time: 30 minutes

1 cake firm tofu (16 ounces), pressed*

1 tablespoon peanut oil or other vegetable oil

3 scallions, cut on the severe diagonal into ¼-inch slices

3 garlic cloves, minced or pressed

1 tablespoon grated fresh ginger root

2 tablespoons fermented black beans, very well rinsed and minced**

½ teaspoon Chinese chili paste

1 teaspoon dark sesame oil

2 tablespoons soy sauce

6 tablespoons dry sherry (or 3 tablespoons sherry and 3 tablespoons sake)

⅓ cup water or vegetable stock mixed with 1 tablespoon cornstarch

1 tablespoon minced fresh cilantro

* Sandwich the tofu between two plates and rest a heavy weight (a can or book) on the top plate. Press for about 20 minutes and drain the expressed liquid.
** Cover the fermented black beans with warm water and let sit for 3 to 5 minutes. Drain. Rinse well under running water and drain again. If fermented black beans are unavailable, use 1½ tablespoons of canned Chinese Black Bean Sauce.

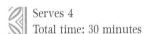

Slice the tofu horizontally into 4 slabs about ½-inch thick. Cut the stacked slabs of tofu into eighths as you would cut a pie: First, cut on the two diagonals (making an "X") and then make one vertical slice and one horizontal slice. Use one hand to keep the tofu in its stacked cube shape while cutting. The result will be 32 triangular tofu pieces.

In a large skillet, warm the oil on medium heat, and stir in the scallions, garlic, and ginger. Add the tofu in a single layer and sauté until golden, about 5 minutes on each side, using a spatula to flip the pieces gently.

Meanwhile, stir together the fermented black beans, Chinese chili paste, sesame oil, soy sauce, sherry, and cornstarch mixture and set aside. When the tofu is ready, pour the sauce over the tofu, lower the heat, and simmer uncovered for about 10 minutes, stirring occasionally. Serve topped with the cilantro.

PER 7-OUNCE SERVING: 177 CALORIES, 11 G PROTEIN, 10 G FAT, 10.2 G CARBOHYDRATES, 1.5 G SATURATED FATTY ACIDS, 0 MG CHOLESTEROL, 415.9 MG SODIUM, 1.9 G TOTAL DIETARY FIBER

the intrepid legumes

Beans, peas, and lentils are old friends and good travelers that have nourished humans for thousands of years. Wild indigenous legumes were a staple in the diets of hunter-gatherers in the Americas 12,000 years ago and, eventually, the descendants of these first native people began to cultivate and trade beans. Archaeologists have found four species of legumes native to the Americas: the common bean, limas and sievas, scarlet runner beans, and teparies. These hardy species yield over 1,500 varieties.

The only legume indigenous to Europe is the fava bean, or broad bean. As early as 1493, when Columbus made his second voyage to the Caribbean, conquistadors selected beans to be taken back to Spain, and it wasn't long before the common bean became regular fare in Europe, Africa, Asia, and the Mediterranean. Chickpeas, also called garbanzos and ceci, were probably domesticated in eastern Mediterranean countries about 7500 B.C.

Lentils were cultivated in the Near East about 7000 B.C. and eventually became a staple in early agrarian cultures of Egypt, Europe, and western Asia. Deposits of dried peas dating back to 5700 B.C. have been found in central Turkey. These starchy peas came to the New World with Columbus. Black-eyed peas, so synonymous with Southern cooking, originated in Africa and were taken to the Caribbean during the sixteenth century. Pigeon peas may have been first cultivated in tropical Africa or India, where 95 percent of the world's crop is now grown.

The most widely consumed legume on the globe, the soybean, was cultivated in China in 1100 B.C. and more than a thousand varieties have spread to all parts of the world. Another East Asian bean, the azuki bean, may have been first grown in Japan, where it remains an integral ingredient in traditional Japanese cuisine. The mung bean is believed to have originated in India almost 3,500 years ago.

winter curry

This sweet and spicy curry went west and never turned back once it ventured into the Caribbean and found the tart, puckery fruit of the tamarind tree.

Cut the potatoes and squash into 1-inch cubes to ensure even cooking. If you can't find butternut squash, acorn squash can be used in its place. Use one or more of the recommended garnishes and serve on your favorite rice.

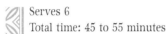 Serves 6
Total time: 45 to 55 minutes

In a 3- to 4-quart saucepan, heat the oil on medium-high heat, and then add the mustard seeds. When the seeds begin to pop, stir in the onions and sauté until translucent, about 10 minutes.

Meanwhile, in a small bowl, combine the garlic, ginger, cumin, coriander, cardamom, salt, and chiles or cayenne. When the onions are translucent, add the spice mixture and cook for 1 minute, stirring constantly. Add the potatoes, squash, and water or stock and bring to a boil. Then reduce the heat, cover, and simmer until the vegetables are barely tender, about 15 minutes.

In a small bowl, dissolve the tamarind in a few tablespoons of the hot cooking liquid and then stir it into the vegetables. Add the tomatoes, chickpeas, and cilantro, cover, and simmer for about 10 minutes, until the vegetables are fully tender.

Serve on rice, topped with any or all of the suggested garnishes.

1½ tablespoons vegetable oil
½ teaspoon black mustard seeds
1½ cups chopped onions
3 garlic cloves, minced or pressed
1 tablespoon grated fresh ginger root
2 teaspoons ground cumin
2 teaspoons ground coriander
½ teaspoon ground cardamom
½ teaspoon salt
1 minced fresh green chile or
    ¼ teaspoon cayenne
4 cups cubed potatoes
4 cups peeled and cubed butternut
    squash
1½ cups water or vegetable stock
1 tablespoon tamarind concentrate
    (page 471)
2 cups fresh or canned chopped
    tomatoes
1½ to 2 cups cooked chickpeas
    (15-ounce can, drained)
2 tablespoons chopped fresh cilantro

cooked rice

plain yogurt, cilantro sprigs, toasted
    cashews, and mango slices; fruit
    chutney (page 383); or raisins

PER 14-OUNCE SERVING: 294 CALORIES, 7.6 G PROTEIN, 5 G FAT, 59 G CARBOHYDRATES, 1.1 G SATURATED FATTY ACIDS, 0 MG CHOLESTEROL, 394.2 MG SODIUM, 6.3 G TOTAL DIETARY FIBER

basic skillet black beans

Here's a supper-in-20-minutes recipe for black beans or any basic bean. Serve it on rice, polenta, or grits, topped with salsa, grated cheese, or sour cream, and chopped fresh cilantro.

Embellish with garlic, ground fennel, thyme, chili powder, chiles, chipotles, or cayenne. Or flavor with cumin only. For the liquid, use orange juice or chopped fresh or canned tomatoes. Add corn, bell peppers, carrots, celery, squash. Serve topped with mango or pineapple salsa, grated cheese, sour cream, or tempeh. Finish with chopped fresh cilantro.

Leftovers? Make chilaquiles or Red & Green Sopa Seca (page 306). Or, make soup in 10 minutes by adding tomato juice or salsa, water, corn kernels, and a topping of cilantro or cheese. Use the beans as a filling for tacos with shredded lettuce, avocado cubes, and salsa or make a taco salad with lettuce, crumbled tortilla chips, salsa, and sour cream.

2 teaspoons olive oil or vegetable oil
1 1/2 cups diced onions
1 teaspoon ground cumin
1/2 teaspoon ground coriander
1 cup salsa or tomato juice
3 cups cooked black beans
  (two 15-ounce cans, rinsed
  and drained)

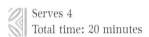
Serves 4
Total time: 20 minutes

In a covered skillet or saucepan, heat the oil on medium-high heat. Add the onions and sauté for 5 minutes, stirring frequently. Add the cumin and coriander and stir for a minute to toast the spices.

Add the salsa or tomato juice, stir well, cover, and simmer until the onions are soft, about 5 minutes. Add the black beans and simmer until slightly thickened, about 5 minutes. If you like, mash a few times with a potato masher.

PER 10-OUNCE SERVING: 218 CALORIES, 11.9 G PROTEIN, 3.3 G FAT, 36.7 G CARBOHYDRATES, 0.5 G SATURATED FATTY ACIDS, 0 MG CHOLESTEROL, 951.4 MG SODIUM, 13 G TOTAL DIETARY FIBER

basque skillet beans

Saffron and extra-virgin olive oil add a complex, sophisticated character to this simply prepared dish. Serve right from the skillet along with chunks of crusty bread and a buttery Havarti or potent French Muenster cheese. If you have time, spoon the beans over piping hot polenta.

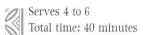 Serves 4 to 6
Total time: 40 minutes

In a small heat-proof bowl, cover the saffron with the boiling water. Set aside.

In a 12-inch skillet, warm the olive oil on medium heat and sauté the garlic, onions, and chiles for about 5 minutes. Using your hands, crush the tomatoes into the skillet. Add the juice from the can, the sherry, and the saffron with its soaking liquid.

Stir in the chickpeas and bring the mixture to a gentle boil. Arrange the spinach on top and reduce the heat to a simmer. Cover and cook for about 5 minutes, until the spinach is wilted but still bright green. Remove from the heat and mix in the spinach. Season with the lemon juice, salt, and pepper to taste.

$^1/_4$ teaspoon crumbled saffron threads
$^1/_4$ cup boiling water
2 tablespoons extra-virgin olive oil
4 garlic cloves, minced or pressed
1 cup chopped onions
1 minced fresh chile (seeds removed
    for a milder hot)
1$^3/_4$ cups canned tomatoes with juice
    (14.5-ounce can)
$^1/_2$ cup dry sherry
3 cups cooked chickpeas
    (two 15-ounce cans, drained
    and rinsed)*
10 ounces fresh spinach, rinsed,
    stemmed, and chopped
2 to 3 tablespoons fresh lemon juice
$^1/_4$ teaspoon salt
ground black pepper to taste

* *Look for excellent-quality chickpeas packed
without salt or preservatives in the natural
food aisles of the market.*

PER 10-OUNCE SERVING: 229 CALORIES, 8.1 G PROTEIN, 6.3 G FAT, 33.9 G CARBOHYDRATES,
0.8 G SATURATED FATTY ACIDS, 0 MG CHOLESTEROL, 562.2 MG SODIUM, 6.5 G TOTAL DIETARY FIBER

variation *Replace the chickpeas with cannellini beans.*

black bean & sweet potato hash

Make this "flash in the pan" Tex-Mex dish into a down-home classic. Use convenient canned beans and frozen corn kernels and vary the spices according to your taste.

Serves 4 to 6
Preparation time: 20 minutes
Cooking time: 20 minutes

1 to 2 tablespoons olive oil

2 cups chopped onions

2 garlic cloves, minced or pressed

6 cups peeled diced sweet potatoes ($\frac{1}{2}$-inch pieces)

1 jalapeño, minced

1 tablespoon ground coriander

1 tablespoon ground cumin

1 teaspoon salt

1 cup frozen corn kernels (or mixed corn and green peppers)

1$\frac{1}{2}$ cups cooked black beans (15-ounce can, drained)

splash of water or orange juice (optional)

dash of salt

cayenne or hot pepper sauce (optional)

minced scallions or chopped fresh cilantro

sour cream (optional)

Heat the oil in a large, deep, nonstick skillet. Add the onions and sauté on medium heat, stirring occasionally, until they begin to soften. Stir in the garlic, cook for a few seconds, then add the sweet potatoes. Cover the skillet and cook for 3 minutes. Add the jalapeño, coriander, cumin, and salt; then use a spatula to turn the potatoes, cover, and cook for another 3 minutes. Add the corn and black beans, cover, and cook for 10 minutes, stirring occasionally.

If the potatoes are still too firm, add a little water or orange juice, cover, and cook on low heat until the potatoes are tender. Add the salt and stir in cayenne or hot pepper sauce to taste.

Serve topped with minced scallions or chopped cilantro and, if you like, a dollop of sour cream.

PER 10.5-OUNCE SERVING: 265 CALORIES, 7.6 G PROTEIN, 3.6 G FAT, 53.3 G CARBOHYDRATES, 0.5 G SATURATED FATTY ACIDS, 0 MG CHOLESTEROL, 667.4 MG SODIUM, 7.9 G TOTAL DIETARY FIBER

chili with tofu or tvp

We've made some good chilis over the years, but this one is by far the most hearty and chewy of them all. Adding ground frozen tofu, an ingredient we use extensively at Moosewood, gives this chili high-quality protein and a traditional meatlike texture. The tofu absorbs a lot of flavor, so you can be generous with the amount of spices you use.

There are several vegetarian meat substitutes, called textured vegetable protein (TVP), that are commercially available and can work well in place of the tofu.

If using a TVP brand that's already highly seasoned, you might want to use a lighter hand with the spices.

Accompany this chili with your favorite crackers or freshly baked cornbread.

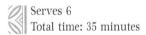
Serves 6
Total time: 35 minutes

Heat the oil in a large nonstick skillet on medium-high heat. Add the onions and garlic and sauté on medium-high heat until soft. Add the cumin, coriander, and chili powder and stir well. Mix in the diced squash and peppers, cover, and continue to cook for about 3 minutes. Stir in the ground tofu or textured vegetable protein and cook for several more minutes until heated through.

Meanwhile, in a soup pot, heat the tomatoes and beans on medium heat. Stir in the tomato paste. Transfer the hot skillet ingredients to the pot and stir well. Add the parsley and season with salsa or Tabasco sauce and salt.

Serve in bowls or mugs, topped with sprinklings of cheese or dollops of sour cream.

3 tablespoons olive oil

1 Spanish onion, chopped

2 garlic cloves, minced or pressed

1 tablespoon ground cumin

1 tablespoon ground coriander

1 to 2 teaspoons chili powder

1 medium zucchini or yellow summer squash, diced

1 large red or green bell pepper, stemmed, seeded, and chopped

1 cake tofu, frozen, thawed, and ground, or 12 to 14 ounces prepared textured vegetable protein (opposite)

3 cups diced tomatoes with juice (28-ounce can)

2 cups cooked pinto beans with liquid (15-ounce can)

2 cups cooked red kidney beans with liquid (15-ounce can)

$2/3$ cup tomato paste (6-ounce can)

2 tablespoons minced fresh parsley

your favorite salsa and/or Tabasco sauce or other hot sauce to taste

salt to taste

shredded Cheddar or Monterey Jack cheese, or sour cream

PER 12-OUNCE SERVING: 376 CALORIES, 21.7 G PROTEIN, 11.7 G FAT, 51.1 G CARBOHYDRATES, 1.6 G SATURATED FATTY ACIDS, 0 MG CHOLESTEROL, 382.1 MG SODIUM, 14.3 G TOTAL DIETARY FIBER

ground frozen tofu

☙ *Fresh tofu has a moist, light, tender texture, like soft scrambled eggs. When frozen, its consistency changes significantly: The water separates into little cells and leaves the tofu like a sponge. When the liquid is squeezed out, the tofu can be crumbled or ground and has a moist chewy texture.*

Since using frozen tofu requires some forethought, you might want to keep some on hand in the freezer. Whole cakes placed on a plate or baking sheet, uncovered, will freeze in 4 to 6 hours, so the simplest method is to freeze the tofu overnight for use the next day. If you're not going to use it right away, wrap it in plastic before freezing. Frozen tofu will thaw in the refrigerator in 10 to 12 hours. If not fully defrosted by the time you're ready to use it, microwave just until you can squeeze it.

To speed up the process, cut fresh tofu into 1-inch-thick slices, arrange it on a plate or baking pan in a single layer, and freeze it, uncovered, for 3 hours. Frozen tofu slices thaw in the refrigerator in 4 to 6 hours. For faster thawing, cover it well and defrost it in a 350° oven for 30 minutes, or zap it in a microwave for 5 to 10 minutes.

When thawed, squeeze out as much water as possible with your hands and discard the liquid. It will feel just like a sponge, and if it breaks or crumbles, it doesn't matter since it's going to be ground or crumbled anyway. The drained thawed tofu can be refrigerated and stored in a well-sealed plastic bag or container for a day, but should be used soon.

To prepare thawed tofu for cooking, shred it in a food processor, crumble by hand, chop with a knife, or mash with a fork or potato ricer. Its chewy texture is similar to chopped meat and it readily absorbs seasonings.

textured vegetable protein (ground meat substitute)

☙ *Several vegetarian meat substitutes are available commercially. They are usually made with some combination of textured vegetable protein, soy protein, and wheat gluten. They range from mildly to highly seasoned and come either ground, shredded, or shaped like sausage. For this recipe, buy a 12- to 14-ounce package. If necessary, chop, shred, or mash it into crumbles the size of ground meat.*

Look for these products in supermarkets or natural foods stores. TVP is often found in the dairy case where soy products are sold.

drunken beans

Whether we need a Mexican main dish that keeps our Moosewood customers hopping or a versatile side dish for a combination platter, Drunken Beans fills the bill.

Traditionally, Drunken beans, or *frijoles borrachos*, hails from Monterrey in northern Mexico, where the renowned Dos Equis beer is brewed. So it's no surprise that Dos Equis is our first choice for this dish. Nevertheless, any amber beer makes delicious beans.

Serve these easy-to-make beans in bowls beside vegetable burritos or cheese enchiladas, incorporate them into chili-and-cheese casseroles and tamale pies, or mash them and serve them in place of refritos. Leftover beans can also be added to Mexican-style soups and stews.

Serves 4 to 6
Total time: 35 minutes

1 tablespoon vegetable oil

1 cup chopped onions

2 garlic cloves, minced or pressed

1/4 teaspoon salt

1 teaspoon ground cumin

12 ounces amber beer

2 teaspoons brown sugar, packed

1 1/2 cups cooked pinto beans
    (15-ounce can, rinsed and
    drained)

1 3/4 cups canned tomatoes with juice,
    chopped (14.5-ounce can)

2 to 3 teaspoons chipotle adobo
    sauce*

2 teaspoons soy sauce

* Canned chipotle peppers in adobo come packed in a tomato sauce that has a sweet, smoky, spicy flavor. On its own the sauce can add a robust flavor without the intense heat of the chipotles. Chipotles in adobo sauce can be found in small cans or jars at Latin American groceries and in the ethnic section of well-stocked supermarkets.

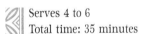Heat the oil in an 8- or 9-inch frying pan. Add the onions, garlic, and salt and sauté on medium-high heat until the onions are translucent, about 10 minutes. Dust the onions with the cumin and continue to cook stirring continuously, for another minute or two.

Stir in the beer, brown sugar, pinto beans, tomatoes, adobo sauce, and soy sauce. Bring to a boil then reduce the heat and simmer gently, uncovered, for about 20 minutes to allow the flavors to mingle and the alcohol to mellow. Stir occasionally.

Ladle into small bowls and serve.

PER 7.25-OUNCE SERVING: 156 CALORIES, 6.1 G PROTEIN, 2.9 G FAT, 24.1 G CARBOHYDRATES, 0.7 G SATURATED FATTY ACIDS, 0 MG CHOLESTEROL, 296.8 MG SODIUM, 5.4 G TOTAL DIETARY FIBER

french ragoût beans

Ragoût is a French word that means "to stimulate the palate." Traditional ragoûts are most often long-simmering affairs, but here is a fast and easy one-dish meal with the same rich flavors.

For a sumptuous springtime feast, serve with roasted asparagus and steamed new potatoes or in colder seasons, ladle over pasta or couscous.

 Serves 2 as a main dish, 4 as a side dish
Total time: 30 minutes

½ cup sun-dried tomatoes
  (not oil-packed)
3 tablespoons extra-virgin olive oil
2 cups diced onions
3 large garlic cloves, minced or
  pressed
1 tablespoon fennel seeds
1 cup diced red bell pepper
1 tablespoon chopped fresh thyme
  (1 teaspoon dried)
2 tablespoons red wine vinegar
3 cups cooked navy beans
  (two 15-ounce cans, drained)
2 ounces plain or herbed chèvre

Place the sun-dried tomatoes in a heat-proof bowl and cover with 1 cup of boiling water. Set aside.

Heat the olive oil in a large skillet. Add the onions and garlic and sauté on medium heat for 5 minutes. Toast the fennel seeds for 1 minute in a toaster oven or small unoiled skillet; then grind in a spice grinder. Add the fennel and bell peppers to the onions and continue to sauté for about 4 more minutes.

Remove the sun-dried tomatoes from the bowl and reserve the soaking liquid. Squeeze out any excess water from the sun-dried tomatoes, chop them, and add them to the sauté. Stir in half of the reserved soaking liquid, the thyme, and vinegar. Gently toss in the beans and cook on medium heat until thoroughly heated.

Transfer the beans to a serving dish and crumble the chèvre on top or spread the cheese on bread or crackers and serve alongside the beans.

PER 11-OUNCE SERVING: 445 CALORIES, 20.6 G PROTEIN, 15.6 G FAT, 60.8 G CARBOHYDRATES, 3.9 G SATURATED FATTY ACIDS, 6.5 MG CHOLESTEROL, 455.3 MG SODIUM, 20.4 G TOTAL DIETARY FIBER

indian skillet black-eyed peas

Create this zippy, spicy Indian dinner in just minutes by combining aromatic spices, fresh tomatoes, spinach, and a good brand of canned black-eyed peas with no preservatives.
Serve it with rice, your favorite chutney, and a cooling dollop of yogurt or raita.

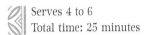
Serves 4 to 6
Total time: 25 minutes

2 tablespoons vegetable oil
1 cup chopped onions
1 garlic clove, minced or pressed
1 tablespoon grated fresh ginger root
1/8 to 1/4 teaspoon cayenne
1/4 teaspoon ground cinnamon
1/4 teaspoon ground cardamom
1/2 teaspoon ground coriander
1 teaspoon salt
1 cup water
1 teaspoon tamarind concentrate
  (page 471)*
3 cups cooked black-eyed peas
  (two 16-ounce cans, rinsed
  and drained)
1/2 cup chopped fresh tomatoes
2 cups rinsed and chopped
  fresh spinach

* *If tamarind is unavailable, use 1 to*
  2 teaspoons of fresh lemon juice instead.

Heat the oil in a skillet or nonreactive saucepan. Add the onions and garlic and sauté on medium-high heat until the onions are soft and beginning to brown, about 10 minutes. Add the ginger, cayenne, cinnamon, cardamom, coriander, and salt and mix well. Stir in the water, tamarind, and the black-eyed peas, cover, and simmer for about 10 minutes. Add the tomatoes and spinach and cook just until the spinach wilts, about 1 minute.

Serve right away.

PER 7.5-OUNCE SERVING: 160 CALORIES, 6.8 G PROTEIN, 5.6 G FAT, 21.8 G CARBOHYDRATES, 1.4 G SATURATED FATTY ACIDS, 0 MG CHOLESTEROL, 785.3 MG SODIUM, 5 G TOTAL DIETARY FIBER

potato & asparagus hash

New green asparagus and crisp hash-brown potatoes make a fast and easy, come-and-get-it meal. If you like, use two pans simultaneously for frying the potato mixture to get to the eating sooner. We find that as soon as we smell those potatoes start to fry, we're suddenly ravenous.

Serve with poached eggs or fish accompanied by your favorite red salsa, ketchup, or Perfect Tomato Salad (page 112).

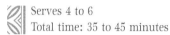 Serves 4 to 6
Total time: 35 to 45 minutes

5 cups peeled diced potatoes
 (1/2-inch cubes)
2 cups chopped fresh asparagus
2 tablespoons vegetable oil
2 cups diced onions
2 garlic cloves, minced or pressed
1 teaspoon salt
1/2 teaspoon ground black pepper
1 tablespoon fresh dill

In a covered soup pot, bring about 6 cups of water to a boil. Add the potatoes and cook for 5 minutes, until the potatoes are tender but still underdone. Remove the potatoes with a slotted spoon or sieve and transfer to a large bowl. Add the asparagus to the still boiling water. Cook for 2 to 3 minutes, until bright green and just tender. Drain and add to the bowl of potatoes.

In a skillet, warm 1 tablespoon of the oil on medium heat. Sauté the onions, garlic, salt, and pepper for about 10 minutes, until the onions are golden. Add the sautéed onions and the dill to the bowl of potatoes and stir well.

In a large nonstick saucepan or lightly oiled cast-iron skillet, heat the remaining tablespoon of oil. Fry the potato mixture in two batches for 5 to 10 minutes, until the potatoes are golden brown.

PER 7.5-OUNCE SERVING: 191 CALORIES, 3.9 G PROTEIN, 5.1 G FAT, 34.2 G CARBOHYDRATES, 1.3 G SATURATED FATTY ACIDS, 0 MG CHOLESTEROL, 405.3 MG SODIUM, 3.7 G TOTAL DIETARY FIBER

peppers & greens skillet hash

The word "hash" can evoke quite a string of culinary associations: diners, cowboys, cook-outs, truck stops, fried potatoes with eggs and toast, fuel to keep you going through the day. Here's a hash with a bit of colorful character. It makes a super dish for lunch, brunch, or supper whether you're in the saddle, riding shotgun, or just lying low.

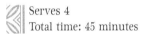

Serves 4
Total time: 45 minutes

4 to 6 cups stemmed sliced Swiss or
   ruby chard, or fresh spinach
3 tablespoons olive oil
2 cups thinly sliced or chopped
   onions
1 large garlic clove, minced or
   pressed
10 cups diced potatoes*
2 cups sliced red bell peppers
1 teaspoon fresh thyme
   (1/2 teaspoon dried)
1 cup sliced mushrooms (optional)
2 tablespoons soy sauce**
4 dashes Tabasco sauce or other hot
   pepper sauce, or to taste

* Four large red-skinned, white, or gold potatoes, peeled and cut into 1/2-inch cubes, will
   yield 10 cups diced. We recommend Yukon
   Gold or Butter varieties.
** We like the mild, mellow flavor of shoyu
   soy sauce.

Rinse the greens well. Blanch them in 1/2 cup of boiling water for 2 to 3 minutes, until wilted. Drain and set aside.

Heat the oil in a large nonstick skillet. Sauté the onions and garlic on medium heat for about 10 minutes, until the onions are translucent. Add the diced potatoes, spread them evenly in the skillet, cover, and cook for about 5 minutes. Uncover and stir well. Cook for another 5 to 8 minutes, until the potatoes are tender and browned.

Add the drained greens, bell peppers, thyme, and, if you like, the mushrooms. Cover and cook for 5 to 10 minutes, stirring frequently, until the peppers are tender. Mix in the soy sauce and Tabasco sauce to taste.

Serve immediately.

PER 21-OUNCE SERVING: 516 CALORIES, 9.9 G PROTEIN, 11.3 G FAT, 97.6 G CARBOHYDRATES,
1.6 G SATURATED FATTY ACIDS, 0 MG CHOLESTEROL, 455.2 MG SODIUM, 9.9 G TOTAL DIETARY FIBER

lighten up & eat well

According to almost every how-to-live-well survey in the last several decades, eating delicious food and staying healthy are priorties for nearly everyone. Unfortunately, there is no cut-and-dried formula for optimum nutrition and establishing definitive guidelines is near impossible, since each one of us is different in the particulars of our bodily strengths, weaknesses, metabolisms and mental outlooks.

There is, however, a growing body of scientific, nutritional findings that can be used as directional "pointers" to help us navigate the sometimes faddish and contradictory mire of health pronouncements. Using common sense and individual experience to sort through the plethora of information and heeding the advice of experts we know personally and trust can really help clarify what will work for us as individuals.

Once we get a handle on the basics, practice makes perfect—or close enough, so start simple. Nutritionists and doctors all agree on one thing: we should be eating less packaged, processed food and more vegetables, grains, and fruits. Beyond that there is widespread consensus that most Americans would benefit from reducing the fat, especially the saturated and hydrogenated fats, in their diets. Many of us could also benefit from lowering our salt and cholesterol intake. We should learn to eat slowly and in moderation, not skip breakfast, not chow down before retiring to bed, and get plenty of exercise and adequate sleep. Developing habits that support healthy choices may well bring about those desirable changes in looks and vigor that we all crave.

American culture often follows the "bigger is better" rule of thumb, and it's no surprise that the size of our food portions has grown as dramatically as car size and so much else over the last few decades. Rediscovering what is a reasonable portion and avoiding excess can make a significant difference in body weight, health, and overall well-being.

When we wrote *Moosewood Restaurant Low-Fat Favorites* in 1996, we worked to create a volume crammed with hundreds of lip-smacking-good recipes and lots of tips that would help us all consume less fat without feeling like we were dieting or depriving ourselves of life's pleasures. During the year it took us to develop the recipes, our diets naturally became lower in fat because we were cooking with less oil and eating fewer high-fat foods. Many of us were encouraged to discover we actually enjoyed eating this way, and—an unexpected bonus—some of us lost weight without trying.

Low-fat eating is certainly not just a flimsy fad diet. Researchers continue to find evidence that a high-fat diet can contribute to the risk of heart disease, various cancers, stroke, hypertension, osteoporosis, obesity, and diabetes mellitus. A low-fat diet, especially an extremely low-fat one, may not be the answer for everyone. But it's worth checking with a doctor and then trying it out if given the go-ahead. A little conscientious effort and sustained attention *can* bring great rewards both immediately and in the long run.

Here are a few key tips for lightening up:

- Sauté with a teaspoon of oil on lower heat rather than using the usual 2 tablespoons on high heat. Invest in at least one good nonstick skillet or 3-quart saucepan with a tight-fitting lid. Use oils such as olive oil that are high in monounsaturated fats, limit your use of butter, and avoid oils high in saturated fats, such as coconut and palm oils. Steer clear of processed foods containing hydrogenated oils. Choose steamed vegetables and baked fish over deep-fried or breaded counterparts. Include in your diet foods that are abundant in health-promoting omega-3 fatty acids, such as salmon, and walnuts.

- Make soups a regular part of your diet. They fill you up, not out. Boost their flavor with extra onions, mushrooms, aromatic herbs, vegetable stock, wine, tomato juice, or a dab of miso. Luscious creamy soups can be made with thick, flavorful, nonfat buttermilk, evaporated skimmed milk, soy milk, nonfat or low-fat yogurt, or Neufchâtel.

- Shop for delicious low-fat and nonfat dairy products and keep them on hand.

- Thicken soups, stews, and sauces using puréed sweet potatoes, powdered rice, blended oats, or puréed bread rather than the traditional and higher-fat butter-flour roux and milk. Substitute fruit purées for the fat in baked goods.

- Try out some of our Moosewood low-fat dressings and experiment to make your own. Turn to herbs and spices for added richness. Replace some of the oil with fruit juice or mild stock and then combine it with flavored vinegars to add oomph. Use only as much dressing as is needed to flavor the dish: Avoid the dump and drench method.

- If you decide to use high-fat toppings such as cheese and nuts, finely shred or grate them to boost flavor using less. Choose sharp cheese and toasted nuts for the most flavor from the least fat.

- Stock the pantry with beans and whole grains. Zippy condiments like mustard, canned chiles, pickles, capers, sun-dried tomatoes, fish sauce, hot sauce, soy sauce, Chinese chili paste, Tabasco, hoisin sauce, horseradish, and Worcestershire sauce lend dishes lots of flavor without adding fat. How you shop can dramatically influence how you eat. Keep an eye out for good lower-fat snack foods such as nonfat and baked tortilla chips, rice cakes, rye crisps, and sourdough pretzels. If they're handy, you'll be more likely to reach for them.

- When you dine out, especially if you do it regularly, be discriminating. And keep in mind that celebrating doesn't have to mean overindulging: Don't feel obligated to opt for more.

We think lightening up is a 100 percent reachable goal, and eating more vegetables, grains, and fruits is a great start. When we truly explore eating well, it evolves in ways we never imagined at first.

showstoppers

showstoppers

✼ Time to put on the pots and make something special? Well, there's no need to take your tux to the cleaners or get your tiara out of the safe-deposit box; these special-occasion recipes taste wonderful and look impressive but aren't particularly fancy.

Our home, Ithaca, is basically very informal, a sweet little city nestled in a beautiful, rural area full of vineyards, orchards, waterfalls, gorges, and truck farms. So when we dream up showstoppers, what we come up with are the makings of homestyle feasts.

A special occasion may ask a little more from the cook, but don't let this intimidate you. Although some of these recipes may take longer or have more steps than other main dishes in this book, they're easy to follow and will make your meal festive and memorable. Shopping for special ingredients that may not be staples in your pantry can be part of the fun and anticipation of the big event.

If you're feeling the least bit nervous, here's some affirming "self-talk" to get you ready for success:

You've impressed the Variety crew.
Just picture the Sunday review:
"Pauline flips her noodle for Kale Pepper Strudel
and Pasta with Sunday Ragù!"

If the new East-West Stuffed Portabellos
make boisterous fans of those fellows,
Just serve them Cioppino with glasses of vino
or Vegan Turnovers so mellow.

"Oh the Batter-fried Veggies & Fish.
How I laughed! How I cried for the dish!"
They're shouting "Olè for Wild Mushroom Sauté
and Pecan-Crusted Fish is deelish!"

A bright diva in search of amoré
prepared Pinenut Pasta Cavalfiore.
Like moths to the flame, came suitors of fame,
with arias from Il Trovatore!

"Pizza with Three Toppings? Wow!"
sang the Three Tenors, mopping their brows.
They made quite a racket for Fish-in-a-Packet
and more Greek Lasagna, and how!

They are liable to dance in the aisle
for Stuffed Eggplant, served Moussaka-style.
They're singing cantatas about Fish Tostadas
and can't help but smile all the while.

Yes, being a celebrity can be a bit of a burden, but just take a deep bow and bask in the applause. Ah, the roar of the crowd! All those wonderful little people out there! Mr. De Mille, it's time for that close-up.

asparagus leek strudel

A whole family of strudels and related tortas and boreks have appeared on the menu here at Moosewood Restaurant and this is one that always wins raves. It has an elegant balance of flavors sure to impress and delight.

Serve this strudel as a main dish with a salad of spinach with Strawberry Dressing (page 385) or in smaller portions as part of a combination platter with Artichoke Soup Provençal (page 70) and Shredded Carrot Salad with Horseradish Dressing (page 111).

Serves 6 to 8
Preparation time: 45 minutes
Baking time: 45 minutes
Sitting time: 15 minutes

filling

8 ounces Neufchâtel or cream cheese

1 tablespoon olive oil

3 cups rinsed and chopped leeks*

5 cups stemmed and thinly sliced asparagus

1 tablespoon chopped fresh tarragon

1 tablespoon unbleached white flour

$3/4$ teaspoon salt

$1/4$ teaspoon ground black pepper

1 cup low-fat or regular cottage cheese

$1/2$ cup grated Gruyère cheese

1 cup grated sharp Cheddar cheese

4 eggs, lightly beaten

filo

$1/2$ to $2/3$ pound filo dough

2 tablespoons butter, melted

2 tablespoons olive oil

2 tablespoons sesame seeds

* *Cut off the root end of the leeks and the tough dark green leaves, leaving only the white and tender green parts of the leek. Immerse the stalks in water to remove obvious sand and grit. Slice vertically down the center of the bulb, separate its layers, and submerge again. Transfer to a colander and rinse again under running water until the sand is gone.*

Preheat the oven to 375°. Lightly oil a 10 x 13-inch baking tray.

Cut the Neufchâtel into several pieces, place in a large bowl, and set aside in a warm place to soften. In a large frying pan, warm the oil. Add the leeks, sprinkle with a pinch of salt, cover, and cook on medium heat for 5 minutes. Stir in the asparagus and sauté for 5 minutes more, until bright green and tender. Toss the sautéed vegetables, tarragon, flour, salt, and pepper with the Neufchâtel. Thoroughly mix in the cottage cheese, Gruyère and Cheddar cheeses, and the eggs.

Lay the filo on a dry surface and cover with a clean, lightly dampened towel (see Note). Combine the butter and oil in a small bowl. Place a pastry brush and the bowl of butter-oil within easy reach. Arrange two sheets of filo pastry in the prepared baking tray, allowing the excess filo to drape over the sides. Lightly brush the top sheet with the butter-oil. Repeat three more times for a total of eight filo sheets.

Spread the filling evenly over the filo in the baking tray. Fold all four sides of the filo up over the filling to make a border, and brush with the butter-oil. Top with the remaining filo, two sheets at a time, brushing each layer as before. Tuck under the edges to fit the baking tray. Sprinkle the top with sesame seeds.

Bake until golden and puffy, about 45 minutes. Let sit for 15 minutes before cutting into squares and serving.

PER 8-OUNCE SERVING: 443 CALORIES, 19.9 G PROTEIN, 33.5 G FAT, 17.2 G CARBOHYDRATES,
13 G SATURATED FATTY ACIDS, 186.2 MG CHOLESTEROL, 683.9 MG SODIUM, 1.9 G TOTAL DIETARY FIBER

note ☙ *Unoiled filo becomes brittle once exposed to the air, so work quickly or keep a damp towel on the not-yet-used filo while you work. It's also helpful to work in a draft-free spot.*

kale & red pepper strudel

We've created a number of recipes in this cookbook that combine tofu and cheese. The tofu adds all of the well-known health benefits of soy foods as well as bulk—but with a lighter texture than cheese. Of course, we still love the rich flavor of cheese, so why not get the best of both worlds?

Our creamy filling boasts the goodness of tofu and the yumminess of cheese. When combined with bright green kale, vibrant red peppers, rosemary, garlic, and parsley, it makes an exquisite filling for the flaky filo.

The amount of filo you need will depend on the size of your baking pan and the size of your filo sheets. A good rule of thumb is to use eight single layers of filo on the bottom, spread on the filling, and top with at least eight more layers of filo. The more layers (within reason), the more puffed and beautiful the strudel will be.

Serves 6
Preparation time: 1 hour
Baking time: 45 minutes
Cooling time: 15 minutes

filling

1 1/2 cups chopped onions

1 tablespoon olive oil

2 garlic cloves, minced or pressed

4 to 5 cups rinsed, stemmed, and chopped kale

1/2 teaspoon salt

1 1/4 cups diced red bell peppers

1 scant teaspoon minced fresh rosemary

1 cake firm tofu (12 ounces), crumbled

1 cup Neufchâtel, at room temperature

1 cup grated sharp Cheddar, Parmesan, or provolone

1 tablespoon unbleached white flour

2 tablespoons chopped fresh parsley

ground black pepper to taste

filo

1/2 to 2/3 pound filo dough

3 to 4 tablespoons vegetable oil or melted butter, or a mixture

1/2 teaspoon sesame seeds (optional)

Preheat the oven to 350°. Lightly butter a 10 x 14-inch baking tray or shallow pan.

Cook the onions in the olive oil on low heat for 5 minutes. Add the garlic, kale, and salt. Cover and cook for about 5 minutes, until the kale wilts, adding 1 to 2 tablespoons of water to prevent sticking, if necessary. Stir in the bell peppers and rosemary. Cover and cook on low heat until the vegetables are tender, about 10 minutes.

While the vegetables cook, combine the tofu, Neufchâtel, grated cheese, flour, and parsley in the bowl of a food processor. Process until smooth and creamy. When the vegetables are ready, drain them if any liquid remains, and stir in the tofu-cheese mixture. Add black pepper to taste and set aside.

Lay the filo on a dry surface and cover with a clean, lightly dampened towel (see Note). Place a pastry brush and a bowl of the oil or melted butter within easy reach. Arrange two sheets of filo pastry in the prepared baking tray, allowing the excess filo to drape over the sides. Lightly brush the top sheet with oil or butter. Repeat three more times for a total of eight filo sheets.

Spread the filling evenly over the filo in the baking tray. Fold all four sides of the filo up over the filling to make a border and brush with oil or butter. Top with the remaining filo, two sheets at a time, brushing each layer with oil or butter. Tuck under the edges to fit the baking tray. Sprinkle the top with sesame seeds, if desired.

Bake until golden and puffy, about 45 minutes. Let sit for 15 minutes before serving.

PER 8.5-OUNCE SERVING: 395 CALORIES, 13.9 G PROTEIN, 31.1 G FAT, 17.9 G CARBOHYDRATES, 9.4 G SATURATED FATTY ACIDS, 34.2 MG CHOLESTEROL, 461.9 MG SODIUM, 1.9 G TOTAL DIETARY FIBER

note *Unoiled filo becomes brittle once exposed to the air, so work quickly or keep a damp towel on the not-yet-used filo while you work. It's also helpful to work in a draft-free spot.*

mushroom cheese & tofu strudel

In a dish this rich and cheesy, it's easy to tuck in some healthful tofu with no one the wiser. And as a lower-cholesterol bonus, the tofu will help bind the filling together, making it unnecessary to use eggs. If you are using dried herbs rather than fresh, add them to the skillet after the onions have sautéed for several minutes to soften them and release their full flavor.

We suggest using about 8 layers of filo for the bottom of the strudel and 8 layers of filo on top of the filling. Since sizes vary, we can't say exactly how many sheets of filo you'll need, but about ⅔ pound should work well. At Moosewood, we use 12 x 17-inch sheets, which fit nicely into a standard baking pan, one sheet per layer. Filo often comes in 1-pound boxes: If you prefer, use all of the filo by adding a few extra layers to the top.

Serves 6 to 8
Preparation time: about 1 hour
Baking time: 45 to 50 minutes
Cooling time: 15 minutes

filling

1½ cups chopped onions

1 tablespoon vegetable oil

3 garlic cloves, minced or pressed

4 cups sliced white or cremini mushrooms

2 tablespoons dry sherry

1 tablespoon soy sauce

1 tablespoon chopped fresh dill (1 teaspoon dried)

1 tablespoon chopped fresh marjoram (1 teaspoon dried)

pinch of ground black pepper

1 cake firm tofu (16 ounces)

1 cup Neufchâtel, at room temperature

1 cup grated extra-sharp Cheddar cheese

1 tablespoon unbleached white flour

½ teaspoon salt

filo

½ to ⅔ pound filo dough

3 to 4 tablespoons butter, melted*

½ teaspoon poppy or sesame seeds (optional)

* *Or use a mixture of melted butter and olive oil.*

✂ Preheat the oven to 350°. Lightly butter a 9 x 13-inch baking tray or shallow pan.

Sauté the onions in the olive oil for 5 minutes on medium-high heat. Add the garlic and mushrooms (see Notes) and cook for another 5 minutes, stirring often. Add the sherry and soy sauce and simmer for about 10 minutes, until the liquid is gone. Remove from the heat and stir in the fresh dill, fresh marjoram, and the pepper. Set the filling aside.

While the vegetables cook, combine the tofu, Neufchâtel, grated cheese, and flour in the bowl of a food processor. Process until smooth and creamy. When the vegetables are ready, stir in the tofu-cheese mixture, add the salt, and set aside.

Unfold the filo onto a dry surface and cover with a clean, lightly dampened towel (see Notes). Place a pastry brush and a bowl of the melted butter within easy reach. Arrange two sheets of filo pastry in the prepared baking tray, allowing the excess filo to drape evenly over the sides. Lightly brush the top sheet with the butter. Repeat three more times for a total of eight filo sheets.

Spread the filling evenly over the filo in the baking tray. Fold all four sides of the filo up over the filling to make a border and brush with the butter. Then top with the remaining filo, two sheets at a time, brushing every second sheet with butter. Tuck the edges under to fit the baking tray. Sprinkle the top with poppy or sesame seeds, if desired.

Bake until golden and puffy, 45 to 50 minutes. Let sit for 15 minutes before cutting into squares and serving.

PER 6-OUNCE SERVING: 294 CALORIES, 11.5 G PROTEIN, 22.9 G FAT, 12.2 G CARBOHYDRATES, 8.6 G SATURATED FATTY ACIDS, 37.3 MG CHOLESTEROL, 484.2 MG SODIUM, 1.2 G TOTAL DIETARY FIBER

notes ❧ *If using dried dill and dried marjoram, add them with the garlic and mushrooms.*
Unoiled filo becomes brittle once exposed to the air, so work quickly or keep a damp towel on the not-yet-used filo while you work. It's also helpful to work in a draft-free spot.

pizza with three toppings

Pizza has become a quintessential American comfort food. Ever since Italian immigrants started making pizzas in their neighborhoods, it's been a hit. Now you find it topped with all sorts of vegetables, cheeses, seafood, meats, and even eggs and fruits. There are pita pizzas, French bread pizzas, English muffin pizzas, taco pizzas, Hawaiian pizzas, and, at Moosewood, our filo pizza with its distinctly Greek or Middle Eastern flair.

Pizza goes great with soup and salad. It's often eaten for breakfast and is probably one of the healthiest fast foods you can buy. For vegan pizza, just go cheeseless.

pizza crust

With this traditional crust, the kind of flour you use will determine the texture. We prefer unbleached white bread flour, which makes for a chewy texture. All-purpose flour is also good, and even pastry flour will work, yielding a tender, lighter crust.

Pizza dough can be frozen after rising. Punch it down and either roll it out or form a ball to be re-kneaded and rolled out into the desired shape after thawing. It takes about 2 hours at room temperature for a ball of dough to defrost. After re-kneading (adding flour if needed) and rolling out the thawed dough, let it rise for about a half hour before baking.

Yields two 12- to 15-inch pizza crusts
Initial preparation time: about 25 minutes
Rising time: 55 to 75 minutes
Baking time: about 25 minutes

1 tablespoon active dry yeast
  (one package)
1 teaspoon sugar
1 1/3 cups warm water (100° to 120°)
3 cups unbleached white bread flour
1/2 cup whole wheat flour
1 teaspoon salt
1/2 teaspoon ground black pepper
3 teaspoons olive oil
1 to 2 cups unbleached white bread
  flour for kneading

Stir the yeast into the sugar and warm water and set aside to proof until it bubbles and foams, usually about 10 to 12 minutes.

Stir in the flours, salt, and pepper and 2 teaspoons of the olive oil. Mix well, adding flour if necessary so that the dough is not sticky, forms a ball, and can be handled. Knead the dough by pressing the ball flat with the heels of your hands, folding it over and pressing down again until flat, and so on for about 10 minutes. Add flour as needed to prevent sticking. (For the health of your back, knead on a fairly low surface if possible, and use the weight of your body to do the work rather than your shoulders and arms.)

Place the ball of kneaded dough in a lightly oiled bowl and cover with a towel. Set aside to rise in a warm, draft-free place until doubled in size, usually 40 to 60 minutes.

While the dough is rising, prepare the topping and preheat the oven to 425° to 450°.

Punch down the risen dough and knead for a couple of minutes, adding flour to keep the dough from sticking to the board or your hands. Cut the dough in half to make two crusts. (If you're going to freeze the dough, now is the time.)

With your hands or a rolling pin, shape each half of the dough into a 12- to 15-inch rectangle or circle. Press down and out from the center of the dough until the crust has reached the desired thickness. Place the dough on a lightly oiled pan and let it rise for about 15 minutes. Add one of the toppings on the following pages. Bake for 20 to 30 minutes, until the bottom of the crust is golden and the dough is firm throughout.

PER 15-OUNCE CRUST: 1,006 CALORIES, 29 G PROTEIN, 10.1 G FAT, 197.7 G CARBOHYDRATES, 1.4 G SATURATED FATTY ACIDS, 0 MG CHOLESTEROL, 1,194.8 MG SODIUM, 10.6 G TOTAL DIETARY FIBER

spinach, artichoke hearts & feta

Yields enough for two 14-inch pizzas.

2 cups thinly sliced onions

2 or 3 garlic cloves, minced

1 teaspoon dried dill weed

1 teaspoon salt

1 tablespoon olive oil

10 ounces spinach, stemmed, rinsed, and chopped

5 artichoke hearts, quartered (14-ounce can, drained)

$\frac{1}{2}$ teaspoon ground black pepper

pizza crust (page 338)

2 cups crumbled feta cheese (optional)

In a large pot, sauté the onions, garlic, dill, and salt in the oil on medium heat until browned, about 10 minutes. Add the rinsed spinach and cook uncovered, stirring frequently, until mostly wilted. Add the artichoke heart quarters and pepper. Allow to cool for a few minutes before spreading onto the pizza crust. Top with the feta cheese, if using, and bake according to the pizza crust instructions.

PER 5-OUNCE SLICE: 208 CALORIES, 6.8 G PROTEIN, 3 G FAT, 39.4 G CARBOHYDRATES, 0.4 G SATURATED FATTY ACIDS, 0 MG CHOLESTEROL, 440.4 MG SODIUM, 4.2 G TOTAL DIETARY FIBER

zucchini & fresh tomatoes with fontina

Yields enough for two 14-inch pizzas.

2 cups thinly sliced onions

2 or 3 garlic cloves, minced or
    pressed

2 teaspoons salt

2 teaspoons olive oil

2 teaspoons ground fennel seeds

4 cups sliced zucchini*

2 cups chopped fresh tomatoes

1/4 cup chopped fresh basil

pizza crust (page 338)

2 cups grated Fontina cheese
    (optional)

* Quarter the zucchini lengthwise, and then
  slice crosswise into bite-sized pieces.

In a skillet or large saucepan, sauté the onions, garlic, and salt in the olive oil on medium heat for 7 to 10 minutes, until translucent. Add the ground fennel and zucchini and cook until the zucchini starts to soften, 3 to 5 minutes. Remove from the heat and add the tomatoes and basil. Allow to cool somewhat and drain any excess liquid before spreading on the pizza crust. Then top with cheese, if you wish, and bake according to the pizza crust directions.

PER 6-OUNCE SLICE: 201 CALORIES, 5.8 G PROTEIN, 2.7 G FAT, 38.9 G CARBOHYDRATES, 0.4 G SATURATED FATTY ACIDS, 0 MG CHOLESTEROL, 602 MG SODIUM, 3.2 G TOTAL DIETARY FIBER

caramelized onions & parmesan cheese

Yields enough for two 14-inch pizzas.

1 tablespoon olive oil

2 or 3 garlic cloves, minced or
    pressed

6 cups thinly sliced onions

1 teaspoon salt

pizza crust (page 338)

1 cup grated Parmesan cheese
    (optional)

In a heavy skillet, combine the oil, garlic, onions, and salt and cook on medium heat until the onions are browned, 10 to 12 minutes. If sticking becomes a problem, add a little water. Let the onions cool a bit before spreading them on the pizza crust. Sprinkle the Parmesan on top, if using, and bake according to the pizza crust directions.

PER 5-OUNCE SLICE: 206 CALORIES, 5.7 G PROTEIN, 3 G FAT, 39.4 G CARBOHYDRATES, 0.4 G SATURATED FATTY ACIDS, 0 MG CHOLESTEROL, 398.8 MG SODIUM, 2.7 G TOTAL DIETARY FIBER

vegan turnovers

These enticing savory turnovers make an impressive appearance at the dinner table—hot, puffed, flaky, and golden brown. The creamy tofu filling is snappy with sun-dried tomatoes, nutritious with greens, and full of herbs and spices. Serve two per plate (or one for those with daintier appetites) with a bright colorful vegetable on the side and it's quite smashing.

We suggest kale, spinach, chard, collards, mizuna, arugula, or some combination of these for the 4 cups of greens in the recipe. Use fresh dill or basil whenever possible. If you must use their dried counterparts, add them earlier in the cooking process along with the thyme and fennel.

Serves 4 to 6
Preparation time: 45 minutes
Baking time: 20 to 25 minutes

1 cake firm tofu (16 ounces)

⅓ cup sun-dried tomatoes, (not oil-packed)*

1 tablespoon olive oil

1 cup chopped onions

¼ teaspoon salt, or less to taste

4 cups rinsed, stemmed, and chopped greens

pinch of dried thyme

½ teaspoon freshly ground fennel seeds

2 garlic cloves, minced or pressed

1 tablespoon fresh lemon juice

1 tablespoon chopped fresh dill or basil (1 teaspoon dried)

¾ pound filo pastry (12 x 17-inch sheets)**

¼ cup olive oil

* If you like, replace the sun-dried tomatoes with chopped, pitted kalamata, Sicilian green, Niçoise, or Spanish olives.
** You can use puff pastry instead of the filo. See our variation at the end of the recipe.

Place the tofu between two plates, weight the top plate with a heavy object, and press for 20 minutes. Place the sun-dried tomatoes in a heat-proof bowl, cover with boiling water, and set aside.

Meanwhile, warm the oil in a large skillet. Add the onions and salt and sauté on medium heat for 8 to 10 minutes, or until translucent. Add the greens, thyme, and fennel; then cover, lower the heat, and continue to cook for another 5 to 10 minutes, stirring often until the greens are tender but still bright green. Drain and set aside.

In the bowl of a food processor (see Notes), crumble the pressed tofu and add the garlic, lemon juice, and the dill or basil. Process until the mixture is smooth and creamy. In a bowl, combine the tofu mixture with the drained cooked greens and mix well. Drain and chop the sun-dried tomatoes and fold them into the filling.

Preheat the oven to 350°. Lightly oil two baking sheets.

Unfold 16 sheets of filo on a clean, dry working surface. Have the filling, the oil, and a pastry brush nearby (see Notes). Take two sheets of filo from the stack and place them with the short sides facing you. Brush lightly with oil and neatly fold in half lengthwise. Brush the strip with oil. Place ¹/₂ cup of filling at the near end of the rectangle. Fold the lower left corner up and over diagonally until the bottom edge is flush with the right side and you have a triangle at the end. Keep folding the triangle up, as you would a flag, to make a triangular pastry. Brush both sides with a little oil and place on the prepared baking sheet.

Repeat to make eight pastries in all. Bake for 20 to 25 minutes, until the turnovers are golden brown and slightly puffed.

PER 6.5-OUNCE SERVING: 355 CALORIES, 9.6 G PROTEIN, 27.8 G FAT, 20.4 G CARBOHYDRATES, 2.1 G SATURATED FATTY ACIDS, 0 MG CHOLESTEROL, 370.9 MG SODIUM, 2 G TOTAL DIETARY FIBER

notes ❧ *If you don't have a food processor, crush the tofu in a bowl with a potato masher and vigorously mash in the garlic, lemon juice, and fresh herbs.*

Unoiled filo becomes brittle once exposed to the air, so keep a damp towel on the not-yet-used filo while you work. It's also helpful to work in a draft-free spot. A new inexpensive 2-inch paint brush works great as a filo pastry brush.

variation ❧ *If you prefer to use puff pastry instead of filo, thaw it according to the instructions on the package. Depending on the type of puffed pastry, divide each strip into 3 equal squarish pieces or cut each large sheet into 4 equal pieces. With a rolling pin, roll each piece into a 7-inch square. Place ¹/₃ to ¹/₂ cup of filling in the center of each square. Fold the 4 corners up and toward the center, twist to form a little topknot, and gently pinch the side seams together. Place each pastry on the prepared baking sheet and bake for 20 minutes.*

wild mushroom sauté

As simple and robust as it is, Wild Mushroom Sauté is still a show-off dish. You get wonderfully deep flavor with this hot sauté method, which sears and browns the surfaces quickly. This is one time you shouldn't use a nonstick skillet, because the pan won't get hot enough to do the job.

Choose a variety of mushrooms. Use a big portabello for its meatiness and bulk and then smaller amounts of several different wild mushrooms. Look for fresh-looking mushrooms with firm, dry stems, unblemished caps, and a pleasant, earthy smell.

Wild Mushroom Sauté is rich and woodsy served over Orange Saffron Rice (page 146), pasta, creamy Low-fat Garlic Mashed Potatoes (page 131), or Breaded Polenta Cutlets (page 282). Leftovers? Use them on crostini or pizza, on a burger, or in omelettes, beans, or tomato sauce.

Serves 4
Total time: 30 minutes

8 cups assorted wild mushrooms*

3 tablespoons olive oil

4 large garlic cloves, minced or pressed

1/2 teaspoon salt

2 tablespoons minced fresh parsley

1 teaspoon dried thyme
(1 tablespoon fresh)

1/3 cup dry wine or sherry, marsala, vegetable broth, or tomato juice

ground black pepper to taste

* *We suggest shiitake, oyster, morels, cremini, chanterelles, portabellos, porcini, or golden trumpets (page ooo). You'll need about 1 1/2 pounds all together.*

Trim the mushroom stem ends. Remove and discard shiitake stems because they don't soften when cooked. Leave small shiitake caps whole; cut the larger ones in half. Separate oyster mushrooms and other mushrooms that grow in clumps into smaller bunches. Chop portabellos into 1-inch pieces. Cut other mushrooms lengthwise, in fairly large halves or quarters. Separate the mushrooms into two groups: the tougher ones, like portabellos, oysters, porcini, and cremini, and the more tender, like shiitake, morels, chanterelles, and golden trumpets. Gently wipe off any grit clinging to the mushrooms with a soft brush or a damp towel without immersing or rinsing them.

If you have a 12-inch skillet, you can cook all of the mushrooms together, pushing the first batch to the sides of the skillet while you sauté the more delicate batch in the middle. If not, use two frying pans and divide the mushrooms and other ingredients between them. Avoid overcrowding; it prevents the mushrooms from searing properly. As a result, they cook too slowly and release too many juices.

Heat the skillet on high heat until just smoking. Add 2 tablespoons of the olive oil and the sturdier group of mushrooms. Sauté on high heat, stirring occasionally, for 5 minutes. Push those mushrooms to the side and add the remaining tablespoon of olive oil, the rest of the mushrooms, and the garlic. Lower the heat and sauté, stirring frequently, for another 5 to 10 minutes, until the mushrooms exude some juice and begin to shrink.

Stir in the salt, parsley, and thyme. Return the heat to high and add the wine or other liquid. Scrape the bottom of the pan to stir up any browned mushroom juices and cook until the liquid is nearly evaporated, about 1 minute. Remove from the heat and add pepper to taste. Serve hot from the skillet or make ahead and reheat gently to serve.

PER 5-OUNCE SERVING: 136 CALORIES, 3.1 G PROTEIN, 10.8 G FAT, 5.6 G CARBOHYDRATES, 1.5 G SATURATED FATTY ACIDS, 0 MG CHOLESTEROL, 307.8 MG SODIUM, 0.9 G TOTAL DIETARY FIBER

vegetarianism crosses the threshold

When we opened our doors in 1973, meatless cuisine was seen by some as innovative and trailblazing and by others as strange and intimidating. Back then, vegetarianism had a whiff of rebellious counterculture about it. Well, it's been a long time in coming, but times have changed and now a vegetarian lifestyle is not the least bit remarkable. In fact, many of the people who come to Moosewood come simply because they like our food, not because they are vegetarians.

It has certainly become easier than it was in the seventies to follow a vegetarian diet. Most restaurants and dining services at least accommodate this choice, if not cater to it. The increase in the number of ethnic restaurants nationwide, the rise of farmers' markets, and a wealth of options at the supermarket all make life easier and more enjoyable for those who prefer not to eat meat either some of the time or all of the time.

Most people who call themselves vegetarians see their food choices as a humane and responsible way of eating and living because a plant-based diet is more beneficial to humans and to the environment. If cropland were used to produce grains and vegetables for human consumption instead of to feed livestock, more people could be fed. An unfortunate consequence of a meat-centered economy is the need for continual expansion of pastureland, which has led to deforestation, desertification, and water contamination.

Current nutritional research and recommendations have also contributed to the increase in vegetarianism. A diet composed of mostly fruits, vegetables, beans, and grains is high in fiber and loaded with vitamins and minerals. So there is a broad mainstream initiative to weight one's diet in the direction of vegetables and to minimize animal foods. And we at Moosewood couldn't be happier.

fish tostadas

When we serve this at Moosewood, the staff always enjoys putting on some catchy samba music to suit the mood. Our crisp tortilla covered with shredded lettuce and teeming with tasty morsels of broiled, spice-rubbed fish will make you want to dance, dance, dance.

We developed Mango Corn Jicama Salsa (page 377) expressly for this dish, but almost any fruit or tomato salsa can add the finishing touch. Other good toppings are Black Bean Mango Salsa (page 372) and Joan's Three-Tomato Salsa (page 375).

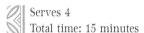 Serves 4
Total time: 15 minutes

1/2 cup vegetable oil*

4 corn tortillas (6 inches across)

1 tablespoon ground cumin

1 tablespoon ground coriander

1/2 teaspoon salt

1/4 teaspoon ground black pepper

1 pound catfish fillets

1 garlic clove, halved

2 tablespoons fresh lemon juice

3 cups shredded romaine, mixed baby greens, or arugula

2 cups prepared salsa

* *The amount of oil needed will depend on the size of the pan.*

Pour an inch of oil into a heavy skillet and heat until a small drop of water flicked into the pan spatters—but don't let the oil begin to smoke. Ease the tortillas one at a time into the hot oil and fry both sides until pale brown and crisp, using metal tongs to flip each one over carefully. Drain on paper towels.

In a small bowl, combine the cumin, coriander, salt, and pepper. Rinse the fish and pat it dry. Rub each fillet with the cut side of the garlic clove and then with the spice mixture. Arrange the fillets on a broiling pan or sheet of aluminum foil and pour the lemon juice evenly over them.

Broil the fish about 3 inches from the flame for 5 to 10 minutes, until its juices run clear. The broiling time will depend on the thickness of the fillets. When the fish is cooked, remove it from the broiler and break it up into bite-sized chunks.

Assemble the tostada by layering each crisp tortilla with one fourth of the greens and fish, and top with the salsa of your choosing.

PER 12-OUNCE SERVING: 472 CALORIES, 20.8 G PROTEIN, 33.1 G FAT, 24.9 G CARBOHYDRATES, 8.2 G SATURATED FATTY ACIDS, 56.6 MG CHOLESTEROL, 906.3 MG SODIUM, 4.3 G TOTAL DIETARY FIBER

east-west stuffed portabellos

Let's face it—we've fallen in love with portabello mushrooms. They're big, easy to use, and delicious in a wide variety of dishes. So, unless you're fungi-phobic, revel in these lavish mushrooms!

We don't know whether Marco Polo took any mushrooms with him to Asia or brought any miso and sesame oil back to Italy, but this dish is what might have happened if he had. For a full meal, serve the portabellos on a bed of rice or on soba or udon noodles, top with steamed broccoli spears, drizzle on the sauce, and scatter scallions and mung sprouts over all. The Simple Sweet & Sour Sauce can be prepared while the mushrooms bake.

Serves 4
Preparation time: 15 to 20 minutes
Cooking time: 35 minutes

1 cake firm tofu (16 ounces)

½ cup diced red bell peppers

⅓ cup diced canned water chestnuts

⅓ cup minced scallions

½ cup cooked brown rice

¼ cup peanut butter

2 to 3 tablespoons light miso,
    to taste

1 teaspoon grated fresh ginger root

4 teaspoons dark sesame oil

1 teaspoon Chinese chili paste with
    garlic (optional)

4 portabello mushrooms
    (about 5 inches in diameter)

1 tablespoon soy sauce

1 recipe Simple Sweet & Sour Sauce
    (page 386)

scallions sliced on the severe
    diagonal

mung bean sprouts

Preheat the oven to 350°. Oil a baking pan large enough to hold the portabellos.

In a bowl, crumble the tofu into small pieces. Add the peppers, water chestnuts, scallions, rice, peanut butter, miso, ginger, 1 teaspoon of the sesame oil, and the chili paste, if using. Mix well and set aside.

Twist off the mushroom stems and gently rinse the caps to remove any dirt. Place the caps gill-side up in the oiled pan. In a small cup, stir together the remaining 3 teaspoons of sesame oil and the soy sauce. Brush the mushrooms with the mixture. Mound one quarter of the filling in each mushroom.

Bake for 35 minutes, until the mushrooms release juice and the filling is firm to the touch. While the mushrooms bake, prepare the Simple Sweet & Sour Sauce. When the mushrooms are ready, top with the sauce, scallions, and/or mung sprouts. Serve immediately.

PER 12-OUNCE SERVING: 322 CALORIES, 16.2 G PROTEIN, 17.3 G FAT, 30.8 G CARBOHYDRATES, 2.9 G SATURATED FATTY ACIDS, 0 MG CHOLESTEROL, 740.1 MG SODIUM, 4.4 G TOTAL DIETARY FIBER

japanese stuffed eggplant

These delicate little eggplants make a nice first course or side dish with steamed vegetables or fish. Select tender young eggplants: they bake more quickly than larger ones, their flavor is mild, and they make attractive individual portions. This is a great way to use leftover rice, but you can also cook the rice while the eggplants bake and add it to the filling just before stuffing the eggplant shells.

The simple rice stuffing can be made with or without the diced tofu. Hijiki seaweed is shaped like pieces of broken vermicelli and has a cooked texture similar to buckwheat noodles. Its color, flavor, and chewiness add striking contrasts to the rice. The Ginger Sherry Sauce is sweet and pungent and can double as a dipping sauce for steamed vegetables or spring rolls.

Serves 3 to 6
Preparation time: 15 minutes
Baking time: 35 to 45 minutes
Total time: 1 hour 10 minutes

3 small eggplants (4 to 5 inches long)
1/2 cup plus 1 tablespoon dry sherry
1/4 cup dried hijiki seaweed
2 or 3 cups cooked brown rice*
1 tablespoon soy sauce
1 tablespoon vegetable oil
1 cup chopped onions
1 large garlic clove, minced or
    pressed
1 cup diced firm tofu (optional)**

ginger sherry sauce

1/4 cup dry sherry
1 tablespoon dark sesame oil
1 teaspoon grated fresh ginger root
2 teaspoons sugar
1 tablespoon rice vinegar
1 to 2 tablespoons soy sauce
1 teaspoon cornstarch
1 tablespoon cold water

chopped toasted pecans or walnuts or
    toasted sesame seeds***
chopped scallions

* 1 cup of raw brown rice will yield about
  3 cups cooked (page 000). If using tofu,
  2 cups of cooked rice will be enough.
** Half of a 3-inch square cake of tofu will yield
  about 1 cup when diced into 1/2-inch cubes.
  If you omit the tofu, use 3 cups of rice.
*** Toast nuts or seeds in a single layer on an
  unoiled baking tray at 350° for a few minutes, until fragrant and golden brown.

✳ Preheat the oven to 375°. Oil a baking sheet (nonstick works best).

Cut the eggplants lengthwise into halves. Place them cut side down on the baking pan. Pour the $1/2$ cup of sherry over them and cover tightly with foil. Bake for 35 to 45 minutes, or until the tops are quite tender and the flesh is lightly browned.

Meanwhile, in a small bowl, cover the hijiki with hot water and set aside to soak for at least 10 minutes, until softened. Mix the rice, soy sauce, and remaining 1 tablespoon of sherry together in another bowl and set aside. In a skillet, heat the oil and sauté the onions and garlic for 3 minutes. Add the tofu, if using, and stir gently. Drain the softened hijiki, add it to the skillet, cover, and cook for 3 to 4 minutes. Stir in the rice and sauté for another 2 minutes. Cover and set aside.

In a small pan on medium heat, bring the sherry, sesame oil, ginger, sugar, vinegar, and soy sauce to a low simmer. Thoroughly blend the cornstarch and cold water in a cup and stir it into the sauce. Continue to stir occasionally on low heat for about 10 minutes, until the sauce slightly thickens. Cover and set aside.

Meanwhile, when the eggplant halves have baked and are cool enough to handle, scoop out the flesh with a spoon, leaving just enough so that the shells hold their shape. Chop the flesh, stir it into the skillet mixture, cover, and cook on medium heat for 2 to 3 minutes. Fill the eggplant shells with the rice stuffing and serve immediately or cover with foil and bake briefly to reheat, if needed.

Serve the stuffed eggplant topped with nuts or sesame seeds and scallions, and pass the sauce separately at the table.

PER 12-OUNCE SERVING: 224 CALORIES, 6.7 G PROTEIN, 6.1 G FAT, 34 G CARBOHYDRATES, 1.3 G SATURATED FATTY ACIDS, 0 MG CHOLESTEROL, 323.1 MG SODIUM, 6.8 G TOTAL DIETARY FIBER

note ❧ *We especially like this recipe with small eggplants, which are often sweeter than the larger ones. But if small eggplants are unavailable, this recipe also works using 2 medium-large eggplants that will serve 4 as a main dish. Adjust the cooking time for baking the eggplants— larger specimens will take longer to become completely tender.*

moussaka-style stuffed eggplant

Greece stretches south into the Aegean and Mediterranean Seas, tantalizingly close to North Africa and just a brief cruise eastward from Italy and France. Inspired by a classic Greek casserole, this dish is a lively blend of these nearby culinary influences.

The spices are typical of the Near East and North Africa. The cheeses are Italian. The vegetables are favorites throughout the region. The custard of whipped egg whites in the topping hints at a French soufflé.

Lovers of feta cheese should feel free to add a bit to the topping or crumble it with the Parmesan to sprinkle on top. Serve the eggplants on a bed of orzo, couscous, or conchigliette and garnish with strips of roasted red pepper or sprigs of fresh dill.

Serves 4
Preparation time: 45 minutes
Final baking time: 30 minutes

2 eggplants (1 to 1 1/4 pounds each)
3 tablespoons olive oil
1 cup chopped onions
2 garlic cloves, minced or pressed
1/2 teaspoon ground cloves
3/4 teaspoon ground cumin
3/4 teaspoon ground cinnamon
pinch of cayenne
1 3/4 cups canned tomatoes with juice,
      chopped (14.5-ounce can)
1 cup chopped green bell peppers
1 cup chopped mushrooms
1 teaspoon salt
1/4 teaspoon ground black pepper
1 cup bread crumbs*
1 3/4 cups ricotta cheese (15 ounces)
2 egg whites
1 cup grated Parmesan cheese

* *Pulverize stale or lightly toasted whole wheat, sourdough, or French bread in a blender or food processor.*

✂ Preheat the oven to 400°. Lightly oil a baking tray.

Slice the eggplants in half lengthwise. Score the flesh of each half with a paring knife, being careful not to pierce the skin. Use a spoon to scoop out the flesh and leave about a 1/2-inch-thick shell. Reserve the flesh to use in the filling.

Brush the eggplant shells with 1 tablespoon of the oil and sprinkle them lightly with salt. Place face up on the prepared baking tray and bake for about 20 minutes, until very tender.

Meanwhile, heat the remaining oil in a nonreactive saucepan. Sauté the onions until translucent, 8 to 10 minutes. Add the garlic, cloves, cumin, cinnamon, and cayenne and continue to sauté for about 1 minute. Cut the reserved eggplant flesh into small cubes and add them. Sauté for about 5 minutes, stirring frequently. Add the tomatoes, bell peppers, and mushrooms. Bring to a simmer and cook for 10 minutes, stirring occasionally. Remove from the heat and mix in the salt, black pepper, bread crumbs, and 3/4 cup of the ricotta cheese. Set the filling aside.

When the eggplant shells are done, remove them from the oven and reduce the temperature to 350°. In a mixing bowl, beat the egg whites until they are stiff and fold them into the remaining cup of ricotta cheese.

Fill each shell with 1 1/4 cups of the vegetable filling. Evenly cover with the ricotta custard and then the grated cheese. Return the baking tray of stuffed eggplant to the oven and bake for about 30 minutes, until puffed and lightly golden on top.

PER 20-OUNCE SERVING: 597 CALORIES, 35 G PROTEIN, 31.6 G FAT, 46.8 G CARBOHYDRATES,
13.6 G SATURATED FATTY ACIDS, 59.5 MG CHOLESTEROL, 1,691.3 MG SODIUM, 8.4 G TOTAL DIETARY FIBER

greek lasagna

Separated only by the Ionian Sea, Greece and Italy share so much history that it's curious how distinct their cuisines have remained. We thought it would be fun to create a dish that combined the two culinary styles. Starting with the classic Italian casserole, lasagna, we switched the cheeses and gave the sauce a Greek touch. The spirited flavors of this fusion played on our palates like a mandolin and bouzouki duet.

We only partially cook the eggplant before layering it into the casserole. This preserves its texture in the finished dish, since it continues to cook as the lasagna bakes. If you're not familiar with our uncooked noodle trick, this is it: don't boil the noodles. As long as they're surrounded by sauce, raw noodles will cook just fine in the oven—so don't bother with all that boiling water!

Serves 8
Preparation time: 50 minutes
Baking time: 45 to 50 minutes
Sitting time: 10 to 15 minutes

tomato sauce

3 tablespoons olive oil

2 cups chopped onions

4 garlic cloves, minced or pressed

2 teaspoons dried marjoram

5 cups undrained canned whole
   tomatoes (three 14.5-ounce cans)

¹/₃ cup chopped kalamata olives

2 teaspoons salt

¹/₂ teaspoon ground black pepper

3 tablespoons chopped fresh dill

1 large eggplant, cut into
   ³/₄-inch-thick rounds
   (1¹/₂ pounds)

olive oil for brushing

3 eggs, beaten

2 cups cottage cheese

1 teaspoon ground fennel seeds

3 cups grated feta cheese

¹/₂ pound uncooked lasagna noodles
   (12 noodles)

In a saucepan, warm the olive oil briefly on medium-high heat. Add the onions and sauté for about 5 minutes, stirring frequently, until the onions have begun to release juices. Stir in the garlic and marjoram and sauté until the onions are translucent. Add the tomatoes, cover, and bring to a simmer; then reduce the heat to medium-low—just enough to maintain a simmer. Add the olives, salt, and pepper. For best flavor, add the dill just before assembling the lasagna.

Preheat the oven to 400°. Lightly oil a large baking sheet.

While the sauce gently simmers, lay the eggplant rounds on the baking sheet, brush them with olive oil, and bake uncovered for about 15 minutes. Remove the eggplant from the oven and reduce the heat to 350°.

Meanwhile, in a bowl, mix together the eggs, cottage cheese, fennel, and 1 cup of the feta and set aside.

Lightly oil a 7½ x 10 x 3-inch casserole dish. Evenly spread 2 cups of the tomato sauce in the bottom of the dish. Top with a layer of noodles and cover with 1 cup of the sauce. Next layer all of the eggplant rounds, 1 cup of the feta cheese, a second layer of noodles, and another cup of the sauce. Finish with all of the egg and cottage cheese mixture, a third layer of noodles, the rest of the sauce, and the remaining cup of feta.

Cover the lasagna with aluminum foil and bake for 45 to 50 minutes. Remove from the oven, uncover the lasagna, and let it sit for 10 to 15 minutes before serving.

PER 15-OUNCE SERVING: 462 CALORIES, 22.9 G PROTEIN, 24.5 G FAT, 39.6 G CARBOHYDRATES, 10.1 G SATURATED FATTY ACIDS, 172.4 MG CHOLESTEROL, 1,827.3 MG SODIUM, 3.5 G TOTAL DIETARY FIBER

pasta with sunday ragù

When Moosewood's Winnie Stein was growing up, she and her sisters were served a Jewish-Italian take on this sauce, courtesy of her Aunt Martha. Martha had married an Italian—a scandalous event for the family in those days—and taught Winnie's mother to make this "gravy," as they called it in South Philly. (Of course, healthful soy crumbles had not yet been invented then).

When the girls arrived home from school and smelled that a "gravy" was simmering, they'd rush into the kitchen for a taste. Winnie's mom would dip pieces of bread in the sauce for each of them, and although they always burned their tongues they immediately begged for more.

Serves 4 to 6
Preparation time: 30 minutes
Cooking time: 30 minutes

3 tablespoons extra-virgin olive oil
1 cup diced onions
$^1/_2$ cup peeled and diced carrots
1 cup diced celery
3 large garlic cloves, minced or
    pressed
2 cups chopped mushrooms
    (cremini are nice)
$^1/_2$ teaspoon salt
2 teaspoons freshly ground fennel
    seeds
2 teaspoons fresh oregano
    (1 teaspoon dried)
1 teaspoon chopped fresh sage
    ($^1/_4$ teaspoon dried)
1 teaspoon minced fresh rosemary
    ($^1/_2$ teaspoon dried)
1 bay leaf
12 ounces soy and/or wheat gluten
    crumbles*
$^1/_2$ cup dry red wine
3 cups crushed tomatoes with juice
    (28-ounce can)
1 cup vegetable stock or water
$^1/_2$ teaspoon ground black pepper
salt to taste
1 pound penne or fettuccine

freshly grated Parmesan cheese

* We like Smart Ground brand soy and wheat
  gluten crumbles. If you wish, use less to taste.

Heat the oil in a soup pot. Add the onions, carrots, celery, and garlic and sauté until the onions are translucent, about 10 minutes. Add the mushrooms and sauté until wilted. Stir in the salt, fennel, oregano, sage, rosemary, bay leaf, and soy or wheat gluten crumbles. Sauté for 5 minutes more. Add the wine, tomatoes, and stock or water, cover, and gently simmer for 20 to 30 minutes. Add the black pepper and more salt to taste. Remove and discard the bay leaf.

Meanwhile, bring a large pot of water to a boil. About 10 minutes before the sauce is done, cook the pasta in the boiling water until al dente. For an Italian touch, stir ½ cup of the pasta cooking water into the tomato sauce. Then drain the pasta and transfer it to a serving bowl. Pour the sauce over the pasta and toss well.

Top with the grated cheese and serve right away.

PER 16-OUNCE SERVING: 505 CALORIES, 25.2 G PROTEIN, 9.1 G FAT, 78.7 G CARBOHYDRATES, 1.3 G SATURATED FATTY ACIDS, 0 MG CHOLESTEROL, 587.8 MG SODIUM, 6.7 G TOTAL DIETARY FIBER

pine nut pasta cavalfiore

Our customers love this traditional Sicilian pasta with ingredients that reflect Arab influence: saffron, currants, and nuts. Our vegetarian version uses sun-dried tomatoes to mimic the salty pungency of the usual anchovies in the dish.

Sicilian cauliflower is green. If your market has broccoflower, a cauliflower relative, try it. For a traditional topping and authentic flair, replace the grated cheese with 1 cup of toasted fine bread crumbs that have been sautéed until crisp in 3 tablespoons of olive oil.

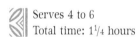 Serves 4 to 6
Total time: 1¼ hours

¹/₃ cup currants

¹/₃ cup chopped sun-dried tomatoes (not packed in oil)

¹/₄ teaspoon crumbled saffron

³/₄ cup boiling water

3 tablespoons olive oil

2 cups chopped onions

3 garlic cloves, minced or pressed

¹/₄ teaspoon red pepper flakes

8 cups bite-sized cauliflower florets

¹/₂ teaspoon salt

¹/₄ cup toasted pine nuts*

1 tablespoon fresh lemon juice

2 tablespoons chopped fresh parsley

12 ounces orecchiette, penne, or other chunky pasta

1 cup grated Parmesan cheese

* *Toast pine nuts in a single layer on an unoiled baking tray at 350° for 3 to 5 minutes, until fragrant and golden brown.*

Place the currants, sun-dried tomatoes, and saffron in a small heat-proof bowl, cover with the boiling water, and set aside. Bring a large, covered pot of salted water to a boil for the pasta.

Meanwhile, warm the oil in a Dutch oven or similar large pot. Add the onions, garlic, and red pepper flakes and sauté on medium-low heat for 10 minutes, until the onions are softened and lightly browned.

Add the cauliflower and salt and sauté for a couple of minutes. Stir in the currants, sun-dried tomatoes, saffron, and their soaking liquid. Cover and continue to cook on low heat, stirring occasionally, until the cauliflower is just tender. Remove from the heat. Add the pine nuts, lemon juice, and parsley, and cover to keep warm.

When the pasta water boils, add the pasta and cook until al dente. Drain it and mix with the sautéed cauliflower to distribute the ingredients evenly.

Serve at once, topped with the grated cheese.

PER 14.5-OUNCE SERVING: 513 CALORIES, 23.3 G PROTEIN, 18.8 G FAT, 66.4 G CARBOHYDRATES, 5.7 G SATURATED FATTY ACIDS, 17.8 MG CHOLESTEROL, 819.4 MG SODIUM, 7.8 G TOTAL DIETARY FIBER

sicilian eggplant pasta

Our Moosewood version of a rustic Southern Italian specialty pairs the crunchiness of fried eggplant with smooth fresh mozzarella that melts into the hot pasta. The eggplant's crisp egg coating prevents it from absorbing excess oil when frying.

Served with Tossed Green Salad Vinaigrette (page 98), this pasta will quickly become one of your favorite meals.

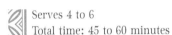

Serves 4 to 6
Total time: 45 to 60 minutes

6 cups peeled and cubed eggplant
   (1-inch pieces)

3 eggs, beaten

1/2 cup olive oil

1 pound chunky pasta, such as shells

2 pints cherry or grape tomatoes,
   halved

4 large garlic cloves, minced or
   pressed

1 cup chopped fresh parsley

1/4 teaspoon crushed red pepper
   flakes, or more to taste

12 ounces fresh mozzarella, cut into
   1-inch cubes

1/2 cup grated Parmesan cheese

6 fresh basil leaves, chopped into
   bite-sized pieces

1 teaspoon salt

grated Pecorino or Parmesan cheese

Bring a large covered pot of salted water to a boil.

Meanwhile, toss together the eggplant and beaten eggs in a large shallow bowl. Heat 1/4 cup of the olive oil in a large skillet on high heat until the oil is hot, but not smoking. Reduce to medium heat and fry the eggplant in two batches. Add 2 more tablespoons of oil to the skillet before cooking the second batch. Fry each batch about 8 minutes, turning to brown lightly on all sides. Remove the eggplant with a slotted spoon and drain on paper towels. Sprinkle with salt and set aside.

Cook the pasta in the boiling water until al dente. While the pasta cooks, heat the remaining 2 tablespoons of oil in a large saucepan and add the cherry tomatoes, garlic, parsley, and red pepper flakes. Sauté for 2 to 3 minutes, stirring gently, and set aside.

When the pasta is al dente, drain it, and transfer to a large, warmed serving bowl. Add the eggplant, tomato mixture, fresh mozzarella cubes, grated cheese, basil, and salt.

Serve immediately, passing additional grated cheese at the table.

PER 18-OUNCE SERVING: 778 CALORIES, 31.8 G PROTEIN, 40 G FAT, 73.7 G CARBOHYDRATES, 13.5 G SATURATED FATTY ACIDS, 185.6 MG CHOLESTEROL, 877.5 MG SODIUM, 6.7 G TOTAL DIETARY FIBER

batter-fried vegetables & fish

Whether it's called tempura, Southern-fried, or fritto misto, batter-fried foods are unsurpassed for their ability to seal in juices and flavors. This simple batter uses carbonated water to make a crisp, light coating with a delicate texture. Using two deep-fryers will save time and ensure that the first fried vegetables are still crunchy and hot by the time the last ones are ready.

The batter works nicely after resting for an hour but is best after 2 hours. Half florets of broccoli and cauliflower and thinly sliced vegetables can be batter-fried raw; thicker slices—1/2 inch—should be blanched first in boiling water for 2 minutes and drained well. Choose a thickness and cut the vegetables uniformly. Be sure they're at room temperature and relatively dry before frying.

Serves 4 to 6
Batter preparation time: 10 minutes
Batter sitting time: 1 to 2 hours
Oil heating time: 20 minutes
Frying time (with two deep-fryers):
    20 to 25 minutes

batter
1 1/3 cups unbleached white flour*
1/2 cup cornstarch
1 1/2 to 2 teaspoons salt
1/4 teaspoon ground black pepper
2 cups seltzer or plain carbonated
    spring water

allow about 1/4 pound per person
peeled and deveined medium whole
    shrimp
whole bay scallops
fish fillets, in bite-sized pieces**

select 3 vegetables (6 cups prepared)
asparagus, cut into 2-inch pieces
bell peppers, seeded and cut into
    2-inch pieces
broccoli, cut into florets
carrots, peeled and diagonally sliced
cauliflower, cut into florets
eggplant, peeled, quartered
    lengthwise, and sliced into
    wedges
fennel bulb, sliced
green tomatoes, sliced
okra, whole small pods
onions, cut into rings and separated
portabello caps, sliced
sweet potatoes, peeled and sliced
white mushrooms, whole or halved
zucchini, cut into rounds

oil for deep-frying
salt and ground black pepper to taste
2 tablespoons fresh lemon juice
Ginger Sherry Sauce (page 348),
    optional

* *If using fish and seafood, you will need additional flour for dredging.*
** *We recommend catfish or tilapia.*

✄ To make the batter, combine the flour, cornstarch, salt, and pepper in a large bowl and slowly whisk in the seltzer until smooth. Be careful not to overbeat. Set aside for 1 to 2 hours. While the batter develops, prepare the fish and/or vegetables.

When you are ready to fry, heat oil in a deep-fryer, large wok, or cast-iron Dutch oven or kettle to about 365°. The oil should be deep enough so that the batter-coated pieces can float at the top without touching the bottom of the pan.

The batter should be the consistency of heavy cream. If it's too thick, add a little seltzer. Dip the vegetables into the batter with tongs or chopsticks and allow the excess to drip back into the bowl. Fry in the hot oil until the coating is crisp and the vegetables tender, 3 to 6 minutes. Dredge the seafood or fish in flour, shake off the excess, dip in the batter, and fry for about 6 minutes, until crisp. Drain everything briefly on paper towels.

Salt the vegetables and sprinkle black pepper and fresh lemon juice on the fish, or offer Ginger Sherry Sauce alongside. Serve immediately.

PER 11-OUNCE SERVING: 268 CALORIES, 25.7 G PROTEIN, 1.7 G FAT, 36.9 G CARBOHYDRATES, 0.4 G SATURATED FATTY ACIDS, 194.6 MG CHOLESTEROL, 845.6 MG SODIUM, 2.8 G TOTAL DIETARY FIBER

variations ❀ *These rubs will coat 1¼ pounds of fish or seafood. Combine all of the ingredients and rub them onto the fish or seafood. Chill for 1 hour and then drain off any accumulated liquid. Next dredge in flour, dip in batter, and fry as above.*

mediterranean-style rub
1 teaspoon dried oregano
1 teaspoon dried basil
2 garlic cloves, pressed or minced
¼ teaspoon salt
pinch of ground black pepper

southern-style rub
1 teaspoon Old Bay seasoning
1 teaspoon dried thyme
2 garlic cloves, pressed or minced

cioppino

Cioppino is a lavish Italian American-style seafood stew with a peppery herbed tomato sauce. It's famous as a specialty dish of the city of San Francisco. Many versions of this dish have developed, using all kinds of seafood, depending upon whatever is available and freshest.

Moosewood cook Michael Blodgett, who trained in New Orleans where the stew is served over pasta, created Moosewood's version. The more usual way to eat cioppino is with a big crusty hunk of garlic bread either on the side or sometimes in the bottom of the bowl.

Serves 6
Total time: 50 to 60 minutes

2 tablespoons olive oil
1 cup chopped onions
1 garlic clove, minced or pressed
1 cup chopped green bell peppers
1 1/2 cups canned tomatoes with juice, chopped (14.5-ounce can)
2 tablespoons tomato paste
1 cup dry red wine
1/2 teaspoon dried thyme
1/2 teaspoon dried oregano
1/2 teaspoon dried red pepper flakes
2 bay leaves
1/4 cup chopped fresh basil
1 teaspoon salt
2 cups vegetable stock or water
1 cup dry white wine

1/2 pound fresh mussels, rinsed and cleaned*
1/2 pound fresh clams, rinsed and cleaned*
1/2 pound large peeled and deveined shrimp, rinsed and drained
1 pound sea scallops, rinsed and drained
1 to 1 1/2 pounds linguine

chopped fresh parsley
lemon wedges

* Discard any mussels or clams that are open or broken, rinse the rest with cold water, and scrub. Remove and discard the stringy "beard" of the mussels. Place the mussels and clams in a bowl, cover with cold water, and refrigerate until ready to use. Rinse and drain again before cooking.

Heat 1 tablespoon of the oil in a large, nonreactive, heavy-bottomed soup pot. Add the onions and sauté on medium heat until translucent, about 10 minutes. Add the garlic and bell peppers and continue to sauté until the bell peppers soften, 2 to 3 minutes. Add the tomatoes, tomato paste, red wine, thyme, oregano, red pepper flakes, bay leaves, basil, salt, and 1 cup of the vegetable stock or water. Bring to a boil, stirring occasionally. Reduce the heat to low and simmer while preparing the other ingredients.

Bring a large pot of salted water to boil.

In a 2-quart saucepan, bring the remaining cup of stock or water and the white wine to a boil. Add the mussels and clams. Cook for 2 to 5 minutes, until the shells open. Remove them with tongs and set aside. Discard any that do not open.

Remove the bay leaves from the simmering tomato sauce and discard. Add the shrimp and scallops and cook until the shrimp turn pink and the scallops are opaque, about 5 minutes. Remove the sauce from the heat.

Add the pasta to the boiling water and cook until al dente. Drain and toss with the remaining tablespoon of olive oil.

Serve the pasta immediately in warmed pasta bowls. Arrange the mussels and clams around the edges of each bowl, ladle the sauce over each serving, and decorate with parsley and lemon wedges.

PER 19-OUNCE SERVING: 495 CALORIES, 29.6 G PROTEIN, 9.2 G FAT, 61.8 G CARBOHYDRATES, 1.4 G SATURATED FATTY ACIDS, 157.2 MG CHOLESTEROL, 781.1 MG SODIUM, 3.3 G TOTAL DIETARY FIBER

elegant oven-poached fish

Low-fat, delicious, fast but impressive, this is an excellent supper dish. The fish stays incredibly moist with this oven-poaching method and the sweet leeks and briny capers add flair. The flavors remain distinct—you can taste each one, yet somehow, they also blend. The dry white wine ties it all together.

Our presentation is handsome enough for quick company fare. And if there are leftovers, well, it's even better the next day. Reheat it or serve it cold on a bed of fresh salad greens and topped with a few fresh herbs.

Serves 4 to 6
Preparation time: 15 minutes
Baking time: 20 to 30 minutes

1 1/2 pounds thick fish fillets, such as sea bass, cod, lake trout, or salmon

2 to 3 leeks, sliced and rinsed well*

1 tomato, coarsely chopped

3/4 cup dry white wine

2 tablespoons capers

2 teaspoons chopped fresh thyme (1/2 teaspoon dried)

salt and ground black pepper to taste

cooked brown rice or orzo

* For this dish, prepare about 2 cups of sliced leeks, using only the tender white bulbs.

Preheat the oven to 425°.

Rinse the fish fillets, pat dry, and set aside.

Spread the sliced leeks on the bottom of a baking dish large enough to hold the fish in a single layer. Scatter the tomatoes over the leeks and pour on the wine. Arrange the fish on top and sprinkle with the capers, thyme, salt, and pepper.

Cover and bake for 20 to 30 minutes, depending on the thickness of the fish. The fish is done when the thickest part is easily pierced with a knife.

Serve each portion on a bed of rice or orzo and spoon some of the pan juices and vegetables over each serving.

PER 6.5-OUNCE SERVING: 152 CALORIES, 24.1 G PROTEIN, 1.1 G FAT, 6 G CARBOHYDRATES, 0.2 G SATURATED FATTY ACIDS, 56.1 MG CHOLESTEROL, 157.1 MG SODIUM, 0.8 G TOTAL DIETARY FIBER

escabeche

This pickled fish, also called *escovitch*, is popular in Latin America, the Caribbean, and in the Mediterranean, especially Spain. Escabeche is usually served chilled after marinating for a few days, but sometimes we just can't wait and eat it warm over rice. The longer it marinates, the more tangy and full-flavored it becomes.

We suggest using fish such as sea bass, ocean perch, catfish, mackerel, or snapper. Or combine fish and shrimp in equal amounts.

Serve chilled escabeche as a main dish or as an appetizer with crackers or crisp bread.

Serves 4 to 6
Preparation time: 50 minutes
Marinating time: 3 to 48 hours

1/2 teaspoon salt

1/2 cup fresh lime juice*

1 pound fish fillets

5 tablespoons olive oil

1 large onion, peeled, halved, and sliced 1/4-inch thick

1 red or green bell pepper, seeded and cut into 1-inch pieces

1 Scotch bonnet or other fresh chile, seeded and minced

2 garlic cloves, minced or pressed

1/2 teaspoon dried thyme

1 to 2 tablespoons capers

1 cup peeled and sliced carrots (1/4-inch-thick rounds)

2 cups bite-sized cauliflower florets

* Distilled vinegar or white wine vinegar can be used for a somewhat sharper flavor.

Dissolve the salt in the lime juice and set aside. Cut the fish into 1 1/2-inch pieces. In a large skillet on medium-high heat, warm 2 tablespoons of the oil until hot but not smoking. Cook the fish for 2 to 4 minutes depending on thickness. Turn with a spatula and cook until just beginning to flake, 2 to 4 more minutes. Transfer the fish to a flat-bottomed large bowl.

Add 2 tablespoons of the oil to the skillet. Sauté the onions, stirring frequently, for about 4 minutes, until they begin to soften. Stir in the bell peppers, chiles, and garlic and sauté for 2 or 3 minutes. Stir in the thyme and capers and sauté for another 2 or 3 minutes, until the bell peppers are tender yet firm. Spoon the vegetables onto the fish in the bowl.

In a nonreactive pot with a lid, warm the remaining tablespoon of oil. Sauté the carrots for about 3 minutes. Add the cauliflower and sauté, stirring frequently, for 2 or 3 minutes. Stir in 3 tablespoons of the seasoned lime juice, lower the heat, cover, and simmer for 3 or 4 minutes. When the vegetables are tender, add them to the bowl. Pour the remaining lime juice over all, cover, and refrigerate. Marinate in the refrigerator, stirring occasionally, for at least 3 hours and up to 48 hours.

PER 7-OUNCE SERVING: 214 CALORIES, 17 G PROTEIN, 12.7 G FAT, 8.9 G CARBOHYDRATES, 1.8 G SATURATED FATTY ACIDS, 37.4 MG CHOLESTEROL, 305.1 MG SODIUM, 2.3 G TOTAL DIETARY FIBER

fish-in-a-packet

A packet of fresh fish and vegetables steamed in savory or spicy flavors is like a gift. Each individually wrapped "present" releases a burst of aromatic steam when opened. The flavors mingle sweet with spicy, hot with salty, briny with piquant. Nothing escapes until the final moment of opening the foil. Inside, the fish is tender and succulent, the vegetables are perfectly cooked, and the sauce has bathed every ingredient.

When cooking in a packet, potatoes take too long and asparagus and snow peas lose their bright color. Carrots, onions, zucchini, yellow squash, and bell peppers are better choices.

Once you prepare all of the ingredients, each packet can be assembled and folded easily and quickly. In general, we don't recommend that you prepare the packets ahead of time because some ingredients may react with the aluminum foil. Serve immediately to avoid overcooking.

gingered salmon-in-a-packet

Serve this Chinese-style fish-in-a-packet with long-grain brown rice.

Serves 4
Preparation time: 45 minutes
Baking time: 20 minutes

4 six-ounce salmon fillets
¼ cup vegetable oil
8 garlic cloves, minced or pressed
¼ cup grated fresh ginger root
¼ cup soy sauce
¼ cup rice vinegar or lemon juice
½ teaspoon dark sesame oil
2 cups peeled and sliced carrots
1 cup sliced water chestnuts
2 cups red bell pepper slices
¼ cup chopped scallions

Preheat the oven to 450°. For each fillet, fold a 12 x 24-inch sheet of aluminum foil in half to make a double-thick 12-inch square; set aside.

Rinse the fish, pat dry, and set aside. Heat the oil in a small saucepan. Add the garlic and ginger and sauté on low heat for about 1 minute. Stir in the soy sauce, rice vinegar or lemon juice, and sesame oil and set the sauce aside.

Place one fourth of the carrots and water chestnuts in the center of each foil square. Drizzle on a bit of the sauce and place a fish fillet on top. Arrange the red peppers on top of each and pour the remaining sauce evenly over all. Fold each square into an airtight packet, crimp the edges shut, and place on an unoiled baking sheet.

Bake for 20 minutes, until the fish flakes easily with a fork. Avoid the steam when opening the packets. Serve topped with the scallions.

PER 13.5-OUNCE SERVING: 499 CALORIES, 32.3 G PROTEIN, 31.5 G FAT, 21.8 G CARBOHYDRATES, 7.1 G SATURATED FATTY ACIDS, 81.4 MG CHOLESTEROL, 924.5 MG SODIUM, 5 G TOTAL DIETARY FIBER

fish with artichokes & capers

Fast enough for an easy work-night supper but elegant enough for a company dinner, this fragrant dish is seasoned with lemon, herbs, and piquant capers.

Serve with Perfect Tomato Salad with Feta Buttermilk Dressing (page 112) for a simple meal. For a dinner party, start with David's Dilled Havarti Spread (page 207) and crudités, serve the fish on Wild Rice Pilaf (page 147), and finish with Fruit Skewers (page 430).

Serves 4
Preparation time: 35 minutes
Bakking time: 20 minutes

4 six-ounce white fish fillets, such as tilapia, haddock, or scrod (¼-inch thick)

2 cups thinly sliced onions

4 cups thinly sliced mushrooms

2 cups sliced artichoke hearts

4 teaspoons capers, drained

¼ cup olive oil

½ cup fresh lemon juice

4 teaspoons Dijon mustard

¼ cup chopped fresh thyme (4 teaspoons dried)

½ teaspoon salt

ground black pepper to taste

4 small sprigs of fresh sage (optional)

¼ cup chopped fresh parsley (optional)

Preheat the oven to 450°. For each fillet, fold a 12 x 24-inch sheet of aluminum foil in half to make a double-thick 12-inch square, and set aside.

Rinse the fish, pat dry, and set aside. Place one fourth of the onions and mushrooms in the center of each square of aluminum foil. Lay the fish fillets on top of the vegetables and top with the artichoke hearts.

In a small bowl, combine the capers, olive oil, lemon juice, mustard, thyme, salt, pepper, and the sage, if using. Pour this sauce evenly over each fish fillet. Fold each foil square into an airtight packet, crimp the edges shut, and place on an unoiled baking sheet with sides to catch any drips.

Bake for 20 minutes, until the fish flakes easily with a fork and is cooked throughout. Use care when opening the packets because steam will be released. Remove the sprigs of sage, if used, and garnish the fish with parsley, if desired.

PER 14.5-OUNCE SERVING: 384 CALORIES, 38.2 G PROTEIN, 16.3 G FAT, 25.1 G CARBOHYDRATES, 2.3 G SATURATED FATTY ACIDS, 44.9 MG CHOLESTEROL, 1,763 MG SODIUM, 8.5 G TOTAL DIETARY FIBER

thai-style scallops-in-a-packet

This seafood packet is hot and citrusy and redolent with cilantro, basil, and mint. Use Thai basil if you have it. Although we like this dish best when made with scallops, it's quite delectable using fillets of scrod or tilapia as well. Four 6-ounce fillets will do just fine.

Serve the scallops on a bed of rice—jasmine rice is nice—alongside your favorite Thai side dishes. As an opener, try creamy but light Thai Coconut Soup (page 66), which has a lovely lemongrass stock for its base.

Serves 4
Preparation time: 35 minutes
Baking time: 20 minutes

¼ cup vegetable oil

½ cup fresh lime juice

1 to 2 teaspoons Chinese chili paste

3 tablespoons brown sugar, packed

½ teaspoon salt

2 cups thinly sliced zucchini or yellow squash

2 cups peeled and thinly sliced carrots

1½ pounds sea scallops

2 cups thinly sliced red bell peppers

¼ cup chopped fresh cilantro

¼ cup chopped fresh basil

¼ cup chopped fresh mint

1 cup mung bean sprouts (optional)

Preheat the oven to 450°. For each fillet, fold a 12 x 24-inch sheet of aluminum foil in half to make a double-thick 12-inch square, and set aside.

In a small bowl, mix together the oil, lime juice, Chinese chili paste, brown sugar, and salt. Set the sauce aside.

Place one fourth of the zucchini and carrots in the center of each square of aluminum foil and drizzle on a little of the sauce. Lay one fourth of the scallops on each serving of vegetables, top with the bell peppers, and pour the remaining sauce evenly over all. Mix together the cilantro, basil, and mint; sprinkle half of it over all of the scallops and reserve the rest. Fold each foil square into an airtight packet, crimp the edges shut, and place on an unoiled baking sheet with sides to catch any drips.

Bake for 20 minutes, or until the scallops are opaque and tender. Use care when opening the packets because steam will be released. Serve dusted with the rest of the fresh herbs and, if you wish, scatter some mung sprouts on top.

PER 12-OUNCE SERVING: 330 CALORIES, 22 G PROTEIN, 16 G FAT, 29.8 G CARBOHYDRATES, 3.8 G SATURATED FATTY ACIDS, 45.1 MG CHOLESTEROL, 431.1 MG SODIUM, 4.7 G TOTAL DIETARY FIBER

pecan-crusted fish

Rich and satisfying, this crunchy topping really dresses up fish fillets for an easily prepared meal. We recommend using fillets such as catfish, snapper, salmon, or tilapia for this dish.

Serve with wedges of lemon or, to be fancy, with Spicy Cantaloupe Salad (page 96) or one of our delightful salsas: Peach Salsa or Summer Melon Salsa (page 381).

 Serves 4
Preparation time: 20 minutes
Baking time: 30 to 45 minutes

4 firm fish fillets (5 to 6 ounces each)
¾ cup buttermilk
¾ cup finely ground pecans*
¾ cup bread crumbs**
3 garlic cloves, minced or pressed
2 tablespoons minced fresh parsley
½ teaspoon dried thyme
½ teaspoon paprika
½ teaspoon salt
pinch of cayenne

Preheat the oven to 375°. Lightly oil a baking pan.

Rinse the fish and place it in a shallow dish. Pour the buttermilk over the fillets. In a separate shallow dish, combine the pecans, bread crumbs, garlic, parsley, thyme, paprika, salt, and cayenne.

* *Grind pecans in a food processor, good blender, mouli-julienne, or in batches in a spice grinder. Or place them in a plastic bag and crush with a rolling pin.*
** *Pulverize stale or lightly toasted whole wheat, sourdough, or French bread in a blender or food processor.*

One at a time, remove the fillets from the buttermilk, allowing the excess to drain off, and then dredge in the pecan mixture to coat all sides. Place each coated fillet in the baking pan.

Bake for 30 to 45 minutes, depending upon the thickness of the fillets, until the topping is lightly browned and the fish is tender and flakes easily with a fork.

PER 7.5-OUNCE SERVING: 397 CALORIES, 35.2 G PROTEIN, 21.6 G FAT, 17.1 G CARBOHYDRATES, 2.3 G SATURATED FATTY ACIDS, 71.6 MG CHOLESTEROL, 566.4 MG SODIUM, 3.9 G TOTAL DIETARY FIBER

salsas,
sauces&
seasonings

sauces, salsas & seasonings ❧

Some of our sauces, salsas, and seasonings are *not* for the faint of heart. If any food will wake you up and make you look twice, it's a fiery salsa, gingery fruit chutney, or a racy salad dressing that packs a wallop. For those who prefer flavors from a more temperate zone, we've interspersed between the spicy options several mild fruit chutneys and salsas, some quick marinades and sauces, and a few moderately seasoned dips and dressings. And, just to please the folks who believe, like us, that some good things never go out of style, we've included Simplest Ever Applesauce and Mushroom Gravy.

There is nothing really tricky or mysterious about any of these accompaniments. With the exceptions, perhaps, of wasabi, garlic scapes, or jicama, the ingredients in these recipes are mostly familiar and are readily available in large supermarkets. We've simply put together good ingredients in new ways that we find exciting. With the generous use of toppings, you can take a dish that is ordinary and familiar and transform its flavor as well as its presentation. It's like wearing sensational new jewelry with a favorite dress that you've had forever. Nobody even recognizes the dress.

So, fill your house with the lively aroma of a spicy Arrabbiata Sauce or Tomato Sauce with Sage. Add sweet-tart Rhubarb Cherry Chutney to your favorite curry. If you're yearning for sunny southwestern cuisine, dip into some Mole, or Joan's Three-Tomato Salsa. Create a hint of the sparkling Caribbean with one of our spectacular fruit salsas. Finally, come back home to back-yard grilled vegetables or baked tofu topped with one of our Two Barbeque Sauces, or to some humble mashed potatoes with Mushroom Gravy.

Old favorites, new accents, simplicity, and a little bit of daring characterize many of these versatile recipes that can be used as side dishes, dips, and toppings, as well as garnishes and flavorings. Most will keep well in the refrigerator for a week or longer. Maybe . . . just maybe, there *is* something new under the sun.

arrabbiata sauce

This will become your new "standard sauce," especially if you like a little spice in your life!

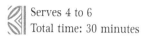 Serves 4 to 6
Total time: 30 minutes

In a 2-quart saucepan, sauté the onions, salt, and garlic in the oil on medium heat until the onions are browned and somewhat caramelized, about 10 minutes. Add the red pepper flakes and the bell peppers and cook for another 2 minutes. Add the chopped tomatoes with their juices and the black pepper and bring to a simmer. Cook, uncovered, for about 15 minutes, stirring occasionally. Stir in the basil and serve.

2 cups diced onions
1 teaspoon salt
2 or 3 garlic cloves, pressed
2 teaspoons olive oil
1 teaspoon red pepper flakes
1 cup diced bell peppers
6 cups canned tomatoes with juice, chopped (two 28-ounce cans)
1/4 teaspoon ground black pepper
2 tablespoons chopped fresh basil

PER 10.5-OUNCE SERVING: 89 CALORIES, 3.2 G PROTEIN, 2.3 G FAT, 16 G CARBOHYDRATES, 0.3 G SATURATED FATTY ACIDS, 0 MG CHOLESTEROL, 687.1 MG SODIUM, 1.2 G TOTAL DIETARY FIBER

creamy tomato sauce

Here's a creamy, simple, and delicious tomato sauce that tastes and looks great.

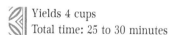 Yields 4 cups
Total time: 25 to 30 minutes

Warm the oil in a saucepan and add the onions, garlic, oregano, salt, and pepper. Cover and cook on low heat for about 10 minutes, until the onions are soft and translucent. Add the tomatoes, cover, bring to a simmer, and cook for about 10 minutes.

In a blender, purée about a cup of the sauce with the Neufchâtel. Stir back into the pan; add the basil. Gently reheat, if necessary.

1 tablespoon olive oil
1 cup diced onions
2 garlic cloves, minced or pressed
1 teaspoon dried oregano
1/2 teaspoon salt
1/8 teaspoon ground black pepper
3 cups canned tomatoes with juice, chopped (28-ounce can)
1/4 cup Neufchâtel or cream cheese
3 tablespoons chopped fresh basil

PER 1-OUNCE SERVING: 14 CALORIES, 0.4 G PROTEIN, 0.7 G FAT, 1.6 G CARBOHYDRATES, 0.2 G SATURATED FATTY ACIDS, 0.7 MG CHOLESTEROL, 73.3 MG SODIUM, 0.1 G TOTAL DIETARY FIBER

avocado wasabi dressing

This is a silky green dressing with an unabashed kick of wasabi—a spicy hot Japanese radish. The uninitiated may want to reduce the amount of wasabi, but we suggest following the recipe fearlessly the first time. You might just like it like that!

Try the dressing on Tofu Hijiki Burgers (page 187) or in a burrito, as a dip for crudités or tortilla chips, or tossed with soba noodles and snow peas. It's also a natural for sushi and can really enliven a spinach-tomato salad or a simple grated carrot salad.

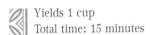
Yields 1 cup
Total time: 15 minutes

1 tablespoon wasabi powder
  (page 474)
3 tablespoons water
1 large ripe avocado, preferably Hass
5 teaspoons rice vinegar
1 teaspoon salt
1 tablespoon vegetable oil

In a small cup, combine the wasabi powder and 1 tablespoon of the water to make a smooth, blended paste. Cover and set aside.

Peel and pit the avocado and cut it into large chunks. In a blender or food processor, purée the avocado, rice vinegar, salt, oil, and the remaining 2 tablespoons of water to form a smooth, pleasantly thick consistency. Blend the reserved wasabi paste into the dressing and adjust the seasonings, if needed.

PER 1-OUNCE SERVING: 60 CALORIES, 0.6 G PROTEIN, 5.8 G FAT, 2.1 G CARBOHYDRATES, 1.1 G SATURATED FATTY ACIDS, 0 MG CHOLESTEROL, 300.2 MG SODIUM, 1.4 G TOTAL DIETARY FIBER

black bean mango salsa

Chunks of bright orange mango and midnight black beans make a gorgeous duet of contrasting colors. Our salsa has a refreshing balance of flavors, but it's easy to vary it to suit your mood: Make it hot with more chiles, really accentuate the cilantro, add more garlic kick, or pucker it up with more lemon.

This versatile salsa is superb on rice dishes, cheese enchiladas, and on Fish with Cornmeal Chipotle Crust (page 298).

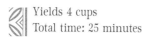
Yields 4 cups
Total time: 25 minutes

1 1/2 cups cooked black beans
(15-ounce can)

1 ripe mango, peeled and diced
(page 461)

1/2 cup diced red bell peppers

2 tablespoons chopped fresh parsley

1 tablespoon chopped fresh cilantro

1 minced fresh green chile (seeded
for a milder hot)

1 garlic clove, pressed

1/3 cup orange juice

1 tablespoon fresh lemon juice

1/4 teaspoon salt

nasturtium flowers and mint leaves
(optional)

Rinse the canned beans and drain well. Transfer to a large bowl and add the mango, bell peppers, parsley, cilantro, chile, garlic, orange juice, lemon juice, and salt. Mix thoroughly.

Top with the nasturtiums and mint leaves, if desired.

PER 1-OUNCE SERVING: 17 CALORIES, 0.8 G PROTEIN, 0.1 G FAT, 3.5 G CARBOHYDRATES, 0 G SATURATED FATTY ACIDS, 0 MG CHOLESTEROL, 60.7 MG SODIUM, 0.9 G TOTAL DIETARY FIBER

four cheese sauce

Wondering what to do with those bits and pieces of assorted cheese you may have on hand? This velvety, elegant, versatile sauce can make short work of them—and to good end. The cheese listed below are just suggestions. About eight ounces total of your four cheese choices is all that you need.

Gruyère, Fontina, sherry, and mustard combine for a taste akin to fondue. And like fondue, this sauce can be the centerpiece of a meal in which everyone dips coarse-grained bread and lightly steamed vegetables into the luscious sauce and swoons.

Try Four-Cheese Sauce on fettuccine or on a chunky pasta, such as penne or shells, topped with diced Roma tomatoes. Use it to create a pasta casserole with steamed cauliflower or broccoli. Or kick off a creamy soup or chowder by adding body with a cup of the sauce.

2 1/2 cups milk

1/4 cup butter

1/4 cup unbleached white flour

1/2 cup grated Gruyère

1/2 cup grated Fontina

3/4 cup grated Parmesan

1/2 cup grated aged provolone

1 teaspoon Dijon mustard

1/4 cup dry sherry

1/8 teaspoon salt, or to taste

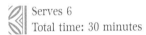

Serves 6
Total time: 30 minutes

In a small saucepan, heat the milk until steaming, but don't let it boil or form a skin. While the milk heats, melt the butter in a heavy 2-quart saucepan on low heat. Add the flour and whisk to form a smooth roux. Continue to cook and whisk for 3 to 4 minutes to thoroughly cook the flour.

Increase the heat to medium and whisk the hot milk into the roux in a thin, steady stream. Continue to cook until the sauce is smooth and has thickened slightly. Never stop whisking, since white sauces can burn in an instant.

Lower the heat, add the cheeses, mustard, and sherry, and whisk until the cheeses melt. Using a double boiler or a heat diffuser, gently cook on very low heat for about 10 minutes, stirring occasionally. Add salt to taste.

PER 5.5-OUNCE SERVING: 295 CALORIES, 15.4 G PROTEIN, 21.2 G FAT, 9.3 G CARBOHYDRATES, 13.5 G SATURATED FATTY ACIDS, 62.6 MG CHOLESTEROL, 552.5 MG SODIUM, 0.1 G TOTAL DIETARY FIBER

garlic scape pesto

In our cool climate of Ithaca, New York, the new growth of garlic is among the first greens to emerge in late winter. When the local farmers' market opens for the season, garlic greens abound and are perfect for an early-season pesto.

The greens have a milder flavor than the bulbs, but are nicely assertive. Later in the season, the young unopened flower stalks, or scapes, can also be used. Both are good only when tender and nonfibrous; the scapes, in particular, quickly outgrow their culinary use.

Our resident organic gardener, David Hirsch, snips his greens from plants that were accidently missed in the previous summer's harvest. If you cut greens from new unharvested bulbs, it will weaken the plants and result in smaller heads of garlic. Non-gardeners can look for scapes and greens at farmers' or specialty produce markets.

1 1/2 cups coarsely chopped garlic scapes or greens, lightly packed

1/3 cup grated Parmesan cheese*

3 tablespoons olive oil

1/3 cup toasted pine nuts**

1 to 2 tablespoons water (optional)

salt and ground black pepper to taste

* *If you want to freeze the pesto for later use, omit the cheese.*
** *Toast pine nuts in a single layer on an unoiled baking tray at 350° for 3 to 5 minutes, until fragrant and golden brown. Or use toasted sunflower seeds, if you prefer.*

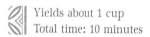
Yields about 1 cup
Total time: 10 minutes

Combine the garlic scapes or greens, cheese, oil, and nuts in the bowl of a food processor and process until fairly smooth. Add water as needed to make a spreadable paste. Add salt and pepper to taste.

PER 1-OUNCE SERVING: 96 CALORIES, 3.2 G PROTEIN, 6.6 G FAT, 7 G CARBOHYDRATES, 1.3 G SATURATED FATTY ACIDS, 2.9 MG CHOLESTEROL, 74.4 MG SODIUM, 0.4 G TOTAL DIETARY FIBER

joan's three-tomato salsa

This is the quintessential end-of-summer salsa, best made when there is a bonanza of tomatoes. Although the salsa is prettiest made with three colors of tomatoes, it's just as tasty made with plain old red ones. If you prefer a milder salsa, remove the seeds from the chile before chopping.

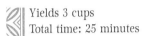 Yields 3 cups
Total time: 25 minutes

1 cup chopped red tomatoes

1 cup chopped yellow tomatoes

1 cup chopped unripe green tomatoes

2 tablespoons chopped fresh cilantro

4 teaspoons olive oil

2 tablespoons fresh lemon or
    lime juice

1 fresh green chile, minced

2 garlic cloves, minced or pressed

2 scallions, chopped

½ teaspoon salt, or to taste

Combine all of the ingredients in a bowl and mix well. Serve at room temperature or chilled.

PER 1-OUNCE SERVING: 13 CALORIES, 0.3 G PROTEIN, 0.9 G FAT, 1.5 G CARBOHYDRATES, 0.2 G SATURATED FATTY ACIDS, 0 MG CHOLESTEROL, 3.5 MG SODIUM, 0.4 G TOTAL DIETARY FIBER

variation ☙ *Replace the green tomatoes with fresh tomatillos that are husked and finely chopped.*

light sour cream

This is delicious, easy to make, and a more healthful alternative to straight sour cream. Sealed and stored in the refrigerator, it will keep for up to 10 days. Use it as a garnish on soups and stews or to top French toast, tacos, chili, and fresh fruit.

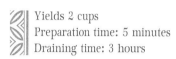 Yields 2 cups
Preparation time: 5 minutes
Draining time: 3 hours

2 cups plain nonfat yogurt, without gelatin
1 cup sour cream

Line a colander with overlapping paper coffee filters or several layers of cheesecloth. Place it over a large bowl. Spoon in the yogurt, cover, and refrigerate.

After an hour or so, empty the liquid collected in the bowl to ensure that it doesn't reach the bottom of the colander. After 3 hours, the yogurt will have thickened considerably. Mix together the drained yogurt and sour cream and transfer to a tightly covered container.

PER 1-OUNCE SERVING: 31 CALORIES, 1.4 G PROTEIN, 2 G FAT, 1.9 G CARBOHYDRATES, 1.3 G SATURATED FATTY ACIDS, 4.5 MG CHOLESTEROL, 19.6 MG SODIUM, 0 G TOTAL DIETARY FIBER

mango lime sauce

Take a taste of this sweet-tart sauce, close your eyes, and you'll swear you're in San Juan—it's pure heaven. Mango Lime Sauce is superb on bitter salad greens or as a dip for roasted or grilled vegetables, fish, tofu, or tempeh. It keeps well, covered and refrigerated, for 2 weeks.

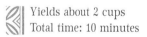 Yields about 2 cups
Total time: 10 minutes

1 mango
2 limes
2 tablespoons olive oil
1/2 teaspoon salt
pinch of ground black pepper

Prepare the mango (see headnote, opposite). Zest the limes and juice them. Place the mango, lime zest and juice in a blender with the oil, salt, and pepper. Purée until smooth.

PER 1-OUNCE SERVING: 35 CALORIES, 0.2 G PROTEIN, 2.4 G FAT, 4 G CARBOHYDRATES, 0.3 G SATURATED FATTY ACIDS, 0 MG CHOLESTEROL, 100.1 MG SODIUM, 0.6 G TOTAL DIETARY FIBER

mango corn jicama salsa

More elaborate than most salsas, this refreshing orange-scented dish does double duty as both a salad and a topping—as nourishment and accent. Dice small when using as a topping, cut into larger cubes for a side dish. It's a perfect side for any simple bean dish and lovely on baked fish.

Mangos have large pits and the pulp is slippery. A shallow slice from end to end along the two broad, flat sides works best. Score the mango flesh of each slice into cubes and pare them away from the skin. Peel the remaining skin around the pit, then carefully cut the tender pulp away from the pit and dice it.

 Serves 4 to 6
Preparation time: 20 minutes
Sitting time: 15 minutes

1 cup peeled and diced jicama

1 cup fresh or frozen corn kernels, cooked to crisp-tender

1 1/2 cups peeled, pitted, and diced mango

1 cup diced red bell peppers

1 tablespoon minced fresh chiles

dressing

1 tablespoon freshly grated orange peel

1/2 cup fresh orange juice

1 tablespoon fresh lemon juice

1 tablespoon olive oil

1 teaspoon minced fresh thyme (pinch of dried thyme)

1/4 teaspoon salt

In a medium bowl combine the jicama, corn, mango, bell peppers, and chiles. Whisk together all of the dressing ingredients and pour over the mango and vegetables.

Allow the salsa to sit at room temperature for about 15 minutes so that the flavors will have a chance to marry.

PER 5-OUNCE SERVING: 105 CALORIES, 1.7 G PROTEIN, 2.9 G FAT, 20.6 G CARBOHYDRATES, 0.4 G SATURATED FATTY ACIDS, 0 MG CHOLESTEROL, 106.8 MG SODIUM, 3.7 G TOTAL DIETARY FIBER

miso lemon marinade

Whether you're grilling or roasting, this marinade is a cinch for enlivening fish or vegetables with classic Asian flavorings. Use it as a drizzle to create a quick rice salad, or splash it on steamed vegetables. We use a light or rice miso, although any miso will do. With a stronger miso, you may want less soy sauce.

Yields 3/4 cup
Total time: 10 minutes

- 1 tablespoon miso
- 2 tablespoons water
- 2 tablespoons fresh lemon juice
- 2 tablespoons dark sesame oil
- 1 tablespoon peeled and grated fresh ginger root
- 2 garlic cloves, minced or pressed
- 1/4 cup mirin or sweet sherry
- 1 tablespoon soy sauce

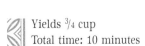

In a bowl, whisk together the miso and water until smooth. Whisk in the remaining ingredients until well blended.

PER 1-OUNCE SERVING: 77 CALORIES, 0.6 G PROTEIN, 4.9 G FAT, 8.1 G CARBOHYDRATES, 0.7 G SATURATED FATTY ACIDS, 0 MG CHOLESTEROL, 228.6 MG SODIUM, 0.2 G TOTAL DIETARY FIBER

thai marinade

Here's a zesty blend of spicy hot, sweet, aromatic, and garlicky flavors. If you can get Thai basil, it will give your marinade the most authentic flavor. If not, Italian basil can substitute. Soy sauce can replace the fish sauce for a good, but noticeably different, marinade.

Yields 1 1/4 cups
Total time: 15 minutes

- 2 tablespoons vegetable oil
- 6 garlic cloves, minced or pressed
- 2 teaspoons minced fresh chiles
- 2 teaspoons freshly grated lime peel
- 1/3 cup fresh lime juice
- 1/4 cup chopped fresh Thai basil
- 2/3 cup mango nectar
- 1 tablespoon fish sauce or soy sauce

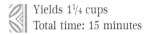

In a bowl with a whisk or in a blender, mix all of the ingredients until well combined. Thai Marinade will keep refrigerated for 1 or 2 weeks.

PER 1-OUNCE SERVING: 38 CALORIES, 0.2 G PROTEIN, 2.9 G FAT, 3.6 G CARBOHYDRATES, 0.7 G SATURATED FATTY ACIDS, 0.9 MG CHOLESTEROL, 115.6 MG SODIUM, 0.1 G TOTAL DIETARY FIBER

mole

The Aztec word *mole* means mixture or sauce, and moles often include chiles, nuts, seeds, and vegetables. This Moosewood mole features three traditional Mexican ingredients: tart and lemony tomatillos, pumpkin seeds, and *guajilla* peppers, named "little gourds" because their seeds rattle in the dried pod like the gourds that are used as rhythmic shaker instruments. If you can't find pumpkin seeds, use almonds instead.

Mole is typically used to flavor and enrich a soup, stew, quesadilla, or bean and rice dish. See our Mexican Baked Tofu (page 224) for an innovative use for mole that really hits the spot.

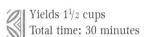 Yields 1¹/₂ cups
Total time: 30 minutes

1 teaspoon whole cumin seeds

1 teaspoon whole coriander seeds

2 dried guajilla peppers, seeded*

2 garlic cloves, peeled and coarsely chopped

1 cup chopped onions

4 or 5 tomatillos, husks removed*

¹/₄ cup shelled raw pumpkin seeds

¹/₄ teaspoon dried thyme

2 teaspoons salt

2 tablespoons sugar

2 tablespoons vegetable oil

¹/₄ cup water

¹/₄ teaspoon cayenne (optional)

* *Find guajilla peppers and canned whole tomatillos in the Latin American sections of well-stocked supermarkets. Pasilla chiles can replace the guajilla peppers, if you like. Use 4- to 5-inch-long peppers.*

In a dry skillet or a toaster oven, toast the cumin and coriander seeds for 1 to 2 minutes, until brown and fragrant. Stem and coarsely chop the guajilla peppers. In a spice grinder, grind the peppers with the toasted cumin and coriander into a powder. In a food processor, whirl the ground spices, garlic, onions, tomatillos, pumpkin seeds, thyme, salt, sugar, oil, water, and the cayenne, if using, until smooth.

Transfer the mole to a saucepan and cook on medium heat for 10 to 15 minutes to mellow the flavors. Serve warm as a condiment, or let cool and store in the refrigerator in a tightly sealed container.

PER 1-OUNCE SERVING: 46 CALORIES, 1 G PROTEIN, 2.7 G FAT, 5.5 G CARBOHYDRATES, 0.6 G SATURATED FATTY ACIDS, 0 MG CHOLESTEROL, 268.6 MG SODIUM, 1.3 G TOTAL DIETARY FIBER

mushroom gravy

This easy, delectable gravy lends the perfect finishing touch to almost any comfort-food meal. Tender sautéed mushrooms and onions are seasoned with a savory herb sauce spiked with sherry. For a glistening dark brown hue, we thicken the gravy with cornstarch rather than flour.

Our recipe calls for white mushrooms, but you can experiment with other varieties and experience their subtle distinctions. Serve with Tofu Stuffed Portabellos (page 286) or one of our Mashed Potato recipes (pages 130–134).

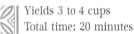 Yields 3 to 4 cups
Total time: 20 minutes

1 tablespoon vegetable oil
1 1/2 to 2 cups diced onions
4 cups sliced mushrooms
1/4 teaspoon dried thyme
1 bay leaf
pinch of salt
1/4 cup dry sherry
2 tablespoons soy sauce
1 3/4 cups water or vegetable stock
1/4 teaspoon ground black pepper
2 tablespoons cornstarch dissolved in
    1/4 cup cold water
salt or additional soy sauce to taste

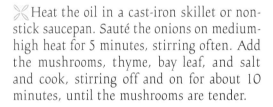 Heat the oil in a cast-iron skillet or non-stick saucepan. Sauté the onions on medium-high heat for 5 minutes, stirring often. Add the mushrooms, thyme, bay leaf, and salt and cook, stirring off and on for about 10 minutes, until the mushrooms are tender.

Add the sherry, soy sauce, and the water or stock, cover, and bring to a simmer. Stir the pepper and the dissolved cornstarch into the gravy and cook, stirring constantly, until the gravy is clear and thickened. Remove from the heat. Discard the bay leaf.

Add salt or additional soy sauce to taste and serve right away.

PER 5-OUNCE SERVING: 65 CALORIES, 1.6 G PROTEIN, 2.6 G FAT, 8.2 G CARBOHYDRATES, 0.6 G SATURATED FATTY ACIDS, 0 MG CHOLESTEROL, 292.7 MG SODIUM, 1.2 G TOTAL DIETARY FIBER

peach salsa

This is a peach of a salsa! Sweet, tart, and spicy, it complements grilled fish, beans and rice, quesadillas, and much more. If you prefer, replace the fresh chile with ¼ teaspoon of cayenne.

Yields 4 cups
Preparation time: 20 minutes
Sitting time: 10 minutes

4 ripe peaches, peeled and chopped
1 ripe tomato, chopped
1 bell pepper, seeded and chopped
1 garlic clove, minced or pressed
2 tablespoons chopped cilantro
2 tablespoons fresh lemon juice
½ to 1 fresh chile, seeded and minced
¼ teaspoon salt
dash of ground black pepper

In a large bowl, mix together all of the ingredients.

Set aside for 10 minutes to allow the flavors to meld. Covered and refrigerated, this salsa will keep for 2 or 3 days.

PER 1-OUNCE SERVING: 9 CALORIES, 0.2 G PROTEIN, 0 G FAT, 2.2 G CARBOHYDRATES, 0 G SATURATED FATTY ACIDS, 0 MG CHOLESTEROL, 19.3 MG SODIUM, 0.4 G TOTAL DIETARY FIBER

summer melon salsa

Here's a wonderful snack with chips and a refreshing topping for bean or fish dishes. For color, use both yellow and red cherry tomatoes or bell peppers. If you like, make the salsa with just a single type of melon.

Yields 3 to 4 cups
Preparation time: 15 minutes
Sitting time: at least 15 minutes

¼ cup fresh lime juice
1 tablespoon vegetable oil
2 teaspoons grated fresh ginger root
1 fresh chile, minced
1 tablespoon minced fresh basil
½ teaspoon salt
1 cup diced cantaloupe
1 cup diced honeydew
1 cup halved cherry tomatoes
½ cup diced bell peppers

In a bowl, whisk together the lime juice, oil, ginger, chiles, basil, and salt. Toss in the cantaloupe, honeydew, tomatoes, and peppers. Let sit for 20 minutes, so the flavors will blend. Serve at room temperature and store chilled.

PER 1-OUNCE SERVING: 13 CALORIES, 0.2 G PROTEIN, 0.6 G FAT, 2 G CARBOHYDRATES, 0.1 G SATURATED FATTY ACIDS, 0 MG CHOLESTEROL, 44.8 MG SODIUM, 0.3 G TOTAL DIETARY FIBER

quick tomato sauce

Moosewood's Tony Del Plato learned to make this tomato sauce from his mama. The speed and ease of the basic recipe, which uses canned tomatoes, reflects the simplicity and economy of much Italian home cooking.

Store-bought tomato sauce may be convenient for the cook in a hurry, but it just can't match the flavor of this Quick Tomato Sauce. Italian canned tomatoes often taste better than domestic ones, so we advise using "pomodori pelati" in juice.

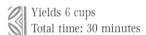 Yields 6 cups
Total time: 30 minutes

2 teaspoons olive oil

2 cups finely chopped onions

2 to 3 garlic cloves, minced or pressed

1 teaspoon salt, or more to taste

6 cups canned tomatoes with juice, chopped (two 28-ounce cans)*

¼ teaspoon ground black pepper

* Chopped whole tomatoes will produce a chunky sauce. If you prefer a smooth sauce, briefly whirl the tomatoes in a blender or food processor or use crushed tomatoes.

Warm the oil in a nonreactive 2-quart saucepan. Add the onions, garlic, and salt and sauté on medium heat for about 7 minutes, until golden. Add the tomatoes, their juice, and the pepper and bring to a simmer. Cook for 10 to 15 minutes, stirring occasionally.

Add more salt to taste. Serve immediately or chill or freeze for later use.

PER 9.5-OUNCE SERVING: 80 CALORIES, 2.8 G PROTEIN, 2.1 G FAT, 14 G CARBOHYDRATES, 0.2 G SATURATED FATTY ACIDS, 0 MG CHOLESTEROL, 686.3 MG SODIUM, 0.6 G TOTAL DIETARY FIBER

rhubarb cherry chutney

Unusual fruit combinations make great low-fat chutneys. Here tart rhubarb and sweet dried cherries create a rosy-hued chutney that's superb with Caribbean or Indian dishes.

Rhubarb is a long-lived perennial with ornamental wavy green and red leaves. Its long, crimson, tart stalks, available in May and June, are a wonderful foil for sweetness. Rhubarb leaves contain toxic amounts of oxalic acid and should not be used, raw or cooked. The stalks are edible only when cooked.

Try this chutney inside Indian Curried Potato Wrap (page 160) or Caribbean Beans & Greens Wrap (page 159). Or use a dollop of it to dress up Winter Curry (page 316) or simple baked or grilled fish fillets.

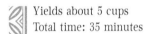
Yields about 5 cups
Total time: 35 minutes

1 tablespoon vegetable oil
1 1/2 cups diced red onions
1 tablespoon grated fresh ginger root
pinch of salt
1/4 cup cider vinegar
1/4 cup sugar
1/2 teaspoon ground coriander
1/2 teaspoon ground cardamom
1 teaspoon ground cinnamon
1/2 cup dried cherries
1 1/2 cups cherry or apple juice
4 cups sliced rhubarb (1-inch pieces)*

* About 1 1/2 pounds of rhubarb will make
  4 cups of bite-sized pieces.

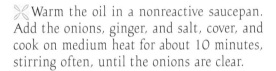 Warm the oil in a nonreactive saucepan. Add the onions, ginger, and salt, cover, and cook on medium heat for about 10 minutes, stirring often, until the onions are clear.

Add the vinegar, sugar, coriander, cardamom, cinnamon, cherries, and juice and bring to a boil; then reduce the heat and simmer for 5 minutes. Stir in the rhubarb and simmer on medium heat for 10 minutes, until the rhubarb is tender and the chutney somewhat thickened.

Serve at room temperature. Stored in a sealed container in the refrigerator, the chutney will keep for at least 2 weeks.

PER 1-OUNCE SERVING: 20 CALORIES, 0.2 G PROTEIN, 0.4 G FAT, 4.2 G CARBOHYDRATES, 0.1 G SATURATED FATTY ACIDS, 0 MG CHOLESTEROL, 4.1 MG SODIUM, 0.5 G TOTAL DIETARY FIBER

simplest ever applesauce

If you have a food mill, this method relieves you of peeling the apples and produces a smooth, blended sauce. If you don't have a food mill, you can purée the cooked, unpeeled apples in a good blender, or peel the apples before cooking: that way, you have the option of leaving the sauce chunky or mashing it once it's cooked.

No matter which way you do it, you'll have fragrant, sweet, delightful applesauce far superior to any commercial sauce. The applesauce, stored in a sealed container, will keep in the refrigerator for at least a week.

Yields 5 cups
Total time: 25 minutes

3 pounds cooking apples*

1 cup water

sugar or pure maple syrup to taste
(optional)

ground cinnamon or nutmeg to taste
(optional)

* We recommend Empire, McIntosh, Ida Red, Crispin, or Cortland apples.

Rinse the apples and remove the stems. Slice the apples into wedges and cut out the cores. Place the apple wedges and water in a heavy saucepan, cover, and bring to a boil on medium heat; then stir, reduce the heat to low, and simmer for 15 to 20 minutes, until soft.

In batches, spoon the apples into a food mill (see Note). Press the sauce into a deep bowl, discarding the skins from the mill. After pressing all of the apples, stir the sauce. Taste for sweetness and, if too tart, add a little sugar or maple syrup. At Moosewood, we serve our applesauce plain, but you can add a dash of cinnamon or nutmeg, if you like.

Serve warm or cold.

PER 4-OUNCE SERVING: 51 CALORIES, 0.3 G PROTEIN, 0.3 G FAT, 13.2 G CARBOHYDRATES, 0.1 G SATURATED FATTY ACIDS, 0 MG CHOLESTEROL, 1 MG SODIUM, 2.3 G TOTAL DIETARY FIBER

note ❧ *Use either a mill with a rotating blade or one with handles that squeeze together. Be careful not to overfill the food mill: the apples can squirt out through the holes and burn you.*

strawberry dressing

We developed this recipe on a whim one day when the produce delivery came with more perfectly ripe strawberries than the dessert-maker could use. The gorgeous fuchsia color and sweet-tart taste of this dressing are delightful over fresh greens, especially spinach. And when fresh berries are out of season, frozen berries work fine. For low-fat dressing, reduce the oil to 1 to 2 tablespoons.

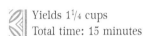 Yields 1¼ cups
Total time: 15 minutes

✂ Combine all of the ingredients in a blender and purée until smooth. Refrigerated in a sealed container, this dressing will keep for 3 days.

1 cup fresh strawberries, rinsed and stemmed
¼ cup olive oil
¼ teaspoon salt
2 tablespoons white or regular balsamic or cider vinegar
1 tablespoon chopped fresh basil
1 tablespoon water
pinch of ground black pepper

PER 1-OUNCE SERVING: 56 CALORIES, 0.1 G PROTEIN, 5.7 G FAT, 1.3 G CARBOHYDRATES, 0.8 G SATURATED FATTY ACIDS, 0 MG CHOLESTEROL, 60.1 MG SODIUM, 0.4 G TOTAL DIETARY FIBER

what's balsamic vinegar?

The art of producing balsamic vinegar is as respected and cherished as that of making fine wine. Juice from ripe grapes is slowly reduced over wood fires, then fermented and acidified in a series of barrels—oak, chestnut, mulberry, ash, or juniper. For white balsamic vinegar, the grape skins are not used. During the aging process, some vinegar is siphoned from each barrel into the next to mingle the flavors. Traditionally, it is stored in clean, drafty attics or lofts where summer heat supports fermentation and winter cold allows the liquid to clarify. The vinegar develops gradually into the dark, flavorful, high-priced product so valued in Italy and abroad.

Italian law requires that true balsamic vinegar (labeled Aceto Balsamico Tradizionale di Modena or di Reggio Emilia) be aged at least twelve years and bottled in 100 cc bottles. At the lofty price of $75 to $400 apiece, it's no wonder people use it a drop at a time and give it as wedding gifts.

The balsamic vinegar you find at the supermarket usually contains grape juice and caramel coloring. Most of these pedestrian balsamics are not fermented in wooden barrels and they have not been aged for twelve years. Not to be dismissed, however, they are certainly acceptable for everyday salad dressings, marinades, and sauces.

tofu sour cream

A tasty vegan alternative to its dairy counterpart, this topping has a texture like that of sour cream. Add your favorite herbs and seasonings for a great dip or try it on Tofu Stroganoff (page 313) or baked potatoes.

Yields about 1¹/₂ cups
Total time: 5 minutes

Combine all of the ingredients in a food processor or blender and purée until smooth and creamy. Scrape down the sides with a rubber spatula as needed. Tofu Sour Cream is best served right away, but it will keep covered and refrigerated for a day or two.

1 cake silken tofu, crumbled
    (12 ounces)*
3 tablespoons olive oil
2 tablespoons rice vinegar
2 tablespoons fresh lemon juice
¹/₄ teaspoon salt

* Low-fat or "lite" silken tofu works, but we prefer regular.

PER 1-OUNCE SERVING: 40 CALORIES, 1.5 G PROTEIN, 3.7 G FAT, 0.6 G CARBOHYDRATES, 0.5 G SATURATED FATTY ACIDS, 0 MG CHOLESTEROL, 41.8 MG SODIUM, 0.1 G TOTAL DIETARY FIBER

simple sweet & sour sauce

This sauce can perk up almost any Asian-style stuffed vegetable. Ladle it over rice, barley, millet, or couscous; add steamed or sautéed vegetables, and you'll have a nice light meal. If you want the sauce sweeter, add a little sugar. Pear or pineapple juice can replace the apple juice.

Serves 4
Total time: 10 minutes

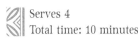In a small nonreactive saucepan, combine the apple juice, soy sauce, vinegar, ginger, and the sugar, if using, and bring to a boil. Stir the dissolved cornstarch into the boiling sauce. Reduce the heat and stir for about 1 minute, until the sauce thickens and becomes clear. Serve hot.

1 cup unsweetened apple juice
1 tablespoon soy sauce
1 tablespoon rice vinegar or cider
    vinegar
1 teaspoon grated fresh ginger root
1 to 2 teaspoons sugar (optional)
1 tablespoon cornstarch dissolved in
    1 tablespoon cold water

PER 2.5-OUNCE SERVING: 39 CALORIES, 0.4 G PROTEIN, 0.1 G FAT, 9.1 G CARBOHYDRATES, 0 G SATURATED FATTY ACIDS, 0 MG CHOLESTEROL, 200.5 MG SODIUM, 0.1 G TOTAL DIETARY FIBER

tomato sauce with sage

This sauce has a sweetness and smooth texture that make it as elegant as it is simple. Fresh sage is the very best choice for this recipe, but dried sage, which maintains aroma and flavor better than many dried herbs, will also work. Feel free to add even more sage if you like.

 Serves 4 to 6
Total time: 30 minutes

1 tablespoon butter, at room temperature

2 teaspoons olive oil

2 cups diced onions

2 or 3 garlic cloves, minced or pressed

1 teaspoon salt

1 tablespoon chopped fresh sage (1 teaspoon dried)

¼ teaspoon ground black pepper

6 cups canned tomatoes with juice, chopped (two 28-ounce cans)

In a nonreactive 2-quart saucepan, heat the butter and oil until the butter melts. Add the onions, garlic, and salt and sauté on medium heat for about 10 minutes, until the onions are translucent. Add the sage, pepper, and the tomatoes and bring to a simmer. Cook for 10 to 15 minutes, stirring occasionally.

Serve hot or refrigerate for later use. The tomato sauce will keep, stored in a sealed container in the refrigerator, for at least a week.

PER 9-OUNCE SERVING: 99 CALORIES, 2.9 G PROTEIN, 4.1 G FAT, 14.3 G CARBOHYDRATES, 1.5 G SATURATED FATTY ACIDS, 5.2 MG CHOLESTEROL, 705.9 MG SODIUM, 0.9 G TOTAL DIETARY FIBER

two barbeque sauces

The big advantage of making barbeque sauce instead of buying a commercially prepared product is that you can play with the ingredients and make your sauce exactly the way you like it.

Sweet and pungent, these sauces can be used on tofu or grain burgers (pages 182–188), tempeh, portabello mushrooms, roasted potatoes, or shrimp. Use them as a basting sauce before baking, roasting, or grilling, or afterward as a condiment.

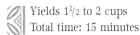 Yields 1½ to 2 cups
Total time: 15 minutes

Combine all of the ingredients for the sauce of your choice in a bowl and mix well. Store in a jar or other sealed container. Refrigerated, either of the sauces will keep for at least a month.

AMERICAN: PER 1-OUNCE SERVING: 35 CALORIES, 0.7 G PROTEIN, 0.2 G FAT, 8.5 G CARBOHYDRATES, 0 G SATURATED FATTY ACIDS, 0 MG CHOLESTEROL, 363.8 MG SODIUM, 0.3 G TOTAL DIETARY FIBER

CHINESE: PER 1-OUNCE SERVING: 55 CALORIES, 0.7 G PROTEIN, 2.5 G FAT, 8 G CARBOHYDRATES, 0.3 G SATURATED FATTY ACIDS, 0 MG CHOLESTEROL, 221.7 MG SODIUM, 0.2 G TOTAL DIETARY FIBER

american-style barbeque sauce

2 tablespoons spicy brown mustard

¼ cup brown sugar, packed

1 cup ketchup

2 teaspoons cider vinegar

2 garlic cloves, minced or pressed

½ cup minced onions

3 tablespoons soy sauce

1 tablespoon Worcestershire sauce

ground black pepper to taste

4 or 5 dashes of Tabasco sauce or other hot red pepper sauce

chinese-style barbeque sauce

½ cup tomato paste

1 tablespoon grated fresh ginger root

2 tablespoons dark sesame oil

¼ cup mirin or unsweetened apple juice

1 to 2 teaspoons Chinese chili paste to taste

2 tablespoons soy sauce

2 garlic cloves, minced or pressed

2 tablespoons brown sugar, packed

2 tablespoons rice vinegar

½ teaspoon five-spice powder

yogurt tahini dressing

Along with brown rice, tofu, and miso soup, yogurt tahini dressing crossed over into main-stream cuisine about twenty-five years ago and never left. To make a delicious lower-fat version, just use nonfat yogurt.

Serve this creamy, tangy sauce on Falafel Burgers (page 184), Tofu Burgers (page 182), or Tofu Hijiki Burgers (page 187), on Moroccan Fish with Cumin (page 299), or on your favorite cucumber salad or greens.

1 cup plain yogurt

2 tablespoons tahini

1 to 2 garlic cloves, minced
    or pressed

1 tablespoon fresh lemon juice

2 teaspoons chopped fresh dill

salt and ground black pepper to taste

 Yields about 1¼ cups
Preparation time: 5 minutes
Sitting time: at least 15 minutes

Combine all of the ingredients and let sit for at least 15 minutes for the flavors to marry. Serve cold.

PER 1-OUNCE SERVING: 30 CALORIES, 1.8 G PROTEIN, 1.6 G FAT, 2.4 G CARBOHYDRATES, 0.3 G SATURATED FATTY ACIDS, 0.4 MG CHOLESTEROL, 19.3 MG SODIUM, 0.3 G TOTAL DIETARY FIBER

breads

breads

Whoever invented leavened bread was a genius, and we bow down in humble gratitude. Mixing flour, liquid, and some kind of leavening agent, shaping dough with your hands, witnessing its metamorphosis as it rises and then bakes crisp and golden, is like dabbling in magic. Fresh-baked biscuits, rolls, and quick breads communicate love and goodness; one whiff can bring comfort and joy. Here are a few yummy things from the oven, the lovely legacy of that original genius.

Bread-baking is satisfying work and it needn't be terribly involved. Cornbread, muffins, and biscuits can be mixed up in a jiffy and bake quickly. Versatile, handsome accompaniments such as Three Seed Whole Wheat Rolls or Savory Cheddar Thyme Biscotti may take a little longer to make than other quick breads, but they add a very special touch to any meal. Most of our recipes are for savory breads to enjoy with soup, stew, or salad; a few, like Walnut Raisin Bread, Flaxseed Banana Bread, and Fruited Quickbread, are sweeter and make a lovely breakfast or a snack with tea. (For more sweet baked goodies, try the muffins, scones, and fruit butters in the Breakfast & Brunch section.)

Needless to say, you and your family, friends, and neighbors will be enticed by the aroma of home-baked treats. You could *try* to bake a little something for yourself, but once you open the oven you'll probably have to share.

biscuits à la focaccia

Here's an innovative and easy way to enjoy the classic flavors of focaccia. For lunch, try filling these biscuits with Italian Tofu Spread (page 178) or serve them alongside Italian Bean & Squash Soup (page 79) or with any of the flavorful risottos in this book.

 Yields 6 biscuits
Preparation time: 15 minutes
Baking time: 20 to 25 minutes

2¹/₂ tablespoons olive oil

2 garlic cloves, minced or pressed

1 teaspoon ground black pepper

1 tablespoon chopped fresh rosemary
   (¹/₂ tablespoon dried)

2 cups unbleached white flour

2 teaspoons baking powder

¹/₂ teaspoon salt

¹/₂ teaspoon baking soda

2 tablespoons cold butter

³/₄ cup buttermilk

Preheat the oven to 425°. Lightly oil a baking sheet.

In a small skillet, heat 2 tablespoons of the oil. Add the garlic, pepper, and rosemary and simmer for about 1 minute. Remove from the heat.

Sift the flour, baking powder, salt, and baking soda into a mixing bowl. Using a pastry cutter or two knives, cut the butter into the flour until evenly distributed. Add the seasoned oil mixture and mix well. Quickly stir in the buttermilk to form a dough that's soft and a little sticky.

On a lightly floured surface, pat the dough into an 8-inch circle about ¹/₂ inch thick. Cut into six equal pie-shaped wedges and transfer them to the prepared baking sheet with a spatula. Brush the tops with a little olive oil.

Bake for 20 to 25 minutes, until the biscuits are firm and golden brown. Serve immediately.

PER 2.75-OUNCE SERVING: 238 CALORIES, 5 G PROTEIN, 10.4 G FAT, 30.9 G CARBOHYDRATES, 3.4 G SATURATED FATTY ACIDS, 11.3 MG CHOLESTEROL, 464.8 MG SODIUM, 1.2 G TOTAL DIETARY FIBER

blue cornmeal muffins

The gray-blue hue of blue cornmeal is eye-catching and the flavor of the muffins, with their bell peppers and cheese, is intriguing. Blue cornmeal, usually organic and stone-ground, can be found in many health food stores and well-stocked supermarkets.

 Yields 12 muffins
Preparation time: 25 minutes
Baking time: 20 to 30 minutes

1 cup blue cornmeal

1 1/2 cups unbleached white flour

2 teaspoons baking powder

1 teaspoon salt

2 tablespoons sugar

1 1/2 cups shredded Cheddar or
    Monterey Jack cheese,
    lightly packed

2 eggs

1/2 cup vegetable oil

1 1/4 cups milk

1 1/2 cups minced red bell peppers

1 fresh green chile, seeded and
    minced

Preheat the oven to 350°. Prepare a standard 12-cup muffin tin by either lightly brushing the cups with oil or lining them with paper liners.

In a large bowl, sift together the cornmeal, flour, baking powder, salt, and sugar. Stir in the cheese. In a separate bowl, lightly beat the eggs. Stir in the oil, milk, peppers, and chiles. Make a well in the dry ingredients and pour in the liquid mixture. Stir just to combine without overmixing. Spoon about 1/3 cup of batter into each muffin cup.

Bake for 20 to 30 minutes, until golden brown and a knife inserted in the center of a muffin comes out clean. Cool on a rack.

PER 3.75-OUNCE SERVING: 281 CALORIES, 8.4 G PROTEIN, 16.1 G FAT, 25.7 G CARBOHYDRATES, 6.1 G SATURATED FATTY ACIDS, 60.7 MG CHOLESTEROL, 365.1 MG SODIUM, 1.6 G TOTAL DIETARY FIBER

bread sticks

Add a little spice to a cocktail party or a touch of elegance to a simple pasta dinner! Our bread sticks can be served beside soups and salads, or as part of an appetizer combo with one or more dips. Since they're prepared in batches, several different toppings can be made to adorn a single recipe of dough.

Our pizza dough recipe is perfect for these bread sticks. Prepare it without the black pepper called for in the original recipe—we add red pepper flakes here instead. After about 1 hour of rising, when the dough has doubled in size, you're ready to begin the bread sticks.

2 teaspoons dried oregano

1 tablespoon dried basil

1/2 teaspoon fennel seeds

1/4 teaspoon red pepper flakes

1/2 to 1 teaspoon kosher salt

1 recipe Pizza Crust dough
 (page 338)

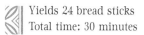

Yields 24 bread sticks
Total time: 30 minutes

Preheat the oven to 425°. Lightly oil a baking sheet.

In a small bowl, combine the oregano, basil, fennel seeds, red pepper flakes, and salt. Divide the dough into four parts. Working with one part at a time, press the dough into a rectangle about 8 x 6 inches. Sprinkle both sides with one fourth of the spice mix and lightly press it into the dough.

Cut the rectangle lengthwise into 6 equal 1-inch-wide strips. Working on a lightly oiled surface, roll each of the strips with your fingertips into a 10-inch-long bread stick with a 1/2-inch diameter. Arrange the strips on the baking sheet 1 inch apart.

Bake for 8 to 10 minutes, turning the sticks after 4 minutes, until brown. While one batch bakes, roll out the dough for the next six bread sticks, and repeat until all of the bread sticks are baked.

PER 1.25-OUNCE SERVING: 85 CALORIES, 2.5 G PROTEIN, 0.9 G FAT, 16.6 G CARBOHYDRATES, 0.1 G SATURATED FATTY ACIDS, 0 MG CHOLESTEROL, 149.5 MG SODIUM, 1 G TOTAL DIETARY FIBER

variations *Replace the herbs and spices in the recipe with 1/2 cup of sesame seeds and 1/2 to 1 teaspoon of kosher salt. Or use 1/2 cup of chopped fresh dill and 1/2 to 1 teaspoon of kosher salt. For a spicy treat, try 3/4 cup of Parmesan cheese, 1/4 teaspoon of cayenne, 1 teaspoon of paprika, and 1/2 to 1 teaspoon of kosher salt.*

cornbread

Freshly baked cornbread is a perennial favorite at Moosewood. For this slightly sweet version, we use a rich, nutty whole wheat flour and a nice whole grain organic cornmeal.

There are many kinds of cornmeal, but the best is usually found in natural foods stores or in the natural foods aisle of supermarkets. In Ithaca, we are fortunate to have Iroquois brand white cornmeal, which we hope will soon be more widely available. It makes an absolutely wonderful cornbread.

Leftover cornbread, cut into bite-sized cubes and mixed with sautéed herbs and minced vegetables, can be a delicious stuffing for winter squash. It also makes very tasty bread crumbs.

Serves 8
Preparation time: 15 minutes
Baking time: 20 to 25 minutes

1 cup cornmeal

1 cup whole wheat pastry flour or whole wheat flour

2 teaspoons baking powder

1/2 teaspoon baking soda

1/2 teaspoon salt

2 eggs

1/4 cup vegetable oil

1/4 to 1/3 cup brown sugar, packed

1 cup nonfat plain yogurt or buttermilk

Preheat the oven to 400°. Butter a 9-inch square or 7 x 11-inch baking dish.

Sift together the cornmeal, flour, baking powder, baking soda, and salt in a large bowl. In a separate bowl, whisk together the eggs, oil, brown sugar, and yogurt or buttermilk. Make a well in the dry ingredients and stir in the wet ingredients until just blended: be careful not to overmix.

Spread the batter evenly in the prepared pan. Bake for 20 to 25 minutes, until golden brown and a knife inserted in the center comes out clean.

PER 3.25-OUNCE SERVING: 246 CALORIES, 7.1 G PROTEIN, 9.4 G FAT, 34.3 G CARBO-HYDRATES, 2.5 G SATURATED FATTY ACIDS, 66.6 MG CHOLESTEROL, 341.4 MG SODIUM, 3.16 G TOTAL DIETARY FIBER

flaxseed banana bread

Flaxseed Banana Bread is a moist, sweet, and healthful treat. Recent research suggests that flaxseeds, rich in omega-3 fatty acids, may help protect against heart disease and certain types of cancers. There is evidence that they are best utilized by our bodies when ground, so try grinding flaxseeds to replace some of the flour in breads that you bake. The ground flax may slightly darken the bread, but it bakes up and tastes just fine. Look for flaxseeds in well-stocked supermarkets and natural foods stores. They have a high oil content, so store them in a well-sealed container in the refrigerator or freezer.

Whole wheat pastry flour is our choice for this bread—it makes a tender, delicate bread that's more nutritious than one made with white flour. You may want to double the recipe to have an extra loaf to give away or to freeze.

Yields 1 loaf
Preparation time: 15 to 20 minutes
Baking time: 1 hour
Cooling time: 25 minutes

1/3 cup vegetable oil

1/2 cup brown sugar, packed

2 eggs

1/3 cup nonfat plain yogurt

1 cup mashed bananas

1/2 cup rolled oats, ground into flour*

1/4 cup flaxseeds, ground into flour*

1 cup whole wheat pastry flour

1 teaspoon baking powder

1/2 teaspoon baking soda

1/2 teaspoon salt

Use a spice grinder or blender to make the flours. We prefer the blender because it can grind the oats and flaxseeds simultaneously. To save time, put the rest of the dry ingredients in the blender with the ground flours and whirl for 1 minute.

Preheat the oven to 350°. Butter or oil a 5 x 9-inch bread pan.

In a mixing bowl, combine the oil and brown sugar. Add the eggs and beat well. Mix in the yogurt and bananas. In a separate bowl or a blender, combine the three flours, the baking powder, baking soda, and salt. Add the dry mixture to the banana mixture and stir just until combined.

Pour the batter into the prepared baking pan and bake for about 1 hour or until a knife inserted in the center comes out clean. Remove from the oven and place the pan on a rack to cool for 10 minutes. Tip the bread out of the pan onto a platter to cool completely.

PER 1-OUNCE SERVING: 86 CALORIES, 2.1 G PROTEIN, 3.6 G FAT, 11.9 G CARBOHYDRATES, 0.9 G SATURATED FATTY ACIDS, 17.7 MG CHOLESTEROL, 77.6 MG SODIUM, 1.3 G TOTAL DIETARY FIBER

fruited quickbread

Apricots and oranges contribute fragrance and flavor to this lightly sweet bread that is also a good source of fiber and vitamins. Enjoy it warm from the oven with butter or cream cheese, or lightly toast it later in the week, if it lasts that long.

 Yields two 8-inch round loaves
Preparation time: 25 to 30 minutes
Baking time: 40 to 45 minutes

1 ½ cups chopped dried apricots

1 tablespoon freshly grated
   orange peel

1 ½ cups fresh orange juice

¼ cup vegetable oil

¾ cup rolled oats

2 ½ cups unbleached white flour

1 tablespoon baking powder

1 teaspoon baking soda

1 teaspoon salt

½ teaspoon ground cinnamon

½ cup melted butter

½ cup mild-flavored honey

2 eggs

1 cup milk

confectioners' sugar, apricot jam, or
   Neufchâtel (optional)

Preheat the oven to 350°. Lightly oil two 8-inch cake pans.

Place the apricots in a nonreactive saucepan and add the orange peel and ¾ cup of the orange juice. On high heat, bring almost to a boil. Remove from the heat and set aside to cool. In a small bowl, combine the remaining ¾ cup of orange juice and the oil. Thoroughly stir in the oats and set aside to soak for 5 to 10 minutes.

In a large bowl, sift together the flour, baking powder, baking soda, salt, and cinnamon. In a separate bowl, whisk together the butter, honey, eggs, and milk to make a smooth custard. Mix the cooled apricots and the softened oats into the custard; then add the custard mixture to the dry ingredients and stir briefly until just combined.

Spoon half of the batter into each of the prepared cake pans. Bake for 40 to 45 minutes, until a knife inserted into the center comes out clean. If desired, dust with confectioners' sugar and serve with apricot jam or Neufchâtel.

PER 1-OUNCE SERVING: 73 CALORIES, 1.4 G PROTEIN, 3 G FAT, 10.9 G CARBOHYDRATES, 1.3 G SATURATED FATTY ACIDS, 13.2 MG CHOLESTEROL, 94 MG SODIUM, 0.8 G TOTAL DIETARY FIBER

lemon thyme biscuits

Kip Wilcox has been a Moosewood dessert maker for over twelve years and has a quiet but unmistakable confidence and ease, especially when she's in the kitchen baking. She developed all of the recipes for biscuits in this chapter, and although they all melt in your mouth, this one got especially rave reviews.

Lemon and thyme are an absolutely sterling combination of tart and assertive flavors—and certainly a classic pairing of European cuisine. Here they come together beautifully in a biscuit. Be sure to use only fresh thyme.

 Yields 6 biscuits
Preparation time: 25 minutes
Baking time: 20 minutes

¹/₄ cup cold butter, cut into
    small pieces
1 tablespoon freshly grated
    lemon peel
2 cups unbleached white flour
1 tablespoon sugar
2 teaspoons baking powder
¹/₂ teaspoon baking soda
¹/₂ teaspoon salt
2 to 3 tablespoons chopped fresh
    thyme
³/₄ cup plus 2 tablespoons buttermilk
buttermilk for brushing

Preheat the oven to 425°. Lightly oil a baking sheet.

Place the butter pieces and lemon peel in a medium bowl or in a food processor. Sift the flour, sugar, baking powder, baking soda, and salt over the butter. By hand or with the food processor, mix the butter into the flour until evenly distributed. Add the thyme and mix well. Add the buttermilk and stir or pulse briefly. The dough will be soft and a little sticky.

On a lightly floured surface, pat the dough into a 9-inch circle that is about ¹/₂ inch thick. Slice it into six pie-shaped wedges. Place the wedges on the prepared baking sheet and brush the tops with a little buttermilk.

Bake for 20 minutes, until the biscuits are firm and golden brown. Serve immediately.

PER 3-OUNCE SERVING: 229 CALORIES, 5.1 G PROTEIN, 8.3 G FAT, 33.4 G CARBOHYDRATES, 5 G SATURATED FATTY ACIDS, 21.8 MG CHOLESTEROL, 508.7 MG SODIUM, 1.4 G TOTAL DIETARY FIBER

pumpkin cornmeal biscuits

These hearty drop biscuits are not a dainty teatime nibbler; they have plenty of heft, flavor, and sweetness. Non-vegans may use butter instead of soy margarine.

Yields 12 biscuits
Preparation time: 30 minutes
Baking time: 20 minutes

¼ cup soy margarine
1½ cups unbleached white flour
½ cup cornmeal
2 teaspoons baking powder
¼ teaspoon baking soda
½ teaspoon salt
2 tablespoons brown sugar, packed
½ cup pumpkin purée
¾ cup plus 2 tablespoons apple cider
    or apple juice

Preheat the oven to 425°. Generously oil a baking sheet.

Cut the soy margarine into small pieces and place in a medium bowl. Sift in the flour, cornmeal, baking powder, baking soda, and salt. Add the brown sugar and mix until lump-free.

In a blender or food processor, combine the pumpkin purée and the cider or juice. Pour into the flour mixture and stir briefly, just until well blended. Drop the biscuits by ¼ cups onto the baking sheet 1 to 2 inches apart.

Bake for about 20 minutes, until puffed and very slightly brown around the edges and a toothpick tests clean. Serve immediately.

PER 2-OUNCE SERVING: 129 CALORIES, 2.2 G PROTEIN, 4.1 G FAT, 20.9 G CARBOHYDRATES, 0.7 G SATURATED FATTY ACIDS, 0 MG CHOLESTEROL, 245.7 MG SODIUM, 1.2 G TOTAL DIETARY FIBER

savory cheddar thyme biscotti

Our notion when we dreamed this up was to create a savory accompaniment for a soup or main dish. So we combined the essence of a cracker, crouton, or biscuit and the convenient form of an Italian cookie to make a not-sweet "biscotti" suitable for dunking into soup or chili.

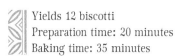 Yields 12 biscotti
Preparation time: 20 minutes
Baking time: 35 minutes

$^1/_2$ cup butter, melted
3 eggs
$^1/_2$ teaspoon minced garlic
1 teaspoon minced fresh thyme
$^1/_2$ cup grated Cheddar cheese
2 cups unbleached white flour
1 $^1/_2$ teaspoons baking powder
$^1/_2$ teaspoon salt

Preheat the oven to 350°. Lightly oil a baking sheet.

In a large bowl, beat together the butter and eggs with an electric mixer or a whisk. Mix in the garlic, thyme, and cheese. Sift the flour, baking powder, and salt directly into the wet ingredients. Fold in until the dough is uniform. Press together with lightly floured hands.

Use a spatula and your floured hands to scoop the dough onto the oiled baking sheet. Form the dough into a 12 x 3-inch diameter log shape; then press down on the log, flattening it to a thickness of about an inch. The flattened log should be about 14 x 4 inches.

Bake on the top rack of the oven for 25 to 30 minutes, until the dough is firm and just slightly brown. Remove from the oven and carefully transfer the log to a cutting board. When cool enough to handle, slice on the severe diagonal into about 1-inch pieces. Arrange the biscotti cut side down on the baking sheet. Bake for about 5 minutes on each side, using tongs to flip them gently. Cool completely on a rack and then store in an airtight container for up to 2 weeks.

PER 3.5-OUNCE SERVING: 361 CALORIES, 10.4 G PROTEIN, 22.1 G FAT, 29.7 G CARBOHYDRATES, 12.6 G SATURATED FATTY ACIDS, 183.5 MG CHOLESTEROL, 533.4 MG SODIUM, 1 G TOTAL DIETARY FIBER

variation ❧ *For Scarborough Fair Biscotti (named for that old Simon and Garfunkel song), omit the cheese and add 1 tablespoon chopped fresh parsley, $^1/_4$ teaspoon dried sage, and $^1/_4$ teaspoon crumbled dried rosemary.*

three seed whole wheat rolls

What could be better than fresh bread, warm from the oven, for a dinner party or an everyday family meal? These rolls are jeweled with poppy, sunflower, and sesame seeds, which add nutrition and attractiveness, but they can be made with fewer kinds of seeds. We suggest always using sunflower seeds, however, which are particularly nice because of their crunch.

 Yields 12 rolls
Preparation time: 25 minutes
Rising time: 30 to 40 minutes
Baking time: 15 to 20 minutes

1 tablespoon dry yeast
¼ cup warm water (105° to 115°)
1 tablespoon sugar
¾ cup milk
¼ cup vegetable oil
1 teaspoon salt
1 cup whole wheat bread flour
1¼ cups unbleached white flour
¼ cup sunflower seeds
1 tablespoon poppy seeds
1 tablespoon sesame seeds

Lightly oil a baking sheet.

In a small bowl, mix the yeast, warm water, and sugar and set aside to proof. In a small pan, warm the milk, oil, and salt to between 105° and 115° and then transfer to a large bowl. When the yeast has dissolved and is foamy, add it to the milk mixture. Add the whole wheat and white flours and the sunflower, poppy, and sesame seeds and mix well.

Turn the dough out onto a floured surface and knead for 5 to 10 minutes, until smooth and elastic, adding more flour as necessary. Divide into 12 equal pieces and roll into balls. Place the balls of dough a couple of inches apart on the prepared baking sheet. Cover with a clean, damp towel and put in a warm place for 30 to 40 minutes, until almost doubled in size.

When rising is almost complete, preheat the oven to 400°. Bake the rolls for 12 to 15 minutes, until golden brown. Cool on a rack.

PER 1.8-OUNCE SERVING: 152 CALORIES, 4.1 G PROTEIN, 7.2 G FAT, 18.7 G CARBOHYDRATES, 1.7 G SATURATED FATTY ACIDS, 1.1 MG CHOLESTEROL, 206.2 MG SODIUM, 2 G TOTAL DIETARY FIBER

vegetable & cheese cornbread

Everybody loves cornbread, and this version provides even more reasons to eat it up. It's savory, n sweet, and it's packed with vegetables. Serve with Basic Skillet Black Beans (page 317) or Drunken Bea (page 322) and with citrusy Jicama Orange Salad (page 95) for a delicious hearty meal.

 Preparation time: 30 minutes
Baking time: 50 minutes

1 1/2 cups cornmeal

1 1/2 cups unbleached white flour

3/4 teaspoon salt

2 teaspoons baking powder

1/2 teaspoon baking soda

1 tablespoon sugar

1 cup grated smoked cheese or
    Cheddar cheese, lightly packed*

2 eggs

1 1/2 cups buttermilk

1/3 cup vegetable oil

1/3 cup minced scallions

1 garlic clove, minced or pressed

1 cup diced red bell peppers

1 fresh chile, seeded and minced

1 cup fresh or frozen corn kernels

Preheat the oven to 375°. Butter or oil a 10-inch glass pie plate, a 7 x 11-inch baking dish, or an ovenproof 10-inch skillet.

In a large bowl, sift together the cornmeal, flour, salt, baking powder, baking soda, and sugar. Stir in the cheese.

In a separate bowl, lightly beat the eggs. Stir in the buttermilk, oil, scallions, garlic, bell peppers, minced chiles, and corn. Make a well in the dry ingredients and pour in the buttermilk mixture. Stir just to combine and pour into the prepared pie plate, baking dish, or skillet.

* If you use smoked cheese, we recommend a naturally smoked, not processed cheese. We like the Smoked Cheddar Cheese, naturally smoked with apple and hardwood, produced by Red Apple Marketing LLC, Farmington, CT 06034.

Bake for about 50 minutes, until a knife inserted in the center comes out clean and the cornbread is golden brown.

PER 6-OUNCE SERVING: 396 CALORIES, 12.5 G PROTEIN, 17 G FAT, 48.9 G CARBOHYDRATES, 6.3 G SATURATED FATTY ACIDS, 82.5 MG CHOLESTEROL, 529 MG SODIUM, 3.6 G TOTAL DIETARY FIBER

walnut raisin bread

A loaf of Walnut-Raisin Whole Wheat Bread from Bittersweet Baking in Jacksonville, Vermont, made its way to Ithaca with Patti Harville, the sister of Moosewood cooks Susan Harville and Nancy Lazarus. Nancy loved the bread so much that she called Janet McGrath in Vermont to ask for the recipe. We made some adjustments to accommodate home baking, and we thank Janet for graciously sharing her expertise.

 Yields two 9-inch round loaves
Prep and kneading time: 35 minutes
Rising time: about 2¹/₂ hours
Baking time: about 30 minutes

1 cup warm milk
1 cup warm water
2 packages dry yeast
3 tablespoons sugar
3 tablespoons vegetable oil or butter, at room temperature
2 teaspoons salt
2 teaspoons coarsely ground black pepper
2 cups whole wheat flour
¹/₂ cup cornmeal
2 to 3 cups unbleached white flour
1 cup chopped walnuts
1¹/₂ cups raisins

In a large bowl, combine the milk, water, yeast, and 1 tablespoon of the sugar until the yeast dissolves. Set aside in a warm place until the yeast foams, about 10 minutes.

With a large spoon, mix in the remaining sugar, the oil or butter, salt, pepper, whole wheat flour, and cornmeal. Vigorously stir in 2 to 3 cups of white flour, one cup at a time, until a soft ball forms. Turn the dough out onto a lightly floured board and knead for about 10 minutes, adding more flour as needed to prevent sticking.

Add the walnuts and raisins to the dough and knead until well incorporated and evenly distributed, about 3 minutes. Place the dough in a large oiled bowl, cover with a clean, damp cloth, and set in a warm place to rise until doubled in size, about 1 to 1¹/₂ hours.

Punch down the dough, and divide it into halves. Press each half into a buttered 9-inch round cake pan. Set in a warm place to rise until doubled, about ¹/₂ to 1 hour.

Preheat the oven to 350°. Then bake for about 30 minutes, until golden on top and hollow-sounding when tapped on the bottom. Cool on a rack.

PER 1-OUNCE SERVING: 85 CALORIES, 2.4 G PROTEIN, 2.8 G FAT, 13.8 G CARBOHYDRATES, 0.5 G SATURATED FATTY ACIDS, 0.4 MG CHOLESTEROL, 103.2 MG SODIUM, 1.4 G TOTAL DIETARY FIBER

desserts

desserts

Desserts delight. They can celebrate an art opening or open house, mark a holiday, or pick you up in the middle of a routine day. It's not hard to think of occasions at which to serve dessert: book groups, baby showers, business meetings, birthdays, post-theater or after-movie dates. The list is endless. Eat dessert when you feel like it, and if you need to, you can always think up a reason later.

Desserts offer a fresh, sweet finish to the savory dishes of a meal. From sweetly simple to richly sweet, desserts span a broad spectrum: ripe fruit, flaky pastry, buttery chocolate, nuts, and cream. Follow your mood, find inspiration in the occasion, complement the simplicity or richness of a meal. Think of fresh fruit, cakes, cookies, puddings, tarts, compotes, or pies.

Some of our desserts are simple and quick, others fussier and more complicated. Try homey cookies or elegant biscotti, good keepers that can be made ahead of time. For a birthday, bake an old-fashioned Caramel Layer Cake. The most popular desserts at Moosewood are fruit pastries and chocolate desserts, especially our ever-popular Deep Chocolate Vegan Cake, which we frequently put on our dessert list. Customers call to request this dark, moist chocolate cake for birthdays and special occasions.

Here you'll find variations on favorite classics, including pound cakes, oatmeal cookies, chocolate chip cookies, and puddings. On the other hand, we always have an eye out for new ethnic and regional flavors that invite us to venture into new territory: purple-hued Thai Black Rice Pudding, Muhallabia Massawa from the cuisine of Eritrea, a takeoff on Mexican fare with Apple Quesadillas, and Pistachio Cardamom Cake from the Middle East. If you're not a baker, try easy party-ready Fruit Skewers, a familiar Caramel Sauce for your favorite ice cream, Winter Fruit Compote, or simply fresh, ripened fruit in season served elegantly on a small plate.

Eating dessert can be an occasion in itself. Usually dessert is accompanied by an unsweetened beverage. Black tea, herbal tea, and coffee come to mind. (See our Drinks & Snacks section for ideas.) These beverages all cleanse the palate and maximize the enjoyment of each sweet morsel. Savor every bite and top off dessert with conversation, laughter, and stories.

big chocolate chip cookies

Moosewood cook Jenny Wang bakes colossal cookies for Cinemopolis, the local independent film theater a block from our restaurant. There, sitting in the darkened theater, patrons slowly nibble the generous cookies, trying to make them last while they soak up the culture. Jenny's big cookies are rich and hearty thanks to the dark brown sugar, whole wheat pastry flour, sweet butter, and extra vanilla. The size of the cookies is really up to you: the more batter, the bigger the cookie.

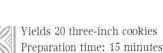
Yields 20 three-inch cookies
Preparation time: 15 minutes
Baking time: 10 minutes per batch

¾ cup butter, at room temperature
1½ cups dark brown sugar, packed
2 eggs
1½ cups unbleached white flour
¾ cup whole wheat pastry flour
1 teaspoon baking soda
1 teaspoon salt
2 teaspoons pure vanilla extract
2 tablespoons water
2 cups chocolate chips
1 cup chopped walnuts and/or raisins (optional)

Preheat the oven to 375°. Lightly butter a baking sheet.

In a large bowl, cream the butter and sugar together until smooth. Beat in the eggs until well blended. In a separate bowl, sift together the white flour, whole wheat flour, baking soda, and salt. Stir the dry ingredients into the butter mixture, mixing well. Add the vanilla and water. Stir in the chocolate chips and, if you wish, the nuts and/or raisins.

For 3-inch cookies, drop the batter by scant ¼ cups onto the baking sheet, leaving 2 inches of space between the cookies. Bake for about 10 minutes, or until the edges and bottoms are light brown and the tops golden. Check after 8 minutes to avoid overbaking.

Remove the cookies to a rack to cool.

PER 2.25-OUNCE SERVING: 263 CALORIES, 3 G PROTEIN, 12.8 G FAT, 37 G CARBOHYDRATES, 7.5 G SATURATED FATTY ACIDS, 45.1 MG CHOLESTEROL, 258.3 MG SODIUM, 1.8 G TOTAL DIETARY FIBER

black forest biscotti

These admittedly rich and decadent biscotti can provide the perfect cover-up for a sweets lover. While you project the very picture of mature restraint dipping your dry biscotti into an elegant little cup of espresso, you can indulge your inner Cookie Monster.

Add $\frac{1}{2}$ cup of chopped toasted almonds, if you dare.

Yields about 20 biscotti
Preparation time: 20 minutes
Baking time: 35 to 40 minutes

$\frac{1}{2}$ cup dried cherries (2 $\frac{1}{4}$ ounces)

1 cup water

$\frac{1}{4}$ cup butter, at room temperature

$\frac{3}{4}$ cup sugar

2 eggs

1 teaspoon pure almond extract

1 teaspoon pure vanilla extract

$\frac{1}{2}$ cup semi-sweet chocolate chips

2 cups plus 2 tablespoons unbleached white flour

$\frac{1}{3}$ cup unsweetened cocoa powder

$\frac{1}{2}$ teaspoon salt

1 $\frac{1}{2}$ teaspoons baking powder

Preheat the oven to 350°. Lightly oil a baking sheet.

In a small saucepan, heat the cherries and water just to boiling, and then remove from the heat and set aside. In a bowl, cream together the butter and sugar until light and well combined. Blend in the eggs and almond and vanilla extracts. Fold in the chocolate chips. Drain the cherries, place them on a paper towel to absorb any extra moisture, and then stir them into the egg mixture.

In a separate bowl, sift together the flour, cocoa, salt, and baking powder. With a rubber spatula, fold in the wet ingredients until the dough is uniform and holds together when pressed with lightly floured hands.

Use the spatula and your floured hands to scoop the dough onto the oiled baking sheet. Form the dough into a 12-inch x 3-inch-diameter log shape; then press down on the log, flattening it to a thickness of about an inch. The length and width of the flattened log should be about 14 x 4 inches.

Bake on the top rack of the oven for 25 to 30 minutes, until the dough is firm and just slightly brown. Remove from the oven and transfer the log to a cutting board. When cool enough to handle, slice crosswise into $\frac{3}{4}$-inch pieces. Lay each biscotti cut side up on the baking sheet. Bake for about 5 minutes on each side, using tongs to flip them. Cool completely on a rack and then store in an airtight container for up to 2 weeks.

PER 1.75-OUNCE SERVING: 137 CALORIES, 2.6 G PROTEIN, 4.7 G FAT, 22.6 G CARBOHYDRATES, 2.6 G SATURATED FATTY ACIDS, 32.6 MG CHOLESTEROL, 116.4 MG SODIUM, 0.8 G TOTAL DIETARY FIBER

almond biscotti

We began making biscotti at Moosewood some years ago when we opened our sunny, beautiful new cafe/bar. We knew biscotti would be perfect for dunking in our new coffees, teas, and dessert wines. We thought it might take a while before biscotti caught on with our clientele, but, boy, were we behind the curve. Everyone already knew and loved biscotti and was thrilled to get them freshly baked. Little kids were bellying up to the bar for another glass of milk in which to dunk these treats.

These biscotti are easily made and one of our favorites. Although a departure from traditional biscotti ingredients, butter creates a softer texture and deeper flavor, and the orange zest is a nice counterpoint to the nuts.

Yields about 20 biscotti
Preparation time: 20 minutes
Baking time: 30 minutes

1/4 cup butter, at room temperature

3/4 cup sugar

2 eggs

1 teaspoon pure vanilla extract

1/2 teaspoon pure almond extract

2 teaspoons freshly grated orange peel

1/2 cup toasted and coarsely chopped almonds*

2 1/4 cups all-purpose flour

1 1/2 teaspoons baking powder

1/8 teaspoon ground nutmeg

1/4 teaspoon salt

* *Toast almonds in a single layer on an unoiled baking tray at 350° for 5 to 10 minutes, until fragrant and golden brown.*

Preheat the oven to 350°. Lightly oil a baking sheet.

In a small bowl, using an electric mixer or a whisk, cream together the butter and sugar until light. Add the eggs, vanilla, almond extract, and grated orange peel and mix well. Fold in the almonds.

In a mixing bowl, sift together the flour, baking powder, nutmeg, and salt. With a rubber spatula, fold in the wet ingredients until the dough is uniform and holds together when pressed with lightly floured hands.

Use the spatula and your floured hands to scoop the dough onto the oiled baking sheet. Form the dough into a 12-inch x 3-inch-diameter log shape; then press down on the log, flattening it to a thickness of about an inch. The length and width of the flattened log should be about 14 x 4 inches.

Bake on the top rack of the oven for about 20 minutes, until the dough is firm and just slightly brown. Remove from the oven and transfer the log to a cutting board. When cool enough to handle, slice crosswise into ¾-inch pieces. Lay each biscotti cut side up on the baking sheet. Bake for about 5 minutes on each side, using tongs to flip them. Cool on a rack.

When completely cool, store in an airtight container. Biscotti will easily keep for a couple of weeks.

Serve with your favorite hot beverage.

PER 1.25-OUNCE SERVING: 127 CALORIES, 2.8 G PROTEIN, 4.8 G FAT, 18.3 G CARBOHYDRATES,
1.8 G SATURATED FATTY ACIDS, 32.6 MG CHOLESTEROL, 85.4 MG SODIUM, 0.8 G TOTAL DIETARY FIBER

old-fashioned molasses drops

You could work your way down the whole supermarket aisle devoted to packaged cookies and not find anything as simple and appealing as these. This is a chewy delight that's quick to make, packs a wallop of molasses flavor, and keeps well, too. For a vegan version, use vegetable oil in place of the butter.

 Yields 3½ dozen 2½-inch cookies
Preparation time: 20 minutess
Baking time: 12 to 15 minutes

½ cup butter, at room temperature

½ cup brown sugar, packed

¾ cup unsulphured molasses

1 teaspoon freshly grated
  orange peel*

⅛ cup water or unsweetened
  apple juice

1 teaspoon pure vanilla extract

1 egg

2 cups unbleached all-purpose
  white flour

1 teaspoon baking powder

½ teaspoon ground cinnamon

½ teaspoon salt

¼ teaspoon ground ginger

¼ teaspoon ground allspice

½ cup wheat germ

Preheat the oven to 350°. Lightly oil two large baking sheets.

In a large bowl, stir together the butter, brown sugar, molasses, orange peel, and water or apple juice. Beat in the vanilla and egg. In a separate bowl, sift together the flour, baking powder, cinnamon, salt, ginger, and allspice. Stir in the wheat germ. Add the dry ingredients to the molasses mixture and blend well.

Drop by rounded teaspoonfuls onto the prepared baking sheets about 2 inches apart. Bake for 12 to 15 minutes, until slightly puffed and golden brown. The cookies will still be soft to the touch in the middle. If using two baking sheets at once, it's a good idea to switch the position of the trays in the oven after about 7 minutes to keep the lower tray of cookies from scorching on the bottom.

Be sure to grate only the very surface of the peel, because deeper grating will mix the bitter pith in with the peel.

Cool for a few minutes on the the baking sheets, then transfer the cookies to wire racks to cool completely. Hidden in a cookie jar, they'll keep for at least 1 week.

PER 0.75-OUNCE SERVING: 72 CALORIES, 1.2 G PROTEIN, 2.5 G FAT, 12.3 G CARBOHYDRATES, 1.4 G SATURATED FATTY ACIDS, 12.2 MG CHOLESTEROL, 63.4 MG SODIUM, 1.3 G TOTAL DIETARY FIBER

sweet pumpkin cookies

These cookies are a wonderful treat to make when the pumpkins come in with the fall squash harvest. But if you like them as much as we do, you'll be happy to hear that the cookies can be made with home-canned or store-bought cooked pumpkin purée as well. That means you can make them any time of year.

If you don't have peanuts on hand, any chopped nuts will do; and although the chocolate chips are optional, they're a great foil to the pumpkin flavor and we highly recommend the addition.

Yields about 42 cookies
Preparation time: 25 minutes
Baking time: 10 to 15 minutes

1 cup butter, at room temperature

1 cup sugar

1 cup pumpkin purée

1 egg, lightly beaten

1 teaspoon pure vanilla extract

2 cups unbleached all-purpose white flour

1 teaspoon baking powder

$1/2$ teaspoon baking soda

1 teaspoon ground cinnamon

$1/4$ teaspoon ground allspice

$1/2$ teaspoon salt

1 cup chopped toasted peanuts

1 cup raisins

$1/2$ cup chocolate chips (optional)

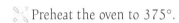 Preheat the oven to 375°.

In a large mixing bowl, cream together the butter and sugar. Add the pumpkin, egg, and vanilla and mix until well blended. Sift together the flour, baking powder, baking soda, cinnamon, allspice, and salt, and add to the mixing bowl. Stir well to form a soft batter. Stir in the chopped nuts, raisins, and, if you like, the chocolate chips.

Drop by rounded teaspoonfuls onto a large, unoiled baking sheet (or two smaller ones), allowing a little space for the cookies to spread as they bake. Bake for 10 to 15 minutes, until a toothpick inserted into the center comes out clean and the cookies just begin to brown slightly on the bottom. Use a spatula to transfer to a cooling rack or plate. Store in your favorite cookie jar.

PER 1-OUNCE SERVING: 111 CALORIES, 1.7 G PROTEIN, 6.2 G FAT, 13 G CARBOHYDRATES, 3 G SATURATED FATTY ACIDS, 18.1 MG CHOLESTEROL, 110 MG SODIUM, 0.7 G TOTAL DIETARY FIBER

wholesome oatmeal raisin cookies

One of these cookies is big enough to share with a friend, and with the combination of oats and oat bran, you'll still respect yourself in the morning when they beckon at breakfast time. They are officially kid-approved by Moosewood's Ned Asta's son Taz and his friends—the second generation of Moosewood taste-testers and fans!

Remember to take the butter out of the fridge ahead of time so that it can soften. Or, if there's just not time for that, put it in the microwave and zap it for a few seconds to soften it up.

Yields 10 to 12 large cookies
Preparation time: 15 minutes
Baking time: 15 minutes
Cooling time: 15 minutes

1/2 cup light brown sugar, packed

1/4 cup sugar

1/2 cup butter, preferably unsalted, at room temperature

1 large egg

1 teaspoon pure vanilla extract

1 1/4 cups rolled oats

1/2 cup unbleached white flour*

1/2 cup oat bran

1 teaspoon ground cinnamon

1/2 teaspoon baking powder

1/2 teaspoon baking soda

1/4 teaspoon salt

3/4 cup raisins

*   *It's important to use all-purpose flour, not pastry flour. With pastry flour, the cookies spread out all over the pan—nice and lacy, but out of control.*

Preheat the oven to 350°. Lightly oil two baking sheets.

In a large bowl, cream together the brown sugar, granulated sugar, and butter with an electric mixer or by hand until light and fluffy. Add the egg and vanilla and mix until well combined.

In a separate bowl, combine the oats, flour, oat bran, cinnamon, baking powder, baking soda, and salt. Add to the butter mixture and stir just until blended. Mix in the raisins.

Drop the dough in scant 1/4-cup mounds about 3 inches apart, and flatten slightly with moistened fingers. Each sheet will hold six cookies. Bake for about 15 minutes, until golden and just firm to the touch. When the cookies first come out of the oven, they're soft and a little delicate, so carefully transfer them to racks. Cool for 15 minutes.

PER 2.25-OUNCE SERVING: 243 CALORIES, 4.7 G PROTEIN, 9.6 G FAT, 37.8 G CARBOHYDRATES, 5.2 G SATURATED FATTY ACIDS, 42.7 MG CHOLESTEROL, 121 MG SODIUM, 2.9 G TOTAL DIETARY FIBER

winter fruit compote

This sauce is tangy with the flavors of cherries and apricots, freshly grated ginger, and orange peel, and balanced with the rich sweetness of hazelnut liqueur. At Moosewood, we use apricots that are imported from Turkey and sun-dried, so they're pure, quite juicy for dried fruit, and very delicious. Look for plump, tender unsulphured apricots in the bulk section of supermarkets, naturals food stores, and Middle Eastern groceries.

Serve our compote sauce warm over shortcake, pound cake, bread pudding, or vanilla ice cream.

Yields 2 cups
Preparation time: 20 minutes
Simmering time: 15 minutes
Sitting time: 5 minutes

1 cup chopped unsulphured dried apricots

1 cup dried cherries

$\frac{1}{2}$ cup dark raisins

1 teaspoon grated fresh ginger root

1 teaspoon freshly grated orange peel

$1\frac{2}{3}$ cups orange juice or apple juice

$\frac{1}{4}$ cup sugar

$\frac{1}{4}$ cup Fra Angelico or other hazelnut liqueur

In a small saucepan, combine the apricots, cherries, raisins, ginger, orange peel, juice, and sugar. Bring to a simmer and continue to gently simmer for about 15 minutes.

Add the Fra Angelico and simmer for 1 minute. Remove from the heat and set aside for the flavors to meld.

PER 1-OUNCE SERVING: 66 CALORIES, 0.7 G PROTEIN, 0.5 G FAT, 15.5 G CARBOHYDRATES, 0.2 G SATURATED FATTY ACIDS, 0.4 MG CHOLESTEROL, 4.6 MG SODIUM, 1.4 G TOTAL DIETARY FIBER

fra angelico (frangelico) Fra Angelico is a hazelnut liqueur made in Italy and used in desserts and beverages. Legend has it that Brother Angelico, a monk who lived three centuries ago as a hermit along the Po River, loved wild hazelnuts, berries, and flowers, which led him to create this sweet treat.

caramel layer cake

When Moosewood cook Lisa Wichman was searching for a new dessert idea, her mom Vera George's caramel recipe suddenly popped into her head. When she called her mother for the recipe, they got to chatting, and Lisa discovered that all those childhood sweets her mother always made were thanks to her grandmother, who worked in a West Virginia candy factory some seventy-five years ago.

Grandma clearly brought her "work" home with her (we bet no one complained), and two generations later we're still reaping the rewards. Lisa developed the Caramel Frosting for this lovely traditional Southern layer cake from that old family recipe.

For easiest spreading, frost the cake as soon as the frosting is ready. Since the cake takes 40 minutes to cool and the frosting takes about 20 minutes to make, you can begin to make the frosting after the cake has cooled for at least 20 minutes. Waiting longer is okay, but if you're trying to get to the finish line as fast as possible, now you know the whole scoop. Cake à la mode, anyone?

Serves 12
Cake preparation time: 30 minutes
Baking time: 30 to 35 minutes
Cooling time: 40 minutes
Assembling time: 10 minutes

cake

- 2½ cups unbleached white flour
- 2 teaspoons baking powder
- ¼ teaspoon salt
- 1 cup unsalted butter, at room temperature*
- 2 cups brown sugar, packed
- 5 large eggs
- ¾ cup milk
- 2 teaspoons pure vanilla extract

caramel frosting

- 2 cups brown sugar, packed
- 3 tablespoons unsalted butter*
- 1 cup half-and-half
- 1 teaspoon pure vanilla extract

* *Unsalted butter is often a higher-quality butter, and many of us prefer it for baking. Salted butter will also work fine.*

Preheat the oven to 350°. Butter two 9-inch round cake pans and lightly dust with flour.

In a bowl, sift together the flour, baking powder, and salt and set aside. Using an electric mixer, cream together the butter and brown sugar. Add the eggs, one at a time, beating well after each. Stir together the milk and vanilla in a measuring cup. Add the milk and flour mixtures alternately to the creamed mixture and beat well after each addition to form a smooth batter.

Divide the batter evenly between the prepared pans. Bake for 30 to 35 minutes, until a knife tests clean and the cake begins to pull away from the sides of the pan. Cool the layers in the pans for about 5 minutes and then turn out onto a rack to cool completely.

In a 2½ or 3-quart suacepan, preferably nonstick, combine the sugar, butter, and half-and-half. Bring to a rolling boil, stirring often. Cover and boil on medium-high heat for 3 minutes. Uncover and continue to boil until the caramel begins to thicken and coats a spoon, about 4 minutes. Keep watch—the sauce can burn in a heartbeat. Remove from the heat and pour into a large mixing bowl.

Add the vanilla and beat with an electric mixer on high speed until creamy, thick, and a good spreading consistency, about 10 minutes.

While the frosting is still warm, fill and frost the cake. If the frosting gets too thick to spread easily, thin it with a bit of half-and-half.

PER 6-OUNCE SERVING: 607 CALORIES, 6.9 G PROTEIN, 23.6 G FAT, 93.7 G CARBOHYDRATES, 13.7 G SATURATED FATTY ACIDS, 167.3 MG CHOLESTEROL, 182.8 MG SODIUM, 0.6 G TOTAL DIETARY FIBER

equipment tips ❧ *A large saucepan is necessary for the frosting because it expands a lot while cooking. To beat the frosting, we prefer the mobility of a hand-held electric mixer.*

french chocolate almond cake

This is a French-style cake, which is to say, a rich, melt-in-your-mouth cake with a soft center and a very thin crackly crust. Adapted from a favorite recipe of Julia Child's, it's sure to become a sought-after recipe among chocolate cake lovers.

The cake is made in an 8-inch springform pan using equal parts of flour and finely ground almonds. The secret to its heavenly texture is a lot of elbow grease with a wire whisk or a good amount of whipping with an electric mixer. Be sure the ingredients are at room temperature—including the eggs, which can be warmed in a bowl of hot tap water for 10 minutes. For an unusual (not French) twist, try adding a little cinnamon and black pepper.

Yields a single 8-inch layer cake
Preparation time: 40 minutes
Baking time: 25 minutes
Cooling time: 10 minutes

1 teaspoon instant coffee granules

2 tablespoons hot water

4 ounces good-quality bittersweet chocolate or semi-sweet chocolate chips*

1/3 cup butter, at room temperature

1/2 cup sugar

3 eggs, separated**

1/3 cup unbleached white flour

1/3 cup finely ground almonds

1/4 teaspoon ground cinnamon (optional)

1 teaspoon ground black pepper (optional)

1/4 teaspoon cream of tartar

pinch of salt

2 tablespoons sugar

2 tablespoons confectioners' sugar

* *A good choice is Ghirardelli, which comes in 4-ounce bars.*
** *The egg whites must not contain even a speck of the yolk for them to whip properly. If you're using the same beaters for the egg whites as for the butter and chocolate mixture, be sure they're scrupulously clean and dry.*

✂ Preheat the oven to 350°. Butter an 8-inch springform pan and dust with flour.

Stir together the coffee and water in a small saucepan. Add the chocolate and warm on low heat, stirring with vigilance until smooth and blended (see Note). Remove from the heat and set aside.

In a medium bowl, beat together the butter and sugar with an electric mixer or a whisk, until light and creamy. Add the egg yolks one at a time, beating well after each addition. Beat in the reserved melted chocolate mixture. In a small bowl, stir together the flour and ground almonds. If using, add the cinnamon and pepper. Set aside.

Using an electric mixer or a whisk, whip the egg whites in a sturdy bowl until white and foamy. Add the cream of tartar and salt and whip until the whites form soft peaks when the beaters are lifted. Add the sugar and continue to whip until the whites are stiff and glossy.

Now combine the mixtures. Fold the flour mixture and the beaten egg whites alternately into the chocolate mixture in two or three batches. Use a gentle, thorough touch so the batter is blended but light and airy. This is what gives the cake its melt-in-your-mouth texture.

Pour the batter into the prepared pan. Bake the cake in the center of the oven for about 25 minutes. When done, the top of the cake will be slightly cracked, a few crumbs will adhere to a toothpick inserted about 2 inches from the edge of the pan, and the center of the cake will be soft and slightly puffed. Cool on a rack for about 10 minutes.

Run a knife around the outside of the cake and remove the sides of the springform pan. Invert the cake onto the rack to remove the bottom of the springform pan. Then invert back onto a serving plate, cracked side up. Sprinkle with the confectioners' sugar and serve at room temperature. This cake is at its very best when served the same day.

PER 2.75-OUNCE SERVING: 293 CALORIES, 5.2 G PROTEIN, 17.8 G FAT, 31 G CARBOHYDRATES, 8.5 G SATURATED FATTY ACIDS, 119.6 MG CHOLESTEROL, 124.6 MG SODIUM, 0.7 G TOTAL DIETARY FIBER

note ❧ *You can also melt the chocolate in the coffee using a double boiler or the microwave.*

orange pound cake

There are many, many recipes for pound cakes, but we think we have the very best—rich, buttery, dense, and finely textured. We've been making a wide variety of pound cakes in great profusion since 1974 at Moosewood, all adapted from a recipe we found in *Family Circle* magazine that year for a pound cake that won a blue ribbon for Mrs. McCollum at the Rockingham County Fair. Our hats off to you, Mrs. McCollum, wherever you are!

Orange Pound Cake, pristine in its simplicity, is perfect unadorned, but it's also good with orange slices or maybe with strawberries and fresh whipped cream.

Serves 16
Preparation time: 30 minutes
Baking time: 60 to 75 minutes
Cooling time: 20 to 30 minutes

cake

2 cups unsalted butter, at room temperature

3 cups sugar

2 teaspoons pure orange extract

6 eggs

4 cups unbleached white pastry flour

1/2 cup orange juice*

2 teaspoons baking powder

orange glaze

1 teaspoon pure orange extract

2 to 3 tablespoons orange juice

1 1/2 cups confectioners' sugar

* *If you use frozen orange juice concentrate, mix 1/4 cup of the concentrate with 1/4 cup of water.*

Preheat the oven to 350°. Butter and flour a 10-inch Bundt pan (see Note).

With an electric mixer, cream the butter and sugar. Beat in the orange extract and the eggs. Add 2 cups of the flour and beat well. Add the orange juice and beat. In a separate bowl, or measuring cup, stir the baking powder into the remaining 2 cups flour. Add to the batter and beat well.

Spoon the batter into the prepared Bundt pan and bake until the cake pulls away from the sides of the pan and a knife inserted in the center comes out clean, about 60 to 75 minutes. Cool the cake in the pan on a rack for 10 minutes. Invert onto a serving plate, leaving the pan on top so the cake holds its shape. Cool for another 10 or 20 minutes.

Meanwhile, prepare the glaze. Stir the orange extract and the orange juice into the sugar with a fork, adding the orange juice a tablespoon at a time; use just enough to produce a thick, smooth mixture. Spread the glaze over the cake with a pastry brush while the cake is still warm, or drizzle it on in a lacy pattern.

PER 5-OUNCE SERVING: 546 CALORIES, 6.2 G PROTEIN, 25.8 G FAT, 73.8 G CARBOHYDRATES, 15.1 G SATURATED FATTY ACIDS, 161.2 MG CHOLESTEROL, 73.3 MG SODIUM, 0.8 G TOTAL DIETARY FIBER

note ✳ *Not every 10-inch Bundt pan holds the same number of cups. There are differences in shape and the slope of the sides. For this recipe, use a Bundt pan that holds at least 12 cups, or the batter is likely to overflow and make an oven mess.*

If your Bundt pan is smaller, spoon a portion of the batter into a miniature loaf pan or a 6-inch round cake pan and bake it alongside your big Bundt cake. Check the small cake earlier: It will bake in less time. The dessert makers do this regularly at Moosewood and serve the small cake to the staff—who have come to love those warm-hearted dessert chefs.

variations ✳ *Pound cake lends itself to invention. If you stick with these proportions of ingredients, you can use any flavor of extract you like or use brown sugar instead of white. For the 1/2 cup of liquid, you can choose milk, yogurt, sour cream, coconut milk, fruit juice, or liqueur. Sometimes we add nuts, dried fruits, chocolate chips, or spices when dreaming up a new pound cake flavor.*

upside-down skillet cake

The cake in this easy, rustic treat is packed with whole grain goodness and is not too sweet. It's the seasonal fruit glistening on top that gives this dessert such visual appeal. Choose a single favorite fruit or a colorful combination. When peach and blueberry season is over, make it with cranberries paired with apples or pears.

This is a nice dessert for a homey meal, such as skillet beans or soup and salad. It's also lovely served warm for breakfast or as part of a special brunch.

Serves 12
Preparation time: 40 minutes
Baking time: 40 to 45 minutes

¹/₂ cup butter

1 cup brown sugar, packed

3 cups pitted and sliced fruit*

2 eggs

2 teaspoons pure vanilla extract

¹/₂ cup oat flour**

¹/₂ cup cornmeal

1 cup whole wheat pastry flour

1 tablespoon baking powder

¹/₂ teaspoon ground cinnamon

¹/₄ teaspoon ground nutmeg

¹/₄ teaspoon salt

²/₃ cup milk

* *Try apricots, plums, peaches, or pears or a full pint of blueberries or raspberries.*
** *You can whirl ¹/₂ cup rolled oats in a blender or spice grinder to make the oat flour.*

Melt ¹/₄ cup of the butter in a 10-inch cast-iron skillet. Stir in ¹/₂ cup of the brown sugar, mixing well. Arrange your choice of fruit in the skillet and set it aside.

Preheat the oven to 350°.

With an electric mixer, cream together the remaining ¹/₄ cup of butter and ¹/₂ cup of brown sugar. Add the eggs and vanilla and beat well. In a separate bowl, stir together the oat flour, cornmeal, whole wheat pastry flour, baking powder, cinnamon, nutmeg, and salt. Alternately mix the flour mixture and the milk into the egg mixture to form a uniform batter. Spoon the batter evenly over the fruit in the skillet.

Bake for 40 to 45 minutes, until a knife inserted into the center of the cake comes out clean. Cool in the skillet on a rack for 5 to 10 minutes; then invert onto a serving plate. If any fruit sticks to the skillet, just pull it off and arrange it on the cake.

This cake is best served warm from the oven, but it can also be served at room temperature.

PER 4.5-OUNCE SERVING: 265 CALORIES, 4.8 G PROTEIN, 9.6 G FAT, 41.6 G CARBOHYDRATES, 5.4 G SATURATED FATTY ACIDS, 65.7 MG CHOLESTEROL, 237.7 MG SODIUM, 3.1 G TOTAL DIETARY FIBER

presto! chocolate cake

This is a moist, quick, easy chocolate cake for every day and a great dessert to make with kids. It has a rich, gooey, super-simple, semi-sweet chocolate and fruit glaze that's ready in 5 minutes. We especially like to eat this cake warm from the oven with a cold glass of milk.

 Serves 8
Preparation time: 20 minutes
Baking time: 30 to 35 minutes

cake

1 cup unbleached white flour

$1/3$ cup unsweetened cocoa powder

$1/2$ teaspoon baking soda

$1/4$ teaspoon salt

$1/2$ cup butter, at room temperature

1 cup sugar

2 large eggs

$3/4$ cup water

1 teaspoon pure vanilla extract

glaze

$1/2$ cup semi-sweet chocolate chips*

$1/3$ cup fruit jam or spread**

2 tablespoons milk, cream, or water

* *We recommend a good-quality chocolate, such as Ghirardelli.*
***Cherry, raspberry, or apricot preserves or orange marmalade are good choices.*

✂Preheat the oven to 350°. Butter and dust with flour an 8- or 9-inch square or round cake pan.

In a large bowl, sift together the flour, cocoa, baking soda, and salt. In a separate bowl, cream the butter and sugar with an electric mixer. Add the eggs to the butter one at a time, beating well after each addition. In a small bowl, combine the water and vanilla. Add the flavored water by thirds to the creamed mixture, alternating with the flour mixture and beating after each addition.

Pour the batter into the prepared pan and bake until a knife inserted in the center comes out clean and the cake begins to pull away from the sides, 30 to 35 minutes.

About 5 minutes before the cake is done, combine the chocolate chips, jam, and milk in a small pan and warm on low heat, stirring constantly until melted. When the cake is done, glaze the top right in the pan. Serve warm or at room temperature.

PER 4.25-OUNCE SERVING: 368 CALORIES, 4.8 G PROTEIN, 17.3 G FAT, 52.2 G CARBOHYDRATES, 10 G SATURATED FATTY ACIDS, 97.4 MG CHOLESTEROL, 284.8 MG SODIUM, 1.1 G TOTAL DIETARY FIBER

pistachio cardamom cake

Dense, syrup-soaked cakes are classics in the Middle East and North Africa. Because we regularly serve food inspired by these regions, this type of cake (served in triangular pieces) often appears on our menu—and our customers love it. It's a deceptively plain cake that is anything but.

Pistachio Cardamom Cake is textured with semolina and pistachios and soaked with lemon syrup. When grinding the pistachios, don't worry about getting rid of every last chunk of nut, or you're apt to end up with nut butter instead of ground nuts. A few little chunks of nuts are really just fine, even welcome, in the cake.

Pistachio Cardamom Cake is the perfect ending to Israeli Za'atar Salad (page 94), or Middle Eastern Lentils & Pasta (page 254), or served alongside Falafel Burgers (page 184).

Serves 12
Preparation time: 30 minutes
Baking time: 30 minutes

cake

¹/₂ cup unsalted butter, at room
 temperature

³/₄ cup sugar

3 eggs

1 teaspoon pure vanilla extract

1 cup semolina (page 469)

¹/₂ teaspoon ground cardamom

¹/₂ teaspoon ground cinnamon

¹/₄ teaspoon salt

¹/₂ cup unsalted pistachios,
 plus 12 whole pistachios

¹/₂ cup nonfat plain yogurt

syrup

¹/₄ cup water

¹/₄ cup sugar

1 teaspoon freshly grated lemon peel

1 tablespoon fresh lemon juice

Preheat the oven to 350°. Butter a 7 x 11-inch baking dish.

With an electric mixer, cream the butter and sugar. Add the eggs, one at a time, beating after each addition. Add the vanilla. In a separate bowl, combine the semolina, cardamom, cinnamon, and salt. Grind ¹/₂ cup of the pistachios in a spice grinder to the consistency of a coarse meal and stir into the dry ingredients. In alternating batches, add the yogurt and the dry ingredients to the creamed mixture, beating well after each addition, to form a smooth batter.

Spread the batter into the prepared pan. Bake for about 30 minutes, until a knife inserted in the center comes out clean.

About 5 minutes before the cake is done, combine the water, sugar, lemon peel, and lemon juice in a saucepan and bring to a boil. Boil rapidly for about 2 minutes and then remove from the heat and set aside.

When the cake is ready, cut it in half lengthwise and then cut it into thirds crosswise to form six square pieces. Cut each square on the diagonal to make 12 triangular pieces. Pour the syrup evenly over the cake and gently press one whole pistachio into the center of each triangle of cake.

PER 2.5-OUNCE SERVING: 236 CALORIES, 5 G PROTEIN, 12.9 G FAT, 26.2 G CARBOHYDRATES, 5.6 G SATURATED FATTY ACIDS, 87 MG CHOLESTEROL, 77.9 MG SODIUM, 0.5 G TOTAL DIETARY FIBER

deep chocolate vegan cake

Loved by vegans and non-vegans alike, this extraordinarily popular Moosewood dessert can be made more quickly than any chocolate cake we know. Use a stainless-steel or glass 8-inch round or square nonreactive cake pan. For easy removal of the cake from the pan, oil the pan and place a piece of parchment paper on the bottom.

Dust the top of the finished cake with confectioners' sugar or prepare a glaze or frosting of your choice. For some of our favorite vegan frostings, see pages 426 and 427.

Serves 8
Preparation time: 15 minutes
Baking time: 25 to 30 minutes

1 1/2 cups unbleached white flour
1/3 cup unsweetened cocoa powder
1/2 teaspoon baking soda
1/2 teaspoon salt
1 cup sugar
1/2 cup vegetable oil
1 cup cold water or chilled brewed coffee
2 teaspoons pure vanilla extract
2 tablespoons cider vinegar

Preheat the oven to 375°. Generously oil an 8-inch square or round baking pan and dust with a little sifted cocoa or line the bottom with parchment paper.

In a medium bowl, sift together the flour, cocoa, soda, salt, and sugar. In another bowl, combine the oil, water or coffee, and vanilla. Pour the liquid ingredients into the dry ingredients and mix until well blended and smooth.

Add the vinegar and stir briefly; the baking soda will begin to react with the vinegar right away, leaving pale swirls in the batter. Without wasting any time, pour the batter into the prepared baking pan.

Bake for 25 to 30 minutes. Serve the cake right from the pan or, when it's cool, transfer it to a plate.

PER 3.5-OUNCE SERVING: 315 CALORIES, 2.9 G PROTEIN, 15.1 G FAT, 43.9 G CARBOHYDRATES, 4.1 G SATURATED FATTY ACIDS, 0 MG CHOLESTEROL, 217.2 MG SODIUM, 0.6 G TOTAL DIETARY FIBER

vegan oil pie crust

Fran Welch, a friend and former Moosewood employee, gave us this recipe. She's probably made hundreds of these crusts, which come together quickly and are surprisingly easy to roll out. Use this recipe anytime you want a vegan crust.

Yields one 10-inch pie shell
Total time: 10 minutes

2 cups unbleached white flour or
    whole wheat pastry flour
    (or a mixture)
$^1/_2$ teaspoon salt
$^1/_2$ cup vegetable oil
$^1/_2$ cup water

Stir together the flour and salt in a large bowl. With a fork, stir in the oil and water. Shape the dough into a ball. On a lightly floured surface, roll the dough out into a 13-inch circle. Place in a 10-inch pie pan and crimp the edges. Chill until ready to use.

PER 16-OUNCE CRUST: 1,828 CALORIES, 23.4 G PROTEIN, 115.6 G FAT, 173 G CARBOHYDRATES, 29.7 G SATURATED FATTY ACIDS, 0 MG CHOLESTEROL, 1,199.8 MG SODIUM, 6.1 G TOTAL DIETARY FIBER

lizzie's choice

During the last decade, a growing number of people have chosen to be vegans (vēg′uns). A vegan diet consists solely of foods from the plant world and most vegans oppose animal slaughter and the living conditions of most commercial livestock. So they do not wear leather, wool, silk, shells, feathers, pearls, or bone, and they avoid milk, eggs, honey, meat, poultry, and fish.

Here's a very familiar scenario these days. The phone rings at the restaurant. On the other end is a very pleasant woman from New Jersey, who is driving up for her daughter Lizzie's birthday. Lizzie is a student at Ithaca College and they'd like to come to Moosewood for dinner. There's just one problem—Lizzie's a vegan. Do we have anything that Lizzie can eat and what about something that *resembles* a birthday cake?

Lizzie's mom needn't worry. At Moosewood, we've seen a continuous increase in veganism, with its emphasis on beans and grains. There are always delicious vegan choices on our menu: tofu or tempeh, plenty of cooked vegetables, and fresh fruit and vegetables in the form of salad. Vegan meals offer lots of opportunity for creativity; they need never be dull or repetitive.

Within these pages you'll find vegan turnovers, lasagna, stroganoff, and bean dishes galore. For breakfast, there are tofu scrambles, vegan pancakes and waffles, and a week's worth of "burgers" for lunch. Dessert: Try Thai Black Rice Pudding or Fruit Skewers. So how about Lizzie's birthday cake? No problem—Deep Chocolate Vegan Cake with Chocolate Raspberry Glaze is always a hit. How many candles for her cake?

four vegan frostings

To dress up our popular Deep Chocolate Vegan Cake we've developed a variety of glazes and frostings that make it "different than last time" for our regular customers. Here are four of our favorites. The "glazes" are all rich and thick and will be as good as the chocolate chips you use.

chocolate peanut butter frosting

2 ounces unsweetened chocolate
¼ cup peanut butter
3 to 4 tablespoons water
1 teaspoon pure vanilla extract
1 cup confectioners' sugar

In a double boiler or small heavy saucepan melt the chocolate on medium heat. While it melts, beat together the peanut butter, water, and vanilla until smooth. Beat in the confectioners' sugar and add the melted chocolate, mixing until blended. Spread the frosting on the cooled cake.

PER 1-OUNCE SERVING: 117 CALORIES, 1.7 G PROTEIN, 4.9 G FAT, 17.9 G CARBOHYDRATES, 1.7 G SATURATED FATTY ACIDS, 0 MG CHOLESTEROL, 26.8 MG SODIUM, 0.3 G TOTAL DIETARY FIBER

orange glaze

1½ cups semi-sweet chocolate chips
3 tablespoons fresh orange juice
1 teaspoon freshly grated orange peel

In a double boiler or small heavy saucepan melt the chocolate chips with the orange juice and peel on medium heat, blending thoroughly. Spread the glaze over the cooled cake, and allow the glaze to cool before cutting the cake.

PER 1-OUNCE SERVING: 125 CALORIES, 1.1 G PROTEIN, 7.7 G FAT, 16.7 G CARBOHYDRATES, 4.5 G SATURATED FATTY ACIDS, 0 MG CHOLESTEROL, 2.9 MG SODIUM, 1.6 G TOTAL DIETARY FIBER

chocolate coconut glaze

3 tablespoons unsweetened grated coconut
1 1/2 cups semi-sweet chocolate chips
3 tablespoons coconut milk
1/4 teaspoon pure coconut extract

Preheat the oven or toaster oven to 325°.

Sprinkle the coconut on a small baking tray and lightly toast it for 1 to 3 minutes, until golden.

In a double boiler or small heavy saucepan combine the chocolate chips with the coconut milk and coconut extract. Melt on medium heat, and whisk until smooth. Spread the glaze over the cooled cake and top with the toasted coconut. Allow the glaze to cool before cutting the cake.

PER 1-OUNCE SERVING: 140 CALORIES, 1.3 G PROTEIN, 9.5 G FAT, 16.6 G CARBOHYDRATES, 6.1 G SATURATED FATTY ACIDS, 0 MG CHOLESTEROL, 4 MG SODIUM, 1.7 G TOTAL DIETARY FIBER

chocolate raspberry glaze

1/3 cup plus 1/4 cup raspberry fruit spread or jam
1 1/2 cups semi-sweet chocolate chips
1 tablespoon water

In a double boiler or small heavy saucepan on medium heat, melt 1/3 cup of the fruit spread with the chocolate chips and blend thoroughly. In another small saucepan, mix 1/4 cup of the fruit spread with the water and warm on low heat until it liquifies. Brush the liquid fruit spread over the cooled cake, then spread on the chocolate glaze. Allow the glaze to cool before cutting the cake.

PER 1-OUNCE SERVING: 115 CALORIES, 0.8 G PROTEIN, 5.5 G FAT, 18.5 G CARBOHYDRATES, 3.2 G SATURATED FATTY ACIDS, 0 MG CHOLESTEROL, 5.2 MG SODIUM, 1.2 G TOTAL DIETARY FIBER

apple quesadillas

Quicker than apple crêpes and lower in fat too, apple quesadillas can be a lovely dessert or the main attraction at a brunch. These crisp, flaky wheat tortillas wrapped around juicy cinnamon-spiced apples will satisfy any yen for apple pie on the spot. If you make the apple filling ahead, or have any left over, it will keep, covered, for about 4 days in the refrigerator. Just reheat the filling while warming the oil for the quesadillas, and in minutes you're ready to eat.

True apple lovers will want to savor the quesadillas unadorned, but for a fancy dessert, try Caramel Sauce (opposite), a dollop of vanilla ice cream, maple syrup, or fresh whipped cream.

Serves 6
Preparation time: 15 to 20 minutes
Cooking time: about 25 minutes (see Note)

5 large or 8 medium Crispin or other trim, medium-tart apples, peeled, cored, and sliced into 1/4-inch-thick slices (about 8 cups)
2 tablespoons fresh lemon juice
1 teaspoon ground cinnamon
3 tablespoons butter
1 tablespoon pure maple syrup

6 wheat tortillas (8- or 9-inch)*
cooking spray or vegetable oil

* We recommend MexAmerica Flour Tortillas. They are a generous 9-inch size, come 10 to a package in a resealable bag, and are both delicious and pliable. They are in the refrigerated section of many supermarkets.

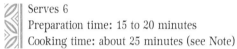

In a large bowl, toss the sliced apples with the lemon juice and cinnamon. Melt the butter in a deep 10- or 12-inch skillet. Stir in the apples, cover, and cook on medium heat for 5 to 10 minutes, stirring occasionally, until tender but still firm enough to retain their shape. Stir in the maple syrup, cover, and set aside.

Warm a lightly oiled, preferably nonstick skillet on high heat. Place a tortilla in the skillet and heat for 1 to 2 minutes. Flip it over, place 1 scant cup of cooked apples on one half and cook for another 1 1/2 minutes, until the tortilla is crisp and lightly browned. Fold in half, transfer to a warm serving platter, and cover with a clean towel. Make 5 more quesadillas the same way, then serve immediately.

PER 5.5-OUNCE SERVING: 273 CALORIES, 3.4 G PROTEIN, 8.8 G FAT, 48.4 G CARBOHYDRATES, 4.3 G SATURATED FATTY ACIDS, 15.5 MG CHOLESTEROL, 211.6 MG SODIUM, 6.3 G TOTAL DIETARY FIBER

note ❦ *Use two skillets simultaneously to cut the quesadilla cooking time in half.*

caramel sauce

The key ingredient in caramel sauce is browned white sugar, which has a distinctive, compelling flavor and fragrance. Although our Moosewood version is rich, sweet, and buttery, believe it or not, it has less butterfat than most caramel sauces because we use half-and-half rather than heavy cream. Be sure to use a heavy saucepan to avoid scorching the caramel, and resist the urge to stir as you melt the sugar.

Try the sauce on ice cream, crêpes, waffles, pancakes, bread or rice puddings, and poached or baked apples or other fruit. It's a good accompaniment to dress up our Apple Quesadillas (opposite).

1 cup sugar
3 tablespoons water
1 1/2 teaspoons cornstarch
1 cup half-and-half
1/4 cup unsalted butter, cut into small pieces
1 teaspoon pure vanilla extract

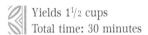
Yields 1 1/2 cups
Total time: 30 minutes

In a small heavy saucepan, stir the sugar and water until the sugar is somewhat dissolved. Cook on medium-high heat, uncovered and *without stirring*, for 10 to 15 minutes, until the syrup begins to turn golden brown, bubbles, and is fragrant.

Meanwhile, in a small bowl, thoroughly mix the cornstarch with about 2 tablespoons of the half-and-half and set aside.

As soon as the syrup browns, remove the pan from the heat. Gradually pour in the rest of the half-and-half; the mixture will sputter and hiss and begin to form a solid mass. Immediately return the pan to medium heat, whisking vigorously for 5 to 10 minutes. The sauce may froth and expand, but just keep whisking until the sugar mass melts again and the sauce is a uniform consistency.

Cook and stir for 4 more minutes to slightly thicken the sauce, then gradually whisk in the butter pieces. When the butter has melted, add the cornstarch mixture, lower the heat, and simmer for 1 1/2 minutes. Remove from the heat and stir in the vanilla.

Serve the sauce warm or chill. In a sealed container the sauce will keep in the refrigerator for up to 4 or 5 weeks. To serve, rewarm it in a double boiler over boiling water, zap it in a microwave, or stir it constantly in a saucepan on medium-low heat.

PER 1-OUNCE SERVING: 126 CALORIES, 0.6 G PROTEIN, 6 G FAT, 18.1 G CARBOHYDRATES, 3.7 G SATURATED FATTY ACIDS, 17.3 MG CHOLESTEROL, 8.5 MG SODIUM, 0 G TOTAL DIETARY FIBER

fruit skewers

Festive and fun, colorful fruit on a stick is great for buffets and parties and can play the role of a dessert, side salad, or appetizer. Twenty 10-inch bamboo skewers work perfectly for this recipe. The fruit can be arranged on the skewers up to 3 hours before serving. If you like, dispense with the skewers and serve the guava-coated fruit in a bowl as a salad.

The guava-lime glaze brings out the jewel-like colors of the fruit and adds a delectable sweetness that is amazingly drip free. Try adding about 2 tablespoons of rum to the glaze.

 Yields 20 skewers
Total time: 25 minutes

½ ripe cantaloupe or honeydew melon, peeled and seeded

½ ripe pineapple, peeled and cored

1 pint fresh strawberries, hulled

1 small bunch of seedless green grapes (about 20)

1 small bunch of seedless red grapes (about 20)

⅓ cup guava paste*

2½ tablespoons fresh lime juice

Guavas are a native Central American fruit with a distinctive, refreshing flavor that ranges from sweet to somewhat sour. The paste is made from the guava pulp collected during jelly making. Find guava paste in Latin and Asian groceries and in the ethnic section of well-stocked supermarkets.

✂ Cut the cantaloupe or honeydew melon into 1-inch, bite-sized cubes and place them in a large bowl. Cut the cored pineapple half into 6 or 8 long wedges and then into bite-sized chunks—you should get at least 40 pieces. Add the pineapple to the bowl along with the strawberries and grapes.

In a blender, purée the guava paste and lime juice into a smooth, thick dressing. Pour the dressing into the bowl and toss with the fruit.

On each bamboo skewer, spear 7 or 8 pieces of fruit: begin and end with grapes because they're the firmest anchors. One possible order could be grape, pineapple, melon, strawberry, pineapple, melon, grape. Arrange the finished fruit skewers side by side on a large oval platter. Make a second layer with the skewers perpendicular to the first layer. Continue the crisscross pattern for as many layers as needed.

Serve immediately or cover well and refrigerate until serving time.

PER 2-OUNCE SERVING: 27 CALORIES, 0.3 G PROTEIN, 0.2 G FAT, 6.7 G CARBOHYDRATES, 0 G SATURATED FATTY ACIDS, 0 MG CHOLESTEROL, 1.2 MG SODIUM, 0.7 G TOTAL DIETARY FIBER

better apple pie

In Ithaca, we are fortunate to have a wide assortment of dried fruits readily available in our supermarkets, and we've found that adding even a small amount of dried berries or cherries will give an impressive burst of sweetness and flavor to baked goods, like good old apple pie.

Making well-balanced fruit pies can be a bit tricky. The sweetness and juiciness of fruit varies, so it is important to adjust the amount of sugar, lemon juice, and any thickening agent—such as cornstarch, flour, or tapioca—in relation to the fruit. It's best to start with less sugar, mix it with the apples, and taste an apple slice. Then use your best judgment to make adjustments. It's hard to tell for sure, but you can usually get a good idea. Practice helps.

This recipe is especially good for sprucing up apples that are out of season or not at their best. And, of course, it's fabulous with the perfectly crisp, juicy apples of autumn.

fruit filling

8 cups peeled and sliced apples

1 teaspoon freshly grated lemon peel

1 tablespoon fresh lemon juice

1/2 cup sugar

1/3 cup dried cranberries

1 tablespoon unbleached white flour

10-inch pie crust, unbaked
(page 291 or 425)

crunchy streusel topping

1/2 cup unbleached white flour

1/4 cup sugar

1/4 cup butter or margarine

1/2 cup rolled oats

1/2 cup toasted and coarsely chopped almonds*

Yields one 10-inch pie
Preparation time: 35 minutes
  (not including crust)
Baking time: about 1 hour

* *Toast almonds in a single layer on an unoiled baking tray at 350° for 5 to 10 minutes, until fragrant and golden brown.*

Preheat the oven to 400°.

In a large bowl, mix together the apples, lemon peel, lemon juice, sugar, cranberries, and flour. Spoon the mixture into the pie crust and set aside.

In a small bowl, combine the flour and sugar for the topping. Work the butter into the flour mixture with a pastry cutter or your fingers until the mixture resembles coarse meal. Add the oats and almonds and mix well. Spread the topping evenly over the apples.

Bake for 55 to 60 minutes, until the apples are tender and the crust is golden brown. For easier serving, let the pie sit for at least 10 minutes before cutting.

PER 9-OUNCE SERVING: 495 CALORIES, 6.7 G PROTEIN, 22.9 G FAT, 70 G CARBOHYDRATES, 11.3 G SATURATED FATTY ACIDS, 46.5 MG CHOLESTEROL, 178.4 MG SODIUM, 6.7 G TOTAL DIETARY FIBER

rustic plum tart

This country-style, free-form tart is easy to put together. There's no fussing with fancy edges or a top crust. The crust is rolled out flat and folded up over the top of the tart to partially cover the filling. Bake it in a 10-inch pie plate or on a flat baking sheet with rims to catch any juices: It may need to bake up to 30 minutes longer when prepared in a pie pan rather than spread on a baking sheet.

For flaky pastry, start with cold ingredients and avoid overhandling. Be sure to let the dough relax in the refrigerator while making the filling.

Serve our plum tart unadorned or with fresh whipped cream, indoors or on the terrace. Pretend you're in France.

Serves 8
Preparation time: 35 to 45 minutes
Baking time: 45 to 75 minutes
Cooling time: 30 minutes

crust

1 1/3 cups unbleached white flour

2 tablespoons sugar

1/2 teaspoon salt

3/4 cup chilled unsalted butter

1/4 cup chilled cream cheese

2 teaspoons fresh lemon juice*

2 tablespoons ice water

filling

1 1/2 pounds plums

2/3 cup sugar

3 tablespoons cornstarch

1 teaspoon freshly grated lemon peel,
   or more to taste*

1 egg (optional)

* Zest the lemon before juicing it and reserve
  the grated peel for the filling.

Preheat the oven to 400°. Butter a 10-inch pie plate or large rimmed baking sheet.

Mix the flour, sugar, and salt in a large bowl or in a food processor. Cut the butter and cream cheese into 1-inch pieces and incorporate them into the flour mixture by hand or by pulsing in the food processor until they are the size of peas. Mix in the lemon juice and ice water until the mixture begins to form a dough. Shape the dough into a ball, flatten it into a disk, wrap in plastic, and refrigerate until ready to roll out.

Cut the plums in half, remove and discard the pits, and slice the plums into 1/2-inch-thick wedges to make about 5 cups of prepared fruit. Place the wedges in a medium bowl and sift the sugar and cornstarch over them. Add the lemon peel and mix well. Set aside.

Lightly flour a clean dry surface, a rolling pin, and the chilled dough. Roll the dough from the center out into a 14-inch circle. Lift and rotate it from time to time to prevent sticking, dusting with more flour as needed. If the dough seems too soft or sticky, refrigerate for about 10 minutes.

Transfer the dough to the prepared pie plate or baking sheet and arrange the plums on the dough in concentric circles. Begin at the center and layer until all the fruit is used. If you're using a baking sheet, end the outermost ring of plums 2 inches from the edge of the dough. Fold over the dough to make a border. For a golden sheen whisk the egg with a tablespoon of water and brush it on the pastry edges.

Bake for 15 minutes. Then reduce the oven temperature to 350° and continue to bake for 30 to 60 minutes, until the crust is browned and the juices bubble up. Remove from the oven and let cool on a rack for 30 minutes. Serve while still warm.

PER 5.5-OUNCE SERVING: 382 CALORIES, 3.3 G PROTEIN, 20.4 G FAT, 48.5 G CARBOHYDRATES,
12.4 G SATURATED FATTY ACIDS, 54.3 MG CHOLESTEROL, 173.7 MG SODIUM, 1.8 G TOTAL DIETARY FIBER

muhallabia massawa

Muhallabia is a refreshing dessert from the Red Sea port city of Massawa in Eritrea. There, it is commonly served for dessert during Ramadan, the Islamic month of fasting. Claudia Roden, herself an exemplar of Middle Eastern cooking, calls it "the most regal and delicious of puddings."

Our pudding has a creamy, smooth texture and the winning combination of cinnamon, cardamom, and vanilla makes it an instant favorite of anyone who tries it. And what's more, it's a cinch to make.

 Serves 6
Preparation time: 30 minutes
Chilling time: about 45 minutes

1 cup sugar

¼ cup cornstarch

½ teaspoon ground cinnamon

½ teaspoon ground cardamom

4 cups milk

2 eggs, well beaten

2 tablespoons butter, at room temperature

2 teaspoons pure vanilla extract

In a medium saucepan, combine the sugar, cornstarch, cinnamon, and cardamom. Gradually add just enough milk to make a paste, and then whisk in the remaining milk. Add the beaten eggs.

Cook on medium heat, stirring often, for 12 to 15 minutes, until the mixture thickens. As it begins to thicken, stir constantly to prevent sticking and to ensure a smooth texture. Remove from the heat and add the butter and vanilla.

Pour into six wine glasses or dessert cups and refrigerate about 45 minutes, or until cold.

PER 8-OUNCE SERVING: 301 CALORIES, 7.7 G PROTEIN, 9 G FAT, 47.4 G CARBOHYDRATES, 4.9 G SATURATED FATTY ACIDS, 109.8 MG CHOLESTEROL, 141.5 MG SODIUM, 0.2 G TOTAL DIETARY FIBER

muhallabia ice cream

When we first tasted Muhallabia Massawa, everyone just loved it. Then as if with one mind, we all thought—what about ice cream? We experimented, and, sure enough, the cinnamon-cardamom pudding flavorings make a sublime ice cream. So get out your ice cream maker 'n' crank 'er up (or plug it in, perhaps?).

Serve this fragrant ice cream as a fine finishing course to a Middle Eastern or Indian dinner or as a wonderful companion to freshly baked apple pie.

1 ¹/₂ cups whole milk

¹/₄ to ¹/₂ teaspoon ground cinnamon

¹/₂ teaspoon ground cardamom

¹/₂ cup sugar

4 egg yolks

1 cup heavy cream

1 teaspoon pure vanilla extract

Serves 4 to 6
Preparation time: 30 minutes
Ice cream making: 1 to 1¹/₂ hours

Combine the milk, cinnamon, cardamom, and ¹/₄ cup of the sugar in a saucepan and heat until almost boiling. Remove the pan from the heat, cover, and set aside for at least 15 minutes to allow the flavors to develop.

Meanwhile, in a large heat-proof bowl, combine the egg yolks and the remaining ¹/₄ cup of sugar. Using an electric mixer, beat until pale and thick, about 1 minute. Bring the milk mixture back to near boiling, and then slowly pour it into the egg yolks and sugar while beating constantly.

Return the custard to the saucepan and cook on low heat, stirring constantly until thickened, about 8 to 10 minutes. Do not let the custard boil. Remove from the heat and stir in the heavy cream and vanilla.

Allow the custard to cool to room temperature. Make ice cream according to your ice cream maker's directions. Store in a sealed container in the freezer. If your freezer is very cold, let the ice cream sit at room temperature for a few minutes before serving.

PER 4.5-OUNCE SERVING: 291 CALORIES, 5.3 G PROTEIN, 20.9 G FAT, 21.1 G CARBOHYDRATES, 11.5 G SATURATED FATTY ACIDS, 259.6 MG CHOLESTEROL, 49.1 MG SODIUM, 0.1 TOTAL DIETARY FIBER

oya's peaches & pistachios

Our friend and loyal customer Oya Reiger is a wonderful and imaginative cook who made up this quick and refreshing salad of juicy fruit and crunchy nuts. We thank her and add our own bit of orange and lemon zest to it.

This is best made and served in the late summer when peaches and melons are juicy and sweet, but if you make this salad out of season or use frozen fruit, add a little sugar to liven it up.

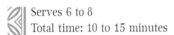 Serves 6 to 8
Total time: 10 to 15 minutes

6 cups peeled, pitted, and sliced
   peaches
8 cups cubed cantaloupe
2 tablespoons fresh lemon juice
1 teaspoon freshly grated lemon peel
2 teaspoons freshly grated orange
   peel
1/4 teaspoon ground cardamom
   (optional)
1 teaspoon sugar (optional)
1 cup shelled unsalted pistachios

In a bowl, toss the peaches and cantaloupe with the lemon juice, lemon peel, and orange peel. Add the cardamom and sugar, if you like. Refrigerate until ready to serve. Stir in the pistachios just before serving.

PER 11.5-OUNCE SERVING: 217 CALORIES, 5.6 G PROTEIN, 9.3 G FAT, 33.1 G CARBOHYDRATES,
1 G SATURATED FATTY ACIDS, 0 MG CHOLESTEROL, 15.6 MG SODIUM, 4.3 G TOTAL DIETARY FIBER

raspberry lemon pudding cake

When they bake, pudding cakes magically separate into a cakey layer and a custardy pudding layer. This old American dessert classic that many of us knew as kids has thankfully re-emerged in recent years. Now we're enjoying a pudding cake renaissance at Moosewood, as our dessert makers regularly invent brand-new versions with different flavors.

This pudding cake is easy to make, light, and deliciously low-fat. If you prefer, blackberries or blueberries will work fine in place of the raspberries. For an elegant presentation, run a paring knife around the outside of the baking cups, invert the cakes onto beautiful plates, and serve topped with fresh berries.

1 tablespoon fresh lemon juice*

2 teaspoons cornstarch

12 ounces fresh or frozen raspberries**

1 cup sugar

3 large eggs, separated

1 cup buttermilk

1 teaspoon freshly grated lemon peel

1/2 teaspoon pure vanilla extract

pinch of salt

1/2 cup unbleached white flour

1/2 teaspoon baking powder

* Before you juice the lemon, grate and reserve a teaspoon of the peel.
** 1 1/2 to 2 cups of fresh raspberries equals 12 ounces.

Serves 6
Preparation time: 20 minutes
Baking time: 40 to 50 minutes

Preheat the oven to 350°. Lightly oil six ovenproof custard cups or six 8-ounce ramekins. Place the cups in a 2-inch-deep baking pan. Begin to heat water to add to the pan just before baking.

In a bowl, combine the lemon juice with the cornstarch. Add the raspberries and 1/2 cup of the sugar and toss lightly. In a separate bowl, with an electric mixer or a whisk, beat the egg whites until stiff. Set aside. In a large bowl, beat the egg yolks and buttermilk with the remaining 1/2 cup of sugar. Beat in the lemon peel, vanilla, salt, flour, and baking powder. Gently stir in the raspberry mixture, then fold in the beaten egg whites.

Spoon the batter evenly into the prepared cups. Pour very hot water into the baking pan until the water reaches about halfway up the sides of the cups. Bake until puffed, firm on top, and golden, 40 to 50 minutes.

Refrigerate and serve chilled.

PER 6-OUNCE SERVING: 263 CALORIES, 6.7 G PROTEIN, 4 G FAT, 51.1 G CARBOHYDRATES, 1.3 G SATURATED FATTY ACIDS, 133.5 MG CHOLESTEROL, 129.4 MG SODIUM, 4.2 G TOTAL DIETARY FIBER

thai black rice pudding

The multi-colored black and brown grains of sweet black rice turn almost purple when cooked. And from the flavor, you would swear that this simple vegan pudding has some sort of berry in it.

You can find sweet black rice at gourmet specialty shops and Asian markets. It's sure to spark conversations at ethnic dinner parties.

1 cup sweet black rice
$^1/_2$ teaspoon salt
$^1/_2$ cup sugar
$3^1/_2$ cups cold water
1 cup coconut milk

Serves 6 to 8
Preparation time: 15 minutes
Simmering time: $1^1/_2$ to $1^3/_4$ hours

Rinse and drain the rice in a sieve. In a medium saucepan with a tight-fitting lid, stir together the rice, salt, sugar, and water and bring to a boil. Stir well, reduce the heat to low, cover, and simmer very gently for $1^1/_2$ hours or longer, until all of the water has been absorbed and the rice is tender.

Stir in the coconut milk and serve immediately or chill and serve cold.

PER 5.5-OUNCE SERVING: 145 CALORIES, 1.8 G PROTEIN, 6.4 G FAT, 21.9 G CARBOHYDRATES, 5.4 G SATURATED FATTY ACIDS, 0 MG CHOLESTEROL, 153.2 MG SODIUM, 0.5 G TOTAL DIETARY FIBER

note *If you have a heat diffuser, it's a good idea to use it for simmering the rice. Then there's less chance of scorching the rice at the end of cooking.*

tropical tapioca

If you haven't eaten tapioca since your grandmother forced a bowl on you years ago, it's time to give it another try. With mangos, strawberries, and coconut milk, it makes a quick, delicious dessert that is also totally vegan. Be adventuresome and try other fresh fruit, such as kiwi, pineapple, bananas, and orange or grapefruit sections.

Serves 6
Preparation time: 30 minutes
Chilling time: 1 hour

½ cup instant tapioca

3 cups vanilla soy milk

½ cup sugar

1¾ cups reduced-fat coconut milk
(14-ounce can)

pinch of ground cinnamon

2 ripe mangos

1 pint fresh strawberries

1 to 2 tablespoons confectioners'
sugar

Combine the tapioca, soy milk, sugar, coconut milk, and cinnamon in a saucepan and let it sit for 15 minutes. This allows the tapioca granules to begin to thicken even before you start to cook.

On medium heat, bring the tapioca mixture to a boil, stirring constantly to prevent lumps and sticking. Lower the heat and cook for 5 minutes. Remove from the heat and let sit for 5 minutes to cool slightly. Pour into individual dessert cups and chill for at least 1 hour.

About 10 to 15 minutes before serving, cube the mangos. Mangos have large pits and the pulp is slippery. A shallow slice from end to end along the two broad, flat sides works best. Score the mango flesh of each slice into cubes and pare them away from the skin. Peel the remaining skin around the pit, then carefully cut the tender pulp away from the pit and dice it. Rinse, stem, and slice the strawberries. In a bowl, combine the mangos and strawberries with the confectioners' sugar to taste, and set aside.

When ready to serve, top each dessert cup with the fruit.

PER 11.5-OUNCE SERVING: 286 CALORIES, 5.1 G PROTEIN, 8.4 G FAT, 51.1 G CARBOHYDRATES, 3.8 G SATURATED FATTY ACIDS, 0 MG CHOLESTEROL, 94.8 MG SODIUM, 3.9 G TOTAL DIETARY FIBER

using leftovers

At Moosewood, we view leftovers not as poor planning but as an opportunity for creative cooking, either as the basic building block or as the crowning touch. Best of all, cooking with leftovers can be a real time-saver. It is not uncommon for a Moosewood cook to have to tell a customer that we can't explain exactly how to make that gumbo they're calling the "best ever," because we threw it together without a recipe. And we did, starting with last night's Jambalaya and leftover Creole Beans, then adding some stock and tomato juice, a splash of lemon juice, and some fresh herbs.

Take leftover roasted vegetables. They make a fabulous omelet filling or, rewarmed, add panache to a plate of scrambled eggs or a quick-sautéed fillet of fish. Add them to tomato sauce and, with no extra effort, pasta that night will be a treat. Roasted vegetables improve any stew and, whole or puréed, give flavorful depth to many soups. Tossed with balsamic or red wine vinegar and topped with a sprinkling of feta, they become an appetizer. This is just the beginning: leftover tangy cucumber and tomato salads can be blended into gazpachos, this noon's rarebit can be tonight's nacho plate. Truly, the examples are endless and we discover new possibilities daily.

At Moosewood, we regularly plan a pasta casserole that combines extra cooked pasta with a steamed or sautéed vegetable (sautéed garlicky greens is a favorite), plus a layer of leftover béchamel or Italian or Greek tomato sauce, and grated cheese. Other times, we layer leftover rice or couscous with roasted eggplant or zucchini, ladle on tomato sauce, and top with grated cheese. We make a casserole moussaka-like by topping it with leftover béchamel sauce whisked together with eggs for a puffy, golden crown.

Perhaps our favorite use of leftovers is transforming them into soups. Almost any stew, whether a curry, mole, or ragoût, is a ready-made template for soup. We cut the stew vegetables into smaller pieces and add stock or water and perhaps a thickener. The ingredients we use to thicken and give body include tomato paste, cooked beans, and grains—a leftover like brown rice or a grain that will cook right in the simmering broth, such as bulghur, couscous, or a tiny pasta. Sometimes the new soup cries for an extra bit of minced garlic and an herb sautéed in a little olive oil. Sometimes it needs a splash of lemon juice, some zest, or a handful of chopped fresh herbs at the end. It can be fun to figure out just what is needed when you're almost there.

Another great base for soup is leftover beans. Chilis, black bean dishes, and lentil or split pea dhals can easily be the foundation for an all-bean soup or can be an ingredient that gives a soup interest or extra flavor. Leftover beans can be added to a pot of steamed or sautéed vegetables along with stock, water, or juice, and voilà, soup! Beans can be puréed with a liquid and herbs or spices for a smooth soup. Puréed beans can thicken a soup.

Day-old potatoes, white or sweet, steamed, boiled, mashed, or roasted, are the most coveted ingredient for puréed and creamy soups. Potatoes puréed with a liquid (stock, milk, cream, soy milk) and sometimes cheese is an almost fail-safe medium for soup. Add sautéed leeks and you have a classic potato-leek soup; chill it and it becomes a vichyssoise. Sometimes we purée sautéed onions, cooked vegetables, and fresh herbs with the potatoes until smooth, and at other times we blend in only a portion so the soup will have texture.

Sauces are also a boon to soups. White sauce, béchamel, or cheese sauce makes a creamy soup more delicious and can be its primary thickener. That leftover salsa or hot sauce may be just what is needed in a Mexican bean soup; leftover tomato sauce for pasta may be a perfect base for a Mediterranean soup or stew. Spicy peanut sauce, with a squeeze of lime and some cilantro, gives an African twist to a simple vegetable soup.

It is probably most satisfying when we can morph one entrée into another. We often serve tostadas at Moosewood, crisp corn tortillas layered high with refried beans, a tomato-chile sauce, grated cheese, and a variety of other condiments. We always plan to have leftovers because the next day our lunch customers will be glad to see the menu board offering chilaquile casserole, a baked and bubbling strata of tortillas, refried beans, chile sauce, and cheese. And it may seem obvious, but any leftover Mexican-style bean dish can also become the filling for a taco, enchilada, or burrito.

Leftover grains are another spark for our creativity. Chilled cooked grains, such as brown rice, white rice, couscous, bulghur, barley, and wheatberries, can be incorporated into pilafs, soups, casseroles, stuffings, puddings, or salads. In *Sundays at Moosewood Restaurant* Bob Love, a longtime Moosewood cook, describes his favorite Philippine breakfast using leftover rice: "fried eggs on garlicky fried rice topped with coarse salt and fresh chilies in white vinegar." For a gentler wakeup in the morning, mix an egg into leftover rice and cook it in a little oil and butter. We've learned that it's best to steam or rewarm grains for salads; the softened grains have a better texture and absorb marinades better. Add diced marinated vegetables (leftover or not), adjust the seasonings, add a fresh herb or two, and the salad is finished.

When you make intentional leftovers—a big pot of rice, extra beans for a stew tomorrow, more-than-enough-for-tonight roasted vegetables—be sure to handle them properly. The most important thing is to cool them down quickly and all the way through, especially rice, beans, and high-protein foods. Quick cooling prevents growth of bacteria and preserves texture and color. Pour out or spread the leftovers into a shallow baking pan and refrigerate until cool, then transfer to a more compact, lidded storage container. If you're cooling down something that can be stirred, put the pot into a sink of cold water and stir it every few minutes, then when it's cool, refrigerate it. When the first meal is over, put the leftovers into the refrigerator as soon as you can; don't let food sit on the table or counter.

going sustainable & growing organic

"In living nature, nothing happens which is
unconnected to the whole."
-Goethe

The technology of growing, harvesting, preserving, handling, and distributing foods is becoming more complex. While global trade has brought us exotic and out-of-season foods from distant places, how these foods are grown and processed remains a mystery to most of us. The joy of being able to eat a peach at any time of the year is tempered by the knowledge that we're producing and consuming in ways that surpass and negate the earth's ability to regenerate.

In the last few years, many food professionals have become involved in an emerging idea called "sustainable cuisine." The main focus of sustainable cuisine is to support agricultural and food distribution methods that help to save and improve our soil and water, reduce reliance on fossil-fuel-based chemicals, develop cause-based rather than symptom-based solutions to agricultural problems, and encourage direct producer-to-consumer links.

One of the key aspects of sustainable cuisine is organic farming, which has one primary goal: to optimize the health and productivity of interdependent communities of soil life, plants, animals, and people. A healthy, nutritionally balanced and microbially active soil results in healthier plants and more nutritious food. Unlike large industrial farms, which use monocropping techniques and large amounts of chemicals, organic farms use methods that minimize air, soil, and water pollution. Using crop rotation, organic matter additions, and careful soil management all contribute to the long-term well-being of the farm and the farmer and, ultimately, each consumer.

To be successful, organic farming has developed new problem-solving and management stategies. Klaas Martens, an organic farmer on 1,100 acres in the Finger Lakes region of New York, explains, "We try to understand the root cause of a problem and then adjust our agronomic practices so we no longer create the conditions for it. This takes a much higher level of management than simply buying a product to spray on the field. But a detailed cost analysis of our farm has shown that organic methods achieve equal or greater yields of equal quality produce at a much lower cost, while conserving soil and water quality."

The National Food Production Act and the National Organic Program (NOP) have taken steps to assure consumers that the organic foods they purchase are produced, processed, and certified within consistent national standards. The labeling requirements apply to raw, fresh products and processed foods that contain organic ingredients. Foods that are sold, labeled, or represented as organic must be produced and processed in accordance with the NOP standards. The rules prohibit the use of most synthetic pesticides on crops, ban antibiotics from meat, and require that dairy cows have access to pasture. Organic farmers cannot use excluded agricultural practices or sewage sludge, and organic processors and distributors are not permitted to use ionizing radiation (irradiation).

So now, you may wonder what the story is on irradiation. Well, it's a process that exposes fruit, vegetables, and other food products, including meat, to large amounts of ionizing radiation. Irradiation extends the shelf life of food and destroys bacteria, insects, fungi, and other pathogens that may cause food-borne illnesses. It also destroys beneficial bacteria and creates new chemicals in food, such as benzene and formaldehyde. Irradiation was first used extensively on wheat and potatoes in the mid-1960s, but today spices are the most commonly irradiated foods. On labels, the radura symbol (a benign-looking circle containing a flower and sun) indicates irradiated products. Labels must also include a statement such as "treated with irradiation."

The use of irradiation has prompted both health and environmental concerns. According to Public Citizen, a consumer advocacy organization, "No studies have been done to show that a long-term diet of irradiated foods is safe." Because irradiation uses radioactive substances, issues include hazardous waste disposal, the dangers of mining the minerals, and the effects of working with the technology in food processing factories. While, at first glance, irradiation appeared to be a boon to the food industry, there's reason to take a closer look and reassess the benefits in light of the hazards and the unknowns.

Learning, sharing information, and making informed decisions are crucial activities, and we're glad that more Americans are becoming aware of the complex aspects of food production and taking part in personally supporting a more sustainable cuisine. Many local and regional "food" groups have cropped up across the country and we applaud these efforts.

Moosewood is a member of Chefs Collaborative,* an association of chefs and food producers that tries to bring together producers and consumers in the United States and works to promote sustainable cuisine by teaching children, supporting local farmers, educating one other, and inspiring consumers to choose locally produced whole foods. Moosewood cook Tony Del Plato has participated in the Chefs Collaborative's adopt-a-school program. In two-hour sessions throughout the school year, he met with groups of elementary school children to cook and to talk about cultures, the environment, and the sources of food. Every little bit helps.

*Chefs Collaborative, 282 Moody Street, Suite 207, Waltham, MA 02453, (781) 736-0635

federal organic standards, 2001

In the autumn of 2000, the USDA approved national standards for the production and labeling of organic foods. Foods that meet these standards and are certified by USDA-accredited agents may bear the "USDA Organic" seal. Genetically engineered foods, irradiated foods, and foods from farms that use sewage sludge may not be labeled "organic." This latest USDA ruling also removes restrictions on truthful claims such as "no drugs or growth hormones used," "free range," or "sustainably harvested."

❦ Products labeled "100 percent organic" must contain only organically produced ingredients (excluding water and salt).

❦ Products labeled "organic" must consist of at least 95 percent organically produced ingredients (excluding water and salt). Any remaining ingredients must consist of nonagricultural substances approved on the National List or non-organically produced agricultural products that are not commercially available in organic form.

❦ Processed products that contain at least 70 percent organic ingredients may be labeled "made with organic ingredients."

❦ Processed products that contain less than 70 percent organic ingredients cannot use the term organic anywhere on the principal display panel, but may identify the specific ingredients that are organically produced on the ingredients statement.

For more information on labeling, call the FDA toll free at 1-888-463-6332 or visit their web site: www.cfsan.fda.gov/label.html. Nongovernmental organizations that provide information on labeling and food safety concerns include:

Center for Food Safety
66 Pennsylvania Ave SE, Suite 302
Washington, DC 20003
(202) 547-9359
www.centerforfoodsafety.org

Organic Consumers Association
6101 Cliff Estate Road
Little Marais, MN 55614
(218) 226-4164
www.purefood.org

a note about GMOs
in the year 2001

In our cookbooks, at our restaurant, and in our home kitchens, we celebrate and love food. We certainly don't want to associate food with danger, but the current controversy concerning genetically modified organisms (GMOs) is important, and we think it needs to be acknowledged.

Biotechnology isn't new. Farmers, gardeners, and scientists have developed the foods we eat today by observing how nature works. Ancient Egyptians used principles of biotechnology when they developed yeast cultures for baking bread and brewing beer. Mayans developed corn from wild grasses. The breeding of seeds for color, size, and flavor, and for increased nutritional qualities and plant yields has been going on for about twelve thousand years.

Today, agricultural chemicals, irradiation, and genetic engineering are all part of biotechnology. The current revolution in biotechnology has set the stage for going beyond natural boundaries by transferring genes from one species to another species with which it could not breed in nature. (Introducing fish genes into tomatoes for frost resistance is an example.) Through genetic engineering, we can change genetic codes to produce food and medicine with desirable traits such as pest and herb resistance, greater yields, and modified nutritional qualities. At first glance, these discoveries and advances appear to be benignly beneficial, but genetic engineering comes with a multitude of challenges. Both the benefits and the risks of genetically modified crops are inconclusive because the crucial studies have not yet been done. The unintended effects of genetic manipulation may pose the most challenging problems.

So, many knowledgeable people are saying that we need to evaluate this new technology before we proceed further. In 2001, the United States still does not require labeling or premarket testing of genetically engineered foods, whereas the European Union enforces strict regulations and refuses to accept genetically modified crops from the United States.

GMOs cannot be recalled. They grow, mutate, and travel. It is too soon to know the unintended outcomes that may develop. People from all walks of life are demanding that we employ a precautionary approach to the development of transgenic products. Critical issues include ownership and patenting of genetic materials, the labeling of GMOs and our "right to know," access to the technology, and the speed of its introduction to the marketplace. Staying informed and understanding the potential long-term, far-reaching effects of GMOs is of paramount importance in the new millennium

herbs are it

Herbs are an integral part of vegetarian cuisine. Pesto and basil, salsa and cilantro, pickles and dill, roasted potatoes and rosemary are inseparable duos. When possible, we at Moosewood use fresh herbs, which provide a fuller, more complex flavor than dried herbs. It's nice to snip fresh herb sprigs for cooking year round. Potted herb plants brighten up a windowsill, terrace, or balcony. Chives, mint, oregano, bay, parsley, rosemary, and thyme do well in pots, but cilantro and dill go to seed quickly. Little-leafed basils are best for smaller pots. Standard basil requires a container at least a foot wide and deep, as does tarragon.

Gardeners with more space can grow enough to store for use later. Herbs add fragrance and visual interest to flower or vegetable gardens. While the plants are growing, it's good to harvest a bit regularly; snipping the tips keeps the plants bushy and compact and encourages growth. If allowed to flower, annuals like basil and cilantro lose flavor and foliage, so pinch off flowering spikes as they appear.

Fresh herbs keep best refrigerated and loosely wrapped in plastic; their leaves should be dry. Bunches of parsley, cilantro, mint, and dill keep well when refrigerated in a small container of water, stems wet, leaves dry. While all herbs can be dried, some taste better frozen, among them basil, cilantro, dill, parsley, and tarragon. Pack stemmed whole leaves in Ziploc bags and freeze. When cooking, break off only as much as you need and return the rest to the freezer. Dried herbs with good flavor retention include mint, oregano, rosemary, savory, sage, and thyme. Store the dried leaves in a closed container in a cool dark spot.

cooking with herbs

- The rule of thumb for converting dried herbs to fresh is to use 3 to 4 times as much fresh as dried for leafy plants like dill and basil and 2 to 3 times as much for resinous herbs, such as rosemary, thyme, and savory.

- The essential oils of the following fresh herbs and herb seeds are released over time and can be added at the beginning of cooking: bay, oregano, rosemary, sage, savory, thyme, caraway, cumin, coriander, dill, fennel, and mustard. Fresh herbs with volatile essential oils lose flavor with exposure to heat and are best added toward the end of cooking; these include basil, chervil, chives, cilantro, dill, marjoram, mint, parsley, and tarragon. For maximum flavor, chop or mince fresh herbs to release the essential oils.

- Dried herbs are more tolerant of heat and can be added early in the cooking process.

- Fresh sprigs from feathery foliaged herbs like dill, chervil, and cilantro make nice garnishes.

- Be judicious in your use of strongly flavored herbs such as oregano and thyme.

guide to ingredients

amaretto ☙ This Italian almond liqueur is made by soaking seventeen herbs and fruits in apricot kernel oil to extract their essences. According to the producers of Amaretto di Saronno, Bernardino Luini was commissioned in Saronno, Italy, to paint a fresco of the Madonna. The talented painter searched for the perfect model and found a beautiful young innkeeper. For the next few months, they worked closely in intimate settings and the girl fell deeply in love. To express her love, she created a sweet, almond-flavored liqueur—the first bottle of di Saronno. It's been used in desserts and as an apéritif ever since.

arborio rice ☙ See *Rice* (page 467).

artichokes ☙ Rich in vitamins and minerals, artichokes are considered a tonic and aphrodisiac by some. Spring is their peak season. The globe artichoke is the most widespread in America, while at least a dozen varieties are popular in Italy. Look for artichokes with bright green, tightly packed leaves. To keep raw artichokes freshest, stem them within an inch of the bottom, set stem end down in shallow water, and refrigerate.

To cook, snap off the small outer petals at the base, slice off the stem and ¹/₂ inch of the top cone of clustered petals, trim any prickly leaf tips with scissors, and rinse well. Boil or steam in flavored water (vinegar and garlic are nice) until the base is tender and a leaf can be easily pulled free.

Eat the artichoke leaf by leaf, dipping in a lemon-butter or other sauce and scraping off the thin layer of flesh with your teeth. The most tender inner leaves can be eaten whole. When you reach the heart, scoop out the fuzzy, bitter, inedible choke down to the firm, tender heart. Now savor eating the delicious heart. Most baby artichokes have not developed a choke and can be completely eaten once peeled down to the yellow inner leaves and cooked until tender. See page 123 for a great recipe.

artichoke hearts ☙ Those succulent, meaty, center bottom parts of artichokes are available marinated, packed in brine, and frozen. At Moosewood, we prefer the ready-to-use, salty, tangy, brine-packed variety. Marinated canned artichoke hearts usually contain oil in the marinade—so they have added fat—and frozen ones are quite bland.

arugula ☙ Originally a staple in southern Italian cooking and harvested wild, arugula has become a standard gourmet addition to salads in both Europe and North America. Also known as *ruchetta* and *rucola*, or "garden rocket," this calcium-packed, nutritious green grows almost any time of year, and within three weeks of planting, the sweet, tender little leaves can be harvested. More mature leaves are peppery and sharp-tasting and add piquancy to salads and soups. With the stems immersed in water, arugula will keep for a few days in the refrigerator.

avocados ☙ This creamy, satisfying fruit of the tropical lauraceous tree is rich in B vitamins and minerals, and most of its fat is monounsaturated. We recommend Hass avocados, a variety with dark green pebbly skin and a smooth yellowish-green interior. A hard avocado will ripen and soften somewhat in 3 to 4 days at room temperature, slower if refrigerated. To cube, slice around the avocado lengthwise, gently twist the halves apart, and remove the pit. Cut the flesh in a criss-cross pattern or in slices right in the skins and scoop out the cubes with a serving spoon.

azuki beans (*aduki, adzuki*) ❦

Small, oval, high-protein, low-fat, burgundy beans that originated in China but are also popular in Japan. They are used in soups, side dishes, teas, and in Japanese sweet red bean paste confections. See page 449 for cooking instructions.

baking powder ❦

The idea for mixing alkalis and acids to produce rising came with the use of wood ash and sour milk to moisten corn cakes in the American colonies. Later came the American invention of baking powder. Modern baking powder is a combination of baking soda, aluminum sulfate, and calcium acid phosphate. Drying agents such as flour or cornstarch are added to absorb moisture and inhibit the release of carbon dioxide during storage, thus increasing shelf life. Nonetheless, an opened and recapped can of baking powder will absorb some atmospheric moisture—it's generally good for 3 to 12 months when stored in a cool, dark place.

When the acids and the alkaline baking soda in baking powder are activated by liquid and/or heat, they release carbon dioxide and the trapped gas causes the dough or batter to rise. To insure that rising isn't exhausted before the batter is in the oven, most of today's baking powders are "double acting": They contain two acids, a fast-acting one that reacts to liquid and a slower-acting one that reacts to heat.

To test your baking powder for activity, dissolve 1 teaspoon in $1/2$ cup of warm water. If the water bubbles vigorously, you're in business. If not, a good substitute is a mixture of 1 part baking soda to 2 parts cream of tartar. Mix only as much as you need, because it doesn't keep. With only one acid (cream of tartar), the mixture is single acting and will produce CO_2 as soon as moistened, so pop the batter into the oven as soon as the wet and dry ingredients are mixed together.

A metallic aftertaste may be evident if the baking powder contains aluminum acid salts. Rumford Baking Powder is one brand that is aluminum-free.

baking soda (*bicarbonate of soda, sodium bicarbonate, sodie saleratus*) ❦

A water-soluble, alkaline powder often used to neutralize or reduce acidity. It's also a main component of baking powder. If a recipe calls for both baking soda and baking powder, the soda's purpose is to mellow an acidic ingredient. Always sift it to remove lumps before adding it to a batter. The right amount will pleasingly deepen the color of cocoa and chocolate during baking, but too much can turn a white cake yellow or negatively affect the aroma and flavor of any baked good. Baking soda can soften the skins of peas and beans, and a pinch added to boiling water will make some green vegetables, like cabbage and broccoli, greener. Baking soda keeps indefinitely.

barley ❦

Cultivated as far back as the Stone Age, barley must be the grandmother of grains. For centuries, it was ground to make bread before the development of more cold- and disease-resistant wheat. Although barley is lower in protein and gluten than wheat, it is low-fat, easily digested, may inhibit cholesterol production, and has a mild, sweet, chewy texture. Products made from barley include barley grits, barley flour, barley extracts, barley grass juice, and barley malt sugar and syrup.

hulled barley ❦ The most nutritious barley available and a good source of protein, calcium, and iron. The outermost protective husk has been removed, but the vitamin-rich endosperm and germ remain intact. It takes $1 1/4$ hours to cook using about a 5:1 ratio of water to barley. One cup of raw hulled barley yields about $3 3/4$ cups cooked.

pearled barley ❦ The protective husk, the endosperm, and the germ have been removed. It is little more than pure starch. It cooks in 50 minutes using a 2:1 ratio of water to barley.

cooking beans

variety	water-bean ratio	cooking time after soaking	cooked quantity of 1 cup dried
Azuki	3:1	$3/4$ to 1 hour	3 cups
Black beans (turtle)	3:1	$1^{1}/_{2}$ hours	3 cups
Black-eyed peas	3:1	$1/2$ hour	$2^{1}/_{2}$ cups
Chickpeas (garbanzos)	4:1	$1^{1}/_{2}$ hours	3 cups
Kidney beans	3:1	1 to $1^{1}/_{2}$ hours	$2^{3}/_{4}$ cups
Lentils, brown	2:1	$1/2$ hour	3 cups
Lentils, red	2:1	15 to 20 minutes	3 cups
Lima beans	3:1	1 hour	3 cups
Mung beans	3:1	$3/4$ hour	3 cups
Pinto beans	3:1	$3/4$ hour	$3^{1}/_{4}$ cups
Soybeans	4:1	2 hours	$2^{3}/_{4}$ cups
Split peas, green	3:1	$3/4$ to 1 hour	$1^{3}/_{4}$ cups
Split peas, yellow	3:1	$1/2$ hour	$2^{1}/_{4}$ cups
White beans (Navy, pea, cannellini)	3:1	$3/4$ to 1 hour	$2^{3}/_{4}$ cups

partially pearled barley ❧ Only part of the endosperm has been removed, so it's nutritionally richer than the completely pearled variety. It usually cooks in about 1 hour.

instant barley ❧ Pearled barley that has been steamed and dried. It cooks in 15 minutes.

beans ❧ One of the oldest cultivated foods, beans have provided satisfying, nutritious food for millennia throughout the world. Most beans contain nearly twice the amount of protein as cereals and, when eaten with other foods—particularly grains—can create a perfect protein. The phytochemicals and isoflavones in beans may help to maintain the health and well-being of the heart and may possibly inhibit the growth of cancer cells. They are an excellent source of fiber, complex carbohydrates, B vitamins, calcium, iron, and zinc.

Look for unbroken dried beans with a deep, vibrant color, which means they are from the current year's crop. The fresher they are, the more quickly and evenly they will cook. Store in airtight containers in a cool, dry, dark place.

Beans must be fully cooked to get the maximum benefits of protein, minerals, and vitamins, and to avoid digestive distress. At Moosewood, we cook dried beans from scratch. Before cooking, sort dried beans to discard stones and shriveled specimens; then soak in plenty of cold water for 6 to 8 hours (overnight works well) and drain. Cooked beans will keep for four or five days in the refrigerator or two to three months in freezer bags in the freezer. When pressed for time, look for Eden, Goya, Randall, Sahadi, or Westbrae brand canned beans without preservatives.

See pages 116 and 460 for more information.

black mustard seeds ✿ To draw out
the nutty flavor of this Indian spice, briefly heat the seeds in a dry skillet and then grind them, or sauté them in a small amount of oil until they begin to make a popping sound and then drain them and add them whole to your dish. Look for them in Indian, Asian, or specialty food stores.

black peppercorns ✿ Grown commercially in Burma, India, Indonesia, Madagascar, and Brazil, peppercorns vary in aroma and pungency depending upon growing conditions. Black pepper adds flavor to dishes, stimulates saliva flow, and aids digestion. For best flavor, grind whole peppercorns just before using.

black turtle beans ✿ These relatives of
kidney beans are actually very deep purple. They are popular in the cuisines of Cuba, Brazil, Mexico, and the southern United States. See page 449 for cooking instructions.

black-eyed peas (cow peas) ✿
Beige with a black scar at the spot where they were attached to the pod. Black-eyed peas originated in Africa around 3000 B.C., and seventeenth-century Spanish and Portuguese explorers introduced them to the Americas. They are generally available dried, frozen, and canned. Dried black-eyed peas, soaked overnight, cook in 1/2 hour. Unsoaked, they must simmer for about an hour. We often substitute black-eyed peas for the harder-to-find pigeon peas and field peas. See page 449 for cooking instructions.

blue cheese ✿ See Cheese (page 452).

bok choy (chinese cabbage, pak choi, bak choi, chard cabbage) ✿ One of the most popular and nutritious
cabbages in China. Both the leaves and the stalks are tasty, and they complement each other: soft and chewy, sweet and slightly bitter. The white crisp stalks grow from a single base and bear broad deep green leaves. Bok choy is packed with calcium and vitamins A and C.

bouillon ✿ The French word for "broth," the
liquid that results from simmering vegetables, herbs, spices, and/or meats. While broths and stocks are made the same way, broths are served as is, whereas stocks are intended to provide the base of a dish.

Vegetable bouillon is available in packages of soft cubes or in jars. Ingredients include dehydrated vegetables, herbs, spices, and proteins and starches from wheat, corn, beans, and potatoes. The salt/sodium content varies considerably and many brands contain artificial ingredients, so check the nutrition labels.

In the past few years, we've seen the emergence of "no-chicken" and "no-beef" broths packaged aseptically and have tried both Imagine and Pacific brands. Although pricey, these mock stocks can help make cooking a soup or stew a breeze. Both brands are fat free and use organic ingredients.

broccoli rabe (rapini, rappi, broccoli de rape) ✿ This small-headed
broccoli is closely related to turnips and has a strong bitter taste. In Italian cooking, it's often mellowed by first sautéing it with olive oil and garlic and then accompanying it with mashed beans or hearty bread, sharp cheese, and wine.

bulghur (bulgur) ✿ Quick-cooking and
nutty-flavored, made from wheatberries that have been steamed or parboiled, dried, and cracked. A staple from the Middle East to Morocco, it is probably

best known in America as the grain in tabouli. Bulghur comes in four grades from fine to extra coarse. Soak it in an equal amount of water for 20 to 30 minutes until tender. At Moosewood, we use medium-grade bulghur and steep it in boiling water for at least 20 minutes.

butter ☙ Its rich flavor, lovely texture, and unparalleled contribution to baked goods gives butter a strong edge over all of its look-alikes and competitors. Studies report that margarines and solid vegetable shortenings all contain transfatty acids formed during hydrogenation that contribute to elevated cholesterol levels and may increase the risk of heart disease and some cancers. So at Moosewood, we use butter. Butter contains vitamin A and is available salted and unsalted. To keep freshest, enclose in the original wrapper and store in the coldest part of the refrigerator for up to 2 weeks. Sealed in a freezer bag, frozen butter can keep for up to 6 months.

buttermilk ☙ Creamy and low-fat or nonfat, this virtual wonder food is made by fermenting 1% or skim milk with a bacterial culture. Its acidic quality inhibits the development of the gluten present in wheat flour and that makes it a natural tenderizer for desserts. Buttermilk has a mildly tangy flavor great for creamy soups, sauces, and baked goods.

cabbages ☙ One of the most hearty, economical vegetables cultivated throughout the world, cabbage comes in many shapes, colors, and textures. Rich in calcium, magnesium, vitamins A and C, and beta carotene, the light and dark leaf crucifer family includes arugula, bok choy, broccoli, broccoli rabe, Brussels sprouts, cauliflower, collards, daikon, kale, kohlrabi, mizuna, mustard greens, red cabbage, turnips, and watercress among others.

See *Arugula* (page 447), *Bok Choy* (page 450), *Broccoli Rabe* (page 450), *Collards* (page 455), *Daikon* (page 456), *Kale* (page 460), *Mizuna* (page 462), *Mustard Greens* (page 463), *Napa Cabbage* (page 463), *Savoy Cabbage* (page 468), and *Turnips* (page 473).

cannellini ☙ Originated in Peru or Mexico 2,000 to 3,000 years ago. Cannellini made their way from the Americas into Italian cuisine as facilely as did tomatoes, corn, zucchini, and peppers. Cannellini vary in size from pea beans to kidney beans and are available dried and canned in most supermarkets. See page 449 for cooking instructions.

capers ☙ The tiny, green buds of a flowering Mediterranean plant. Capers are sharp, piquant, and simply adorable. Processing and importing—not to mention labor-intensive harvesting—drives up their price. They are packaged either in a vinegar-based brine or in sea salt. At Moosewood, we use the brine-packed variety, which is less salty and comes in jars. Rinse capers well before using, use sparingly, and add toward the end of cooking for the best flavor.

caramelized onions ☙ When the sugars in onions are released by cooking, the sweet browned onions that result are called caramelized. To caramelize onions, cook them in oil on medium heat for at least 20 minutes, stirring occasionally, until brown and creamy. Be careful not to scorch, or the sweetness will be lost.

chanterelles ☙ See *Mushrooms* (page 462).

chapati ☙ Common in India and Pakistan, this unleavened flatbread is made from water and finely ground whole wheat flour that is often mixed with unbleached white flour. It is usually baked and flipped once on a hot dry griddle, but sometimes oil or butter is used. *Phulka*, meaning "puffed," is a thicker version of chapati that is cooked for a second time over a flame to puff it up. Chapati are available in the Indian section of many supermarkets.

chard Enjoyed since the fifteenth century in France, red-veined Ruby chard (often called red or rhubarb chard) and green Swiss chard are both relatives of beets. Chard is high in calcium and vitamins A, B, and C. Its leaves and stems can be simmered or sautéed, and small leaves are sometimes used in mesclun salad mixes. Look for fresh leaves with bright tender stems and veins.

chayotes See *Squash* (page 469-470).

cheese Fresh cheeses are soft, young, mild, and occasionally seasoned with black pepper or herbs. Goat's-milk cheese, or *chèvre,* is most often ripened by surface mold, can sometimes be tolerated by people who are lactose intolerant, and requires no pasteurization since goats don't carry the tuberculosis bacteria. Farmer's cheese is a dry white cheese similar in taste to cottage cheese but with no curds. It is pressed into blocks for slicing and is a good choice for crêpe and pastry turnover fillings.

Cheeses that have a white-mold rind, such as Brie and bucheron, are ripened cheeses usually made with cow's milk and have a smooth, buttery texture and flavor. They are most often used as spreads for crackers or bread.

Marbled blue cheeses can be blue- or green-veined depending on the molds introduced during cheesemaking. They come in a wide variety of strengths and textures. The main types include Italian Gorgonzola, Danish blue cheese, English Stilton, French Roquefort, and domestic blue cheese made in Canada and the United States. Most are made with cow's milk except Roquefort which is always from sheep's milk.

Edam is a mild, buttery semi-firm Dutch cheese and is an interesting alternative to Cheddar or Swiss cheese. Feta cheese is a sharp, white, salty cheese made with either goat, sheep, or cow's milk. Most American-made feta is lower in fat than Cheddar, provolone, Swiss, or Muenster. Havarti, named after a farm in Denmark, is a semi-soft, creamy cheese with irregular holes. Mascarpone is a sweet, 75% fat, creamy white cheese—a by-product of making Parmesan in Lombardy, Italy.

Smoked cheeses are infused with a smoky flavor either by exposure to a hickory wood fire, by the addition of smoked salt, or by adding a chemical called "liquid smoke" during cheesemaking. The most readily available smoked cheeses are Cheddar, Gouda, Swiss, and mozzarella. Look for naturally smoked cheeses in natural foods stores and gourmet cheese shops.

Hard cheeses are dry, aged, sharp cheeses that are usually grated and used in small quantities as flavorings or toppings. One of the most common is Parmesan, which is made from skim milk and originated in Parma, Italy. Others include Romano and Pecorino Romano.

chèvre See *Cheese* (above).

chickpeas (*garbanzo beans*) Round beige legumes used whole in Mediterranean soups and stews and puréed in the familiar chickpea spread, hummus. Chickpea flour is often used in Indian and Mediterranean cuisines for making crêpes and pancakes. See page 449 for cooking instructions.

chiles (*hot peppers, chili peppers*) Members of the *Capsicum* family, an enormous variety abounds with new hybrids constantly appearing. The heat of a chile can vary wildly even among chiles of the same type, so taste to determine how many chiles to use and remove the seeds and membrane, which are the hottest parts, if you want to tone down the heat.

Look for chiles with taut smooth skins. Refrigerated in a plastic bag, fresh chiles will keep for about 5 days. Whole chiles can be frozen for up to a year, chopped ones for 6 months.

Chiles we regularly use at Moosewood:

anaheims (*green chiles*) Bright green, slender, long chiles that tend to be mild, adding flavor without a strong kick.

anchos ✿ The biggest though not the hottest chiles around. A type of poblano chile, anchos are dark green to dark purple, juicy, shiny, and heart-shaped like a miniature green bell pepper. They're the most commonly used chiles in Mexico.

arbols✿ Bright red, slim, 3- to 5-inch curved pods. They are similiar in heat and flavor to cayenne and are used in barbeque sauce, curry, and chili. Arbol chiles are often used in the production of hot pepper oil and vinegar.

banana peppers ✿ Pale yellow, short, fat, curved oval chiles, usually quite hot.

guajillos ✿ A medium-hot, red variety of mirasol chiles, which are yellow hot peppers. When dried, the seeds in guajillos rattle when shaken, giving it the nickname "little gourd."

habaneros *(scotch bonnets)* ✿ Crown-shaped yellow, red, or green chiles, often mercilessly hot.

jalapeños ✿ Short, green, oval chiles that vary from not-so-hot to very hot. Sometimes the more mature red jalapeños are available.

serranos ✿ Small, thin, green, sleek, pointed chiles. Often extremely hot, they are *the* chile in Mexico for guacamole and salsas. We always keep these fresh chiles on hand at Moosewood to use as our general all-purpose chile.

thai peppers ✿ Ranging from green to red to reddish-black, Thai peppers are tiny oblong peppers that mean business: very hot to fiery hot.

chinese chili paste (*chili paste with garlic*) ✿ A wonderful condiment to spark up an Asian stir-fry, stew, sauté, or sauce. Supermarkets usually carry a wide variety of chili pastes and most include crushed, fermented chiles, salt, soy oil, and garlic. We've found that the simpler the ingredient list, the better. Look for bottled brands without preservatives. Tightly capped and refrigerated, Chinese chili paste keeps indefinitely.

chipotles in adobo sauce ✿ Chipotles are jalapeño peppers that have been smoked and packed in a fragrant, thick tomato purée called adobo sauce. Different varieties of adobo sauce are traditional in the Philippines, Spain, and Mexico. Most canned chipotle adobo sauces include tomatoes, vinegar, onions, ground chiles, sugar, spices, and herbs. We like La Torre brand canned chipotles in adobo sauce.

chives ✿ The mildest member of the onion family. Chives are a hardy garden plant whose long, thin, hollow green stems can be snipped raw into soups, salads, and dressings, and whose pretty purplish white flowers are very mild, edible, and gorgeous as garnishes. Chives are available in supermarkets fresh, frozen, and freeze-dried.

chocolate ✿ The generic name of the cocoa tree means "food of the gods" and chocolate, which is derived from cocoa tree beans, certainly tastes heavenly to many. In 1502, Columbus captured a canoe laden with cocoa beans and other produce, and, although he saw commercial value in the cargo, he never knew that a drink was made from the "black almonds," as cocoa was first called. The Aztecs saw cocoa as a drink for warriors, while Catholics debated whether it was "a woman's drink" or could be drunk during lent. The Spanish created the word *chocolatl* by combining the Mayan word for hot, *chocol*, and the Nahuatl word for water, *atl*.

The journey from cocoa beans to "chocolate kiss" is awesome. First, cocoa beans are fermented, dried, roasted, hulled, ground, and heated to make a chocolate liquor. Then sugar, vanilla or vanillin, lecithin, and additional cocoa butter are added. (For milk chocolate, milk solids are also added). Next, this mixture is "conched" (kongkt). Conching is a process that simultaneously reheats, mixes, grinds, and stirs the mixture for up to 4 full days and produces chocolate's satiny-smooth texture. For gloss and snap, chocolate is then tempered by more heating, cooling, and reheating. Finally, comes the molding and shaping process.

A chocolate's type and quality depend on the amount of cocoa butter and sugar added, the mixture of cocoa beans, the roasting time, and the conching time. Couverture is a French term used to describe chocolates made with a very high percentage of cocoa butter, which due to their high fat content can make smooth thin coatings that harden well. At Moosewood, we use a Belgian chocolate called Callebaut. European chocolates are available in many supermarkets, usually in the candy aisle rather than in the baking section.

Types of chocolate include the following:

unsweetened chocolate (*baking chocolate, bitter chocolate, cooking chocolate*) ❧

Made with chocolate liquor processed from whole cocoa beans and contains only cocoa solids and cocoa butter. No sugar is added, but vanilla may be included.

sweet chocolate ❧

All dark chocolates that have any amount of sugar added and are made with a minimum of 35% chocolate liquor. Most good-quality sweet chocolates are made with 55% to 70% chocolate liquor. German chocolate is a "sweeter than semi-sweet" dark chocolate developed by Samuel German of Bakers Chocolate Company. Subcategories of sweet chocolate include semi-sweet and bittersweet chocolate. The names describe the sugar content, which decreases from sweet to semi-sweet to bittersweet.

semi-sweet chocolate ❧

Made with chocolate liquor, additional cocoa butter, sugar, vanilla or vanillin, and lecithin. It contains less sugar than sweet chocolate and is available in chips and solid blocks. Most European "semi-sweet" chocolates are called bittersweet and contain less sugar than semi-sweet chocolates made in the United States.

white chocolate ❧

Contains no cocoa solids, so technically it's not true chocolate. White chocolate is made of cocoa butter, sugar, vanilla, milk solids, and lecithin. The richest ones contain a high percentage of cocoa butter and less of other fats such as vegetable oil.

milk chocolate ❧

By law contains at least 10% real chocolate liquor and 12% whole milk. A good milk chocolate may contain up to 40% chocolate liquor.

Chocolate is temperature-sensitive—it melts at 80°—so store it in a cool, dry spot between 50° and 60°. Temperatures below 50° or high humidity cause it to bloom: The cocoa butter rises to the top and streaks the chocolate with white, leaving it edible but unattractive. Because it absorbs odors easily, keep chocolate in a sealed container. Well stored, dark chocolate keeps for years. Milk and white chocolates are more perishable, lasting from 3 to 12 months.

cilantro (*green coriander, spanish parsley, chinese parsley*)

❧ The fresh leaves of the coriander plant. It has a strong, heady, distinctive aroma and flavor. An ancient herb in the carrot family, this hardy annual was originally native to southern Europe and the Middle East. Now cilantro is grown on almost every continent and is the most widely consumed culinary herb in the world.

At Moosewood we've found that cilantro can balance both the flavors of rich ingredients and the heat of chiles. Always rinse it well before using. Fresh cilantro will keep refrigerated for about 4 days with the stems or roots immersed in water and a plastic bag loosely covering the leaves. Look for cilantro in the fresh herb section of the produce department. We don't recommend dried cilantro.

cocoa powder ❧ Used to make both cocoa powder and chocolate, cocoa beans are part cocoa butter (fat) and part cocoa solids (rich in protein and carbohydrates). The first stage involves roasting, grinding, and melting ripe cocoa beans. Then the pressed pods are ground to produce the unsweetened cocoa powder used in baking.

Dutch cocoa has a small amount of alkali added to neutralize cocoa's natural acidity, yielding a mellower, more deeply colored, easy-to-dissolve cocoa. However, the absence of acid can affect leavening, so use Dutch-processed cocoa in baking only when specified or when rising is not an issue.

When working with cocoa, crush lumps before measuring. Cocoa is temperature-, humidity-, and odor-sensitive, so store in a tightly sealed container and keep in a cool, dry place.

coconut ❧ Unsweetened coconut flakes are available in Indian, Caribbean, or Southeast Asian groceries, natural foods stores, and many supermarkets. If you must use the very sweet "sweetened shredded coconut" in the supermarket baking section, reduce another sweetener in the recipe. To toast shredded or flaked coconut, spread it on an unoiled baking sheet and bake at 350° for 2 to 3 minutes, until lightly golden.

Coconut milk is neither the liquid in a fresh coconut nor the sweetened coconut cream in tropical beverages and mixed drinks. Coconut milk is a smooth, thick, rich-flavored liquid made from water and grated coconut that has been puréed and strained. It comes canned in regular and reduced-fat versions and is available free of preservatives and additives. Once opened, it will keep for about 3 days covered and refrigerated. Frozen it will last indefinitely.

For more information about using fresh coconut and making homemade coconut milk, see Moosewood Restaurant Daily Special, page 360.

collards (*collard greens*) ❧ Bluish green, paddle-shaped leaves packed with vitamins, minerals, fiber, and almost as much calcium as milk. Collards readily absorb the flavors of vinegars and spices and are often paired with beans in traditional Southern cuisine.

couscous ❧ The North African name for dishes made in a couscousière—a two-tiered clay or ceramic pot specially designed for steaming couscous over a simmering stew. In Moosewood recipes, couscous refers to the ready-to-cook grain alone, which is available in supermarkets and natural foods stores. Commercial couscous is a pre-cooked semolina milled from durum wheat and cooks in just 10 minutes into a light, fluffy grain. Regular couscous looks like tiny yellow pearls similar to millet, and whole wheat couscous is the same size and shape but with a light brown color and nuttier flavor.

cranberry beans ❧ Also called Roman beans, these medium, oval, creamy white and red speckled beans are used in many traditional Italian soups and dishes.

cremini (*brown italian mushrooms*) ❧ See *Mushrooms* (page 462).

currants ❧ In our recipes, currants refer to dried black grapes native to Greece—their largest exporter—and also grown in California, South Africa, and Australia. Sweet and glistening, small, deep black currants don't fade, even when simmered. The dark color provides a lovely visual accent when used as a garnish on curries, stews, or fruit salads.

Many other types of wild and cultivated berries go by the name of currants, such as the red, white, and black currants in the gooseberry family commonly used for making jellies and preserves and the golden currant of North America. These varieties should not be used in our recipes.

curry ❧ The southern Indian Tamil word *kari*, meaning a spiced sauce with a soupy consistency, is the root for our English word curry, which refers to East Indian dishes flavored with curry spices mixed with yogurt, coconut milk, or other cooking liquids.

curry paste ❧ This Southeast Asian condiment combines curry spices and vegetable oils to create a highly concentrated, savory seasoning. Curry pastes can add spark to dressings, rice salads, sauces, sautés, soups, pilafs, and (of course) curries. Like curry powders, curry pastes have a range of flavors and spiciness. Curry pastes are available in jars at Indian groceries and in the ethnic section of many supermarkets. To make your own, see page 365 of *Moosewood Restaurant Low-Fat Favorites*.

curry powder ❧ A mixture that usually includes ground cumin, coriander, turmeric, cardamom, cayenne, and cinnamon. Nutmeg, fenugreek, cloves, anise or fennel, and black pepper are sometimes added. Supermarket blends are often bland. We recommend shopping in Asian markets for a prepared curry powder you like or experimenting at home to make your own.

For homemade curry powder, toast the seeds just before grinding to mellow the sharp edge of uncooked spices and produce the fullest flavor.

daikon (*japanese radish*) ❧ Resembling a giant white carrot or parsnip and measuring up to a foot or more in length, this impressive-looking radish is crisp, mildly peppery, and good for refreshing the palate and adding zest to a dish. Daikon originated in southern Asia and spread east to Japan and west to Europe. Today, Florida is a major producer of daikon, which is frequently used in Caribbean cooking.

dashi ❧ Often the starting point for Japanese soups, sauces, and rice, dashi is a clear, strained, seaweed broth. Traditional dashis are made by simmering kombu in water, and dried bonito flakes (a mackerel-like ocean fish) or dried shiitake (mushrooms) are often included. Dashi is a wonderful base for miso soup. Most natural foods stores or Asian groceries carry the basic ingredients for making dashi. For a simple dashi recipe, see page 64.

dijon mustard ❧ White wine, spices, and vinegar give a distinctive flavor to this yellowish brown mustard flecked with crushed mustard seeds. Named for a city in east central France.

edible flowers ❧ While flower fragrances are important in confections, it's the visual appeal that's most striking when they're used decoratively in salads, soups, and tarts, and as garnishes. The rose is the most widely used edible flower: its petals are good both fresh and dried. Roses can be crystallized or candied and are used to make jams, conserves, fragrant water, and flavored vinegar. Nasturtiums, calendula, violets, marigolds, dianthus, pansies, and day lilies are other edible flowers that can add pizzazz to salads. Zucchini flowers, apple blossoms, and lilacs are often made into delicate fritters. Before using flowers for food or garnishes, be certain of their identity and be sure they have not been sprayed with pesticides or herbicides. Always soak them gently in cold water to remove dirt and drain well.

endive ❧ See *Frisée* (page 459).

escarole ❧ This mildly bitter, juicy member of the chicory family has dark green, wavy leaves with white sweet-tasting midribs. It's delicious sautéed with garlic and oil or chopped raw and added to soups and stews. Avoid wilted, yellow, or brown-edged bunches. Escarole will keep in a perforated plastic bag for several days in the refrigerator.

extracts ❦ Used most often in baking, these strong flavorings are made by cooking the most flavorful part of a plant in alcohol until a thick, syrupy oleoresin is produced, and then diluting the syrup with alcohol in a ratio of 1:4. Flavorings differ from extracts in that they use glycerin instead of alcohol as a medium. Vanilla, chocolate, orange, lemon, maple, almond, and coconut flavors are all available as pure extracts and pure flavorings, and taste far better than artificial ones.

fava beans (*broad beans*) ❦ Small, immature, fresh favas are a springtime delicacy. Enjoy fresh favas as a snack or add them to sauces and soups. To cook more mature fresh favas, blanch in boiling salted water, drain, rinse with cold water, remove the outer skins, and then cook until tender. Dried favas may be found whole or split, the latter being easier to cook and digest. They are also available canned.

fennel ❦ Fresh fennel bulb, or "Florence fennel," is a curious-looking vegetable with a sweet anise/licorice flavor and crunchy texture. Sometimes labeled anise at markets, fresh fennel has a large, white, edible bulbous bottom with green celery-like stalks topped by feathery fronds. The bulb can be sliced raw into salads, cooked as a side dish, or added to stews, and the fronds make nice garnishes. The tough stalks should be discarded.

Fennel seeds share the licorice flavor and fragrance of fresh fennel bulbs, but the seeds are the product of a different plant. Fennel seeds come from a native Mediterranean member of the parsley family, a widely cultivated aromatic perennial with umbrella-like flowers. Toasted and ground just before use, fennel seeds add depth and complexity to dishes—sometimes making them taste surprisingly like meat-based versions.

Wild fennel is bitter, has no anise flavor, and is generally not used for culinary purposes.

feta ❦ See *Cheese* (page 452).

filo (*phyllo*) ❦ *Yufka* is the modern Turkish word for a single sheet of filo, a paper-thin dough that originated in Turkey. Our English word is derived from the Greek word *phyllo* meaning "leaf." The dough, widely available packaged, is used to make strudels and pastries. After opening a package of filo, remove only as much as you plan to use and work quickly, because it dries out rapidly when exposed to air. Look for it in the frozen or refrigerated sections of the supermarket.

fish ❦ Versatile and widely available, fish can make a substantial and delicious meal with the simplest preparation and provide a lean source of protein and essential oils. Choose fish with a sweet, mild odor or a fresh briny aroma and avoid anything that smells strong or offensive. The flesh should be firm, unblemished, elastic, moist, and translucent. It's important not to overcook fish: a good rule of thumb is to cook 10 minutes for each inch of thickness.

Cod, scrod (young cod), flounder, haddock, ocean perch, and whiting are all tender lean sea fish with mild flavors. Halibut, pollock, red snapper, sea bass, turbot, and monkfish (poor man's lobster) are lean sea fish with firm white flesh. Mahimahi found in semitropical waters on both coasts of the United States is a lean sea fish with a strong meaty flavor.

Oil-rich sea fish include bluefish, herring, mackerel, mako, pompano, smelt, swordfish, tuna, and salmon. In general, these fish have a stonger flavor than the lean sea fish. Many are sold as steaks and are excellent for grilling.

Freshwater fish include carp, catfish, perch, striped bass, sturgeon, trout, whitefish, and tilapia. Sturgeon, tilapia, trout, and catfish (sometimes called "tenderloin trout"), are farm-raised in the United States.

Shellfish, which are quick-cooking but take more preparation if not already cleaned and deveined, include clams, mussels, several varieties of scallops, and shrimp. The shells can be used to make fish stock for soups or stews.

fish sauce (*nam pla, nuoc mam, tuk trey*) ❦

A pungent condiment made from salted small fish fermented in vats of brine. The briny liquid is removed, dried in the sun, and then bottled. An essential part of Southeast Asian cooking and popular throughout Asia and the Pacific, fish sauce is used in sauces, stir-fries, and soups and liberally added to foods at the table. In Thailand and Vietnam, this high-protein, vitamin B-filled sauce plays a role similar to soy sauce and tamari in China and Japan. It does not require refrigeration.

five-spice powder ❦

This spicy Chinese seasoning made of ground Szechuan peppercorns, star anise, fennel, cumin, and cloves is available in most Asian markets and adds a distinctive flavor to Asian dishes and marinades.

flour ❦

Technically, any ground cereal, such as wheat, oats, barley, rye, rice, and corn, is called flour, but generally speaking in America and Europe, the term applies to ground or milled wheat. Varieties include whole grain, white, bleached, unbleached, pastry, bread, and all-purpose—a combination of pastry and bread flours. We prefer unbleached flours in which the endosperm is preserved. Whole wheat varieties are higher in fiber, vitamins, and minerals. In India and other parts of the world, beans such as chickpeas are often ground into flours for added texture and flavor.

Flours vary in fineness and gluten according to the type of wheat from which they are made, but all flours should be stored in a cool, dry location in airtight containers. Whole wheat pastry flours should be refrigerated. Flours kept in paper bags or the original sack can

absorb odors from other foods. Here is the lowdown on various types of flour and their uses:

all-purpose flour ❦ Most recipes in our books can be made with this multipurpose blend of hard and soft wheats—especially good for making quick breads, biscuits, cakes, and cookies. It's by far the most versatile and widely available wheat flour and has a protein content ranging from 8 to 12 percent. Unbleached flour is naturally aged and matured without the use of chemical bleaching agents like chlorine dioxide. At Moosewood, we use unbleached flour without preservatives or bromates. When substituting, use 1 cup minus 1 1/2 tablespoons of all-purpose flour per cup of pastry flour.

bread flour ❦ Bread flour is milled from hard wheat, contains the most gluten, and produces the most elastic doughs. It's highest in protein of all the types of flour (at least 12 percent) and should be avoided in dessert baking or any time that a dough with a high gluten content is undesirable.

cake flour ❦ A low-protein, soft wheat flour that is heavily chlorinated or bleached to inhibit its ability to form gluten with liquids. Because it bonds more readily with fats and absorbs liquids faster than other flours, it produces especially light, delicate cakes. At Moosewood, we don't use cake flour because we believe the fewer additives in our food, the better. To approximate cake flour, replace 2 tablespoons of each cup of bleached all-purpose flour with 2 tablespoons of cornstarch.

pastry flour ❦ Milled from soft wheat with a soft, fine texture and very little gluten. Its lower protein content makes a tender crumb ideal for pie and tart doughs, biscuits, muffins, and some cookies and cakes. Cakes made with pastry flour may have less "rise" and cookies tend to be flatter and crisper. When substituting, use 1 cup plus 2 tablespoons of pastry flour for each cup of all-purpose.

self-rising flour ☙ This is flour, common in the southern U.S., contains baking powder and salt. It should not be used in place of all-purpose flour, since the leavening incorporated in it may wreak havoc with the recipe.

whole wheat flour ☙ Contains all of the nutrients in wheat, including fiber, vitamins and minerals. The fat content of wheat germ shortens the shelf life of whole wheat flour, so store it in the refrigerator.

frisée (*endive, curly chicory, curly endive*) ☙ A delicate bitter salad

green that has frilly individual leaves and a crisp texture. Its thin serrated leaves in various shades of lime green can visually enliven a salad and its sharp flavor complements sweeter mixed greens. Frisée will keep refrigerated for about 4 days in a loosely closed plastic bag. Rinse well just before using.

garam masala ☙ Like curry powders, garam masala is a mixture of roasted, ground spices that can vary according to taste and purpose. Here's one of our favorite recipes: 6 inches of crushed cinnamon stick, $1/4$ cup of coriander seeds, 2 tablespoons of cumin seeds, 2 tablespoons of black peppercorns, 1 tablespoon of cardamom seeds, $1^1/2$ teaspoons of whole cloves, and $1^1/2$ teaspoons of fennel seeds. Heat all of the spices on an unoiled baking tray at 200° for $1/2$ hour; cool and grind. Experiment with proportions to find the mix you like best. Other spices sometimes included are nutmeg, mace, and saffron. Convenient blends are often available in Asian markets or in the herb and spice aisle or the specialty foods section of the supermarket. Store in a tightly sealed container in a cool, dark place and use within 3 months for best results.

ginger root ☙ The bronze-colored, knobby, underground branching stem of a perennial rhizome. Its spicy hotness with sweet undertones is milder and distinct from that of chiles. Healthy fresh ginger

has a smooth, taut, tan skin and golden juicy flesh. Peeling is necessary only if the skin is blemished or doesn't grate easily. Ginger root can be finely grated or thinly sliced into rounds for use in Asian, African, and Caribbean dishes. Look for it in the fresh produce section of the market. Fresh ginger root keeps for several weeks refrigerated and for months in the freezer.

greens ☙ This term refers both to raw salad greens and to leafy greens that are usually cooked. Grouping greens into raw and cooked categories, however, is not without quite a bit of overlap. Some salad greens are delicious steamed or sautéed, or added to or blended into soup. Likewise, a good many cooking greens, especially when young and tender, can make a nutritious tasty addition to salads.

Popular salad greens include Boston lettuce, spinach, Belgian endive, mesclun, looseleaf lettuces, radicchio, and arugula (page 447). Cooked greens include beet and turnip greens, chard (page 452), collards (page 455), escarole (page 456), frisée (page 459), kale (page 460), mustard greens (page 463), broccoli rabe (page 450), bok choy (page 450), and watercress.

grits ☙ A popular staple of southern United States cuisine. Yellow and white grits have similar sweetness, flavor, and nutritional value. Commercial grits are made from dried corn with the germ removed and are available in instant, quick-cooking, and regular varieties. We recommend using the quick-cooking or regular grits, which can be found in the cereal section of most supermarkets. Stone-ground grits are dried whole kernels of white or yellow corn crushed between millstones: they are delicious but take longer to cook than commercial regular grits. Stored in the freezer in a well-sealed container, grits will keep for several months. For more about grits, see page 151.

havarti ☙ See *Cheese* (page 452).

herbs ❦ See page 446 for information.

hijiki *(hiziki)* ❦ See *Seaweed* (page 468).

hoisin sauce ❦ Traditionally used in Mu Shu dishes, this sweet Chinese condiment is spread on thin pancakes that are filled with stir-fried vegetables and rolled. Hoisin sauce is a deep chocolate-colored brown purée with a smooth thick texture. It contains soybeans, sugar, vinegar, and spices.

hominy ❦ Made by soaking dried corn kernels in lye wood ash, a process that removes the germ layer and turns the kernel creamy white. Although vitamins are lost, the lye-soaking process enhances the availability of the corn's protein and niacin. Hominy has a firm, smooth, chewy texture and distinctive taste. Whole hominy is in the canned vegetable section of most supermarkets. Look for brands without preservatives or other additives.

horseradish ❦ A pungent condiment popular in Russian, German, and Scandinavian cuisines, a perfect foil for creamy sauces and seafood chowders, and a good source of iron and potassium. Most supermarkets carry jars of grated horseradish mixed with vinegar and salt, either sweetened and colored with beet juice or plain. Freshly grated horseradish root makes an excellent aromatic garnish.

jicama ❦ This clean-tasting, mildly sweet tuber from Mexico and the Amazon has a rather spherical shape and coarse brownish skin. Its crunchy, translucent white flesh is high in potassium, low in sodium, good raw or cooked, and can be combined with fruit, vegetables, or seafood. Jicama can vary in weight from 1/2 to 6 pounds! Thin-skinned jicamas are the most tender and tasty. Store whole jicama unwrapped in a dry spot in the refrigerator. Once cut, it will keep in plastic for about a week.

kale ❦ One of recorded history's oldest vegetables. An exceptionally nutritious food, it's a rich source of fiber and is loaded with vitamins A and C, thiamine, iron, and calcium. Young leaves are tender enough for a raw salad, but most often kale is served cooked. The bluish green, frilly-edged leaves are at their sweetest after the first frost. Kale will keep in the refrigerator for at least a week.

To cook kale, hold each leaf by the stem and run your other hand down the rib to strip off the leaf, chop into bite-sized pieces, and steam or sauté until just tender. One pound of raw kale yields 4 cups cooked.

kombu ❦ See *Seaweed* (page 468).

leeks ❦ A mild relative of the onion and garlic family. They were once a food of the Roman aristocracy and today they're the national vegetable of Wales. Leeks have thick stalks with wide overlapping leaves and resemble giant scallions. Their subtle flavor makes them a renowned delicacy celebrated in many cultures. The Scottish make Cockaleekie soup which contains leeks and chicken. In China, the heart of the leek is used in a popular condiment for Beijing pancakes. And, of course, there's the famous French potato-leek soup, vichyssoise.

To prepare leeks, cut off the root end and the tough part of the leaves and discard. Slice vertically down the center of the bulb, separate its layers, and submerge in water, rinsing well to remove sand and grit.

legumes ❦ A French word for "vegetables." The English term "legume" replaced the older word for beans, *pulse*, in the seventeenth century. Among nutritionists, legumes include beans, lentils, peas, and peanuts. Among botanists, a legume is a fruit that splits into two halves. See *Beans* (page 449).

lemongrass stalks ☙ Amazingly aromatic round reeds with a lemony flavor. They can grow up to 2 feet high and range in color from pale yellowish green to green-gray. To use lemongrass, cut off the tough root end, peel the thick outer layers, and mince the tender core. Lemongrass can be eaten raw, but we usually sauté or simmer it. The tough exterior layers can be used in stock: One stalk of outer leaves and tough stems will flavor about a quart of water. Lemongrass is sold in Asian markets and many supermarkets, and is easy to grow. Although tropical, it will grow in moderate climates, and we have successfully harvested it even with our short upstate New York summers.

lentils ☙ Second only to soybeans in protein content, lentils are quick-cooking, sulphur-free legumes that contain calcium, magnesium, sodium, potassium, and other nutrients. They are a staple in Europe, the Middle East, the Mediterranean, and India. Varieties include red, brown, and French lentils. Red lentils are available whole or split, cook faster when split, and transform into a gorgeous golden purée when cooked. The familiar brown lentils maintain their color and must simmer for 30 to 40 minutes. French lentils are small and stay firm and nutty when cooked. Lentils can be the basis for soups, stews, side dishes, and salads, and they make flavorful crunchy sprouts. In Italian culture, a bowl of lentil soup on New Year's Eve brings good luck for the coming year.

mangos ☙ Originated in Southeast Asia and the tropics. A Vedic legend has it that the mango tree sprang from the ashes of a golden lotus and when a ripe fruit fell to the ground, a king's long lost wife stepped out from it. Mangos were introduced into the Americas in the nineteenth century.

A ripe mango should have a distinct aroma at the stem end, a smooth surface without soft or deflated spots, and apricot colored flesh that's sweet and smooth. Mangos that are odorless or winy are respectively underripe or overripe. A mango has a large, flat central pit that can occupy almost a third of the fruit. To cube, cut the mango lengthwise into two halves, as close to the pit as possible. Score the fruit of each mango half just down to the peel in a crosshatch pattern. Then bend each mango half inside out and slice off the cubes.

marsala ☙ A sweet blended wine from the town of Marsala in the hills of Sicily. To help maintain a consistent flavor, the kegs of wine are stacked so when some is drawn from the bottom keg, the keg above drains into the lower one. At Moosewood, we use marsala to sweeten desserts, sauces, and stews.

Marsala is the setting for Shakespeare's play Much Ado About Nothing. *During the American prohibition, marsala was disguised in medicine bottles because it could pass for cough syrup in appearance.*

mascarpone ☙ See *Cheese* (page 452).

milk ☙ In most cases, whatever milk you have on hand will suffice for our recipes. At Moosewood, we mostly use 2% milk, which has a texture and flavor closer to whole milk than either 1% or skim, but is still considerably lower in fat than whole milk.

Evaporated milk is a canned milk with the moisture content reduced by 60%. Processing slightly caramelizes the natural milk sugar, which produces a somewhat sweet flavor. Skimmed evaporated milk adds a rich, velvety creaminess to dishes without the butterfat. Condensed milk is a highly sweetened, concentrated milk that is also available skimmed.

mirin ☙ This Japanese rice cooking wine has a lovely sweet flavor used to season marinades, sauces, dressings, and glazes. Both hon-mirin (brewed from sake, sweet rice, and rice malt) and aji-mirin (a wine with salt, fructose, and corn syrup) are widely available. If you're caught without mirin, use a mixture of ⅔ cup of dry sherry and ⅓ cup of sugar instead. Find mirin in Asian groceries and the ethnic section of supermarkets. Store in a cool, dry place.

miso ❀ A staple of Japanese cuisine, miso has a wonderful, complex flavor and can give dressings, sauces, stews, and marinades a boost in both taste and nutrition. Made from fermented soybeans, miso types vary greatly in intensity and flavor depending on the grains added to the soybeans and the length of the aging process. Miso is cholesterol-free, low in saturated fat, high in protein, and full of beneficial digestive enzymes. Three basic misos are aged hatcho miso, which is dark and rich; savory dark red barley miso; and amber rice miso, which is more delicate and slightly sweet. All of them make an almost-instant invigorating soup using just water for the broth. It's the soothing restorative "chicken broth" for vegetarians.

mizuna ❀ A mild-tasting Japanese green with white stems and green feathery foliage. When young, this member of the mustard family has a mild bite and is often included in mesclun and other baby green mixes. Mizuna is easy and gratifying to grow: The greens re-grow after snipping and, therefore, can be harvested all season from a single planting.

molasses ❀ Made from sugarcane. Providing sweetness, rich flavor, B vitamins, and iron, it adds moisture to baked goods for better keeping. We use unsulphured molasses because its flavor is assertive without being overpowering. Blackstrap molasses is so strong that it can overwhelm a dish, and sulphured molasses retains unpleasant sulphur odors.

morels ❀ See *Mushrooms* (page 462).

mung beans ❀ These olive-green, bead-like beans are familiar to most Westerners as sprouts, but East Asians are more familiar with them made into cellophane noodles and smooth sweet fillings for pastries. Indians know split mung beans as the staple *moong dhal.* See page 449 for cooking instructions.

mushrooms ❀ Available in all shapes and sizes, both fresh and dried, cultivated and wild. With fresh mushrooms, look for firm, relatively unblemished fungi that are dry to the touch. For best results, store them unwashed in the refrigerator in a paper bag—never in plastic. Store dried mushrooms in a well-sealed glass jar.

button mushrooms (*common, domestic, moonlight*) ❀ The common variety always available in supermarkets and found most often in 8- and 12-ounce containers or with the bulk vegetables. They are white and mostly bite-sized; larger ones make great stuffed hors d'oeuvres.

chanterelles ❀ Most often golden to orange in color, with a trumpet shape and delicate flavor. They are firm and take longer than button mushrooms to release their juices when cooked. They are available seasonally in some supermarkets and are also harvested wild by mushroom "experts."

cremini *(crimini)* ❀ The brown and tan Italian relatives of button mushrooms. While smaller ones hold their shape when cooked whole, more mature larger ones produce a darker juice and fuller flavor. They are sometimes labeled either Baby Portabellos or Baby Bellos.

morels ❀ A sweet, spicy, and nutty variety of wild mushrooms that can be used either fresh or dried. Remove and discard their tough stems before using, and soak dried morels for 15 minutes in water to cover before cooking.

oyster mushrooms ✿ Grown on tree stumps in clusters of cream, gray, or light brown with caps shaped like shells. They are chewy with a flavor somewhat reminiscent of the sea. We especially like them grilled or stir-fried.

porcini ✿ Fleshy imported Italian mushrooms with a rich, woodsy flavor. They can be expensive, but a little goes a long way. Most often, you will find them dried. Soak them in warm water for about 30 minutes before cooking and use the strained soaking liquid for stock.

portabellos ✿ Brown to taupe with almost black gills. Their large size (up to 6 inches across) makes them easy to spot. They are all the rage grilled, roasted, or stuffed and are readily available fresh in most supermarket produce sections.

shiitake ✿ The name comes from the Japanese beech tree or *shii* on which they most commonly grow. Asians value shiitake as health stimulants. They are brown, fleshy mushrooms with woody stems that should be removed before eating the chewy, smoky-flavored caps. They are always eaten cooked, never raw, and fresh ones are often dried for storage. Choose fresh shiitake that are firm, aromatic, and dry but not leathery. Dried shiitake should be soaked in boiling water for at least 20 minutes before sautéing or adding to dishes. Both fresh and dried are available in the United States, although fresh ones can be more difficult to find.

straw mushrooms ✿ Grown in beds of rice straw or husks—thus, their name. They are cone-shaped, beige to brown in color, meaty textured, and mildly flavored. They are available canned or dried.

tree ears ✿ Sometimes called wood ears, these smooth mushrooms with brown caps are mild and crunchy and available dried in packages in Chinese and Southeast Asian groceries.

wild mushrooms ✿ Should be foraged only by experts because most species have poisonous look-alikes. Fortunately, the wild mushroom selection is quite good in many supermarkets. Most of what are called "wild" mushrooms are actually cultivated exotics. Some varieties are rarer and pricier than others but, in general, wild mushrooms are more flavorful than the ordinary white ones.

mustard greens ✿ A spicy, mustardy
green terrific for flavoring and good as a companion to milder greens such as collards or spinach. They are commonly used in Southern cooking and in many parts of Africa, India, and China. Young red mustard greens are often included in mixes of mesclun or baby greens. Wrapped in a damp towel in plastic in the refrigerator, they will keep for about 3 days.

napa cabbage ✿ Crinkly, soft, elongated
leaves that soften quickly for stuffed cabbage. Napa has a mild sweet taste, good for slaws and stir-frys. Look for light green, crisp, tightly packed leaves. Place in a closed plastic bag and store in the refrigerator crisper.

navy beans ✿ This small white bean has
many nicknames: Boston bean, pea bean, white pea bean, haricot. The name "Navy bean" comes from the frequency with which it was served to sailors on ships. Navy beans are perfect for baked beans, soups, and stews and are easily puréed for dips. See page 449 for cooking instructions.

neufchâtel ✿ Here in the United States,
Neufchâtel refers to a low-fat cream cheese widely available in supermarket dairy cases. It's an excellent alternative to full-fat cream cheese. Although the name derives from the place in France where the original French Neufchâtel has been made since the Middle Ages, our low-fat Neufchâtel in America is quite different from the French Neufchâtel.

nori ❦ See *Seaweed* (page 468).

oats ❦ One of the world's most often eaten hot cereal breakfasts. Oats can add flavor and texture to baked goods, as well as holding moisture for good keeping quality. They can also be used as a hidden but effective thickener in soups and stews. Oats are available in three grades: steel-cut, regular, and quick-cooking. Avoid instant oats, which are not worth cooking. Unless otherwise stated, our recipes use regular rolled oats. See pages 30–37 for more information and delicious recipes

oils ❦ A form of liquid fat used to prevent sticking and to add body, flavor, and a rich smoothness to foods. Store oils away from light and use while fresh. Avoid using old, rancid specimens. Olive oil and canola oil are high in monounsaturated fat and low in saturated fat, so good-quality brands of these oils are recommended as the healthiest oils for regular consumption. Canola oil has a very mild flavor and is pressed from the seeds of the rape plant, which is in the *Brassica* family.

Peanut oil is particularly valued for deep-frying and sautéing because it does not scorch until heated above 500°. Sesame oils come in two main varieties, light and dark. Light sesame oil has a mild flavor, is made with unroasted sesame seeds, and is good for dressings and sautéing. Dark sesame oil, pressed from roasted sesame seeds, is used almost exclusively as a rich aromatic flavoring in dressings, sauces, and soups.

A sprinkling of hazelnut or pumpkin seed oil will will nicely flavor a salad dressing, soup, condiment, or dessert and almond and walnut oils are delicious in salads, baked goods, and infused with herbs. Asian chili oils are specialty flavoring oils infused with dried chiles or crushed pepper flakes and will add fire and seasoning to any dish.

olives ❦ Cultivated in the Mediterranean since 3000 B.C., olives were brought to the Americas by the Spanish. They are cured to remove their natural bitterness and then most types are fermented in salt or brine. See pages 213–215 for more information and recipes. Here are a few varieties we keep on hand:

california ripe olives ❦ These black olives are often pitted and canned and have a mild flavor that's less tangy than most olives because they aren't fermented in salt or brine before canning.

green spanish olives ❦ Picked before they're ripe, then cured and preserved in brine. Available jarred, both pitted and unpitted, in most supermarkets, they have a bright tangy flavor.

kalamata olives (*calamata*) ❦ Delicious, meaty, purplish-black olives marinated in wine vinegar and then packed in olive oil and vinegar. Look for them in specialty and Greek groceries and the delicatessen section of well-stocked supermarkets.

onions ❦ In the wild, onions have been natives of Southeast Asia for 4,000 years. Now there are hundreds of varieties thriving in a wide spectrum of conditions. Cultivated onions grown in warm climates tend to be mild and perishable, while cold-climate onions are stronger flavored and better keepers. Choose onions that are firm near the stem and store them in a well-ventilated, cool, dark place. Below we discuss the most common varieties of onions. For other onion relatives, see *Chives* (page 453) and *Leeks* (page 460).

pearl onions ❦ Very small, many-layered onions harvested in the late summer and fall. When they are larger than $1^1/_2$ inches across they are sometimes referred to as "boiling onions." Look for them year round in the frozen vegetable section of supermarkets or in season in the produce section. Fresh pearl onions should be hard with papery white skin. To peel, blanch for about 15 seconds in boiling water, cut off the root end, and slip off the skin.

red onions ☙ These add color and crunch when used raw in salads, and have a milder, sweeter flavor than Spanish or Bermuda onions. They are usually smaller in size than large Spanish onions and release water when cooked. The freshest red onions are available from late summer to early winter.

shallots (*welsh onions*) ☙ A head composed of cloves wrapped in a reddish-brown papery skin. They are eaten cooked and raw and have a delicate flavor. Store in a well-ventilated, cool, dark place.

spanish onions ☙ These large round onions with light amber, papery skin are delicious and juicy either raw or cooked. Most supermarkets carry them year round, but the best-quality ones are available in autumn and winter.

vidalia onions ☙ Correctly pronounced (vi-dah-lyuh) with a long "i" as in "high," this juicy sweet onion is named for a town in the state of Georgia. Vidalias are sweet because they are harvested when slightly underripe, before they develop the strong taste and bite of other onions. Vidalias are in season during May and June.

parchment paper ☙ A thin, translucent, dry paper used as a pan liner to prevent sticking and burning when baking delicate sweet or savory pastries. Parchment paper can be re-used when baking multiple batches. Purchase it at cooking supply stores and in the cooking supply or baking section of many supermarkets.

parsnips ☙ Most parsnips look like slender pale carrots; round "turnip" parsnips also exist. They are a beige-skinned winter root vegetable with a creamy white fibrous interior that's sweet and mild. Choose smooth, firm parsnips during their peak season from December through March. Peel before chopping and adding to soups and stews.

pasta ☙ Many brands of domestic and imported pastas line the shelves of markets today. Because pasta is made with a variety of flours and in every shape imaginable, the discriminating cook can find exactly the pasta that suits the dish. In general, small pastas work best in soups and larger ones in main dishes or salads. Use thin, long strands of pasta for smooth sauces and spirals or shells for chunkier vegetable sauces. Always cook in lots of boiling water until just tender or *al dente.*

Some familiar pasta shapes and descriptive names are conchiglie (conch shells), farfalle (bowties or butterflies), fettuccine (small ribbons), linguine (small tongues), manicotti (small muffs), orecchiette (little ears), rotini (corkscrews), spaghetti (strings), trenette (square-cut strings), tubetti and tubettini (small and tiny tubes), and vermicelli (little worms).

See page 248 for additional information.

peanut butter ☙ Our peanut butter of choice is made from just peanuts with no addition of hydrogenated fats, sweeteners, or stabilizers.

pecorino romano cheese ☙ Produced mostly in Sardinia from November to June, a hard grating cheese made from sheep's milk, enjoyed since the early Roman Empire. It has a fragrant aroma and a slightly gamey, piquant flavor. Nutritionally, it is high in protein, vitamins A and D, and calcium and phosphorous. In $\frac{1}{4}$ ounce of cheese, there are 25 calories, 2 grams of fat (1 gram saturated), 5 milligrams of cholesterol, and 140 milligrams of sodium. Wrap in heavy paper and store in the lower part of the refrigerator.

pesto ❦ A sumptuous paste usually made with olive oil, basil, nuts, garlic, and aged cheese. It's a condiment to add to soups (such as pistou), to wake up steamed vegetables and seafood, to sauce hot pastas, and to spread on crackers or toast.

pine nuts (*pignoli*) ❦ The edible seeds of certain pine trees that grow in Central America, the Mediterranean, and the southwestern United States. These highly perishable nuts are small ecru ovals with a sweet flavor and creamy texture. Store them in a sealed container in the refrigerator for up to 2 months. For the best flavor when used as a garnish, dry roast them in a skillet or 350° oven for 3 to 5 minutes until golden-brown.

pinto beans ❦ In Spanish, pinto means "spirited." This mottled beige and brown bean is used in chilis, refried beans, and southwestern dishes. See page 449 for cooking instructions.

polenta ❦ A cornmeal mush or pudding made most simply with yellow cornmeal, water, and salt. Serve polenta under saucy stews and sautés or as a hot breakfast cereal, or use it to make "cutlets" or a crust for savory pies. See pages 280–285 for additional information and recipes.

porcini ❦ See *Mushrooms* (page 462).

portabellos ❦ See *Mushrooms* (page 462).

potatoes ❦ In many sizes and colors, potatoes range from starchy to waxy. Always store them in a dark, cool location between 35° and 50°. Exposure to light causes potatoes to turn green and green sections, eyes, and sprouts all have high concentrations of a toxic substance that can cause illness if eaten in large quantity. So remove any green sections, eyes, or sprouts before cooking. Storing an apple with the potatoes helps maintain their flavor and texture by preventing them from sprouting.

Look for these outstanding potatoes at your local farmers' market or well-stocked produce section:

caribe ❦ This attractive potato with very white flesh and contrasting violet skin has a high starch content and makes exceptionally fluffy mashed potatoes.

new potatoes ❦ Young tubers harvested before maturity and usually available from early spring through summer. Prized for their delicate flavor and texture, they're sweeter and moister than their older siblings. Look for thin, somewhat fragile skins; sometimes merely small potatoes are peddled as new.

peruvian purple ❦ A fingerling type of blue potato with deep purple skin and flesh. When mashed, they produce a pretty pastel violet dish. When boiling blue potatoes, add 1 to 2 tablespoons of vinegar to the water to keep the color vivid.

rose gold ❦ Pale red skin and yellow flesh, combining the best of red-skinned and golden potatoes. They're firm enough for steaming and creamy enough to bake well.

ruby crescent ❦ With thin pink skin, flavorful yellow flesh, and a firm yet creamy texture, this is one of the best of the fingerlings. Others include Russian Banana, French Fingerling, and Ratte. All are superb roasted or boiled.

yellow finn ❦ A good all-purpose variety with pale yellow skin and deeper yellow flesh, moist and sweeter than most potatoes.

yukon gold ❦ This specialty variety with yellow skin and flesh made a big hit and crossed over from gourmet markets to supermarkets. It has an excellent, buttery texture and flavor for mashed, boiled, or salad potatoes.

quinoa (*keen-wah*) ❧ Indigenous to South America and first cultivated by the Incas, this easily digestible grain is mild, slightly crunchy, nutty-flavored, and rich in vitamins, minerals, and protein. It cooks in just 15 minutes and contains all eight essential amino acids. A little goes a long way: It expands four to five times in cooking. Use a 2:1 ratio of boiling water to quinoa.

red kidney beans ❧ These thick-skinned, long-cooking beans range in color from light red to deep reddish-purple. Kidneys hold their shape well and are popular in chilis. Quicker-cooking small, red chili beans, which are sometimes called Mexican red beans, may also be used. See page 449 for cooking instructions.

rice ❧ A popular worldwide grain grown in tropical, equatorial, and temperate zones across the continents. Raw rice can be stored for months in a capped container in a cool, dark place. Rice that retains its bran, such as brown rice, should be refrigerated to prevent rancidity. Rice is always eaten cooked and can be served hot, at room temperature, or cold.

arborio rice ❧ An Italian short-grain, highly absorbent, starchy white rice used in risottos. Look for arborio rice in the ethnic section of the supermarket or in Italian specialty shops.

basmati rice ❧ Grown in the foothills of the Himalayas, with slender, long grains that are aged for as much as a year before being sold. Its nutty flavor, sweet fragrance, and smooth texture make it an appealing choice. Brown basmati rice is available in natural food stores and white basmati is often found in well-stocked supermarkets. Texmati and calmati are hybrids grown in Texas, California, and Arkansas. RiceTex recently failed in its attempt to patent a genetically engineered variety of basmati rice.

black rice (*oryza sativa*) ❧ With a dark bran covering a milky white endosperm, black rice comes in several varieties. Some brands, like Lundberg Family Farms, combine both a mahogany rice and black japonica. Black rice is available in Asian and specialty markets and natural foods stores.

black thai rice ❧ Semi-polished kernels that are moist, sticky, purple-colored, and pleasantly sweet when cooked, making it good for use in desserts. It is sometimes called black sticky rice. Look for it in cloth sacks or burlap-textured plastic in Asian markets and in supermarkets that have extensive ethnic sections.

brown rice ❧ An excellent rice with a chewy texture and full-bodied flavor, brown rice has only the hull removed—the bran and germ are retained, adding nutrients and the light brown hue. Available in long-grain, medium-grain, and short-grain varieties: the shorter the grain, the smaller, plumper, and moister the cooked rice kernels will be. Long-grain is good when a slightly dry, fluffy rice is preferred. Medium and short-grain are perfect for Asian dishes eaten with chopsticks.

carnaroli rice ❧ One of the choice, oval, short-grain white rices classified as "superfino," used for risotto. It has a hard-grained, glass-like exterior, is resistant to rapid liquid absorption, and produces a creamy risotto. Other risotto rices are arborio, vialone nano, and baldo. The very best risotto rice is grown in Italy's Piedmont and Veneto regions.

jasmine rice ❧ A creamy, Thai long-grain rice with a distinctive aromatic fragrance. It can be found in Asian markets or in the international section of well-stocked supermarkets.

sushi rice ❧ A short-grain, slightly glutinous white rice perfect for making sushi and available in the Asian section of well-stocked supermarkets and in Asian specialty shops.

sweet sticky rice ❧ An Asian rice that goes by many names: glutinous rice, sticky rice, sweet rice, sweet glutinous rice. It has plump, white grains that become translucent when cooked and is mostly used in Asian sweets. It is available in Asian markets.

wehani rice ❧ Developed by Lundberg organic growers in California, this is a long-grain, unpolished, bronze-brown rice with a sweet, nutty flavor and chewy texture. It can be cooked mixed with other types of brown rice, since the water-rice ratio for cooking and the cooking times are the same.

white rice ❧ Also known as polished rice because it has been processed to remove both its hull and bran. "Enriched" white rice has thiamine, niacin, and iron added to it. It is sold in long-grain, medium-grain, and short-grain varieties.

wild rice ❧ Not a rice, but the slim seeds of an aquatic grass related to the rice plant. Hand-harvested wild crops and cultivated wild rice paddies are both sources of wild rice, but cultivated paddies may be treated with pesticides. This rice is pricey, so we often combine it with other rice or grains. Look for organic wild rice in naturals foods stores.

ricotta salata ❧ A hard, salty, dry cheese made from sheep's milk. Despite its name, it is not related to ricotta cheese, but is grated like Pecorino Romano as a topping.

risotto ❧ Plump, short- or medium-grain rice, such as arborio or carnaroli rice, makes the best risotto. Look for packages marked "ai pestelli," which means it was hulled with a mortar and pestle. This leaves a powdery starch on the rice which contributes to a creamy texture. A good domestic rice is a California-grown Cal-Riso, which resembles arborio rice but is faster cooking. See page 238 for additional interesting information.

saffron ❧ Stiff, short, reddish-orange threads that are the dried stigmas of the saffron crocus. Crumbled into saucy dishes near the end of cooking, it imparts a bright yellow color and distinctive flavor. It is popular in Spanish, Portuguese, and Provençal cooking. Saffron is expensive, but no other spice can really replace it. Although turmeric also imparts a yellow-orange color, it is very different and is not a substitute for saffron.

savoy cabbage ❧ A round green cabbage with ruffled leaves, a sweet flavor, and delicate texture. Wrap cut heads in plastic and store in the crisper bin of the refrigerator.

seaweed ❧ Literally tons of seaweed or sea vegetables exist. For some interesting lore and fascinating facts see pages 149 and 186. Here are a few we use most often at Moosewood:

hijiki or hiziki ❧ Belonging to the brown algae family *Phaeophyta*, hijiki has thin, black strands that resemble vermicelli. After soaking, the strands expand up to five times their original size. High in iron, phosphorus, calcium, and protein, hijiki adds an assertive sea flavor to dishes.

kombu or kelp ❧ Long dark green leaves high in calcium, glutamic acid, potassium, iodine, calcium, trace minerals, and vitamins A, B-complex, and C. It is gathered off the coast of Hokkaido, Japan, and is usually sold cut into segments or folded. Use it for soup stock, a vegetable side dish, or a wrapper. Kombu's flavor is near the surface, so don't rinse it—instead, wipe it gently with a damp cloth. For easiest cutting, use scissors. Look for it in natural and specialty foods stores and Japanese groceries.

nori ❧ A marine algae harvested and processed in Japan, Korea, and the northwestern United States. It comes in packages of thin, flat, dark green, slightly salty sheets and is available both toasted and untoasted. It is the wrapper of choice for nori rolls and sushi rolls and can also make a lovely garnish when shredded on salad and rice dishes.

wakame ❦ This member of the *Alaria* family of sea kelp is only available dried in the United States. In Japan, it's eaten most often fresh in season. Soak dried wakame for about 20 minutes in lukewarm water until its leaves unfurl; then chop it into soups or salads.

seitan ❦ When the starch is removed from wheat through a lengthy process involving water and kneading, the gluten remains. This wheat gluten is called seitan, a low-fat and high-protein chewy meat substitute that readily absorbs flavors. Most commercial seitan is wheat gluten that has been boiled and then sautéed in flavorings such as soy sauce and ginger. It is available in sealed packages and canned, both plain and seasoned (with an ever-widening selection of seasonings) and, once opened, will keep refrigerated for about a week.

semolina ❦ A granular, milled product of durum wheat, consisting almost entirely of endosperm particles, used to make couscous.

shiitake ❦ See *Mushrooms* (page 462).

sour cream ❦ Baked goods made with sour cream have a particularly tender, light crumb because of the presence of lactic acid, a by-product of the beneficial bacteria present in sour cream cultures. Conventional sour cream has a butterfat content of 18 to 20%, light sour cream about 10%, and, of course, nonfat is 0%. Nonfat sour cream is creamy due to the inclusion of thickeners and starches.

soybeans ❦ More than 1,000 varieties of soybeans of yellow, green, red, black, white, and mottled hues are cultivated worldwide. Soybeans are used in an extensive array of food products: soy sauce, tofu, textured vegetable protein, miso, soy milk, soy oil, sprouts, tempeh, fermented black beans, and snacks. They are 38% protein, the highest of any legume, and are low in fat and carbohydrates. See page 449 for cooking instructions.

soy margarine ❦ Shedd's Willow Run is our margarine of choice for our vegan desserts and savory pastries. Unlike many margarines on the market, Willow Run is made with essential natural ingredients free of artificial stabilizers, thickeners, and preservatives. Willow Run contains liquid soybean oil and partially hydrogenated soybean oil, water, salt, soy flour, soy lecithin, beta carotene (for color), and vitamin A.

soy milk (*soy drinks*) ❦ Made primarily from soybeans, water, and salt, and often sweetened with rice syrup or barley malt, soy milk is a thick dairyless beverage that can be used in place of regular milk in sauces, soups, desserts, and on cereal. Soymilk is 45% fat (compared to 51% in regular milk) and all of the fat is polyunsaturated. Soy milk is also available in low-fat and flavored varieties. It can be found in natural foods stores and many supermarkets.

soy sauce ❦ The best-tasting, most pure soy sauces are made from four ingredients only: soybeans, water, wheat, and salt—and some wheat-free brands also exist. We recommend avoiding diluted sauces that have caramel coloring, sweetening, and/or preservatives. Soy sauces vary in strength and saltiness, so taste yours before adding it to a dish. Soy sauce is widely available in Asian groceries and supermarkets. See *Tamari* (page 471).

squash ❦ The fruits of various vinelike, tendril-bearing plants of the genus *Curcurbita*. A tremendous variety of squash grows all over the world, many depending upon certain climates and soil conditions. They come in all shapes, sizes, and colors and can be baked, simmered, or in some cases eaten raw. Many (such as acorn, buttercup, crook-neck) derive their names from descriptions of their shapes. Here are a few we use at Moosewood:

buttercup squash ❦ A winter squash shaped like an oversized teacup. It has thick, dark green skin and sweet, moist, orange flesh. Stored in dark, dry, cool conditions, it can last most of the winter.

butternut squash ❦ A dense, club-shaped, thin-skinned winter squash with subdued light orange skin and bright yellowish orange flesh. Its sweet flavor adds natural sugar to soups and stews. It is good plain or with a dab of butter.

chayote ❦ Originated on Mayan and Aztec farms. Its mild taste is a cross between a cucumber and zucchini, but it is prized for its aroma, texture, and ability to absorb flavors. This gourd-like food can replace summer squash, raw or cooked or scooped out and stuffed. Its crisp, fresh taste makes a lively addition to salads and stews. Jamaicans use it like apples in pies, and in New Orleans it is called mirliton. Firmer than other squash, its cooking time is longer.

delicata squash ❦ A tube-shaped, sweet and creamy winter squash with streaks of orange or white on its green skin. It's great in soups or stews and makes a delicious shell for stuffing. It's not always necessary to peel the thin skin of this squash, especially when it's going to be cubed and simmered in a stew or soup.

spaghetti squash ❦ A unique winter squash that will baffle the uninitiated. To prepare, place the whole squash in a pot with water to cover and bring to a boil; then reduce the heat and simmer for 30 minutes, until tender when pierced. Drain and cool. When it can be handled, cut it in half, lengthwise, remove the seeds, and scoop out the spaghetti-like strands. Keep warm and serve the "spaghetti" with your favorite tomato sauce, herbed butter, or pesto. Store like other winter squash—in a cool, dry location with good air circulation between the squash.

summer squash ❦ Thin-skinned with light ivory to tan- or golden-hued flesh. They cook quickly and can be eaten raw, steamed, blanched, sautéed, or baked. Some common types are crook-neck, yellow squash, pattypan, and zucchini. Although a recipe may call for a particular summer squash, any kind that you have on hand or prefer will do fine.

winter squash ❦ A wide variety of green- and orange-skinned gourds that make excellent shells for stuffing and have sweet flesh good for soups, sautés, stews, and pie fillings. Winter squash are best freshly harvested in autumn. Some of the most easy to use types include acorn, buttercup, butternut, delicata, small pumpkins, and turban squash. Avoid overly large specimens, which are usually bland and pulpy. Scoop out and discard the stringy center mass and seeds before cooking. Or save pumpkinseeds and dry-roast and lightly salt them for a really delicious, nutritious snack.

zucchini ❦ A mild-tasting summer squash. The most common variety has a green, subtly speckled skin, although some are gold, gray, and even black! Choose zucchini 4 to 8 inches long: Longer ones are likely to be tough, seedy, and tasteless. Seeding zucchini before adding them to a stew will help maintain their texture.

stock ❦ See *Vegetable Stock* (page 473).

sun-dried tomatoes ❦ These Italian
specialty items are now spreading rapidly to supermarkets all across the United States as their tart-sweet, salty flavor and chewy texture gain popularity. They pop up at deli counters—in salads, in fillings, and even in bagels—as well as in prepared foods. We recommend plain dried tomatoes without sulfites

over the pricier, higher-fat ones packed in oil. Soak dried tomatoes in boiling water for 10 to 15 minutes until softened before chopping and adding to a dish.

tabasco sauce ❧ One of the most widely known and used brands of hot pepper sauce and a constant pantry item in the Moosewood kitchen. It's made with vinegar, red chiles, and salt, and a few serious squirts will add quite a bit of spicy hotness to a dish. Other excellent hot pepper sauces abound, so use any you like in our recipes.

tahini (*sesame tahini*) ❧ Made from unroasted hulled sesame seeds, this thick, smooth, spreadable, creamy beige paste is widely used in Middle Eastern, Mediterranean, North African, and Asian cuisine. It's popular in salad dressings combined with yogurt or fresh lemon juice and can add a wonderful nutty flavor and richness to soups, stews, burgers, and noodles. Don't confuse it with its thicker, heavier, stronger-tasting, and much darker brown relatives, sesame paste and sesame butter.

tamari ❧ Originally, *tamari* was the word used to describe the rich, salty liquid residue from making miso. The word is now often used interchangeably with soy sauce, and most tamari sauces on the market are unrelated to the original tamari. Tamari sauces can be stronger than the average soy sauce, so you may want to use less tamari in a recipe than the called-for amount of soy sauce.

tamarind ❧ Made from the pods of a tropical tree and used to flavor Indian and East African dishes, tamarind comes in concentrate, paste, pulp, and fresh pod form. The concentrate is a tart brown paste that usually comes in jars. Dissolve it in water before stirring into a curry or sauce or add it directly to a simmering soup or stew. If using pulp, mash and soak it and use the soaking liquid. Look for tamarind in Indian and Asian markets.

tarragon ❧ Fresh tarragon has a beguiling licorice taste that is wonderful in a vinaigrette, on grilled fish, or as the star of a piquant sauce. It also combines well in the proverbial French *fine herbes*, a blend of tarragon, parsley, chives, and chervil.

tea ❧ Green, black, oolong, and flavored teas all come from the small leaves and delicate white flower buds of the evergreen *Camellia sinensis*, which can vary in height from 5-meter bushes to 20-meter trees. *Camellia sinensis*, although highly adaptive to differing conditions, thrives most luxuriantly surrounded by misty clouds at high elevations where the mornings are cool and the days hot and humid. The distinct flavor and aroma of each variety is determined by the time of day the leaves are picked and the methods of picking, processing, manufacturing, and storage. It is said that an expert tea "sommelier" or taster can tell the height of the plant, time of day picked, and even the weather on harvest day!

Tea leaves readily absorb flavors and aromas from fruit, spices, and flowers. In China, many teas are scented with flowers including orchids, jasmine, rose petals, honeysuckle, bergamot, magnolia, and gardenia. Tea in Arabia is most often flavored with mint, while tea in India and parts of northeast Africa is usually combined with spices. To create flavors such as vanilla, caramel, banana, or apricot, the leaves are sprayed with granules or liquid flavors before the final step in processing.

Organic teas are strictly controlled by international certification organizations that require three years of inspections, tests, and visits before final certification. We recommend Ambootia, Seeyok, Makaibai, and Banaspaty brands as well as organic tea from Assam. Tea that is labeled "fair trade" indicates that the pickers and factory workers share in the profits and have better working conditions, pensions, and health care.

thai basil (*ocimum sanctum, holy basil*) ❀ A member of the mint family with serrated dark reddish-green leaves, tiny deep purple flower stalks, and a sharper flavor than regular basil. It's delightful as a minced fresh herb in Southeast Asian dishes. If your supermarket doesn't carry it, look for seed packets and cultivate it in your garden or a sunny window.

tofu (*bean curd*) ❀ A high-protein soy product with a creamy, soft, cheese-like texture. It is sold in cakes that can vary in weight from about 10 to 16 ounces and is often water-packed. Fresh tofu is available both refrigerated and in vacuum-packaging at room temperature. At home, store fresh tofu and opened vacuum-packed varieties in a container of water in the refrigerator, change the water daily, and use within a week.

firm tofu ❀ A denser texture than either soft or silken varieties, good to use in dishes where you want cubes or triangles of the tofu to remain intact after baking, sautéeing, or stir-frying. Firm tofu is also best to use when making fillings for stuffed vegetables or when freezing the tofu.

frozen tofu ❀ Can be grated in a food processor to make a crumbly, dense, chewy product good for stuffings, soups, and stews. Place a cake or cakes of firm tofu on a tray, cover with plastic wrap, and freeze for at least 6 hours. Defrost in the refrigerator or other cool place and then squeeze out the water as you would a sponge. Use immediately; defrosted frozen tofu is highly perishable.

silken tofu (*japanese-style tofu*) ❀ Made with a higher ratio of soybeans to water than regular tofu, giving it a higher protein and fat content. With its mild flavor and delicately silky texture, it performs well in dairyless desserts, drinks, and dressings where it absorbs the surrounding dominant flavors and produces a thick, smooth, velvety purée. "Lite" silken tofu with a reduced fat content is also available.

soft tofu ❀ A texture that falls between that of the firm and silken varieties. It is excellent cubed and simmered in brothy soups and stews and blended into sauces, dips, spreads, and thick purées. Soft and silken tofus are best for desserts because of their custard-like consistency.

tofu-kan (*five-spice bean curd*) ❀ The brand name of Moosewood's locally made baked, seasoned tofu. With its spiced and slightly smoky flavor and chewy, dense texture, it's perfect in soups, salads, sandwiches, sautés, and fillings. It is quite similar to Chinese five-spice bean curd, which is named for the five-spice powder used in seasoning. Look for these ready-to-slice-and-eat products in natural foods stores and Asian markets.

tomatillos (*mexican green tomatoes, tomatitos verdes*) ❀ Tomatillos resemble plum-sized green tomatoes with tissue-thin husks and smooth but sticky skin. Their tart, lemony flavor makes them a favorite in Mexican and southwestern United States cuisine. Look for dry, firm fruit with clean, tight husks in the produce section of the supermarket. Tomatillos are high in vitamins C and K and will keep refrigerated for 2 to 4 weeks. To prepare ahead for cooked dishes, husk, stem, and simmer the tomatillos until soft; then drain, cool, and freeze until ready to use.

tortillas ❀ These thin, unleavened flatbreads are made most simply from water mixed with wheat flour or corn flour. They commonly range from $4\frac{1}{2}$ to 11 inches in diameter; packaged corn tortillas in the United States are usually on the smaller end of that range and the wheat ones on the larger end. Tortillas become pliable when heated and make great wraps for sandwiches, burritos, quesadillas, and enchiladas. Look for brands with no added fat or preservatives in the dairy case or frozen food aisle of the supermarket. See pages 158–163 for heating directions and recipes.

tree ears �} See *Mushrooms* (page 462-463).

turnips 🌱 White, beet-shaped, potassium-rich root vegetables tinged with fuchsia-purple coloring near their crowns. Raw turnips are quite pungent and excellent for pickling. When cooked, they become juicy and earthy-flavored but can range in assertiveness from mild and sweet to powerful and slightly bitter. If you're uncertain how you feel about turnips, we suggest using tender young turnips, which have a milder, more balanced flavor. But don't shy away from eventually trying mature ones; for some, a strong turnip taste really hits the spot.

Select smooth firm vegetables with unsprouted tops and store in the refrigerator for up to 2 weeks.

vegetable oil 🌱 When a recipe calls for vegetable oil, we use bland vegetable oils, such as canola, soy, or safflower, all without preservatives. For more information, see *Oils,* page 464.

vegetable stock 🌱 A broth made by simmering vegetables in water until they release their flavors and nutrients. A real enhancement to soups, stews, and sauces, stock adds far more depth and interest than plain water and is the perfect way to use any unattractive vegetables, forgotten but not yet rotten. Most vegetables are fine candidates for stock, but avoid using the assertive cabbage family (broccoli, cauliflower, turnips, kohlrabi) as well as the two nightshades eggplant and bell peppers, which can make stock bitter. Take into account vegetables that bleed color, such as beets, red cabbage, and greens. If using the stock to make a dairy soup, don't add large amounts of acidic fruits or vegetables such as

tomatoes that might curdle the soup. Learn to tailor your stock for the dish you plan to make by adding complementary seasonings. For some of Moosewood's favorite vegetable stocks, see pages 62–63.

A good stock should have the characteristic flavor of its major ingredient: For example, the classic Japanese broth, dashi, should have the rich, aromatic flavor of seaweed. Vegetarian stocks tend to be golden-hued, mild, and sweet. The ratio of ingredients to water will determine the strength of the broth. Simmer gently until the stock has the desired full-bodied flavor.

vinaigrette 🌱 Derived from French, vinaigrette is actually the word for a small, ornamental bottle or box for holding aromatic vinegar or smelling salts. Vinaigrette sauce is defined as a tart mixture of oil, vinegar, and seasonings usually served cold with salads. In present usage, most people just say "vinaigrette" to refer to the sauce and not the container.

vinegar 🌱 When airborne bacteria called *acetobacter* combine with the oxygen in alcohol, acetic acid and water are formed, and from this chemical reaction we get vinegar. Vinegar can be made from the sugar in many fruits, grains, and natural sweeteners and has been used for centuries—the earliest written record dates back to 5000 B.C. The Babylnians made vinegar from dates, the Asians from rice, the southern Europeans from grapes, and the early American colonists from apples. In the mid-1600s the French commercialized the production of wine vinegar, and in Italy the finest balsamic vinegar is regarded as a national treasure.

balsamic vinegar 🌱 Dark, syrupy, and complexly flavored, balsamic vinegar is a favorite for salads, sauces, vinaigrettes, and marinades and is particularly good with fruit, cheese, and mushrooms.

champagne vinegar ❧ A delicate flavor and a slightly lower acidity than other wine vinegars, perfect for making herb and fruit vinegars.

cider vinegar ❧ A traditional North American vinegar made from apple cider and used as an all-purpose flavoring in cooking and salad dressings.

distilled white vinegar ❧ Clear-colored with a crisp bite, good for pickling and general household use. It is made from dilute distilled alcohol.

fruit vinegars ❧ Usually made from wine or champagne vinegars that have been combined with macerated fruit and then filtered. They're delicious in vinaigrettes and sauces.

malt vinegar ❧ Made from fermented malted barley. Malt vinegar is England's national vinegar and is used for pickling and as a condiment, especially on fish and chips.

rice vinegar ❧ This slightly sweet, mild vinegar made in China and Japan from rice wine has a lower acidity than most other vinegars.

sherry vinegar ❧ A medium brown, slightly sweet, aromatic vinegar from Spain, delicious when paired in dressings with nut oils.

wine vinegar ❧ Red wine vinegar is excellent in robust mustard vinaigrettes and in combination with shallots, garlic, and strong herbs such as rosemary, oregano, and thyme. White wine vinegar is perfect with less assertive herbs such as tarragon, basil, chives, and cilantro.

wakame ❧ See *Seaweed* (page 468).

wasabi ❧ The name for a light green powder made from a particular radish root native to Japan. When mixed with water in a 1:1 ratio and used as a condiment for sushi or nori rolls, it has the spicy, sinus-clearing effect often experienced with horseradish and pungent mustards. Mix only as much as you plan to use immediately, since the flavor fades with time. We don't recommend the premade paste, because all brands we've seen have additives.

water chestnuts ❧ Named for their chestnut-colored outer skin, water chestnuts are fleshy underwater stems cultivated throughout China and Southeast Asia. Their flesh is mild, crisp, sweet, and crunchy. While the canned ones available in the United States are well-preserved and tasty, the true fresh item is a rare delicacy. Canned water chestnuts should be rinsed and then briefly cooked.

wheatberries ❧ Whole grains of wheat with only the hulls removed. Most are ground into flour or processed to make bread, pasta, cereal, bulghur, and cracked wheat, but they can also be purchased whole and cooked like barley. They have a unique, slightly sweet, nutty flavor. Look for wheatberries in natural foods stores and the natural foods section of supermarkets.

wonton wrappers ❧ Wontons are the earliest recorded stuffed food, historically documented in the Tang period (A.D. 618 to 907), and still going strong. Today both fresh and frozen packaged wonton wrappers come in varying thicknesses and shapes. They are easy to use, fairly sturdy, and readily form a tight seal when moistened. Once filled, the wontons can be boiled or deep-fried for about 5 minutes and they're ready to eat. Uncooked, well-wrapped wontons will keep in the freezer for up to 2 months. Thaw before frying or just drop them frozen into simmering liquid.

worcestershire sauce, vegetarian ❧ The classic Worcestershire sauce contains sardines, but there are several excellent vegetarian versions available, which taste almost identical to the original sauce. We especially like the Wizard's Vegetarian Worcestershire Sauce produced in California. It's a zesty, savory condiment that is good for dressings, sauces, and grilling.

yeast ✿ One of the oldest leavenings for baked goods, yeast is a live organism that feeds on starch and sugar and produces carbon dioxide, which causes breads, cakes, and pastries to rise. Yeast is available fresh and dried: Fresh, or compound, yeast will keep for up to 2 weeks if properly chilled; dried or powdered yeast can last for up to a year. One 1/4-ounce package (about 2 1/4 teaspoons) of dried yeast granules is equivalent to a standard 3/5-ounce cake of fresh yeast. Store all yeast refrigerated.

Fast rising yeast, also called rapid acting yeast, is a different strain that does not need to be proofed and reduces rising time by about half. Some bakers say the taste and texture of baked goods may suffer from a fast rise; some recipes call for a long rise to develop flavor.

yogurt ✿ Cultured with live, beneficial bacteria, yogurt is a familiar dairy product made from whole, low-fat, or skim milk. Like many "soured" dairy products, it creates a more tender crumb in baked goods. It is an excellent lower-fat alternative to sour cream and makes a wonderful, velvety base for dressings, sauces, and spreads.

yogurt cheese ✿ Soft and creamy, yogurt cheese is easily made at home. When prepared with nonfat or low-fat yogurt, it can serve as a lighter replacement for cream cheese or sour cream.

To make yogurt cheese in the traditional manner, line a colander with overlapping paper coffee filters or several layers of cheesecloth. Place the colander in a large bowl. Spoon in 2 quarts of yogurt and cover with plastic wrap. Refrigerate for 12 to 24 hours. After 3 or 4 hours or overnight, discard the liquid collected in the bowl. The yogurt will thicken to a consistency similar to soft cream cheese will yield from 3 to 5 cups.

For our quick yogurt cheese method, reduce the amount of yogurt to 1 to 1 1/2 quarts. Set up the yogurt to drain as in the traditional method, but place a plate and a heavy object such as a can on top of the covered yogurt. Refrigerate for 2 hours. The weighting will speed the process and produce 3 to 5 cups of yogurt cheese.

zest ✿ Grated citrus peel, most often lemon, lime, or orange. Make zest at home by finely grating around the outermost surface of the fruit's rind. Don't grate long in one spot, because deeper near the white pith the rind becomes very bitter and undesirable. Many cooking supply stores carry specially designed sharp graters with tiny holes for zesting that make the task quick and enjoyable. Freshly grated peel is superior to the bottled zest found in the spice section of the supermarket.

vegan list

Vegans are no longer as rare as they were twenty years ago. Now more people are choosing to eat a diet based solely on plant foods. All of the following recipes adhere to vegan guidelines and contain no animal products, dairy products, or honey.

breakfast & brunch
Gingered Peach Butter
Maple Nut Granola
Plum Butter with Orange
Savory Congee
Stovetop Almond Oatmeal
Sweet Spiced Congee
Tempeh Sausage
Three Tofu Scrambles
Vegan Oat & Walnut Pancakes

soups
Vegetable Stocks
Artichoke Soup Provençal
Asian Cabbage Soup
Carolina Vegetable Soup
Curried Spinach Pea Soup
Fennel Leek Soup
Italian Bean & Squash Soup
Minimalist Miso Soup
Smooth Gazpacho with Greens
Southeast Asian Fruit Soup
Spanish Bean Soup
Spinach Coconut Soup
Squash & Tomatillo Soup
Thai Carrot Soup
Thai Coconut Soup
Vegetable Barley Soup
Zero Soup

salads
Asian Cabbage Slaw
Cucumber Peanut Salad
Cucumber Side Salads
Israeli Za'atar Salad
Jicama Orange Salad
Pretty Beets & Carrots
Spicy Cantaloupe Salad
Spicy Potato Salad
Thai Eggplant & Tomato Salad
Three Peppers Cabbage Slaw
Tomato Salad with Basil Pineapple Dressing

Tossed Green Salad Vinaigrette
Two Shredded Carrot Salads
Vietnamese Root Vegetable Slaw
Warm Potato Salad

side vegetables
Asian Greens & Spring Vegetables
Asparagus with Red Pepper Sauce
Curried Corn
Mixed Greens
Spicy Stir-Fried Savoy Cabbage
Tofu Mashed Potatoes
Turnips with Greens

grains
Bulghur with Caramelized Onions
Bulghur with Spinach
Couscous Pilaf with Pine Nuts
Curried Quinoa
Golden Pineapple Rice
Grits with Quinoa
Mexican Red Rice
Orange Saffron Rice
Sesame Rice
Simple Asian Pilaf
Wehani & Apricot Pilaf
Wild Rice Pilaf

wraps, rolls & burgers
Caribbean Beans & Greens Wrap
Dixie Burgers
Fajitas
Falafel Burgers
Italian Tofu Spread
Mushroom Pecan Burgers
Portabello Spinach & Tomato Sandwich
Thai Tofu Spread
Tofu Burgers
Tofu Hijiki Burgers
Tofu Sloppy Joes
Vegetable Rolls

drinks & snacks
Apple Pie à la Mode Drink
Autumn Smoothie
Baked Tofu Sticks
Basic Popcorn
Curried Lentil Dip
Curried Tofu
Elissa's Egg Cream
Espresso Drink
Flavored Olives
Frozen Jeff
Fruit & Herbal Iced Tea
Green Olive & Artichoke Tapenade
Hot Flash Cooler
Lemongrass Limeade
Lemony Baked Tofu
Mexican Baked Tofu
Simple Baked Tofu
Sparkling Strawberry Lemonade
Tomatillo Guacamole

the lighter side
Antipasto with Spring Vegetables
Greens & Soft Polenta
Israeli Couscous & French Lentils
Mediterranean-style Orzo Salad
Middle Eastern Lentils & Pasta
Moroccan Roasted Vegetables
Roasted Vegetables for Pasta
Roasted Winter Vegetables

casseroles & baked dishes
Caribbean Sweet Potato Gratin
Polenta Cutlets with Olives
Tofu Manicotti
Tofu Stuffed Portabellos
Vegan Lasagna

sautés, stews & hashes
Basic Skillet Black Beans
Basque Skillet Beans
Bibimbop
Black Bean & Sweet Potato Hash
Chilean Bean Stew
Chili with Tofu or TVP
Drunken Beans
Indian Ratatouille
Indian Skillet Black-eyed Peas
Peppers & Greens Skillet Hash
Potato & Asparagus Hash

Sicilian Stir-Fry
Spicy Broccoli Soba Sauté
Tilghman Island Stew
Tofu in Black Bean Sauce
Vegetarian Pozole
Winter Curry

showstoppers
East-West Stuffed Portabellos
Japanese Stuffed Eggplant
Pasta with Sunday Ragù
Pizza with Three Toppings
Vegan Turnovers
Wild Mushroom Sauté

sauces & seasonings
Arrabiatta Sauce
Avocado Wasabi Dressing
Garlic Scape Pesto
Black Bean Mango Salsa
Joan's Three-Tomato Salsa
Mango Corn Jicama Salsa
Mango Lime Sauce
Miso Lemon Marinade
Mole
Mushroom Gravy
Peach Salsa
Quick Tomato Sauce
Rhubarb Cherry Chutney
Simple Sweet & Sour Sauce
Simplest Ever Applesauce
Strawberry Dressing
Summer Melon Salsa
Thai Marinade
Tofu Sour Cream
Two Barbeque Sauces

breads
Bread Sticks
Pumpkin Cornmeal Biscuits

desserts
Deep Chocolate Vegan Cake
Four Vegan Frostings
Fruit Skewers
Oya's Peaches & Pistachios
Thai Black Rice Pudding
Tropical Tapioca
Vegan Oil Pie Crust
Winter Fruit Compote

healthy low-fat favorites

Eating a lower-fat diet can have significant health benefits. Here is a list of delicious recipes that contain only 15 grams or less of fat per serving. Those highlighted with an asterisk(*) derive only 20 percent or less of their calories from fat and fall well within the recommended guidelines for a healthy diet.

breakfast & brunch
Apple Zucchini Muffins*
Cherry Whole Wheat Scones
Gingered Peach Butter*
Greek Wheatberries & Peaches*
Huevos Rancheros
Lemon Ricotta Pancakes
Moosewood Muffins (Basic)
Oatmeal Banana Pancakes
Oven Apple Oats
Peach Oats Brûlée*
Plum Butter with Orange*
Puffy Pancake
Quick Cinnamon Biscuits
Savory Congee
Stovetop Almond Oatmeal
Strawberry Banana Muffins
Sweet Potato Pancakes
Sweet Spiced Congee*
Tempeh Sausage
Up-to-Date Irish Oatmeal*
Vegan Oat & Walnut Pancakes

soups
Vegetable Stocks*
Artichoke Soup Provençal*
Asian Cabbage Soup
Carolina Vegetable Soup
Creamy Chestnut Soup*
Curried Fish Chowder*
Curried Spinach Pea Soup
Fennel Leek Soup
Italian Bean & Squash Soup*
Manhattan Seafood Chowder
Minimalist Miso Soup
Scallop Chowder
Smooth Gazpacho with Greens
Southeast Asian Fruit Soup
Spanish Bean Soup
Spinach Coconut Soup
Squash & Tomatillo Soup*
Thai Coconut Soup
Vegetable Barley Soup

salads
Asian Cabbage Slaw
Avocado & Shrimp Sushi Salad
Celery Salad with Blue Cheese
Cucumber Peanut Salad
Cucumbers with Spicy Peanut Dressing*
Israeli Za'atar Salad
Jicama Orange Salad*
Scandinavian Slaw
Spicy Cantaloupe Salad
Spicy Potato Salad*
Spinach Salad with Peanut Dressing
Thai Eggplant & Tomato Salad
Three Peppers Cabbage Slaw
Tofu Salad
Tomato Salads
Tossed Green Salad Vinaigrette
Two Shredded Carrot Salads
Vietnamese Root Vegetable Slaw*
Warm Potato Salad

side vegetables
Asian Greens & Spring Vegetables*
Cauliflower with Polonaise Topping
Curried Corn
Fennel Leek Mashed Potatoes
Low-Fat Garlic Mashed Potatoes*
Mashed Potatoes with Shallots
Mixed Greens
Pretty Beets & Carrots
Roasted Caramelized Balsamic Onions
Spicy Stir-Fried Savoy Cabbage
Tofu Mashed Potatoes*
Wasabi Mashed Sweet Potatoes

grains

Bulghur with Carmelized Onions
Bulghur with Spinach*
Couscous Pilaf with Pine Nuts*
Curried Quinoa
Golden Pineapple Rice*
Grits with Goat Cheese & Dill
Grits with Quinoa*
Kasha with Red Cabbage
Orange Saffron Rice*
Pan American Grits
Risotto-style Barley
Sesame Rice
Simple Asian Pilaf

wraps, rolls & burgers

Caribbean Beans & Greens Wrap
Cheese Sandwiches with Marinated Feta
Dixie Burgers
Falafel Burgers
Five Ethnic Egg Salads
Indian Curried Potato Wrap
Mushroom Pecan Burgers
Portabello Spinach & Tomato Sandwich
Thai Tofu Spread
Tofu Hijiki Burgers
Tofu Sloppy Joes
Vegetable Rolls

drinks & snacks

Apple Pie à la Mode Drink*
Autumn Smoothie*
Baked Tofu Sticks*
Basic Popcorn
Blueberry Buttermilk Falls Drink*
Chai
Curried Lentil Dip*
Curried Tofu
David's Dilled Havarti Spread
Deviled Eggs Four Ways
Elegant Pimiento Cheese Spread
Elissa's Egg Cream*
Espresso Drink
Flavored Olives
Frozen Jeff*
Fruit & Herbal Iced Tea*
Green Olive & Artichoke Tapenade

Green Tea Smoothie*
Green Tea with Ginger*
Hot Flash Cooler*
Lemongrass Limeade*
Mexican Baked Tofu*
Simple Baked Tofu
Sour Cream Onion Dip
Sparkling Strawberry Lemonade*
Spiced Nuts
Sun-dried Tomato & Chèvre Dip
Tomatillo Guacamole

the lighter side

Aromatic Whole Wheat Pasta
Dressed up Salmon Cakes
Greens & Soft Polenta
Israeli Couscous & French Lentils
Lovely Low-Fat Latkes*
Middle Eastern Lentils & Pasta*
Mixed Greens Frittata
Moroccan Roasted Vegetables
Orecchiette with Butter Beans*
Pasta with Asparagus & Lemon
Pasta with Zucchini & Mascarpone
Red Risotto*
Risotto Milanese
Spinach Feta Risotto
Tabouli with Shrimp & Orange
Vegetable Pho with Shrimp

casseroles & baked dishes

Breaded Polenta Cutlets
Fish with Cornmeal Chipotle Crust
Instant Tamale Pie
Macaroni & Cheese with Tofu
Moroccan Fish with Cumin
Polenta Cutlets with Olives
Spinach Gnocchi
Tofu Manicotti
Vegan Lasagna

sautés, stews & hashes

Arrabiatta Sauce
Basic Skillet Black Beans *
Basque Skillet Beans
Bibimbop
Black Bean & Sweet Potato Hash *
Chilean Bean Stew *
Chili with Tofu or TVP *
Drunken Beans *
Indian Ratatouille
Indian Skillet Black-eyed Peas
Peppers & Greens Skillet Hash *
Potato & Asparagus Hash
Sicilian Stir-Fry
Spicy Broccoli Soba Sauté
Tilghman Island Stew
Tofu in Black Bean Sauce
Tofu Stroganoff
Vegetarian Pozole *

showstoppers

Batter-fried Vegetables & Fish *
Cioppino *
Escabeche
Japanese Stuffed Eggplant
Pasta with Sunday Ragù
Pizza with Three Toppings *

sauces & seasonings

Avocado Wasabi Dressing *
Black Bean & Mango Salsa *
Creamy Tomato Sauce
Garlic Scape Pesto
Joan's Three-Tomato Salsa
Light Sour Cream
Mango Jicama Salsa
Mango Lime Sauce
Miso Lemon Marinade
Mole
Mushroom Gravy
Peach Salsa *
Quick Tomato Sauce
Rhubarb Cherry Chutney *
Simple Sweet & Sour Sauce *

Simplest Every Applesauce *
Strawberry Dressing
Summer Melon Salsa
Thai Marinade
Tofu Sour Cream
Tomato Sauce with Sage
Two Barbeque Sauces *

breads

Biscuits à la Focaccia
Bread Sticks *
Cornbread
Flaxseed Banana Bread
Fruited Quickbread
Lemon Thyme Biscuits
Pumpkin Cornmeal Biscuits
Three Seed Whole Wheat Rolls
Walnut Raisin Bread

desserts

Almond Biscotti
Apple Quesadillas
Big Chocolate Chip Cookies
Black Forest Biscotti
Caramel Sauce
Deep Chocolate Vegan Cake
Four Vegan Frostings
Fruit Skewers *
Muhallabia Massawa
Old Fashioned Molasses Drops
Oya's Peaches & Pistachios
Pistachio Cardamon Cake
Raspberry Lemon Pudding Cake *
Sweet Pumpkin Cookies
Thai Black Rice Pudding
Tropical Tapioca
Upside Down Skillet Cake

low-carbohydrate list

For those who need to watch their carbs, here are the recipes in this book that contain no more than 10.5 grams of carbohydrates per serving.

breakfast & brunch
Plum Butter with Orange
Tempeh Sausage

soups
Vegetable Stocks
Thai Coconut Soup

salads
Celery Salad with Blue Cheese
Cucumbers with Spicy Peanut Dressing
Thai Eggplant & Tomato Salad
Three Peppers Cabbage Slaw
Tossed Green Salad Vinaigrette
Two Shredded Carrot Salads

side vegetables
Asian Greens & Spring Vegetables
Asparagus with Red Pepper Sauce
Mixed Greens
Pretty Beets & Carrots
Roasted Caramelized Balsamic Onions

wraps, rolls & burgers
Five Ethnic Egg Salads
Thai Tofu Spread

drinks & snacks
Baked Tofu Sticks
Chai
Curried Lentil Dip
David's Dilled Havarti Spread
Deviled Eggs Four Ways
Elegant Pimiento Cheese Spread
Flavored Olives
Fruit & Herbal Iced Tea
Green Tea with Ginger
Lemony Baked Tofu
Simple Baked Tofu
Sour Cream Onion Dip
Spiced Nuts
Sun-dried Tomato & Chèvre Spread
Tomatillo Guacamole

the lighter side
Mixed Greens Frittata

casseroles & baked dishes
Moroccan Fish with Cumin

sautés, stews & hashes
Spicy Broccoli Soba Sauté
Tofu in Black Bean Sauce

showstoppers
Escabeche
Wild Mushroom Sauté

sauces & seasonings
Avocado Wasabi Dressing
Black Bean Mango Salsa
Creamy Tomato Sauce
Four Cheese Sauce
Garlic Scape Pesto
Green Olive & Artichoke Tapenade
Joan's Three-Tomato Salsa
Light Sour Cream
Mango Lime Sauce
Miso Lemon Marinade
Mole
Mushroom Gravy
Peach Salsa
Rhubarb Cherry Chutney
Simple Sweet & Sour Sauce
Simplest Ever Applesauce
Strawberry Dressing
Thai Marinade
Tofu Sour Cream
Two Barbeque Sauces
Yogurt Tahini Dressing

desserts
Fruit Skewers

index

about the author
working collectively—flat, fluid & functional

The Moosewood Collective is a group of nineteen people who own and operate Moosewood Restaurant and write cookbooks. This is our ninth book. "Collective" is our group's philosophical identity, not a legal term. Most of us have worked together for more than twenty years and some of us have worked together since Moosewood opened in 1973. Our membership has changed over the years, but basically we are a stable group. When all is said and done, Moosewood is a hard place to leave.

We've tried not only to feed people well, but also to treat people well. Over the last twenty-eight years our company has come to represent something bigger than we ever anticipated, and something better than the usual business. We struggle to hold on to the best of what we've been, and to mature into what we can become, periodically checking in with each other. We fret and sometimes doubt ourselves, hoping always to find safe harbor. We've tried to live up to the expectations people have invested in our image. Sometimes we fall short and sometimes we resist being the least bit famous. Most of us experience the Collective as a kind of second family. We've shared a significant portion of our lives with one another and find Moosewood a loving and supportive place that can drive us crazy too. Sometimes it's easy, sometimes it's hard . . . having so much good food around sure doesn't hurt.

The corporate world is just now being transformed by the realization that cross-training and shared responsibility produce better results. Working collectively at Moosewood has meant a flat, fluid, functional way of sharing work. The experience is like having no boss, or like having nineteen bosses, depending on how you choose to look at it. Both the restaurant and the cookbooks are primarily collective endeavors.

Much of the romance about groups that resist a hierarchical structure rests on the mythology that a group without a boss is a group without leaders. The "leaderless group" is a popular notion, especially among academics exploring ways to organize committees and teams. We can testify that leadership has little to do with title or chain of command. It is a quality that exists within every successful group. Several leaders among us with courage, creativity, self-discipline, principles, and willingness to learn, teach, support, and share, have kept us going. Leadership emerges in the unplanned heroism and grace under fire that every one of us has shown at times. Leadership is irrepressible. It gets passed around depending on the task. Collective work doesn't automatically generate equal voices. When some of our voices dominate, it's important others speak up to add balance. The accommodating ones among us have to resist always going with the flow because it's easier. Sometimes we need to be active and raise conflict. We've had to work at developing diplomatic ways to express ourselves so that interpersonal disagreements don't turn into a test of skill and endurance.

Our meetings, and we do have quite a few, have gotten a lot better over the years. We delegate more responsibility to our boards, teams, and committees. But we still rely on the whole collective to reach major decisions and support big changes. Our tradition has been to strive for consensus. Simple majority is fast and useful, but it's only reliable for less significant issues. Going for high majority or for consensus keeps us together.

Consensus is a widely misunderstood process, and we're still learning how to best use it. It's not just another word for unanimity. The discussions that happen on the way to consensus raise lots of alternatives and disagreement. People have to keep paying attention. Someone has to summarize once in a while to keep ideas alive and available. When someone objects to a proposal, it's not always easy or popular to say so or explain why. We're constantly learning the importance of dissent, listening to each other, and being patient. When we reach agreement, we may not have found the ideal solution, but we believe it's the best we can do for the time being. And when the decision doesn't reflect our personal opinion, the hard part is having the self-discipline to support the group decision and to consciously avoid undermining it. This is a more challenging lesson.

We recognize that we're not all equally good at everything, nor do we have to be. We find ways to accommodate our differences and play to our individual strengths, while keeping opportunities open and accessible. Since the climb up our corporate career ladder isn't very steep, we find ways to stretch out and around. The shy and cautious push through being uncomfortable. The control freaks work at being patient, accepting the influence of others. The self-directed independents strive to be open to shared responsibility. It's been quite a dance.

We think a lot about how to support personal development without sacrificing quality. Exchanging roles and functions was easier years ago when the only choice was between working as a busser, "waitron," cook, or "omni" (someone willing to prepare the fish). Anyone might competently play all of those roles in one week. Writ-

ing books, editing, managing, consulting, developing products, doing publicity tours, starting new ventures—these roles are a different story. The nice part is that we can learn from each other. We're a real do-it-yourself kind of group. We've had to learn to establish standards and then hold ourselves accountable to them. We've had to pioneer in brand-new jobs without the benefit of support or supervision. We've learned that when someone turns out to be good at something, it makes sense to let them keep at it. Or, when they're ready to move on, that we learn from them first. We are individually neither interchangeable nor dispensable. And as we diversify our business, we wrestle with how to value all of the different kinds of work we do.

There are many benefits of working collectively. There's the broad base of support—getting over a hump because people put wind under your wings by pitching in and lifting. We have steady people who come in early, or stay late. Some are calm and level-headed in a storm. Others help us remember our values. There are sensitive ones who speak up for people who aren't present. Those who remember to appreciate and acknowledge others. The explorers, who take risks and step out in front. Those who take on the unpopular and difficult jobs. We feel tremendous gratitude for our collective perseverance and staying power, the incredible commitment to just keep contributing.